Viking Settlements and Viking Society

Delegates of the congress standing in front of the University of Iceland, from the front row left and back, see list of names on page 510.

Viking Settlements and Viking Society

Papers from the Proceedings of the Sixteenth Viking Congress, Reykjavík and Reykholt, 16–23 August 2009

Svavar Sigmundsson

EDITOR

CO-EDITORS:

Anton Holt • Gísli Sigurðsson
Guðmundur Ólafsson • Orri Vésteinsson

Fylgirit Árbókar Hins íslenzka fornleifafélags 2011

HIÐ ÍSLENZKA FORNLEIFAFÉLAG & UNIVERSITY OF ICELAND PRESS
REYKJAVÍK 2011

RITRÝNT

Each chapter in this book has been peer reviewed
by two anonymous reviewers.
We thank our reviewers for their contribution.

This book was sponsored by Nordisk Kulturfond and
The Icelandic Ministry of Education and Culture

Viking Settlements and Viking Society.
Papers from the Proceedings of the Sixteenth Viking Congress,
Reykjavík and Reykholt, 16–23 August 2009

Editor:
SVAVAR SIGMUNDSSON
Co-editors:
ANTON HOLT, GÍSLI SIGURÐSSON,
GUÐMUNDUR ÓLAFSSON AND ORRI VÉSTEINSSON

Layout: Sverrir Sveinsson
Photograph on cover: Ívar Brynjólfsson
Cover design: Helga Gerður Magnúsdóttir

Printed in Iceland by: Prentmet ehf.

Hið íslenzka fornleifafélag and University of Iceland Press

Reykjavík 2011

U2011139
ISBN 978-9979-54-923-9

Table of Contents

Delegates standing in front of Snorralaug in Reykholt, from left to right, see list of names on page 511.

Foreword

At the 15th Viking Congress in Cork in 2005 it was decided that the next Congress would be held in Iceland in 2009. Accordingly, preparations for the 16th Viking Congress were progressing well when Iceland's economy came crashing down in October 2008. The banks collapsed one after the other and the whole country came to a standstill. Suddenly all plans were turned upside down. To the Organising Committee the future now looked pretty grim and uncertain. After the initial shock had been overcome, the committee came to the conclusion that in spite of gloomy economical aspects, the Congress had to be held at all cost. The organisation went ahead as planned, in accordance with Icelandic optimism that everything would fix itself in the end – and surely it did.

The location of the Congress was divided between the University of Iceland in Reykjavík and Snorrastofa in Reykholt.

Besides the regular planning of the Congress, the Organising Committee opened a new official webpage for the Viking Congress (http://www.vikingcongress.com), provided and cared for by Snorrastofa. It contained the history of the Viking Congress, Congress diaries, photos and additional information from all earlier Viking Congresses. Here, for the first time laid out in writing was the framework for the organisation of the Viking Congress that before had only existed in oral tradition, thanks to the generous help of many members of the Congress Council. The final version of the organisation framework was approved at the Congress Council meeting in Reykholt.

Through the website, delegates could also register and make all other Congress reservations.

The organising committee is now proud to present select papers in the *Proceedings of the Sixteenth Viking Congress*. The main theme of the Congress was Viking Settlements and Viking Society and that is also the name of the Proceedings. Sixty-four papers were presented at the Congress and thirty-one papers are published in this volume. In accordance with the written Congress organisation statutes, all articles were peer reviewed. The articles are organised in alphabetical order by author.

As in 1956, when the Third Viking Congress was also held in Iceland, the proceedings are published by Hið íslenzka fornleifafélag, now in cooperation with Háskólaútgáfan who produced this volume.

Guðmundur Ólafsson
Reykjavík, August 2011

Acknowledgements

The Organising Committee of the Sixteenth Viking Congress would like to thank all the wonderful people and institutions who helped to make the Congress such a great success. First we mention Mr. Ólafur Ragnar Grímsson, president of Iceland for his patronage. A generous financial backing from the Icelandic Ministry of Education and Culture was crucial for making of the Congress in Iceland, as the good cooperation and support from Þjóðminjasafn Íslands, Háskóli Íslands, Stofnun Árna Magnússonar í íslenskum fræðum, Snorrastofa, Fornleifavernd ríkisins, Reykjavíkurborg and Minjasafn Reykjavíkur, Clara Lachmanns Fond, Letterstedtska föreningen, Seðlabanki Íslands, The Scandinavian embassies, Gestamóttakan, Vífilfell and many others institutions colleges and student assistants, who helped to make the Congress such a success. Our special thanks go to Þóra Pétursdóttir, the general manager of the Congress preparations, who solved every problem and made it look so effortless.

Our warmest thanks go also to Nordisk Kulturfond and Icelandic Ministry of Education and Culture whose grant and financial support made this publication possible.

The Organising Committee

Anton Holt
Gísli Sigurðsson
Guðmundur Ólafsson
Orri Vésteinsson
and Svavar Sigmundsson

Members and Associates

PATRON:

Ólafur Ragnar Grímsson, President of Iceland

NATIONAL REPRESENTATIVES:

Denmark: Else Roesdahl and Niels Lund
England: Judith Jesch and †Richard Hall
Faroe Islands: Símun V. Arge and Eivind Weyhe
Greenland: Claus Andreasen and Georg Nygaard
Iceland: Guðmundur Ólafsson and Svavar Sigmundsson
Ireland: John Sheehan and Patrick Wallace
Norway: Else Mundal and Dagfinn Skre
Scotland: Doreen Waugh and Olwyn Owen
Sweden: Anne-Sofie Gräslund and Henrik Williams
Wales: John Hines

HONORARY MEMBERS OF THE CONGRESS:

Ólafur Ragnar Grímsson, President of Iceland; Katrín Jakobsdóttir, Minister of Education and Culture; Bergur Þorgeirsson, Director of Snorrastofa; Guðný Gerður Gunnarsdóttir, Director of The Reykjavik City Museum; Guðrún Nordal, Director of The Árni Magnússon Institute for Icelandic Studies; Jónas Kristjánsson, Director emeritus of The Árni Magnússon Institute for Icelandic Studies; Kristín Ingólfsdóttir, Rector of the University of Iceland; Kristín Huld Sigurðardóttir, Director of The Archaeological Heritage Agency; Margrét Hallgrímsdóttir, Director of the National Museum; Ólafur Halldórsson, member of the 3rd Viking Congress; Vésteinn Ólason, Director emeritus of The Árni Magnússon Institute for Icelandic Studies; Þór Magnússon, Director emeritus of the National Museum.

DELEGATES OF THE 16TH VIKING CONGRESS IN ICELAND 2009:

Denmark: Andres S. Dobat, Claus Feveile, Else Roesdahl, Eva Andersson Strand, Lasse Sonne, Lisbeth Imer, Silke Eisenschmidt, Søren Sindbæk, Unn Pedersen.

Schleswig-Holstein: Joachim Schultze, Sven Kalmring, Volker Hilberg.

England: Christina Lee, Christopher Callow, David Griffiths, Dawn Hadley, Garreth Williams, James Graham-Campbell, Jane Kershaw, Judith Jesch, Lesley Abrams, Marjolein Stern, †Mark Blackburn, †Richard Hall.

Faroe Islands: Helgi Michelsen, Símun V. Arge.

Greenland: Jette Arneborg, Mogens Skaaning Høegsberg, Poul Baltzer Heide, Sarah Croix.

Iceland: Adolf Friðriksson, Anton Holt, Elisabeth Ward, Gavin Lucas, Gísli Sigurðsson, Guðmundur Ólafsson, Guðný Zoëga, Guðrún Sveinbjarnardóttir, Gunnar Karlsson, Haki Antonsson, Helgi Þorláksson, Hildur Gestsdóttir, Jesse Byock, Ragnheiður Traustadóttir, Rúnar Leifsson, Steinunn Kristjánsdóttir, Svavar Sigmundsson, Vala Björg Garðarsdóttir, Þórgunnur Snædal.

Ireland: Donnchadh Ó Corráin, John Sheehan, Maire Ní Mhaonaigh, Patrick Wallace, Ruth Johnson.

Norway: Anne Pedersen, Dagfinn Skre, Else Mundal, Frans-Arne Stylegar, Frode Iversen, Ingvild Øye, James Knirk, Jón Viðar Sigurðsson, Svein Harald Gullbekk, Sæbjørg Walaker Nordeide.

Scotland: Arne Kruse, Barbara Crawford, Clare Downham, Colleen Batey, Elizabeth Pierce, Erin-Lee McGuire, Julie Bond, Kevin Edwards, Neil Price, Olwyn Owen.

Sweden: Anne-Sofie Gräslund, Birgitta Hårdh, Daniel Sävborg, Kenneth Jonsson, Staffan Fridell, Torun Zachrisson.

Wales: Alan Lane, John Hines, Nancy Edwards.

SPECIAL DELEGATES:

James Graham-Campbell, England; Thomas McGovern, USA; Przemysław Urbańczyk, Poland; Birgitta Wallace, Canada.

STUDENT ASSISTANTS:

Ásta Hermannsdóttir, Jakob Orri Jónsson, Katrín Dröfn Guðmundsdóttir, Margrét Sigvaldadóttir, Sigrún Antonsdóttir.

16th VIKING CONGRESS 2009

REYKJAVÍK AND REYKHOLT, ICELAND

Congress Diary

Delegates arrived in Reykjavík on Sunday, August 16th 2009. At 17:00 they were welcomed by Guðný Helgadóttir, from the Ministry of Education and Culture, and Margrét Hallgrímsdóttir, director of the National Museum, in a reception at the National Museum of Iceland. Following the reception, at 20:00, Birgitta Wallace, archaeologist emeritus at Parks Canada, opened the congress by giving the first lecture in the University's Main building. The lecture, on L'Anse aux Meadows research project, was the first of five public lectures and was well attended.

Formal proceedings began early the following morning, August 17th, with an opening speech by Mr. Ólafur Ragnar Grímsson, President of Iceland and Patron of the 16th Viking Congress. This was followed by a busy day of lectures on the theme "Settlements and Viking Society". At 12:00 Else Roesdahl, professor in Medieval Archaeology at Aarhus University, gave the second public lecture, called "Scandinavia in the Melting Pot, c. 950–1000".

The first day was closed with a reception at Bessastaðir, the presidential residence, hosted by Mr. Ólafur Ragnar Grímsson. The President gave a talk welcoming the guests, and before leaving, Patrick Wallace said a few words and thanked the President on behalf of the congress delegates. When back in central Reykjavík many of the participants continued with the social program at the congress bars, Fjalakötturinn and Uppsalir.

On Tuesday morning papers were still devoted to the first theme of "Settlements and Viking Society". At noon Przemysław Urbańczyk, Professor of Archaeology at the Polish Academy of Science in Warsaw gave a public lecture on the formation of an Icelandic identity based on archaeological information. After lunch at the University's restaurant Háma, and a hasty group-photo opportunity, two buses left for an excursion to Krýsuvík and Húshólmi, south of the capital.

The first stop was at the Seltún geothermal area in Krýsuvík. There participants enjoyed the smell of sulphur, bioling mud pots and water, as well as spectacular scenery. From Seltún, the journey continued on good roads for a few kilometres when suddenly the buses turned onto a narrow mud track leading, along the edge of the lavafield, towards the southern shoreline in the distance. For a critical hour or so, it was uncertain whether or not all the participants, or in fact the buses, would make it to the end. However, after several incidents, both buses succeeded. The participants were welcomed by Agnes Stefánsdóttir, from the Archaeological Heritage Agency of Iceland, who escorted the parade into the lavafield towards Húshólmi. After a refreshing walk through the rough lava in weather typical of the south coast, the party was rewarded with a warm welcome and re*fresh*ments, in the form of fermented shark and Icelandic brennivín, by Kristín Huld Sigurðardóttir, Kristinn Magnússon and Gunnar Bollason, at the AHA's mobile bar. While enjoying these traditional delicacies, Agnes explained the archaeology and nature of the buildings in the lavafield at this Viking Age site.

From Húshólmi, the drivers again managed the impossible and the whole group was delivered safely to the Reykjavík 871±2. Museum in central Reykjavík, where the Reykjavík City Museum hosted a reception. A welcoming talk was given by Guðný Gerður Gunnarsdóttir, director of the Reykjavík City Museum, and after enjoying the museum's outstanding exhibition, James Knirk thanked her and her staff for the wonderful reception on behalf of the guests. Afterwards, many of the participants continued socializing at the congress bar conveniently located above the museum.

Wednesday, August 19th, was a day packed with lectures starting early in the morning. Before the lunch break, lectures were devoted to the theme "Settlements and Viking Society", while after lunch to the theme of "Viking Age Iceland". At noon James Graham-Campbell, professor emeritus of Medieval Archaeology at University College London, gave a public lecture on silver hoards from Viking Age Iceland. Lectures went on until 15:30, when the social program took over and delegates attended the Manuscript exhibition in the Culture House, guided by Gísli Sigurðsson. After an interesting visit, a reception across the street at the Central Bank of Iceland and The National Museum's Numismatic Collection followed. Anton Holt, curator at the banks' collection, welcomed the guests who could then look through the collection while enjoying the refreshments, kindly provided by the bank. Again the socializing continued at the congress bar into the night.

On the fourth day, Thursday August 20th, the congress moved its venue from the capital of Reykjavík to the medieval centre of Reykholt, home to chieftain and writer Snorri Sturluson. After being loaded with luggage, food and other *Viking*-necessities, the buses left Reykjavík early in the morning. The first stop on the way was made on the outskirts of the city, at Þingnes by lake Elliðavatn, perhaps the earliest assembly site in Iceland. After Guðmundur Ólafsson had explained the site, the buses stopped at Hrísbrú in Mosfellsdalur, where Jesse Byock described the Viking Age site and explained the Mosfell project.

At Þingvellir the Congress was welcomed by Einar Á. E. Sæmundsen, the interpretive officer of the National Park, who gave a presentation and an excellent guided tour of the World Heritage Site. From Þingvellir the tour went on over a rocky mountain road to the Surtshellir cave, where surprisingly many dare-devils followed, at their own risk(!); with Guðmundur Ólafsson taking a truly adventurous trip deep into the lava cave, to see the unique Viking Age remains. Fortunately, despite a few close calls, no one got seriously injured.

Finally the buses stopped at the beautiful Hraunfossar and Barnafoss waterfalls before entering Reykholt. After a chaotic and at times stressful check-in at the hotel, all participants were grateful for a bed to sleep in, and the formal program could proceed.

Friday the 21st was filled with lectures all day, devoted to various themes. At noon, Thomas McGovern, professor at Hunter College, CUNY, New York, gave a public lecture about Vikings in the International Polar Year: bloodthirsty, sustainable and educational.

After the day's sessions, Guðrún Sveinbjarnardóttir gave a tour of the archaeological site of Reykholt and The Rev. Geir Waage gave insight into the history of Reykholt. In the exhibition sites under the church, Bergur Þorgeirsson, director of Snorrastofa, introduced Snorrastofa to the Congress while delegates enjoyed red and white wine – and other *Viking* beverages, generously donated by the Danish, Norwegian and Swedish embassies. Afterwards, the Reykholt Church choir gave a most memorable concert in the church.

After a lovely dinner at the Reykholt hotel restaurant, the socializing continued at the hotel bar (and not in Snorralaug) into the night.

On Saturday the 22nd the Congress went on a Saga trail to Snæfellsnes peninsula and Breiðafjörður fjord. The first stop was at Eiríksstaðir, where the archaeology of the site and the reconstructed hall of Eirikur the Red's farm were explained by Sigurður Hrafn Jökulsson, the keeper of the site, and Guðmundur Ólafsson.

On the bus, driving through the Saga landscapes between stops, congress members were entertained with appropriate passages from the Sagas read by a carefully selected group of readers. After lunch at Hotel Stykkishólmur, the congress delegates had the opportunity to walk around the town during the interesting local festival of "Danish Days". Then it was time to board the boat for a trip around Breiðafjörður fjord, noted for its rich bird life, beautiful rock formations and many historical sites. Delicious seafood was hauled in and, in contrast to national tradition, enjoyed fresh with a glass of good wine.

On the journey back towards Reykholt a short stop was made at Borg, where John Hines read Egill Skallagrímsson's poem Sonatorrek.

Back in Reykholt the Congress Council met for a second brief meeting to discuss the draft version for the Organisation of the Congress, as well as accepting an invitation from Scotland to host the next congress.

The Congress Dinner, enjoyed at the Reykholt hotel restaurant, included several surprise performances and talks. Afterwards all delegates, as well as the staff of Snorrastofa and Reykholt church, were invited to a *Viking*-party at the old school building where they once again enjoyed surprising amounts of *Viking* brew in cans and bottles, now well familiar to all delegates. After discussing the matter of bathing with The Rev. Geir Waage a joint verdict was reached that bathing in Snorri's laug was "not allowed – but not forbidden". Socializing thus continued at various locations on the Reykholt manor into the night and early morning.

Sunday 23rd, the last day of the Congress continued with mixed theme presentations, until lunchtime. After a communal lunch, the Congress ended with a formal invitation by Olwyn Owen to the next Viking Congress in the Hebrides in 2013.

At 14.00 most Congress delegates went back to Reykjavik, while a brave flock of some 30 people, equipped with a still surprising amount of *Viking* brew, took the Post Congress Tour bus to North Iceland. After a stop at the natural hill fort of Borgarvirki, the group got a well-deserved rest at Hólar in Hjaltadalur, bishopric of Northern Iceland.

On the following morning the flock awoke to heavy rain and dark skies at Hólar. Despite this, a few brave souls, began the day with a horribly cold bath in the Hólar swimming pool. After conferring with the guides of the day, Ragnheiður Traustadóttir, director of the Hólar Archaeological Project, Jennica Einebrant Svensson and Guðný Zoëga, head of the Archaeological department of the Skagafjörður Museum, the programme was rearranged and the result was that all sites were visited in good and dry weather.

The old local assembly at Hegranes, and the Keldudalur site were visited under the guidance of Ragnheiður, Jennica and Guðný. At Víðimýri turf church Einar Örn Einarsson, keeper of the church, showed the group around and after a lovely lunch at Áskaffi in Glaumbær, the group was welcomed to the Glaumbær museum by Guðný Zoëga on behalf of Museum director Sigríður Sigurðardóttir.

In the afternoon Ragnheiður lead the group to the medieval harbour at Kolkuós, the reconstructed medieval Auðunarstofa and the archaeological sites at Hólar as well as the Viking Age remains at Hof in Hjaltadalur. After dinner many spent the evening at the archaeological lab at Hólar. Some explored the turf house farm at Hólar, with torches, and experienced the darkness in these old dwelling houses.

On the 25th the tour went on to Eyjafjörður. A first stop was made at the medieval monastery site Möðruvellir where Professor Bjarni E. Guðleifsson welcomed the group in the Möðruvellir church and introduced it to the history of the farm and manor. After enjoying coffee and "kleinur" at the old Möðruvellir theatre, the journey continued to the medieval harbour at Gásir where Þóra Pétursdóttir explained the site and the Gásir excavation project.

Haraldur Þór Egilsson, director of the Akureyri Museum, welcomed the group to the Akureyri City Museum. After a lunch picnic in the Museum garden Haraldur introduced the museum exhibitions. Before leaving Akureyri the group had a quick stroll through the town centre. From Akureyri the bus headed for Mývatnssveit with a short stop at the old Laufás turf house farm and Goðafoss waterfall.

At Hofstaðir, Adolf Friðriksson presented the excavations of the large Viking Age hall, pit house and other remains at the site.

After a fantastic dinner buffet at Narfastaðir guesthouse in Reykjadalur, many participants went for a visit to the geothermal baths in Mývatnssveit to relax their weary bones. Some wished they could have stayed there longer ... perhaps forever.

On Wednesday August 26th, the last day of the Post Congress Tour, the unusual and dramatic lava formations at Dimmuborgir and the smelly geothermal area at Námaskarð were visited. Leaving the Mývatnssveit area the tour headed towards Laxárdalur through the Hólasandur sand desert where the beautiful old turf house farm at Þverá in Laxárdalur, with the indoor creek, was inspected.

After a short stop at Grenjaðarstaður turf farm, the group headed back to Akureyri where the Post Congress Tour came to a formal end with a garden party and BBQ at Þóra's inlaws. Some took the plane back to Reykjavík, while most of the participants took the bus and arrived in the capital around midnight. Many even got a few hours sleep before catching the early flight the following morning, bringing them back to "normal life".

Með góðum kveðjum frá Íslandi!

Þóra Pétursdóttir
Guðmundur Ólafsson

Opening Address by the President of Iceland Ólafur Ragnar Grímsson at the 16th Viking Congress in Iceland 17 August 2009

Distinguished scholars,
Dear friends,

It gives me great pleasure to open the proceedings of the 16th Viking Congress in Iceland and welcome this distinguished gathering of scholars and academics from so many countries. I hope that your time of deliberation and dialogue in Reykjavik and Reykholt, the seat of the chieftain and author Snorri Sturluson, will be both fruitful and inspiring.

The Viking Congress has a long and remarkable history. The first of these interdisciplinary meetings was held close to 60 years ago in Shetland, and since then, they have been convened in many countries in northern Europe: Denmark, Sweden, Norway, Ireland, the Isle of Man, Orkney and England, the Faroe Islands and in Iceland for the first time more than half a century ago, in 1956, at the invitation of the University of Iceland and the National Museum. The chairman of the organizing committee for that congress was Dr. Kristján Eldjárn, at the time Iceland's State Antiquary and later the third president of the Republic. I believe you will be following in the footsteps of participants at that congress by travelling to some of the same locations as they did on your excursions later this week.

The eminent Icelandic scholar Hermann Pálsson, professor in Edinburgh, who with Magnus Magnusson was so tireless in introducing the Icelandic sagas to English readers in the last century, somewhere used the term *paper viking*. We could take this as meaning that the Icelandic Vikings, unlike their Scandinavian relatives and ancestors, performed their heroic deeds not so much in reality as on vellum, in the medieval literature that flourished in Iceland.

When the war-weary Vikings sailed to our coasts in the 9th and 10th centuries, they had already conquered extensive regions. They had established their presence in Russia, the British Isles, France, Italy, including Sicily, and also traded with the Arabs in the East, but were yet to sail westward to discover a new world – and have the good sense to lose it again, as Oscar Wilde is said to have remarked.

The men who staggered ashore in Iceland, trembling after their long voyage, were full of curiosity and had with them various things apart from livestock, tools and weapons. They brought with them across the ocean tales of their forefathers and their glorious deeds all over Europe, mythological and heroic poetry in ancient meters, including the Eddic poetry that was later to be written down in the famous manuscript *Codex regius;* last but not least, they brought with them their vast collective experience of life.

All these elements shaped the society they formed and the unique literature that was to flourish in the new country where they settled down as farmers. We could say that Iceland became a kind of shelter for elderly Vikings: a sanctuary. Here, men like Skalla-Grímur and Egill took residence and became skilled farmers who also cultivated their poetic arts.

It is remarkable how vigorous and lively the interest in this heritage has been in the modern era, even now in our strange and fragmented times. Here in Iceland we have witnessed a keen popular interest in the new findings of archaeologists and historians, philologists and literary scholars; the excavations carried out in recent years here in Reykjavík and in Reykholt, Hólar, Mosfellsbær, Gásar, Skriðuklaustur and elsewhere in Iceland have drawn thousands of visitors every summer. The publication of the Complete Sagas of Icelanders a decade ago by Leifur Eiriksson Publishing House – the first complete publication of the sagas in English – was extremely well received by readers and critics on both sides of the Atlantic and led to the issue by Penguin of a special volume of ten sagas and also of individual sagas in seven new books.

One of the many events prepared for the Frankfurt Book Fair in 2011, where Iceland will be the Guest Country of Honour, is a comprehensive publication by Fischer Verlag of the Icelandic sagas and tales in new German translations. The Icelandic publishing house, Saga Publishing, is also preparing new editions of the complete sagas and tales in Danish, Norwegian and Swedish translations.

All these editions will be similar in scope to the recent English publication, with translations that are true to the original, but at the same time readable and accessible to a modern audience. They will be a solid indication of the strong position of this heritage in our modern times.

I found it highly illuminating to witness the great interest in the legacy of the Viking explorations, when in the year 2000 the Nordic Countries, together with the United States and Canada, celebrated the millennium of the discovery of America. I had discussed some of the ideas for these celebrations with President Clinton in the White House in 1997, including the great Viking Exhibition which was subsequently opened at the Smithsonian in Washington, with Icelandic manuscripts on display, together with many artifacts from northern Europe and the North American continent. It was memorable to be present at the opening of that exhibition in Washington, and then in New York, and also, two years later, in Minneapolis, when the exhibition completed its journey to many cities across North America. It generated extensive coverage of the historical heritage of the Vikings in prestigious periodicals, magazines, newspapers, television and radio.

Furthermore, one of the great attractions in that celebratory year was the voyage by the replica Viking ship *Íslendingur,* "the Icelander", built by Gunnar Marel Eggertsson, an idealistic sailor who created this remarkable enterprise on his own and was also the captain on the voyage. The ship sailed from western Iceland to Brattahlíð in Greenland, and then onwards to Canada and the United States to commemorate the journeys made a thousand years earlier by Leifur Eiríksson, Þorfinnur karlsefni, Guðríður Þorbjarnardóttir and other Icelandic explorers. It was truly memorable to be present at the arrival of the ship in Greenland together with Queen Margaret II of Denmark and Jonatan Motzfeld, the Premier of Greenland, but even more remarkable was to see it reach New York and go for a short cruise on the Hudson River where we offered a group of famous and distinguished American passengers some traditional Icelandic cuisine: dried haddock, smoked lumpfish and of course rotten shark.

When the *Íslendingur* finished its journey the ship returned to Iceland and the town council of Reykjanes decided to build a special museum, designed by one of our best architects, to house the vessel together with the core of the Smithsonian exhibition. To close the circle, one of the creators of the display in Reykjanes is Elisabeth Ward, who also was one of the main curators of the Viking Exhibition in the Smithsonian in Washington.

I strongly recommend that you visit this new museum and also the other interesting exhibitions and new museums that have recently been opened in different parts of Iceland. In Borgarnes Kjartan Ragnarsson, one of our leading playwrights and theater directors, and Sigríður Margrét Guðmundsdóttir have created an original and lively exhibition which focuses on the Saga of Egill Skalla-Grímsson and the Settlement of Iceland. In the same way many other communities, for example in the West Fjords, the northwestern region and on the south coast, have been drawing on the sagas and this medieval heritage to create new types of celebrations, exhibitions and replica houses, thus hoping to make the Viking heritage a pillar in their regional culture and their share of the 21st century tourism.

On the many occasions where we commemorated the millennium anniversary of the Viking explorations in America, I often referred to Guðríður Þorbjarnardóttir, who was surely the most widely travelled person in the world around the year 1000 – and would remain so for another five hundred years. She was born in Iceland, married in Greenland, gave birth to a son in North

America, then came back to Iceland, made a pilgrimage on foot to Rome, and ended her days as a nun and anchoress on her farm in Skagafjörður in Northern Iceland. Her life spanned almost the whole known western world at that time. She was an independent woman, the architect of her own fate, who with characteristic modesty took her place among the great explorers and female heroes of history.

Ten years ago, when I visited the Vatican and met His Holiness Pope John Paul the Second, I explained that five hundred years before Christopher Columbus, Guðríður, this remarkable Icelandic woman, had become the first person and also the first Christian in world history to visit both Rome and America. Since she brought priests with her, as is described in the Saga of Eirik the Red and the Saga of the Greenlanders, her missionary journey had brought Christianity to the shores of the American continent five hundred years before Christopher Columbus set out to sea.

It was memorable to witness the reaction of His Holiness when he realized that through the Viking journeys, Christianity had indeed arrived in North America at the end of the first millennium, and that it could be argued that the Vatican's mission had thus received critical support from the Vikings. Earlier this year, on my visit to Guðríður's home district on Snæfellsnes, I discussed with enthusiastic local leaders the idea of taking a small statue of Guðríður, a replica of the one which now stands at her birthplace, to the Vatican and thus allowing her finally to take her proper place within the walls of the Holy See.

Yes, the Viking heritage indeed offers many opportunities for interesting endeavors and enterprises in the modern era. But in all of those undertakings it is important that the foundations be strengthened by vigorous research and scholarly debates. Therefore, people at many different levels of society share an interest in your work and deliberations; local communities and public associations, study-groups and individuals continue to turn to the Viking era for both wisdom and enjoyment.

This Congress is thus an important contribution to our modern mission and it is in that spirit that I welcome you again and wish you success in your dialogue and deliberations.

Tools and Textiles – Production and Organisation in Birka and Hedeby

EVA ANDERSSON STRAND

ABSTRACT

The textiles produced in Viking Age Scandinavia were not only a twofold system of spun fibres. They were a result of complex interactions among resources, technology and society and moreover the Viking societies' needs, desires and choices. Naturally, the accessibility of resources and the state of technology conditioned the choices of this society (Andersson Strand et al., 2010). In this article, textile production and its organisation in Birka and Hedeby will be compared and discussed. This will be done via studies of textiles and textile tools, and a model of various organisational modes presented. The results of tool analyses demonstrate that, the majority of the textiles from the two places could also have been produced there. The general assumption that most of the textiles were imported to Birka is questioned.

Keywords: Textile, production, tools, spindle whorls, loom weights, Birka, Hedeby.

Textiles, above all types of garments, have always been an important part of people's lives, from the cradle to the grave. Dress is one way to display status, group affiliation, and so on. This is not unique to the Viking Age. There is significant evidence for the importance of textiles in different regions of the world, in many different periods, and occasionally it is also possible to find information about the organisation of textile production (e.g. Hoffmann, 1974; Herlihy, 1990; Barber, 1991; Waetzoldt, 2010; Gleba, 2008; Michel & Veenhof, 2010).

From an archaeological perspective, it is, of course, not possible to directly apply insights into the organisation of textile production in other periods and regions to the analysis of the organisation of textile production in Viking Age Scandinavia. However, what is interesting is the number of different ways the production of textiles could be set up in ancient times – and that textiles were produced in different types of organisations in the same region, at the same period.

In Viking Age Scandinavia the need for textiles of different types was substantial. There is archaeological evidence for a variety of different fabrics for clothing. These range from very fine textiles made in complicated weaving techniques with thin threads and many threads per centimetre, to coarse textiles woven with thick and unevenly spun yarn. Whether the settlement was large or small, textile manufacture for everyday use must have taken up a great deal of time. It has been estimated that about 6 kg of wool and approximately 42.000 m of spun yarn was needed to make a complete male and a complete female Viking Age costume in a coarse quality, and that it would take one spinner around 800 hours to spin this amount of thread (Andersson, 2003a; Andersson et al., 2008). More than one individual in a community must have had the knowledge and ability to produce textiles, and several people would have been involved in the various production processes. These would have included the harvesting of fibres, preparing them for spinning, weaving, various finishing processes and finally sewing them into clothing and other products (e.g. Walton Rogers, 2007; Andersson, 2003a; Geijer, 1994).

In my opinion, the value of textiles during the Viking Age, as in other regions of the world and in different eras, cannot be underestimated. The work that had to be performed in order to cover simple household requirements for textiles would have been quite substantial. We also know that textiles were considered valuable gifts during this time. The need for sailcloth should not be underestimated either. In order to meet the demand for different types of textiles, is it plausible that textile production during the Viking Age in Scandinavia was organised in different ways?

Thanks to the information available on the range of textile products, we have the opportunity to study textile manufacture and the organisation of textile crafts in this period (e.g. Geijer,1938, 1965, 1980; Hald, 1980; Hoffmann, 1974; Hägg, 1974; 1983, 1984, 1986, 1991; Bender Jørgensen, 1986, 1992). In the following, the organisation of textile production in Birka and Hedeby will be discussed, based on a consideration of different organisational methods, earlier investigations of the preserved textiles and, above all, new analyses of the textile tools uncovered at these sites. The detailed analysis of the tool assemblages makes it possible to shed light on the textile production at these two settlements, and the available knowledge of tool types and their functions is sufficient to give a good idea of how textile manufacture was performed (e.g. Hoffmann, 1974; Hald, 1980; Walton Rogers, 1996; Andersson, 2003a, Andersson, 2007; Andersson et al., 2008; Mårtensson, Nosch & Andersson Strand, 2009; Cutler et al. in press). However, it is important to note that the textile tools from both Hedeby and Birka are only dated to the Viking Age in general, and do not have a more specific date. The results can therefore only indicate what could have been produced at these sites during the Viking Age as a whole. Furthermore, in this article, the focus will be on the textiles that hitherto have been considered as imported goods.

To develop the discussion and increase our knowledge of the craftsmen/craftswomen and their organisation, and to facilitate the discussions on how can we discern household production from that intended for a wider market, I have in earlier studies proposed the following model, consisting of four different levels of production: *household production*, *household industry* and/or *putting out system*, *attached specialised production* and *workshops* (Fig. 1). (Andersson 2003b, 2007; after Costin, 1991; Olausson, 2000).

Even if most of the textiles were produced in a household context, it is possible that there were spinners and weavers manufacturing textiles in their homes either in a household industry mode or in a putting out mode. In a putting out organization mode the work is done on a household level where

Household production	**Household industry / putting out system**
The production solely covered the household's own needs Household members possessed general knowledge and skills Raw materials were commonly accessible They did not work full time on the production of textiles	The production scale was beyond the needs of the producers It was organised at household level The household members possessed general knowledge and skills There was a surplus of raw material and/or the buyers gave them raw material They did not work full time on the production of textiles
Attached specialist production High quality products, such as those used for desirable gifts were produced Production was performed by craft specialists and their skills were enhanced by full time occupation within textile production Craftsmen/women were supported by and dependent on patrons They worked on a full time basis The raw materials were of a better and/or higher quality	**Workshops** Production for direct market That the items were practical and standardized The production volume was high. There was a great demand for products Craftsmen/women worked on a full time basis

Fig 1. Model of four different levels of production.

the output of production is based on orders from external sources and the craftspeople of the household are provided with the raw material and/or the tools needed. Some textiles are extremely complicated to produce and the craftsmen and women who make them need specialised knowledge and ability, as well as time to focus: it is therefore likely that crafts people manufacturing these types of textiles would work full time, and such textiles may thus have been produced in an attached specialist production mode. In my opinion, the manufacturing of sailcloth (like the ships themselves) must also have been well organised in, for example, a household industry/putting out mode. The material used for sailcloth in the Viking Age was probably wool. The processes of producing a sail is the same as that of producing other textiles (fibre procurement, processing fibers, spinning weaving and finishing), but on a far larger scale. The cloth varied in weight between 500 g to 1000 g per m^2 (Andersen et al., 1989, 12). If the sail had 10 threads per cm in warp and weft, more than 2000 m of yarn was needed per m^2. If the sail was 50 m^2 one has to spin more 100 000 m of yarn. Furthermore, it would have taken time not only to weave but also to warp the loom and to carry out finishing treatments on the fabric after it had been woven. To have completed a sailcloth, it has been calculated that it would have taken at least 2 years full-time work for one person to produce a sail of 25 m^2 (Andersen & Nørgård, 2009, Nørgård, personal communication). To conclude, the production of a sail demands considerable amounts of raw material and moreover takes a very long time to produce. It is therefore reasonable to believe that the production of a sail is likely to have been organized in a household industry/putting out mode.

In order to use the model, one needs detailed knowledge of the original sources. The challenge is that we have no written sources for this period that describe the organisation of the Viking Age Scandinavian textile production. However, we do have, in contrast to many other regions and periods, *textile tools* and *preserved textiles*.

TOOLS FOR TEXTILE PRODUCTION

In earlier work, 2318 textile tools from Birka and 5235 tools from Hedeby, a total of 7553 tool finds, have been recorded (Fig. 2) (Andersson, 2003a). Besides spindle whorls, loom weights and bone needles, needle boxes, metal needles, tablets for tablet weaving etc were also recorded.

Tool studies can become even more informative when used in combination with experimental archaeology, which tests the function and efficiency of textile tools and equipment. As such, experimental archaeology forms a link between textiles and textile tools and contributes to a better understand-

	Birka	Hedeby
Spindle whorls	429	939
Loom weights	Complete 69	Complete 514
	Fragments 1406	Fragments 3480
Bone needles	414	302
Total number	2318	5235

Fig. 2. The number of spindle whorls, loom weights and bone needles recorded.

ing of textile production and its complexity. In recent years I have worked closely with experienced textile crafts women, in other tool projects, who have performed several spinning and weaving tests that are applicable for the interpretation of the function of the Birka and Hedeby tools (Andersson, 2003a; Andersson et al., 2008; Mårtensson et al., 2009; Cutler et al. in press; Andersson Strand & Nosch in press).

However, when comparing the results from analysed textiles with the results from the analysed tools, it is important to take into consideration that all archaeological textiles have been affected in some way. One can only estimate, for example, how much a textile has shrunk or how many warp threads the fabric had in the loom setup. Furthermore, one can never give exact information on the fabrics produced with a certain spindle whorl or loom weight. It is only possible to give a range of the types of textiles that it would be most optimal to produce with a certain tool. One can suggest what types of yarn a certain spindle is suitable to produce, or what types of fabric a specific loom weight could have been used to make, but there will always be a variation, since one spindle can be used to produce different types of yarn, depending on the fibre quality, and a loom weight can be used in different setups with different types of yarn, which will result in different types of fabrics.

SPINDLE WHORLS AND SPINNING

We know from experiments that it is primarily the weight of the spindle, the fibre material and to a certain extent the spinner that affects the outcome. It is clear that it is preferable to spin a thin thread with a light spindle and to spin a thick thread with a heavy spindle (Fig. 3). It is also clear that it takes more time to spin a thin thread with few fibres than a thicker thread (Andersson et al., 2008).

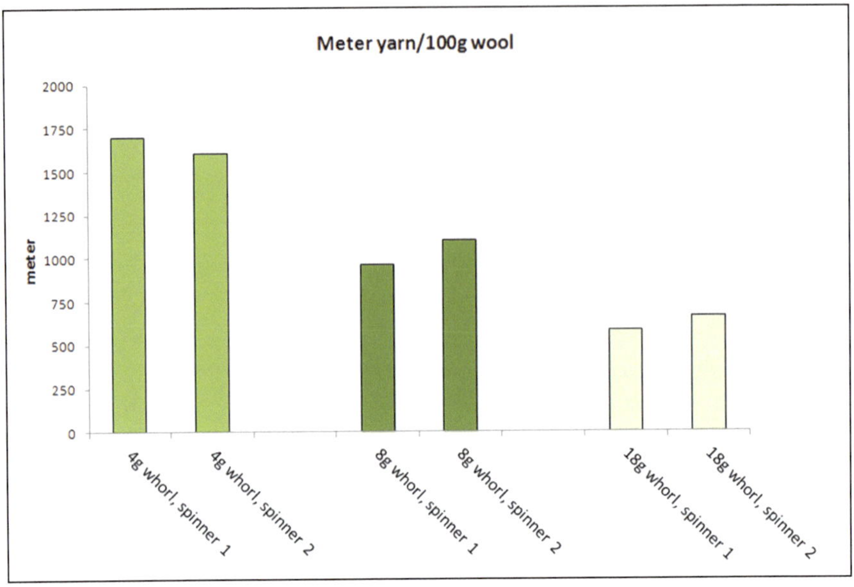

Fig. 3. Calculation of metre yarn per 100 g spun wool, 4 g, 8 g and 18 g whorls.

A comparison of the materials from which spindle whorls were made shows that ceramic whorls are most common in Hedeby (88%), while the largest group of spindle whorls in Birka are made from various types of stone (50%) (Fig. 4). However the registration shows that despite the great difference in the material, the weight is concentrated in the same groupings. As is demonstrated in Fig. 5, the distribution of the weight of spindle whorls shows that yarn was produced in several different thicknesses. Furthermore, registration and comparison of spindle whorls from Birka and Hedeby show that the whorls from Birka vary slightly more in weight.

Even if the whorls from Birka vary slightly more in weight and diameter the results clearly demonstrate that there were spinning tools in Birka and Hedeby for producing all the qualities of textiles of wool and linen evidenced in the analyses of the textile finds. Furthermore, it confirms that people in Birka and Hedeby had a similar yarn production.

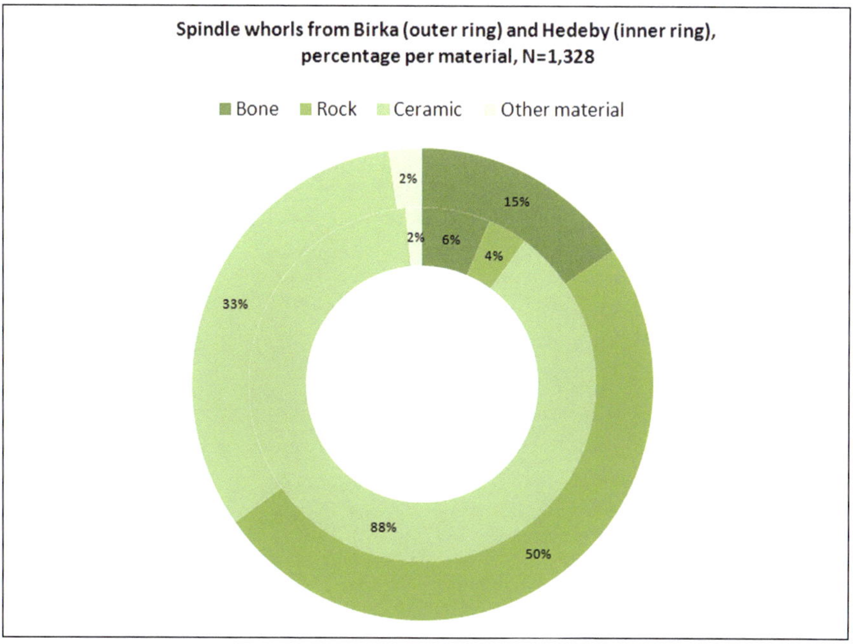

Fig. 4. All registered spindle whorls from Birka and Hedeby, material.

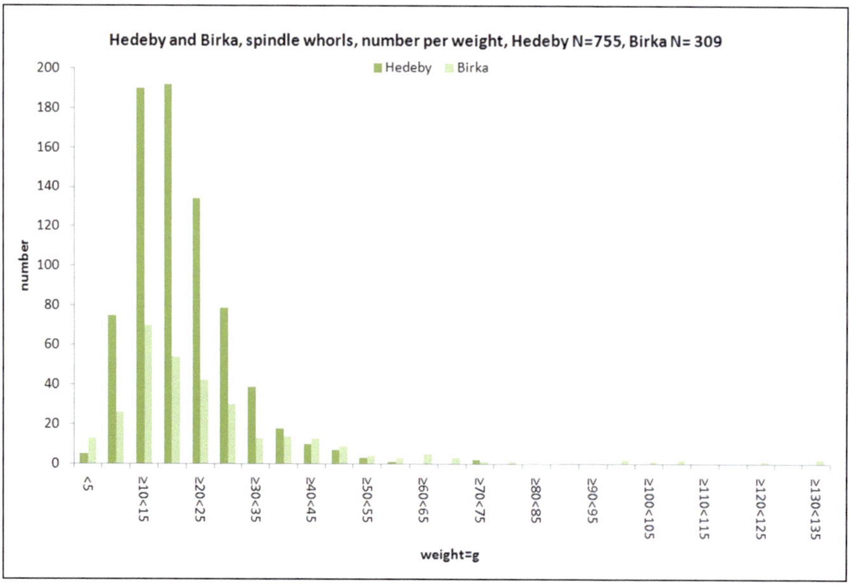

Fig. 5. All spindle whorls from Birka and Hedeby with preserved weight.

Fig. 6 (i)

Fig. 6 (ii)

Fig. 6. A 2/2 twill weave woven on a warp-weighted loom with four rows of loom weights. The fabric has 15 warp threads and 15 weft threads per cm. 15 warp threads are attached to each loom weight (i) the warp-weighted loom with the setup (ii) the four rows of loom weights. Please note that the warp threads are fastened to a yarn loop that is attached to the loom weight; i.e. the warp threads are not directly attached to the loom weight. Please also note that the loom has three heddle rods (for creating four sheds) one heddle rod on the top heddle rods holders and two heddle rods on the same lower heddle rods holders.

(By courtesy of Ulla Lund Hansen and the Vorbasse project, photo by Linda Olofsson).

LOOM WEIGHTS, WEAVING AND WEAVING TECHNIQUES

A fabric is the result of weaving two thread systems, which cross each other at right angles. One of the systems, the warp, runs parallel to the side of the loom and is kept stretched during weaving. On a warp-weighted loom the vertically hanging warp threads are kept taut by the weight of the attached loom weights. The other system, the weft, runs alternately over and under the warp threads (e.g. Andersson, 2003a). Different types of fabrics can be produced on a warp-weighted loom depending on the type of weaving technique (tabby, twill etc) and how many rows of loom weights are used.

In order to calculate a possible loom setup and the type of fabric that a particular loom weight may have been used to produce, it is first necessary to define the various possibilities and limitations. This has been achieved by combining the mathematics of weaving with weaving tests and weavers' experience, thereby making it possible to describe the range of textiles that can be produced using different loom weights. Different types of yarn need different amounts of tension when they are used in the warp on a loom. To a large extent it is the thread diameter/weight per meter that defines the appropriate warp tension, but the amount of tension required is also affected by how hard the thread is spun, the fibre quality, and the degree of fibre preparation. If too much tension is applied, the thread will break. If the tension is not sufficient, the thread will not be held taut enough and this will affect the weaving process, since it will be more difficult and time consuming to change the shed (Mårtensson et al., 2009; Cutler et al. in press; Andersson Strand & Nosch forthcoming).

Since different types of yarn need different tensions, this limits how many warp threads can be attached to an individual loom weight. If the yarn needs 20 g tension per warp thread, and the loom weight weighs 500 g, the weaver can attach 25 warp threads to the weight. If, however, the weaver uses yarn that requires 50 g tension, only 10 warp threads can be attached to the same loom weight. The weight of a loom weight therefore dictates how many threads of a given type can be fastened to it.

Another key parameter, however, is the thickness of the loom weight. Weaving experiments have demonstrated that the width of the finished cloth is determined by both the width of the starting borders and the total width of the loom weights in each row (Mårtensson et al., 2007a; Mårtensson et al., 2007b). If these widths differ, the width of the fabric will vary and/or the weaving process will become unnecessarily complicated. The thickness of the loom weights, in combination with the number of warp threads attached to an individual weight and the number of rows of loom weights used, also governs the thread count per cm of fabric on the loom (Mårtensson et al., 2009; Cutler et al. in press; Andersson Strand & Nosch in press).

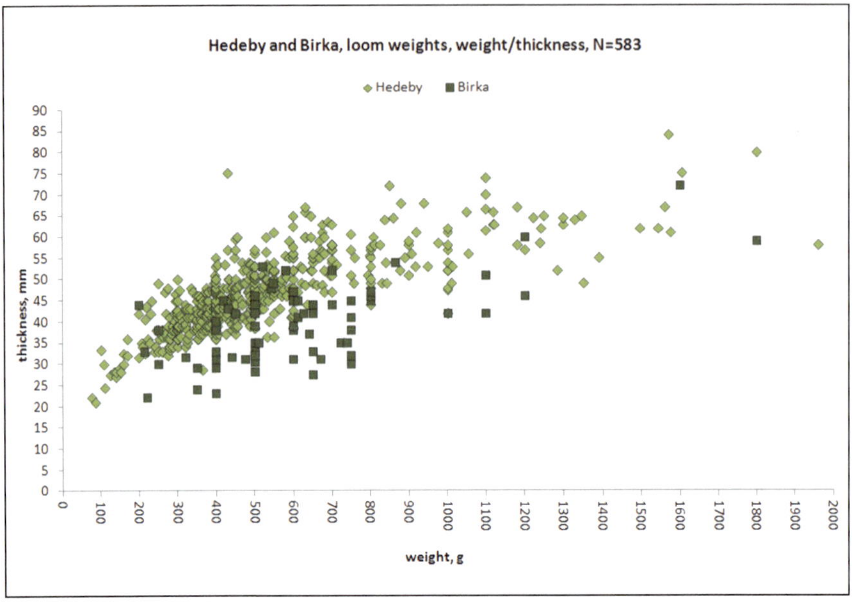

Fig. 7. All loom weights from Birka and Hedeby with preserved weight and thickness, weight/thickness.

Complete loom weights from Birka and Hedeby have been analyzed according to this new method and calculations with weight tensions from 5 to 70 g have been done. Furthermore, calculations with different types of setups using two, three and four rows of loom weights have been carried out. 514 loom weights from Hedeby are included in these analyses. However, the loom weights from Birka are very badly preserved and therefore only 69 of the Birka weights are included (Fig. 7).

The analyses clearly demonstrate that the loom weights in Hedeby and Birka could have been used for producing many of the types of textiles from the sites. Moreover, the majority of the loom weights from Hedeby could have been used with threads needing between 15 g and 45 g tension, while a smaller number could have been used for threads needing 5–10 g tension and 50–70 g tension. Furthermore, the analyses demonstrate that tabbies with 3–21 warp threads per centimetre and twills with 6–43 warp threads per centimetre could have been produced. Finally, they show a possible production of a 2/1 twill with 5–31 warp threads per centimetre woven with 3 rows of loom weights. However, it is important to note that the number of loom weights suitable for the denser fabrics, both tabbies and twills, is significantly smaller. The loom weights from Birka are in general thinner (Fig. 7) which indicates a production of slightly denser but still similar fabrics to those used at Hedeby.

Summary

It is important to note that a tool, for example a loom weight, can be used for producing different types of fabric. The analyses of the spindle whorls and loom weights clearly demonstrate a production of various types of textiles in many different qualities that would meet all the demands of the Vikings in Hedeby and Birka. The most interesting result is that some of the textile types that have been considered as imports could actually, according to the new tool analyses, have been produced at the sites. Therefore, in the following I will focus on these types of textiles.

THE TEXTILES

A large number of textile fragments have been found at Birka and Hedeby. The analyses of these finds, carried out by Agnes Geijer and Inga Hägg, have yielded unique information about various costume details, as well as raw materials, techniques, and manufacture (Geijer, 1938, 1965, 1980; Hägg, 1974; 1983, 1984,1986, 1991).

The textile discoveries from Hedeby are unique not only by virtue of their quantity, but also because textiles have been found in several contexts; not only in the cemetery, but also in the settlement site, as well as the harbour. The textile fragments in graves generally demonstrate a higher quality of textiles than the textiles from the settlement and harbour area (Hägg, 1991). From Birka, approximately 4800 textile fragments are preserved, all of which are from burials (Hägg, 1983, 205). The most detailed analyses on the Birka textiles were carried out by Agnes Geijer in the 1930s. The analyses of the textiles from Birka and Hedeby were done in slightly different ways, and the results are therefore not directly comparable. However, the textiles from Birka and their provenance have been discussed to a larger extent (e.g. Geijer, 1938, 1965; Hoffmann, 1964; Ingestad, 1980; Bender Jørgensen, 1986; Hedeager Krag, 1994), and I have therefore decided to focus on the results of textile analyses made on those from Birka by Geijer and more generally compare these with the Hedeby material. The textiles that have been discussed are: "group II – patterned twill fabrics of high quality" (Gemusterte Köpergewebe von zarter Qualität, Geijer, 1938, p. 22), "group III – ribbed fabrics and other tabby weaves of fine quality" (Rips und andere Gewebe in Leinwandbindung zarter Qualität, Geijer, 1938, p. 34) and finally "group IV – diagonal twills" (Schlichte Stoffe in Köperbindung, Geijer, 1938, p. 37).

• Group II. The patterned twill fabrics of high quality are generally made of fine-fibre wool and the yarn is evenly spun. According to the analyses, the number of warp threads is much higher per centimetre than the number of weft threads, and the thread count varies between 24/15 threads/cm and

55–60/17 threads/cm. Both warp and weft threads are always Z-spun of hair. These textiles are made of various 2/1 and 2/2 diamond twills. Geijer considers them as "standard ware" since, proportionally, there are many more examples of this type of textile in Birka and also because they have a high and uniform standard (Geijer, 1938, p. 22). The 2/1 twills are generally finer and thinner than the 2/2. Several fragments are dyed; for example, with woad, which gives a blue colour, and weld, which gives yellow (Geijer, 1938, p. 22). These types of textiles are also found in Hedeby (Hägg, 1984, 1991). The number of finds from Hedeby is smaller than the number from Birka (6–7 as against 40). Also, the fabrics from Birka generally have a higher thread count (Hägg, 1991b, p. 234).

• Group III. In the ribbed fabrics the warp threads are usually more thinly spun than the weft threads, with the result that the weft covers the warp in the weave. The yarn used for weaving ribbed fabric is strikingly smooth and firm, mostly Z-spun. The thread count for the warp varies between 14 and 25 threads/cm but is on average around 18–22 threads/cm. The weft ranges from 8 to 12 threads/cm. The quality of the wool in nine of the analysed fragments of ribbed fabric corresponds to the type of wool used in the manufacture of the textiles in group II. Finally, this group includes two fragments of a ribbed fabric made of a more coarse-fibred wool and a linen fabric where the warp is striped in blue and reddish-brown while the weft is reddish-brown (Geijer, 1938, p. 36). The number of textiles in this group is quite small in both Birka and Hedeby (Geijer, 1938; Hägg, 1984, 1991).

• Group IV. The diagonal twill fabrics are woven in 2/2 twill (one fragment is a 2/1). A characteristic feature of these textiles is the professional execution with regard to both the spinning of the yarn and the weaving of the cloth (Geijer, 1938, 37). In most cases the fabric received some kind of treatment after weaving; for example, by being washed, fulled or smoothed. The thread count in both directions varies between 11/8 threads/cm and 20–22 threads/cm. The warp and weft threads are spun in different directions, that is to say, S-spun in one direction and Z-spun in the other (Geijer, 1938, p. 37). The quality of the wool differs from the textiles in groups II and III in that both hair and wool were used (Geijer, 1938, p. 38). This type of fabric is common in both Birka and Hedeby (Geijer, 1938, Hägg, 1984, 1991).

In textile research, professional production has been defined by the criterion of a homogeneous product of a high and uniform standard (Hoffmann, 1974, p. 227; Geijer, 1994, p. 98; Bender Jørgensen, 1986, p. 168, 1995, p. 76). Several different factors are necessary to be able to produce the final product. The wool should be of a specific quality. It should be produced, cut, sorted, cleaned, if necessary dyed, and combed. The yarn then has to be spun evenly, woven, and finished. Geijer concluded that the textiles in group II and III as well as most of those in group IV were imports. She considered that the textile workers in Birka did not have access to a homogenous and selected raw material. Neither did they have the knowledge or ability, and therefore not the possibility or tradition, to organize this type of production (Geijer, 1938, p. 40). The conclusion was, therefore, that only the coarsest woollen fabrics were produced in Birka in household organisation mode.[1] However, the analyses of the textile tools from these sites partly contradict this assumption.

TEXTILE PRODUCTION AND ORGANISATION

The results of the tool analyses demonstrate that the majority of the high quality textiles in Group II could not have been produced in either Birka or Hedeby. According to the result of the spindle whorl analyses, extremely thin thread could have been produced with the light spindle whorls. However, the analyses of the loom weights demonstrate that there are none that are suitable for producing twills with more than 43 warp threads per centimetre. The analyses of the loom weights from Hedeby demonstrate that 6,5% of them would function for a production of fabrics with up to 30 warp threads per centimetre, but only 1,5% would be suitable for a production of textiles with more than 31 warp threads per centimetre. It should also be noted that these types of textiles were made of a wool type that differed from the majority of other woollen textiles.

The number of ribbed fabrics (group III) is very small. Likewise, the analyses of the loom weights indicate a possible small scale production of this type of textiles. The analyses of the loom weights from Hedeby demonstrate that only 2,2% would function for this type of production (and none would be suitable to produce fabrics with more than 21 warp threads per centimetre). Finally, the wool fibres correspond to the type of wool used in the manufacture of the textiles in group II. Even if one cannot exclude a small scale production of the "coarsest" of these textiles I would strongly suggest that the majority of the textiles in group II and III were imported to both Birka and Hedeby.

However, the tool analyses demonstrate that one cannot exclude that some of these textiles were produced in Birka and Hedeby. If so, it is most likely that they were produced in an attached specialised production mode. To produce them it would have been necessary to have specialised knowledge and skills. The raw material used was homogenous and was very well prepared, and the crafts people must have had access to high quality raw material. It is also important to bear in mind that it would have taken much more time to produce these types of textiles in all stages, and it is therefore plausible that the

[1] The discussion on where the textiles were imported to Birka from, has continued since 1938 (see e.g. Geijer, 1938, 1965, 1980; Hald, 1950; Hoffmann, 1974; Ingstad, 1980; Hägg, 1974; 1983, 1987; Bender Jørgensen, 1986, 1987). However, the textile production in Hedeby and/ or imports has not been discussed as intensively, even if there are very large similarities within the textiles.

crafts people were supported so that they could work full time. These products could have been used either by the sponsors on a basis of need and/or given as gifts, or used in exchanges.

Group IV is comprised of the "simplest twills". There is strong evidence that the majority of these textiles could have been produced in Hedeby and Birka. The majority of both spindle whorls and loom weights (54%) are suitable for this production and it is also clear that most of the tools could not have been used for a production of coarser textiles. The textiles could of course have been produced in a household production organisation mode, but Geijer's observation that these textiles are very standardised also suggests that they could have been produced in other organisation modes like a household industry, or a putting out system. Of course, these textiles could also have been produced in an attached specialist organisation. However, the number of tools uncovered in both Hedeby and Birka indicates that this production was on a large scale and would have involved a number of people. These products could also have been used either for the producers on a basis of need and/or given as gifts, or used in exchanges.

CONCLUSION AND FURTHER DISCUSSION

In this presentation I have, via earlier analyses of textiles and new analyses of textile tools, argued that some textiles that in the past have been considered imports to Birka were manufactured in both Birka and Hedeby. Furthermore, I suggest a partly organised textile production in Birka and Hedeby, based on analyses of the tools. There is no archaeological evidence for textile workshops, but the analyses of the tools support the suggestion of textile production organised in a household industry and/or in a putting out system. If there was also a production of very high quality textiles, I would suggest that they were produced in an attached specialist production mode, since this demands that the craft people work full time. In this paper the "domestic" textiles have been excluded from the discussion, but it is clear that this production was also on a large scale and would have demanded a lot of raw-material and work. Furthermore, the production of more specialised products like tablet woven bands, sprang etc have not been discussed, but it is likely, according to the tools, that such textiles also could have been produced at these two Vikinge Age sites.

It is evident that Viking Age textiles were generally produced on a domestic handicraft basis at various levels, although the larger households, manors, royal estates and the Viking towns like Birka and Hedeby doubtless provided scope for differentiation and professional specialisation, and were probably producing more specialised textiles on a minor scale. The result from the Birka and Hedeby tool analyses supports this hypothesis.

Extensive analysis and much work has been done, but there is still much to do. It is extremely important to do new and modern analyses on the textiles from both Birka and Hedeby. These results will inevitably give fresh and valuable information, and might change the existing results. More details of the contexts and stratigraphy of the textile finds are also needed in order to continue the discussion.

In this article I have also argued for the potential of combining information on textiles, textile tools and the organisation of textile production, not just for textile research itself, but for archaeological Viking Age research in general. By including the textiles and the textile production we make an important part of Viking Age life visible.

ACKNOWLEDGEMENTS

I wish to express my warmest thanks my colleagues and friends Ulla Mannering, Joanna Cutler, and Marie-Louise Nosch at the Danish Research Foundation's Centre for Textile Research for providing constructive criticism and wise viewpoints. I also thank my colleagues in our research project Engendering Central Places. I am also grateful to Joanna Cutler who has proof read this paper. I thank my colleagues Ulla Lund Hansen and Linda Olofsson for collaboration and the use of the results from the Vorbasse research programme supported by The Danish Council for Independent Research | Humanities (FKK). Finally I would like to thank the anonymous reviewer for constructive criticism.

This research was carried out with the support of, Denmark; Culture Programme of the European Union, the Danish National Research Foundation and the Swedish Research Council.

BIBLIOGRAPHY

Andersen, E., Miland, J. & Myhre, E. 1989 *Uldsejl i 1000 år.* Vikingeskibshallen, Roskilde.

Andersen, E. & Nørgård, A. (2009). *Et uldsejl til Oselven.* Arbejdsrapport, Vikingeskibsmuseet. Roskilde.

Andersson, E. (2003a). *Tools for Textile Production, from Birka and Hedeby,* Birka studies volume 8. Stockholm.

Andersson, E. (2003b). Textile production in Scandinavia. In L. Bender Jørgensen, J. Banck-Burgess & A. Rast-Eicher (Eds.), *Textilien aus Archäologie und Geschichte, festschrift Klaus Tidow,* pp. 46–62. Neumünster.

Andersson, E. (2007). Engendering Central Places: some aspects of the organisation of textile production during Viking Age. In A. Rast-Eicher & R. Windler (Eds.), *Archäologische Textilfunde – Archaeological Textiles NESAT IX,* pp. 148–153. Braunwald.

Andersson, E., Mårtensson, L., Nosch, M-L. & Rahmstorf, L. (2008). New Research on Bronze Age Textile Production. *BICS*-51 2008. *Bulletin of the institute of classical studies*, pp. 171–174.

Andersson Strand, E., Frei, K. M., Gleba, M. Mannering, U., Nosch, M.-L. & Skals, I., 2010. Old Textiles – New Possibilities, *European Journal of Archaeology V 13, 2,* pp. 149–173.

Andersson, E. & Nosch, M.-L. (Eds.). In print. *Tools, Textiles and Contexts. Investigations of textile production in the Bronze Age Eastern Mediterranean.* Oxford: Oxbow Books.

Barber, E. J. W. (1991). *Prehistoric Textiles. The Development of Cloth in the Neolithic and Bronze Ages.* Princeton.

Bender Jørgensen, L. (1986). *Forhistoriske tekstiler i Skandinavien – Prehistoric Scandinavian Textiles,* Nordiske Fortidsminder serie B. Bind 9. Copenhagen: Det Kgl. Nordiske Oldskriftselskab.

Bender Jørgensen, L. (1987). Metoder og kildekritik i textilforskningen, Et svar på et debatoplæg, *Tor 21*, pp. 263–282.

Bender Jørgensen, L. (1992). *North European Textiles until AD 100.* Aarhus: Aarhus Universitetsforlag.

Bender Jørgensen, L. (1995). Karl den Store, Muhammed og Uldsækken. In H. Gjøstein Resi (Ed.), *Produksjon og samfunn,* Varia 30, pp. 73–83. Oslo.

Costin, C. L. (1991). Craft Specialization: Issues in Defining, Documenting and Explaining the Organization of Production. In M. B. Schiffer (Ed.), *Archaeology, Method and Theory*, pp. 1–56. Tuscon.

Cutler, C., Andersson Strand, E., Nosch, M.-L., Firth, R., Poursat, J.-C. & Rougemont, F. in print. Textile production in Quartier Mu. In J.-Cl. Poursat (Ed.), Le Quartier Mu V (Études Crétoises), Athens: EFA.

Geijer, A. (1938). *BIRKA III. Die Textilfunde aus den Gräbern.* Stockholm: KVHAA.

Geijer, A. (1965). Var järnålderns "frisiska kläde" tillverkat i Syrien? Reflektioner i anslutning till ett arbete om tyngdvävstolen. *Fornvännen 60*, pp. 112–132.

Geijer, A. (1980). The textile finds from Birka, *Acta Archaeologica 50*, pp. 209–222.

Geijer, A. (1972/1994). *Ur textilkonstens historia.* Stockholm.

Gleba, M. (2008). *Textile production in Pre-Roman Italy.* Ancient textiles Series Vol. 4. Oxford: Oxbow.

Hald, M. (1980). *Ancient Danish Textiles from Bogs and Burials. A Comparative Study of Costume and Iron Age textiles.* Copenhagen: The National Museum.

Hedeager Krag, A. (1994). *Dragtutviklingen fra 8.–10-århe. Kr. i Sydskandinavien – med udgangspunkt i skålformede spænder.* Lag 5. Århus.

Herlihy, D. (1990). *Opera Muliebria Women and Work in Medieval Europe.* Baskerville.

Hoffmann, M. (1964 (1974)). *The Warp-Weighted Loom.* Oslo.

Hägg, I. (1974). *Kvinnodräkt i Birka* (Aun 2). Uppsala.

Hägg, I. (1983). Birkas orientaliska praktplagg, *Fornvännen 78*, pp. 204–233.

Hägg, I. (1984). *Die Textilfunde aus dem Hafen von Haithabu*, mit Beiträgen von G.

Grenander Nyberg und H. Schweppe. Berichte über die Ausgrabungen in Haithabu 20. Neumünster.

Hägg, I. (1985). Textilhistoria, statistik och källkritik, *Tor 20*, pp. 259–278.

Hägg, I. (1986). Die Tracht, *Birka II:2*. KVHAA, pp. 51–72. Stockholm.

Hägg, I. (1987). Textilhistoria, statistik och källkritik, *Tor 21*, pp. 283–296.

Hägg, I. (1991a). *Textilfunde aus der Siedlung und aus den Gräbern von Haithabu. Beschreibung und Gliederung.* Berichte über die Ausgrabungen in Haithabu 29. Neumünster.

Hägg, I. (1991b). Rangsymboliska element i vikingatida gravar. In Iversen, M., Näsman, U. & Vellev, J. (Eds.), *Mammen. Grav, kunst og samfund i vikingetid.* Jysk Arkæologisk Selskabs Skrifter 28, pp. 155–162. Århus.

Ingstad, A. S. (1980). "Frisisk klede"? En diskusjon omkring noen fine tekstiler fra yngre jernalder, *Viking 43*, pp. 81–95.

Michel, C. & Veenhof, K. R. (2010). *The Textiles traded by the Assyrians in Anatolia (19th–18th Centuries BC)* in C. Michel & M.-L. Nosch (Eds.), *Textile Terminologies in the Ancient Near East and the Mediterranean Area from the 3rd to the 1st millennium BC*, Ancient Textiles Series 8, pp. 210–271. Oxford: Oxbow Books.

Mårtensson, L., Andersson, E., Nosch, M.-L. & Batzer, A. (2007a). *Technical Report Experimental Archaeology, Part 3: Loom weights, 2007.* Tools and Textiles – Texts and Contexts Research Program. The Danish National Research Foundation's Centre for Textile Research, University of Copenhagen. http://ctr.hum.ku.dk/research/tools_and_textiles_/.

Mårtensson, L., Andersson, E. & Nosch, M.-L., (2007b) *Technical Report Experimental Archaeology, Part 4 Spools, 2007.* Tools and Textiles – Texts and Contexts Research Program. The Danish National Research Foundation's Centre for Textile Research, University of Copenhagen. http://ctr.hum.ku.dk/research/tools_and_textiles_/.

Mårtensson, L., Nosch, M.-L. & Andersson Strand, E. (2009). Shape of Thing: Understanding a Loom Weight, *Oxford Journal of Archaeology 28(4)*, pp. 373–398.

Olausson, D. (2000). Talking Axes, Social Dagger. In D. Olausson & H. Vandkilde (Eds.), *Form, Function & Context, material culture studies in Scandinavian archaeology*, pp. 121–133. Lund.

Pedersen, A., Widgren, M., & Welinder, S. (1998). *Jordbrukets första femtusen år, 4000 f. Kr.–1000 e. Kr.* Stockholm.

Waetzoldt, H. (2010). *The Colours of Textiles and Variety of Fabrics from Mesopotamia during the Ur III Period (2050 BC).* In C. Michel & M.-L. Nosch (Eds.), *Textile Terminologies in the Ancient Near East and the Mediterranean Area from the 3rd to the 1st millennium BC*, Ancient Textiles Series 8, pp. 201–209. Oxford: Oxbow Books.

Walton Rogers, P. (1996). *Textile Production at 16–22 Coppergate.* The Archaeology of York AY17/11. York.

Walton Rogers, P. (2007). *Cloth and Clothing in Early Anglo-Saxon England, AD 450–700.* York.

Hofstaðir: Does the Artefact Assemblage Reflect its Special Status?

COLLEEN BATEY

ABSTRACT

Excavations at the major settlement site of Hofstaðir in Northern Iceland by the Archaeological Institute of Iceland and NABO (North Atlantic Biocultural Organisation) have demonstrated that there are a number of factors which could be used together to confirm the special status of the site. Amongst these are the large size of the *skáli* itself and the potential for a very large catchment for natural resources, most particularly cattle. The artefactual assemblage however, if seen in isolation, would not suggest anything extraordinary, representing as it does commonly identified elements of household activities. It does however demonstrate that the *Primary Tool Kit* of imports from Scandinavia with the earlier settlers, such as whetstones, steatite vessels, iron tools etc is modified as a secondary stage by the increased use and replacement by the use of locally available resources (such as whetstones, iron tools and repairs to copper alloy vessels, Icelandic spar and jasper). This underlines the lack of dependency on contact with the Scandinavian homelands and the self-sustaining capabilities of the new Icelandic settlers.

Keywords: Artefact, status, Iceland, Primary Tool Kit.

INTRODUCTION: HOW DO WE DEFINE STATUS?

There are a number of potential inter-connected indicators which can assist in the identification of the status of a site. These can be applied regardless of whether the site is of high or low status, of special status with perhaps a religious function or a political centre. The range of indicators is large, and probably differs through geography or through cultural requirements, but for this case study the following are considered to be significant. The size of the structure(s) involved, the activities taking place there, the location and the local resource base, the presence in the immediate locality of rich graves, and the identification of a broad-ranging artefact assemblage which includes exotic or quasi-exotic items which have been imported to the site during the lifetime of the settlement. Defining the specific status of a site requires both detailed

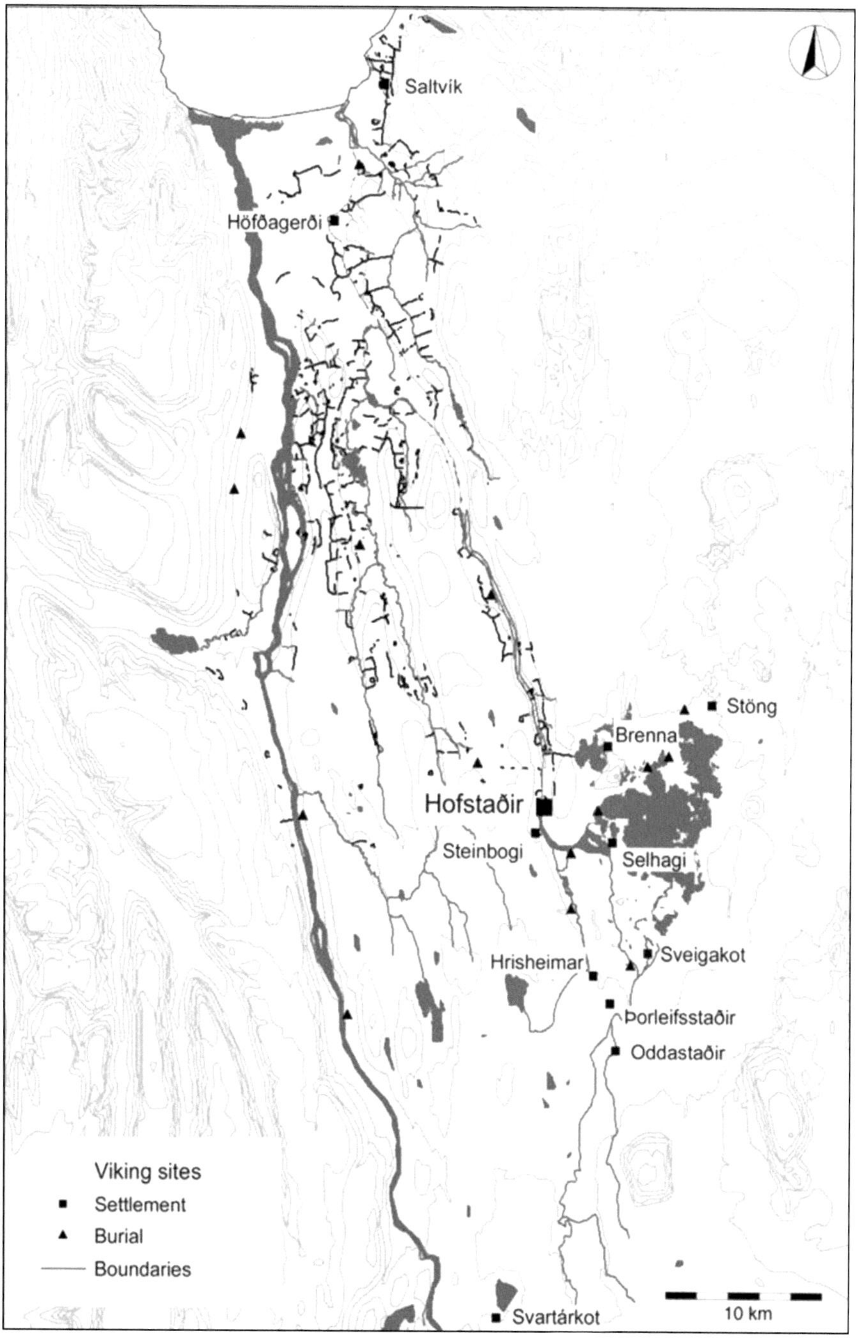

Fig. 1. Map of Hofstaðir in relation to known contemporary sites in the area (Lucas 2009, 403).

information about the site itself, but more particularly detailed information about the contemporary situation in the region. In the context of Hofstaðir in Mývatnssveit, an intense landscape survey in combination with a programme of settlement excavations provide a basis for this consideration. Fig. 1.

IS HOFSTAÐIR A SITE OF SPECIAL STATUS?

Through a consideration of these elements, we can begin to assess, at least in part, whether Hofstaðir did indeed have a special status, both locally and more widely. The exceptional size of the *skáli* at Hofstaðir (38 m; Fig. 2) in relation to the normal range in Iceland of between 12 and 16 m (Lucas, 2009, 376), has long excited comment. The scale of the building, in combination with the place name element *hof*, ensured that an identification as a pagan temple dominated the earlier interpretations (as discussed in Lucas, 2009, pp. 1–4). Excavations commencing in 1991 confirmed the dating of the site to the 9–11th centuries and indeed revealed that the structure is "the largest known settlement from the Viking period in Iceland" (Lucas, 2009, 4). Additionally, Lucas has drawn attention to the possible foundation deposits recovered during excavation, including a crucible fragment and human tooth from a posthole opposite the primary hearth (*op cit*, 394). The consistency of the faunal record through each of the main phases indicates a household economy geared to the production of young pigs, goat milk products and young sheep (McGovern, 2009, 252) which can be interpreted as representing the provisioning of seasonal gatherings. The increased hall size available from Phase II onwards, may bespeak of an increased size of such gatherings, and the concomitant increase in suckling pigs within the faunal remains is significant in this context. The presence of 14 young bull skulls, which were placed in the open air at the end of the settlement of the site (in the 11th century) could support a ritualistic closure of the structure at Hofstaðir (McGovern, 2009, pp. 236–237; Lucas, 2009, 399).

The nature of potentially specialist ritual centres or cultic landscapes is an interesting issue to explore and there is no doubt that elite residences such as Uppsala in Sweden (Hedlund, 1993), Lejre in Denmark (Christensen, 1991) and Borg in Lofoten, Arctic Norway (Munch et al., 2003) could be identified as such on the basis of their size (e.g. the hall at Lejre is 48 m; and Borg a massive 64 m), and which could have acted as focal points for religious activity. However, as Lucas cautions, the evidence for ritual activity is often textual not archaeological (*op cit* 10), so perhaps size is not the most significant aspect of the special status identification. It is however significant that at Borg for example, there are several exotic imports to the site, including fine glass ware, Germanic

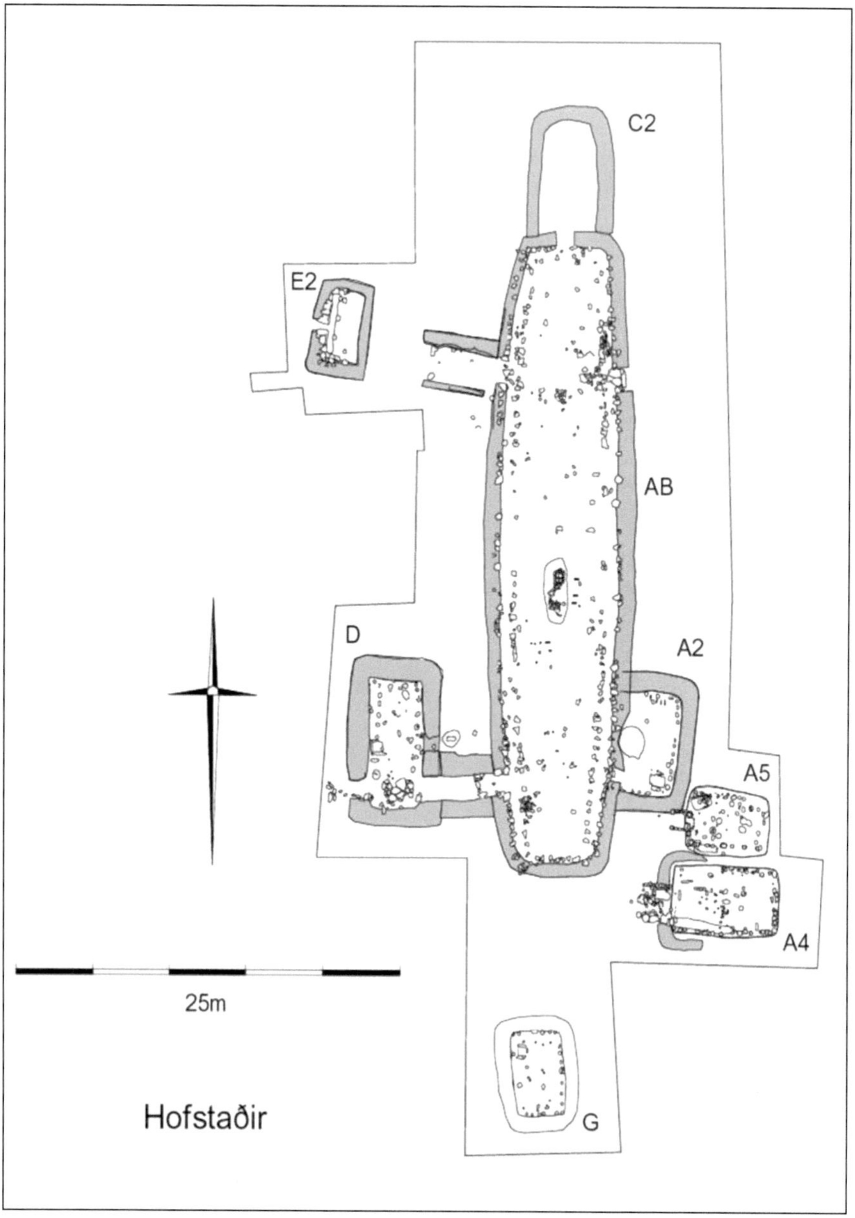

Fig. 2. Overall Plan of Hofstaðir.

ceramics and distinctive votive *gullgubber* plaques (Holand, 2003; Munch, 2003) which coupled with an extensive integral byre to the hall suggest considerable wealth focussed at that one site. At Borg, although the majority of the assemblage is related to normal everyday activity (such as textile working, cooking, fishing etc) there can be no doubt that the site is of special status due to the "large number of objects, displaying wealth, power and prestige" (Näsman & Roesdahl, 2003, 286). Other sites are however only really identifiable as being of higher status through the survival of specific literary sources. The high status site at The Biggings on Papa Stour, Shetland was initially identified solely through the rare survival of a document dated to 1299. This document was drawn up by the lawthingmen of Shetland, and recorded a dispute between Duke Hakon's bailiff Thorvald Thoresson and Ragnhild Simunsdatter of Papa Stour which took place in the principal room (*i stofuni i hertugaboenum*) of the duke's house on Papa Stour (Crawford & Ballin Smith, 1999, chapter 4). Location of the specific site and the identification through excavation of the wooden *stofa* mentioned in the source, confirmed the status of a structure which, without the chance survival of the wooden structural elements themselves, would otherwise have been unremarkable. Indeed the artefactual record alone would not have automatically confirmed such a status.

Other aspects can denote the special status of a settlement. The location of the specific site and its access to resources – human and material – from the local and wider environments, could be of equal significance. In a recent discussion of the site at Sveigakot, located on the south shore of Lake Mývatn, Vésteinsson makes particular reference to its economic status and availability of land for grazing, highlighting that the vegetated land available to that site was only about 20% of that which Hofstaðir could command (1.2 square km versus 15 square km; Vésteinsson, 2010, 497). Sveigakot seems to have been particularly poor in this resource, and Hofstaðir relatively rich. The interesting feature of this is that they are in the same region and potentially part of the same much larger integrated network of land use. Ongoing isotopic studies by McGovern et al. indicate that Hofstaðir has cattle remains which are from a considerably wider geographical area than any existing models had contemplated (pers comm Tom McGovern). At sites such as Borg, in Arctic Norway where a substantial integral byre indicates the housing of many cattle, and is thus an obvious indicator of material wealth, the on-site presence of cattle suggests relatively local pasturage, whereas the lack of a byre at Hofstaðir, could be taken to indicate that cattle are not being nurtured at the site.

Related to this new discovery in the faunal material at Hofstaðir, is the realisation that a relatively broad hinterland would also be required to supply the turf for the walls of the large *skáli*, the bog iron for the extensive local working of iron, and scrubby woodland for the charcoal required in processing the iron for replacement items and repairs to equipment etc. Other resources from the hinterland included trout from the Laxá River, one of the best in Iceland, as well as strong coastal connections noted in the faunal material from the primary phase (Lucas, 2009, 395). Also grazing lands perhaps for dairying (and related shieling activity) and the less obvious – but integral – resource of the human population in the area which would have been required to service the requirements of the farm at Hofstaðir. An understanding of the nature of the contemporary social network in Iceland has been very much focussed on the potential number of slaves within the population, brought in from the British Isles or elsewhere, but Vésteinsson suggests that the relationship may have been more akin to that of a serf than a slave (*op cit*, pp. 503–505). Whatever the nature of this relationship between the main farmer (or chieftain?) and his workers or even co-workers, the resources of the land can be tracked in the archaeological record from the site at Hofstaðir which has seen detailed multi-disciplinary methodologies brought to fruition (Lucas, 2009).

The proximity of wealthy pagan Viking graves could shed light on the disposable wealth of the local population, and obviously of those involved in the burying: material wealth in death may be a mirror of wealth in life, and the inclusion of horses commonly within the graves of Iceland (albeit in several cases older beasts, pers comm Rúnar Leifsson) displays a close affinity with the working of the land through life and into death. The seminal study of the Icelandic pagan graves, undertaken by Kristján Eldjárn and updated by Adolf Friðriksson (2000) revealed over 300 graves across the country. In more recent years there have been notable new finds to add to this (e.g. Litlu-Núpar and Ingiríðarstaðir, pers comm Adolf Friðriksson and Guðrún Alda Gísladóttir). It is interesting to note however, that although there are a number of graves from the general vicinity of the Hofstaðir site, there is no notable concentration close to the site itself (see Lucas, 2009, Fig. 8.18, 403). Further south, however in the vicinity of Lake Mývatn and nearer to Sveigakot and Hrísheimar, one of the richest of all pagan graves from Iceland was recovered at Baldursheimur (Eldjárn & Friðriksson, 2000, pp. 200–203).

THE ARTEFACTUAL ASSEMBLAGE FROM HOFSTAÐIR

That the settlement at Hofstaðir is of a special status cannot be denied. The discussion above demonstrates this on several levels (see also Lucas and McGovern this volume). The overall assemblage from Hofstaðir, numbering in the region of 1200 individual items, however, is confined to the standard range of artefact types from a typical Viking Age settlement, albeit biased towards recovery from midden deposits which had in most cases been cleared from the floor areas.

The floor deposits, zones of active wear and attrition, are essentially lacking within the main *skáli* (Area AB) and within the small annexed hall (Area D). A large proportion of the available artefactual material was redeposited at various stages in the pit-house (Area G), most particularly in the primary phases of the site's use.[1] However, within the artefacts studied from the site, it is clear that in the first stages of the settlement, an imported tool kit was in use and this was supplemented by local resources where possible almost from the very beginning. This was in turn followed by the careful curation of both imports and hard-won local commodities, with the repair and re-modelling of various items as required. This was still a settlement which required to be virtually self-sufficient, and in this it was hardly different from any other site. The difference lay mainly in which resources it could call on, but not necessarily in the quantity of those resources.

THE PRIMARY TOOL KIT

It is clear that in the primary phase, there are items which are part of the initial package of imports (UC *Primary Tool Kit*), presumably arriving with the settlers and soon afterwards, while contacts with the homeland were still actively taking place. Through usage and the passage of time, these items were used up and discarded or replaced by items made from locally available materials, presumably as regular contact with Scandinavia was less frequent.

The primary tool kit of imports to Iceland is well-represented in this assemblage, mostly from Phase I and II (with a few items being recovered from Bruun's later backfilling of his trench which disturbed primary layers in the *skáli*). Amongst the more culturally and chronologically sensitive pieces, are personal items such as beads in both amber (Hreiðarsdóttir, 2009a, e.g. 98–123 and possible amulet 98–122 from Area G) as well as glass (Hreiðarsdóttir, 2009b, e.g. 01–045 and 98–226) and antler combs (such as the single-sided example 00–141 and the comb case segment 98–227). Household items such as steatite bowls are represented in this assemblage by a single steatite sherd from Brunn's backfill (01–061) and spindle whorls, three were newly made in steatite and finely worked (e.g. 99–264 and 99–263) and others were made from re-used vessel sherds (such as 01–002 Fig. 4) and may belong to the period when settlement had been established for some time. Norwegian whetstones, identified by Alsvik as being of two types of schist (a light grey fine-grained muscovite quartz schist of Eidsborg type and a darker grey very fine-grained muscovite quartz schist) with probable origins in S Norway in the Nappe area (Alsvik & Batey, 2009, pp. 293–296) and which are used until they

1 The designation of excavation areas on the site is illustrated in Lucas, 2009, Fig. 1.14, 16. (See Fig. 2).

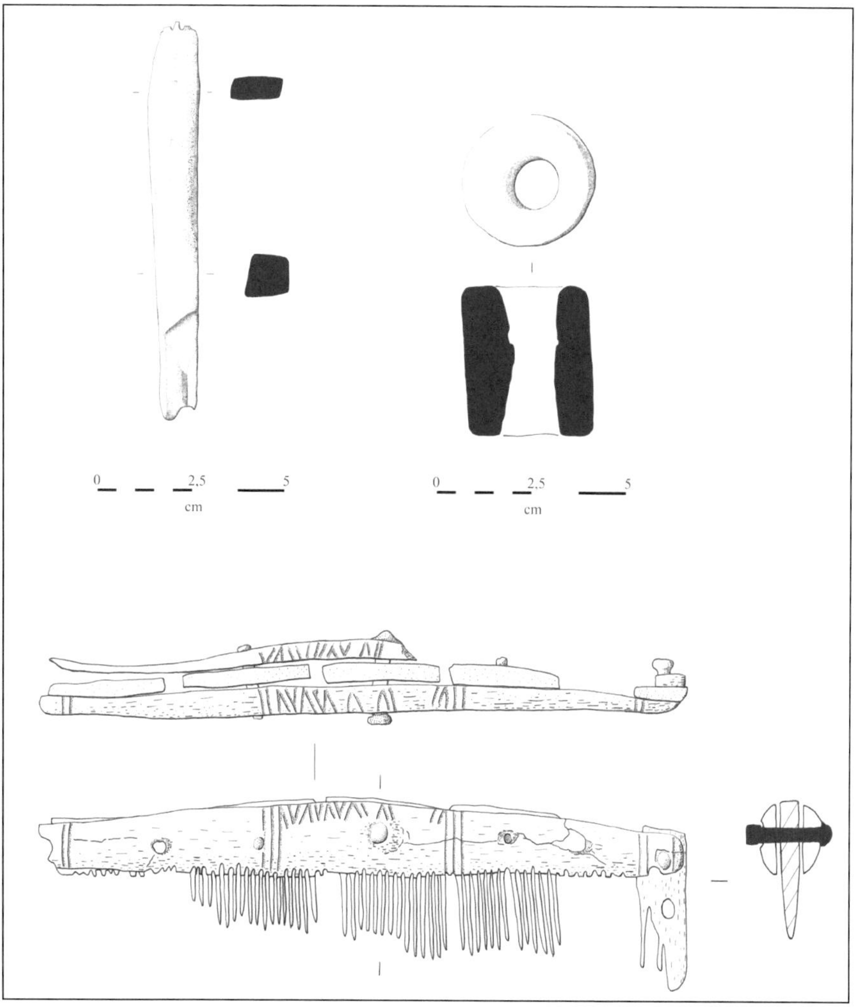

Fig. 3. Elements of the Primary tool kit: whetstone SF 98–119, grinding stone SF 00–014 and antler comb SF 00–141 (illustrations by Stefán Ólafsson).

become too worn in many cases (Fig. 3). These cannot readily be replaced like for like within Icelandic resources, and there is only one potential Icelandic native whetstone in the assemblage (92–004, which is unfortunately from an unstratified context). The distinctive rotary grind stone (00–114) which is so closely paralleled at York in the Viking Age was recovered from Phase VII, Bruun's backfill but is likely to be part of this initial package at the site (Fig. 3). The 12 flint fragments which served as strike-a-lights are also likely to have arrived from Scandinavia to Iceland in this first phase of activity (e.g. 01–293 and 02–127). Although relatively small in number, iron tools such as punches (e.g. 00–149), chisels (e.g. 01–024), rasps or files (e.g. 01–076), and awls (e.g. 98–050) are all represented in early phases from the site and are presumed to be primary imports. Such finds are commonly under-represented in Viking Age domestic assemblages, but every farmstead must have been undertaking minor repair works, if not to buildings, then to equipment. Elsewhere amongst the metalwork, highlights of the assemblage include three silver finds, amongst which is a pendant (01–008, from Phase I–II Area AB) and some silver wire from the same area and phase (02–061) as well as a silver alloy coin blank (97–012) from Phase II, Area G. All of which would seem likely to have been brought to Iceland at the beginning of the settlement phase at Hofstaðir.

THE SECOND STAGE: MODIFICATION AND LOCAL SUPPLY

This category of material covers two specific activities which could have been taking place at the same time. The few items which have been made from reworked broken steatite vessel sherds can be included, but also the distinctive import from Britain of a ring headed pin (01–181) whose shaft has been filed down and remodelled after breakage, potentially after its arrival in Iceland

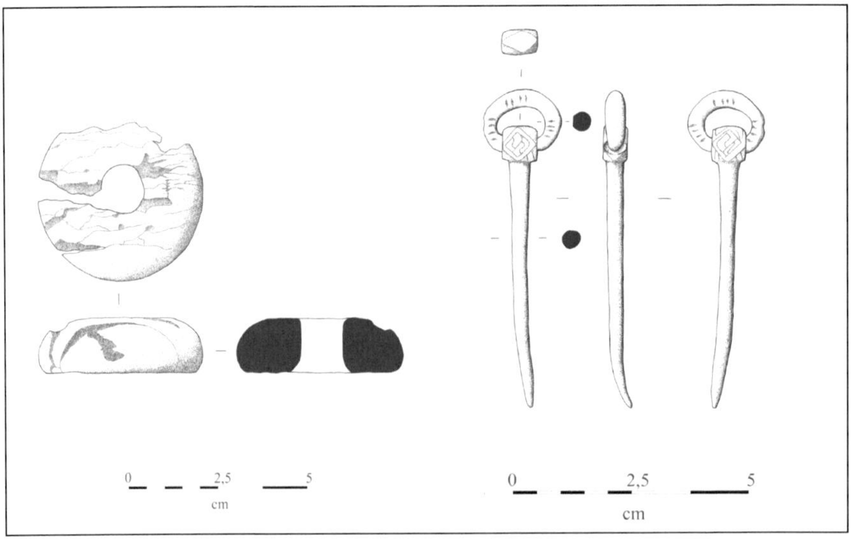

Fig. 4. Import objects, subsequently modified: spindle whorl of re-worked steatite vessel sherd, SF 01–002 and ringed pin SF 01–181 (illustrations by Stefán Ólafsson).

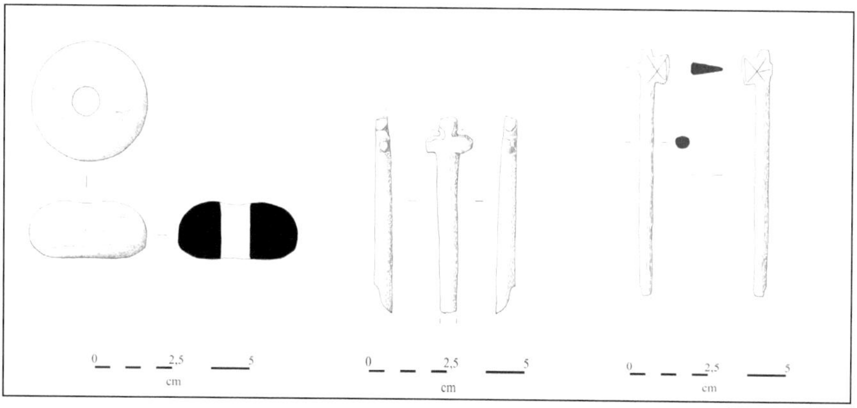

Fig. 5. The working of local materials: red sandstone spindle whorl SF 95–001, bone pins SF 98–127 and SF 99–278 (illustrations by Stefán Ólafsson).

(Fig. 4). The major part of this group however is made up of items made from materials available in Iceland and some of these are also from the early phases. Amongst these, the casual whittling of animal bones to create simple pins (e.g. 98–127 of Phase II and 99–278 of Phase III) may well have provided a welcome reminder of homeland activities (Fig. 5). Basaltic pebbles made good expedient loomweights (such as 00–116 and 00–131 from the primary phase of Area G) but further afield in the stone record, the earliest record of the exploitation of Icelandic Spar (97–027) is noted at Hofstaðir. Originating from the East of Iceland, and only known from two sources there, this stone with its double refraction attribute was used in the optical industry from the 19–20th centuries, but its earliest known utilisation prior to the Hofstaðir find was in the 17th century (Batey & Hauptfleisch, 2009, 302). In addition to the Icelandic Spar, Jasper was also brought to the site, the nearest source being between Bárðardalur and Eyjafjörður to the west (e.g. 98–117 and 02–130). The utilisation of local stone for the production of spindle whorls would have been an efficient expedient, and the local red sandstone was readily available (e.g. 95–001, Phase I–II; Fig. 5) as was the tuff (e.g. 98–115, Phase III). This exploitation may well have come into force shortly after the arrival of settlers.

Within the metal assemblage, the replacement and reworking of iron for knives etc and the repair of copper alloy vessels, some of which may have been early arrivals, enabled a longer life span for both knives and cooking pots. This extended the biography of the artefacts beyond the regular timeframe and ensured the careful curation of the artefacts wherever possible within the new and vibrant colony of Iceland. This is explicable in terms of self-sufficiency rather than a wider general supply source. Iron finds dominate the assemblage, with nails scattered across phases, some likely to be structural and re-deposited in G, bolts and knives, horse gear of various forms and most particularly tools. The maintenance and making of such tools, is reflected in the metallurgical evidence at Hofstaðir. Detailed examination of the metallurgical debris by McDonnell and Maclean (2009) identified slags and residues, mainly ferrous in origin (both smithing and smelting, with hearth linings and bases), although there are signs of non ferrous materials being worked, including the presence of a small number of crucibles (McDonnell & Maclean, 2009). Of the total assemblage nearly two thirds by weight is smithing slag. Chemical analysis suggests the smelters were maximising the amount of iron to be extracted from the ores, and McDonnell interprets this as an adaptation to the limitations of the immediate landscape and its resources, which would have included charcoal production as noted by Church et al. (2006) in the Mývatn area. There is minor iron smelting activity in Phase 1 in Area G, but more significant quantities of evidence in Phase II, with the building of a new smithy and evidence of bloom refining in this phase, and the making of objects at a workshop on site. The production of iron bars may be significant in relation to observations by Kevin Smith, in relation to evidence from the site at Háls, in Western Iceland that spatulate bars have close similarities with Viking Age currency bars (Smith, 2005, Fig. 11.6, 205). The similarities in both date and range of evidence at the Háls site is important, including as it does furnaces and low furnace stacks which differ from those identified by Martens in Norway where there are clay resources to allow such construction (Martens, 1987): the paucity of readily available Icelandic clay resources is an issue throughout the assemblage. Amongst the limited copper alloy assemblage are few identifiable items, such as pins, keys, sheet metal and a small quantity of non-ferrous metalworking indicated in the industrial assemblage which might simply be for the patching of vessels.

This is an image of enforced and perhaps inevitable self-sufficiency, extending to the textile evidence and mirrored eloquently within the faunal assemblage from the site. The potential for Hofstaðir to be seen as a site of special significance, a site of a substantial and powerful farm considered to be a centre of ritual and high status, sadly cannot readily to be supported by this artefact assemblage. A broader issue within Iceland might relate to how one can define higher status within the archaeological record of this period. There has been considerable discussion about the identification of Central Places within Iceland (e.g. Vésteinsson et al., 2004) and it would certainly seem that this site falls within that category. However, such a site may also have had a regular way of life as a major farm, gaining special status as much by its topographical location as by its size and wealth. In artefactual terms this may not be distinguishable from any regular site. Defining personal status is a problematic area of discussion, perhaps distinguishable through continued contact with the homelands, whereby the continued supply of resources needed in the new settlement was effectively channelled through a specific site or group of people: this would empower them both financially and politically. Although in contrast to this, the independence from imported goods might also indicate a status in the new lands where the local resources have been brought together from a wide hinterland dominated by the new settlement. The picture at Hofstaðir is clearly one of a short-lived contact with the homelands following settlement. The artefactual material is of interest and of significance because it has a good contextual record, but it is neither an unusually large assemblage in size or extensive in scope nor indeed is it packed with riches from the homelands: the site's status is better represented in its landscape setting and in the richness of its natural resource base.

ACKNOWLEDGEMENTS

The work which forms the basis of this brief discussion has been undertaken by several individuals and I am particularly grateful to the following: Helge Alsvik, Gerry McDonnell, Amanda Forster, Ramona Harrison, Elín Hreiðarsdóttir, Stefán Ólafsson (for finds illustration). Detailed discussions with, and encouragement from, Orri Vésteinsson, Adolf Friðriksson, Gavin Lucas, Ian Simpson, Tom McGovern and Guðrún Alda Gísladóttir have made the pleasure of working with colleagues in Iceland all the greater, and for that I am most grateful.

BIBLIOGRAPHY

Askvik, H. & Batey, C. E. (2009). The Whetstones: Petrography and Provenance. In G. Lucas (2009), pp. 293–296.

Batey, C. E. (2009). Chapter 5. The Artefactual Material. In G. Lucas (2009), pp. 253–321.

Batey, C. E. & Hauptfleisch, U. (2009). Miscellaneous Stone. In G. Lucas (2009), pp. 301–307.

Christensen, T. (1993). Lejre Beyond the Legend – The Archaeological Evidence. *Journal of Danish Archaeology* 10, pp. 163–185.

Church, M. J., Vésteinsson, O., Einarsson Á. & McGovern, T. H. (2006). Charcoal production pits at Höskuldsstaðir, Mývatnsveit. Unpublished report for the National Museum of Iceland.

Crawford, B. E. & Smith, B. Ballin (1999). *The Biggings, Papa Stour, Shetland: the history and archaeology of a royal Norwegian farm*. Society of Antiquaries of Scotland Monograph Series Number 15. Edinburgh.

Eldjárn, K. & Friðriksson, A. (2000). *Kuml og haugfé úr heiðnum sið á Íslandi.* Reykjavík: Mál og menning.

Forster, A. K. (2009). Soapstone. In G. Lucas (2009), pp. 297–301.

Hedlund, G. (1993). Södra kungsgårdsplatån utgrävningen 1992. In *Arkeologi och miljögeologi i Gamla Uppsala. Studier och rapporter 1.* W. Duczko (ed.). Occasional Papers in Archaeology 7. Uppsala.

Holand, I. (2003). Glass Vessels. In G. S. Munch, O. S. Johansen and E. Roesdahl (Eds.) (2003), pp. 211–227.

Hreiðarsdóttir, E. (2009a). Amber and Stone Beads. In G. Lucas (2009), p. 307.

Hreiðarsdóttir, E. (2009b). Glass Beads. In G. Lucas (2009), pp. 309–312.

Lucas, G. (2009). *Hofstaðir. Excavations of a Viking Age Feasting Hall in North-Eastern Iceland.* Institute of Archaeology Monograph Series 1. Reykjavík.

Martens, I. (1987). Iron Extraction, Settlement and Trade in the Viking and Early Medieval Ages in South Norway. In J. E. Knirk (ed.) *Proceedings of the Tenth Viking Congress Larkollen, Norway 1985.* Universitetets Oldsaksamlings Skrifter Ny Rekke Nr 9. Oslo, pp. 69–80.

McDonnell, G. & P., Maclean (2009). The Metalworking Slags and Residues. In G. Lucas (2009), pp. 271–289.

McGovern, T. H. (2009). Chapter 4, The Archaeofauna. In G. Lucas (2009), pp. 168–252.

Munch, G. S. (2003). Jet, amber, bronze, silver and gold artefacts. In Munch et al. (Eds.) (2003), pp. 241–263.

Munch, G. S., Johansen, O. S. & Roesdahl, E. (Eds.) (2003). *Borg in Lofoten. A chieftain's farm in North Norway.* Trondheim: Tapir Academic Press.

Näsman, U. & Roesdahl, E. (2003). Scandinavian and European perspectives – Borg I:1. In G. S. Munch et al. (Eds.) (2003), pp. 283–299.

Smith, K. (2005). Ore, Fire, Hammer, Sickle: Iron production in Viking Age and Early Medieval Iceland. In R. Bork (Ed.), *De Re Metallica: The Uses of Metal into the Middle Ages,* AVISTA Studies in the History of Medieval Technology, Science and Art, Vol 4 Aldershot, pp. 183–206.

Vésteinsson, O. (2010). Ethnicity and class in settlement-period Iceland. In J. Sheehan and D. Ó. Corráin (Eds.) *The Viking Age: Ireland and the West* (Proceedings of the Fifteenth Viking Congress). Dublin, pp. 494–510.

Vésteinsson, O., Einarsson, Á. & Sigurgeirsson, M. A. (2004). A New Assembly Site in Skuldaþingsey, NE-Iceland. In *Current Issues in Nordic Archaeology. Proceedings of the 21st Conference of Nordic Archaeologists 6–9 September 2001 Akureyri, Iceland.* Ed. G. Guðmundsson, Society of Icelandic Archaeologists. Reykjavík, pp. 171–179.

The Biggins *Stofa*
A Colonial Feature of North Atlantic Society

BARBARA E. CRAWFORD

ABSTRACT

The wooden buildings known as *stofa* (pl. *stofur*) were introduced in the North Atlantic in the centuries after they were first built in Norway in the late 10th century and became a standard feature of urban housing in the 11th and 12th centuries. The historical and archaeological record for such log-timbered houses in Shetland, Faeroe and Iceland is examined, with particular emphasis on the site at the Biggins, Papa Stour, Shetland. The existence of a timber *stofa* is documented here at the very end of the 13th century and the author's own programme of excavations discovered the remains of a wooden building of the same century. Examples of such houses of status are known in Faeroe, where the bishops' *stofa* at Kirkjubøur is still standing, and in Iceland where the episcopal *stofa* at the northern see of Hólar is recorded in the early 14th century. The value of such timber buildings in Norse Atlantic societies and the significance of the status which they conveyed is discussed.

Keywords: Archaeology, medieval *stofa,* Papa Stour, Shetland, social status.

Study of the 1299 document,[1] Shetland's earliest document, led to a long-running research project which has focussed on a type of log-timbered building known as *stofa* (pl. *stofur*) in Old Norse. This project has been both historical and archaeological, using the documented evidence of a *stofa* on the island of Papa Stour in Shetland (in the 1299 document) to search for the site of such a building.[2] The likely location of the recorded *stofa* was tracked down through place-name analysis and settlement topography, and excavation of the site resulted in the discovery of what had been a timber building with the remarkable survival of pieces of a planked wooden floor.[3] In the past two years a successful partial restoration of the log-timbered house on the site of the Biggins

1 *Testimony of the lawthingmen of Shetland recording the allegations made by Ragnhild Simunsdatter against Thorvald Thoresson*, and with a statement about the land prices and rental rates on the island of Papa Stour (AM 100,3). See refs. in footnote 7.

2 The 1299 document and the Duke's house on Papay was first discussed in Crawford 1971, 357; the preliminary results of excavation are in Crawford, 1985, 128–58.

3 Full details can be found in the excavation report by Crawford and Ballin Smith, 1999, 77–81, 216–8.

stofa has been achieved through the initiative and financial support of NHU (Norsk Handverksutvikling), and this has led the excavators to think more widely about the place of such wooden buildings in the Norse societies which grew out of the Viking settlement of the Atlantic islands (Crawford & Ballin Smith, 2008; Crawford, 2009). This particular type of building, constructed out of notched logs imported into the islands, was an alien element among the stone-built (and turf-built) houses of Orkney and Shetland, Faeroe and Iceland, which was constructed by the ruling political and ecclesiastical elite. Such *stofur* were imported and built by the powerful administrators and bishops, and were very visible symbols of status.

The building of notched-log *stofur* seems to have developed in forested districts of central and eastern Europe, and spread north to Scandinavia.[4] The earliest examples from Norway have been excavated in Trondheim, dating from the late tenth century (Christophersen & Nordeide, 1994, 274–77). There have also been excavations of *stofa* buildings at urban Gamlebyen, Oslo, dating to the eleventh and twelfth centuries, where a standard type of urban *stofa* develops *c.*1100; a two-roomed house with an almost square main room and an ante-room (*forstue*) through which the building was entered. On average the whole measured 7.3 m x 5.3 m. (Fett, 1989, 29; Schia, 1993, 300). The majority of these houses were 'lafted'.[5] Dwelling-houses of this kind, timber built, without central posts, were known by the ON word *stofa*, which is thought to have meant in origin an insulated warm building (Stoklund, 1984, 101). The English word 'stove' has the same origin, but has of course become identified with the means of warming such a room. The way in which the Norwegian *stofa* was heated varied from central hearths to wall-hearths to corner fire-places, but the latter became the norm for the urban *stofur* in Gamlebyen, where the majority of the houses were furnished with corner stone-built hearths and wooden floors. In rural areas the central hearth (*åre*) continued longer and led to the term *roykstova* becoming the usual word for this main building in the community, deriving from the smoke haze which permeated the room from the open hearth in the centre of the floor (Lærum & Brekke, 1990, 58–66).

This building development meant that in many areas of Norway there was a move away from the long, rectangular houses (*skáli*) with parallel rows of load-bearing posts down the middle of the living space, which had been a feature of late Iron Age/Viking Age culture. Once the notched-log method of construction was introduced this did away with the internal rows of posts, which supported the roof timbers, and led to narrower buildings, where the roof rested

4 Stoklund, 1984, 101; 1993, 211; 1996, 111, quoting Konrad Bedel and Joachim Hägel on the appearance of the *Stube* in central Europe in the early Middle Ages, and the origin of the term.

5 The anglicised form of the Norwegian *å lafte* 'to notch logs together at the corner' as used in Crawford, 1996, 139 and Crawford & Ballin Smith, 1999, 61.

on the log walls. This had other consequences, for the wide benches down the long walls were replaced by narrow benches *(moldbenker)* made of earth and stones but covered by wooden seating and fronting. This fixed feature of *stofa* buildings is usually recognisable under excavation, especially as the wooden flooring stops short of the timber walls, where there is a gap of about 40 cms. Wooden flooring is a normal feature of a *stofa* in urban locations, but in the countryside the floor was usually of beaten earth with some stone paving in areas where there was much wear.

The new building style and timber structure were very different from the single long-house of the earlier age where all domestic activities were carried out under one roof. It led to the proliferation of different houses on the Norwegian farm, each with a different function (KLNM XVII, 242, sub *stove*), kitchen *(eldhus),* sleeping-hall *(skáli),* guest-house *(gjeste-hus),* storehouse *(búr)* and the living-room *(stofa).* The latter was the main dwelling, especially in the winter, where the family gathered in the evenings. However, the pattern was not absolutely uniform throughout the country, for geographical conditions varied widely, and in the western coastal districts the long-house survived in some shape or form, with the log-built *stofa* added on at one end, or located in the middle and joined to the other rooms under the same roof .[6]

It would not be surprising if the classic log-timbered *stofa* appeared in the Norwegian skattlands (those areas brought under Norwegian royal authority in the twelfth and thirteenth centuries) in a very different guise, considering the very different environment in the islands where the Vikings established their settlements. Remarkably, however, we do find evidence that log-timbered *stofur* were imported, in kit form and re-erected. First of all we will examine the evidence for a *stofa* which is known to have existed on the island of Papa Stour, at the very end of the thirteenth century.

THE *STOFA* IN PAPA STOUR

Historical evidence

The evidence is in the record of an altercation which took place on the island at Easter time, 1299, between Thorvald Thoresson and a woman on the island, Ragnhild Simunsdatter.[7] Thorvald was the sysselman *(sysselmaðr)*, or bailiff, of Duke *(hertogi)* Hakon Magnusson, who succeeded to the Norwegian throne

6 Lærum & Brekke, 1990, ch. 6 'Rekketun og langhustradisionar. Byggeskikken på strilelandet'; full discussion in Myhre, 1982, 210–11, where all the different theories about house-development are brought together; Myhre, 1993, 293.

7 *Dip. Norv.*1, no. 89; *Orkney-Shetland Recs*, vii, 38 (with English translation); *Orkney Recs.* xxviii (with English translation); Hødnebø, 1960, no. 66 (with modern Norwegian translation); Ballantyne & Smith, 1999, no. 2 (English translation); Bibire, 2002, 9–11 (with English translation).

later in the year. Thorvald was accused by Ragnhild of cheating the duke, his master, and the imputation was that he had been embezzling taxes or rents. The document was drawn up by the lawthingmen of Shetland at the Lawthing later in the year, addressed to Duke Hakon specifically, in order to refute Ragnhild's accusations and setting out the standard rates for the assessment of rents and taxes. In describing the events which had taken place it is noted that the two had met in the *stofa* on the ducal farm on the island. This is a very early reference to such a building in a Norwegian source, and it is remarkable to have written evidence that one existed on such a peripheral island as Papa Stour, which lies off the west side of Shetland, and separated from the Mainland of Shetland by strong tidal currents making contact hazardous (Fig. 1).

However, Papa Stour's remote position today belies its former importance, for it was probably a centre of administration for Norwegian royal officials (Crawford & Ballin Smith, 1999, 29–31). This island had many advantages as a residence for the political authorities in a period of time when contacts by sea were the usual and preferred way of travelling. Papa Stour was above all a fertile island, especially in the context of most of Shetland, and its valuation was always remarkably high (Smith, 2002, 39–42). It had possibly been a possession of the earls of Orkney before Shetland was taken from the earls by King Sverre as a result of the involvement of Earl Harald Maddadson in the Eyjaskeggjar rising of 1193, after which it was taken into the royal estate. In 1299 Shetland was held by Duke Hakon Magnusson as part of his ducal appanage. The existence of a *stofa* on the ducal farm relates therefore to the status of the island as a royal possession, built to function as the meeting-place for occasions when officials were visiting the island, as indeed it was in 1299. Most probably it was constructed after Shetland had been taken under direct Norwegian control in 1195.

Archaeological evidence

Documentary evidence provided the historical information about such a building. Excavated evidence provided the material reality in this inter-disciplinary project, and a brief account of the excavations will be given to describe the discovery of a building which was of an undeniable *stofa* type (and which is likely to have been the site of the ducal *stofa* of 1299).[8] The documentary reference was the inspiration which led to the series of excavations carried out in six seasons between 1977 to 1990 at the Biggins. This has always been the centre of settlement on the island, lying at the head of the best land, and near the church. In the mid-nineteenth century there were 30 families living at the Biggins, but in the 1870s many of the buildings were torn down as the population declined. In their place one house was constructed, called 'da Gørl', and

[8] For the excavation report and description of the evidence see Crawford & Ballin Smith, 1999.

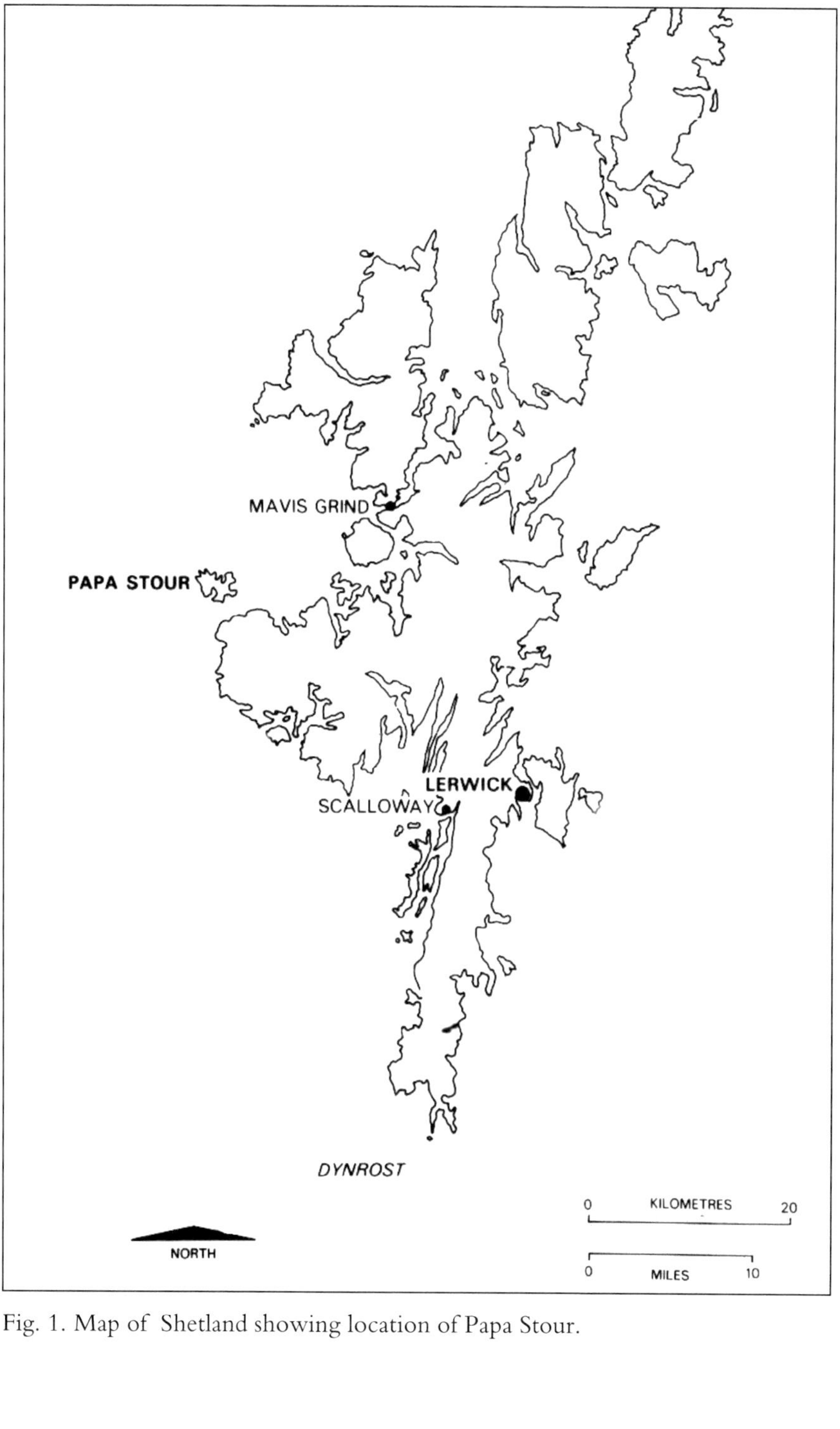

Fig. 1. Map of Shetland showing location of Papa Stour.

Fig. 2. Part of the excavated wooden floor at the Biggings, Papa Stour, showing the planking and joists.

it was under the location of this building (abandoned in the 1930s) that the remains of a medieval wooden *stofa* were uncovered.

Local place-names in the area indicated that the yard at the rear of the Biggins had been where older houses had stood, and this area was available for excavation as the older houses had been destroyed. However the destruction in itself and the intensive settlement over the centuries meant that the archaeological sequences in this area were difficult to interpret. Only at the side of the yard where the Gørl stood were earlier sequences undisturbed. The wooden *stofa* lay right under the Gørl which had been built using the remains of the stone sills and protective walls as its own foundation. The pressure it imposed had preserved the timber flooring and other organic material by creating an anaerobic layer (Fig. 2).

The *stofa* was only one phase in a long building history on that site, but it was the most exciting one because of the evidence it provided of the existence of the type of building mentioned in 1299. How did we recognise that it was a wooden *stofa* building? The parts of the wooden floor which survived

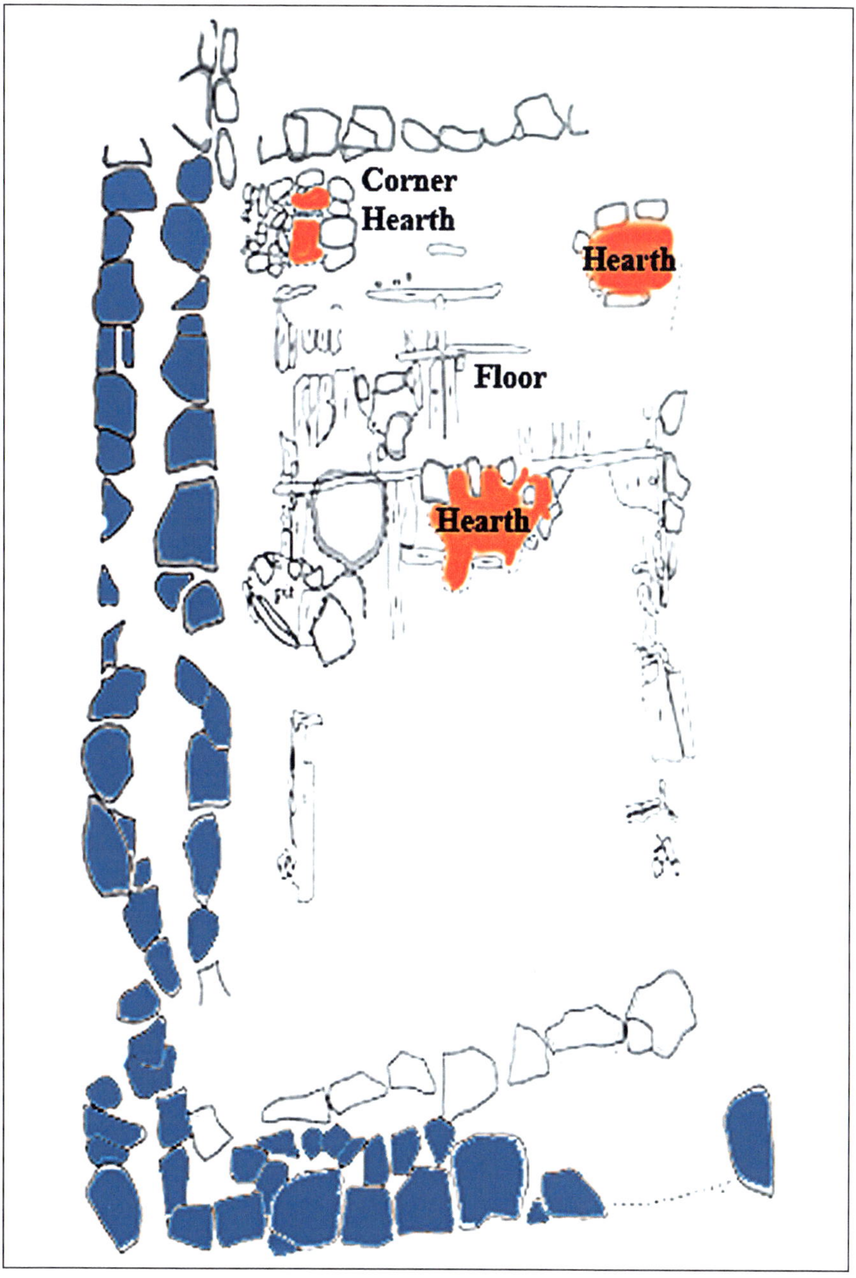

Fig. 3. Plan of the surviving planked floor of the excavated 'stofa' with the protective stone walls (*vernemurer*) (in blue) along the south-west side and north-east gable. Hearths shown in red.

revealed first of all that we were dealing with an unusual building. There were some well-preserved pieces of floor planking running lengthways (E-W) with underlying joists running across the building (N-S). The wood was pine with a carbon 14 date-range of *c.*1000−1214 (Crawford & Ballin Smith, 1999, Table 1, p.76).

The dimensions and internal features also indicated, indeed proved, that it was a building of *stofa*-type, *c.*7.7 m long by *c.*5.0 m wide, which accords with the dimensions of many of the urban *stofa* houses at Gamlebyen, Oslo and Bryggen, Bergen. Moreover, a narrow seating bench (*moldbenk*), which is a required feature of *stofa* buildings, was recognised along the south wall. Fragments of the wooden front of the bench survived, as did the wooden pegs which had held the front of the bench in place and were found rammed down into the subsoil. A series of remarkably well-preserved hearths were also uncovered, which included a paved central *åre*, and a wall hearth, which were succeeded by a classic corner hearth (*hjørneildsted*).[9] The corner hearth lay in the south-west corner of the room, next to the entrance, which was in the centre of the west gable, just as with the lay-out of the Gamlebyen houses (Fig. 3).

One striking and well-preserved feature was dominant throughout the excavation; a stone-built wall (1.10 m–1.40 m wide) which ran the length of the south-west side but which was probably not connected to the wooden house. This survived 2–3 courses high and a similar wall had evidently existed along the N-E gable of which only the foundation stones survived in situ.[10] Their function was apparently to protect the timbers, as is known in western Norway, where protective stone walls (*vernemurer*) are constructed to shelter wooden structures from the effects of the weather in exposed maritime conditions. Such walls are also a feature of the Faeroese wooden houses, and have been excavated around a series of wooden churches at Sandur in Sandoy.[11]

A small annex had been built against the west gable wall, probably stave-built, because the sill-stones for the upright timbers to rest on were still in situ. It measured 1.30 m x 1.50 m and enclosed a pit which was filled with large stones and capped with gravel, evidently functioning as a 'sump' or soakaway. It has therefore been interpreted as a privy or latrine, conveniently placed adjacent to the main entrance into the *stofa,* and a very remarkable survival in a medieval rural context. West of the *stofa* and privy two more buildings from this period were found, although so badly destroyed that it was difficult to be certain of their function, or how they were constructed. They have

9 Under the wooden floor in phase 2 there was a large fire-pit, paved and sealed with clay, and lined with large stones.

10 This was not fully recognised in the excavation report (Crawford & Ballin Smith, 1999), but confirmed when the reconstruction project got underway in 2007.

11 Stoklund, 1996, Fig. 58 after Krogh, 1975.

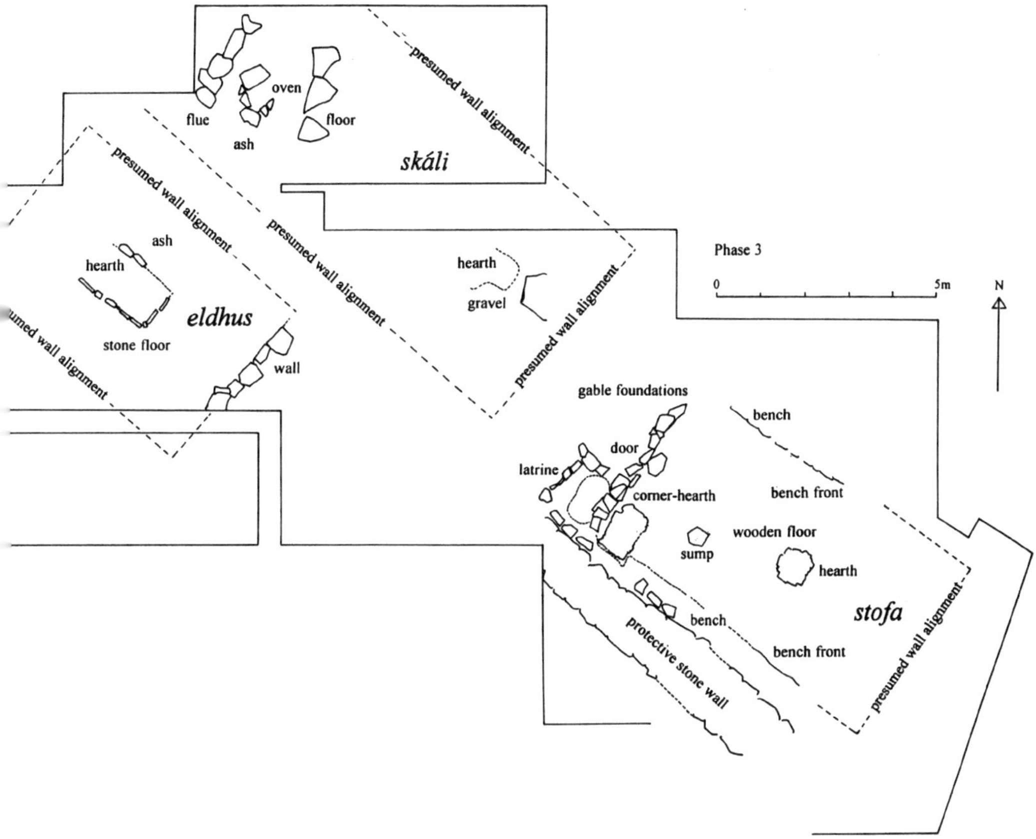

Fig. 4. Overall plan of the site at the Biggins showing the relationship of *stofa*, *skáli* and *eldhus* (Crawford & Ballin Smith, 1999, illus. 122).

been interpreted as *skáli* (hall) and *eldhus* (cook-house); along with a *stofa* these three buildings make up the standard components of medieval Norwegian and Icelandic farms.[12] The *skáli* ran on the same alignment as the *stofa* (NW-SE) and was at least 10 m in length, and *c*.5 m wide. The *eldhus* lay alongside the *skáli* and was much smaller and squarer (4 x 6 m) with a large central hearth (2 x 1 m). There were hearths also in the *skáli* and an oven with a flue, so these

12 From documentary sources the *stofa, eldhus,* and *búr* (= 'store-room') are listed, but in Iceland the term *skáli* or *eldaskáli* appears to be retained (Myhre, 1982, 210). The term *skáli* was used for the third building at the Biggins because of its length. It seems likely that this building was still in use when the *stofa* was constructed.

two buildings were where the main cooking activities and domestic work were carried out (Fig. 4).

Despite the excavating difficulties and devastation caused by the continuous habitation at the Biggins, the medieval settlement evidence which was uncovered proved to be exceptionally interesting and important for our knowledge of the Norwegian period in Shetland's history. It fully justified the impetus of attempting to follow up the historical evidence about a *stofa* which was contained in the 1299 document. Of course many questions remain. Was this the actual *stofa* referred to in that document? I have argued tentatively that the likelihood is high, but it can never be conclusively proven that it was (Crawford, 2001, 243). Another question-mark lies over the actual construction of the *stofa,* for it is exceedingly difficult to be certain of the type of wooden superstructure when nothing has survived of the wall timbers. There is no doubt that this was a *stofa* building from its dimensions and lay-out, but does its designation as a *stofa* in 1299 mean that it would have been constructed of notched-logs, or might it have been constructed in some other way? There were alternative ways of fitting timber houses together, and as Bjarne Stoklund explains, from his experience of Faeroese houses, 'the log-timbered *stofa* also seems to have had a further influence by being imitated in other techniques', such as a frame or box construction (Stoklund, 1984, 104). So the walls could be built of horizontal boards, or logs, set in grooves in both sides of upright corner posts ('bole' construction), or made of vertical boards set in grooves in sills above and below ('stave' construction).[13] Both these types were originally built with posts dug into the earth, but from the Middle Ages the houses were built of horizontal logs, either 'lafted' or with corner posts, neither method of which would leave any post-holes. Therefore it is very difficult to know on excavating a wooden house which method had been used, as no traces of the construction are visible in the underlying ground.[14] The best way of coming to a conclusion about this is to look to other known *stofa* buildings in the skattlands for comparative material.

'STOFA' BUILDINGS IN THE NORTH ATLANTIC ISLANDS

In Faeroe some 'lafted' timber buildings have survived, remarkably, up to the present day. This gives visible proof that large notched logs were imported from Norway to the remote Atlantic islands, and 'lafted' *stofur* were able to

13 This kind of construction must be the principle behind the later Shetland house term 'Stokk-stove', Smith, 1980; Stoklund, 2002, 149.

14 The difficulty of coming to a definite conclusion on which method of timber construction was used on the Biggins *stofa* is discussed in the excavation report. Crawford & Ballin Smith, 1999, 59–60; 225–27, 243.

survive the adverse weather conditions for centuries. The most famous is the Roykstovan at Kirkjubøur, but there were others. J. Christian Svabo (who wrote a report from his travels in Faeroe in the 1780s), says that of the houses built in the Norse way, called 'stokkastovur', *hvis Vægge bestaae of Bjelker, vandret lagde hinanden (Stokkastova) findes nu kan faae Exempler i Færoe, endskjønt dei i ældre Tider have været almindeligere'*(whose walls consist of beams, laid horizontally on each other, only a few examples can now be found in Faeroe, although in former times they were much commoner').[15] The complex of buildings at Kirkjubøur is changed, due to damage caused by landslips, and the present Roykstovan has been moved and placed on a stone cellar undercroft. It may be that this was the original site of the Bishop's palace, a two-storeyed stone building, and after the destruction of the upper storey lafted log-houses were imported and placed onto the lower storey (Dahl, 1968, 192). This is likely to have happened before the mid fourteenth century and the disruption caused by the Black Death, and tradition says that these houses were brought from Norway *c.*1300 after a catastrophic fire (Christie, 2002, 136). There are the remains of two 'lafted' buildings, the Roykstovan and Stokkastovan, the former with a square ground plan 7 m x 7 m. The latter now measures 8 m x 4 m, but excavation in 1953–4 exposed the foundations of the main room of this large hall which had been 8 m x 11 m (with the surviving southern part forming the *forstue* of an original three-roomed *stofa* building) (Ibid.139 and Fig. 8.10; Berg, 1995, 256–57). The excavated (and unpublished) remains of another wooden building lying parallel to the Roykstovan was apparently stave-built, and had a planked floor (Thorsteinsson, 1982, 155). This complex of wooden buildings at the episcopal residence is striking evidence of the status of the bishop in Faeroese society.

However, it is not the only evidence for wooden, log-timbered buildings in the Faeroese islands. There is a tradition that the stone foundations of 'Husfruens gård' at Húsavík in Sandoy once supported a wooden building. The existing 'Stokkestuen' at Tinganes in Tórshavn, the centre of government and trading operations, is not medieval, having replaced an older (and medieval?) 'blokkestuen' in the late 1600s (Stoklund, 1996, 67). Historical sources indicate that there were several wooden houses at Tinganes in the early 1600s, and also in the main part of the town in the 1700s. The continued use of imported wood for house-building in Faeroe is remarkable, and the concept of the 'roykstova' continued to be an important element in the domestic dwelling right up to modern times, although built of planks and conjoined with the 'glasstova' which had windows. Frequently these houses were surrounded by protective stone and turf walls (Stoklund, 1996, Fig. 63).

Further excavated evidence has discovered a stave-built house at Tjörnuvík

15 Quoted in Stoklund, 1996, 66–7.

dating from the medieval period, surrounded also by a large stone wall (Thorsteinsson, 1982, 155). It was 4.20 m wide although only 4.50 m of its length could be excavated, and it had been sub-divided into different rooms, all of which had planked floors. The upright planks of the walls rested on sill stones along all the walls, with corner staves dug into the earth and placed on stones. The main room had a corner hearth, with traces of stone-built benches along three sides, fronted with remains of horizontal planking, typical of the Norwegian *stofur*, and showing that such a 'high medieval' stave-built *stofa* was imported into the Faeroe islands, as well as the log-timbered 'lafted' variety.[16] It was no doubt a matter of wealth and status which dictated whether one or the other was chosen.

Iceland

In Iceland the excavated evidence of medieval houses is extensive, and the developmental changes very marked. Restricting our discussion to the *stofa* we have evidence that this made an appearance on ordinary farms as an extension to the *skáli*, and 'never built as a unit completely separate from other farmhouses' (Jóhannesson, 1974, 341). However, there is now an exception to this general picture, recently excavated at the episcopal see of Hólar, as we will see. The usual pattern was indeed, as can be seen at Stöng, to have the smaller, narrower *stofa* leading off from the *skáli* (or *eldaskáli* as it was known in Iceland). The site at Stöng is generally considered to have been abandoned after being covered with ash from a volcanic eruption in 1104.[17] The excellent preservation gives a completely indisputable picture of the standard fitments and plan of the *stofa*. Over 4 m in width and about 8 m in length internally which is the standard size, it had the standard sitting benches round the walls and a central hearth pit.[18] It was, however, lined internally with wainscot panelling, as can be seen from the sill stones along the walls behind the benches. The walls themselves were constructed of turf, and there is no possibility that log-timbering was used here.

Jóhannesson gives the clearest, and most plausible analysis of the origin and function of the *stofa* in Icelandic medieval society. It was, he says, probably a replacement of the earlier sunken bower (*dyngja*), where the women did their handiwork. 'Later it became the most important part of the farmhouse, serving as the main living quarters, where people would dine, receive visitors, celebrate festive occasions, and even sleep if circumstances so required'. Across

16 Presumably this house dates to *c.*1300, and certainly pre-1350.

17 This has however been disputed by V. Vilhjálmsson from the evidence of artefacts dating later than the early 12th cent. and carbon dates (Vilhjálmsson, 1991, 98).

18 This hearth pit is unusual in a *stofa* but is remarkably similar to the fire pit in the Biggins phase 2 house, which was interpreted as a slightly sunken *dyngja* (Crawford & Ballin Smith, 1999, 71–6).

the inner gable of the *stofa* was a dais (*pallr*), constructed of timber planking where the women worked, and on festive occasions this was the part of the room especially reserved for them. 'The high-seat was in the middle of the benches. It gradually became the most sumptuous of the rooms in the house' (Jóhannesson, 1974, 341).

If the word sumptuous is justifiably used then certainly this *stofa* development would only happen on the wealthier farms. The way in which it was developed as an extension of the main *eldaskáli* and built with the same materials as the rest of the farmhouse meant that it would not be too costly to construct in terms of materials, particularly wood. The wealthiest section of Icelandic society may, however, have had more ambitious aspirations where wood was concerned, which is evident regarding Snorri Sturlason's residence at Reykholt. Snorri was a very powerful chieftain, and after he was made a *lendr maðr* by King Hakon in Norway *c.*1220 he may well have wanted to flaunt his position with a prestigious building project. Evidence from Sturlunga Saga tells that in 1233 Snorri's steward went to Skagafjörður in northern Iceland for wood for a new *stofa* at Reykholt (Guðrún Harðardóttir, 2006, 49: *Sturlunga saga* 1988, 349). It seems very likely that a visit to Skagafjörður was for the purpose of going to the harbour at Kolkuós to collect wood imported from Norway. Would this have been 'lafted' timber for a notched-log *stofa*, or planking for a stave-built structure? Excavations at Reykholt have not revealed any evidence of this wooden building, although plenty of other interesting features (Guðrún Sveinbjarnardóttir, 2006). However, the visit to the north coast to collect wood for the new *stofa* is indication in itself that a prestigious new building was going to be constructed, in which high quality wood from Norway was an important component.[19]

Wooden stofur *at Hólar*

Just under a hundred years later, there is another historical reference to the importing of timber for a *stofa* at the northern bishopric of Hólar. Bishop Auðun the Red (1313–1322), a Norwegian, is said in Bishop Laurentius Saga to have imported timber from Norway for a *stofa* building at his episcopal seat (*Laurentius saga biskups*, 66). Known as *Auðunarstofa,* for many centuries it served as a residence for the bishops. Only in the early nineteenth century was it dismantled and the wood sold off – still usable after 500 years.[20] The Lögmannsannáll (E) under the years 1300–1315 says of Bishop Audun *hann let reisa fyrstr manna timbrstofu a Island*, ('he was the first man to cause a timber *stofa*

[19] Most likely a hall for formal occasions, called a *veislustofa,* which could be expected to have been stave-built, 'with a timber floor and at least a good timber lining', Guðrún Harðardóttir, 2006, 52.

[20] Information drawn from a diocesan leaflet on 'Auðun's House' (www.holar.is).

Fig. 5. *Auðunarstofa* at Hólar, the reconstructed *stofa* of Bishop Auðun, built as a joint Norwegian – Icelandic project, completed in 2006 (photo B.E.Crawford).

to be built in Iceland') (Storm, 1888, 265) and from that comment there can be little doubt that this was indeed a 'lafted' stofa building[21] (Fig. 5).

However, it may not have been the first wooden *stofa* built at Hólar. South of the cathedral, where the episcopal residence and domestic buildings were located, recent excavations have uncovered the traces of an earlier timber hall (Fig. 6). It measured 7.7 m by 4.5 m (internal measurements), and the main entrance was in the north gable which had been built of timber resting on a row of sill stones. The other wooden walls appear to have been supported on large pad stones (33–43 cms in diameter), five down each side, and this may indicate that the construction had consisted of upright planks slotted into the ground sill beam, which rested on the large pad stones. The wooden structure had been surrounded by turf protective walls (1.32–1.45 m wide) which survived best at the south-west corner. There were the remains of several hearths down the central axis of the earth floor, and the finds indicate that this

21 A magnificent replica of Bishop Audun's *stofa* was built at Hólar as a millennium project (Þorsteinn Gunnarsson, 2004). The same Norwegian craftsmen built the Biggins *stofa* partial reconstruction in 2007–8.

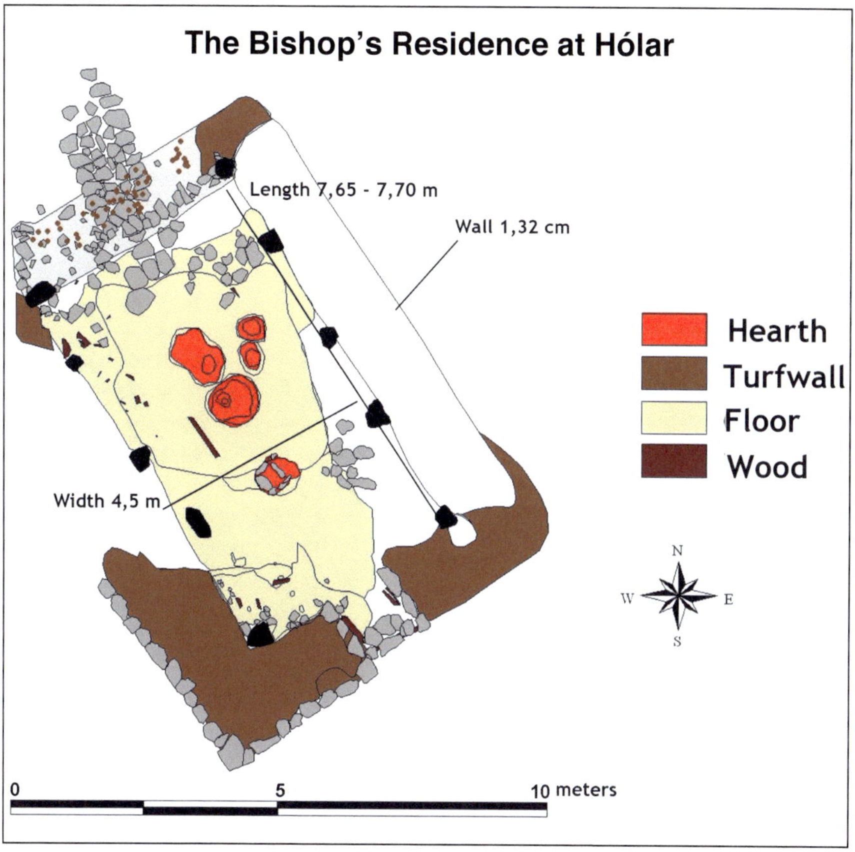

Fig. 6. Plan of House 10, *Biskupstofa,* at Hólar, dating to 12th-13th centuries, excavated in 2006 (Traustadóttir, 2009).

was a hall which had been used for feasting and public occasions (Ragnheiður Traustadóttir, 2009, 19–21). It is dated broadly to the twelfth-thirteenth centuries, and was therefore the predecessor of Bishop Audun's log-timbered *stofa*.

General Conclusions

The Biggins *stofa* which is recorded in 1299 can be seen from the evidence from the other 'skattlands' to be a symbol of Norwegian influence in a period when the kingdom was at its greatest extent. The known timber *stofur* in the skattlands were very certainly associated with the powerful ecclesiastical and secular leaders of Norse society. The Faeroese Røykstovan and Stokkastovan complex is the most dramatic survival, providing startling evidence for the

Fig. 7. Viking Congress delegates sitting on the wall benches in *Auðunarstofa* at Hólar during the post-Congress tour, August 2009.

status of the bishops of Faeroe. Perhaps this is because in these islands there was no resident secular ruler. The Hólar situation is rather similar with the documentary evidence of Bishop Audun's *stofa* and the excavated evidence of an older episcopal *veislustofa*. On the secular side we know that Snorri Sturlason imported wood for a *stofa* in the 1230s, which is the period of time when the Biggins *stofa* is likely to have been built for the use of royal officials who were ruling Shetland as part of the Norwegian administration.

The ambience of such a building therefore appears to have provided the rulers in these island societies with suitable accommodation of status which they needed and desired. Was this to do with the interior space which the *stofa* provided? As well, perhaps, as with the association with wooden buildings known to be used by the powerful in Norway?[22] It seems probable that the *stofa* design and form was appropriate for gatherings and formal occasions when those summoned to meetings could sit on the benches around the walls

22 The surviving *Lagmansstova* at Aga on Sørfjorden (Hardanger) (Berg, 1995, 174–5) provides a dramatic example of a log-timbered *stofa* built probably for Sigurd Brynjolfsson of Aga, Lawman of Gulating in the 1290s, and from its size (7.50 m x 7.50 m) very suitable for the official occasions over which Lawman Sigurd would have presided (Crawford, 2002, 169–72).

(Fig. 7), and those conducting affairs would preside from the *pallr* (dais) at the far end. The earlier hall (*skáli)* with two rows of internal roof-bearing posts was far less convenient for such arrangements. This is a possible motivation lying behind the importation of wooden *stofur* into the Atlantic islands and their construction by the bishops and administrators.[23]

The provision of a timber-lined room with more central space and seating around the walls – the *stofa* ideal – was attractive to the island populations and 'caught on' as a desirable component of the ordinary farm (those owned by the wealthier section of society). It became a feature of medieval housing throughout the 'skattlands'. In Iceland the concept was adapted to becoming a unit under the same roof as the older *eldaskáli*, as is evident from the excavated houses at Stöng and Gröf. The use of the term *stofa* clearly entered into the language, as it is a component of place-names in Faeroe, Orkney and Shetland (although hardly recorded in Iceland).[24] This presumably indicates a distinct, separate, timber building on a farm, one which gave its name to a new division or unit, or replaced an older name. Only further excavation will reveal whether these may have been 'lafted' timber buildings or stave-built ones. But, as with the excavations at the Biggins, that may not be simple to discern, even though the standardised *stofa* plan can be easily recognised.

Note: The excavations at Bessastaðir revealed interesting remains of a medieval wooden building that have been interpreted as belonging to a *stofa*. (Guðmundur Ólafsson, 2010, 105–109).

BIBLIOGRAPHY

Ballantyne, J. & Smith, B. (1999). *Shetland Documents 1195-1579*, Lerwick.

Berg, A. (1995). *Norske Tømmerhus frå Mellomalderen*, V, *Hus for Hus i A. Agder … Sør Trøndelag*. Riksantikvaren, Oslo.

Bibire, P. (2002). 'The 1299 Shetland document, AM 100,3. Transcription and Translation' in Crawford, (Ed.), 9–11. Also in *Collegium Medievale,* vol 15 (2002), 9–11.

Christie, H. (2002). 'The *stofa* in Nordic Building Tradition' in Crawford, (Ed.), 2002, 127–140. Also in *Collegium Medievale,* vol.15 (2002), 127–140.

23 In this respect the situation in Shetland which was no longer part of the earldom of Orkney was more akin to Faeroe and Iceland. Shetland's bishop, however, was not resident, being based in Orkney, so that the administrator (*sysselman)* was the leader of island society, perhaps in association with the archdeacon, who is named in 1299 as having been a member of a commission appointed to investigate the fiscal assessments in the island of Papa Stour (see refs. in n.7 above).

24 Info. from Svavar Sigmundsson.

Christophersen, A. & Nordeide, S. W. (1994). *Kaupangen ved Nidelven* Riksantikvarens Skrifter nr. 7. Trondheim.

Crawford, B. E. (1971). *The Earls of Orkney-Caithness and their Relationship with Norway and Scotland, 1158–1471.* St. Andrews Ph.D. thesis, unpublished.

Ibid. (1985). 'The Biggings, Papa Stour – A multi-disciplinary investigation', in B. Smith, (Ed.) *Shetland Archaeology,* Lerwick, 128–58.

Ibid. (1996). 'The Excavation of a Wooden Building at the Biggins, Papa Stour, Shetland' in D. Waugh, (Ed.), *Shetland's Northern Links. Language and History.* Lerwick, 136–56.

Ibid. (2001). 'The history and excavation of a royal Norwegian farm at the Biggings, Papa Stour, Shetland', *Det Norske Videnskaps-Akademi Årbok,* 1997, 231–44.

Ibid. (2002). 'Afterword', in Crawford, (Ed.), 2002, 167–73. Also in *Collegium Medievale,* 15, 167-73.

Ibid. (2009). 'The "stofa" Project at the Biggins, Papa Stour, Shetland' in *Living Crafts.* Maihaugen, 128–37.

Ibid. (Ed.) (2002). *Papa Stour and 1299. Commemorating the 700th anniversary of Shetland's first document.* Lerwick. Also in *Collegium Medievale,* vol.15 (2002).

Crawford, B. E. & Ballin Smith, B. (1999). *The Biggings. Papa Stour, Shetland. The History and Excavation of a Royal Norwegian Farm* (Society of Antiquaries of Scotland Monograph no. 15; published jointly with The Norwegian Academy).

Ibid. (2008). 'The stofa reconstruction on the island of Papa Stour, Shetland. From historical research and archaeological investigations to cultural asset' in C. Paulsen & H. D. Michelsen, (Eds.), *Símunarbók. Heiðursrit til Símun V. Arge á 60 ára degnum.* Tórshavn, 42–57.

Dahl, Sverri (1968). 'Kirkjubøur', *Fifth Viking Congress,* (Ed.) B. Niclasen, 187–92. Tórshavn.

Dip.Norv.= Diplomatarium Norvegicum (Kristiania 1849-1919).

Fett, H. (1989). 'Bygninger og bygningsdetaljer' in Schia E. (Ed.), *De Arkeologiske utgravninger i Gamlebyen, Oslo,* bind 6. *Hus og gjerder.* Øvre Ervik.

Guðmundur Ólafsson (2010). Bessastaðarannsókn 1987. Aðdragandi og upphaf. Uppgraftarsvæði 1–11. In S. Kristjánsdóttir (Ed.), *Skýrslur Þjóðminjasafns Íslands 2010/1.* Reykjavík: Þjóðminjasafn Íslands.

Guðrún Harðardóttir (2006). 'The physical setting of Reykholt according to Sturlunga saga' in E. Mundal, (Ed.), *Reykholt som makt- og lærdomssenter i den islandske og nordiske kontekst.* Reykholt: Snorrastofa, 43–64.

Guðrún Sveinbjarnardóttir (2006). 'Reykholt, a centre of power: The archaeological evidence' in E. Mundal, (Ed.), *Reykholt som makt- og lærdomssenter i den islandske og nordiske kontekst.* Reykholt: Snorrastofa, 25–42.

Hødnebø, F. (Ed.) (1960). *Norske Diplomer til og med år 1300.* Oslo.

Jón Jóhannesson (1974). *Íslendinga Saga. A History of the Old Icelandic Commonwealth.* University of Manitoba Press.

KLNM = *Kulturhistorisk Leksikon for Nordisk Middelalder* XVII. Oslo: Gyldendal, 1972.

Krogh, K. J. (1975). 'Seks kirkjur heima á Sandi', *Mondul* 2, 21–54.

Lærum, O-D. & Brekke, N-G. (1990). *Røykstova – bustad gjennom tusen år*, Universitetsforlaget.

Laurentius saga biskups (1969), Á. Björnsson (Ed.), Reykjavík.

Myhre, B. (1982). 'Synspunkter på huskonstruksjon i sørvestnorske gårdshus fra jernalder og middelalder' in Myhre, B., Stoklund, B., Gjærder P., *Vestnordisk byggeskikk gjennom to tusen år*, AmS-skrifter 7. Arkeologisk museum i Stavanger, Stavanger, 98–118.

Myhre, B. (1993). 'Houses,1. Rural' in Pulsiano, P., (Ed.), *Medieval Scandinavia. An Encyclopedia,* New York and London, 292–3.

Orkney Recs.= Records of the Earldom of Orkney, (Ed.) J. S. Clouston (Scottish History Society) 1914.

*Orkney-Shetland Recs.= Orkney and Shetland Records,*vol.1, (Ed.) A. W. Johnston & others (Viking Society, London, 1907–13).

Ragnheiður Traustadóttir (2009). 'Ekki í kot vísað' in Guðmundur Ólafsson, Steinunn Kristjánsdóttir, (Eds.), *Endurfundir. Fornleifarannsóknir styrktar af Kristnihátíðarsjóði 2001–2005*, Reykjavík, 16–29.

Schia, E. (1993). 'Houses, 2. Urban' in Pulsiano, P., (Ed.), *Medieval Scandinavia. An Encyclopedia,* New York and London, 293–301.

Smith, B. (1980). 'Stock-stove Houses', *Shetland Folk-Book*, 7, 22–27.

Ibid. (2002). 'The 1299 letter about Papa Stour; a note' in Crawford (Ed.), 37–43. Also in *Collegium Medievale,* vol.15, 37–43.

Stoklund, B. (1984). 'Building Traditions in the Northern World' in Fenton, A. & Pálsson, H. *The Northern and Western Isles in the Viking World, Survival, Continuity and Change,* Edinburgh, 96–115.

Ibid. (1993). 'On the Concepts of *Eldhus* and *Stova*: The Faroese evidence' in Cheape, H. (Ed.), *Tools and Traditions. Studies in European Ethnology presented to Alexander Fenton.*

Ibid. (1996). *Det Færøske Hus i kultur-historisk belysning,* København.

Ibid. (2002). 'The Riddle of the Stock-Stove Houses; An Attempt at an Explanation' in Crawford, (Ed.), 127–40. Also in *Collegium Medievale*, vol. 15,127–40.

Storm, G. (1888). *Islandske Annaler indtil 1578*, Christiania.

Sturlunga saga (1988), (Ed.) Örnólfur Thorsson. Reykjavík: Svart á hvítu.

Thorsteinsson, A. (1982). 'Færøske huskonstruktioner fra vikingetid til 1800-årene' in Myhre, B., Stoklund, B., Gjærder, P., (Eds.), *Vestnordisk byggeskikk gjennom to tusen år,* AmS Skrifter 7, 149–161.

Vilhjálmur Vilhjálmsson (1991), 'The application of Dating Methods in Icelandic Archaeology'. *Acta Archaeologica* 61 (1990), 97–107.

Þorsteinn Gunnarsson, (Ed.) 2004. *Um Auðunarstofu.* Reykjavík: Hólanefnd.

Memorialisation of Vikings and National Identity in the 'Old Statistical Account' of Scotland, 1791–1799[1]

CLARE DOWNHAM

ABSTRACT

The Old Statistical Account, published between 1791 and 1799, was the first national survey of Scotland. It includes information on the history and antiquities of every parish, and preserves significant number of local commentaries on the Viking Age. This information gives a fascinating insight into attitudes towards the 'Old North' before the writings of Walter Scott popularised an enduringly romantic image of Vikings in Scotland's past. This paper has focused on records from the adjoining counties of Aberdeenshire, Banffshire and Moray. This region of relatively few Scandinavian place-names or antiquities provides a conservative barometer to analyse interest in Vikings across the nation. From the area survives a vivid collection of tales about battles, kings, subterfuge and a wronged princess, interwoven with folkloric explanations of features in the landscape. The account shows how local and national identities in late eighteenth century Scotland were tied together with the memorialisation of Vikings.

Keywords: Vikings, Scotland, antiquarians, identity, Enlightenment, Statistical Account.

The Statistical Account of Scotland, published between 1791 and 1799 was the first national survey of Scotland. It was compiled under the direction of Sir John Sinclair of Ubster, an MP and lay member of the General Assembly of Scotland. The compilation was an ambitious undertaking with questionnaires being sent out to the ministers of all 938 Scottish parishes in the spring of 1790. It is a great credit to Sinclair's tenacity that he was able to get a comprehensive set of results published in twenty-one volumes over nine years. The 160 questions addressed to ministers mainly concerned geography and natural history, population, and economy of each locality (Sinclair, 1790). Nevertheless, tucked away in the 'Miscellaneous' section of the questionnaire were four

1 Many thanks are owed to Lisa Collinson, Christina Lee, Susan Marshall and Ralph O'Connor for commenting on a draft of this paper, and the anonymous reviewers. I would also like to thank Andrew Newby, Colin Wallace and Elizabeth Platt for bibliographic assistance. I am grateful to the students of my 'Vikings in Scotland' course for getting me interested in this subject through their stories of local traditions. This article is written for them.

queries relating to the history and antiquities of each parish. The responses to these enquiries provide the basis for the present paper.

In this paper I hope to show the importance of the Statistical Account as a source for analysing memories of Vikings in the Scottish past.[2] At the time when the parish reports were being written there was a growing interest to record and preserve ancient monuments and oral traditions in Scotland. The Account was soon utilised by historians seeking insights into Scotland's medieval past. The memories of Vikings varied significantly from region to region, and even at a local level conflicting traditions were recorded. In this paper I have focused on the counties of Aberdeenshire, Banffshire and Moray. This area of north east Scotland was little affected by Viking settlement. The representation of interest in Vikings in this region in the Statistical Account therefore provides a conservative barometer to analyse interest in Vikings across the nation as a whole. It will be illustrated how matters of local and national identity went hand in hand with the memorialisation of Vikings.

The aims of John Sinclair in compiling the Statistical Account were focused on current affairs. His intention was to generate a body of national data which could be used to inform government decisions. The enthusiasm of some ministers to record historical or antiquarian matters in their parish accounts provoked Sinclair to circulate the message in December 1791 that 'deep researches of antiquity are far from being considered as equally essential' (Sinclair, 1978-83, I.52). Despite this lack of encouragement many ministers were evidently interested in the past. As Sinclair edited parish contributions with a light hand a significant body of information on antiquarian matters is preserved within the Statistical Account.

The Old Statistical Account is a useful source in that it presents attitudes towards the past from across Scotland. It provides a perspective on the relationship of history and identity beyond the literary circles of Edinburgh and the writings of celebrated authors. In the late eighteenth century a number of scholars were working to rehabilitate attitudes towards Vikings as civilised but un-English inhabitants of north Britain. Montesquieu, in his *De l'esprit des lois* (1748, §§ XIV.2, XVI.2, XVII.2–4) argued that the cold northern climate was better for societal and personality development than the heat of the south and so challenged the hegemony of Mediterranean Classical culture in European history. Paul Henri Mallet subsequently claimed in his *Introduction a l'Histoire de Dannemarc* (1755) that the ancient Scandinavians were descended from Trojan refugees who established an outpost of classical culture and learning in Northern Europe (Clunies Ross, 1998, p. 43). Mallet's *Introduction* was translated and expanded for a British audience by Thomas Percy in 1770. Scandinavia

2 This paper was composed to fit the theme of 'Memory' at the Viking Congress. For the meaning and use of this concept within historical discourse, see Klein, 2000.

was thereafter feted in translations of Old Norse poetry as an important source of European culture. Scottish authors were prominent within this movement and the *Scots Magazine* and the *Edinburgh Magazine* included discussions and translations of old Scandinavian literature during the 1790s (Cowan, 1972, pp. 118–19; Clunies Ross, 1998, pp. 240–42). In the Old Statistical Account the positive impact of Scandinavian culture was only accepted in a minority of parish accounts (focused in the Northern Isles), but the general level of interest in Vikings is significant. The Statistical Account gives testimony to the vitality of local traditions which may have nurtured a growing academic interest in Scotland's Scandinavian heritage.

The Old Statistical Account can be used to study the reception of texts (for example, Torfaeus's *Orcades*, or Macpherson's *Ossian*).[3] A further dimension to these accounts is that ministers were long term residents within their parishes, so they were often familiar with local opinions and folklore. It can be calculated that over a third of Statistical respondents had been in their parishes for more than two decades (Withrington, 1983, I.xxv). The information the ministers obtained was inevitably filtered and edited to suit their own opinions and religious perspectives. Nevertheless the records offer a unique glimpse into the views of a class of Scottish people which could have otherwise been lost from history. It was characteristic of eighteenth century enquiries into antiquities that the local knowledge of the lower ranks was collected (Fox, 2010, p. 600). In this respect we must be grateful where ministers described folktales and popular names for historical sites, although sometimes they were dismissed in favour of more bookish interpretations. In sum, the Old Statistical Account provides a valuable insight into attitudes towards the 'Old North' shortly before the writings of Walter Scott's popularised a romanticised image of the Vikings as heroic players in British history (Wawn, 2000, pp. 60-88).

As a statistician John Sinclair had his eyes fixed on the Scottish future, others were more curious to gather records of Scotland's past. David Stuart Erskine, Earl of Buchan, was instrumental in the creation of the Scottish Society of Antiquaries in 1780. In that year Buchan gave a speech laying out a plan for a national survey of antiquities including descriptions and drawings of the old buildings and remains of every parish. The level of contemporary interest in Scotland's historic connections with Scandinavia is illustrated by Buchan's reference to 'many Danish remains ... some of which have not been well described or represented by drawings' (Smellie, 1782, p. 8). This project was superseded by the Statistical Account. While medievalists must lament that Buchan's plan was not fully realised, we do have in the Old Statistical Account a less ambitious but nationwide response to questions regarding the antiquities and historic events of Scotland's parishes.

3 Macpherson, 1765; Torfaeus, 1697; Cord iner, 1780, pp. 128–73.

The enthusiasm of Buchan and a number of his contemporaries to record relics of the past may be seen as a response to rapid changes in Scottish society through economic development, clearances and migration. Awareness of social change is indicated in the Statistical Account in remarks (sometimes giving way to nostalgic laments) by individual ministers. The changes in eighteenth century Scottish society threatened the survival of historic monuments which lay in the way of agricultural improvement or which provided a useful source of stone. The extent of destruction becomes apparent in the Old Statistical Accounts. For Aberdeenshire and Banffshire alone there is record of 'druid circles' recently destroyed at Keith, Rathven and New Deer (Sinclair, 1978–83, XV.115, XVI.262, 390). The stones from the circle at New Deer were used to lay the foundation of the new Manse. In addition to utilitarian plundering the hooliganism of bored youths in rural Scotland was another threat to historic sites. At Mortlach (Banffshire) three 'Danish' skulls were said to have been embedded in the wall of the church. According to the minister 'no longer than about thirty years ago was the last of these picked out and tossed around by the school boys' (Sinclair, 1978-83, XVI.351)! In the face of wilful destruction or neglect, a written account of surviving antiquities was considered to be an important undertaking.[4]

The movement of people and altering social values could be seen to herald the loss of old ways and ancient knowledge. A drive to record oral traditions as well as monuments features in the Old Statistical Account and in contemporary literature. To some these traditions may have seemed to be at the edge of extinction (as represented in Walter Scott's *Minstrelsy of the Scottish Border*).[5] To their recorders, folktales were often regarded like verbal artefacts passed down from generation to generation, occasionally showing cracks and signs of repair, but remaining essentially unchanged. Folklore associated with antiquities was seen to be particularly valuable and worthy of record. For example, one of Sinclair's original questions sent to the Scottish clergy was 'Are there any … remains of antiquity? and what traditions or historical accounts are there of them?' (Sinclair, 1790, question 146). This emphasis on 'traditions' can be related to Enlightenment ideas about memory and the associative mind (Jones, 2000, p. 32). The Edinburgh scientist William Cullen had argued that memory

4 Needless to say early antiquarian investigations of ancient monuments could also be very destructive, but this opinion was not widely held by contemporaries.

5 Scott, 1806, I.cxxxviii 'it has been my object to throw together, perhaps without sufficient attention to method, a variety of remarks, regarding popular superstitions, and legendary history, which, if not now collected, must soon have been totally forgotten. By such efforts, feeble as they are, I may contribute somewhat to the history of my native country; the peculiar features of whose manners and character are daily melting and dissolving into those of her sister and ally. And, trivial as may appear such an offering, to the manes of a kingdom, once proud and independent, I hang it upon her altar with a mixture of feelings, which I shall not attempt to describe'.

depended on associations (Cullen, 1775, pp. 51–54). It then followed that a memory linked with a location or object was more reliable and could convey important historical information. These eighteenth century views differ from modern approaches to folklore as cultural memories which are remoulded or reinvented in successive generations to suit contemporary perceptions or agenda (Bottigheimer, 1989, p. 343). There was also a risk of circularity in accepting a folkoric explanation for a monument or place name, when the monument or place-name could then be invoked to verify the story. Nevertheless as we shall see contemporaries were not always uncritical in drawing on oral traditions as a historical source.

While some ministers who contributed to the Old Statistical Account had no discernable interest in Scottish history, many supported the record of local antiquities and oral traditions. Their efforts complement a broader movement to record and celebrate the past in late eighteenth century Scotland. It was perhaps a matter of national pride. The Scottish philosopher David Hume developed the idea that identity depended on a relationship of ideas which were in turn founded on memory and imagination.[6] In the rational mind, memory was regarded a conscious act contributing to perceptions of the self (Jones, 2000, p. 34). Generalising Hume's theory from the rational individual to the rational community, it could be argued that national identity therefore depended on shared recollections of the past and a collectively imagined vision for the future (Cf. Anderson, 1991, pp. 5–6). The Act of Union in 1707 risked the erosion of a distinctive Scottish identity. By preserving and reviving memories of the Scottish past, patriots could save their heritage from being subsumed within the dominant narratives of British historiography.

The Old Statistical Account was treated as a source by nineteenth century historians writing about the medieval Scottish past. This ensured that some information and stories about early monuments gathered at a parish level reached a national audience. Examples of historians who were quick to draw information from the Old Statistical Account include George Chalmers (author of *Caledonia*, 1807) and James Aikman (translator of George Buchanan's 'History of Scotland', 1827–29). There seems to have been a perception that stories associated with monuments could help fill a gap left by the restricted supply of early medieval documents in Scotland. The Old Statistical Account

6 Hume, 1999, pp. 16, 182–4; cf. Alison, 1790, pp. 23–28, at p. 28, 'There is no man in the least acquainted with the history of antiquity, who does not love to let his imagination loose on the prospect of its remains, and to whom they are not in some way sacred, from the innumerable images which they bring. Even the peasant, whose knowledge of former times extends but to a few generations has yet in his village a monument of the deeds or virtues of his forefathers and cherishes with a fond veneration of those good old times to which his imagination returns with delight, and of which he loves to recount the simple tales that tradition has brought him'.

therefore had an impact on attitudes towards national history as well as being an important collection of local records (Graham-Campbell, 2004, pp. 212–13).

In terms of what the Old Statistical Account reveals about attitudes towards Vikings, it is not surprising that opinions varied, but they also had a marked regional character. In the 1790s the word 'viking' was not yet current. According to the *Oxford English Dictionary* the term made its debut in Chalmer's *Caledonia* in 1807. The label was to gain wide currency in the Victorian era (Graham-Campbell, 2004, p. 218). In the Old Statistical Account, the word 'Norse' only appears nine times. Seven examples appear in parish accounts of the Northern Isles, showing a marked regional usage. This term originally meant 'nordic' in Standard English but in the Scottish tongue 'Norse' meant 'Norwegian' (Downham, 2009, pp. 140–41). The word 'Norwegian' appears forty-nine times in the Old Statistical Account. Just over half of the examples appear in parish accounts of the Northern Isles with the north mainland counties of Caithness, Ross and Cromarty, and Inverness accounting for most other occurrences. Outside the Northern Isles, the word 'Dane' was most commonly used across Scotland to refer to Vikings. In the eighteenth century this word was used fairly loosely to mean 'Scandinavian'. The regional usage of the different terms 'Norse', 'Norwegians' and 'Danes' in the Old Statistical Account is interesting. It seems to reflect a distinction between Vikings who settled in Scotland (who might be regarded as ancestors) and those who raided from outside (who could be perceived as enemies).

The terms 'Norse' and 'Norwegian' in the Old Statistical Account tend to be used in a relatively neutral or positive way, especially in the derivation of place names, while the term 'Danes' has more negative connotations and is frequently used in referring to historic conflicts. This nuanced use of the term 'Danes' could even apply to hostile actions between Norwegians and Scots. For example in a report of the famous Battle of Largs the forces of the Norwegian King Hakon IV are called 'Danes' (Sinclair, 1978–83, VI.431–32, VIII.297). The term 'Dane' may therefore imply that the Vikings under discussion are 'others', a foil to the identity of Scottish defenders. A similar phenomenon can be observed in Macpherson's collection of Ossianic poems published in the 1760s. Macpherson provided a romantic re-conceptualisation of the Gaelic past which obtained a wide readership. In his poem *Fingal*, Norway is represented as an exotic land of fierce enemies and beautiful princesses, and 'Fingal' the Scottish hero battles against the armies of 'Swaran king of Lochlin' (Macpherson, 1765, I.3–123). The past was co-opted to reinforce modern regional identities. In the north mainland and Northern Isles, parishioners were aware of their Scandinavian heritage, but outside these areas the Vikings were often regarded as 'other'.

Regional differences can be seen in the interpretation of antiquities in the

Scottish landscape. An example is the broch. These Iron Age stone towers are distributed across the Atlantic seaboard of Scotland (Armit, 2003, p. 14). In the 1870s a debate raged across the pages of the *Proceedings of the Society of Antiquaries of Scotland* as to whether these were Pictish or Scandinavian in origin (Anderson, 1876–78; Ferguson, 1876–78). In the Old Statistical Account they are attributed to Danish invaders in the Western Isles and Scottish mainland, but to Picts in the Northern Isles.[7] It seems that in observing the brochs as a curious feature in the landscape the inclination was to assign them to historic cultures which were obsolete or exotic. Despite the long involvement of Scandinavia in Hebridean history, the Vikings were treated as foreigners in Gaelic literature and folklore (Christiansen, 1931). In the Northern Isles the inhabitants were strongly aware of their Scandinavian heritage but it was the Picts who were a people of folklore (Kunin & Phelpstead, 2001, p. 8; Bruford, 1991). Rather than rejecting the influence of alien cultures on the Scottish landscape, the stories in the Old Statistical Account appear to embrace the idea that strange and wonderful peoples had roamed the land leaving monuments and a trail of stories behind them.

The different types of memories of Vikings in the Old Statistical Account vary according to the history and heritage of each region. Aberdeenshire, Banffshire and Moray are areas with few Norse place-names or Viking antiquities.[8] Nevertheless Vikings occupy a significant place in accounts from the north-east littoral. As in the west of Scotland, Vikings tend to be perceived as enemies with reference made to frequent incursions and innumerable battles. However, for the coastal communities of north east Scotland the Vikings were not the only cultural 'other' against which local identities could be pitched. Highlanders were also viewed as outsiders, and various comments portray them as poor, hardy and potentially dangerous.[9] What seems to emerge from these portrayals is that some north-east coastal dwellers regarded themselves as a distinctive group hemmed in between strangers on sea and land. This complements Andrew Blaikie's analysis of north-eastern fisher families in the nineteenth century highlighting their fairly exclusive interaction, with few marriages conducted between coastal dwellers and outsiders (Blaikie, 2002, pp. 23, 28). Contemporary social and economic concerns may have fostered a desire for north-easterners to retain a discrete identity. It may be that the stories in the Old Statistical Account reflect a desire to protect the close knit character of these communities by rooting their particularism in the past.

Language was (and still remains) an important vehicle for expressing iden-

7 E.g. Sinclair, 1978-83, XIX.140-41, 285, XX.164, 186, 218; cf. Pinkerton, 1814, II.249-50; Martin, 1999, p. 33.

8 The reasons for this include coastal topography and Viking Age politics.

9 Sinclair, 1978–83, XV.483, XVI.156, 256, 511. The image of the feminized mystical Celt we are familiar with from the nineteenth century had not yet taken hold: Kidd, 1999, p. 185.

tity. Distinctive dialects of Scots are spoken north-east coastal lowlands of Scotland which are still broad enough to cause occasional confusion to outsiders (myself included). At the end of the eighteenth century Scottish Gaelic was rarely spoken within twenty miles of the northeastern littoral but it was used more frequently as one travelled further inland. Some ministers saw the coastal Scots dialects as vulgar or uncouth (Sinclair, 1978–83, XV.298–99). Nevertheless two ideas about the origin of Scots are presented in the Old Statistical Account which promoted a sense of local pride. One view was that Scots was the language of the English who fled Norman tyranny in the eleventh century (Sinclair, 1978–83, XVI.203–04). It was therefore portrayed as a purer form of English than that spoken in England. The origins of this idea can be traced back to the early seventeenth century (L'Isle, 1623, p. 17). Another view, more relevant to the title of this paper, was that Scots was a Gothic language once spoken by the Picts. The idea that the Picts originated in Scandinavia emerged as a matter of debate among early eighteenth century Scottish antiquaries (Nicolson, 1702, p. 64; Ritchie, 1994, p. 17). John Pinkerton enthusiastically promoted this view in the 1780s (Pinkerton, 1787). He regarded the Picts as a Gothic people who migrated to eastern Scotland before the Gaels arrived in the west.[10] The reception of these ideas is witnessed in the Old Statistical Account in the reports of Aberdeen and St Fergus, Aberdeenshire (Sinclair, 1978–83, XIV.256, XVI.415). The incredible derivation of Scots from Pictish was an attractive theory for it offered a language and identity to Scots speakers which was un-English and un-Gaelic but nonetheless linked to ancient inhabitants of North Britain.[11] The argument implied that speakers of Scots were distant cousins of the Scandinavians even if the two groups did not get along in the Viking Age.

The Old Statistical Account seems to present a divided view of the Scottish people along regional lines. However the reports of the ministers are often concerned to link local events to national history. From these accounts an image of dual allegiance emerges in which Scottish identity is shown to be as significant as local loyalties. A number of cairns, earthworks and carved stones which were (often erroneously) associated with Vikings were described with reference to meta-narratives of Scottish history. In some cases this may be because a story has passed from text to folklore. In some instances ministers may be interpreting local tradition to fit in with accounts that they have read.

Two examples may be drawn upon to illustrate links between local antiquities and national history in Aberdeenshire, Moray and Banffshire. The first

[10] Pinkerton, 1814, I. lii-liii, 103, 121, 172. These views were very contentious, see Lane Buchanan, 1997, p. xii; Ferguson, 1998, pp. 252–64.

[11] See for example, Abercromby, 1711–15, p. 124: 'tis erroneous to think that the modern *Scots* have borrow'd their Language from the *English Saxons*'.

related to the Scottish King 'Indulf'. According to medieval kinglists he was killed near the River Cullen by Vikings in the year 962 (Woolf, 2007, pp. 193–94). The story of Indulf's demise was elaborated upon in later histories, including George Buchanan's *Rerum Scoticarum historia*, published in 1582 (Buchanan, 1827–29, I.289–90). Buchanan's history continued to be regarded as an authority by antiquarians and historians working in the eighteenth century, including Alexander Gordon and Patrick Abercromby (Abercromby, 1711–1715, I.84; Gordon, 1726, p. 147). It was claimed that a Viking fleet first sought to land at the Firth of Forth, but failed and travelled north, eventually taking harbour at Boyne near the mouth of the River Cullen. Here a battle was fought in which Indulf was killed, but the 'Danes' were defeated (Abercromby, 1711–15, p. 147).

In the Old Statistical Account parish landscapes and antiquities are tied in with the story of Indulf. At Bellie (Banffshire) a field with entrenchments 'to which tradition has given the name Danish Camp' is linked with the conflict. However the informant James Gordon preferred to interpret it as a Roman camp (Sinclair, 1978–83, XVI.87). At Rathven, just west of Cullen, a heap of stones called 'King's cairn' was identified by 'tradition' as the grave of Indulf. The minister George Donaldson reported that the conflict is said to have taken place at Bauds 'and it is believed erroneously ... that by it the Danes were finally expelled from Scotland' (Sinclair, 1978–83, XVI.391n). Close to the alleged battle site were cairns 'supposed to be the burial places of the Danes' and an eye witness account is presented of a stone coffin being recovered from one of these (Sinclair, 1978–83, XVI.391–92n). Cairns were also recorded at Fordyce to the east of Cullen where a rival claim is put forward Indulf's last stand (Sinclair, 1978–83, XVI.157). It was commonly held in the Old Statistical Account that large cairns were the burial places of kings and groups of cairns represented war graves. It is not surprising that conflicting traditions could arise regarding the location of momentous recorded incidents. There was an abundance of local monuments with which such traditions could be correlated.

Stories relating to Malcolm II were written even more vividly across the Scottish landscape. Malcolm was said to have fought numerous engagements against Viking invaders. There are no surviving contemporary records of these conflicts although it is known that Malcolm met Canute, king of Denmark and England, in 1031 and that he lost control of Moray (Hudson, 1992). These facts may have provided a framework for later historians to develop their account of Malcolm's reign. According to George Buchanan and his eighteenth century followers, two Viking leaders 'Olaus' and 'Enetus' conquered Moray and travelled to Mortlach (Banffshire) where Enetus was slain. On hearing of this setback, the Scandinavian king 'Sueno' raised an army commanded by 'Camus' which landed at Redhead in Angus. A battle was fought at Panbride (Forfarshire) and Camus was killed soon after.[12] Further engagements took place in Forfarshire and Buchan where the Danes were defeated.[13] The Scandinavian king Sueno responded to these setbacks by sending his son Canute to invade Scotland. According to Abercromby, Canute landed at Cruden Bay (Aberdeenshire) where a battle was decisively won by Malcolm. In the resulting treaty, the Vikings agreed to leave Scotland.[14] Numerous antiquities were associated with these narratives in the Old Statistical Account.

At Mortlach (Banffshire) features of the landscape echo the story of King Malcolm. The battle between Malcolm II and Enetus was ascribed to the year 1010. The minister George Gordon provides a list of 'traditional and pretty sure memorials of this famous battle' (Sinclair, 1978–83, XVI.350). They include earthworks 'called by the neighbourhood the Danish camp'.[15] A number of cairns are said to represent the graves of the fallen and the skulls of three unfortunate Danes were said to have formerly filled three niches in the church wall (Sinclair, 1978–83, XVI.351). The grave of the Viking leader Enetus was represented by a massive stone and this was unfortunately broken up during the nineteenth century. [16] A Pictish stone which currently stands in a field below Mortlach churchyard was also anachronistically associated with the battle.[17] George Gordon reported that a local river, the Dullan, was dammed overnight and then unleashed 'on the surprised Danes' (Sinclair, 1978–83, XVI.350). The lengthy description given in the Old Statistical Account presents the image of a landscape (literally!) saturated with legends of Malcolm's victory.

Regarding the fate of the Viking leader Camus, in the Old Statistical Account no fewer than three parishes claimed to witness his final defeat and burial. In Barrie (Angus) a number of tumuli and earthworks were linked with his downfall (Sinclair, 1978–83, XIII.66). Although it is not recorded in the Old Statistical Account, a Pictish stone at Camuston (in the neighbouring parish of Monikie) was identified as Camus's grave stone from the sixteenth century onwards.[18] At Kintore (Aberdeenshire) the Old Statistical Account records

12 Abercromby, 1711–15, pp. 205-07. Cf. Buchanan, 1827–29, I.317–319.

13 Abercromby, 1711–15, p. 208. Cf. Buchanan, 1827–29, I.319.

14 Abercromby, 1711–15, pp. 209. Cf. Buchanan, 1827–29, I.320.

15 http://canmore.rcahms.gov.uk/en/site/16381/details/dailuainine+danish+dyke (accessed 11/11/09), National Grid Reference NJ 2391 4106.

16 http://canmore.rcahms.gov.uk/en/site/16862/details/dufftown+aquvitae+stone (accessed 11/11/09), National Grid Reference NJ 3231 4072.

17 http://canmore.rcahms.gov.uk/en/site/16800/details/mortlach+the+battle+stone (accessed 11/11/09), National Grid Reference NJ 3237 3928. A gold chain recovered in the glebe field is considered to have been an ornament of one of the warriors. Sinclair, 1978–83, XVI.351.

18 Buchanan, 1827–29, I.319; Gordon, 1726, p. 154. Patrick Maul's manuscript history of Scotland is quoted by Gordon in support of this identification, and Maul reported that ploughing near the 'obelisk' revealed a skeleton and grave goods. http://canmore.rcahms.gov.uk/en/site/34552/

the 'tradition of a battle' at a local estate called Cammiestane, where 'Camus or Cambus was slain, and is buried' (Sinclair, 1978–83, XIV.577). A prehistoric standing stone at Duffus in Moray was also identified as Camus's grave.[19] This is close to the village of Kaim which was said to have taken its name from the Viking leader.[20] It is therefore possible to observe different parishes competing in their claims to associate local antiquities with famous national events.

The rivalry between Malcolm II and the Vikings was alleged to have culminated in a battle at Cruden Bay in 1012. According to Buchanan and subsequent historians, Canute and the Vikings agreed to leave Scotland after a stunning defeat. In the Old Statistical Account of Cruden, a black marble stone in the local churchyard was said to have lain over a Danish king who fell in the encounter. The comment that an inscribed copper plate had once been attached to it highlights the anachronism of this record (Sinclair, 1978–83, XV.78–79n). The old parish church at Cruden was dedicated to St Olaf, allegedly at the behest of Malcolm II in honour of the foreign dead although St Olaf did not die until some years after the supposed battle (Sinclair, 1978–83, XV.78). There is also some disagreement in the fanciful etymologies put forward for Cruden. One minister derived the name from 'Croju Dane' meaning 'slaughter of the Danes' (Sinclair, 1978–83, XV.79). Another derived the name from Cruthen, first king of the Picts (Sinclair, 1978–83, XVI.416). It appears that the record in the Old Statistical Account for Cruden derived from successive retellings of a story about a decisive battle. Individual monuments and topographical features were creatively drawn into a narrative as the storyteller's eye ranged across the landscape. This place-lore evidently gave rise to anachronistic and whimsical interpretations of monuments and names. At Cruden and at other locations, multiple and divergent narratives could arise in associating historic events with a particular place, and these matters invited debate as one party sought to promote its version of the story over another.

Other monuments in the north east of Scotland were drawn into anecdotes of Malcolm's defence of the realm against Vikings (Sinclair, 1978–83, XV.475n). Perhaps the most famous of these is the so-called 'Sueno's Stone' at Forres (Sinclair, 1978–83, XVI.350; XVI.634). This is one of the most elaborate Pictish stones in Scotland standing over twenty feet high and it is conventionally dated to the ninth century.[21] The popular association of the

details/camus+s+cross/ (accessed 10/11/09). National Grid Reference NO 51962 37907.

19 http://canmore.rcahms.gov.uk/en/site/16128/details/camus+s+stone+inverugie (accessed 10/11/09), National Grid Reference NJ 2391 4106. (accessed 10/11/09). National Grid Reference NJ 1529 6838.

20 Sinclair, 1978–83, XVI 498. This tradition may be based on a variant translation of Buchanan, 1827–29, I.319.

21 http://canmore.rcahms.gov.uk/en/site/15785/details/forres+sueno+s+stone (accessed 11/11/09), National Grid Reference NJ 04655 59533.

stone with a battle against King Sweyn ('Sueno') of Denmark is recorded by the sixteenth century historian Hector Boece, but different opinions as to the stone's origin were circulated. One rival view reported in the Old Statistical Account of Grange (Banffshire) was that the stone commemorated a conflict between Donald III of Scotland and Vikings in the late ninth century (Sinclair, 1978–83, XVI.204). The historian John Pinkerton reported its association with a clash between Malcolm IV and the people of Moray. Pinkerton considered the monument to be Pictish and was critical of the view that 'engraven obelisks ... in Scotland are sometimes attributed to the Danes' (Pinkerton, *Enquiry*, II.254–55). This opinion had been ventured decades before by Alexander Gordon in his *Itinerarium Septentrionale* of 1726 (Gordon, 1726, p. 160). What is revealed in these debates is that Pictish stones were commonly associated with Viking Age battles and royal murders.

Many disagreements and anachronisms relating to memories of Vikings are revealed in the Old Statistical Account. These often relate to the proud recollection of ancient deeds. One example which can be explored in the space allowed is the claim recorded in numerous parish accounts that the Vikings were expelled from their patch. Perhaps the most striking of these traditions is linked to the promontory fort at Burghead (Moray). According to the Old Statistical Account, this had been erected by Vikings. In the words of the local minister John Reid (Sinclair, 1978–83, XVI.507):

> A fabulous story prevails among the country people, that a daughter of the King of Scotland was married to a Danish prince who used her ill, upon which the Scots King threatened revenge for the affront and ... brought a number of pigeons and other birds, besmeared their feathers with tar and oil, set them on fire, and let them loose to fly through the different parts of the garrison; and how soon the Danes saw the flames, they fled with what valuables they could transport with them.

Archaeological evidence has indicated that the fort at Burghead was Pictish and therefore pre-Viking Age (Carver, 1999, pp. 29–31). Nevertheless, many 'facts' which we nowadays take for granted were unknown or unproven in the eighteenth century. In their wake legends developed to explain features in the landscape in literature and folklore.

A longstanding theory which has been used to analyse historical discourse, is that the past is often interpreted in two major ways, either as disjunctions or continuities (Foucault, 1980, pp. 111–14). One of the fascinating aspects of the Old Statistical Account is that it combines these two modes of thought. The events reported in parishes follow a model of disjunction. Often they are decisive events involving battles, death and expulsion. Nevertheless, the features of the landscape which were said to commemorate these deeds represent continuity. They are visible reminders of the past which have altered slowly over time. As monuments can be perceived as a meeting place between the present and the past, they could serve as important foci for narratives about bygone times.

A further striking feature of the Old Statistical Account is that memories were not fixed but that they were matters of debate. An active dialogue concerning the past is witnessed reflecting local perceptions and flourishing beyond (but not disengaged from) academia. The learning of books and the learning of folktales are intermingled in these narratives, each seemingly feeding off the other. It could be argued that the creation of the Old Statistical Account, as a national survey compiled from parish reports, encouraged expressions of local identity linked with a wider national consciousness (Withers, 2001, pp. 142–48). The antiquities of the community were therefore linked to the records of the nation. The Old Statistical Account committed memories to text thereby sharing and preserving them for a national audience. It also became an authority to be cited by others as witnessed in Chalmer's *Caledonia* and numerous nineteenth-century local histories. In this way, the writing of the Statistical Account founded memories for the Scottish public, just as the parish accounts had been influenced by the writings and publications of previous authors.

In sum, the Old Statistical Account provides a fascinating record of local attitudes towards Vikings in Scotland at the end of the eighteenth century. The records reflect contemporary interests in recording monuments and traditions in the face of social change. They highlight the significance of narratives about the past as a tool for defining local and national identities. Across large areas of Scotland in the eighteenth century 'Danes' or Vikings were cast in a negative light, although in the Northern Isles and Caithness the 'Norse' were regarded as praiseworthy ancestors. However in the nineteenth century as a result of the popular works of Walter Scott and others, a greater pride in Scotland's Scandinavian heritage would emerge (Wawn, 2000, pp. 93–116).

BIBLIOGRAPHY

Abercromby, P. (1711–15). *The Martial Atchievements* (sic) *of the Scots Nation* (Vols. 1–2). Edinburgh: Robert Freebairn.

Alison, A. (1790). *Essays on the Nature and Principals of Taste*. Edinburgh: Bell and Bradfute.

Anderson, B. (1991). *Imagined Communities: Reflections on the Origin and Spread of Nationalism*. (2nd ed.). London: Verso.

Anderson, J. (1876–78). Notes on the Structure, Distribution and Contents of the Brochs with Special Reference to the Question of their Celtic or Norwegian Origin. *Proceedings of the Society of Antiquaries of Scotland*, 12, 314–55.

Armit, I. (2003). *Towers in the North: the Brochs of Scotland*. Stroud: Tempus.

Blaikie, A. (2002). Coastal Communities in Victorian Scotland: What Makes Northeast Fisher Families Distinctive? *Local Population Studies*, 69, 15–31.

Bottigheimer, R. B. (1989). Fairy Tales, Folk Narrative Research and History. *Social History*, 14, 343–357.

Bruford, A. (1997). Trolls, Hillfolk, Finns and Picts: The Identity of the Good Neighbours in Orkney and Shetland. In P. Narváez (Ed.), *The Good People: New Fairy Lore Essays* (pp. 116–41). Lexington KY: Kentucky University Press.

Buchanan, G. (1827–29). *The History of Scotland* (J. Aikman, Trans.) (Vols. 1–4). Glasgow: Blackie, Fullerton and Co. (Original work published 1582).

Carver, M. (1999). *Surviving in Symbols: A Visit to the Pictish Nation*. Edinburgh: Canongate.

Chalmers, G. (1807). *Caledonia: or, an Account, Historical and Topographic of North Britain from the Most Ancient to the Present Times.* London: Cadell and Davies.

Christiansen, R. T. (1931). *The Vikings and the Vikings Wars in Irish and Gaelic Tradition*. Oslo: J. Dwybad.

Clunies Ross, M. (1998). *The Norse Muse in Britain, 1750–1820*. Trieste: Parnaso.

Cordiner, C. (1780). *Antiquities and Scenery of the North of Scotland in a Series of Letters to Thomas Pennant*. London (n.s.).

Cowan, E. J. (1972). Icelandic Studies in Eighteenth and Nineteenth Century Scotland. *Studia Islandica*, 31, 107–51.

Cullen, W. (1785). *Institutions of Medicine. Part I: Physiology* (3rd ed.). Edinburgh: Charles Elliot.

Downham, C. (2009). 'Hiberno-Norwegians' and 'Anglo-Danes': Anachronistic Ethnicities and Viking-Age England. *Mediaeval Scandinavia*, 19, 139–69.

Ferguson, J. (1876–78). On the Norwegian Origin of the Scottish Brochs. *Proceedings of the Society of Antiquaries of Scotland*, 12, 630–69.

Ferguson, W. (1998). *The Identity of the Scottish Nation: A Historic Quest*. Edinburgh: Edinburgh University Press.

Foucault, M. (1980). *Power/Knowledge: Selected Interviews and Other Writings 1972–1977* (C. Gordon Ed. & Trans.). New York: Pantheon.

Fox, A. (2010). Printed Questionnaires, Research Networks, and the Discovery of the British Isles, 1650–1800. *Historical Journal*, 53 (2010), 593–621.

Gordon, A. (1726). *Itinerarium Septentrionale, or a Journey thro' Most of the Counties of Scotland, and Those in the North of England*. London: G. Strahan *et al.*

Graham-Campbell, J. (2004). '*Danes* ... in this Country': Discovering the Vikings in Scotland. *Proceedings of the Society of Antiquaries of Scotland*, 134, 201–39.

Hudson, B. (1992). Cnut and the Scottish Kings. *English Historical Review*, 107, 350–60.

Hume, D. (1999). *A Treatise of Human Nature: Being an Attempt to Introduce the Experimental Method of Reasoning into Moral Subjects*. Kitchener, Ont.: Batoche Books (Original work published 1739-40).

Jones, C. A. (2000). Scott's *The Heart of Midlothian* and the disordered memory.

In J. Labbe, M. Campbell & S. Shuttleworth (Eds.), *Memory and Memorials, 1789–1914: Literary and Cultural Perspectives* (pp. 30–45). London: Routledge.

Kidd, C. (1999). *British Identities before Nationalism: Ethnicity and Nationhood in the Atlantic World 1600–1800*. Cambridge: Cambridge University Press.

Klein, K. L. (2000). On the Emergence of *Memory* in Historical Discourse. *Representations* 69, 127–150.

Kunin, D. (Trans.) & Phelpstead, C. (Ed.) (2001). *A History of Norway and the Passion and Miracles of the Blessed Óláfr*. London: Viking Society for Northern Research.

Lane Buchanan, J. (1997). *Travels in the Western Hebrides from 1782 to 1790*. Waternish, Skye: Maclean press (Original work published 1793).

L'Isle, W. (1623). *A Saxon Treatise Concerning the Old and New Testament*. London: John Haviland, London.

Macpherson, J. (1765). *The Works of Ossian the Son of Fingal* (3rd ed.) (Vols. 1-2). London: T. Becket & P.A. Dehondt.

Martin, M. (1999). *A Description of the Western Isles of Scotland circa 1695*. Edinburgh: Birlinn (Original work published 1703).

Nicolson, W. (1702). *The Scottish Historical Library*. London: T. Childe.

Pinkerton, J. (1787). *Dissertation on the Origins and Progress of the Scythians or Goths*. London: John Nichols.

Pinkerton, J. (1814). *Enquiry into the History of Scotland Preceding the Reign of Malcolm III* (2nd ed.) (Vols. 1–2). Edinburgh: Bell and Bradfute.

Ritchie, A. (1994). *Perceptions of the Picts from Eumenius to John Buchan*. Rosemarkie: Groam House.

Scott, W. (1806). *Minstrelsy of the Scottish Border* (3rd ed.) (Vols. 1–3). Edinburgh: Longman, Hurst Rees and Orme.

Sinclair, J. (1790). Queries Drawn up for the Purpose of Elucidating the Natural History and Political State of Scotland. Retrieved from http://edina.ac.uk//stat-acc-scot/

Sinclair, J. (Ed.). (1978–83). *The Statistical Account of Scotland, 1791–1799* (Vols. 1–20). Wakefield: EP Publishing (Original work published 1791–99).

Smellie, W. (1782). *Account of the Institution and Progress of the Society of the Antiquaries of Scotland*. Edinburgh: Society of Antiquaries of Scotland.

Torfaeus, T. (1697). *Orcades, seu Rerum Orcadensium Historiae Libri Tres*. Copenhagen: J. Hög.

Wawn, A. (2000). *The Vikings and the Victorians. Inventing the Old North in Nineteenth Century Britain*. Woodbridge: D. S. Brewer.

Withers, C. W. (2001). *Geography, Science and National Identity: Scotland since 1520*. Cambridge: Cambridge University Press.

Withrington, D. (1983). General Introduction. In J. Sinclair (Ed.), *The Statistical Account of Scotland, 1791-1799* (I. ix-xlv). Wakefield: EP Publishing.

Woolf, A. (2007). *From Pictland to Alba, 789–1070*. Edinburgh: Edinburgh University Press.

Is there a Norse 'footprint' in North Atlantic Pollen Records?

KEVIN J. EDWARDS, EGILL ERLENDSSON
& J. EDWARD SCHOFIELD

ABSTRACT

The movement of the Norse across the North Atlantic has left a legacy which may be investigated in many ways, including floristically. Palynology – the science of pollen and spore analysis – is a key method for investigating the presence and scale of vegetation-based impacts of human communities upon landscapes. We explore the concept of a pollen 'footprint' for Norse age records covering a variety of plant types and communities. There appear to be no specific indicators in the Faroese or Icelandic pollen data, but suites of taxa do respond to the Norse presence. This also applies partly to Greenland. Although spatially differentiated, *Rumex acetosella* (sheep's sorrel) would seem to either indicate a Norse presence in the Eastern Settlement, or to expand upon Norse arrival in the Western Settlement. Microscopic charcoal and fungal spores are considered to be useful non-pollen indicators.

Keywords: Palynology, vegetation, Norse, landnám, Faroe Islands, Iceland, Greenland, North Atlantic.

INTRODUCTION

The Norse diaspora from Scandinavian homelands across the North Atlantic has left a legacy which may be investigated in many ways – linguistically, archaeologically, historically and biologically to name the most obvious. Biological approaches have yielded a wealth of data, including information ranging from insects to genetics and from agriculture to diseases. Palynology – the science of pollen and spore analysis – is a key method for investigating the presence and scale of impacts of human communities upon landscapes, and the associated environmental contexts. Early successes include Firbas's (1937) exposure of cereal pollen in the fossil record and Iversen's (1941) demonstration of woodland clearance phenomena in the Neolithic 'landnam'[1] levels of Danish pollen

1 The term 'landnam' (or occupation, clearance, disturbance or interference phases – Edwards, 1979) has been applied widely to such sequences in the palynological literature of Europe; this should be differentiated from the use of the italicized word *landnám*, as here, to denote initial Norse settlement in the largely unoccupied North Atlantic area.

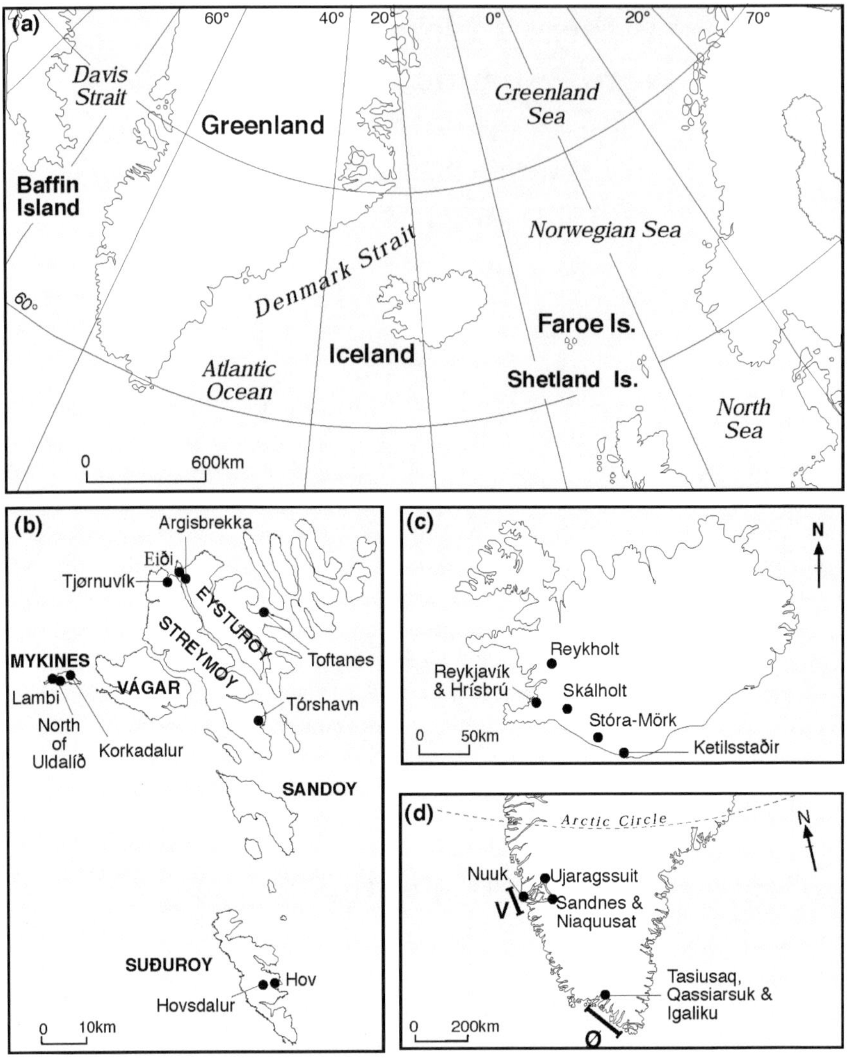

Fig. 1. Location maps showing sites mentioned in the text: (a) The North Atlantic area; (b) The Faroe Islands; (c) Iceland; (d) Greenland.

diagrams. The latter investigation especially was able to show how detailed pollen-analytical work revealed the removal of woodland, the use of fire, the growth of cereal crops and the spread of weeds such as *Plantago lanceolata* (ribwort plantain), before woodland regeneration occurred.

Indicator taxa such as *Plantago lanceolata* (in Europe), *Ambrosia* (ragweed; North America) or *Pteridium esculentum* (bracken; New Zealand) represent important guides to humanly-related ecological change. Although they are seldom viewed in isolation from their reconstructed plant communities, thus necessitating a consideration of suites of associated pollen, spores and other palynomorphs (especially microscopic charcoal), the desirability of identifying what might be termed a pollen 'footprint' – a key palynomorph which acts like a diagnostic fingerprint or gene marker – will be as obvious as it is perhaps elusive. Nevertheless, in this paper we have undertaken to explore the Norse palynological legacy in the fossil records of the Faroe Islands, Iceland and Greenland (Fig. 1a).[2]

THE FAROE ISLANDS

The lack of an extensive woodland cover for this archipelago (Fig. 1b) throughout the Holocene means that any marked reduction in its palynological representation cannot be expected, thus removing an otherwise useful palaeovegetational indicator. So, is any anthropogenic palynological footprint in evidence, let alone a Norse one? Discussing the site of Tjørnuvík, Jóhansen (1985, p. 54) maintained that 'The changes reflecting man's arrival are numerous', yet most pollen diagrams display rather muted changes ascribable to human activity (cf. Hannon & Bradshaw, 2000; Edwards et al., 2005; Borthwick et al., 2006; Borthwick, 2007; Lawson et al., 2005, 2008). The taxon which has perhaps seen the greatest attention is cereal-type, confidently assigned to Cerealia by Jóhansen (1979, 1985; cf. Hannon et al., 2001; Edwards & Borthwick, 2010). Even *Elymus* (*Leymus*) *arenarius* (lyme-grass) is suggested as a possible human introduction by Jóhansen (1985, p. 55), as large Cerealia size pollen grains are not found early in pollen sequences, and it was grown as a corn crop in Iceland. It is a rare plant in the Faroes at the present day (Jóhansen, 2000). The finds of cf. cereal pollen remain contentious, but it is instructive that 'rapid scanning' (searching for cereal-type grains using optimizing techniques

[2] No attempt is made to examine data from other areas such as the Northern or Western Islands of Scotland or Canada. The former area experienced human impacts from prehistoric times (Edwards & Whittington, 1997) and a specifically Norse palynological signal is probably impossible to detect at most sites. A number of pollen diagrams exist for the lakes, bog and fens surrounding the ruins of the short-lived former Norse settlement at L'Anse aux Meadows, Newfoundland (e.g. Henningsmoen, 1977; Davis et al., 1988), but these diagrams demonstrate little, if any, human impact on the local vegetation around the time of settlement (*c.*AD 1000).

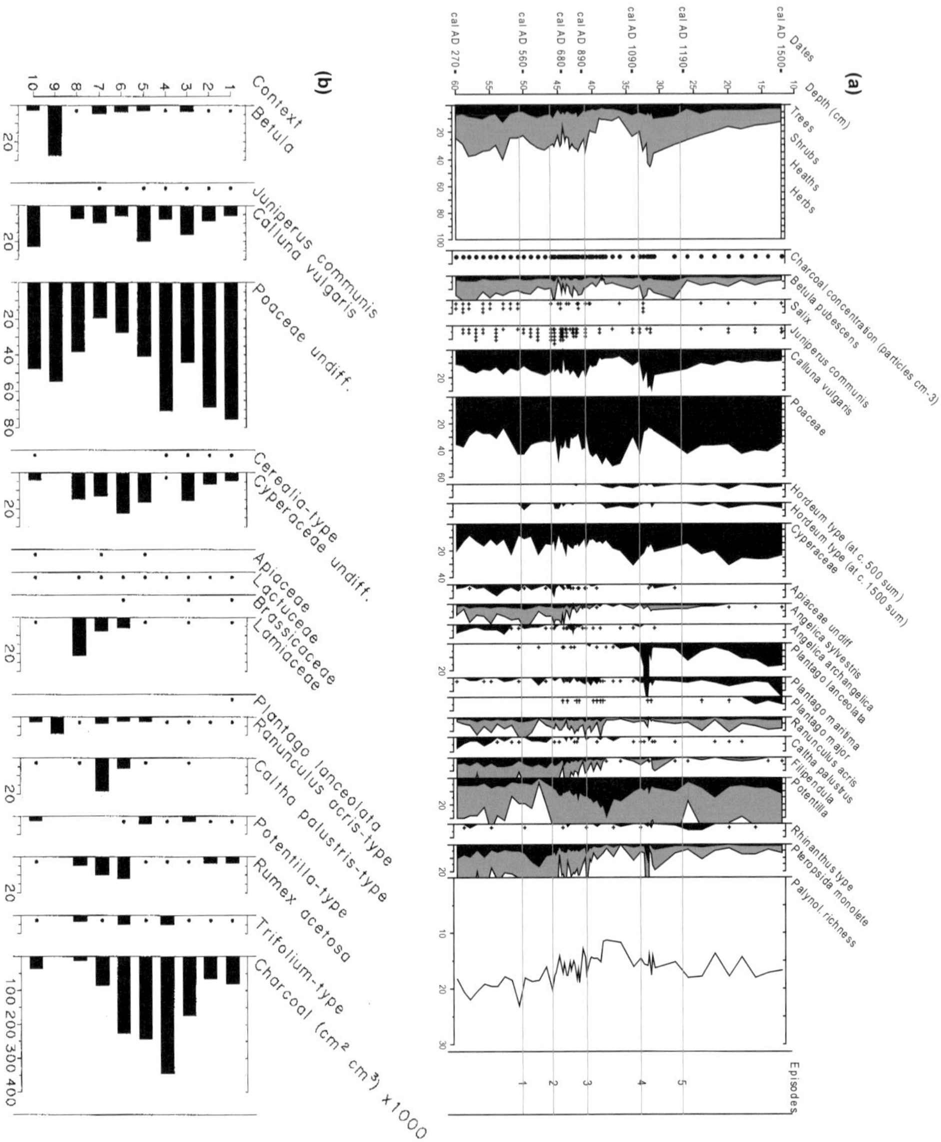

Fig. 2. Selected taxa percentage pollen diagrams from the Faroe Islands: (a) Hov (Edwards et al., 2005). Exaggeration curves are x5. + indicates <2% total land pollen. Dates derive from ^{14}C dates (indicated on graphs) which use the mid-point of the 2σ calibrated AD ranges; (b) Toftanes (Edwards et al., 1998). Dots indicate <2% total land pollen.

[Edwards & McIntosh, 1988]) at Hov revealed no such grains (barley-type in this instance) prior to AD 540 (Fig. 2a). Arguably, such examples of cereal-type pollen from conventionally pre-Norse contexts, may signify colonization by *papar* (Irish anchorites) or early Norse settlers (Edwards & Borthwick, 2010).

Rumex longifolius (northern dock) and *R. obtusifolius* (broad-leaved dock) were considered to be 'among the first anthropochors (*sic.*)' (Jóhansen, 1985, p. 55 and cf. Guldager Christiansen & Fosaa, 2009). *R. acetosa* (common sorrel) is noted as expanding from *landnám*. Palynologically, however, only *R. acetosa* is presented in several of Jóhansen's diagrams where it is combined with *Oxyria digyna* (mountain sorrel). The latter is presumed to be the dominant pollen producer of the two, but both grew in lowland and mountain areas, and the pollen group (labeled as *R. acetosa*) is shown to expand at Hovi B after *landnám,* as it is at Lambi. The Mykines site, though, alongside that of nearby North of Uldalíð, has just as much (more at Lambi) *R. acetosa* pollen prior to *landnám*. The site of Tjørnuvík seems to have a clearly demarcated rise in (cf.) *R. acetosa* pollen at *landnám*. Interestingly, Hannon et al. (2001) have enhanced representation of *Rumex* cf. *longifolius* pollen following *landnám* at Tjørnuvík, Eiði and Korkadalur, although this is unremarked.

Plantago lanceolata (ribwort plantain) was not found at the outset of *landnám* at Tjørnuvík, but it did occur regularly, if sporadically, thereafter. Jóhansen (1985, p. 55) considered it to be transported from long distances, but it is commonly recorded elsewhere (Edwards et al., 2005; Lawson et al., 2008). At the Mykines sites of Lambi and North of Uldalíð, it is *P. maritima* (sea plantain) that rises and Jóhansen regarded it as an introduced species there along with *Avena* (oats) at Lambi. Sea plantain is evident long before this in other pollen profiles from the Faroe Islands (Jóhansen, 1985; Lawson et al., 2008).

A common phenomenon around the time of *landnám* is the expansion in the pollen of Poaceae (grasses) and/or Cyperaceae (sedges). These ubiquitous taxa have frequent fluctuations and declines throughout the Holocene spectra and cannot, alone, be designated as providing anthropogenic 'footprints'. Seen less consistently are the increases for *Potentilla* (cf. *P. erecta* [tormentil]) as at Hov and Argisbrekka, Brassicaceae (perhaps reflecting *Capsella bursa-pastoris* [shepherd's purse]) at Lambi, *Ranunculus acris*-type (meadow buttercups) and *Rhinanthus*-type (cf. yellow rattle) at Hov, and the aquatics *Myriophyllum alterniflorum* (alternate-flowered water milfoil) and *Potamogeton* (pondweed) at Eiði.

Just as some sites display expansions in a number of herbs, others show reductions in tall herbs, heaths and ferns. The sites of Hov/Hovi alone see falls in e.g. Apiaceae (carrot family), *Angelica archangelica* (garden angelica), *A. sylvestris* (wild angelica), *Filipendula ulmaria* (meadowsweet), *Caltha palustris* (marsh marigold), *Sedum/Rhodiala rosea* (roseroot), *Calluna vulgaris* (heather) and undifferentiated ferns (*Pteropsida* monolete indet.). These plants are variously attractive to people or animals as well as being susceptible to grazing and trampling pressures. Many of these taxa were evident in the archaeologically-related pollen samples from inter-building contexts at Toftanes (Fig. 2b; Edwards et al., 1998, 2005). Although such data cannot necessarily be interpreted after the manner of the off-site peat and lake profiles which form the purview of this paper, the Toftanes results are of interest in that they are likely to derive from habitation, infield and outfield areas with palynomorphs arriving as a result of normal aerial pollen deposition as well as on feet and hoofs and within peat carried to the site. Conjecturally, an initial episode of grazing and small-scale cereal cultivation could have resulted in over-grazing (decreased flowering of grasses) or even some abandonment as other plants (e.g. sedges, thyme [Lamiaceae], sorrel) invaded formerly grazed areas. A successful effort may then have been made to re-intensify use of the land and more charcoal was produced (either from burning of the land surface to encourage the renewed spread of grass, and/or as a product of more domestic activity); this latest phase might also have seen further barley cultivation.

The supposed decline of *Juniperus communis* ssp. *alpina* (dwarf juniper) at *landnám* as a result of browsing by goats introduced by the Norse, in addition to other uses (e.g. as a flavouring agent or for ropes) was posited by Small (1991). An evaluation of the evidence by Edwards (2008) produced no support for this argument. Similarly, the settlement horizons of Faroese pollen sequences have also shown falls in *Betula pubescens* (downy birch) or *Salix* (willow) (Edwards et al., 2005; Hannon & Bradshaw, 2000, 2007; Hannon et al., 2005) which may be anthropogenically related.

Given the highly variable pollen histories of the Faroese palaeoflora, it would seem that the most productive indication of cultural impacts on the past vegetational landscapes are to be seen at the community scale with considerations of suites of pollen and spores, combined where possible with records of microscopic charcoal (as an indicator of fire incidence – related to domestic activity as much as land management), sedimentology and radiocarbon-dating (cf. Edwards et al., 2005; Edwards & Borthwick, 2010). The few studies of 'palynological richness' in the Faroes do not reveal that the arrival of the Norse led to an increase in floristic diversity. It might be supposed that the development of an infield/outfield system and shielings would create environmental heterogeneity, resulting in an increase in plant habitat types. At the sites of Hov and Hovsdalur on Suðuroy (Edwards et al., 2005), however, there are overall declines in diversity as tree, shrub, heath, tall herb, and some wetland taxa are reduced by grazing and drainage (Fig. 2a). It would seem that any increase in floristic diversity associated with the addition of anthropogenic taxa is offset by losses of marginal tree and shrub components, and eventually heaths and the taller palatable herbs.

ICELAND

The role of the Norse settlement of *c.*AD 870[3] in providing a new immigration process for plants, is uncertain. Þórhallsdóttir (1996) compiled a list of 62 species from Steindórsson's (1962, 1964) and Kristinsson's (unpublished) records as probable post-settlement components, out of which 7 are considered very rare. From the remaining 55 species, only 11 can be palynologically identified to species level, of which just *Rumex acetosella* (sheep's sorrel) and *Polygonum aviculare* (knotgrass) are common in Icelandic pollen diagrams. The remaining species (*Rumex longifolius*, *Plantago major* [greater plantain], *Capsella bursa-pastoris*, *Urtica dioica* [common nettle], *Valeriana officinalis* [common valerian], *Viola tricolor* [wild pansy], *Prunella vulgaris* [selfheal]) occur sporadically in some of the more detailed, settlement-orientated pollen diagrams (Hallsdóttir, 1987; Erlendsson, 2007; Lawson et al., 2007). Considerations as to which plants have been humanly-introduced are highly speculative. Botanically, assumptions are typically made from plants' preferred habitats and distribution patterns, while palynologically intermittent finds of specific pollen grains hardly allow for rigorous interpretations.

Other possible footprint taxa are the domesticated plants possibly introduced by the Norse, including *Hordeum vulgare* (barley), *Avena sativa* and *Linum usitatissimum* (flax). Of these the pollen of *Hordeum*-type is most common in Icelandic pollen records (Hallsdóttir, 1996; Erlendsson, 2007). As in the Faroe Islands, *Elymus arenarius* could be indicated, and it is a more common plant in Iceland where it was also used as a cereal in times of famine (Guðmundsson, 1996). *Avena*-type pollen is rare in Icelandic pollen profiles but it has been recorded in late-medieval natural sediments at Ketilsstaðir, Stóra-Mörk and in cultural contexts at Reykholt (Figs 1c, 3a and 3b; Erlendsson et al., 2009; Sveinbjarnardóttir et al., 2007). The Icelandic pollen record contains only a single mention of pollen from *L. usitatissimum* (Einarsson, 1963), but flax pollen is likely to be restricted to the fields where it was cultivated (modern cultivars are largely self-pollinating and sometimes insect-pollinated) and its pollen is produced in very low quantities (Gennard, 1985).

The possible domestic importance of two other plants has been suggested. Þórarinsson (1944, p. 127) identified pollen as that of *Myrica gale* (bog myrtle) and considered it possible that it had been cultivated for brewing. He also found *Artemisia* (mugwort) pollen (p. 129) and listed historical records for its growth in Iceland before AD 1600 and near Skálholt between 1791 and 1794. From a palynological viewpoint, the case of the *Myrica* pollen is highly doubtful, as it is hardly separable from *Corylus* (hazel) pollen (Edwards, 1981) by

[3] Culturally-based pollen studies in Iceland are greatly assisted by the spatially extensive distribution of the settlement tephra (dated to AD 871±2 [Grönvold et al., 1995]).

standard methods and hazel pollen may have reached Iceland as a long-distance airborne arrival. As far as can be seen from Þórarinsson's photos of the alleged *Myrica* pollen (p. 126), *Betula* spp., may be a better candidate, in particular the *Betula pubescens/B. nana* hybrid (cf. Karlsdóttir et al., 2007). Given the historical accounts for *Artemisia* and its multiple functions as, for example, spice and medicine, it would seem possible that it was cultivated in Iceland. *Artemisia* spp. are, however, powerful invaders and *Artemisia vulgaris* thrives in both Alaska and Greenland and should thus have been able to maintain itself in Iceland.

Increasingly, research is showing that the major woodland in Iceland was often declining prior to *landnám* (Erlendsson & Edwards, 2009) or was not always dominant at this time (Erlendsson et al., 2009). Ari the Wise's claim in the 12th century *Íslendingabók* (Benediktsson, 1968) that woodland at the time of *landnám* stretched from the mountains to the seashore may be an over-statement. Saga evidence (Gunnarsdóttir, 2001) certainly demonstrates variability in Iceland's past arboreal cover.

It would seem that a conventional palynological approach is unlikely to provide any single 'indicator' which unequivocably signifies Norse colonization. This leaves us with the task of attempting to track the Norse by using suites of pollen taxa. In fact the majority of pollen profiles from farms with an early settlement record display the decline of woody taxa and tall, grazing-sensitive herbaceous plants and sometimes *Sphagnum* (bog moss). This is often followed by the expansion of apophytes (native species expanding into humanly-created habitats) of which Poaceae is usually the predominant taxon but often in association with such pollen taxa as *Thalictrum alpinum* (alpine meadow-rue), *Plantago* spp., and *Galium* (bedstaws), and the spores of *Equisetum* (horsetails) and *Selaginella selaginoides* (lesser clubmoss) (Fig. 3; cf. Hallsdóttir, 1996). Such major transformations of vegetation are well recorded from sites adjacent to major farms like Reykholt, Stóra-Mörk and Hrísbrú (Fig. 3) where woodlands existed before the settlement.

Fig. 3. Selected taxa percentage pollen diagrams from Iceland: (a) Stóra-Mörk (Erlendsson & Edwards, 2009; Vickers et al., 2011); (b) Reykholt (Erlendsson et al., in press); (c) Hrísbrú (present authors, unpublished). Exaggeration curves are x5. + indicates <1% total land pollen, but for cereal-types they represent numbers of pollen encountered. Dates derive from tephrochronology and from ^{14}C dates (indicated on graphs) which use the mid-point of the 2σ calibrated AD ranges.

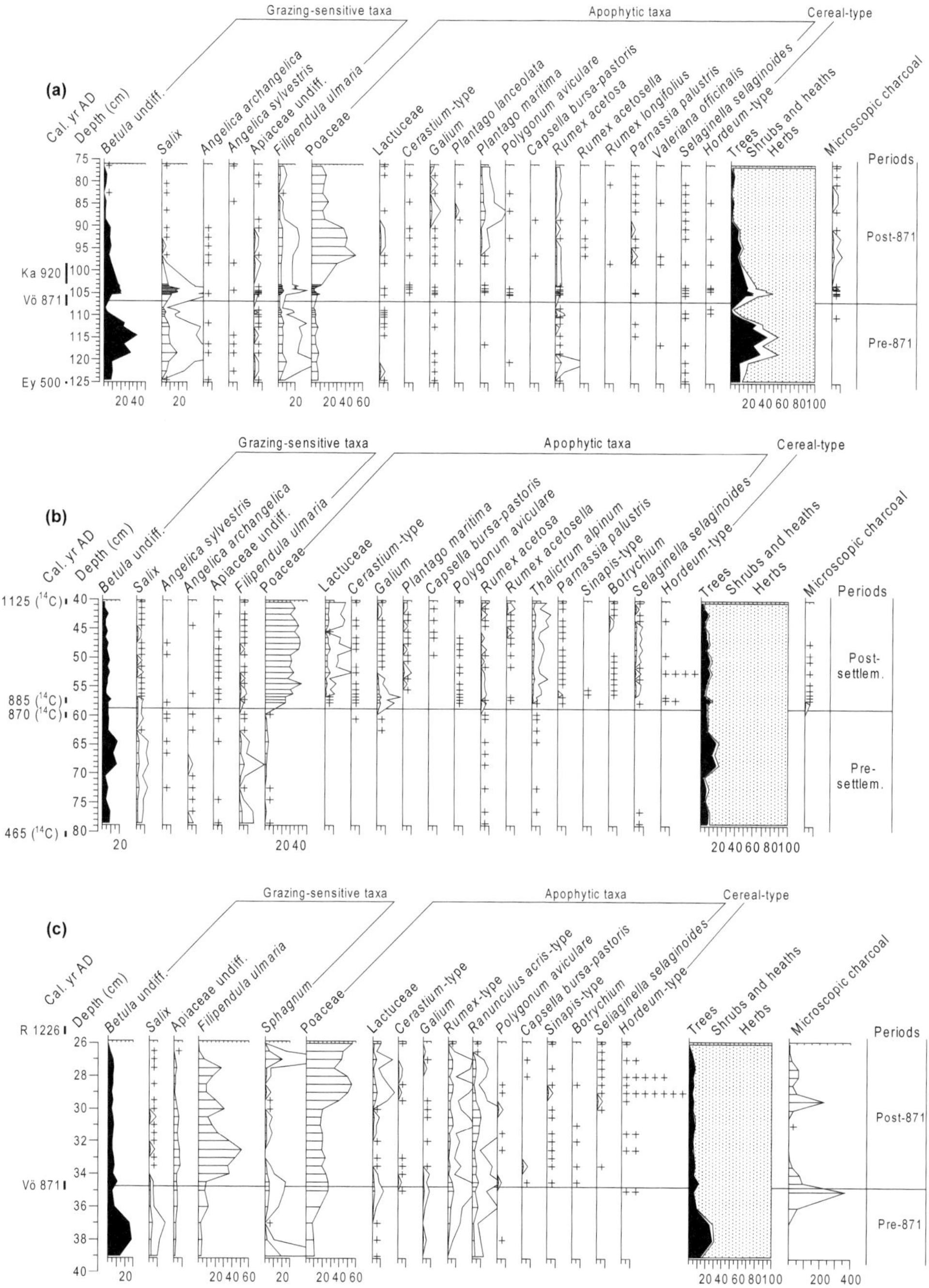
(a)
Grazing-sensitive taxa
Apophytic taxa
Cereal-type
Cal. yr AD
Depth (cm)
Betula undiff.
Salix
Angelica archangelica
Angelica sylvestris
Apiaceae undiff.
Filipendula ulmaria
Poaceae
Lactuceae
Cerastium-type
Galium
Plantago lanceolata
Plantago maritima
Polygonum aviculare
Capsella bursa-pastoris
Rumex acetosa
Rumex acetosella
Rumex longifolius
Parnassia palustris
Valeriana officinalis
Selaginella selaginoides
Hordeum-type
Trees
Shrubs and heaths
Herbs
Microscopic charcoal
Periods
Post-871
Pre-871
Ka 920
Vö 871
Ey 500
(b)
Grazing-sensitive taxa
Apophytic taxa
Cereal-type
Cal. yr AD
Depth (cm)
Betula undiff.
Salix
Angelica sylvestris
Angelica archangelica
Apiaceae undiff.
Filipendula ulmaria
Poaceae
Lactuceae
Cerastium-type
Galium
Plantago maritima
Capsella bursa-pastoris
Polygonum aviculare
Rumex acetosa
Rumex acetosella
Thalictrum alpinum
Parnassia palustris
Sinapis-type
Botrychium
Selaginella selaginoides
Hordeum-type
Trees
Shrubs and heaths
Herbs
Microscopic charcoal
Periods
Post-settlem.
Pre-settlem.
1125 (14C)
885 (14C)
870 (14C)
465 (14C)
(c)
Grazing-sensitive taxa
Apophytic taxa
Cereal-type
Cal. yr AD
Depth (cm)
Betula undiff.
Salix
Apiaceae undiff.
Filipendula ulmaria
Sphagnum
Poaceae
Lactuceae
Cerastium-type
Galium
Rumex-type
Ranunculus acris-type
Polygonum aviculare
Capsella bursa-pastoris
Sinapis-type
Botrychium
Selaginella selaginoides
Hordeum-type
Trees
Shrubs and heaths
Herbs
Microscopic charcoal
Periods
Post-871
Pre-871
R 1226
Vö 871

Problems remain in identifying on pollen evidence the exact stratigraphic horizons of particular events, like the establishment of permanent settlement. Recent high-resolution studies from Stóra-Mörk and Ketilsstaðir (Erlendsson et al., 2009) have revealed tentative evidence for anthropogenic impact through *Hordeum*-type pollen from just before the deposition of the settlement tephra, enhanced between AD 870 and 920 by the reduction of tall herbs, probably through grazing. At the inland settlement of Stóra-Mörk, it is not until after 920 that the pollen record shows the typical settlement impact of a permanent birch decline and a rise in weedy taxa and apophytes. At Ketilsstaðir the situation is somewhat complicated by the apparent absence of woody taxa and strong pre-settlement representation for typical open-environment taxa. There, it is not until the middle of 11th century that Poaceae enters a long-term trend of increase and the weed taxa (mainly *Plantago* spp.) become prominent.

GREENLAND

There has been considerable debate concerning which plants may have been introduced to Greenland by Norse settlers (e.g. Ostenfeld, 1926; Pedersen, 1972). Early theories on this subject were driven primarily by a consideration of contemporary species distribution patterns and how these related to the former areas of Norse colonization (the Eastern and Western Settlements, Fig.1d). On this basis, for example, Porsild (1932) estimated that the 'Old Norse' element of the flora of Greenland was probably in the region 1.5-5.0%. The emergence of palynology added an extra dimension to this debate by not only providing the necessary historical perspective that had hitherto been absent, but also by giving some indication as to which native plants appeared to be favoured by human (Norse) activity.

Fig. 4. Percentage pollen diagrams from the Eastern Settlement of Greenland showing selected Norse 'indicators': (a) Ø2 Tasiusaq (Edwards et al., 2008); (b) Ø47 Igaliku/*Garðar* (Buckland et al., 2009); (c) Ø39 Qinngua (Schofield & Edwards, 2011). All dates are mid-points of calibrated 2σ age ranges. + indicates <1% total land pollen. Charcoal data are presented as charcoal to pollen ratios. The columns headed LPAZ (= local pollen assemblage zones), on the right-hand sides of the diagrams, display areas of palynomorph homogeneity designated by a letter/number system which relates to fuller pollen profiles than can be presented here.

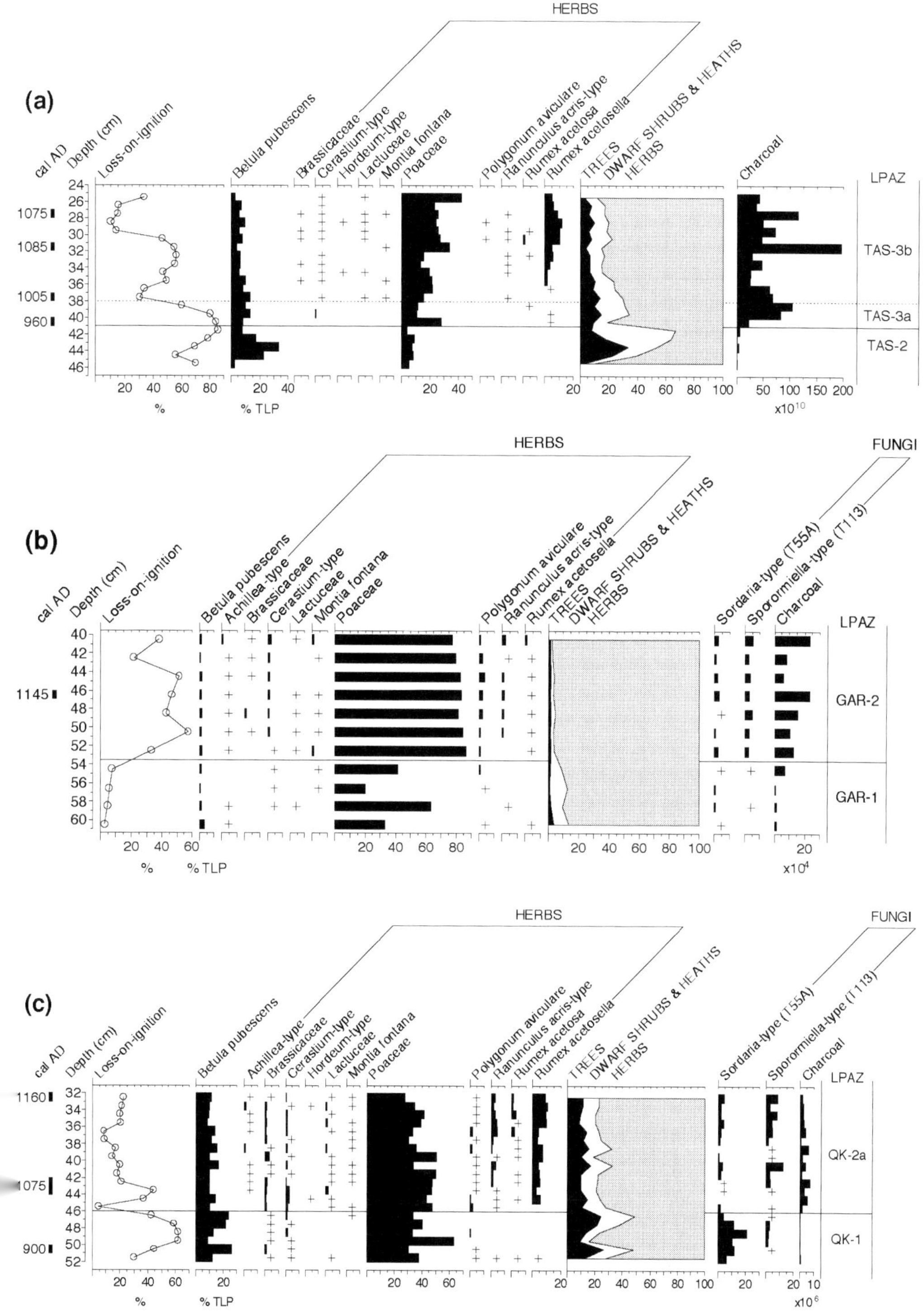
(a)
HERBS
cal AD
Depth (cm)
Loss-on-ignition
Betula pubescens
Brassicaceae
Cerastium-type
Hordeum-type
Lactuceae
Montia fontana
Poaceae
Polygonum aviculare
Ranunculus acris-type
Rumex acetosa
Rumex acetosella
TREES
DWARF SHRUBS & HEATHS
HERBS
Charcoal
LPAZ
TAS-3b
TAS-3a
TAS-2
1075
1085
1005
960
%
% TLP
x10^10
(b)
HERBS
FUNGI
cal AD
Depth (cm)
Loss-on-ignition
Betula pubescens
Achillea-type
Brassicaceae
Cerastium-type
Lactuceae
Montia fontana
Poaceae
Polygonum aviculare
Ranunculus acris-type
Rumex acetosella
TREES
DWARF SHRUBS & HEATHS
HERBS
Sordaria-type (T55A)
Sporormiella-type (T113)
Charcoal
LPAZ
GAR-2
GAR-1
1145
%
% TLP
x10^4
(c)
HERBS
FUNGI
cal AD
Depth (cm)
Loss-on-ignition
Betula pubescens
Achillea-type
Brassicaceae
Cerastium-type
Hordeum-type
Lactuceae
Montia fontana
Poaceae
Polygonum aviculare
Ranunculus acris-type
Rumex acetosa
Rumex acetosella
TREES
DWARF SHRUBS & HEATHS
HERBS
Sordaria-type (T55A)
Sporormiella-type (T113)
Charcoal
LPAZ
QK-2a
QK-1
1160
1075
900
%
% TLP
x10^6

The first palynological investigations of Norse-age material from Greenland were undertaken by Iversen (1934). Pollen analysis of a peat profile near ruin group V7[4] (*Anavík*/Ujaragssuit) in the Western Settlement revealed that a reduction in *Betula* pollen and an increase in grasses followed the inferred Norse *landnám*, indicating scrub clearance and the extension of grazing land. Also of significance was an increase in pollen from *Rumex* spp. (otherwise rare before *landnám*) and a charcoal layer, the latter supposedly indicative of clearance of vegetation by burning.

Investigations by Fredskild (1973, 1978) shifted the focus of attention to the Eastern Settlement where pollen diagrams were constructed for two lake basins – Galium Kær and Comarum Sø – and several peat deposits in and around ruin group Ø29/29a at Qassiarsuk (the favoured location for Erik the Red's farm estate, *Brattahlíð*). At these sites the Norse *landnám* was accompanied by very clear changes to pollen assemblages. Clearance of birch woodland and birch/willow scrub was indicated, whilst an increase in microscopic charcoal was evident. Visible macroscopic charcoal layers were not observed in the peat profiles, suggesting that unlike in the Western Settlement, the clearance process may have been a result of felling rather than burning of the vegetation cover (Fredskild & Humle, 1991). Fredskild (1973) noted the emergence of *Achillea millefolium* (yarrow) pollen at *landnám*, but the most prominent feature of the pollen diagrams, as at V7, was the appearance and expansion of *Rumex acetosella/acetosa*. With only two grains of this aggregated type recorded prior to the Norse *landnám*, Fredskild (1973) concluded that both species must have been introduced – at least to south Greenland – by the Norse settlers (note that *R. acetosella* had already spread to the Western Settlement by the mid-Holocene; Fredskild, 1983).

In addition to undertaking pollen analyses, Fredskild (1978) examined the plant macrofossils preserved in the peat deposits around Qassiarsuk. Norse 'cultural' horizons within the peat revealed huge numbers of seeds from aggressive 'weeds' of disturbed or waste ground, most notably *Poa annua* (annual meadow grass), *Stellaria media* (common chickweed), *Capsella bursa-pastoris* and *Polygonum aviculare* – plants identified as likely Norse introductions. Increased numbers of seeds of the native *Montia fontana* (blinks, a plant that flourishes under conditions of nutrient-enrichment yet is palynologically sparse) were also conspicuous in the Norse horizons; in one assemblage zone (from section QDB) around 4000 *M. fontana* seeds were recorded but only two pollen grains.

4 The prefix letters V and Ø are used to designate the Norse Western (Vesterbygd) and Eastern (Østerbygd) Settlement ruin groups, respectively, under the number registration system developed by Daniel Bruun at the end of the 19th century (cf. Berglund, 1986). Although these have been superseded by a more comprehensive set of map sheet-based preservation codes, the old system is still widely used and understood.

More recently, consideration of the Norse palynological signal in Greenland has extended beyond Qassiarsuk to some of the other farms in the Eastern Settlement (e.g. Edwards et al., 2008; Schofield et al., 2008; Buckland et al., 2009). At each site, although the fine details vary slightly, the same general patterns emerge (Fig. 4). At the community scale the introduction of pastoral farming at *landnám*, and the associated expansion in hayfields and grazing land at the expanse of heathland and scrub, can be traced through an increase in herbaceous pollen (notably grasses) and a decline in pollen from trees and shrubs. Without exception the charcoal to pollen ratio (C:P) also increases, although the absence of visible charcoal layers in the stratigraphy, and sustained high levels of charcoal recorded throughout the settlement period, suggests that the charcoal particles may largely be derived from domestic fires (e.g. for heating, cooking, etc.) rather than being a by-product of land management practices. Loss-on-ignition (LOI) measured from natural contexts (Ø2 and Ø39, but not Ø47) may be regarded as a proxy for soil erosion, and the decrease in LOI that is in most cases evident at (or shortly after) *landnám* suggests that farm construction, scrub clearance and the extension of grazing led to widespread destabilization of soils around the Norse farms – a situation which would favour taxa that colonize disturbed areas (ruderals).

Sometimes apparent at *landnám* is a decline in pollen of *Betula pubescens*, the only tree that is native to south Greenland, which could represent the destruction of localized patches of woodland at the time of settlement in order to provide timber for the construction of buildings (cf. Edwards et al., 2008). More ubiquitous, however, are the emergence of a suite of herbaceous pollen types (Fig. 4) – annual 'weeds' which thrive around habitations, and perennials of short, grazed turf, meadows and field margins – which given the timing of their appearance are undoubtedly ascribable to the impacts of Norse settlement and pastoral farming. In addition to those indicators already described, these include pollen of *Ranunculus acris*-type and Lactuceae, a tribe of the Asteraceae which includes *Leontodon autumnalis* (autumn hawkbit), a plant which both Böcher et al. (1968) and Feilberg (1984) promote as Norse on the basis of its modern distribution. Furthermore, it seems probable that the increase in *Cerastium*-type and Brassicaceae pollen could represent the expansion in *Stellaria media* and *Capsella bursa-pastoris* that were evident during Fredskild's (1978) study.

Generally speaking, increased numbers of coprohilous fungal spores – linked to the presence of grazing animals (cf. van Geel et al., 2003) – also occur in post-*landnám* pollen assemblages, although the patterns revealed do vary according to context. At Ø47 Igaliku/*Garðar* (the site of the cathedral, farm and former residence of the bishops of Greenland) large numbers of T55A and T113 spores were recorded in a 'plaggen-type' deposit containing a significant dung component (Buckland et al., 2009). Yet in a peat profile (a natural context) from Ø39 Qinngua (~10 km north of Qassiarsuk), T113 and T55A display conflicting patterns. In this case the reduction in T55A after *landnám* could suggest that the fungus was growing largely upon dead/decaying wood that was cleared at the onset of settlement.

Regarding any possible palynological evidence for arable, the climate of Greenland during the Norse period is generally regarded as having been unsuitable for growing crops, yet occasional grains of *Hordeum*-type do appear in Norse-age horizons from the Eastern Settlement (e.g. Ø2, Ø39). *Hordeum*-type are, however, near-palynologically inseparable from grains of the native *Elymus arenarius,* and, on the basis of current evidence, the argument as to whether the Norse ever attempted to grow cereals in Greenland still remains a case unproven (for further discussion see Krogh, 1967; Schofield et al., 2007; Edwards et al., 2008). A few pollen grains of *Linum usitatissimum* have been reported from V48 (Niaquusat) and V51 (Sandnes) which may indicate the growing and/or processing of flax (Fredskild & Humle, 1991).

CONCLUSIONS

So, are there convincing palynological indicators of a former Norse presence in the North Atlantic region? A response may be summarized thus:

- There appear to be no specific indicators in the Faroese or Icelandic pollen data; but suites of taxa do respond to the Norse presence.
- This also applies partly to Greenland, but although spatially differentiated, *Rumex acetosella* (sheep's sorrel) would seem to either indicate a Norse presence in the Eastern Settlement or to expand upon Norse arrival in the Western Settlement.
- Microscopic charcoal and fungal spores are useful non-pollen indicators.

ACKNOWLEDGEMENTS

The Leverhulme Trust is thanked for financial support.

BIBLIOGRAPHY

Benediktsson, J. (Ed.) (1968). *Íslendingabók. Landnámabók* (Book of Icelanders, Book of Settlements). Íslenzk fornrit 1. Reykjavík: Hið íslenzka fornritafélag.

Berglund, J. (1986). The decline of the Norse settlements in Greenland. *Arctic Anthropology*, 23, 109–135.

Borthwick, D. M. (2007). *The timing and impact of the Norse landnám on the vegetation of Hovsdalur, Faroe Islands.* Unpublished PhD thesis, University of Aberdeen.

Borthwick, D. M., Edwards, K. J., & Cook, G. (2006). Shieling activity during the Norse period in the Faroe Islands: a palynological approach. In J. Arneborg & B. Grønnow (Eds.), *The dynamics of northern societies* (pp. 299–306). Copenhagen: Proceedings of the SILA/NABO Conference on Arctic and North Atlantic Archaeology, Copenhagen, 2004; PNM, Publications from the National Museum, Studies in Archaeology and History, Vol. 10.

Buckland, P. C., Edwards, K. J., Panagiotakopulu, E., & Schofield, J. E. (2009). Palaeoecological and historical evidence for manuring and irrigation at *Garðar* (Igaliku), Norse Eastern Settlement, Greenland. *The Holocene*, 19, 105–116.

Böcher, T. W., Holmer, K., & Jakobsen, K. (1968). *The flora of Greenland.* Copenhagen: P. Haase & Son.

Davis, A. M., McAndrews, J. H., & Wallace, B. L. (1988). Palaeoenvironment and the archaeological record at the L'Anse aux Meadows site, Newfoundland. *Geoarchaeology*, 3, 53–64.

Edwards, K. J. (1979). Palynological and temporal inference in the context of prehistory, with special reference to the evidence from lake and peat deposits. *Journal of Archaeological Science*, 6, 255–270.

Edwards, K. J. (1981). The separation of *Corylus* and *Myrica* pollen in modern and fossil samples. *Pollen et Spores*, 23, 205–218.

Edwards, K. J. (2008). Juniper, goats and the Norse: did the decline of *Juniperus* in the Faroe Islands have a human cause? In C. Paulsen & H. D. Michelsen (Eds.), *Símunarbók. Heiðursrit til Símun V. Arge á 60 ára degnum* (pp. 58–71). Tórshavn: Fróðskapur, Faroe University Press.

Edwards, K. J., & Borthwick, D. B. (2010). Peaceful wars and scientific invaders: Irishmen, Vikings and palynological evidence for the earliest settlement of the Faroe Islands. In J. Sheehan & D. Ó Corráin (Eds.), *The Viking Age: Iceland and the West. Proceedings of the XVth Viking Congress, Cork* (pp. 66–79). Dublin: Four Courts Press.

Edwards, K. J., Borthwick, D., Cook, G., Dugmore, A. J., Mairs, K.-A., Church, M. J., Simpson, I. A., & Adderley, W. P. (2005). A hypothesis-based approach to landscape change in Suðuroy, Faroe Islands. *Human Ecology*, 33, 621–650.

Edwards, K. J., Buckland, P. C., Craigie, R., Panagiotakopulu, E., & Stummann Hansen, S. (1998). Landscapes at landnám: palynological and palaeoentomological evidence from Toftanes, Faroe Islands. *Fróðskaparrit*, 48, 229–244.

Edwards, K. J., & C. J. McIntosh (1988). Improving the detection rate of cereal-type pollen grains from *Ulmus* decline and earlier deposits from Scotland. *Pollen et Spores*, 30, 179–188.

Edwards, K. J., Schofield, J. E., & Mauquoy, D. (2008). High resolution paleoenvironmental and chronological investigations of Norse *landnám* at Tasiusaq, Eastern Settlement, Greenland. *Quaternary Research*, 69, 1–15.

Edwards, K. J., & Whittington, G. (1997). Vegetation change. In K. J. Edwards & I. B. M. Ralston (Eds.), *Scotland: environment and archaeology, 8 000 BC–AD 1 000* (pp. 63–82). Chichester: John Wiley & Sons.

Einarsson, Þ. (1963). Pollen analytical studies on the vegetation and climate history of Iceland in late and post-glacial times. In Á. Löve, & D. Löve (Eds.), *North Atlantic biota and their history* (pp. 355–365). Oxford: Pergamon Press.

Erlendsson, E. (2007). *Environmental change around the time of the Norse Settlement of Iceland.* Unpublished PhD thesis, University of Aberdeen.

Erlendsson, E., & Edwards, K. J. (2009). The timing and causes of the final pre-settlement expansion of *Betula pubescens* in Iceland. *The Holocene*, 19, 1083–1091.

Erlendsson, E., Edwards, K. J., & Buckland, P. C. (2009). Vegetational response to early human colonisation of the volcanic and coastal environments of Ketilsstaðir, southern Iceland. *Quaternary Research*, 72, 174–187.

Feilberg, J. (1984). A phytogeographical study of south Greenland. Vascular plants. *Meddelelser om Grønland, Bioscience*, 15, 1–69.

Firbas, F. (1937). Der pollen analytische nachweis des Getreidebau. *Zeitschrift für Botanik*, 31, 447–478.

Fredskild, B. (1973). Studies in the vegetational history of Greenland. *Meddelelser om Grønland*, 198, 1–245.

Fredskild, B. (1978). Palaeobotanical investigations of some peat deposits of Norse age at Qagssiarssuk, south Greenland. *Meddelelser om Grønland*, 204, 1–41.

Fredskild, B. (1983). The Holocene vegetational development of the Godthåbsfjord area, West Greenland. *Meddelelser om Grønland, Geoscience*, 10, 1–28.

Fredskild, B., & Hulme, L. (1991). Plant remains from the Norse farm Sandnes in the Western Settlement, Greenland. *Acta Borealia*, 1, 69–81.

van Geel, B., Buurman, J., Brinkkemper, O., Schelvis, J., Aptroot, A., van Reenen, G., & Hakbijl, T. (2003). Environmental reconstruction of a Roman Period settlement site in Uitgeest (The Netherlands), with special reference to coprophilous fungi. *Journal of Archaeological Science*, 30, 873–883.

Gennard, D. E. (1985). Observations on the evidence for flax growth in Ireland provided by pollen analysis. *Circaea*, 3, 159–162.

Grönvold, K., Óskarsson, N., Johnsen, J., Clausen, H. B., Hammer, C. U., Bond, G., & Bard, E., (1995). Ash layers from Iceland in the Greenland GRIP ice core correlated with oceanic and land sediments. *Earth and Planetary Science Letters*, 135, 149–155.

Guðmundsson, G. (1996). Gathering and processing of lyme-grass (*Elymus arenarius* L.) in Iceland: an ethnohistorical account. *Vegetation History and Archaeobotany*, 5, 13–23.

Guldager Christiansen, H., Fosaa, A. M. (2009). Færøernes ældste kulturplanter. *Fróðskaparrit*, 57, 128–149.

Gunnarsdóttir, B. (2001). Gróðurfarslýsingar í Íslendingasögum bornar saman við núverandi gróðurfar (E. Descriptions of vegetation in the Icelandic Sagas compared to present vegetation). *Skógræktarritið*, 2001, 63–77.

Hallsdóttir, M. (1987). *Pollen analytical studies of human influence on vegetation in relation to the Landnám tephra layer in Southwest Iceland.* Lund: Lundqua Thesis 18, Lund University.

Hallsdóttir, M. (1996). Frjógreining. Frjókorn sem heimild um landnámið. In G. Á. Grímsdóttir (Ed.), *Um landnám á Íslandi – fjórtán erindi* (pp. 123–134). Reykjavík: Vísindafélag Íslendinga.

Hannon, G. E., & Bradshaw, R. H. W. (2000). Impacts and timing of the first human settlement on vegetation of the Faroe Islands, *Quaternary Research*, 54, 404–413.

Hannon, G. E., & Bradshaw, R. H. W. (2007). Human impact and landscape change at Argisbrekka. In D. L. Mahler, *Sæteren ved Argisbrekka – Økonomiske forandringer på Færøerne i vikingetid og tidlig middelalder* (pp. 306–323). Tórshavn: Annales Societatis Scientiarum Færoensis Supplementum, 47; Faroe University Press.

Hannon, G. E., Bradshaw, R. H. W., Bradshaw, E. G., Snowball, I., & Wastegård, S. (2005). Climatic change and human settlement as drivers of late Holocene vegetation change in the Faroe Islands. *The Holocene*, 15, 639–647.

Hannon, G. E., Wastegård, S., Bradshaw, E., & Bradshaw, R. H. W. (2001). Human impact and landscape degradation on Faroe Islands. *Biology and Environment: Proceedings of the Royal Irish Academy*, 101B, 129–139.

Henningsmoen, K. E. (1977). Pollen-analytical investigations in the L'Anse aux Meadows area, Newfoundland. In A. S. Ingstad (Ed.), *The discovery of a Norse settlement in America* (pp. 289–340). Oslo: Universitetsforlaget.

Iversen, J. (1934). Moorgeologische Untersuchungen auf Grönland. *Meddelelser fra Dansk Geologisk Forening*, 8, 341–358.

Iversen, J. (1941). Landnam i Danmarks stenalder (Land occupation in Denmark's Stone Age). *Danmarks Geologiske Undersøgelse*, Series II, 66, 1–68.

Jóhansen, J. (1985). *Studies in the Vegetational History of the Faroe and Shetland Islands.* Tórshavn: Annales Societatis Scientiarum Færoensis Supplementum, 11; Føroya Fróðskaparfelag.

Jóhansen, J. (2000). *Føroysk flora.* A. M. Fosaa & S. Rasmussen (Eds.). Tórshavn: Føroya Skúlabókagrunnur.

Karlsdóttir, L., Thórsson, Æ. Th., Hallsdóttir, M., Sigurgeirsson, A., Eysteinsson, Th., & Anamthawat-Jónsson, K. (2007). Differentiating pollen of *Betula* species from Iceland. *Grana*, 46, 78–84.

Krogh, K. J. (1967). *Viking Greenland.* Copenhagen: National Museum.

Lawson, I. T., Church, M. J., McGovern, T. H., Arge, S. V., Woollet, J., Edwards, K. J., Gathorne-Hardy, F. J., Dugmore, A. J., Cook, G., Mairs, K.-A., Thomson, A. M., & Sveinbjarnardóttir, G. (2005). Historical ecology on Sandoy,

Faroe Islands: palaeoenvironmental and archaeological perspectives. *Human Ecology*, 33, 651–684.

Lawson, I. T., Edwards, K. J., Church, M. J., Newton, A. J., Cook, G. T., Gathorne-Hardy, F. J., & Dugmore, A. J. (2008). Human impact on an island ecosystem: pollen data from Sandoy, Faroe Islands. *Journal of Biogeography*, 35, 1130-1152.

Lawson, I. T., Gathorne-Hardy, F. J., Church, M. J., Newton, A. J., Edwards, K. J., Dugmore, A. J., & Einarsson, Á. (2007). Environmental impacts of the Norse settlement: palaeoenvironmental data from Mývatnssveit, Northern Iceland. *Boreas*, 36, 1–19.

Ostenfeld, C. H. (1926). The flora of Greenland and its origin. *Biologiske Meddelelser Kongelige Danske Videnskabernes Selskab*, 6, 1–70.

Pedersen, A. (1972). Adventitious plants and cultivated plants in Greenland. *Meddelelser om Grønland*, 178, 1–99.

Porsild, M. P. (1932). Alien plants and apophytes of Greenland. *Meddelelser om Grønland*, 92, 1–85.

Schofield, J. E. & Edwards, K. J. (2011). Grazing impacts and woodland management in *Eriksfjord*: *Betula*, coprophilous fungi and the Norse settlement of Greenland. *Vegetation History and Archaeobotany* 20, 181–197.

Schofield, J. E., Edwards, K. J., & Christensen, C. (2008). Environmental impacts around the time of Norse *landnám* in the Qorlortoq valley, Eastern Settlement, Greenland. *Journal of Archaeological Science*, 35, 1643–1657.

Schofield, J. E., Edwards, K. J., McMullen, J. A. (2007). Modern pollen-vegetation relationships in subarctic southern Greenland and the interpretation of fossil pollen data from the Norse *landnám*. *Journal of Biogeography*, 34, 473–488.

Small, A. (1991). The juniper decline during the Norse landnam in the Faroe Islands, *Acta Borealia*, 9, 3–6.

Steindórsson, S. (1962). On the age and immigration of the Icelandic flora. *Rit Vísindafélags Íslendinga*, 35, 1–157.

Steindórsson, S. (1964). *Gróður á Íslandi*. Reykjavík: Almenna bókafélagið.

Sveinbjarnardóttir, G., Erlendsson, E., Vickers, K., McGovern, T. H., Milek, K., Edwards, K. J., Simpson, I. A., & Cook, G. (2007). The palaeoecology of a high-status Icelandic farm. *Environmental Archaeology*, 12, 197–216.

Vickers, K., Erlendsson, E., Church, M. J., Edwards, K. J., & Bending, J. (2011). 1000 years of environmental change and human impact at Stóra-Mörk, southern Iceland: A multiproxy study of a dynamic and vulnerable landscape. *The Holocene* 21, 979–995.

Þórarinsson, S. (1944). *Tefrokronologiska studier på Island: Þjórsárdalur och dess förödelse*. Copenhagen: Munksgaard.

Þórhallsdóttir, Þ. E. (1996). Áhrif búsetu á landið. In G. Á. Grímsdóttir (Ed.), *Um landnám á Íslandi – fjórtán erindi* (pp. 149–170). Reykjavík: Vísindafélag Íslendinga.

The Viking Age Graves from Hedeby

SILKE EISENSCHMIDT

ABSTRACT

At Hedeby, approximately 1350 graves have been excavated between 1812 and 1970. They are spread out over six cemeteries. The most important are two cemeteries with more than 300 graves inside, and approximately 1000 burials south of the semicircular rampart. The article discusses the chronological and spatial development of each cemetery. There are both cremation and inhumation burials. Most of the graves contain none or only a few grave goods. Only a few burials are richly furnished chamber graves. The graves date from the 8th to the 10th century, suggesting a horizontal stratigraphy from west to east. At last, questions concerning the ethnic and social division in the population of Hedeby, as well as their religious beliefs in a time of profound change, are discussed.

Keywords: Hedeby, graves, burial customs, ethnicity, social division, Christianization.

Between 1812 and 1970, approximately 1350 graves have been identified and investigated in and around Hedeby. The graves represent a small fraction of the burials from the 300 years of Hedeby's existence. H. Steuer (1974, pp. 19f.) estimates that there may be as many as 10,000 burials in the area. Geomagnetic investigations in 2002 suggest that the whole south-western area of Hedeby has been used for burials (Hilberg, 2007, pp. 198f.). If so the number of graves is probably significantly higher than 10,000.

Most of the finds have been unavailable to researchers until now. U. Arents from the University of Kiel used the material for her PhD thesis, which has only been available on microfiche (Arents, 1992). During the last year this PhD has been updated and supplemented (Arents & Eisenschmidt, 2010).

The 1350 graves are spread out over six cemeteries (Fig. 1):

– North of the semicircular ramparts, on a distinct hill named Hochburg, which means Hillfort, about 60 small burial mounds have been identified. South of Hochburg burials with well preserved coffins were found.

– Within the semicircular rampart, three cemeteries have been identified, containing approximately 350 graves: Chamber graves were found in the western part. In the centre as well as near the harbour, inhumation graves with or without coffins were discovered.

– The largest coherent excavation was carried out south of the semicircular rampart. Here nearly 1000 graves were found.

Fig. 1. Hedeby, Kr. Schleswig-Flensburg. Excavated areas between 1900 and 1980. 1 Burial mounds at „Hochburg“, 2 Northern cemetery, 3 Inhumation cemetery, 4 Chamber graveyard, 5 Graves near harbour (Noor), 6 Southern cemetery with the boat chamber grave (B) (Map: V. Hilberg, Archäologisches Landesmuseum Schleswig).

Fig. 2. Hedeby, northern cemetery. 1 Golden filigree brooch found in 1855/56; 2 Carolingian strap mounting found in 1812/13 (Foto: 1 Archäologisches Landesmuseum Schleswig, 2 Nationalmuseet Copenhagen). 1 M. 3:2; 2 M. 1:1.

GRAVES NORTH OF THE SEMICIRCULAR RAMPART

The graves north of the semicircular rampart have not been documented in a systematic way and very little information remains. The Hochburg rises to a level of 26 meters a.s.l. The plateau is surrounded by an earthen wall where 57 small mounds were registered in 1969. The mounds are randomly distributed in the north-western part of the plateau, whereas the south-eastern part is badly disturbed by the removal of marl. Six mounds were excavated in 1889 and 1896 by W. Splieth from the Museum in Kiel and another four in the 1930s initiated by H. Jankuhn (Loewe, 1998, pp. 51–53). The excavated burial mounds were 7–10 meters in diameter and 0.8–1.0 meters tall. The graves contained cremation deposits without grave goods. As the graves resemble the early Viking Age graves in Scandinavia, it is assumed that the burial mounds on Hochburg are from the 8–9th century.

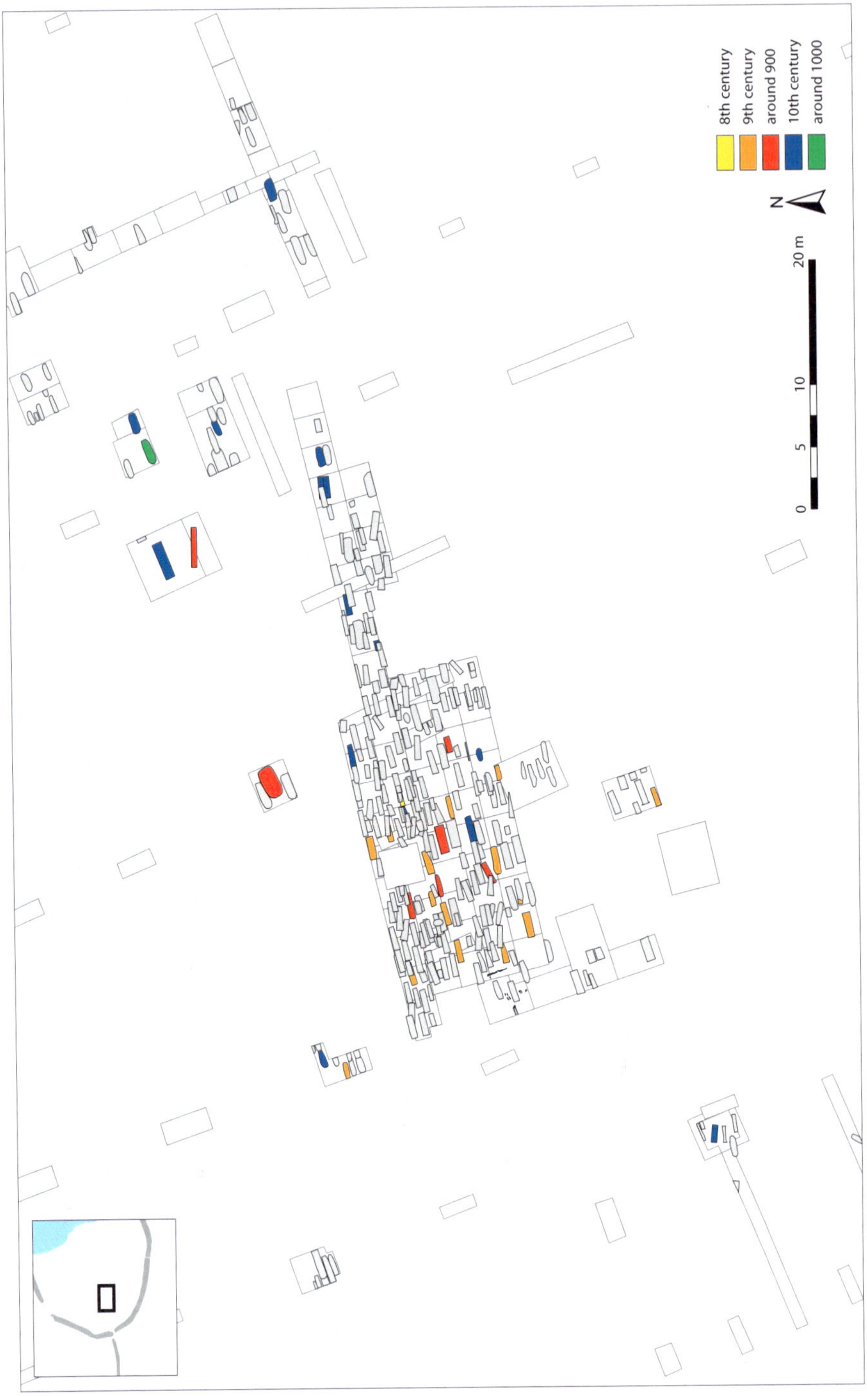

Fig. 3. Hedeby, inhumation cemetery inside the semicircular rampart. (Drawing: J. Schüller, Archäologisches Landesmuseum Schleswig, after Arents & Eisenschmidt, 2010, p. 220).

The wet area south of the Hochburg has clay suitable for making bricks. The removal of clay has disturbed the area since the 17th century. This has continually revealed burials and single objects such as two oval brooches – type JP 37 and 51, a golden filigree brooch, a Carolingian strap mounting and sword type JP V (Fig. 2). The finds can be related to individual inhumation graves, some of which still had remnants of a burial mound. Also a row of six coffins in a west-east direction have been reported. The few descriptions and preserved finds suggest that the area between the Hochburg and the semicircular rampart was used as a cemetery from the mid 9th to the mid 10th century.

GRAVES WITHIN THE SEMICIRCULAR RAMPART

Within the semicircular rampart excavations carried out between 1900 and 1969 three large sections of cemeteries were revealed with a total of 353 graves.

The majority were found between 1900 and 1912 in a 900 m^2 area south of the creek. This excavation revealed approximately 320 inhumation graves, mostly oriented westsouthwest-eastnortheast (Fig. 3). Many of them had traces of coffins. The graves were so tightly spaced that there was no room for burial mounds. 21% of the graves contained grave goods, but rarely more than one item. The most common grave goods were brooches and knives. Only two female graves contained more than six grave goods, one of which was a chamber grave. More than half of the 39 datable graves were dated to the second half of the 9th century and the first half of the 10th century. A coin – an Otto-Adelheid-Pfennig – dates the youngest grave to around 1000. The earliest burials were probably in the south western part of the area around mid 9th century and later expanding to the east, north and west. The area has been reused over time. Contrary to the opinion of H. Jankuhn (1986, pp. 105–108) the alignment and the type of graves (inhumation graves with or without coffins, with and without nails) gives no clue to their chronology. The oldest graves to the west were covered by a later culture layer. The younger graves to the east lay on top of an earlier settlement layer.

About 50 meters southwest of the inhumation cemetery, a group of nine chamber graves, a simple inhumation and a cremation grave were discovered in 1930–1931 at the highest point east of the rampart. A further 40 meters east, another chamber grave and an inhumation grave were found (Fig. 4). The chamber graves were established in two rows. Segments of circular ditches suggest that some graves were originally covered by small burial mounds. Almost all the chamber graves contained grave goods unlike the majority of inhumation graves with and without coffins. Nine of the 13 graves contained datable

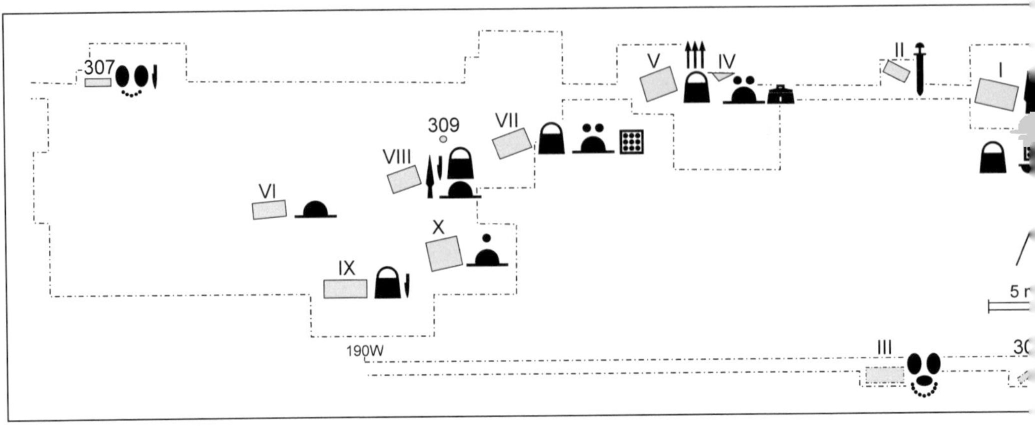

Fig. 4. Hedeby, chamber graveyard (Symbols: H. Dieterich, University of Kiel).

artifacts. Seven graves contained weapons, especially shields, rarely spears and only once a sword or a set of arrows. Coins were found in three of these graves. Two female graves were furnished with oval brooches. The majority of the graves were established in the first half and middle of the 9th century and not in the 10th century, as previously suggested (Aner, 1952, p. 99). The only exception is chamber grave X, dated to or shortly after 900. During the 10th and 11th century, a few pit-houses were built in the area (Jankuhn, 1986, pp. 93–95).

Near the harbour, the 1963–1969 excavations revealed a disturbed cemetery (Fig. 5). Apart from 18 more and less intact skeletons, a number of skeletal remains were found spread over a larger area. Eight graves were closely spaced, presumably in rows. The wet soil has preserved organic material. In one grave enough details of the coffin were preserved to illustrate how the coffin was built (Schietzel & Ulbricht, 1977, pp. 61f.). Also a maple staff – the only grave goods – was preserved. The stratigraphy is complex (Schultze, 2008, pp. 72ff.), but a re-evaluation of the documentation shows that all the skeletal remains were situated in, or connected to, the upper layers[1]. Dendro dates from the layers beneath suggest that this cemetery was established after 900 and not as previously suggested before 900 (Schietzel & Ulbricht, 1977, pp. 60f.).

1 Joachim Schultze has been very helpful introducing the digitized excavation documentation and discussing the stratigraphy.

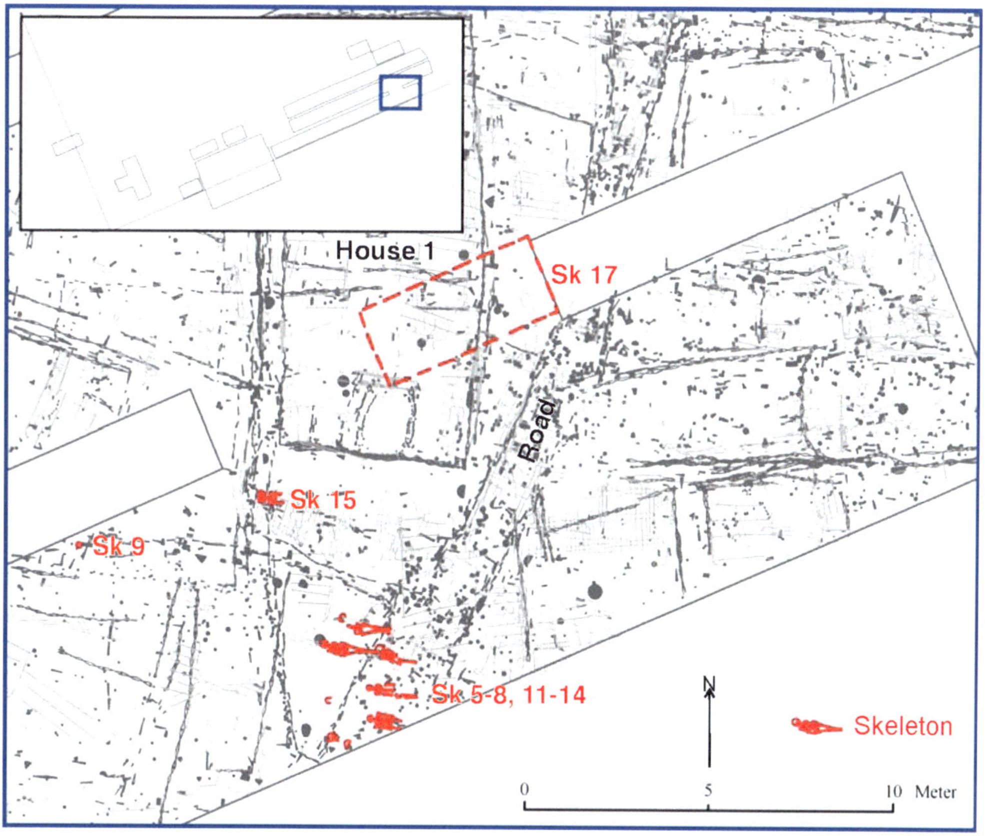

Fig. 5. Hedeby, graves near harbour (Noor). Area with skeletons 5–9, 11–15 and 17 above settlement structures (Drawing: J. Schultze, Archäologisches Landesmuseum Schleswig).

GRAVES SOUTH OF THE SEMICIRCULAR RAMPART

The largest cemetery was excavated south of the ramparts. In the years between 1957 and 1970 a 16.600 m^2 large area was excavated, revealing approximately 1000 graves. The western limit of this large cemetery is undetermined. To the south a creek defines a natural border. Today the cemetery is bisected into an eastern and a western area by the so-called Church road.

A total of 450 inhumations and 90 cremation graves were found to the west of the Church road (Fig. 6). The famous boat chamber grave, excavated in 1908, situated only 20–30 m southeast of the field, is associated with this cemetery (Müller-Wille, 1976; Wamers, 1994). Unfortunately, parts of the area have been disturbed by deep plowing and road tracks. Only 12% of the 540 burials contained grave goods, mainly knives and whetstones. Jewelry is

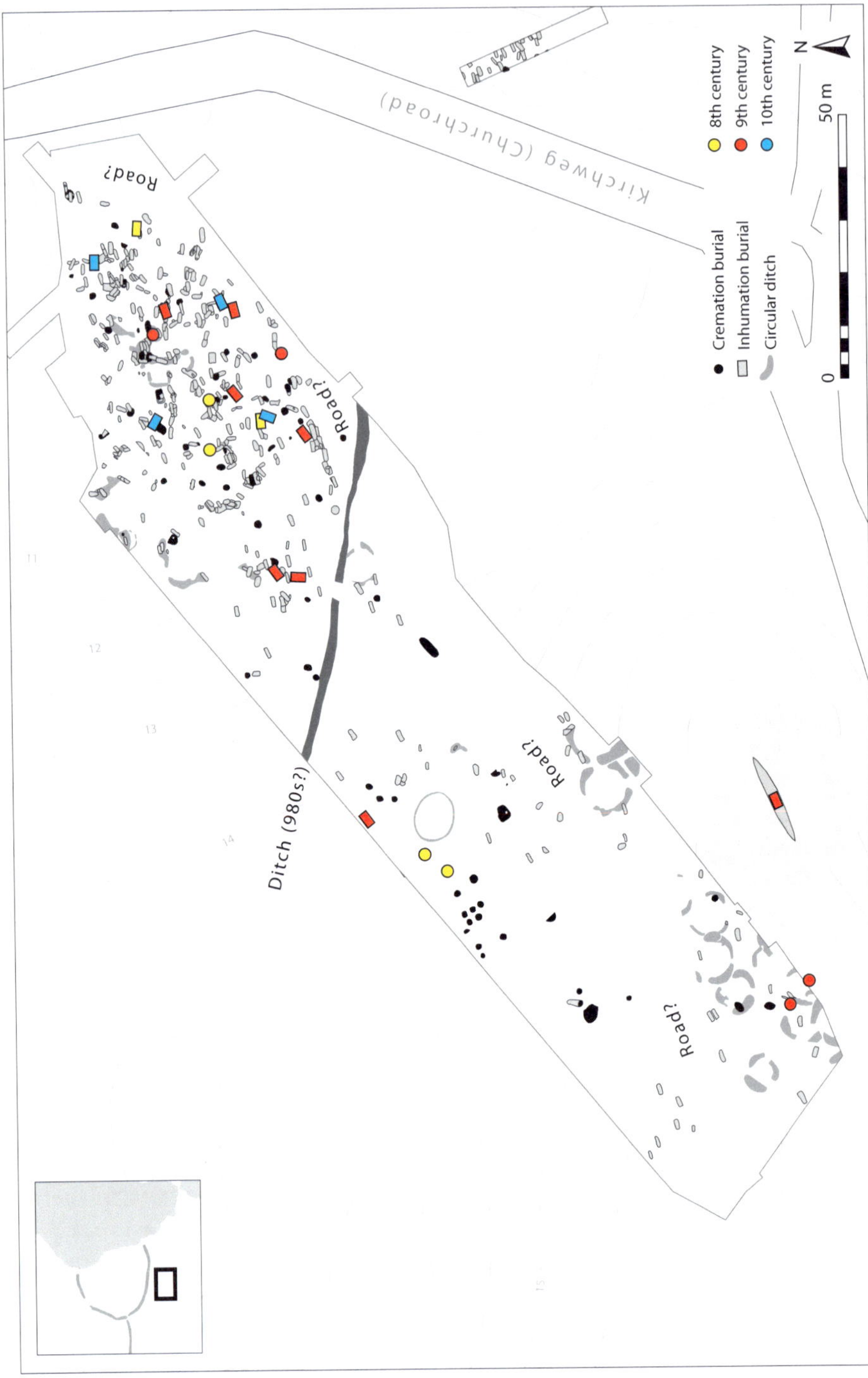

Fig. 6. Hedeby, southern cemetery, western part (Drawing: J. Schüller, Archäologisches Landesmuseum Schleswig, after Arents & Eisenschmidt, 2010, p. 250).

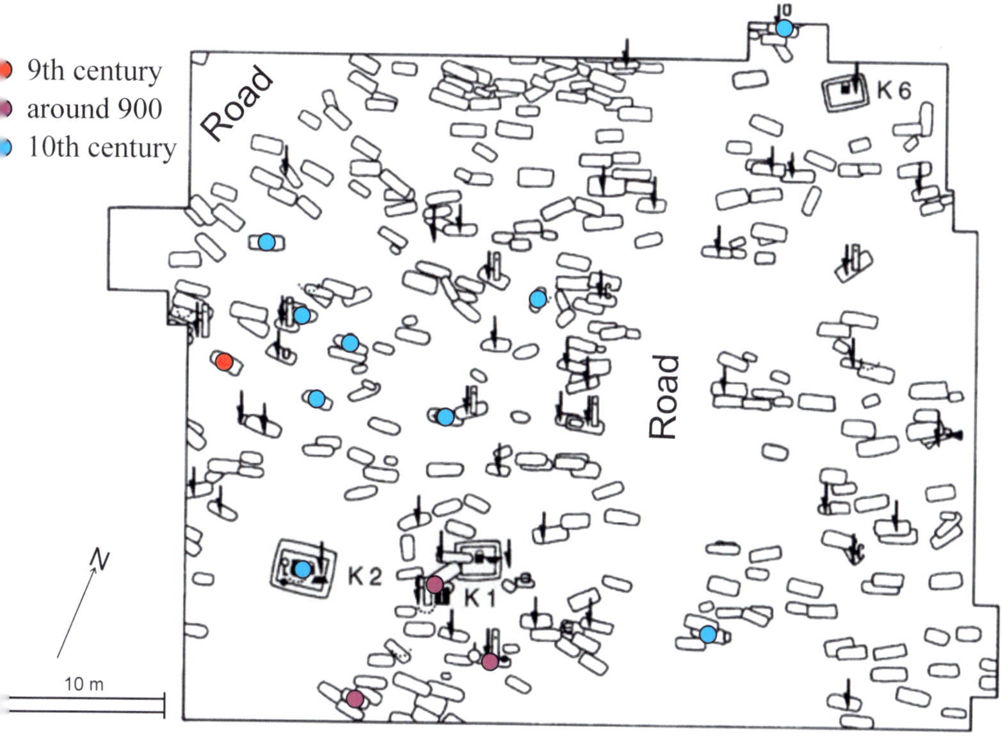

Fig. 7. Hedeby, southern cemetery, eastern part. Excavated area near shore (Noor) with chamber graves (K) 1, 2 and 6 and burial mounds (after Steuer, 1984b, p. 356).

infrequent compared to the cemetery inside the rampart. The only exceptions are the boat chamber grave and a coffin grave with a female (grave 497). These were both furnished with tableware, as well as riding gear in the boat chamber and jewelry in the female grave.

East of the Church road the excavation revealed approximately 430 inhumation graves and five chamber graves (Fig. 7). Artifacts were found in 18% of the graves. The number of grave goods was usually restricted to one, most often a knife, more rarely jewelry. Only one weapon grave with an axe was found. Better equipped graves with tableware and jewelry were restricted to the five chamber graves. Notably, chamber graves 2 and 5 were the largest and best furnished. The chamber graves were covered by small burial mounds. The younger inhumation graves in between the burial mounds were oriented approximately east west. The direction of the roads, which already existed when the area was occupied by pit-houses, seems to have influenced the position of the graves.

Only 39 graves revealed datable artifacts. The graves are evenly distributed over the investigated area which makes it possible to describe the evolution of the cemetery. The oldest burials – cremation pits and urns – were established in the 8th century west of the church road, in the central and northeastern part of the excavated field. Circular ditches indicate the former presence of small burial mounds covering cremation graves. Also, contemporary north-south and to some extent, west-east oriented inhumation graves were found. During the early 9th century the cemetery expands to the southwest towards the vicinity of the boat chamber grave. At the end of the 9th century, the areas around the roads going south and southwest from Hedeby were covered by small burial mounds. Later, inhumation graves, largely west-east oriented, were placed in between the burial mounds, especially in the northern section. The youngest grave is dated to around the mid 10th century.

After abandoning the pit-house area at the Noor in the late 9th century, this area was also used for burials (Steuer, 1974, p. 161). As before the roads leading away from Hedeby seem to have influenced the positioning of the graves, marked with small burial mounds along the roads. Some of these graves were well-equipped chamber graves. Shortly thereafter, the space in between the mounds was used for inhumation graves with or without coffins. These are now dominantly west-east orientated. The defense system of Hedeby was strongly reinforced during the second half of the 10th century (Steuer, 1974, p. 23; Andersen, 1998, p. 146). Parallel to the semicircular rampart, two ditches were dug that cut several graves in the southern cemetery. It is not possible to determine if the area continued to be used for burials after the defense system was expanded because of the lack of grave goods. The youngest datable graves are late 10th century.

BURIAL CUSTOMS IN HEDEBY

An overview of the Hedeby graves suggests a horizontal stratigraphy going from west to east (Fig. 8) although some parts of the cemeteries were used for centuries. In general, the older graves from the 8–9th century are located in the west, several hundred meters away from the settlement, and the shore of the Noor, while the youngest 10th century burials were found near the shore in the east. The southern cemetery is a good example of older graves found to the west on higher ground, while the younger graves were found in the lower area to the east towards the Noor. This area close to the shore had previously been occupied by pit-houses dating to the 8th and 9th centuries (Steuer, 1974, p. 161). A horizontal stratigraphy can also be observed within the semicircular rampart. The oldest graves are the chamber graves on the plateau close to the rampart. In the 10th century houses were built here. This is also visible in the relatively small excavated area of the inhumation cemetery, with the

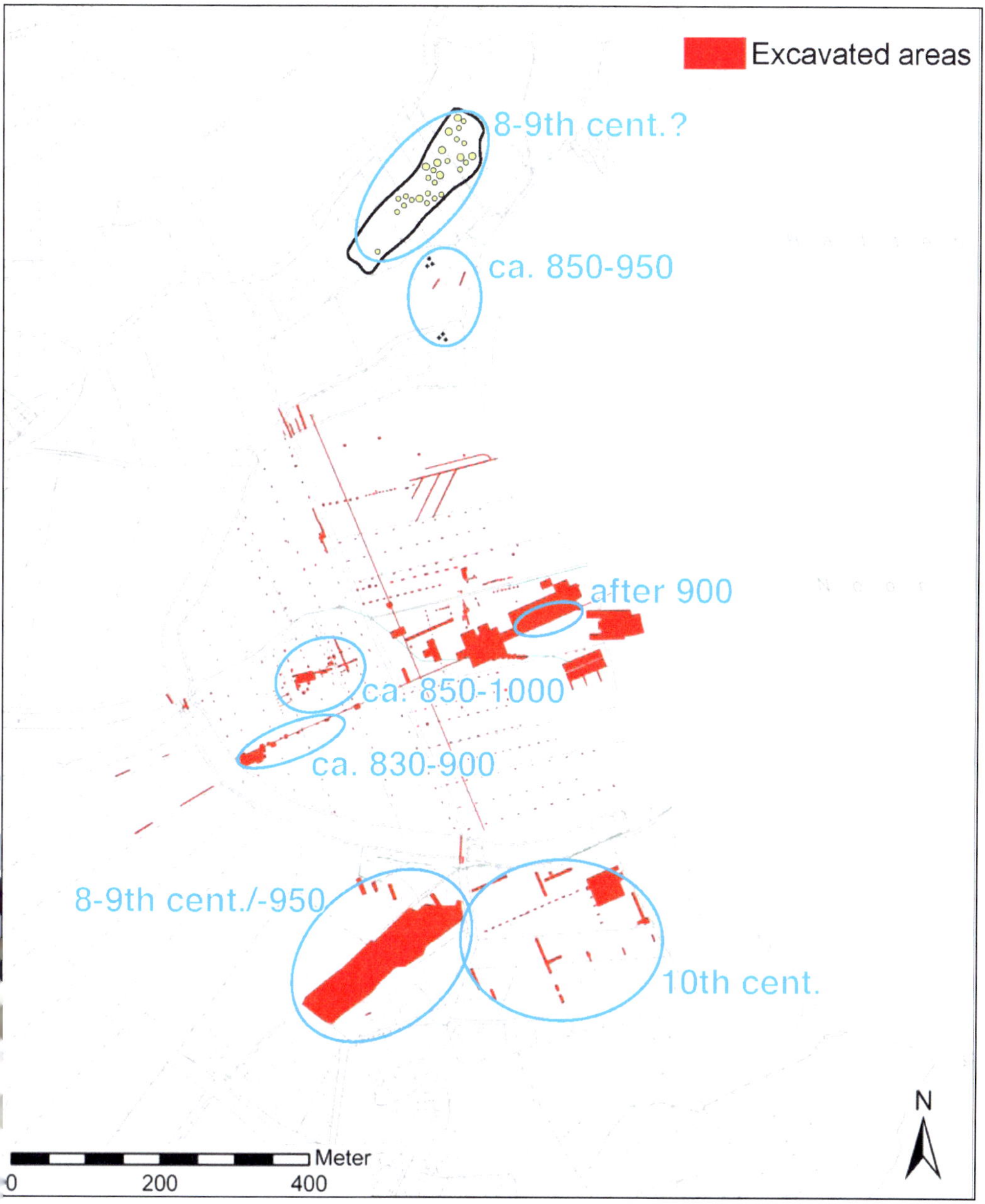

Fig. 8. Hedeby. Dating of the individual graveyards (Map: V. Hilberg, Archäologisches Landesmuseum Schleswig).

Fig. 9. The political situation in Central-Europe in the Viking Age.

older graves in the west and the slightly younger to the east. According to the excavator, F. Knorr, the older graves in the west are partly covered by 10th century settlement deposits while the graves to the east overlie earlier settlement layers. This development ends close to the Noor where inhumation graves without grave goods are found. The underlying settlement has been dendro-dated to the very late 9th century. North of the semicircular rampart there are cremation burials, presumably early Viking Age on the Hochburg and the well equipped inhumation graves dating to the second half of the 9th and 10th century near the Noor.

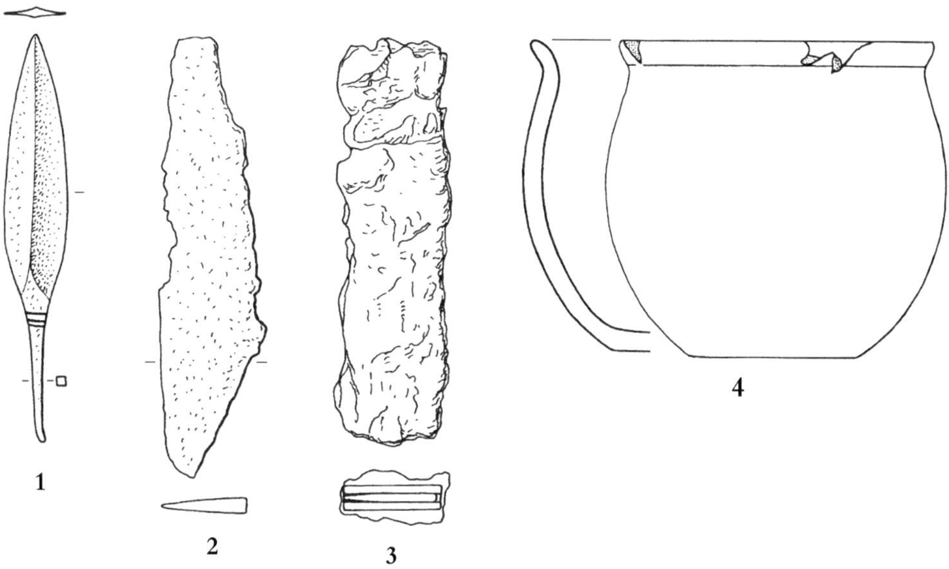

Fig. 10. Hedeby, southern cemetery. Cremation grave 320 with a typical Frisian egg-shaped urn, pocketknife and knife (after Arents & Eisenschmidt, 2010, pl. 60). 1–3 M. 1:2, 4 M. 1:3.

INTERPRETATION

When interpreting the graves one must keep in mind that probably less than 10% of the original burials are known. None of the graveyards have been completely excavated. A large part of the investigated areas were already disturbed prior to excavation and standards have changed considerably since the beginning of excavations. Only 20% of the graves contained grave goods at all, and only a few of these were well equipped with grave goods.

ETHNICITY

Hedeby was the largest Danish Viking Age *emporium* or proto-town, located close to the Carolingian and later Ottonian empires and the Slavonic region (Fig. 9). According to written sources, Hedeby was inhabited by Danes, Saxons, Frisians and Slavs. A longstanding question is: can the ethnic origin of the inhabitants be detected in the burial habits? The grave goods are mostly Scandinavian, while the house types and pottery point to the Saxon area. The fact that Saxons and Frisians stopped furnishing their graves with grave goods

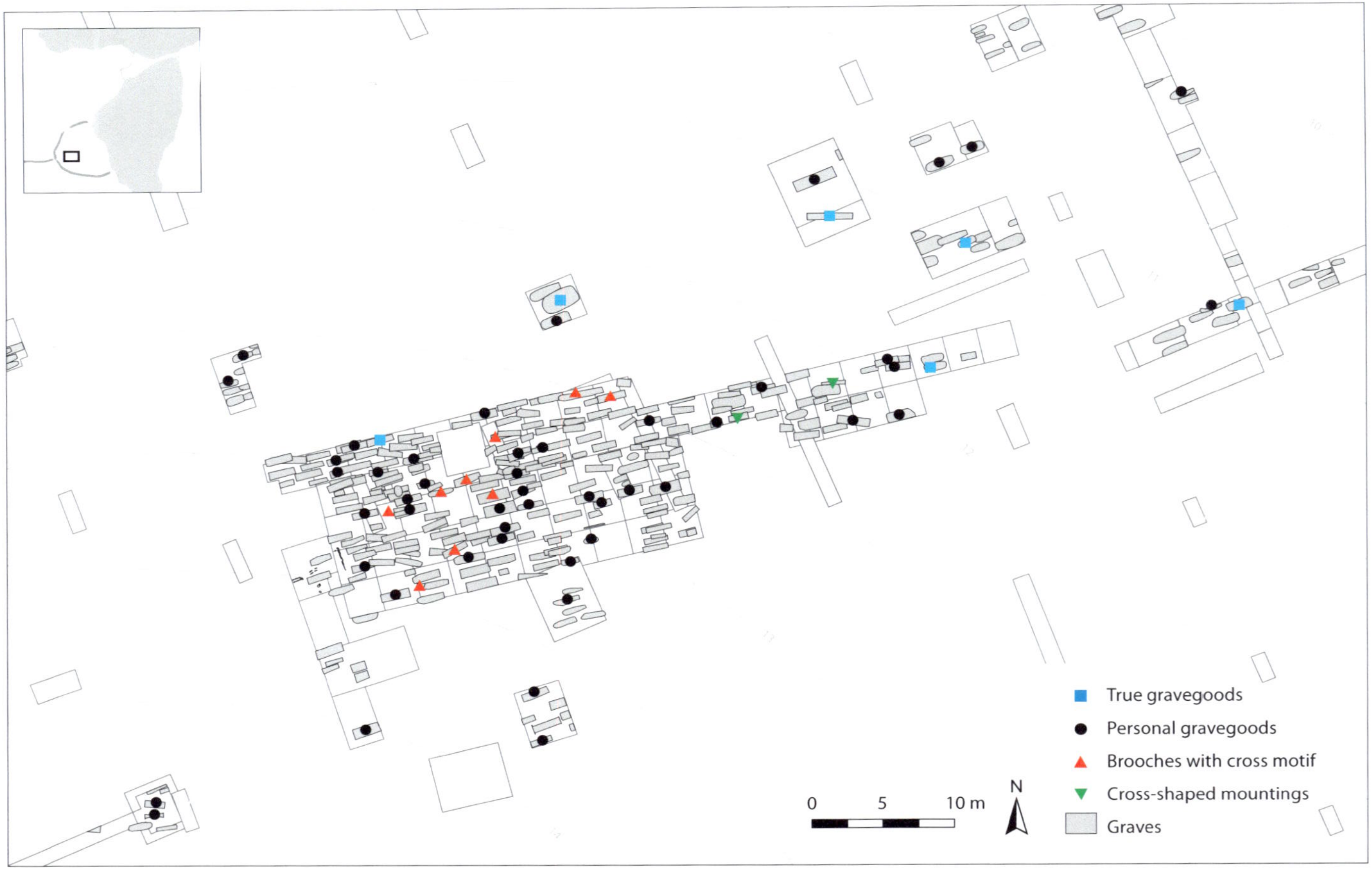

Fig. 11. Hedeby, inhumation cemetery inside the semicircular rampart. Only few graves have "true" grave goods like weapons or tableware (Drawing: J. Schüller, Archäologisches Landesmuseum Schleswig, after Arents & Eisenschmidt, 2010, p. 295).

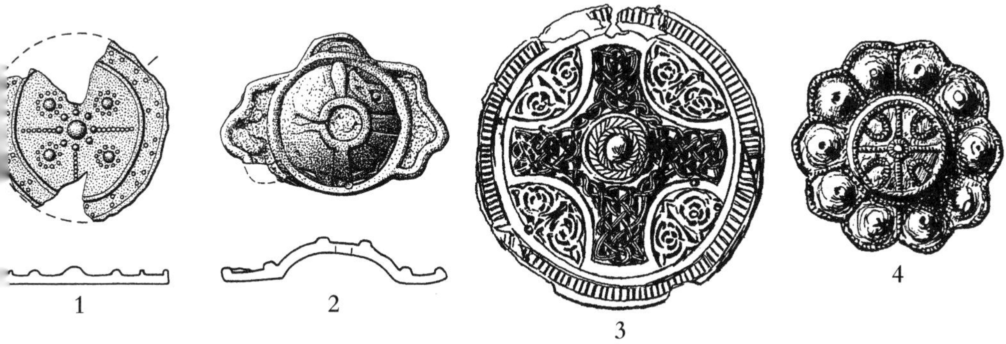

Fig. 12. Hedeby, inhumation cemetery. Brooches with cross motif. 1 grave 147, 2 grave 255, 3 grave 77, 4 grave 270 (after Arents & Eisenschmidt, 2010). M. 2:3.

in the first part of the 9th century at the latest (Kleemann, 2002, p. 345), makes it impossible to distinguish their ethnicity from the numerous other inhumation graves lacking grave goods, as is the custom in contemporary graves in the cemeteries of the rural Danish areas. In conclusion, only when it comes to graves dating to the early Viking Age can the grave give information about the ethnicity of the deceased.

The 8th century urn cremations are almost certainly Frisian (Fig. 10). The egg shaped urns, knives with angular backs and pocketknives are found in abundance along the southern North Sea coast. Possibly the circular ditches and north south oriented inhumation graves can be explained by the presence of Saxons in the 8th and early 9th century. It is questionable, if cremation pits can be associated with Slavs and cremation deposits with the Danes. Since the first half of the 9th century inhumation dominates, regardless of ethnicity.

CHRISTIANIZATION

The transition to inhumation happens significantly earlier in Hedeby than in the rest of Denmark where this change is first seen in the late 9th century. This can probably be explained by Ansgars missionary attempts, which start around the year 830 in the trading places Hedeby, Ribe and Birka (Rimbert, cap. 7–8). During the 10th century more and more Christian influence can be observed in burial customs. The construction of mounds ceases during the first half of the 10th century. The majority of burials with grave goods are dated from the mid 9th to the first half of the 10th century. The decrease in the number of grave goods in the second half of the 10th century could be explained by the

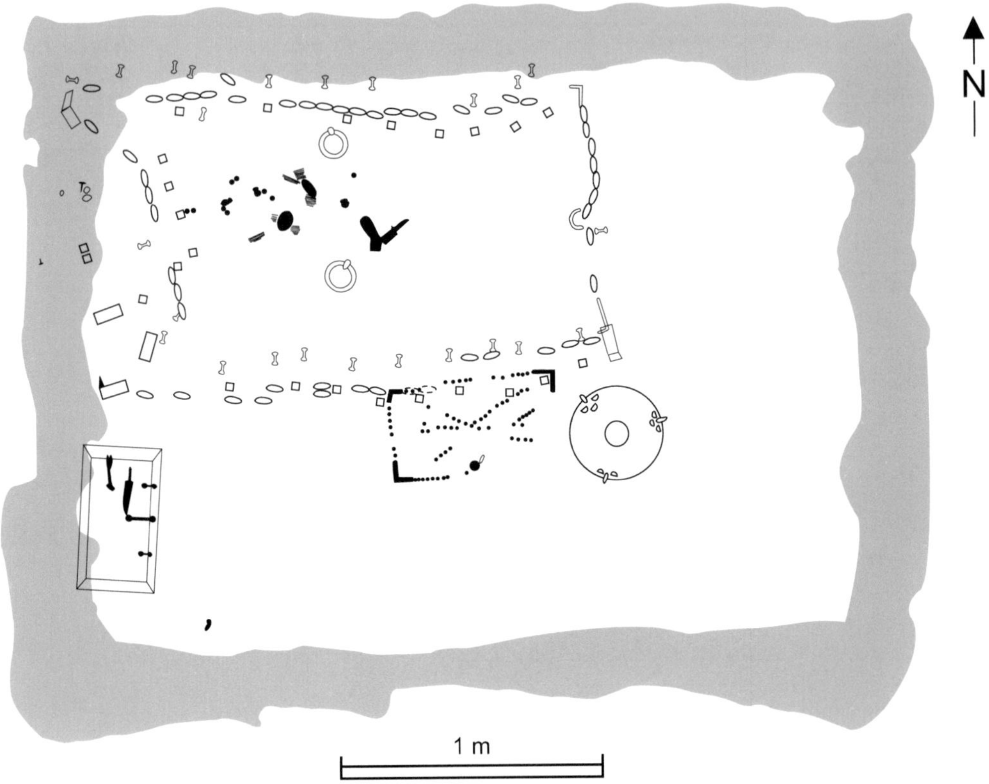

Fig. 13. Hedeby, southern cemetery, eastern part. Chamber grave 5 (Drawing: N. Kossmer, Museum Sønderjylland, Haderslev, after Steuer, 1984a, p. 204).

conversion of the Danes, announced by Harold Bluetooth around the year 965 (Skovgaard-Petersen, 1991, 324). Graves dated to the 11th century cannot be recognized with certainty. Probably more and more Christians were buried in the churchyard. In written sources, a church in Hedeby is mentioned as early as 850 (Rimbert, cap. 24; Lund, 2004, 26), but the remains of the church have not been located yet. Possibly it lies beneath the medieval church located 700 meters north of the rampart.

The cemeteries within the semicircular ramparts show several features of Christian cemeteries (Fig. 11). The inhumation burials are closely spaced, west-east oriented and are nearly arranged in rows. On the other hand, two important elements are missing: the church and an enclosure. Notable are a group of graves with brooches with a cross motif and two coffins with cross-shaped mountings (Fig. 12).

Fig. 14. Hedeby, southern cemetery, eastern part. Jewelry from chamber grave 5 (Photos: Archäologisches Landesmuseum Schleswig). 1–2 M. 1:1; 3–5 M. 3:2.

SOCIAL ASPECTS

A small number of graves in Hedeby contain a complete set of grave goods suggesting a more complex burial with chamber and an overlying mound. These graves most probably represent members of the elite in the area. The variation in grave goods and type of burial, cannot be used to make finer distinctions of social status and rank. The majority of these outstanding graves date to two periods. The first period covering the first half to mid 9th century, with the boat chamber grave and the chamber graveyard. The second period covering from around 900 and the first half of the 10th century with the chamber graves in the southern cemetery. The boat chamber grave dating 830–850 AD stands out among the graves in Hedeby and the whole of Denmark and it has been suggested that it may be the grave of a king (Wamers, 1994, p. 33; Staecker, 2005, pp. 6–9).

In Hedeby, chamber graves already appear approximately 100 years earlier than in the rural areas of Danmark. This could explain why the Hedeby chamber graves lack riding gear, unlike the numerous 10th century chamber graves known especially in the western part of Denmark (Pedersen, 1997, p. 128). At the same time, a feature of high-status-female graves is the use of wagon bodies as coffins. Chamber grave 5 in the southern cemetery and possibly grave 45 in the inhumation cemetery inside the rampart, are the only examples of this special coffin-type found in Hedeby (Fig. 13). The graves were established around 900, which make them the oldest known graves of this type.

Chamber grave 5 is also interesting because of the woman's dress. The deceased was buried with two unique oval brooches made of silver with filigree ornamentation as well as two golden pendants, showing the earliest known Terslev motif (Fig. 14; Eilbracht, 1999, p. 142). Slightly younger high-status female graves, for instance chamber grave 2 and other graves in the vicinity of Hedeby, only contain a single small round brooch made of gold or silver with the Terslev motif. The lack of 10th century oval brooches in Hedeby and the southern part of Jutland, suggest that the transition from the traditional Scandinavian women's dress with three fibulas to the continental with only one fibula takes place shortly after 900.

CONCLUSION

Contact with the southern neighbours, whether peaceful or violent, resulted not only in the exchange of goods, but also in a transfer of knowledge, lifestyle as well as rituals, and ceremonies. Specifically, the 200 years of Christianisation led to a profound change. The inhabitants of Hedeby played a key-role in this process. This is expressed in the burial customs. The transition to inhumation is significantly earlier here, as are the high-status-graves in the 9th century. The rapid introduction of the one fibula-dress is another example.

BIBLIOGRAPHY

Andersen, H. H. (1998). *Danevirke og Kovirke. Arkæologiske undersøgelser 1861–1993*. Højbjerg: Jysk Arkæologisk Selskab.

Aner, E. (1952). Das Kammergräberfeld von Haithabu. *Offa*, 10, 61–115.

Arents, U. (1992). *Die Grabfunde von Haithabu, Kr. Schleswig*. Unpubl. ph.d.-thesis, Univ. Kiel.

Arents, U., & Eisenschmidt, S. (2010). *Die Gräber von Haithabu*. Die Ausgrabungen in Haithabu (Vol. 15). Neumünster: Wachholtz.

v. Carnap-Bornheim, C., Hilberg, V., Kalmring, S., & Schultze, J. (2007). Hedeby's settlement and harbour: recent research in a Viking age trading center. C. J. C. Reuvenslezing (Vol. 19). Amsterdam: Spinhex & Industrie.

Eilbracht, H. (1999). *Filigran- und Granulationskunst im wikingischen Norden. Untersuchungen zum Transfer frühmittelalterlicher Gold- und Silberschmiedetechniken zwischen dem Kontinent und Nordeuropa*. Zeitschrift für Archäologie des Mittelalters Beiheft (Vol. 11). Köln: Rheinland Verlag.

Hilberg, V. (2007). Haithabu im 11. Jahrhundert. Auf der Suche nach dem Niedergang eines dänischen *emporiums* der Wikingerzeit. In Posselt, M., Zickgraf, B., & Dobiat, C. (Eds.), *Geophysik und Ausgrabung. Einsatz und Auswertung zerstörungsfreier Prospektion in der Archäologie*. Internationale Archäologie: Naturwissenschaft und Technologie (Vol. 6, pp. 187–203). Rahden, Westfalen: Leidorf.

Jankuhn, H. (1986). *Haithabu. Ein Handelsplatz der Wikingerzeit* (8th Ed.). Neumünster: Wachholtz.

Kleemann, J. (2002). *Sachsen und Friesen im 8. und 9. Jahrhundert. Eine archäologisch-historische Analyse der Grabfunde*. Veröffentlichungen der urgeschichtlichen Sammlungen des Landesmuseums Hannover (Vol. 50). Oldenburg: Isensee.

Loewe, G. (1998). *Archäologische Denkmäler Schleswig-Holsteins: Kr. Schleswig (seit 1974 Kreis Schleswig-Flensburg)*. Veröffentlichungen des Archäologischen Landesamtes Schleswig-Holstein (Vol. 8). Neumünster: Wachholtz.

Lund, N. (2004). Mission i Danmark før Harald Blåtands dåb. In Lund, N. (Ed.), *Kristendommen i Danmark før 1050*. Roskilde: Roskilde Museums Forlag. Symposium Roskilde 2003.

Müller-Wille, M. (1976). Das Bootkammergrab von Haithabu. In Schietzel, K. (Ed.), *Berichte über die Ausgrabungen in Haithabu (Vol. 8)*. Neumünster: Wachholtz.

Pedersen, A. (1997). Weapons and riding gear in burials - evidence of military and social rank in 10th century Denmark. In Nørgård Jørgensen, A., & Clausen,

B. L. (Eds.), *Military Aspects of Scandinavian Society in a European Perspective AD 1–1300*. PNM Studies in Archaeology & History (Vol. 2, pp. 123–135). Copenhagen: National Museum of Danmark. Symposium Copenhagen 1996.

Rimbert. *Vita Anskarii*. Quellen des 9. und 11. Jahrhunderts zur Geschichte der Hamburger Kirche und des Reiches. Translated by W. Trillmich. Ausgewählte Quellen zur deutschen Geschichte des Mittelalters (Vol. 11, pp. 16–133). Freiherr vom Stein-Gedächtnisausgabe. Darmstadt: Wissenschaftliche Buchgesellschaft.

Schietzel, K., & Ulbricht, I. (1977). Bemerkungen zu Bestattungen und verstreuten Skelettresten der Ausgrabung Haithabu (1963–1969). In Schietzel, K. (Ed.), Untersuchungen zur Anthropologie, Botanik und Dendrochronologie. *Berichte über die Ausgrabungen in Haithabu* (Vol. 11, pp. 57–63). Neumünster: Wachholtz.

Schultze, J. (2008). *Haithabu – Die Siedlungsgrabungen. I. Methode und Möglichkeiten der Auswertung*. Die Ausgrabungen in Haithabu (Vol. 13). Neumünster: Wachholtz.

Skovgaard-Petersen, I. (1991). Konge – småkonge – høvding – vasal. En vurdering af de skriftlige kilder. In Iversen, M., Näsman, U., & Vellev, J. (Eds.), *Mammen. Grav, kunst og samfund i vikingetid*. Jysk Arkæologisk Selskabs Skrifter (Vol. 28, pp. 321–328). Viborg Stiftsmuseum (Vol. 1). Højbjerg: Jysk Arkæologisk Selskab.

Staecker, J. (2005). The Concept of *imitatio* and *translatio*: Perceptions of a Viking-Age Past. *Norwegian Archaeological Review*, 38, 3–28.

Steuer, H. (1974). *Die Südsiedlung von Haithabu. Studien zur frühmittelalterlichen Keramik im Nordseeküstenbereich und in Schleswig-Holstein*. Die Ausgrabungen in Haithabu (Vol. 6). Neumünster: Wachholtz.

Steuer, H. (1984a). Zur ethnischen Gliederung der Bevölkerung von Haithabu anhand der Gräberfelder. *Offa*, 41, 189–212.

Steuer, H. (1984b). Soziale Gliederung der Bevölkerung von Haithabu nach archäologischen Quellen. In Jankuhn, H., Schietzel, K., & Reichstein, H. (Eds.), *Archäologische und naturwissenschaftliche Untersuchungen an ländlichen und frühstädtischen Siedlungen im deutschen Küstengebiet vom 5. Jahrhundert v. Chr. bis zum 11. Jahrhundert n. Chr.* 2 Handelsplätze des frühen und hohen Mittelalters (pp. 339–366). Weinheim: Acta Humaniora.

Wamers, E. (1994). König im Grenzland. Neue Analyse des Bootkammergrabes von Haiðaby. *Acta Archaeologica (Copenhagen)*, 65, 1–56.

'The Serpent's Bed': Gold and Silver in Viking Age Iceland – and Beyond

JAMES GRAHAM-CAMPBELL

ABSTRACT

The Viking Age gold and silver finds from Iceland – both hoards and single-finds – are surveyed in this paper in the context of comparative material from Britain and Scandinavia. There is discussion of what is known – or can be deduced – from literary and historical sources about how precious metal was used in Iceland during the Viking Age, and why it came to be deposited in the ground. Given that no coinage was struck in Iceland during this period, individual coins were mounted as pendants, whereas others were hoarded for their value as bullion, when not melted down for conversion into ornaments. Rings and brooches played a vital role in the so-called 'display economy' and provided the means for prestigious gift-giving. The 'bullion economy', for making payments, is also represented not only by hack-silver hoards, but also by finds of the scales and weights needed for making such transactions. Chance losses of gold and silver items are rare finds on settlement sites, but not unknown – and those from Hofstaðir are briefly considered.

Attention is drawn to the need for more detailed publication than hitherto of the silver hoards from Keta and Sandmúli, the latter being the larger and more important with some close similarities to the well-known hoard from Skaill, in Orkney. Likewise, the more recent find of the Miðhús hoard requires further specialist research, in particular given the problem presented by a neck-ring fragment seemingly made from mechanically manufactured rods – instead of being hammered as was the method used during the Viking Age.

Keywords: Iceland, gold, silver, hoards, rings, brooches, pendants, coins.

When I was invited to deliver a public lecture, during the 16th Viking Congress, on the subject of Viking Age gold and silver in Iceland (and beyond), I chose to title it the 'The Dragon's Bed', after one of the many kennings for gold. In this case, it was taken from Arnórr Þórðarson's *Magnússdrápa*, cited in *Heimskringla* (ch. 1 of the *Saga of Magnús the Good*), as brought to my attention by Judith Jesch (2000, p. 32), in whose translation the young king Magnús is referred to as 'disburser of the dragon's bed'. However, given the absence of 'true' dragons from Viking Age art (that is of beasts with two legs, wings and a

Fig. 1. An eleventh-century depiction of the Sigurd legend, at Ramsundsberget, Sweden.

long tail; cf. Hicks, 1993, pp. 254–255), it is better to follow Anthony Faulkes in translating *ormr* as 'serpent', as in the section of the *Edda* (*Skáldskaparmál*, ch. 40), which ends with Snorri's words: 'Now the story has been told that is the origin of gold being called lair or abode of Fafnir …' (Faulkes, 1987, p. 102).

It would have been well known that it was for the legendary hero Sigurd to kill the serpent Fafnir in order to obtain the gold, which was nevertheless to end up in the Rhine; hence another kenning for gold, 'Rhine's rock', as in the half-stanza by Einar skálaglamm, quoted by Snorri (in *Skáldskaparmál*, ch. 46), which ends 'I do not think the ruler's men will run short of Rhine's rock' (Faulkes, 1987, p. 113).

Various depictions of the Sigurd 'cycle' are known from the tenth century onwards, as on some of the Manx cross-slabs (Margeson, 1983). Other well-known examples include the eleventh-century carving (Fig. 1) on Ramsundsberget, Sweden (A. Andersson in Anker, 1970, pp. 196 & 198, Fig. 67; Fuglesang, 1980, p. 185, no. 80, pl. 46a), and the portal of Hylestad stave-church, Norway (Anker, 1970, pp. 408–10, pls. 219–222). However, by gaining the (cursed) gold, Sigurd only brought himself to his own death. Part of the continuing popularity of this story is thus explained because it contains the Christian moral that to gain great wealth is no guarantee of good fortune – and certainly not of living happily ever after – if only because 'we brought nothing into this world, and it is certain we can carry nothing out' (Paul's 'First Epistle to Timothy', 6:7).

Skalds loved to speak of gold (cf. Jesch, 2000, p. 35); the saga-writers were, however, somewhat more circumspect. They certainly knew of gold finger-rings, and even of gold arm-rings, but it would appear that it was

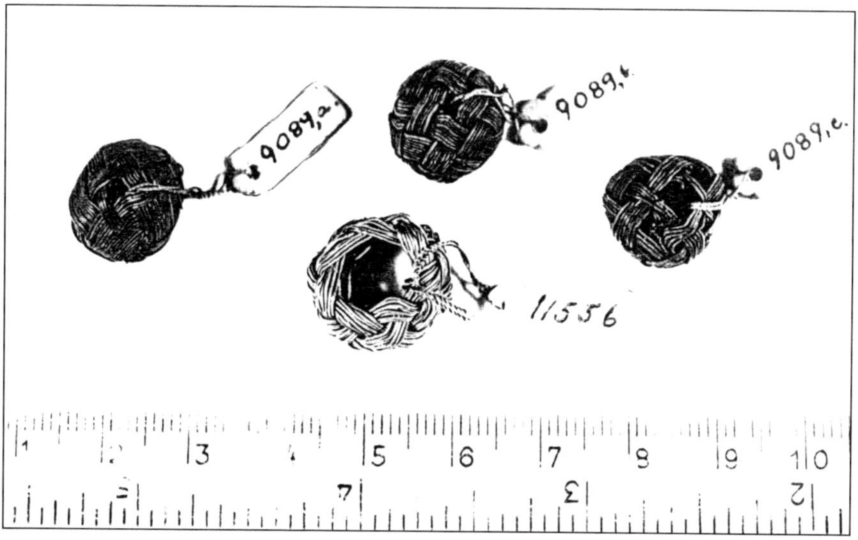

Fig. 2. The four decorative wire balls from the site of the cemetery at Kápa, with the gold ball at the bottom; the other three are made from silver wires. (Photo: James Graham-Campbell.)

silver that they knew best, including silver coins. Indeed, only three small objects of gold are known (to date) to have survived from the Viking Age in Iceland. First, a (now lost) stray-find of a twisted-rod gold finger-ring, from Skarð in Haukadalur (Eldjárn & Friðriksson, 2000, p. 392). A second gold ornament takes the form of a small wire ball found, together with three such balls of silver, (Fig. 2) eroding from a pagan cemetery site at Kápa (ibid, pp. 46–49, 392, illus. 314). These are believed to be from the Irish Sea region, where they appear to have served as costume accessories in the tenth century (Graham-Campbell, 2005, pp. 132–133, Fig. 5; cf. Graham-Campbell, forthcoming). The third piece is a small filigree-decorated mount of Irish workmanship, probably from a so-called 'kite-brooch' (cf. Whitfield, 1997), found, in a late tenth-century midden, during the recent excavations at the farm of Vatnsfjörður, where it was presumably in secondary use as a pendant (*Fornleifastofnun Íslands. Ársskýrsla 2005*, p. 28, Fig.).[1]

Returning to Sigurd, his lack of good fortune serves as a reminder of a tale told of Eirik the Red (*Eiríks saga rauða*, ch. 5). Eirik, who had just been persuaded to participate in a voyage to Vinland, is said (on the morning of his departure) to have first taken

1 Another such gold filigree fragment, seemingly also from an Irish kite-brooch, found its way to York, where it was deposited at Coppergate in the late ninth/tenth century (Mainman & Rogers, 2000, pp. 2574–2575, no. 10535, Figs. 1270–1271).

> … a small chest containing gold and silver. He hid the money and then went on his way. After going only a short way he fell from his horse, breaking several ribs and injuring his shoulder, so that he cried out, 'Ow, ow!'. Because of this mishap he sent word to his wife [Thjodhild] to retrieve the money he had hidden, saying he had been punished for having hidden it. (Kunz, 2000, p. 662).

Eirik had clearly not wanted his wife and family to have access to his wealth while he was away on his travels, but then he felt himself punished by the gods for his mean behaviour.

The implication of this tale is that he normally kept his wealth readily available to him 'in a small chest' – and not routinely buried for safety. Similarly, Hrafn (in *Vápnfirðinga saga*), who was 'a Norwegian by birth, rich and fabulous for his treasures, but a miserly man', is said to have 'possessed a gold ring which he wore constantly on his arm, and a small strongbox which he never let out of his sight and was reputed to be full of gold and silver' (Jones, 1961, p. 43).

Eirik, who felt that he had angered the gods, was thus somewhat at odds with the so-called 'Odin's Law', which provides the basis for advancing a ritual explanation for some Viking Age hoards deposited by 'pagans'. 'Odin's Law', as recounted by Snorri Sturluson in *Heimskringla* (*Ynglinga saga*, ch. 8), states that men would enjoy in their after-life the treasures which they had themselves buried:

> Thus he [Odin] ordered that all the dead men were to be burned on a pyre together with their possessions, saying that everyone would arrive in Valholl with such wealth as he had with him on the pyre and that he would also enjoy the use of what he himself had hidden in the ground. (Hollander, 1964, pp. 11–12).

There naturally exists some uncertainty as to whether or not hoards were actually buried anywhere in the Viking world for this reason. It is possible that Snorri's statement may, to some extent, reflect a religious rationalisation to provide an explanation for the occasional discovery of Viking Age hoards in Icelandic soil. Nevertheless, it does provide some justification for advancing a ritual explanation for hoarding in some cases, although Snorri was clearly mistaken in the first part of his statement, when he supposed that cremation of the dead had been standard practice in Iceland.[2]

Few hoards have, in fact, been interpreted within a ritual framework (Zachrisson, 1998; Graham-Campbell & Sheehan, 2009). The overall tendency has been to interpret hoards within an economic framework, with the

2 The only certain cremation grave known from Iceland is that recently excavated from the Hulduhóll mound, at the seaward entrance to the Mosfell Valley (Byock et al., 2005, pp. 214–217).

occasional correlation of individual hoards with crisis events – approaches that are, of course, not necessarily mutually exclusive. It is worth noting that there could have been practical social benefits connected with ritual hoarding. The deposition of wealth for the gods might have been a strategy designed to reinforce the status of the donor among his peers. Gift-giving, of rings (for example), was an important social institution, within which the donor's status and authority was enhanced. So-called 'ritual hoarding' might have been a way of achieving the same objective, without the problem of entering into a competitive gift-giving cycle, but with the benefit of gaining the reputation for having established a good relationship with the gods.

As a possible example of the ritual deposition of silver in Viking Age Iceland, Torun Zachrisson reminded us at the Congress, during discussion of my paper,[3] of a passage in *Svarfdœla saga*, ch. 11 (cf. Zachrisson, 1998, pp. 198–199), which Judith Jesch has kindly translated for me:

> Þorsteinn svörfuðr now went between mountain and shore and claimed all the valley [i.e. Svarfaðardalr] on the other side of the river. He went up into the mountains and made a marker [*kennimark*] in the furthest place he reached, and there he broke his comb into pieces and threw down the comb fragments and left behind silver in three places, half a *mörk* in each place, and that land is now called *at Kambi*; and Þorsteinn named witnesses, and by this means he made the valley his legal domicile and named it after himself and called it Svarfaðardalr.

I am also grateful to Judith Jesch for the information that this passage, together with most of the saga, is preserved only in a seventeenth-century manuscript, although copied from a medieval one, and for her suggestion that the story of the broken comb might simply be an invention to explain a place-name. Given that a broken comb does not amount to much by way of an offering, one might suppose that the silver could have been an addition to try and add conviction to an otherwise somewhat unlikely tale – with a medieval *mörk* and a half amounting to about 300 gm.

Archaeological evidence throughout the Viking world reflects the distinction made here between grave-goods and separately buried wealth (in the form of hoards), given that Viking Age grave-goods only rarely include silver or gold objects. It has, however, been argued that, in the case of Scotland, at least, 'Odin's Law' cannot be considered relevant as an explanation for hoard depo-

[3] Also during the post-lecture discussion, Przemysław Urbańczyk drew attention to his (then) forthcoming paper on 'The Polish discussion on medieval deposits of hack-silver' (Urbańczyk 2009). This takes a radically different view of the interpretation of hack-silver to that expressed by myself in this paper, as also by most other archaeologists and numismatists of the period – as, for example, in the papers in the volume recently edited by Dagfinn Skre (2008).

sition, given that this practice appears to have become established only after so-called 'pagan' burial had ceased (Graham-Campbell, 1995, p. 61; Graham-Campbell & Batey, 1998, p. 245); such would also appear to have been the case on the Isle of Man (cf. Wilson, 2008). It must, however, be remembered that the end of pagan burial practices does not necessarily imply the contemporary demise of all related beliefs.

There are several instances in the Icelandic sagas which might be considered to lend some literary support to the notion of hoarding contained in 'Odin's Law'. In *Egils saga*, there are two accounts of particular relevance: one concerns Skallagrim, Egil's father (ch. 59), and the other is about Egil himself (ch. 87). Before Skallagrim died, he is said to have ridden away from home one evening, with 'a fairly large chest [of silver] on his knees, and ... an iron cauldron under his arm'. 'People have claimed ever since that he put either or both of them in the Krumskelda Marsh with a great slab of stone on top.' (Scudder, 2000, p. 108). The saga goes on to relate how Egil buried him in a mound 'with his horse and weapons and tools', with no mention of 'whether any money was put into his tomb'; but, at the same time, it is told that Egil 'inherited his father's lands *and valuables*' (ibid; my italics). Not long before Egil died himself, he is likewise said to have buried 'his chests of silver', with the aid of two slaves whom he killed (ibid, p. 182). These were the two chests full of money that Egil had brought back from England – in addition to three gold arm-rings – as gifts from King Athelstan (ibid, pp. 90–91). Then Egil, in his turn, was dressed 'in fine clothes' and buried in a mound 'along with his weapons and clothes' (ibid, p. 183).

It is not possible, however, to judge whether accounts of this type were written by way of recalling actual (ancient) ritual practices or were simply literary devices to demonstrate the (pagan) religious character of the saga heroes. After all, as noted above, there needed to be some explanation for both the existence of burial mounds and the occasional discovery of silver in Iceland during the medieval period.[4] For example, *Egils saga* (ch. 88) tells us that:

> East of the farm [of Mosfell] is a gully leading down from the mountain. It has been noticed that English coins have been found in the gully when the river recedes after floods caused by sudden thaws. Some people believe that Egil must have hidden his treasure there. (Scudder, 2000, p. 183).

And then, there is the story told in *Landnámabók* (ch. 142 of the *Sturlubók* version) of how:

4 Eyvind, in *Haralds saga Gráfeldar* (ch. 1), is described by Snorri as having 'owned a large and valuable gold ring called Moldi. It had been dug out of the ground long ago.' (Hollander 1964, p. 131).

> On his way back home the Norwegian found some silver buried in the ground and took twenty coins from it, assuming he'd find the treasure again. But when he went to look for it he couldn't find it. Ljot caught him when he was digging for it and forced the Norwegian to pay him three hundreds for each coin he'd taken (Pálsson & Edwards, 1972, p. 69).

By way of archaeological illustration for these two stories, it is worth considering the hoard from Gaulverjabær (Fig. 3), which contains *c.*360 coins and weighs almost 0.5 kg (Eldjárn, 1948; Eldjárn & Friðriksson, 2000, pp. 424–425, illus. 354; Magnússon, 1996, p. 8, Fig.; Graham-Campbell, 2005, pp. 133–134; Holt, 2005). Most of these coins come from Anglo-Saxon England, but from no specific region; they have a clear cut-off date of *c.*1002/03. Slightly fewer coins are from German mints, but these are later in date, continuing through to *c.*1010. These factors suggest that it is a savings hoard which may, initially at any rate, have been assembled in Norway, given that there are also eight Scandinavian imitations of Anglo-Saxon coins, four coins of Olof Skötkonung of Sweden (994–1022) and five half-bracteates attributed to Harald Bluetooth. In addition, there are two Hiberno-Norse coins (from Dublin), and the remains of five Cufic coins; a deposition date of *c.*1010–15 has been suggested. Nine of the coins are recorded as having been pierced for suspension, but none is fitted with a loop. In, addition, there are the cut and broken remains of three 'flans', or circular blanks, which show no signs of having been actual coins, as well as a broken fragment of a sheet silver ornament with zig-zag decoration.

It follows that, if some hoards were consigned to the ground in accordance with Odin's so-called 'Law', then they were obviously not intended for recovery and such might, therefore, be reflected archaeologically in some way, either inherently or contextually. A prime example of this is represented by hoards from graves, which are known in small numbers in both Scandinavia and the West. For instance, a coin hoard, dated to *c.*870, was found 'in a coffin' in the churchyard of St Mary's Minster, Reading, which presumably relates to the fact the 'Great Army' had its winter-quarters there during 870/71 (Graham-Campbell, 2004a, p. 380).

In general terms, Viking Age hoards from 'pagan' graves are almost the only ones that were, without doubt, deposited for reasons of ritual. There is, however, an obvious Christian exception in the case of the coin hoard which was deposited as an offering, *c.*1035, in a foundation-trench for a stone church in Roskilde (Glob (ed.), 1980, no. 38; Jensen (ed.), 1995, no. 9).

Objects of silver or gold, including coins (other than those converted into pendants), are only rarely encountered in graves. The reason for this may have been to avoid grave-robbing, a practice well-documented archaeologically

Fig. 3. General view of Gaulverjabær hoard. (Þjms. 8.7.1930. Photo: Ívar Brynjólfsson, Þjóðminjasafn Íslands.)

in Scandinavia; however, it appears more likely that silver was not usually abandoned in the form of grave-goods so as to avoid placing this increasingly important means-of-exchange beyond permanent use. I have previously suggested that silver may have come to be 'considered too valuable an asset to be abandoned to the dead, regarded perhaps as farm or family wealth to be inherited like land' (Graham-Campbell, 1982, p. 33).

In Scandinavia, and elsewhere in the Viking world, both hoards and single-finds (particularly of complete gold ornaments) are on record as having been found in bogs and other watery places, and it has been suggested that these circumstances imply that such were ritual offerings. Probably the most spectacular collection of such finds is from Lake Tissø, in Sjælland, Denmark, which were presumably deposited as offerings to the god, Tyr (Jørgensen, 2003, p. 183). Is it possible that Skallagrim's deposition of his chest of silver in a marsh reflects the practice of hoards being deposited in wet locations for ritual reasons?

The saga literature contains two most interesting accounts of the function of silver in Viking Age Iceland – and there would seem to exist no reasons for not accepting them both as genuine reflections of past practices. In discussing Viking Age silver, it has become common practice (e.g. Graham-Campbell, 1982, pp. 32–33; 2007, p. 216; Williams, 2007, pp. 182–183) to quote Snorri's story, from *Heimskringla* (in *Haralds saga Gráfeldar*, ch. 1), of how the Althing awarded the tenth-century Icelandic poet, Eyvind Finnsson, a large silver cloak-pin which had been made especially for him (following a collection of silver pennies, which were 'white when scratched'), only for him to have it 'cut into pieces' because he needed to buy cattle for himself (Hollander, 1964, p. 143). This episode provides the clearest possible example of how the so-called 'display' economy operated alongside the bullion economy.

Another example of the prestige function of silver in Iceland during the 'pagan' period is the use of 'oath rings', for which there exists independent contemporary evidence, as in the *Anglo-Saxon Chronicle* s.a. 876 (Page, 1995, p. 30; see also Graham-Campbell, 2000, pp. 7–8). Here, I return to *Landnámabók*, although there is also a reference in *Eyrbyggja saga* to one such oath/arm-ring being kept at Hofstaðir for wear by 'the temple priest' (Page, 1995, pp. 29–30). The passage (ch. 268 of the *Hauksbók* version) states, in part:

> A ring of at least two ounces should lie on the altar of every main temple. Every priest should have such a ring on his arm at all legal moots that he had to inaugurate himself ... [and] every man who needed to take part in pleading before the court must first swear an oath on the ring ... (Page, 1995, p. 174).

Moving on from the social, legal and economic importance of silver, it is desirable to consider a few Viking hoards found well 'beyond' Iceland, so as to provide some context for the Icelandic treasures themselves. Five hoards have been selected for brief mention here, two deposited during the second half of the ninth century, and three from the tenth. The first is the largest of all, that from Spillings in Gotland, given that the two separate parcels into which it had been divided (and buried 3 m apart) together weigh over 60 kg of silver. The contents include over 14,000 coins which indicate that the hoard(s) were hidden in the 870s (Östergren, 2008; 2009). The Gotlanders proudly (and correctly) proclaim that this is the largest Viking Age silver hoard 'in the world' – and, although it contains many complete arm-rings (for instance), it is clearly a currency hoard, given the manner in which groups of arm-rings have been bundled up together, combined with the presence of hack-silver (that is fragmentary coins, ingots and ornaments, deliberately cut-up to produce smaller pieces of silver for economic reasons).

It is interesting to contrast this amazing treasure with the largest gold hoard yet known from Viking Age Scandinavia – the Hoen hoard, from south-east Norway (Fuglesang & Wilson (Eds.), 2006). There are immediate and obvious contrasts – and not only between gold and silver, although the two precious metals did seem to move, for the most part, in separate ways in Viking Age Scandinavia (and beyond). Hoen is certainly not a currency hoard in the manner of Spillings. It is a hoard consisting exclusively of personal ornaments; for example, all its coins have been mounted for use as pendants (and the few which are of silver have been gilded to make up the set).

The two parcels of silver which together constitute the Spillings hoard were buried beneath the floor of one and the same house, presumably for security, although Zachrisson has argued in her thesis (1998) that some such unrecovered farmstead/household hoards were buried as a way 'of guarding the farm domain'. On the other hand, the Hoen hoard was deposited in a bog in the open countryside, so a different case could be made for suggesting that this might have been done for ritual reasons.

Another example of what might be called a 'house-hoard' is provided by the well-known find from Birka, which was deposited *c.*970 (Graham-Campbell, 1980, p. 87, no. 302). The Birka hoard weighs almost 2.2 kg and consists of a mixture of complete ornaments and hack-silver, together with Cufic coins, as well as one from Byzantium. This accords well with what one might suppose to have been the likely contents of a late tenth-century merchant's 'chest', in central Sweden (although in this case it was deposited on an iron dish).

Moving from an urban to a rural context, my next silver hoard for consideration is from Grimestad, Vestfold, Norway, with a *terminus post quem* of 921 for its deposition (Hårdh in Skre (ed.), 2007, p. 104, Fig. 5.7).[5] Birgitta Hårdh states that Grimestad should not be called a 'hack-silver hoard', even though it does contain some such pieces of fragmentary silver. This is because the majority of the silver in the hoard is stored in the form of complete (and therefore, wearable) rings and complete ingots, as well as coins (for the provision of small change), even if some of the latter have been perforated for use as pendants. The Grimestad hoard thus belongs to my category of 'chieftain's wealth' – the working capital of a large farm or estate – wealth not to be buried with the dead, but to be kept safe for use as and when necessary (cf. the hoard from Skaill, Orkney, below p. 115).

Last, for brief mention, is the large treasure found at Cuerdale in north-west England. This is truly a hack-silver hoard, containing over 1,000 pieces of bullion, most of which (apart from numerous ingots) are fragmentary; in addition, there were *c.*7,500 coins which demonstrate that it was deposited *c.*905–10 (Graham-Campbell, 1987; forthcoming, hoard no 1). Its total weight was *c.*42 kg, the same as the larger of the two parcels from Spillings. This remarkable find serves as reminder that the bullion economy depended on the use of scales (see below), together with various procedures for testing the surface appearance and quality of the silver by nicking the edges of ingots and ornaments, and by bending and/or pecking coins (cf. Skre (ed.), 2007).

Returning to Iceland, we might first consider the small hoard of three coins found at Mosfell, in 1725 (Eldjárn, 1948, p. 42; Eldjárn & Friðriksson, 2000, pp. 425–426). This has most properly been described as 'a somewhat uncertain find', and Mark Blackburn (2005, p. 147) has cautioned against necessarily accepting the proposed mid-tenth-century date for its deposition, but it is likewise only speculation on his part that this may have taken place as late as the eleventh century. *Egils saga*, as quoted, tells of the English coins that were said to wash out in the gully 'to the east of the farm' at Mosfell (Byock et al., 2005, Fig. 1). So does this eighteenth-century discovery represent just a coincidence? Or might, indeed, these coins represent part of Egil's treasure, given that he appears to have buried it somewhere nearby just before he died in about 990?

Leaving such speculation aside, there are two other, undoubted, eleventh-century coin hoards from Iceland, both with mixed contents, one of which – from Gaulverjabær – has been discussed above (p. 109). The second is the small hoard from Keta, weighing only 135 gm (Eldjárn, 1953; Eldjárn & Friðriksson, 2000, p. 426, illus. 355; Graham-Campbell, 2005, p. 134). This consists for the most part of hack-silver, together with the remains of five coins; four of these are Cufic (one in two pieces), dating from 883/4-913/32 (Blackburn, 2005, p. 147), and one is German (from *c.*1000). This indicates that the hoard

5 It should be noted that the ball-type brooch terminal at the centre of this photograph of the Grimestad hoard does not belong to it.

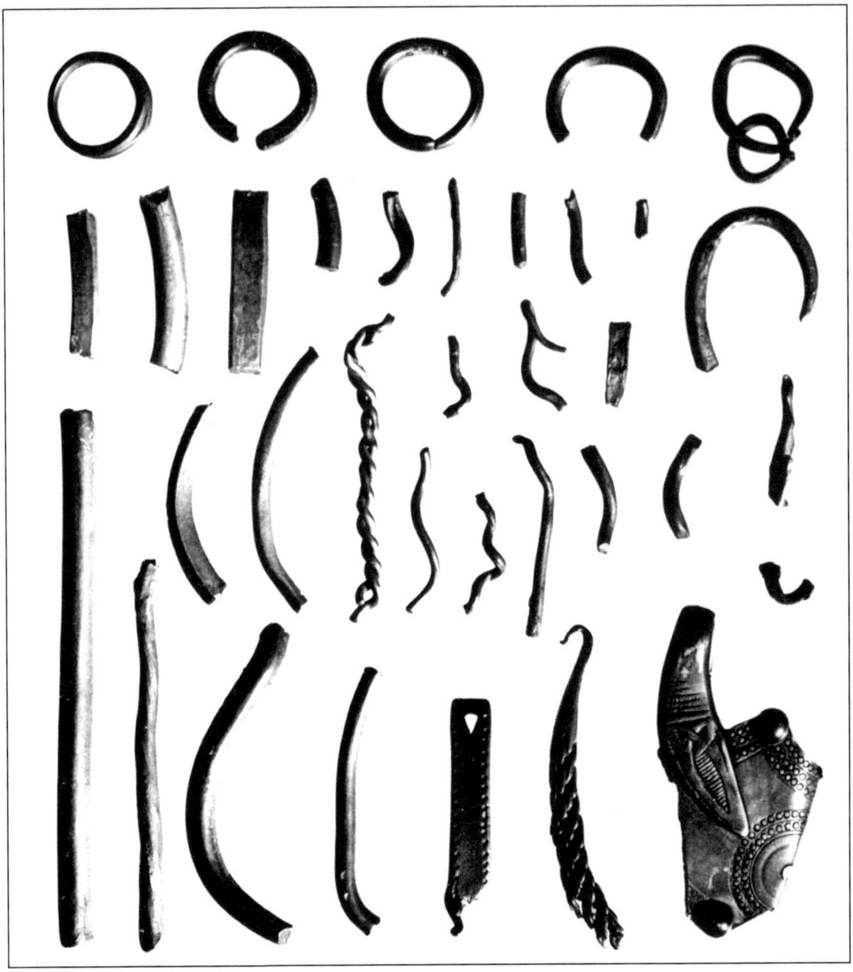

Fig. 4. The coinless silver hoard from Sandmúli, weighing 304 gm. (© Þjóðminjasafn Íslands).

was deposited in the early eleventh century, and so it is broadly contemporary with that from Gaulverjabær. It differs most obviously from the latter in that it contains much more hack-silver, amounting to a total of thirty-five fragments, although these have yet to be published in detail. However, they mostly appear to be of Scandinavian origin, including a terminal fragment from a penannular brooch, with stamped decoration. The other major difference between these two hoards, as pointed out to me by Mark Blackburn, is that the Cufic coins in Keta represent 80% of the total, but only 1% in the case of Gaulverjabær.

There are also two coinless hoards, from Sandmúli and Miðhús, which are most probably of somewhat earlier date than these two mixed hoards – both seemingly deposited in the mid/late tenth century. The Sandmúli hoard (Fig. 4) is slightly larger than Keta, but still weighs only 304 gm (Eldjárn & Friðriksson, 2000, p. 426, illus. 356; Roesdahl & Wilson (Eds.), 1992, no. 332; Graham-Campbell, 2005, pp. 134–135, Fig. 6). It consists for the most part of hack-silver, but does include some plain finger-rings (Fig. 4, top). There are thirty-six pieces in all, of which only one fragment, from an Irish bossed brooch (Fig. 4, bottom right, & Fig. 5), has so far been subject to detailed discussion (see below), but it is also important to note the presence of a small piece of another type of Insular brooch, in the form of a tiny C-shaped fragment cut from the pin-head or terminal of a so-called 'ball-type' brooch (Fig. 4, right). In addition, a massive straight rod, broken at both ends (Fig. 4, bottom, left), is most likely to be the remains of the pin of another such penannular brooch, both having parallels in the well-known hoard from Skaill in Orkney (Graham-Campbell, 1995, pp. 34–48 & 108–127, no. 24, pls. 8–49). The Skaill hoard consisted of *c.*8 kg of silver, comprising more than 100 items of bullion, together with a few coins, but sufficient to indicate that it was deposited *c.*960–80 (the date range currently proposed by Gareth Williams).

A further important similarity between the Sandmúli and Skaill hoards is the prevalence in both of the simple type of plain silver arm-rings known as 'ring-money', which were in widespread circulation in Scandinavian Scotland during the tenth and eleventh centuries (Graham-Campbell, 1995, pp. 38–40

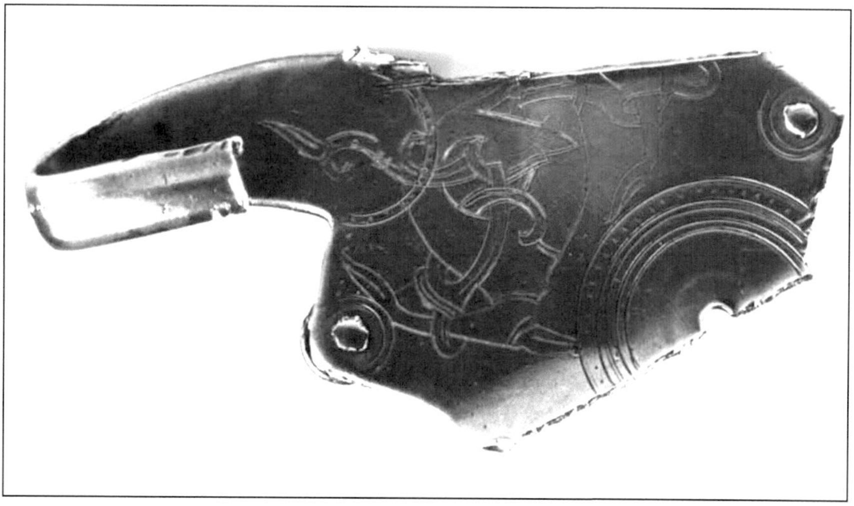

Fig. 5. Mammen-style animal on the reverse of the Sandmúli bossed brooch fragment. (Þjms. 1909:265. Photo: Ívar Brynjólfsson, Þjóðminjasafn Íslands.)

& 57–59). Furthermore, the presence of an ingot fragment in Sandmúli is matched by the presence of a few fragments (and four complete ingots) in the larger Skaill hoard. In other words, the Sandmúli hoard could readily disappear (as it were) into the Skaill hoard, so that there is every reason to suppose that it was likewise deposited sometime within the same two decades (that is during the middle of the second half of the tenth century).

In addition to the close similarities in content between these two hoards, from Iceland and Orkney, there is a close stylistic link which returns us to the Irish brooch fragment. This has attracted particular attention because of the fine Mammen-style animal (Fig. 5) that has been sketched, in a secondary position, on its reverse (Graham-Campbell, 1995, pp. 41–43, Fig. 22). Alas, the (original) incorrect reconstruction of the brooch itself has been reproduced once again in the revised edition of Eldjárn (Eldjárn & Friðriksson, 2000, illus. 272), despite Shetelig (1937, pp. 215 & 219, note 15) having correctly identified this piece as cut from the terminal of a 'bossed' penannular brooch of the particular type

Fig. 6. General view of Miðhús hoard. (Þjms. 1980:96. Photo: Ívar Brynjólfsson, Þjóðminjasafn Íslands.)

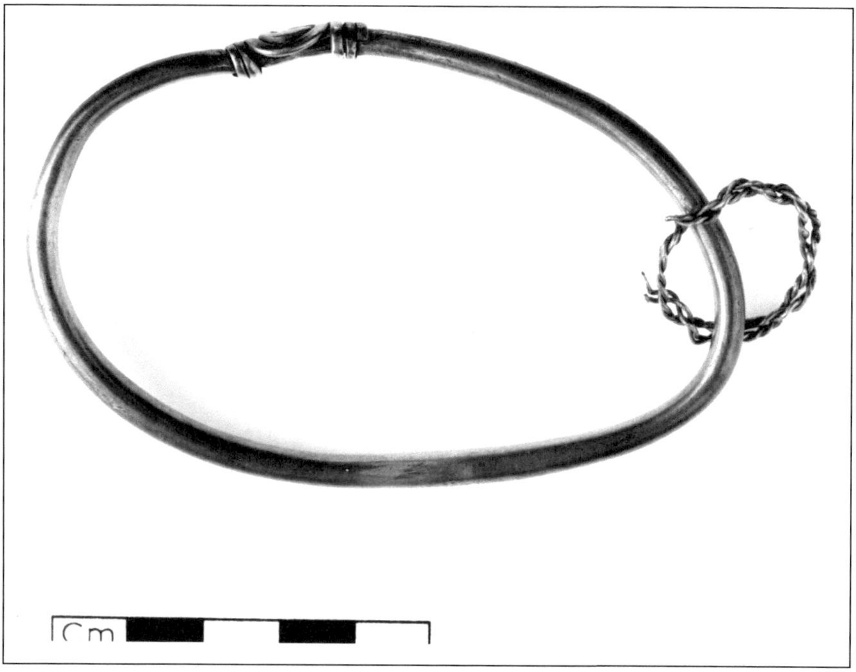

Fig. 7. Complete rod arm-ring from the Miðhús silver hoard, with attached twisted-wire rod ring. (© Þjóðminjasafn Íslands).

represented in the British Museum by an unprovenanced example from Ireland, and now also by a recent find from near Penrith, in north-west England, where it forms part of a hoard that consists exclusively of a mixture of bossed and ball-type Insular brooches (Graham-Campbell, forthcoming, hoard no. 2).

The most recent silver hoard to have been discovered in Iceland, at Miðhús (in 1980),[6] is so far the largest in weight, weighing 653.5 gm (Magnússon, 1980; 1996, p. 6, Fig.; Eldjárn & Friðriksson, 2000, p. 426, illus. 357; Graham-Campbell, 2005, pp. 135–136). It was 'uncovered by a power shovel, which by a stroke of luck barely touched it, and there is good reason to think that nothing was lost of the hoard' (Magnússon, 1980, p. 20). This hoard is coinless, consisting of over forty items of bullion (Fig. 6), which include a small number of complete rings. There is a fine example of a single rod arm-ring (Fig. 7), with a small ring of twisted wires attached to it (Magnússon, 1980, pp. 9 & 12, no. 4, Figs. 3–4 & 6), and also other rings which are characteristically made from twisted rods; however, the Miðhús hoard consists mostly of hack-silver, with close parallels to that from Sandmúli.

[6] That is before the small hoard newly discovered in 2009, as reported to the Congress (by Adolf Friðriksson).

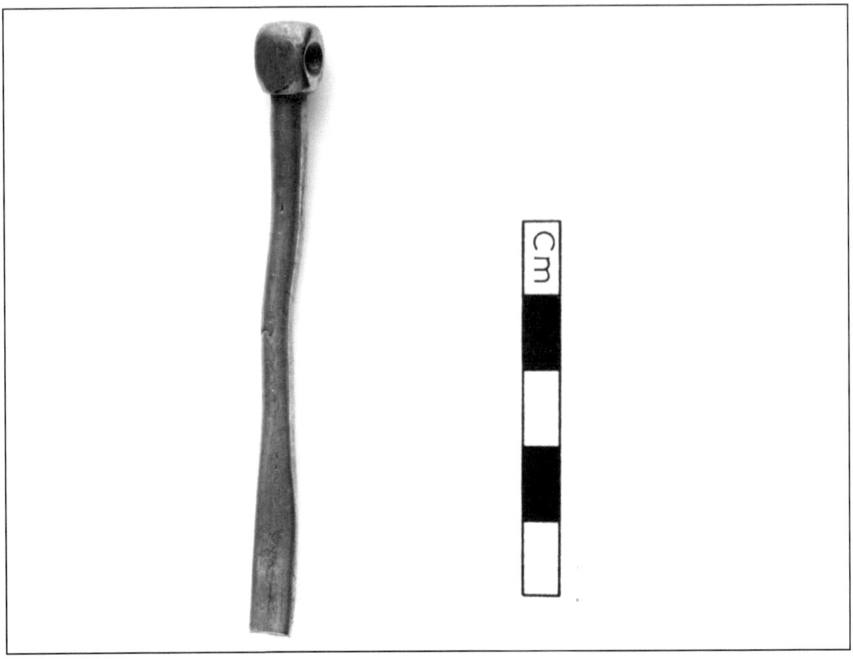

Fig. 8. The Insular ringed-pin fragment (ring missing) from the Miðhús silver hoard. (© Þjóðminjasafn Íslands).

The Miðhús hoard contains a complete example of a piece of the so-called 'ring-money' (Magnússon, 1980, p. 12, no. 6, Fig. 3), together with some fragments of others – all most probably from Scandinavian Scotland (see above), as well as a couple of plain rod finger-ring fragments (ibid, nos. 23 & 24), and the terminal of a small ingot (ibid, no. 30). Although there are no remains of bossed or 'ball-type' brooches in this hoard, it is possible to identify the hoops of two simple penannular brooches; one of these, which is complete, with plain terminals (ibid, p. 12, no. 8, Figs. 3–4), is paralleled in the Skaill hoard (Graham-Campbell, 1995, p. 113, no. 24:9, pl. 24). Also of particular interest is part of an Insular ringed pin (Fig. 8), with a polyhedral head socketed to take the tapered ends of its (lost) penannular ring (Magnússon, 1980, p. 12, no. 10, Fig. 4). Silver ringed pins are rare, but this fragment is exactly matched by a complete example in the Skaill hoard, even to the faint remains of a lightly incised step-pattern on one face of its flattened shaft (Graham-Campbell, 1995, p. 117, no. 24:51, pl. 46a–b).

Taken as a whole, therefore, it may be suggested that the Miðhús hoard is broadly contemporary with the Sandmúli hoard and may thus, by reference to the Skaill hoard, also be dated to the second half of the tenth century.

One of the neck-rings in the Miðhús hoard, although somewhat small in size is of a standard type (Fig. 9) made by twisting together three silver rods (Magnússon, 1980, p. 9, no. 1, Fig. 5), each rod being thickest in the middle, tapering towards the hooked terminals (in this case from a maximum diameter of 0.5 cm down to 0.3 cm). This tapering is the direct result of the way in which such rods were produced during the Viking Age – that is by hammering out ingots, which are in themselves most often thicker in the middle than they are at the ends.

Another neck-ring in the hoard, of similar small size, was also manufactured by twisting together three silver rods, although in this case they are much slighter (Fig. 10). This ring is catalogued as being complete but in three pieces (Magnússon, 1980, p. 9, no. 3, Figs. 3–4). It is unusual (although not unknown) to find a complete ring in three pieces in a Viking Age hoard, but there is one such from Ballacamaish, Isle of Man (Graham-Campbell, 1983, pp. 63, 68 & 76–78, no. 19, Appendix C, Fig. 7; forthcoming, hoard no. 12). The reason for cutting/breaking a piece off a ring was in order to make a payment (thus leading to its disposal). In fact, there is a difference in appearance and finish between the two terminals in the Miðhús hoard: the longer, and more elegant, of the two is far less shiny than the other, and so (on both accounts) it seems unlikely to me that they do, in fact, belong to the same ring.

The reason that the three Miðhús pieces have been grouped together is because their rods are the same size, with a diameter of 0.2 cm (at the terminal of the larger hook), which is where the rods are necessarily going to be at their most tapered. It is thus remarkable that all three of the rods from which the ring itself is manufactured measure exactly 0.2 cm throughout their entire lengths. Indeed, laboratory examination has confirmed that they were not made in the normal Viking Age way by hammering – rather they were manufactured by drawing.[7] Viking Age silversmiths were of course capable of drawing silver and gold wire, using draw-plates (Duczko, 1985, pp. 16–17, Figs. 1–2; Lønborg, 1998, pp. 51–52, Fig. 55; Whitfield, 1990); indeed, there is a little hank of silver wire amongst the contents of the rich Icelandic grave excavated at Kaldárhöfði (Eldjárn & Friðriksson, 2000, p. 90, illus. 28). They did not, however, have the equipment with which to draw rods – the technology for which is generally considered to have been the product of the Industrial Revolution.

This silver neck-ring (excluding the long terminal) is thus unique in all the Viking Age hoards I have examined – as also in all those examined by Birgitta

7 This was established during scientific examination in the laboratory of the National Museum, Copenhagen (unpublished report, 1995).

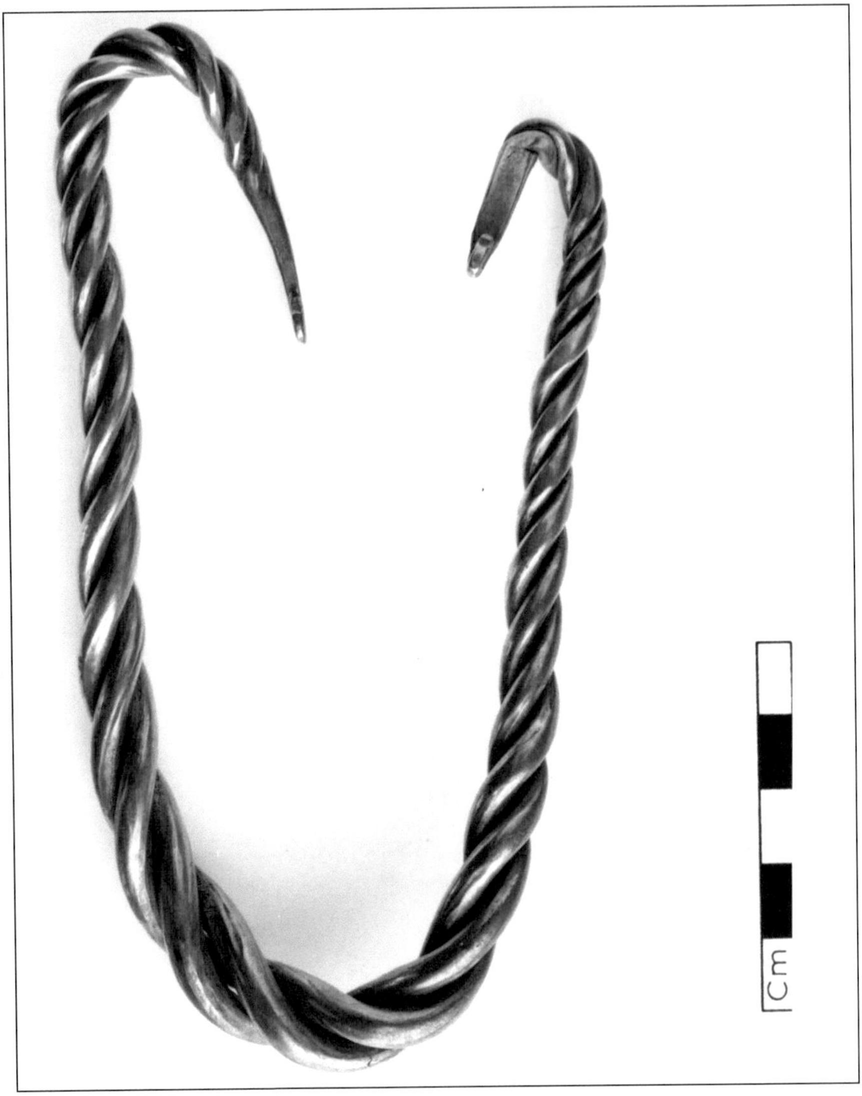

Fig. 9. Small intact neck-ring of twisted rods, with hooked terminals, from the Miðhús silver hoard. (© Þjóðminjasafn Íslands).

Hårdh – and so it leaves us with a problem yet to be solved.[8] It is, therefore, important that the Miðhús hoard, together with the Keta and Sandmúli hoards, should soon be subject to modern specialist examination and publication for the importance of their interesting contents extends well beyond Iceland.

8 I am most grateful to Professor Birgitta Hårdh for lengthy discussions of the Miðhús hoard, as well as of Viking Age silver in general.

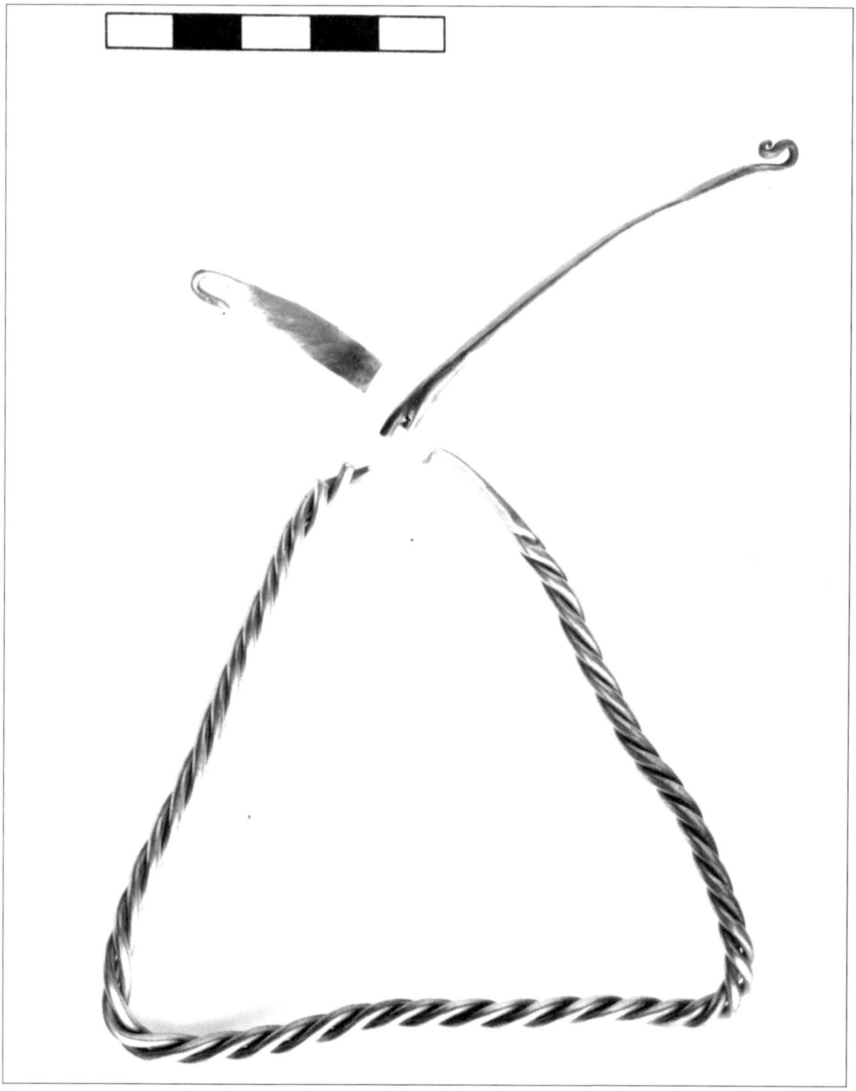

Fig. 10. The terminals and incomplete neck-ring, of twisted rods, from the Miðhús silver hoard. (© Þjóðminjasafn Íslands).

Moving forward, to an even more recent find – a single piece of hack-silver has been excavated at Thingvellir (*Fornleifastofnun Íslands. Ársskýrsla 2005*, p. 24, Fig.). This was cut from a band-shaped arm-ring, with two rows of characteristic stamped decoration (Fig. 11), as on a complete example from Denmark, in the hoard from Vaalse, Falster, which has a *terminus post quem* for its deposition of *c.*991 (Graham-Campbell, 2005, p. 130, Fig. 4). It is noteworthy that one

Fig. 11. Recently excavated hack-silver fragment from Thingvellir (not to scale), with a complete arm-ring from the Vaalse, Falster, hoard (Denmark).

such complete arm-ring, with a slightly more elaborate stamped decoration, was already known from Iceland, as a stray-find; it is unprovenanced, although 'probably from Skagafjörður' (Eldjárn & Friðriksson, 2000, pp. 391 & 605, illus. 311–312). This new fragment, taken together with the stray-finds of eleventh-century coins also known from Thingvellir (Graham-Campbell, 2005, p. 133; *Fornleifastofnun Íslands. Ársskýrsla 2006*, p. 28, Fig.), serves as a reminder that meetings of the Althing were not just occasions for decision-making, but also for doing business.

Silver from Viking Age settlement sites in Iceland is rare, but except for the fine silver brooch (a stray-find) from the deserted farm of Tröllaskógur, to be described below (Fig. 15), it was only in the form of coins (in print, at least) until the publication of the modern excavations at Hofstaðir (Lucas, 2009). By 2005, six coins had been published from five sites, of which the majority have seen use as ornaments, as is evident from the fact that they have been pierced for suspension (e.g. Eldjárn & Friðriksson, 2000, illus. 301), although that from Valþjófsstaðir is fitted with a loop (ibid, p. 426; Graham-Campbell, 2005, p. 133)[9]. On the other hand, both of the two coins recently excavated from the tenth/eleventh-century site at 'Pálstóftir', in Kárahnjúkar, are twice pierced in a manner suggesting that they may once have formed part of a more elaborate coin-necklace (*Fornleifastofnun Íslands. Ársskýrsla 2005*, pp. 32–33, Fig.; cf. Graham-Campbell, 1980, pp. 45–46, no. 156, from Äspinge, Skåne).

Three pieces of silver were found in the Viking Age occupation levels during the re-investigation of Hofstaðir, represented by Phase I (*c.*940–980) and Phase II (*c.*980–1030), as catalogued and discussed by Colleen Batey (2009, pp. 253–255). Two were excavated from the main 'Aisled Hall', but their deposition cannot be more closely dated than to the combined Phases I–II (*c.*940–1080). One is in the form of a small pendant (01-008) and the other is 'a piece of silver wire' (02–061). Unfortunately, the catalogue entries for the Hofstaðir artefacts contain no descriptions and most of them are not illustrated. The diameter of the silver wire is not recorded, but it may be supposed, from its discussion (pp. 254–255), that it is fine enough to have been manufactured by drawing – and so to be similar to the little hank of silver wire from Kaldárhöfði and to the small twisted wire ring attached to an arm-ring in the Miðhús hoard (as referred to above); (Fig. 7).

9 The worn (cut and pierced) coin found by Kristján Eldjárn at the settlement site of Hrossatunga, in Þjórsárdalur (Eldjárn 1979; Eldjárn & Friðriksson 2000, p. 425), is that correctly identified as a probable dirham by Blackburn (2005, p. 147, no. 5), but wrongly listed by Graham-Campbell, in the same volume (2005, p. 133).

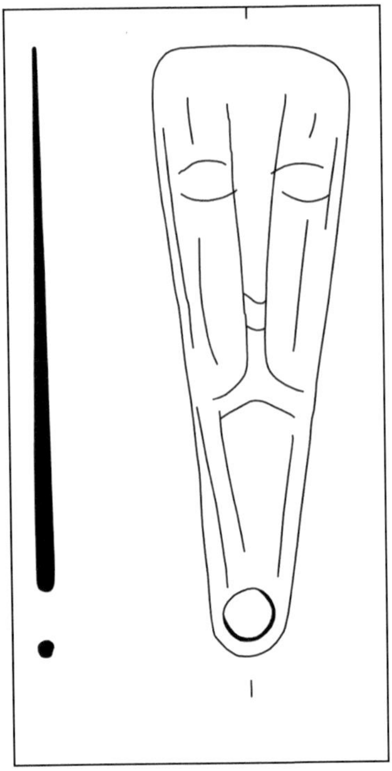

Fig. 12. Silver pendant from Hofstaðir, inverted to show the incised human face-mask. (Drawing: Letty Ten Herkel, after Lucas, 2009).

The third piece of silver found at Hofstaðir is catalogued (on the advice of Anton Holt) as 97-012, A semicircular silver alloy planchet with no visible markings corroded and fragmented ca.15mmø, 0.19g, 1, [0005b], Area G, Phase II.

This is interpreted (ibid, p. 255) as 'a silver alloy coin blank or planchet ... from midden dump [0005b] in Structure G', but without further comment. Structure G is the 'pithouse', constructed during Phase I, which was being used for dumping during Phase II (*c.*980–1030). Table 3.42 (ibid, p. 141) reveals that this 'coin blank' is from 'the later sequence of midden dumps in the pithouse', and one must assume, therefore, that it is unlikely to have been deposited much before *c.*1000. This is of some interest given the remains of the three coin 'flans', or circular blanks, in the Gaulverjabær hoard (discussed above, p. 109), with its suggested deposition date of *c.*1010–15. However, in the absence of an illustration – and without knowing its thickness – it is unclear as to whether this is something of a rarity, as an example of such a coin blank (which has been cut in half), or just a rounded terminal cut from a slight ingot.

Of greatest interest is the Hofstaðir sheet-metal pendant (01–008), both because it is complete and has incised ornament on its front face. It is sub-triangular in form, with a rounded apex (perforated for suspension), and rounded corners at its base; it is 2.8 cm long, measured from its illustration (Batey, 2009, Fig. 5.1). According to Batey (p. 253), the incised decoration is 'in the form of a cross and a possible Thor's hammer', but it is difficult to determine which lines are the ones supposed to form these motifs. On the other hand, if the pendant is viewed the other way up (as it would have been by the person wearing it), then the incised lines may be seen to represent a human face-mask, with plain oval eyes, to either side of an elongated nose, a down-turned moustache and a pointed beard (Fig. 12).

Fig. 13. Grave-goods from Vatnsdalur boat burial, including the silver Thor's hammer pendant, the perforated coin and a scale-weight. (Þjms. 1964:122; Þjms. 1964:120. Photo: Ívar Brynjólfsson, Þjóðminjasafn Íslands.)

All the Icelandic pendants, as known from before the end of the twentieth century, have been discussed as a group by Eldjárn & Friðriksson (2000, pp. 380–385, illus. 287–300). Among them is one example, from a grave at Rangá (ibid, p. 382, illus. 293–294), of a triangular face-mask type which is well known from Scandinavia. This displays, in the normal orientation (facing the viewer), the same tapered face, with plain oval eyes and downturned moustache. It would appear, therefore, that the unique Hofstaðir pendant represents a local variant of this imported type. Given its thin section, it could readily

Fig. 14. Foss pendant. (Þjms. 1910:195. Photo: Ívar Brynjólfsson, Þjóðminjasafn Íslands.)

have been hammered out from just such a small lump of imported silver as that represented at Hofstaðir by the 'coin blank'.[10]

Silver from Viking Age graves has already been mentioned – or rather the lack of it. In the case of Iceland, only twelve out of the total of over 316 graves, which had been recorded in Iceland up to the year 2000, contain objects of silver (as listed in Graham-Campbell, 2005, p. 132, after Eldjárn & Friðriksson, 2000). These are mostly small and simple objects, sometimes just a single coin (perhaps worn as a pendant) – a recent example is the fragment of an Anglo-Saxon penny (955–75) from the male grave excavated, in 1995, at Eyrarteigur (Kristjánsdóttir, 1998; Eldjárn & Friðriksson, 2000, pp. 231–232, no. 144). What is just as important for our knowledge of the bullion economy in Viking Age Iceland is, however, the presence of weights and scales in as many as twenty-one graves (cf. Fig. 13), in addition to some stray-finds (ibid, pp. 411–415, illus. 344–347).

The best known Viking Age burial from Iceland to contain silver ornaments is the well-equipped boat-grave at Vatnsdalur, Patreksfjörður (Eldjárn & Friðriksson, 2000, pp. 115–119, no. 54). This contains two silver pendants (Fig. 13): one a simple Thor's hammer and the other a Cufic coin, now fragmentary, but probably dating from between *c.*870–930 (ibid, p. 117, illus. 44, & p. 385, illus. 299). In any case, it serves to introduce the splendid silver pendant from Foss (a stray-find), which is a Thor's hammer to some and a cross to many others (Fig. 14); whichever, it is a matter of note that the symbol is guarded by a fierce animal head, forming the suspension-loop (Graham-Campbell, 1980, p. 156, no. 526; Magnússon, 1996, p. 7; Eldjárn & Friðriksson, 2000, p. 384, illus. 297–298).

10 Colleen Batey (2009, p. 254) describes this silver pendant as being 'very similar to 01-009 which is also from the primary phase [= also from Phases I–II] of the aisled hall and made of copper alloy'. They are certainly both 'very simply formed', from sheet metal, and are perforated at their apex, but the copper-alloy example, which is plain, differs in its profile (ibid, fig. 5.1), having a slightly concave 'neck' (below its suspension hole), before expanding to what would presumably have been a spatulate end, whereas the silver example is straight sided, so that it is more nearly triangular in form. Their general similarity does, however, serve to reinforce the suggestion that both could well be local products of much the same date.

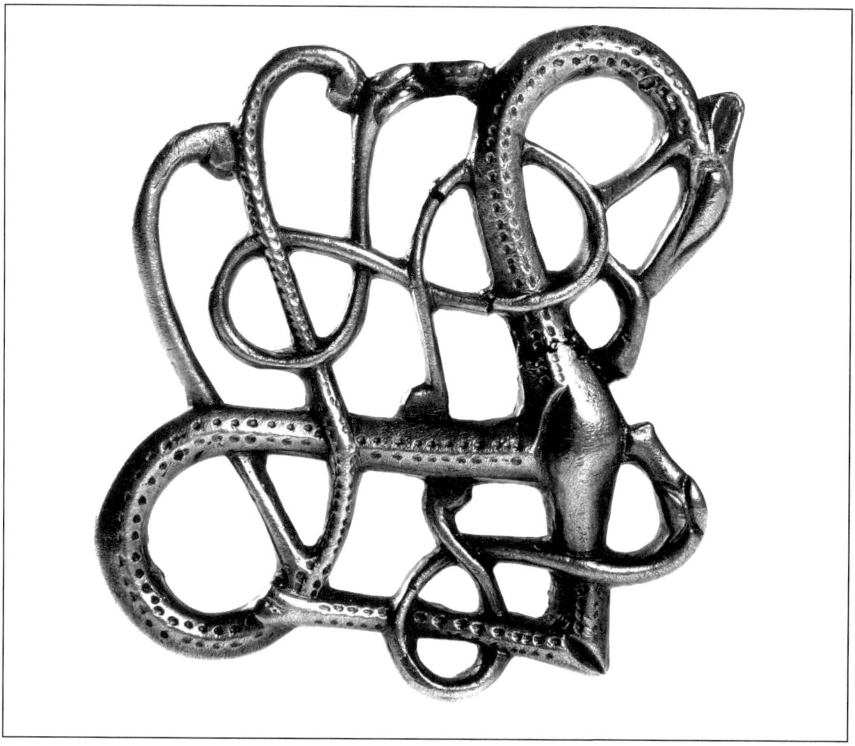

Fig. 15. Tröllaskógur Urnes-style animal-brooch. (Þjms. 1913:100. Photo: Ívar Brynjólfsson, Þjóðminjasafn Íslands.)

Iceland has, however, not yet produced an eleventh-century Crucifix pendant like those of the type found throughout much of Scandinavia, including the two well-known examples from the Trondheim hoard, deposited *c.*1029–35 (Fuglesang, 1980, pp. 158–159, no. 30, pl. 17c; Graham-Campbell, 1980, p. 157, no. 530). But there is doubtless one waiting to be discovered!

Having begun this paper with an imaginary serpent, it needs to end with an Icelandic one – or perhaps, Danish – because elegant Urnes-style brooches, depicting the so-called 'Great Beast', are commonest in southern Scandinavia (e.g. that from Lindholm Høje, Jutland: Graham-Campbell, 1980, p. 149, no. 502). The well-known silver example from Iceland – a stray-find from the deserted farm of Tröllaskógur – does, however, differ enough from the Danish brooches to suggest that it might indeed be of Icelandic workmanship (Shetelig, 1937, pl. xxix, no. 4; Magnússon, 1996, p. 7; Eldjárn & Friðriksson, 2000, pp. 461–462, illus. 382–383; Graham-Campbell, 2004b, pp. 224–225, Fig. 6). The 'Great Beast', which is not itself a dragon, is attempting to bite the body of the snake that entwines its body, in a figure-of-eight loop, while a second snake fetters its front leg.

In contemplating such a fine product of a late Viking Age silversmith, in the form of a brooch created (once again) for ostentatious display, one would do well to recall not only the quotation from Paul's Epistle (cited above), but also the words of the dying Fáfnir to Sigurd (*Fáfnismál*, st. 9; Larrington, 1996, 159):[11]

> the resounding gold and the glowing red treasure,
> those rings will be your death!

BIBLIOGRAPHY

Anker, P. (1970). *The art of Scandinavia*, Vol. 1. London: Paul Hamlyn.

Batey, C. E. (2009). The artefactual material. In G. Lucas (2009), 253–321.

Blackburn, M. (2005). Coinage and contacts in the North Atlantic during the seventh to mid-tenth centuries. In A. Mortensen & S. V. Arge (Eds.), 141–151.

Byock, J., Walker, P., Erlandson, J., Holk, P., Zori, D., Guðmundsson, M., & Tveskov, M. (2005). A Viking-age valley in Iceland: The Mosfell Archaeological Project. *Medieval Archaeology*, 49, 195–218.

Duczko, W. (1985). *Birka V. The filigree and granulation work of the Viking Period.* Stockholm: Kungl. Vitterhets Historie och Antikvitets Akademien.

Eldjárn, K. (1948). Gaulverjabær-fundet og nogle mindre islandske møntfund fra vikingetiden. *Nordisk numismatisk årsskrift 1948*, 39–62.

Eldjárn, K. (1953). Fundinn forn silfursjóður í Ketu á Skaga. *Árbók hins íslenzka fornleifafélags 1953* (1954), 87–90.

Eldjárn, K. (1956). *Kuml og haugfé úr heiðnum sið á Íslandi.* Akureyri: Norðri.

Eldjárn, K., & Friðriksson, A. (Ed.). (2000). In K. Eldjárn (1956), *Kuml og haugfé úr heiðnum sið á Íslandi*; (2nd edition). Reykjavík: Mál og menning.

Faulkes, A. (1987). *Snorri Sturluson, Edda* (Everyman's Library). London: J. M. Dent & Sons Ltd.

Fuglesang, S. H. (1980). *Some aspects of the Ringerike style.* Odense: Odense University Press.

Fuglesang, S. H., & Wilson, D.M. (Eds.) (2006). *The Hoen hoard: A Viking gold treasure of the ninth century* (Acta ad Archaeologiam et Artium Historiam Pertinentia, 14; Norske Oldfunn, 20). Rome: Det norske institutt; Oslo: University of Oslo.

Glob, P. V. (Ed.) (1980). *Danefæ.* Copenhagen: Nationalmuseet.

Graham-Campbell, J. (1980). *Viking artefacts: A select catalogue.* London: British Museum Publications.

[11] I am most grateful to Professor Judith Jesch and to Sir David Wilson for their considerable advice and assistance in the process of converting this paper from public lecture to a publication.

Graham-Campbell, J. (1982). Viking silver hoards: An introduction. In R. T. Farrell (Ed.), *The Vikings*, 32–41. Chichester: Phillimore.

Graham-Campbell, J. (1983). The Viking-age silver hoards of the Isle of Man. In C. Fell, P. Foote, J. Graham-Campbell & R. Thompson (Eds.), *The Viking Age in the Isle of Man*, 53–80. London: Viking Society for Northern Research.

Graham-Campbell, J. (1987). Some archaeological reflections on the Cuerdale hoard. In D. M. Metcalf (Ed.), *Coinage in ninth-century Northumbria* (British Archaeological Reports, British Series 180), 329–44. Oxford: BAR.

Graham-Campbell, J. (1995). *The Viking-age gold and silver of Scotland (AD 850–1100)*. Edinburgh: National Museums of Scotland.

Graham-Campbell, J. (2000). The power of silver. In E. Roesdahl & P. M. Sørensen (Eds.), *Beretning fra nittende tværfaglige vikingesymposium*, 7–20. Højbjerg: Forlaget Hikuin.

Graham-Campbell, J. (2004a). The archaeology of the 'Great Army' (865–79). In E. Roesdahl & J. P. Schjødt (Eds.), *Beretning fra treotyvende tværfaglige vikingesymposium,* 30–46. Højbjerg: Forlaget Hikuin.

Graham-Campbell, J. (2004b). Viking art at the millennium in the North Atlantic. In S. Lewis-Simpson (Ed.), *Vinland revisited: The Norse world at the turn of the first millennium*, 219–226. St John's, NL: Historic Sites Association of Newfoundland and Labrador.

Graham-Campbell, J. (2005). The Viking-age gold and silver of the North Atlantic region. In A. Mortensen & S. V. Arge (Eds.), 125–140.

Graham-Campbell, J. (2007). Reflections on 'Silver economy in the Viking age'. In J. Graham-Campbell & G. Williams (Eds.), 215–223.

Graham-Campbell, J. (forthcoming). *The Cuerdale hoard and related Viking-age silver and gold, from Britain and Ireland, in the British Museum*. London: British Museum.

Graham-Campbell, J., & Batey, C. E. (1998). *Vikings in Scotland: An archaeological survey*. Edinburgh: Edinburgh University Press.

Graham-Campbell, J., & Sheehan, J. (2009). Viking age gold and silver from Irish crannogs and other watery places. *Journal of Irish Archaeology*, 18, 77–93.

Graham-Campbell, J., & Williams, G. (Eds.) (2007). *Silver economy in the Viking age*. Walnut Creek, CA: Left Coast Press.

Hicks, C. (1993). *Animals in early medieval art*. Edinburgh: Edinburgh University Press.

Hollander, L. M. (1964; reprinted 2002: American-Scandinavian Foundation). *Snorri Sturluson, Heimskringla: history of the kings of Norway*. Austin, Texas: University of Austin Press.

Holt, A. (1998). Mynt frá víkingaöld og miðöldum fundin á Íslandi á síðari árum. *Árbók hins íslenzka fornleifafélags 1998* (2000), 85–92.

Holt, A. (2005). Gaulverjabæjarsjóðurinn. In A. Mortensen & S. V. Arge (Eds.), 217–228.

Holt, A. (forthcoming). *Sylloge of the Coins of the British Isles: Viking-age coins found in Iceland.*

Jensen, J. S. (Ed.) (1995). *Tusindtallets Danske Mønter fra Den kongelige Mønt- og Medaillesamling.* Copenhagen: Nationalmuseet.

Jesch, J. (2000). The power of poetry. In E. Roesdahl & P. M. Sørensen (Eds.), *Beretning fra nittende tværfaglige vikingesymposium*, 21–39. Højbjerg: Forlaget Hikuin.

Jones, G. (1961). *Eirik the Red and other Icelandic sagas* (The World's Classics). London: Oxford University Press.

Jørgensen, L. (2003). Manor and market at Lake Tissø in the sixth to eleventh centuries: the Danish 'productive' sites. In T. Pestell & K. Ulmschneider (Eds.), *Markets in early medieval Europe: Trading and 'productive' sites, 650–850*, 175–207. Macclesfield: Windgather Press.

Kristjánsdóttir, S. (1998). The last Viking in Iceland. *Viking Heritage Newsletter*, 3, 1–5.

Larrington, C. (1996). *The Poetic Edda.* Oxford: Oxford University Press.

Lucas, G. (2009). *Hofstaðir: excavations of a Viking Age feasting hall in north-eastern Iceland* (Institute of Archaeology, Reykjavík, Monograph No. 1). Reykjavík: Fornleifastofnun Íslands.

Lønborg, B. (1998). *Vikingetidens metalbearbejdning* (Fynske studier, 17). Odense: Odense Bys Museer/Odense Universitetsforlag.

Magnússon, Þór (1980). Silfursjóður frá Miðhúsum í Egilsstaðahreppi. *Árbók hins íslenzka fornleifafélags 1980* (1981), 5–20.

Magnússon, Þór (1996). Silfur á Íslandi. In *Silfur í Þjóðminjasafni*, 6–31. Reykjavík: Þjóðminjasafn Íslands.

Mainman, A. J. & Rogers, N. S. H. (2000). *Finds from Anglo-Scandinavian York* (The Archaeology of York: The small finds, 17/14). York: Council for British Archaeology (for York Archaeological Trust).

Margeson, S. (1983). On the iconography of the Manx crosses. In C. Fell, P. Foote, J. Graham-Campbell & R. Thompson (Eds.), *The Viking Age in the Isle of Man*, 95–106. London: Viking Society for Northern Research.

Mortensen, A., & Arge, S. V. (Eds.) (2005). *Viking and Norse in the North Atlantic.* Tórshavn: The Faroese Academy of Sciences.

Oddy, W. A. (1984). Ancient jewellery as a source of technological information – a study of techniques for making wire. In *Fourth international restorer seminar*, Vol. 2. *Investigation of museum objects and materials used in conservation*, 241–252. Budapest.

Page, R. I. (1995). *Chronicles of the Vikings.* London: British Museum Press.

Roesdahl, E., & Wilson, D. M. (Eds.) (1992). *From Viking to Crusader: The Scandinavians and Europe 800–1200.* New York: Rizzoli.

The Sagas of Icelanders: a selection (2000). London/New York; Penguin Books/Viking Penguin. Reprinted (with minor alterations) from *The Complete Sagas of Icelanders*, Vols. IV (1997). Iceland; Leifur Eiríksson Publishing Ltd.

Scudder, B. (2000). Egil's saga (trans.). In *The Sagas of Icelanders*, 3–184.

Shetelig, H. (1937). Islands graver og oldsaker fra vikingetiden. *Viking*, 1, 205–219.

Skre, D. (Ed.) (2007). *Means of exchange: Dealing with silver in the Viking Age* (Kaupang Excavation Project Publication Series 2: Norske Oldfunn XXIII). Oslo: University of Oslo.

Sturluson, Snorri. See Faulkes (1987) and Hollander (1964).

Urbańczyk, P. (2009). The Polish discussion on medieval deposits of hack-silver. In S. Brather, D. Guenich & C. Huth (Eds.), *Historia Archaeologica*, 70, 501–523. Berlin: Walter de Gruyter.

Whitfield, N. (1990). Round wire in the early middle ages. *Jewellery Studies*, 4, 13–28.

Whitfield, N. (1997). The Waterford kite-brooch and its place in Irish metalwork. In M. F. Hurley, O. M. B. Scully & S. W. J. McCutcheon, *Late Viking age and medieval Waterford: Excavations 1986–1992*, 490–517. Waterford: Waterford Corporation.

Williams, G. (2007). Kingship, Christianity and coinage: monetary and political perspectives on silver economy in the Viking age. In J. Graham-Campbell & G. Williams (Eds.), 177–214.

Wilson, D. M. (2008). *The Vikings in the Isle of Man*. Aarhus: Aarhus University Press.

Zachrisson, T. (1998). *Gård, gräns, gravfält: Sammanhang kring ädelmetalldepåer och runstenar från vikingatid och tidig medeltid i Uppland och Gästrikland*. Stockholm Studies in Archaeology, 15; Stockholm University.

Östergren, M. (2008; 2009: English edition). Spillings – världens största vikingatida silverskatt. In A.-M. Pettersson (Ed.), *Spillingsskatten – Gotland i vikingatidens världshandel*, 11–40. Visby: Gotlands Museum.

Interpreting Power and Status in the Landscape of Viking Age Orkney

DAVID GRIFFITHS & JANE HARRISON

ABSTRACT

Landscape is seen as the key to unlocking past patterns of visibility, consumption and deposition which indicate strategies for social and economic control. Much of this paper consists of a detailed summary of fieldwork and excavations at the Bay of Skaill (on the Atlantic west-facing coastline of West Mainland, Orkney), together with Marwick and Birsay Bay immediately to the north. Excavations in 2008–2010 revealed a substantial (26.3 m x 4.5 m) longhouse, which artefacts and radiocarbon dates show was occupied in the tenth to twelfth centuries AD. The role of this building, and its ancillary complex of smaller buildings and metalworking areas, is explored. The excavation is seen as an example of mounded settlement (of which a number of other examples are offered) occupying politically-strategic points in the landscape. Feasting, hospitality, and the place-name *Skáli* (as in *Skaill*) are discussed.

Keywords: Landscape, settlement, mounds, consumption, deposition, visibility, status, excavations.

Defining archaeological signatures of power and status is as fundamental an interpretative challenge as recognising the complexities of identity and ethnicity. Perceptions of status in the archaeological record hinge in material terms on the relative size, complexity and quality of buildings, proximity to other important sites such as churches, together with the discovery of traded items of precious metal, glass, imported/exotic materials or those which are perceived to be rare or valuable, and manufacturing evidence in bone or metal. Longhouse dimensions in excess of 20 m, such as those at Jarlshof, Shetland (Hamilton, 1956) are almost instinctively perceived to be indicative of high social status, whereas smaller-sized buildings are apportioned a lower social rank by reason of this factor alone. Where the historical record is present, saga references add to perceptions of status (but conversely, should their absence imply lower status?). Later historical documents such as the later medieval Orkney rentals (Thomson, 2001) may be used to infer earlier status, but this approach must be used with caution. Archaeologists are increasingly aware of the role of 'agency': of the active part played by material culture in the shaping of human status and identity (Kopytoff, 1986; Hodder, 1993; Jones, 1997;

Edgeworth, 2006, etc.). Less often stressed is the role of landscape in articulating ideas, beliefs, identity or status.

Distinguishing high from medium or low status is a subjective exercise, and is compromised by the completeness of survival rates of structures, finds and biological remains. 'High status' is most often claimed or suggested, but subtler gradations are less frequently illustrated. An example of a considered distinction in settlement hierarchy is the juxtaposition, within under five miles, of a modest-sized and equipped farmstead occupied between *c.*1000–*c.*1300 AD at Cille Pheadair, South Uist (Scotland) with a 'much larger settlement at Bornais', which in the words of the excavator was 'one of the bottom rung of small (but by no means poor) single farmsteads, above which were the larger farming complexes, and at the top, a large community in the island's "capital" at Bornais – the difference was not only in terms of size. Bornais seems to have possessed a hall-like building which would have given an importance in administrative terms' (Parker-Pearson, 2005, 253; Sharples, 2005). Yet missing from this short, pragmatic characterisation of status are less 'archaeologically demonstrable' factors – the size, commodification, complexity and geographic reach of the site's rural economy (see e.g. Barrett, 2007), its spiritual or ancestral power, and the call it had upon its surrounding population in terms of family or social obligation.

THE BIRSAY-SKAILL LANDSCAPE ARCHAEOLOGY PROJECT

We have attempted to explore the subtle complexities of status in Viking Orkney by moving beyond the traditional indicators to investigate a settlement's relationship with its landscape and how that expresses local role and significance. Investigating how a settlement's use of – and place – in the landscape might define status is central to the Birsay-Skaill Landscape Project. Since 2003, Oxford University, with the support of Historic Scotland and Orkney Islands Council, has been undertaking landscape-scale archaeological research on the west-facing coastal areas of Orkney's north-west Mainland: the 'Birsay-Skaill Landscape Archaeology Project'.[1] The project has provided an arena for experimentation in landscape method and interpretation. Of the present authors, Griffiths is the originator and director of the project, while Harrison supervises the excavations and is writing an Oxford D.Phil [PhD] thesis on Viking-Norse coastal settlement mounds in the North Atlantic, focusing on Orkney Skaill (*Skáli)* sites.

At Birsay, the major concentration of early historic archaeology on landward-facing side of the tidal island known as the Brough of Birsay was exten-

1 Project website: http://www.conted.ox.ac.uk/research/projects/Birsay-Skaill.

sively excavated in the 1930s by A.O. Curle, in the 1950s by C.A. Ralegh Radford and S. Cruden, and the 1970s and early 1980s by C.D. Morris and J.R. Hunter (Hunter, 1986; Morris, 1996; Morris, forthcoming). The common assumption that the pre-Viking Brough was a high-status Pictish site has recently been re-examined and questioned (Brundle, 2005). The Brough's highly visible yet conditionally-accessible geography endows it with an enduring sense of distinctiveness and semi-isolation in full view of the Mainland, which has prompted continual re-evaluation of its spiritual and temporal status (see also the Brough of Deerness, Barrett & Slater, 2009). A magnetometry and resistivity survey covering the full extent of the areas previously part-excavated was completed in 2003–2007 (Griffiths, 2006). On the Buckquoy Peninsula, the narrow point of the Mainland facing the Brough, excavations by F.T. Wainwright, Anna Ritchie and C.D. Morris between 1960 and 1982 took place at ten individual locations within the cliff erosion zone (Ritchie, 1977; Morris, 1989). Survey and excavation at Marwick Bay began in 2007 and continues. This is aimed at further understanding two scheduled sites, a settlement mound on the foreshore with protruding collapsing stone walls and exposed middens, together with a nearby stone building which was scheduled as a chapel site.

However, most of the work of the Birsay-Skaill Landscape Project has so far been concentrated on the north side of the Bay of Skaill, where fewer indications of archaeological potential were previously known. A swathe of land measuring 300 m by 200 m (6 ha) on the northern edge of the extensive sandy links surrounding the centre of the bay has been subjected to geophysical, topographic and remote-sensing survey and mapping, supplemented by coastal survey and documentary research. These investigations have identified and mapped an extensive cluster of sandy mounds of archaeological character, which number at last four (and if the morphology of two of these is taken as suggesting a coalescence of more than one individual mound, their number may be up to seven). The mounds are located in an arc around the bay hinterland on the edge of a grassed zone of windblown sand (The Links of Skaill) links, fronting a system of freshwater streams connecting dune slacks within the Links to the sea. The most prominent mound, although not the most extensive in area, is the only one to have a name – the 'Castle of Snusgar', attested in records going back at least to the *Old Statistical Account* of Scottish parishes (OSA 16:458) of 1795 (which also recorded some stone masonry exposed on the flank of the mound), and the earliest Ordnance Survey maps.[2] The Skaill Hoard, found near

[2] The 'Castle' appellative is an interesting hint of former status (see below) but lacks the antiquity of a saga or medieval reference. The OSA refers to 'the ruins or remains of a large building, which yet bears the name of Castle of Snusgar'. 'Snu' or 'Snoo' refer elsewhere in Orkney to nose-like headlands and promontories (e.g. the point of Snooshan, Birsay), possibly coupled with ON *Garðr* (enclosure).

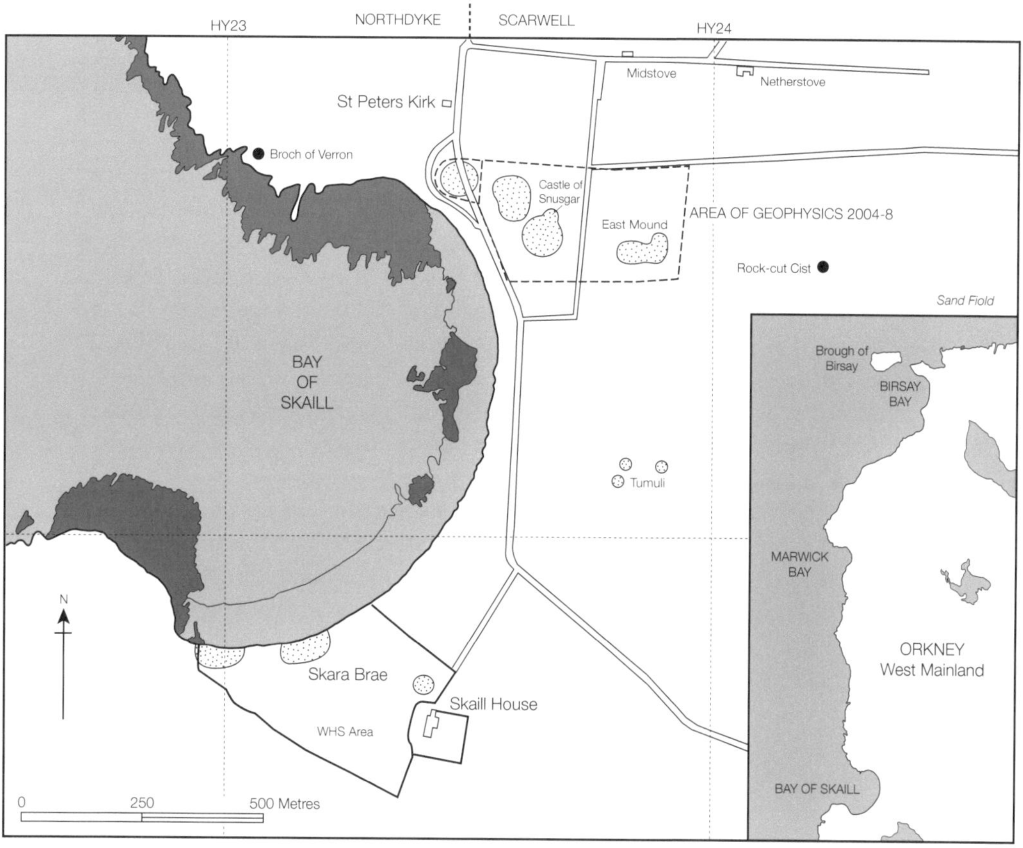

Fig. 1. The Bay of Skaill: survey and excavation areas: mound sites shaded.

here in 1858, remains the largest Viking silver hoard yet found in Scotland. It was composed of at least 115 pieces of bullion and 21 coins, the date of which suggests a date of deposition between AD 950 and 980 (Graham-Campbell, 1995,108–127). The precise location of the hoard was not accurately recorded at the time, however, and it is not possible to determine the location except within an area (measuring roughly 300 m north-south) between the 'Castle of Snusgar' and the Parish kirk of St. Peter.

In order to explore the nature of the geophysical anomalies further, selective excavation was undertaken on the top and flanks of Snusgar in 2004–2006, which revealed a badly eroded and robbed-out, but nonetheless impressive, series of masonry features including an east-west wall of 1.3 m width with external facings and a rubble core. Associated with these features were extensive midden layers, rich in Norse-period finds, sandwiched between lenses of wind-blown sand. There had been an extensive building complex here; its reduced and partial state of preservation is probably partly due to stone robbing for the construction of field dykes (walls) in the eighteenth and nineteenth centuries. The stratigraphy of Snusgar was investigated in deeper section in another trench on the south-eastern flank of the mound in 2005–2006. This confirmed that the mound was constructed of layers of domestic refuse and peat ash, with intermittent episodes of clean windblown sand. It is clear that the struggle to maintain stability and fertility against blanketing influxes of sand was an unremitting one for the inhabitants. The layers were generally flat in profile, and soft surfaces vulnerable to erosion had been deliberately stabilised by the admixture of stones and organic material. The latter has provided a significant return of archaeobotanical, archaeozoological and micro-artefactual data, and residues such as hammerscale from metalworking, through systematic soil sampling and floatation. Ten radiocarbon (AMS) dates taken from charred grain and short-lived wood species date the principal build-up of deposits to between 900 and 1050 Cal AD, a picture confirmed by a series of Optically-Stimulated Luminescence (OSL) dates taken in 2006 on midden deposits and the windblown sand layers. The lowest buried land surface sampled on the north-east flank of the mound produced a cormorant bone, which was dated as 1710±35 BP (Cal AD 610–780 at 95.4% probability).

Another, slightly less prominent, but more extensive, mound inland 200 m to the east of Snusgar, now termed the 'East Mound' was also subjected to geophysical survey in 2004. A test trench here in 2005 was extended and deepened to a full-scale area excavation in short summer seasons between 2006–2008 and 2010. In 2010, the most extensive exposure yet, the heart of the complex was revealed as a stone-built east-west aligned longhouse measuring 26.3 m in length and 4.5 m in width (Fig. 2). Remarkably well-preserved under its protective blanket of wind-blown sand, the shape of the exterior walls shows evidence for the classic Scandinavian 'bow-sided' morphology, although there is evidence for several phases of construction and reconfiguration (post-excavation analysis of these is pending).

The longhouse has a central internal division between domestic and byre areas, marked by a stub wall and an internal entrance passage. The byre, which occupies the eastern end of the building, shows evidence for animal stalling, and has a substantial central stone-flagged passageway with a network of drains beneath. As wind-blown sand was removed from the earth floors of the byre, animal hoof-prints were revealed *in situ*. The domestic area, in the central and western portions of the longhouse, is laid out in two zones. The central part of the building has a wide uncluttered floor, narrow side benches constructed from stone slabs, and a small but well-defined hearth which has produced met-

Fig. 2. 'East Mound' excavations 2010 from NW, the longhouse is orientated E–W in the foreground with the ancillary buildings and metalworking areas to the S.

alworking residues. The western end, constructed in a manner suggesting an extension to the original structure, has much wider side benches and a series of hearth deposits, the finds and environmental samples from around which suggest food preparation. We have begun, provisionally, to interpret the central area as a 'meeting room' with the main living quarters – and cooking area – at the western end. South of, but linked to, the main building, through its principal entrance in its south wall and via a stone-flagged yard and staircase, is a complex of small ancillary buildings, which probably housed domesticated animals and some craft-working. A small stone-walled yard area on the south west of the complex produced extensive ferrous and limited non-ferrous metalworking residues from four bowl hearths, which are undergoing further analysis.

Forty-one radiocarbon dates obtained from carbonised grain and other short-lived flora have given a date range for the occupation of the longhouse and its associated structures between 950 and 1150 Cal AD, although further statistical analysis of these is expected to result in considerable refinement of their detailed chronology.

The structures briefly outlined above are rich in finds. Surrounding the building complex are extensive midden deposits which were used in conjunction with spreads of stone to stabilise exterior ground surfaces. The artefacts, which almost all fall within the material culture repertoire characteristic of the Viking/Norse period, provide a parallel chronology to the radiocarbon dates. Amongst the earliest independently datable objects are three beads provisionally identified by Birgitta Hoffmann (in Griffiths, Harrison & Hanshaw, 2009). A biconical blue glass bead provisionally identified as Callmer type A176 is paralleled in Scandinavian contexts dating to AD 790–860. Even earlier is a white opaque glass bead with crossing blue swags. Scandinavian white beads of the period AD 800–1000 usually have red or brown swags, whereas an earlier type of white glass bead which does have blue swags, known from Anglo-Saxon England but commoner in the Rhineland and Northern France (Guido Group 3iiia, or alternatively Koch 34 blue), dates to the period AD 580–650. An incomplete flat concentric reddish amber bead from an occupation layer within the domestic area of the 'East Mound' major building is paralleled by an example from a child's grave in a small Viking cemetery at Cnip, Lewis (Dunwell et al., 1995, 726, Fig. 725, 721), is of likely Baltic provenance and probably dates to the ninth or tenth century. A further glass object from the site is a black bun-shaped linen smoother, of a type recognised principally from female graves throughout the Viking world.

Bracketing the date range of finds at the later end is a series of sherds of imported colour-decorated pottery, some of which is decorated with decorative orange appliqué pads. Derek Hall and the late Alan Vince have both examined the pottery, and have suggested that the pottery is probably sourced from northern France or the Low Countries, dating from the twelfth century at the earliest. The predominant material used for vessels and containers here was steatite, of which over fifty examples have been found to date, including both Norwegian and Shetland-sourced vessels. Small bone pins and needles, and decorated antler comb fragments, fall into type groups of the tenth to twelfth centuries associated with Viking/Norse sites elsewhere in Orkney and the western Viking world. The combs are exclusively of iron-riveted rather than copper-riveted types, strengthening their date attribution to the earlier phase of the Viking comb tradition (S. Ashby: pers. comm.). Metal finds have predominantly been small iron objects such as ties and nails, many of which arguably formed part of the wooden superstructure. Keys, hammers and clench-bolts are also present. Non-ferrous metal artefacts are rarer, but include a complete crutch-headed ringed pin, several small copper-alloy clasps, strips, wires, and small blobs of secondary tap slag. The latter, when coupled with evidence for willow charcoal, hammerscale and other metalworking residues, strongly suggests that metalworking was a significant part of the economy here, and four fine small whetstones or polishers (two pierced) contribute to this picture.

Environmental archaeological sampling points towards the Snusgar and East Mound settlements as 'consuming' rather than 'producing' sites in economic terms. The improvement of soil by the admixture of seaweed and burnt peat is evident, as is the predominance of oat, flax and barley cultivation (the latter including the six-row hulled *Hordeum Vulgare* variety). The archaeozoological material favours cattle, sheep/goat and pig (with in many cases evidence of butchery), together with lower incidences of red deer, cat, dog, horse and seal. The bird bone is predominantly from marine species, such as the gannet, and the presence of a large number of fractured gannet humeri in a particular midden context (1504)[3], has led Ingrid Mainland to suggest that systematic seabird exploitation was occurring (in Griffiths, Harrison and Hanshaw, 2008). Fish remains occur in most of the midden and occupation deposits but are not disproportionately abundant. No 'fish-processing' type middens such as those at Freswick and Quoygrew (Barrett, 2005) have been exposed here, although cod head-bones are common in the assemblage, suggesting the possible preparation of stockfish, albeit on a more pluralistic and less industrial scale than at these sites.

3 (1504) is dated by AMS on carbonised barley grain to Cal AD 940–1050 at 95.4% probability (SUERC 17850).

EXPRESSIONS OF SOCIAL AND POLITICAL STATUS IN THE ORCADIAN LANDSCAPE

By traditional standards of interpretation (large buildings, proximity to an important church and a major silver hoard, imported finds, fine metalworking), the above evidence seems strongly to favour a high-status interpretation for the Viking-Norse sites on the north side of the Bay of Skaill. But by investigating the landscape context of the mounds can we reach a more nuanced depiction of the operation of standing and power in their locality? There are many forms in which power and status might have been expressed. In an oral, early medieval culture, social significance was of course rooted in the local for most people. For almost all contemporary Orcadians, power was symbolised by, and operated most potently through, people and places they encountered or saw as they went about their daily lives. *Orkneyinga Saga* depicts a culture articulated by personal alliances, gift-giving, tribute and formalised feasting: and although the Saga deals mainly with the Earls and their retinues, the same sorts of face-to-face relationships, in which power was often embodied in physical, visual symbols, operated at all social levels.

Known or suspected Viking-Norse settlements in Orkney are frequently found on mounds in sandy bays. Excavated examples include Skaill, Deerness; Pool, Sanday; Saevar Howe, Birsay, and Tuquoy, Westray (Buteux, 1997; Hunter, 2007; Morris, 1989 and 1996; Owen, 1993). Many more such sites exist but have not yet been studied as a group across Orkney, or excavated under modern conditions. Interest in mounded settlement sites was stimulated by research on 'farm mounds' by (amongst others) Donald Davidson, Raymond Lamb and Reidar Bertelsen (Bertelsen & Lamb, 1993). Two to three decades on, however, it is clear that the initial definition of 'farm mound', drawing mainly on evidence from sites on Sanday, Orkney, was unduly reductive. On the basis of relatively small investigations the mounds were interpreted as accumulations of richly organic midden sediments only – and therefore as evidence for the failure of early medieval farmers to make full use of available fertiliser (e.g. Davidson et al., 1986). More recent research and larger-scale excavation has shown that some coastal mounds were carefully controlled constructions of superimposed buildings, yards, middens, paths and small cultivation plots over long periods of time. Norse settlers invested considerable effort in staying precisely in one place, embarking on the characteristic complexities of rebuilding on the same site (Batey, 1987). In layering and reconfiguring these deposits, as excavation on the Skaill sites and at sites such as Pool and Tuquoy has demonstrated, considerable preparation was required: structures were demolished, surfaces levelled or built-up, and walls strengthened or shored. An archaeological 'layer-cake' or tell resulted, comprising structural stone, turf

Fig. 3. Bay of Skaill mound sites under excavation: East Mound (foreground, right) and 'Castle of Snusgar' (intermediate, left) with St Peter's Kirk in (background, centre), looking north-west.

and peat, ash, byre cleanings and domestic rubbish. This superimposition of structures and surfaces gradually creating or further embellishing a mound was apparently a deliberate policy; not simply the result of reluctance to move, or the unthinking piling up of manure and stone. Understanding the significance of these actions brings us to the heart of a rich social landscape in which status was defined in reference to the mounds.

Visually dominating an area was an obvious statement of power in the landscape. Some of the mounds, such as the Marwick site excavated in 2009, whilst less visible from the land, are especially dominant when approached from the sea. Visual authority across the seascape was almost certainly as relevant to bolstering and proclaiming status as dominating the sweep of the land. In this respect it is notable that most of the settlement mounds are associated with beaches which would have been suitable landing places for ships.

However, the profiles of the mounds did not only provide a visual statement in the landscape, they demonstrated mastery of the cultural and economic resources of the bay – human, agricultural and marine. Organic additions created fertile and well-drained garden plots but also made enlarging and building on a sandy mound practicable. We would concur with our colleagues in prehistoric archaeology that, as many would suggest for early farmers, there was "no such thing as rubbish"; but we would also argue that the "rubbish" of the landscape and its plants and animals was integral to expressing status and would have been appreciated as such. It is interesting in this respect to recall the extraordinary feasting middens of the Iron Age such as Chisenbury Warren, England; which are also testaments to the physical demonstration of status through conspicuous consumption and deliberate accumulations of organic material (McOmish, 1996).

Settling on an existing coastal mound also provided incoming Viking settlers with an immediate connection to the past of that area. The settlement mounds excavated in the Bay of Skaill are close to and physically reference earlier settlement. Other significant settlements were either on or close to prehistoric foci. Skaill, Deerness; Tuquoy in Westray; the Birsay Bay sites and Marwick Bay provide other examples of Viking groups occupying existing mounds in areas clearly marked by previous settlement. In these already well-settled and organised agricultural and social landscapes, new leaders needed rapidly to establish a dominance which was both physical and linked to existing landscape symbolism. Occupying existing settlement eminences and creating new ones in visual reference to older prominences linked the new leaders into a long-standing tradition of inscribing the landscape. The appropriation or foundation of a church or chapel may have been initiated in the spirit of religious conversion, but was also an astute acquisition – a status-enhancing symbol and increasingly part of a politically useful organisational structure (cf.

Anglo-Saxon England; Blair, 2005). St Peter dedications may be linked to the earliest established chapels (Lamb, 1993), and many settlement mounds are in close association with other known or suspected early church sites: in addition to the St Peter Kirk in the Bay of Skaill, are, for example: the Crosskirk at Tuquoy, and the chapel in Backaskaill Bay, Sanday and a mound site in Marwick Bay where the chapel is a matter of metres from the considerable settlement revealed by geophysics in 2009 and in the eroding mound (Griffiths & Harrison, 2010).

Skaill or *Skáli* settlement names, most often combined with *Lang* prefix (Thomson, 1995), provide another possible indication of higher-status associations with these coastal mound landscapes. *Skáli* is accepted in Orkney as denoting a significant longhouse or drinking hall which acted as an arena for social and political gatherings, and the collection of tribute (Thomson, 2008). Other settlement names in *Bu* and *Huseby* (Housebay) may have performed similar roles at different times (Crawford, 2006) – a comparison at Bornais has been noted above. The *Skáli* names are particularly numerous in Orkney (at least 40), and are arguably associated with the tribute-gathering or 'hospitality' role (ON *veizla*) required by peripatetic Earls, Bishops and their retinues (Thomson, 2008, pp. 16–17; Lamb, 1997). There are references in the *Orkneyinga Saga* to important political players being *á veizlu* in Skaill locations as part, for example, of the negotiation of alliances and attempts to heal quarrels (e.g. Pálsson & Edwards, 1978, ch. 16 dealing with Earl Einar and Skaill, Deerness, chs 65 and 74 dealing with Earl Paul Håkonsson and Skaill, Rousay). *Skáli* names have already been related to significant Viking-Norse settlement areas in mound landscapes such as in Marwick Bay, the Bay of Skaill and Skaill, Deerness and further work is underway to investigate the less well-understood Skaill landscapes across the Orkney Islands.

The conjunction of place-names and mounded settlements has more to offer in analyses of status in the landscape. Individual higher status sites connect to communal political processes and traditions. Mounds are recognised as having symbolic meanings, and have a clear association with authority and decision-making through *Thing* (ON *Þing*) assemblies (Skre, 1997; Skre, 2007, pp. 403–405); examples in Orkney include Dingieshowe, and Tingwall (which is focused on a prominent Iron Age broch site). Mound symbolism is redolent with ideas of assembly, status and communal focus; settlements on mounds will have gained from that linkage in landscape status vocabulary. The visible statements made by mounds and the associations established with control of the land, feasting and abundance, with religious, political and economic authority and with communal organisation, were part of a very long tradition of constructing status in the landscape. There is a considered notion of architecture applicable to the mounded settlement sites: in particular that the use of midden and domestic refuse (symbolic of abundance and consumption) in creating visual symbols in the landscape is an active expression of agency, and also factor common to many places across the Viking world. As a physical expression of status, its significance has long been underestimated and overlooked.

BIBLIOGRAPHY

Barrett, J. H. (2005). Economic Intensification in Viking Age and Medieval Orkney, Scotland: Excavations at Quoygrew. In A. Mortensen and S. V. Arge (Eds.), *Viking and Norse in the North Atlantic, Select Papers from the Proceedings of the Fourteenth Viking Congress, Tórshavn, 19–30 July 2001*. Tórshavn: Annales Societatis Scientiarum Færoensis Supplementum XLIV, 264–283.

Barrett, J. H. (2007). 'The pirate fishermen: The political economy of a medieval maritime society'. In B. B. Smith, S. Taylor & G. Williams (Eds.), *West over Sea: Studies in Scandinavian sea-borne expansion and settlement before 1300*. Leiden: Brill, 299–340.

Barrett, J. H., & Slater, A. (2009). New excavations at the Brough of Deerness: Power and religion in Viking Age Scotland. *Journal of the North Atlantic* 2, 81–94.

Batey, C. E. (1987). *Freswick Links, Caithness. A re-appraisal of the Late Norse site in its context. Parts i and ii*. Oxford: BAR British Series 179.

Bertelsen, R., & Lamb, R. G. (1993). Settlement Mounds in the North Atlantic. In C. E. Batey, C. D. Morris & J. Jesch (Eds.), *The Viking Age in Caithness, Orkney and the North Atlantic, Select Papers from the Proceedings of the Eleventh Viking Congress*, (pp. 544–554). Edinburgh.

Blair, J. (2005). *The Church in Anglo-Saxon Society*. Oxford University Press.

Brundle, A., (2005). The Unimportance of Early Birsay. In O. Owen (Ed.), *The World of Orkneyinga Saga* (pp. 75–88). Kirkwall: Orkney Museums and Heritage.

Buteux, S. (Ed.) (1997). *Settlements at Skaill, Deerness, Orkney. Excavations by Peter Gelling of the Prehistoric, Pictish, Viking and later periods 1963–81*. Oxford: British Archaeological Reports, British Series 260.

Crawford, B. E. (2006). Kongemakt og jarlemakt, stedsnavn som bevis? Betydningen av Housebay, Harray og staðir navn på Orkenøyenes West Mainland. *Viking* LXIX, 195–214.

Davidson, D. A., Harkness, D. D., & Simpson, I. A. (1986). The Formation of Farm Mounds on the Island of Sanday, Orkney. *Geoarchaeology* 1, 45–60.

Dunwell, A. J., Cowie, T. G., Bruce, M. F., Neighbour, T., & Rees, A. R. (1995). A Viking Age Cemetery at Cnip, Uig, Isle of Lewis, *Proceedings of the Society of Antiquaries of Scotland* 125, 719–752.

Edgeworth, M. (Ed.) (2006). *Ethnographies of Archaeological Practice.* Lanham MD and Oxford: Altamira.

Graham-Campbell, J. A. (1995). *The Viking-Age Gold and Silver Hoards of Scotland (AD 850–1100).* Edinburgh: National Museums of Scotland.

Griffiths, D. (2006). Birsay and Skaill, Orkney, Landscape Survey 2003–2004. In R. E. Jones & L. Sharpe, (Eds.), *Going over Old Ground: Perspectives on archaeological, geophysical and geochemical survey in Scotland*, (pp. 213–224). Oxford: British Archaeological Reports British Series 416.

Griffiths, D., Harrison, J., & Hanshaw, S. (2007). *Birsay-Skaill Landscape Archaeology Project, Data Structure Report Phase V–VI, 2006.* Oxford: OUDCE.

Griffiths, D., Harrison, J., & Hanshaw, S. (2008). *Birsay-Skaill Landscape Archaeology Project, Data Structure Report Phases VII–IX, 2007.* Oxford: OUDCE.

Griffiths, D., Harrison, J., & Hanshaw, S. (2009). *Birsay-Skaill Landscape Archaeology Project, Data Structure Report Phase X, 2008.* Oxford: OUDCE.

Griffiths, D., & Harrison, J. (2010). *Birsay-Skaill Landscape Archaeology Project, Data Structure Report Phase XI, 2009.* Oxford: OUDCE.

Griffiths, D. (forthcoming). Status and Identity in Norse Settlements: a case study from Orkney. In J. M. Barrett (Ed.), *Maritime Societies in the Viking World*, Cambridge: McDonald Institute of Archaeological Research.

Hamilton, J. R. C. (1956). *Excavations at Jarlshof, Shetland.* Edinburgh: HMSO.

Hedges, J. W. (1983). Trial Excavations on Pictish and Viking Settlements at Saevar Howe, Birsay, Orkney. *Glasgow Archaeological Journal* 10, 73–124.

Hodder, I. (1993). The narrative and rhetoric of material culture sequences. *World Archaeology* 25 (2), 268–281.

Hunter, J. R. (1986). *Rescue excavations on the Brough of Birsay 1974–82.* Edinburgh: Society of Antiquaries of Scotland.

Hunter, J. R., with Bond, J. M., & Smith, A. N. (2007). *Excavations at Pool, Sanday: a multi-period settlement from Neolithic to Late Norse Times*, Investigations in Sanday, Orkney v.1. Kirkwall: The Orcadian, in association with Historic Scotland.

Jones, S. (1997). *The Archaeology of Ethnicity.* London: Routledge.

Kopytoff, I. (2006). The Cultural Biography of Things: commoditization as a process. In A. Appadurai (Ed.), *The Social Life of Things, Commodities in Perspective*, (pp. 64–91). Cambridge.

Lamb, R. (1993). Carolingian Orkney and its Transformation. In C. E. Batey, C. D. Morris & J. Jesch (Eds.), *The Viking Age in Caithness, Orkney and the North Atlantic* (pp. 260–271). Edinburgh: Edinburgh University Press.

Lamb, R. (1997). Historical background to the Norse Settlement (pp. 13–16) in Buteux 1997.

McOmish, D. (1996). East Chisenbury: ritual and rubbish at the British Bronze Age-Iron Age transition. *Antiquity* 70, 68–76.

Morris, C. D. (1985). Skaill, Sandwick, Orkney: preliminary investigations of a mound-site near Skara Brae, *Glasgow Archaeological Journal* 12, 82–92.

Morris, C. D. (1989). *The Birsay Bay Project Volume 1, Brough Road Excavations*

1976–1982. Durham: University of Durham Department of Archaeology Monograph Series 1.

Morris, C. D., (forthcoming). *The Birsay Bay Project Volume 3, The Brough of Birsay, Orkney, Investigations 1957–2007*. Edinburgh: Society of Antiquaries of Scotland.

Old Statistical Account (1791–1799). *The Statistical Account of Scotland, drawn up from the communications of the ministers of the different parishes* 16 *(Orkney)*. Edinburgh.

Pálsson, H., & Edwards, P. (1978). *Orkneyinga Saga*. London: Penguin Books.

Parker-Pearson, M., Smith, H., Mulville, J., & Brennand, M. (2004). Cille Pheadair: The life and Times of a Norse Period Farmstead, c. 1000–1300. In J. Hines, A. Lane & M. Redknap (Eds.), *Land, Sea and Home, Settlement in the Viking Period* (pp. 235–254). Leeds: Society for Medieval Archaeology Monograph 20.

Ritchie, A. (1977). Excavation of Pictish and Viking-Age farmsteads at Buckquoy, Orkney, *Proceedings of the Society of Antiquaries of Scotland* 108, 174–227.

Sharples, N. (2005). *Excavations at Mound 3, Bornais, South Uist*. Oxford: Cardiff Studies in Archaeology, Oxbow.

Skre, D. (1997). Haug og grav. Hva betyr gravhaugene? In A. Christensson, E. Mundal & I. Øye (Eds.), *Middelalderens symboler*. Kulturtekster 11, (pp. 37–52), Bergen.

Skre, D. (Ed.) (2007). *Kaupang in Skiringssal*. Aarhus: Aarhus University Press.

Thomson, W. P. L. (1995). Orkney Farm Names: a re-assessment of their chronology. In B. E. Crawford (Ed.), *Scandinavian settlement in Northern Britain* (pp. 42–63). Leicester: Leicester University Press.

Thomson, W. P. L. (2001). *The New History of Orkney*. Edinburgh: Mercat Press.

Thomson, W. P. L. (2008). *Orkney land and People*. Kirkwall: The Orcadian Limited.

Similarities or Differences? Rune Stones as a Starting Point for Some Reflections on Viking Age Identity

ANNE-SOFIE GRÄSLUND

ABSTRACT

The concept of identity is discussed and the Scandinavian Late Viking Age rune stones are pointed out as a field of research where we can discover how identity was perceived. The famous Jarlabanke of Täby, who raised several stones in memory of himself, is mentioned as an example of a man who obviously had excellent self-confidence and who was certainly aware of his personal identity. It is argued that the reason for using very similar design of runic carvings could be due to a political system comparable to the *goði*-institution of the Icelandic Commonwealth, as a wish from the raiser to show his loyalty to the local chieftain who may have erected the first rune stone with a specific design. The distribution of rune stones of great similarity may thus be an expression of such a social organization.

Keywords: Viking Age, identity, rune stones, ornamentation, political and social system, loyalty.

MATERIAL CULTURE AND IDENTITY

When we talk about material culture as "active" or "laden with meaning", one aspect is that material culture creates identities. Signals are sent out, whether consciously or not. Identity can thus be expressed e.g. through dress customs or through the construction of a specific kind of house or monument, but also through everyday artefacts. In the two first cases, this is probably consciously done; in the latter it may well be an unconscious expression.

During the last decades, identity has been a field of research of great popularity, not least in North European archaeology, and today this is more discussed as cultural ethnicity. However, the concept of cultural identity has increasingly taken over, as identity seems to be a less problematic concept. There is a comprehensive archaeological literature on ethnicity and ethnic and cultural identity, which in many respects is critical and full of scepticism (see e.g. Jones, 1997 and Hillerdal, 2009).

Identity can be collective or individual; archaeologically, it may be easier to distinguish the collective identity, the belonging to a group. When discussing identity, it is important to point out both that identity is based on the person's own perceptions and feelings, and that one individual may have several identities, depending on the actual situation. Such a multiple identity could e.g. be made up of age, gender, household, locality and ethnicity.

Identity means that individuals or groups regard themselves as belonging to a specific culture, to an ethnic group or to a region. We speak about cultural identity, ethnic identity or regional identity. A group of people may share cultural values, material culture and/or having history in common. The cultural identity and perhaps also the regional identity are possible to trace in the archaeological source material, but not the ethnic one, as it postulates a self definition and self understanding, which we as prehistorians cannot get hold of when it concerns the periods from which there are no written sources. The situation becomes a little better for the Viking Age with its runic inscriptions and literary evidence.

Another problem is individual identity, which is difficult to grasp through material culture. An expression of personal identity should probably just be understood as something falling outside the general pattern.

The concept of identity means both similarities and differences: similarities within the group and differences in relation to other individuals and groups. The feeling of identity presupposes the idea of the others and is obviously created in relation to these. But there is also a forced identity, something that has been laid upon people for political reasons, to give them a feeling of solidarity – such as a national identity in the case of politically created national states. There are much better conditions for a voluntary appearance of regional identity. The region is a level between the central power and the local community and people's roots in and belonging to the region are parts of the regional identity, which in all probability is also influenced by the landscape.

ZOOMORPHIC RUNE STONES AS A FIELD OF RESEARCH[1]

Our Late Viking Age rune stones form a field of research where we can reflect on how identity was perceived. There is a personal identity and a collective identity, and sometimes it has been argued that the personal identity does not appear until early modern times, from the end of the 18th century, based on

1 Concerning the terminology, the term "picture rune stone" is sometimes suggested instead of zoomorphic rune stone. In my opinion, however, there is an important difference between a zoomorphic rune stone, where the runes are carved in the band-shaped body of what I call a rune animal, and a picture rune stone, where there is a picture separate from the rune animal, e.g. a man on horseback or an animal, a bird or a quadruped. Additional snakes, intertwined (or sometimes not) with the rune animal are part of the composition (the great beast struggling with a snake) and as well as the crosses, they are not regarded as separate pictures.

Fig. 1. Rune stone U 212 B, Vallentuna church, Uppland. Photo: Anne-Sofie Gräslund.

the appearance of autobiographies at that time. In my opinion, however, the runic inscriptions clearly show that there was already a feeling of a personal identity in the Viking Age (and, I am convinced, long before that). Good examples of this are the stones raised in memory of the raiser himself, such as the famous Jarlabanke stones in southeast Uppland, where the raiser claims (U 165, Täby tä, Täby parish and U 212A, Vallentuna church) that "he alone owned all of Täby", or (U 212B, Vallentuna church), Fig. 1 that "he alone owned all of this Hundred". The stone U 1011, Örby, Rasbo parish in

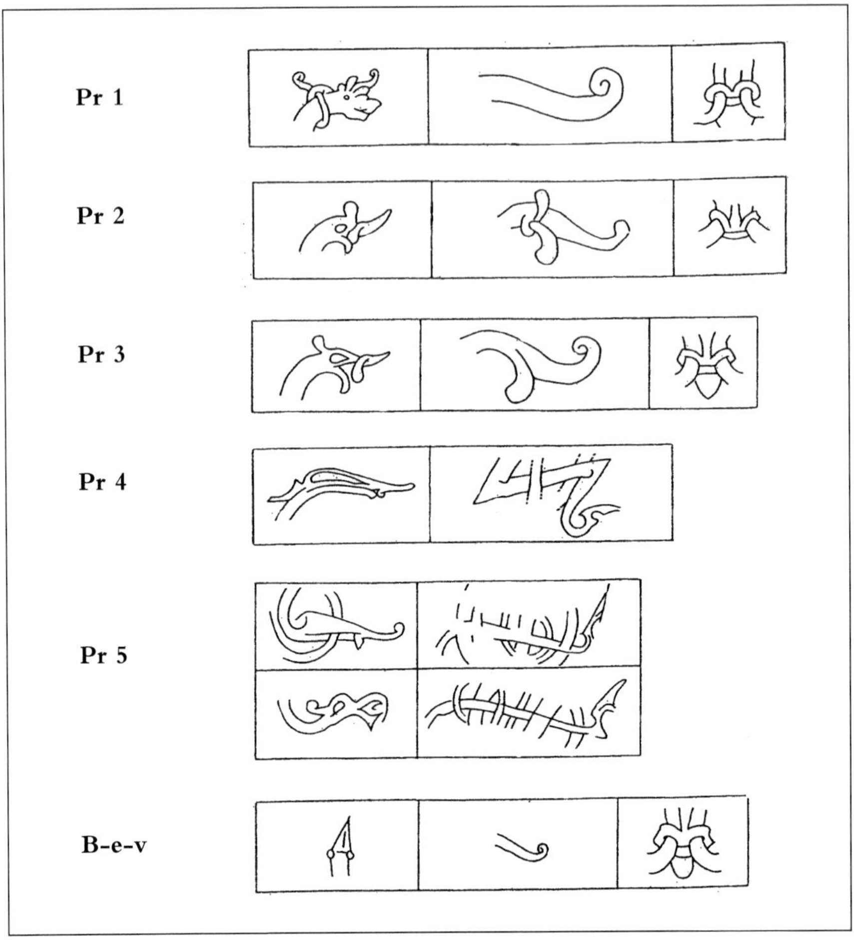

Fig. 2. Stylistic groups of rune animals. Important elements.

Uppland should also be mentioned, where it is said that *Vigmund, shrewdest of men, had the stone cut in memory of himself. God help the soul of Vigmund the steersman. Vigmund and Åfrid cut the memorial in his lifetime.*

Obviously, both Jarlabanke and Vigmund had an excellent self-confidence, and they were certainly aware of their personal identity.

Concerning collective identity, my question is whether this is the reason for the choice of a special design on certain rune stones. Generally, obvious signs of regional sub-groups can be distinguished in the ornamentation in spite of the conformity that has made it possible to stratify the rune stones chronologically on stylistic grounds (Gräslund, 2006 with refs.), Fig. 2. I have studied the zoomorphic carvings from Uppland, both those where the rune-animal's head

Fig. 3a

Fig. 3 a. Rune stone U 485, Marma, Lagga parish, Uppland, signed by Öpir. Photo: Marit Åhlén, Runverket, Riksantikvarieämbetet.

Fig. 3 b. Rune stone 1084, Hämringe, Bälinge parish, Uppland, probably intended as a copy of U485. Photo: Marit Åhlén, Runverket, Riksantikvarieämbetet.

Fig. 3 c. Rune stone 1096, Rörby, Bälinge parish, Uppland, obviously intended as an imitation of U 1084. However, the carver has misunderstood certain elements. Photo: Marit Åhlén, Runverket, Riksantikvarieämbetet.

Fig. 3b

Fig. 3c

is seen from above, in other words from a bird's-eye view, as well as those where the head is seen in profile – this latter group is by far the larger. The material is sorted by stylistic analysis, resulting in a classification into different groups, B-e-v, Pr 1-5, in a certain order (and, of course, many overlaps). The result has then been checked against genealogically dated rune stones. Archaeological dating including dendrochronology has subsequently been used to establish a suggested chronology.

However, even in the chronological style groups there are stones that are more similar than what is normally the case within a specific group. The concept of similarity is not an easy one – there are several degrees, from almost identical to fairly similar.

There are obvious cases of imitations of ornamentation; as an example, three stones are chosen, Fig. 3 a-b-c. The first one, (U 485) Marma, Lagga parish, signed by the outstanding rune carver Öpir, is really a very elegant representative of the youngest stylistic group Pr 5, in my view dated to the beginning of the 12th century. The second one (U1084) Hämringe, Bälinge parish, can be regarded as a good copy of the Lagga stone, while the third one (U 1096) Rörby, Bälinge parish, obviously is meant as a direct imitation of stone number two. However, here the carver has misunderstood certain elements of the ornamentation (as for example the "bump" at the knee, and the projection at the foot). The inscriptions are ordinary memorial formulations and there are no genealogical connections between them. Two more stones may be seen as belonging to this group, (U 914 Ströja, Börje parish and U 1014, Ärentuna church) both of them elegant and very similar to the three mentioned above, but the design is not identical. The distribution of these five carvings is within a distance of *c*.20 km; thus, in this area, which is extremely rich in rune stones, there are several other carvings of this stylistic group without this very close similarity.

In a seminar paper, Annika Hansson has made a detailed analysis of 13 carvings, belonging to the stylistic group Pr 4, with a strong mutual similarity (Hansson, 1993, 50 ff.). All 13 are similar, but two pairs are almost identical (U 281 Smedby, Hammarby parish and U 481 Lagga church, as well as U 660 Norränge, Håtuna parish and U 674 Skadevi, Häggeby parish, Fig. 4). The distance between the two first are *c*.30 km; between the two later ones the distance is much shorter.

It is tempting to interpret a conscious connection between stones with a strong similarity, perhaps seeing a wish from the raiser to show his/her loyalty to the person who raised the first stone with this design, and to mark a community. I would even suppose that the similar carvings were a contribution to the creation of a local/regional identity. Such a group of similar rune stones may be an indication of a social organisation of farmers as a subgroup

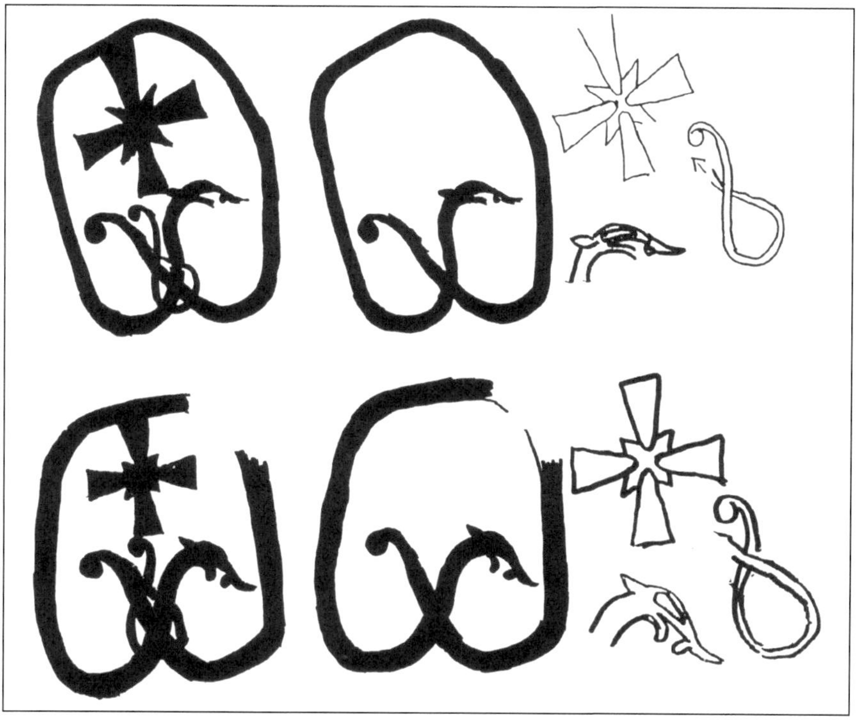

Fig. 4. Analysis of the design of two very similar rune stones, U 660, Norränge, Håtuna parish and U 674, Skadevi, Häggeby parish, both in Uppland. After Hansson 1993.

in the social hierarchy during the Late Iron Age, as suggested by Ulf Näsman (1988, 123 ff.) and Per Ramqvist (1991, 305 ff.), following the knowledge of Germanic tribes in the Migration Period. The local chieftain or magnate may have erected the first stone with a specific design.

Should we see the distance between the similar stones as a problem? Not necessarily, if we compare them with the *goði*-institution in the Icelandic Commonwealth. The *goði* was a chieftain with power over a *goðorð* – a chieftaincy (Sigurðsson, 1999). This was an abstract concept, meaning power over people, not over land, and it was not a geographical unit. Several chieftains could have what is called thingsmen, connected farmers in the same area. In *Grágás*, it is stated that the landowning farmers should elect a *goði* (certainly within the domain where they lived, but in practice, this rule was not followed). The chieftain and the farmers had mutual duties. The chieftain spoke for the farmers at the thing. They were in charge of the local things and had the power at the common Althing. They had also certain religious functions. The chieftain's most important task was to protect the peace among his thingsmen, and the greatness of his power depended on the number of thingsmen that had chosen him. If a farmer was not satisfied with his *goði*, he could change. The *goði* had no power without the loyalty from his farmers and the position of the farmers was precarious without the protection from the *goði*. Personal ties between the *goði* and the farmers were the foundation of the chieftaincy; this could be ties of friendship or of kinship. A long distance between the thingsmen and the *goði* was of course a difficulty, but was also regarded as a sign of strength. I would suggest that the distribution of the rune stones with great similarity may be an expression of a similar social organisation.

In this connection, the so called Ingvar stones are of interest. More than 20 stones (13 in Södermanland, seven in Uppland and one in Västmanland) were raised in the Mälar provinces in memory of men who had died when they followed the chieftain Ingvar on his disastrous expedition to Särkland. Ingvar and all his men died. It has been suggested by Mats G. Larsson (1983, 1987) that the expedition went to Georgia, according to information in the Georgian Chronicle on foreign warriors in the area in 1040. This hypothesis has met severe critique (Fischer, 1999, 21 with refs.). However, the dating to about 1040 corresponds to what is said in the Icelandic Saga about the death of Ingvar the Far-Travelled in 1040 or 1041, and as a suggestion, it may be reasonable. Even if this is more or less a legendary saga, some background information may reflect reality.

No less than 15 of the 21 Ingvar stones are ornamented in the Bird's-eye's-view style and many of them have a similar design, Fig. 5. Six of the seven Upplandic stones have two rune animals, all with very large pop-eyes, laid in open loops, which in only two cases are locked by an "Irish knot". The open loop, in this case made by only one rune animal, is also found on the so called Gripsholm stone (Sö 179) Gripsholm, Kärnbo parish, Södermanland, raised in memory of Harald, who is said to be the brother of Ingvar: *Tola had this stone raised in memory of her son Harald, Ingvar's brother. They fared like men / far after gold / and in the east / gave the eagle food. / They died southward / in Serkland.* We also find it on the interesting Tystberga stone (Sö 173) where the design consists of one edge-following rune animal in stylistic group Pr 2 and another rune animal in the Bird's-eye-view stylistic group, laid in an open loop. The stone was erected in memory of Holmsten who had first been "long in the west", but had then returned and with one of his sons, Rodger, had sailed away with Ingvar, and with him, "they died in the east". This stone is of great importance as it shows that stylistic groups B-e-v and Pr 2 are contemporary. As Pr 2 is often a good representative of classical Ringerike style, it should be dated to the first half of the 11th century, and my suggestion for Pr 2 is *c.*1020–1050. Stylistic group Bird's-eye view seems to start a little earlier and

Fig. 5. Rune stone U 778, Svinnegarn church, Uppland, raised in memory of a man who fell in the East with Ingvar. After Upplands runinskrifter.

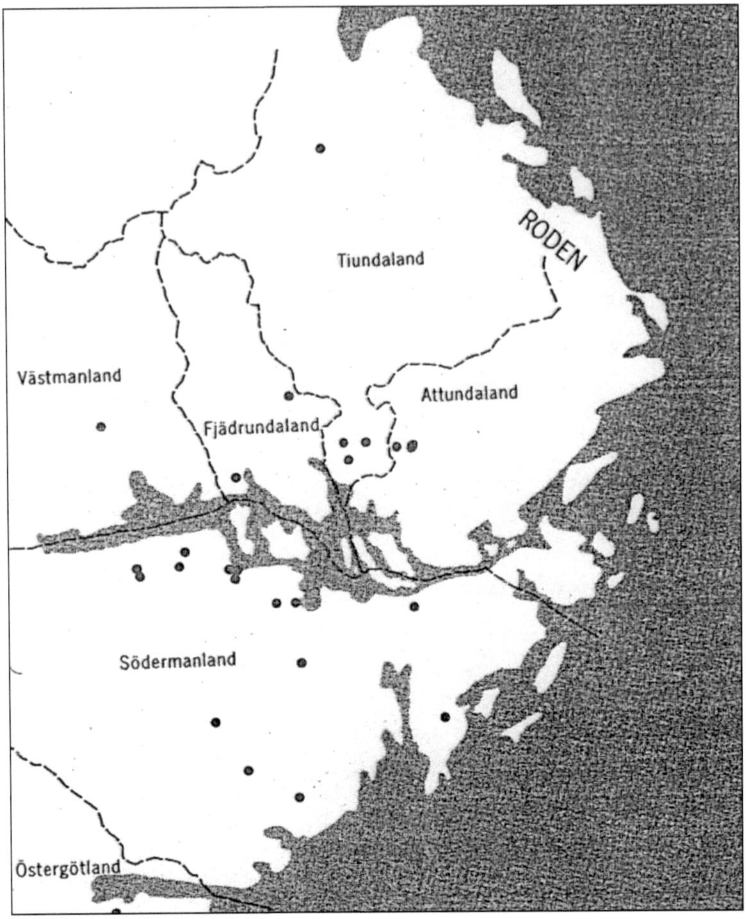

Fig. 6. Distribution map of the Ingvar stones. Redrawn after Larsson 1987 with addition of the stone found at Arlanda in 1990.

thus have a slightly longer lifetime, *c.*1010–1050. Additional snakes with B-e-v heads are frequent and start in fact as early as on the Jellinge stone (DR 42), dated to *c.*970.

There are also 15 stones, decorated in the Bird's-eye-view style, with an extremely uniform appearance, in a limited area in the western part of Uppland, but none of these seems to have any connection to the Ingvar expedition. The design with one edge-following B-e-v animal locked with an "Irish knot" and with a processional cross in the centre is never used on an Ingvar stone, as far as we know. In this case, this seems more to be a regional group, maybe expressing loyalty to a local chieftain in the area.

The Ingvar stones are distributed over a rather large area (Fig. 6). How could it be that the families, who were going to erect rune stones in memory of their dead fathers, brothers and sons, knew that it should be this design when it concerned the Ingvar expedition? At this time, another design, with the rune animal's head seen in profile, was very popular. The families must have got information, perhaps through itinerant rune carvers. Could it be that the mourning families wanted to express a feeling of community in this way? Or was it a way to show solidarity with the Ingvar family, who was probably a powerful magnate family, even if it was not, as has been suggested, a royal family. It lies close at hand to think of some kind of alliance, as inscription after inscription repeats "he went with Ingvar" or "he fell in the East with Ingvar". Such phrases do not occur in other inscriptions.

It has been argued that the rune carver was the one who decided design and ornamentation of the runic monuments. However, as Magnus Sundquist has pointed out, the commissioner obviously had a considerable impact on the design (Sundquist, 1996). Sundquist has analysed a group of stones with the decoration of three large loops in style Pr 4, signed by or attributed to the famous rune carver Öpir, active in Uppland in the later part of the 11th century. Such stones occur above all in two areas, one north of Uppsala and one in the south part of the province. In the northern area, the largest loop is on the top, whereas in the southern area, the top loop is a small one and the two bottom loops are larger. Öpir has carved many more rune stones in other parts of Uppland, but with very few examples of this design of three-loops, an indication that those who ordered a rune stone had a clear idea of which design they wanted.

Evidence that farmers or bailiffs, dependent on or allied to a magnate, might express this iconographically can be found in medieval heraldry. The historian Hans Gillingstam has pointed out that persons recently ennobled into the lower aristocracy might fetch a motif from the coats of arms of their masters, belonging to the high aristocracy (Gillingstam, 1988, 16–19). He shows the seal of Sten Sture the elder with water-lily leaves and compares this with the seals of his clients Lasse Birgersson and Knut Eriksson, both with water-lily leaves. Hemming Gadh, also a client of Sten Sture, was allowed to take over (with some changes) the coat of arms of Sten Sture who died in 1503 without children. In turn, Hemming Gadh's bailiff Måns Gadh has one water-lily leaf in his seal, which is interpreted by Gillingstam as an expression of subordination under Hemming Gadh, who had six such leaves in his seal (Fig. 7).

Looking again at the distribution map of the Ingvar stones, we see that with two exceptions, there are no such stones in Attundaland, and the two exceptions lie at the border between Attundaland and Tiundaland. One explanation, put forward by Mats G. Larsson, might be that the Ingvar expedition

Fig. 7. Seals with water-lily leaves. Top left Sten Sture the elder, right Lasse Birgersson. Bottom left Heming Gadh, right Måns Gadh. After Gillingstam 1988.

was organised in accordance with the ledung system, and that the ledung ships of Attundaland were needed for the defence of the entrance to the Mälar area (Larsson, 1986, 108). I want to suggest another explanation: that central Attundaland was an area at this time dominated by the Jarlabanke family and where the Ingvar family only had very few allies. As Täby-Vallentuna is a region extremely rich in rune stones, it is remarkable that there are no Ingvar stones there. From the evidence of the rune stones, it seems as these two powerful families more or less excluded each other. Was this the reason why the Jarlabanke family could be so dominating and important? We know of no other family of that dignity with such a concentration of rune stones, either from Tiundaland or Fjärdhundraland, Västmanland or Södermanland, where

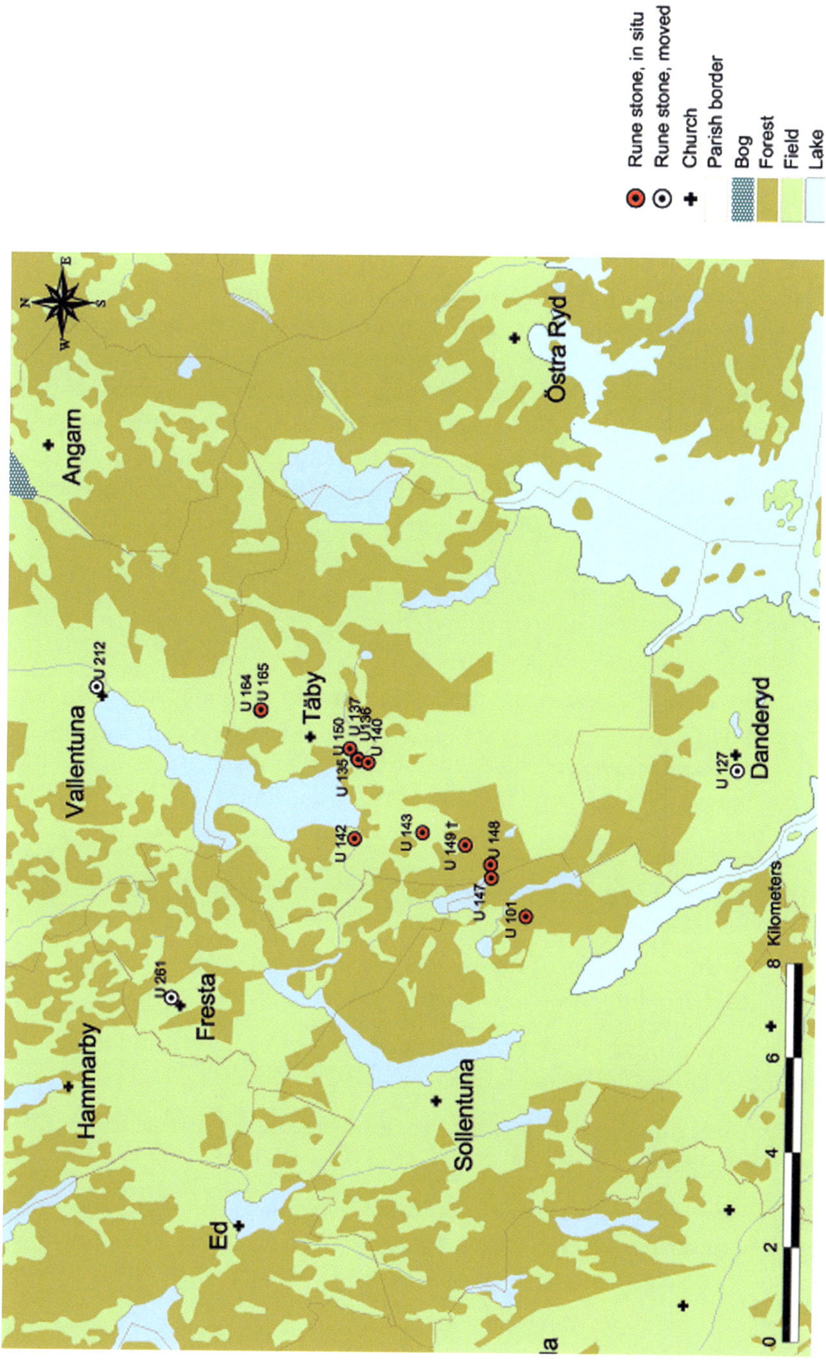

Fig. 8. Distribution map of the Jarlabanke stones. Map: Laila Kitzler Åhfeldt.

the numerous Ingvar stones can be interpreted as a sign that the Ingvar family had a great number of allies.

Such a conclusion presupposes that these two magnate families were contemporary, and there is nothing to contradict that. The Jarlabanke family appears on at least 16, probably 19 rune stones in Täby-Vallentuna (Gustavson and Selinge, 1988, 21–31, 59), Fig. 8; the earliest, with ornamentation in stylistic group Pr 2, raised by Jarlabanke's grandmother and the latest, raised in memory of Jarlabanke after his death, has ornamentation in stylistic group Pr 4. The stones raised by Jarlabanke in memory of himself while he was still alive are decorated in stylistic group Pr 2; in at least one case, U 212 B (see Fig.1) with a certain indication of a transition to stylistic group Pr 3. The other side of the stone, U 212 A, has a clear ornamentation in stylistic group Pr 2. Interestingly, independent of stylistical reasons it has been suggested that U 212 B has been carved later than U 212 A (Gustavson and Selinge, 1988, 45–48). A dating of U 212 B to the 1040s seems to be reasonable. Thus, if we accept the traditional dating of the Ingvar expedition to *c.*1040 and the Ingvar stones to the 1040s, this fits in well with the time when Jarlabanke raised his stones.

CONCLUDING REMARK

I have argued that the design and ornamentation of the rune stones as well as their distribution have a great potential for our understanding of the raiser's feeling of identity. Nevertheless, the question of who decided the design, the carver or the one who ordered the rune stone is not simple, but it seems clear that the raisers had a great influence on the appearance of the carvings.

★★★★

Rune stone numbers refer to the corpus Sveriges runinskrifter, published by Kungl. Vitterhets Historie och Antikvitets Akademien, Stockholm.

Sö = Södermanlands runinskrifter, granskade och tolkade av E. Brate och E. Wessén. Sveriges runinskrifter 3, Stockholm 1924–1936.

U = Upplands runinskrifter, granskade och tolkade av E. Wessén och S.B.F. Jansson. Sveriges runinskrifter 6–9, Stockholm 1940–1958.

Vs = Västmanlands runinskrifter, granskade och tolkade av S.B.F. Jansson. Sveriges runinskrifter 13, Stockholm 1964.

BIBLIOGRAPHY

Fischer, S. (1999). *Ingvarsstenarna i tid och rum.* Seminar Paper, Department of Scandinavian Languages, Uppsala University, Uppsala.

Gillingstam, H. (1988). Några klientvapen från svensk medeltid. In M. von Platen (Ed.) *Klient och patron. Befordringsvägar och ståndscirkulation i det gamla Sverige.* Stockholm: Natur och Kultur, 16–19.

Gräslund, A-S. (2006). Dating the Swedish rune stones on stylistic grounds. In M. Stoklund, M. Lerche Nielsen, B. Holmberg, & G. Fellows-Jensen (Eds.) *Runes and their Secrets. Studies in runology.* Copenhagen: Museum Tusculanum Press, 117–139.

Gustavson, H. & Selinge, K-G. (1988). Jarlabanke och hundaret. Ett arkeologiskt/runologiskt bidrag till lösningen av ett historiskt tolkningsproblem. *Namn och bygd, tidskrift för nordisk ortnamnsforskning,* 76, Uppsala: Kungl. Gustav Adolfs Akademien, 19–85.

Hansson, A. (1993). *Kopior eller likhet. Tolkningsproblem kring runstenars ornamentik.* Seminar Paper, Department of Archaeology, Uppsala University, Uppsala.

Hillerdal, Ch. (2009). *People in Between. Ethnicity and Material Identity, a New Approach to Deconstructed Concepts.* Opia 50, Uppsala: Uppsala University.

Jones, S. (1997). *The Archaeology of Ethnicity. Constructing identities in past and present.* London & New York.

Larsson, M. G. (1983). Vart for Ingvar den vittfarne? *Fornvännen* 78, 95–104.

Larsson, M. G. (1987). Ingvarstågets arkeologiska bakgrund. *Fornvännen* 81, 1986, 98–113.

Näsman, U. (1988). Analogislutning i nordisk jernalderarkæologi. Et bidrag til udviklingen af en nordisk historisk etnografi. In Mortensen, P. & Rasmussen, B. M. (Eds.), *Fra stamme til stat i Danmark 1. Jernalderens stammesamfund.* Jysk Arkæologisk Selskabs skrifter 22 (pp. 123–140), Højbjerg: Jysk Arkæologisk Selskab.

Ramqvist, P. (1991). Perspektiv på regional variation och samhälle i Nordens folkvandringstid. In Fabech, Ch. & Ringtved, J. (Eds.), *Samfundsorganisation og regional variation. Norden i romersk jernalder og folkevandringstid. Beretning fra 1. Nordiske jernaldersymposium på Sandbjerg Slot 11–15 april 1989.* Jysk Arkæologisk Selskabs skrifter 27, (pp. 305–318), Højbjerg: Jysk Arkæologisk Selskab.

Sigurðsson, J. V. (1999). *Chieftains and Power in the Icelandic Commonwealth.* Odense: Odense University Press.

Sundquist, M. (1996). *Treöglerunstenar i Uppland.* Seminar Paper, Department of Archaeology, Uppsala University.

The Reykholt Shieling Project: Some Preliminary Results

GUÐRÚN SVEINBJARNARDÓTTIR, KRISTOFFER DAHLE, EGILL ERLENDSSON, GUÐRÚN GÍSLADÓTTIR & KIM VICKERS

ABSTRACT

This paper gives an overview and some preliminary results of an interdisciplinary project that deals with the keeping of livestock at the summer farms, or *shielings*, belonging to the farm Reykholt in Borgarfjörður, focusing on the 13th century when Reykholt was at the height of its status and wealth. The aim is to investigate how the shielings contributed to the wealth of the farm, by combining archaeological, historical and palaeoenvironmental evidence. The results so far show general environmental signs of the first appearance of man and his grazing animals in the shieling areas, which coincides with the earliest occupation of the home farm in the 11th century, and also the effect on the environment. Historical evidence indicating that one shieling was moved from one site to another is supported by archaeological and environmental evidence, and there is some indication of iron-ore extraction at one site.

Keywords: Iceland, Reykholt, shieling, archaeology, history, palaeoecology.

INTRODUCTION

The economic importance of outfields in Iceland for livestock and summer transhumance is generally acknowledged and there is plenty of evidence to suggest that these areas were exploited for this purpose from the beginning of the settlement period. The evidence comes in the form of references in some of the earliest preserved literature, which admittedly post-dates the settlement period, place names and now also some archaeological remains, although this is still small scale. The practice of keeping livestock at summer farms, shielings (*sel*) is also supported by comparative material from elsewhere in the North Atlantic, the cultural area to which Iceland belongs, namely Norway, where it has been shown to date back to well before the Viking period (Øye, 2002), the British Isles (Gelling,1964), Faroes (Mahler, 1993) and Greenland

(Albrethsen and Keller, 1986). There is every reason to believe that the practice was brought to Iceland from the homeland of the settlers during the Viking period.

This field of study has received increased attention in Iceland in recent years with several area-based surveys being undertaken in different parts of the country (Sveinbjarnardóttir, 1991; Gunnarsdóttir, 2002; Pálsdóttir, 2005; Lárusdóttir, 2006; Guðmundsson, 2008), but so far only one full scale excavation (Lucas, 2008). The identification of shieling sites has been based on written sources, such as place names and the early 18th century Árni Magnússon land survey (*Jarðabók*). In many instances sites identified in this way are clearly multi-period and may have served different functions at different times, including that of small marginal farms. However, deciding what is a shieling rather than a farm is problematic. Criteria such as height above sea level, size of ruins and lack of enclosure banks have been used, and in two cases so far entomological (study of insects) and micromorphological (composition of floor layers) analyses have been applied in an attempt to throw light on this (Buckland & Sadler, 1991; Lucas, 2008; Vickers & Sveinbjarnardóttir, in prep.).

THE REYKHOLT SHIELING PROJECT

The project follows on from extensive archaeological and historical investigations which have been carried out in recent years at the farm site Reykholt in Western Iceland. Historically the site is known as one of the major farms in Iceland during the medieval period. The results of the archaeological investigations show that the site was occupied from *c.*AD 1000 and that a church was erected there not long after the farm was first occupied in the 11th century, or shortly after Christianity was introduced in *c.*AD 1000. The site had become a church centre by the early 12th century growing in wealth and stature, not least during Snorri Sturluson's occupation here in the first half of the 13th century (Sveinbjarnardóttir et al., 2007; Sveinbjarnardóttir, 2009; Sveinbjarnardóttir, forthcoming).

The homeland belonging to Reykholt is neither particularly good nor extensive. In addition to the land surrounding the farm itself, Reykholt owned, certainly by 1206, the farm Hægindi directly south of the river running through the Reykholtsdalur valley, Breiðabólstaður to the east, which was the original farm in the valley according to Landnámabók, and to the north Norðurreykir and the cottage Háfur which was in the care of the church farmer (Íslenzkt fornbréfasafn I, 279–280). A study based on all available written sources and aimed at discovering how the farm was managed in the past has shown that access to extra land resources was crucial for the success of the rise of the farm in wealth and power. The number of livestock reported in the

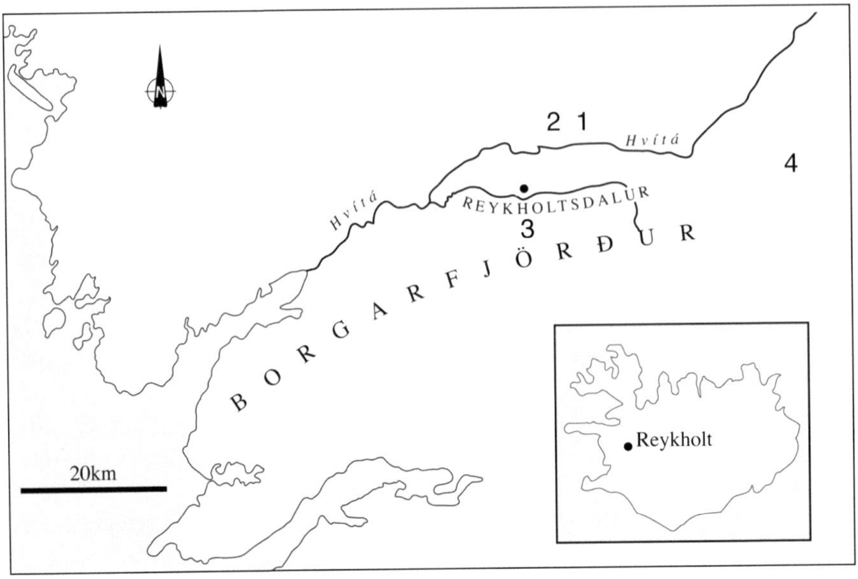

Fig. 1. Map showing locations of the sites studied. 1. Reykholtssel. 2. Norð-tungusel. 3. Faxadalur. 4. Geitland.

sources could never have been kept on the yield of the homeland alone, and but for these extra land resources, Reykholt would probably only have been a farm of medium means (Eyþórsson, 2008).

The Reykholtsdalur valley does not have any natural communal upland grazing areas so these had to be sought further afield. The earliest preserved reference to such resources is a late 12th century church charter where it is stated that Reykholt has the right to a shieling in *kior*, now Kjarardalur (1 & 2 in Fig. 1) which lies parallel and to the north of Reykholtsdalur, together with half of the fishing in the river and the woodland in the nearby valley Þverárhlíð for use at the shieling. The farm also has access to resources in Faxadalur, to the south, (3 in Fig. 1) the nature of which is not specified, and to woods in Geitland (4 in Fig. 1), an inland area *c.*25 km to the east of the farm (Íslenzkt fornbréfasafn I, 280). Three further sites, Reyðarvatnsós, Vestri Fossárhöfði/ Kaldárhöfði and Selhöfði, are mentioned in later sources as resource areas attached to Reykholt, but the nature of their use is uncertain (Þorláksson, 2004).

The main aim of the shieling project, which was launched formally in 2007 and will run until the end of 2011, is to investigate how the shielings which are known to have belonged to Reykholt in the medieval period contributed to the economic success of the farm. This is being done with an extensive programme of palaeoecological analysis on soil samples taken at and in the vicinity of the sites. These analyses have the potential to provide information about the timing of developments in human activity around the shieling sites, the landscape and vegetation surrounding the sites, and the impact of human activity in the areas studied. From this data, inferences can be drawn about questions involving the permanency of occupation, and the activities and land use taking place at shielings. Pollen shows when man and his grazing animals arrived on the scene and gives an indication of the nature of the land use, such as woodland exploitation and whether land use was continuous or not. The same applies to insects. Certain insects are only associated with man and his activities and therefore give a good stratigraphic marker for human settlement. Different types of insects are also associated with different activities, such as hay storage, possibly pointing to permanent occupation (Buckland & Sadler, 1991). They can also tell us about changes in the environment and when these occurred, such as a decline in humus and litter layers which are probably related to the loss of woodland, and the increase of grassland or heath. A decrease in organic carbon and nitrogen in the soil, and soil accumulation caused by erosion are all indications of increased grazing pressure. This may also be evident in the pollen data through a decrease of plant types that suffer badly as a result of grazing, a limited increase of grasses, and an increase in pasture and weed taxa. For more concrete evidence of the nature of occupation at a site, micromorphological analysis of the composition and layering of floor deposits can indicate whether the occupation was permanent or episodic.

By combining the environmental information collected from the sites with the written and archaeological evidence, a good picture should be obtained of the nature and development of human activity in the shieling areas. Emphasis will be put on establishing the functions carried out at the shielings belonging to Reykholt, the natural conditions in which the shieling activity took place and the effect it had on the environment. The data will then be put into a wider Icelandic, Scandinavian and North Atlantic context.

THE FIELDWORK

Two sites are known in Kjarardalur, a valley which lies parallel and to the north of the Reykholtsdalur valley. It does not have much lowland and the only farms ever known to have been there are at the mouth of the valley. The site further inland (1) is now called *Reykholtssel* and the other (2) *Norðtungusel*. Ruins are visible at both sites which have been surveyed. Trial trenches were made in selected places and small scale excavations were carried out in an attempt to throw light on the buildings and get dating material, and samples were taken for environmental analysis of pollen, insects and soil.

The remains at Reykholtssel were overgrown, but clearly those of buildings placed at a height of *c.*160 m a.s.l., at the side of a stream. Two areas of structures were identified on the surface, but attempts to capture the inside of buildings with trial trenches turned out not to be as easy as was anticipated – a reminder of the fallibility of trusting surface outlines of collapsed buildings made of stone and turf. In the main complex a *c.*35 cm thick deposit of heavily layered cultural material was discovered. A 14th century date[1] is suggested for the earliest formation of this deposit the layered nature of which indicates seasonal occupation. Micromorphological analysis which is planned of the material may throw further light on its nature.

The building remains at *Norðtungusel* (no. 2 on Fig. 1), the site further down valley, were considerably clearer, placed on a platform at *c.*166 m a.s.l. The remains were interpreted with the help of a geophysical survey and limited excavation (Fig. 2). The written sources indicate that this was the earlier of Reykholt's two shielings in Kjarardalur and that it was not used by Reykholt after the 16th century, but rented out – last to the farm Norðtunga, the name of which it now carries. In building A1, the main complex, three separate floor layers were discovered with a thin charcoal layer *c.*45 cm below the lowest floor layer, imbedded into the natural. Dates obtained on charred birch from this layer and from a midden just outside the same ruin suggest activity at the site as early as the late 10th or early 11th century. The charcoal lens may indicate woodland clearance before the site was occupied, but could also represent some other human activity before the occupation proper represented by the three successive floor layers discovered within the building. Further excavation is needed to throw light on this since the excavated area where the charcoal lens appeared does not extend all the way to the walls of the building.

In the lowest of the floor layers, which has been dated to the 15th century, a piece of clean iron smelting slag was discovered. The composition indicates that it derives from bog ore and that fuel may have been scarce at the time it was produced, something confirmed by the environmental data (see below). This discovery indicates that iron ore extraction may have been one of the activities carried out at this shieling, in which case a proper upright slag-tapping furnace should be found somewhere in the vicinity of the site, since the slag produced in more primitive pits has a different composition (Rehren, unpublished data). As yet no other evidence for iron working in the valley is available. The nature of the Norðtungusel discoveries is undeniably reminiscent to some extent of the evidence discovered at Háls in Hálsasveit of iron-ore extraction which pre-dates the occupation of the site, although here a smelting furnace base was discovered (Smith, 2005).

1 The overall results of the radiocarbon dates for the project remain to be processed. They will be presented and discussed elsewhere.

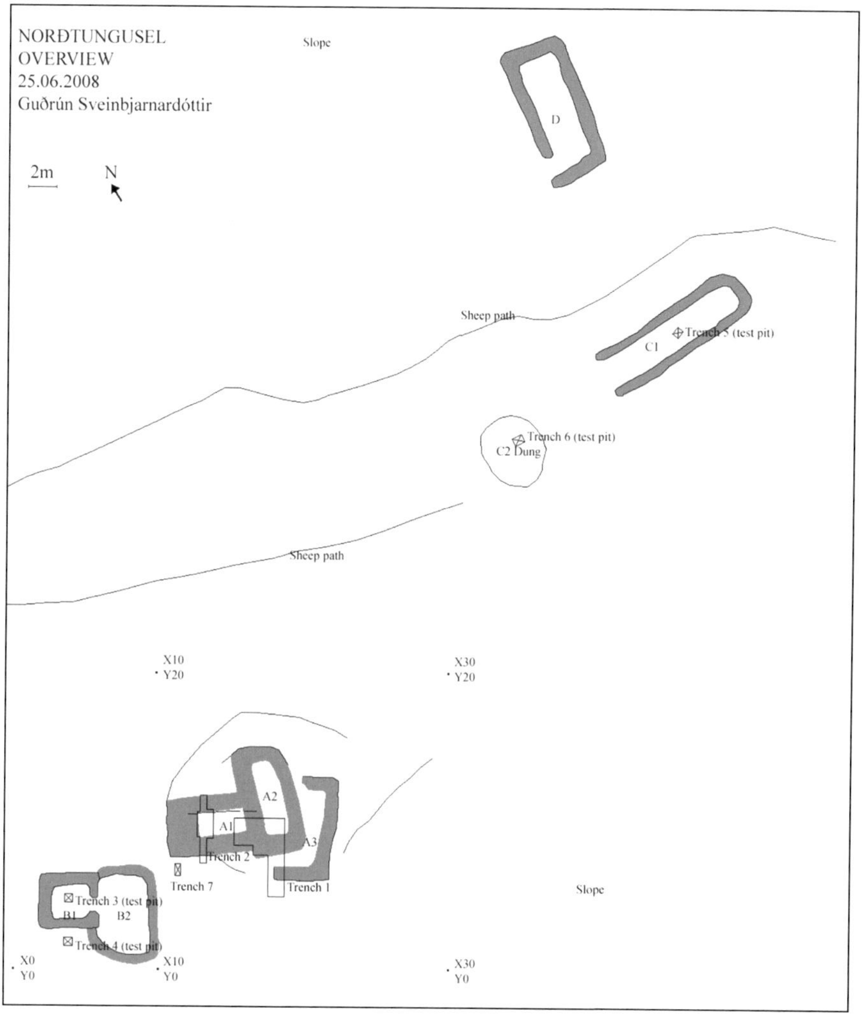

Fig. 2. Site plan of Norðtungusel.

The results of palaeoecological analysis on samples taken in the vicinity of both sites in Kjarardalur have revealed extensive environmental change shortly after the time of settlement, a horizon now conveniently marked by the *landnám* volcanic ash layer dated to AD 871±2 (Grönvold et al., 1995). The birch (*Betula*) woodland for which there is evidence in the pollen record and is supported by the insect remains, as well as in the place name (*kjarr* = brushwood) and actual tree trunks discovered in pre-*landnám* deposits, was soon reduced. The lowered values for the pollen of birch are coincident with more frequent recording of microscopic charcoal fragments, which perhaps indicates charcoal production or other use of fire near the sampling site. Some grazing is also signified by the decrease in plants that suffer badly as a result of grazing. The exploitation of the valley's resources also affected the wider landscape as shown by the decrease of organic carbon and nitrogen, and more rapid soil accumulation caused by erosion. The beetle fauna at Reykholtssel changes after *landnám*. We see the introduction of the dung beetle, which is associated with man, as well as other synanthropic species which live on waste materials, the disappearance of beetles associated with humus – probably on the woodland floor, and an increase in those associated with drier, more open grassland.

These are all general indications of the first appearance of man in the valley and the effect of human activity on the environment. More specific results so far are evidence of heavy grazing at Norðtungusel from the time of settlement until the late 14th century, when the pressure is released, as demonstrated by reduced numbers of spores from dung-loving fungi and a parallel expansion of birch woodland. These results are in keeping with the earliest dating evidence obtained from the sites, which indicate that Norðtungusel was occupied from as early as the 10th century, whereas the earliest dates from Reykholtssel suggest that the site was first occupied in the 14th century. These results also match the historical evidence which indicates that Reykholt's shieling activity was moved from Norðtungusel to Reykholtssel at about that time. Despite this, it is clear that the landscape around Reykholtssel was modified significantly well before the earliest archaeological or historical evidence for occupation, showing that the area was being used, to an intensity strong enough to clear the woodland even if the site was not settled. Microscopic charcoal fragments in the sediments are most frequent between *c.*AD 970 to 1300, perhaps suggesting the involvement of fire in reducing and suppressing woodland growth around the site, or the exploitation of the woodland for charcoal production. On the whole the land around the sites, both of which face to the south, was well suited for shieling activity in the past, and much better than the land on the south side of the river. The area is now heavily eroded, particularly around Reykholtssel.

A shieling in *Faxadalur* (3 on Fig. 1) in Flókadalur, which lies parallel and to the south of Reykholtsdalur, is first mentioned in 16th century written sources (Eyþórsson, 2008, pp. 145–146). By the late 12th century Reykholt was, however, making unspecified use of the area according to the church charter of that date (Íslenzkt fornbréfasafn I, 280). The shieling was in use until the 19th century, which explains why the building remains are so clear. The site is placed in heathland, in a depression close to a stream, at a height of *c.*225 m a.s.l. A complex of three rooms and what is probably a milking fold (*kvíar*) were planned and a trial trench was made into one of the rooms in the com-

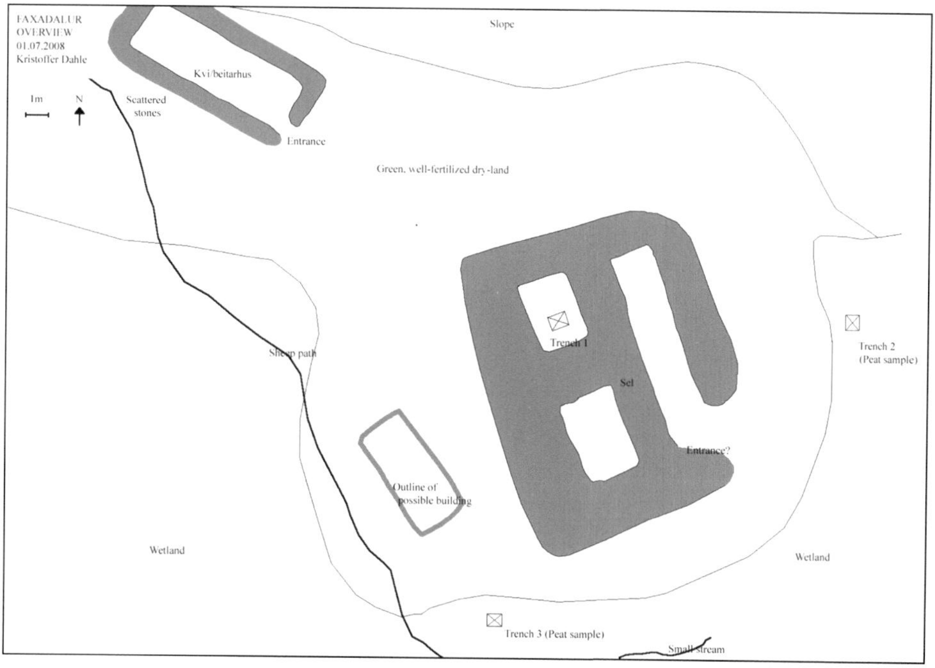

Fig. 3. Site plan of the Faxadalur site.

plex (Fig. 3). It produced a sequence of cultural layers, the earliest of which was radiocarbon dated on charred birch giving calibrated estimates which indicate that there was occupation at the site from as early as the beginning of the 11th century which is well before the site is mentioned as a shieling in the written sources. There is little doubt that this is a shieling rather than a permanently occupied farm. This is supported by the written sources, the sequence of floor layers indicating seasonal occupation, the layout of the buildings and the general setting of the site. The results of palaeoecological analysis of samples taken in a midden close to the buildings and of micromorphological analysis on samples from the floor layers should throw further light on the economy and nature of activities at the site.

The dating of the earliest human activity at the shieling sites in Kjarardalur and in Faxadalur, coupled with the general evidence of human activity in Kjarardalur seen in the soil sections by the onset of erosion and disappearance of woodland, fits well with the archaeological dating of the initial occupation at Reykholt to *c.*AD 1000 or the early 11th century (Sveinbjarnardóttir et al., 2007; Guðrún Sveinbjarnardóttir, forthcoming). The suggestion is that these resource areas were being used from the beginning of the occupation of the farm.

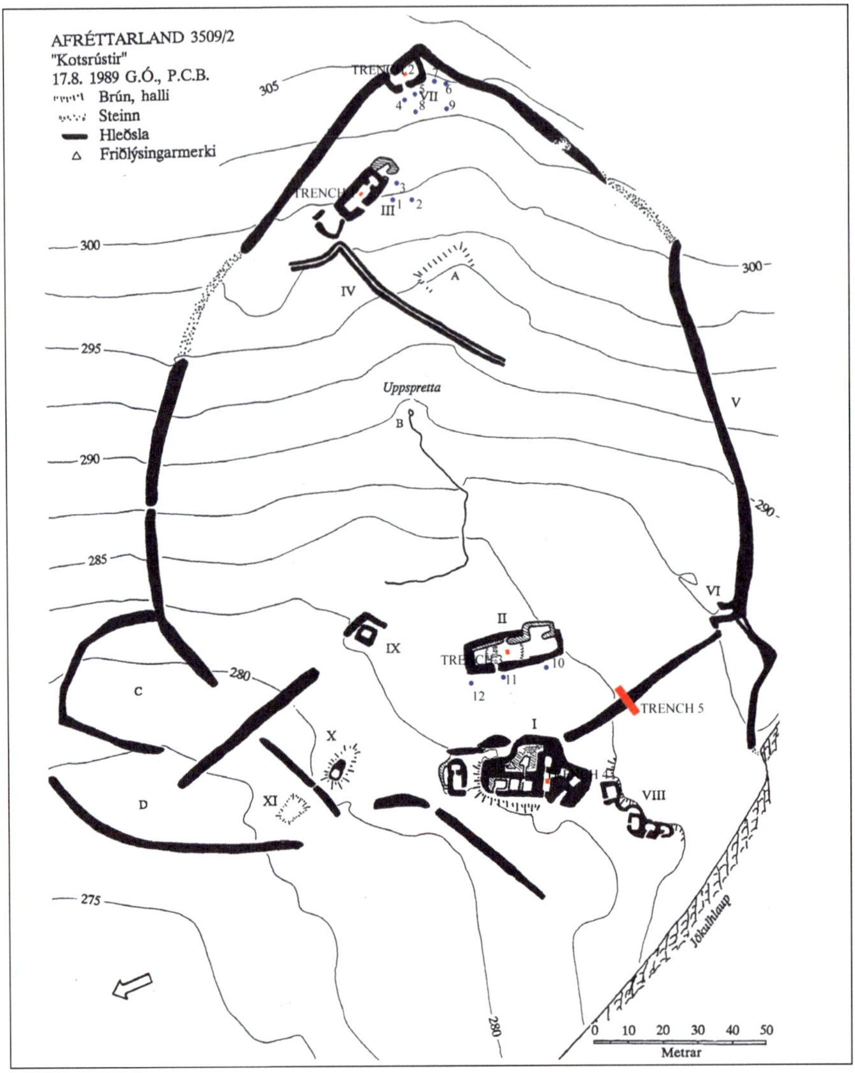

Fig. 4. Site plan of Kot in Geitland.

The third study area is *Geitland* (4 on Fig. 1) which lies *c*.25 km in a straight line inland from Reykholt and is mentioned among its property in the late 12th century church charter. It differs from the other two study areas in that there is no reference to there ever having been a shieling here. Two sites are known in the area, placed at a height of *c*.300 m a.s.l., which contain a number of ruins which are obviously not all contemporary. Geitland is mentioned in Landnámabók as the location of the settlement of one of the earliest settlers.

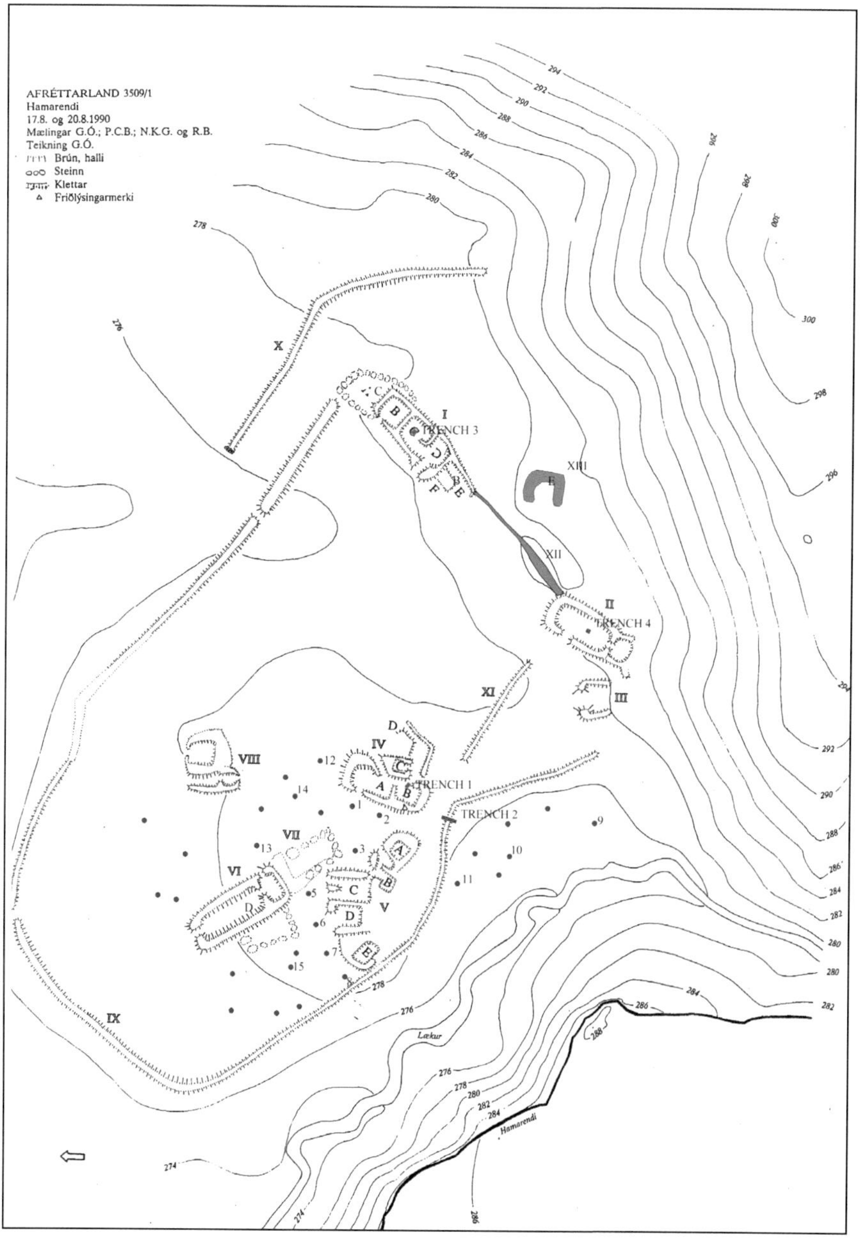

Fig. 5. Site plan of Hamraendar in Geitland.

The two sites, which were surveyed in 1989 (Ólafsson, 1996, pp. 74–81) are physically very different to the three sites discussed above (Figs. 4 and 5). Both contain enclosure banks and a considerably larger number of ruins, including two longhouses at each site inside which trial trenches were dug revealing thick occupation layers. Two layers which have been interpreted as floor layers, separated by a few centimetres of soil, were discovered indicating at least two phases of occupation. Dates on the earlier and clearer floor layers suggest that the sites were occupied already in the 9th century, with the second phase taking place one to two hundred years later. This dating evidence and the nature of the remains rather supports the hypothesis that the sites in Geitland are an example of optimistic initial settlers choosing land which turned out not to be so good for farming in the long run. It is possible that when the occupants left Geitland they went to settle at Reykholt where the archaeological evidence points to initial occupation by *c.*AD 1000 or the early 11th century, and that they kept Geitland as a resource area, as reported in the written sources (Sveinbjarnardóttir, 2010; but see Þorláksson, in press).

Whether the second phase of occupation at these sites belongs to shieling activity remains to be seen. Micromorphological analysis on samples from the floors may throw light on this. This kind of analysis was instrumental in nailing down the interpretation of the only assumed shieling site that has been excavated in Iceland (Lucas, 2008). This interpretation was supported by scant entomological evidence which is already being questioned on the basis of results obtained on material analysed in this project (Vickers & Sveinbjarnardóttir, in prep.). Pollen analysis on samples from the infield at Kot may also throw light on what activities took place there.

The more complicated building complexes, I at Kot and IV at Hamraendar, are not dissimilar to the main complex for example at Norðtungusel. They are clearly made up of components of different dates and are likely to have been the centres for the second and subsequent phases of activity at these sites. In the case of Kot such activity is known to extend to the 16th century when tradition has it that the site was settled. This may also be the time when it acquired its present name, Kot, which in Iceland refers to a minor, dependent farm of a late date (Lárusson, 1960). Around AD 1900 two farmers in Reykholtsdalur grazed sheep at the site and erected a shelter, the remains of which are clearly evident built into complex I. Some of the smaller ruins at both sites also seem to post-date the initial occupation and may belong to subsequent activity there with animals.

THE REYKHOLT SHIELINGS IN A WIDER CONTEXT

Compared to other areas in Iceland where shieling sites have been surveyed, the number known in the Reykholtsdalur valley is very small. A study carried out in Dýrafjörður in the Western peninsula, where there is limited lowland, revealed a great number of shielings, located in the mountain pasture on average at a distance of 2,6 km and at a height above sea level which was 2–3 times that of the home farm (Guðmundsson, 2008). In an area in Eyjafjörður in the North there were also many shielings, located in marginal land above the farms, on steep slopes and at elevations above 200 m a.s.l., while the home farms were on average placed at 159 m a.s.l. (Gunnarsdóttir, 2002). A study in Reykjahverfi, also in the North, on the other hand, showed that shielings were almost completely absent (Lárusdóttir, 2006). Furthermore, a study based on archaeological surveys in the whole of Iceland showed that there were relatively few shielings in Rangárvallasýsla in the south (Pálsdóttir, 2005), the area which has the most extensive lowland and best land for animal husbandry. These examples show that the picture of shieling activity in Iceland is by no means uniform and that many factors are likely to play a part.

There may be several reasons for the small number of shielings known in the Reykholtsdalur valley. Perhaps the grazing areas, which are particularly extensive in the lower part of the valley where it opens out to the lowland plain, were sufficient to sustain the animals at most of the farms. It is also possible that some of the sites of small dependent farms established within the holdings of the larger farms previously served as shielings, although this is difficult to prove without investigating these sites specifically. There are some place names which could support such an interpretation. The fact remains that the high status farm Reykholt was in a position to make use of shieling areas outside the valley, adding to its resource base and thus to its extra wealth.

The results of the project so far are promising in answering the questions posed as to the nature of the shielings of Reykholt, what effect they had on their environment and how they fit into the wider picture. In the next two years we hope to fill in this picture further.

ACKNOWLEDGEMENTS

The project has been supported by grants from the Icelandic Centre for Research, no. 080655023, Kultur- og kirkjedepartementet in Norway, the bank Sparisjóður Mýrasýslu, the Culture and Medieval Centre Snorrastofa, the Ministry of Agriculture in Iceland and the Archaeology Fund in Iceland.

BIBLIOGRAPHY

Albrethsen, S. E. & Keller, C. (1986). The Use of the Sæter in Medieval Norse Farming in Greenlend. *Arctic Anthropology*, 23 (1 & 2), 91–128.

Buckland, P., & Sadler, J. (1991). Farm or Shieling? An Entomological Approach. Appendix to Guðrún Sveinbjarnardóttir (1991), *Acta Archaeologica* 61, 93–96.

Eyþórsson, B. (2008). *Búskapur og rekstur staðar í Reykholti 1200–1900*. Reykjavík, IS: Sagnfræðistofnun Háskóla Íslands.

Gelling, P. S. (1964). Medieval Shielings in the Isle of Man. *Medieval Archaeology*, 6–7 (1962–1963), 156–172.

Grönvold, K., Óskarsson, N., Johnsen, S. J., Clausen, H. B., Hammer, C. U., Bond., G., & Bard, E. (1995). Ash layers from Iceland in the Greenland GRIP ice core correlated with oceanic and land sediments. *Earth and Planetary Science Letters* 135, 149–155.

Guðmundsson, B. (2008). Sel og selstöður við Dýrafjörð. Unpublished manuscript.

Gunnarsdóttir, S. (2002). The transhumant landscape of Saurbæjarhreppur. A study of shielings, dependent farms and their locations in connection to the mother settlements. Unpublished MA thesis, School of Archaeological Studies, University of Leicester.

Hitzler, E. (1979). *Sel – Untersuchungen zur Geschichte des isländischen Sennwesens seit der Landnahmezeit*. Oslo, Norway: Universitetsforlaget.

Íslenzkt fornbréfasafn I. Diplomatarium Islandicum I. Kaupmannahöfn, Denmark, (1857–1876).

Jarðabók Árna Magnússonar og Páls Vídalíns. Copenhagen, Denmark: Hið íslenzka fræðafélag (1913–1943).

Lárusdóttir, B. (2006). Settlement, organization and farm abandonment: the curious landscape of Reykjahverfi, North-East Iceland. In W. Davies, G. Halsall & A. Reynolds (Eds.), *People and Space in the Middle Ages, 300–1300* (pp. 45–64). Brepols, Netherlands: Turnhout.

Lárusson, Ó. (1960). Gårdnavne. Island. *Kulturhistorisk leksikon for nordisk middelalder* V, 642–645.

Lucas, G. M. (2008). Pálstóftir. A Viking Age shieling in Iceland. *Norwegian Archaeological Review* 41(1), 85–100.

Mahler, D. L. (1993). Shielings and their role in the Viking-Age Economy. In C. Batey, J. Jesch & C. Morris (Eds.) *The Viking Age in Caithness, Orkney and the North Atlantic* (pp. 487–505). Edinburgh, Scotland: Edinburgh University Press.

Ólafsson, G. (1996). *Friðlýstar fornleifar í Borgarfjarðarsýslu*. Rit Hins íslenska fornleifafélags og Þjóðminjasafns Íslands 2. Reykjavík, IS: Hið íslenska fornleifafélag og Þjóðminjasafn Íslands.

Pálsdóttir, A. H. (2005). Segðu mér sögu af seli. Fornleifafræðileg úttekt á íslenskum seljum. Unpublished BA thesis. University of Iceland.

Smith, K. P. (2005). Ore, fire, hammer, sickle: iron production in Viking Age and Early Medieval Iceland. In R.H. Bjork (Ed.), *De Re Metallica: The use of Metal in the Middle Ages* (pp. 183–206). AVISTA Studies in the History of Medieval Technology, Science and Art, Vol. 4. Aldershot, Britain: Ashgate Publishing Limited.

Sveinbjarnardóttir, G. (1991). Shielings in Iceland: an archaeological and historical survey. *Acta Archaeologica* 61, 73–96.

Sveinbjarnardóttir, G., Erlendsson, E., Vickers, K., McGovern, T. H., Milek, K. B., Edwards, K. J., Simpson, I. A., & Cook, G. (2007). The palaeoecology of a high status Icelandic farm. *Environmental Archaeology*, 12 (2), 197–216.

Sveinbjarnardóttir, G. (2009). Kirkjur Reykholts. Byggingasaga. In G. Ólafsson and S. Kristjánsdóttir (Eds.) *Endurfundir. Forleifarannsóknir styrktar af Kristnihátíðarsjóði 2001–2005* (pp. 58–69). Rit Þjóðminjasafns Íslands 19. Reykjavík, Iceland: Þjóðminjasafn Íslands.

Sveinbjarnardóttir, G. (2010). The making of a centre: the case of Reykholt, Iceland. In J. Sheehan & D. Ó Corráin (Eds.), *The Viking Age: Ireland and the West* (pp. 483–493). Proceedings of the XVth Viking Congress, Cork, 2005, Dublin, Ireland: Four Courts Press.

Sveinbjarnardóttir, G. (forthcoming). Reykholt. Archaeological investigations at a high status farm in western Iceland.

Vickers, K., & Sveinbjarnardóttir, G. (in prep.) Insect invaders, seasonality and transhumant pastoralism in the Icelandic shieling economy. *Environmental Archaeology.*

Þorláksson, H. (2004). *Sel Reykholts.* Unpublished research proposal for the shielings of Reykholt in Borgarfjörður. Prepared for the Icelandic Ministry of Education, 18th of February 2004. Reykjavík.

Þorláksson, H. (in press). Reykholt vokser fram som maktsenter. In B. Þorgeirsson, (Ed.) *Mellan tekst och materiell kultur.* Reykholt. Snorrastofa, Menningar- og miðaldasetur.

Øye, I. (2002). Landbruk under press 800–1350. I del 2. In B. Myhre & I. Øye (Eds.) *Norges landbrukshistorie I 4000 f.Kr – 1350 e.Kr.* Jorda blir levevej (pp. 215–414). Oslo, Norway: Norske Samlaget.

Money and its Use in the Saga Society: Silver, Coins and Commodity Money

SVEIN H. GULLBEKK

ABSTRACT

The history of money takes a remarkable turn in the Icelandic Saga society after *c.*1100, when silver is replaced by *vaðmál* as the main unit value of account. At the same time silver and coins more or less disappear from archaeological finds: Only three coins have been recorded in finds from *c.*1100 to *c.*1400. While Northern Europe embarked on the road towards monetary economies, the Saga society conserved and enhanced a commodity money system. The Icelandic laws define and regulate carefully the value relations between different commodities and how valuations of commodities should be undertaken when disputes arose.

In the 11th century, however, the number of Icelandic stray finds of coins are not insignificant compared with either Scotland or Norway. In total, 17 stray finds of 11th century coins have been found in Iceland. The equivalent for Scotland is 9 coins and for Norway, 60 coins. In Norway as many as 51 stray finds have been found in archaeological excavations within Trondheim. A comparison between Iceland and Western Norway give a stray find ratio of 17 to 4 coins in favour of Iceland for 11th century coins. This suggests that coins were available and probably used more frequently than has been appreciated in 11th century Iceland. References to use of money in the sagas support this, and particularly coin use of a more seasonal character where the Thing was an arena for coins used for paying fines, compensations, debts and for the purpose of commerce.

All coins from the first half of 11th century in Icelandic finds are Anglo-Saxon, German, Danish and Swedish. In the second half of the century a shift in the composition of coins can be observed: Out of eight coins, seven are Norwegian. This is a parallel development to that which took place within Norway at that time. Harald Hardrade (1047–1066) established a national currency, and foreign coins in circulation were replaced by Norwegian coins. This suggests a strong Norwegian influence on the Icelandic economy in this period.

If we compare the use of money in the saga society in the 11th century with the situation in the 12th, 13th and 14th century, it becomes clear that Iceland did not adopt anything resembling a money economy. In fact a shift from silver to *vaðmál* around the year 1100 and its continuation into the following centuries, makes it clear that the Icelandic economy was organized on the basis of a commodity money system rather than a money economy. This became increasingly more common in societies with which Iceland came into contact.

Keywords: Medieval money, medieval coins, Iceland medieval economy, commodity money system.

The total number of coins found in Viking territory adds up to more than 800,000 coins with an emphasis on Russia, Poland, the islands in the Baltic Sea, and the coastal areas of mainland Sweden, Denmark, then Norway and Finland. In comparison, the total number of coins and coin finds from Iceland are few and far between. It is only on Greenland that Viking Age coins have yet to be found, even though it is likely that coins were there. The late 11th century penny struck in the reign of the Norwegian king Olaf Kyrre (1067–1093) found in Newfoundland reflects the most Western distribution of coins in the Viking world.

A survey of Icelandic Viking and medieval coin finds add up to 389 coins, of which 356 coins derive from the Gaulverjabær hoard deposited *c.*1015 at a farmstead in Árnessýsla (Eldjárn, 1948; Jonsson, forthcoming) and 6 coins deposited together with 135 grams of hacksilver at Keta in Skagafjarðarsýsla, t.p.q. *c.*1000 (Eldjárn, 1953). The rest of the coins have been found as single finds; Islamic, English, German, Danish and Norwegian coins from 10th to 14th century found in different contexts; thing places, market places, farmsteads and graves.[1] As elsewhere in the Northern lands the population of coins and coin finds from the first half of the 11th century include a wide range of currencies; Islamic, Bohemian, German, Anglo-Saxon, Irish, Scandinavian, Swedish, Danish and Norwegian. While German coins appears much more frequent and in higher numbers than Anglo-Saxon coins in Swedish and Danish finds, is the relationships slightly in favor of Anglo-Saxon coins in Norway (Jonsson 1993, pp. 207–208).[2] In the Gaulverjabær hoard the relation between German and Anglo-Saxon coins were respectively 160 and 180 coins, and Anglo-Saxon pennies struck pre-1050 outnumber German pfennigs by nine to two in the Icelandic single finds material. This composition resembles the coin finds in Norway from that period, *c.*990–1050.

In the second half of the 11th century the single find material suddenly take on a different composition. Out of eight single find coins seven are Norwegian and one German while Anglo-Saxon coins disappear altogether. This sudden

1 An unpublished survey of the Icelandic single finds of coins has been made based on Eldjárn, 1948; Eldjárn, 1953; Ólafsson, 1990; Holt, 1998; Kristjánsdóttir, 2005; Institute of Archaeology, annual report 2005; Application for Inclusion in the World Heritage List Þingvellir National Park; Communications from Anton Holt and Ragnheiður Traustadóttir.

2 In the ongoing project Sylloge of Coins from the British Isles: Norway dr. Elina Screen has identified quite a few additional Anglo-Saxon pennies through careful studies of fragments in Norwegian hoards (volume I–II forthcoming).

shift must be understood in relation to the major turn in Norwegian coinage and monetary organization. When King Harald Hardråde (1047–1066) established a national coinage foreign coins were driven out of circulation and replaced by Norwegian coins. This process continued into the reign of his successor Olaf the Peaceful (1067–1093). By the 1080s foreign coins made up less than 10% of the total coins in circulation and Norwegian coins more than 90% (Skaare, 1976, pp. 22–23; Gullbekk, 2009, pp. 29–30 and 42–44).

After the 11th century, in the period *c.*1100 to *c.*1400, the number of coins in Iceland add up to a grand total of three; two English sterlings and one Norwegian bracteat found as single coins. In comparison the Norwegian finds from the same period add up to more than 30,000 coins. The number of coins from Danish and Swedish finds is significantly higher; in Denmark from the period 1241–*c.*1340 in total *c.*157,000 coins (Grinder-Hansen, 2000, p. 23) and in Sweden from the period *c.*1140–*c.*1520 in total *c.*220,000 coins (Stockholm Numismatic Institute).

10th century	5
11th century	17
12th century	1
13th century	2
14th century	0

Tab. 1. Icelandic single finds of coins from the 10th to 14th century. The evidence of coin finds makes a clear distinction between the period before and after *c.*1100. In total 22 single finds of coins from the 10th and 11th century have been found as well as two hoards containing 356 coins. Not one hoard and only three single finds of coins have been found dating from the 12th and 13th century, and none from the 14th century.

It is clear beyond doubt that monetary affairs in Viking Age witnessed a progressive expansion of which the dynamics came primarily from the state and church on the institutional side and towns and trade on the economical side. The underlying reasons for the growth of monetary economy varied over the years, and sometimes the growth was negative. However, over the centuries the overall cumulative effect was great. This monetary development seems to have had little impact on economy and society in Viking Age and medieval Iceland. Icelandic history comprises a remarkable feature in the history of money; around the turn of the twelfth century the number of coins lost or buried decreased and almost disappear according to the archaeological evidence. A decrease in coin finds from the first half of the 12th century was, however, nothing remarkable. At that time less availability of silver in Europe lead to demonetization at places that had embarked on the road to monetization in previous centuries. However, when fresh silver resources were discovered in Europe a sweeping wave of monetization commenced from the second half of the 12th century. Iceland was never part of this monetary development, but the Icelanders followed a different path of economic development in the medieval and early modern period.

In this article I will therefore focus on use of money with the basis in archaeological and numismatic evidence and argue the case for a commodity money system in operation in Iceland on the basis of archaeological, legal and saga evidence. The general trend from silver to commodities in Viking Age and medieval Icelandic economy has, of course, been acknowledged in the literature (Byock, 2001, p. 45). The aim with this study is to develope the understanding of money and its use in Iceland by applying new perspectives to this field of research.

COMMODITY MONEY SYSTEM

In Iceland, as in the rest of the northern world, silver was the first choice of payment and measure of value in the Viking era. The old Icelandic laws (Grágás) explicitly states that "At the time when Christianity came here to Iceland, silver was the currency in all major debts" (Grágás §245).[3] This is probably trustworthy information. However, the availability of silver – both in unminted and minted form – seem to have become increasingly scarce towards the end of 11th century. As availability of silver became insufficient *vaðmál* was introduced as measures of value alongside silver. As silver became increasingly rare it was partly replaced by commodities as means of exchange. In Iceland, as elsewhere, commodities had been used for barter and as money alongside silver ever since commerce became a feature of the society, presumably right from the very start in Iceland. The use of commodities as money was, however, nothing special for Iceland. In Viking and medieval Norwegian economy cattle, butter and crop were used as standard units of value besides silver, and many other types of commodities were also used as means of exchange.

Around the turn of the 12th century the saga society adopted *vaðmál* as

3 This provision states that "white silver which should stand the test of a nick and be more of silver than not and coined to give sixty pennies to a weighed ounce, and then silver counted and silver weighed was all one." In the Norwegian medieval coinage the penny standard has only been of such a standard for a rather short period (1 ounce = 28,35 grams = 60 coins/pennies of 0,48 grams = 28,35 grams). This corresponds to half the weight of a Norwegian penny-standard of the 11th century. Pennies of half-penny standard (*c.*0,45 grams and 90% silver) was introduced in the reign of Magnus Barefoot (1093–1103) (Skaare, 1969, pp. 21–36). This suggests that §245 was recorded in writing after 1093, but presumably before *c.*1115.

main measure of value alongside silver. When *vaðmál* was chosen as a main standard of value the saga society picked a commodity money that was well known and well approved. And, equally important, *vaðmál* was a commodity with an established value relation to silver. By doing so they could continue to make business as usual without having to change a universally accepted standard or come up with a new standard. In spite of silver being rarely available it continued to be an important measure of value, but was increasingly replaced as means of payment by commodities of standard values.

In fact Grágás contains a paragraph on standard values, legal money and the assessment process by lawful valuers (§246). In this lengthy paragraph the standards of value are defined as an ounce unit valued accordingly in homespun, trade cloak, fox-skins, lambs-fleeces, shorn-skins, skins of old tomcats and cats, gold, silver, iron cauldron, scythe-blade, and cast and wrought iron. A cow is a standard value after specific definitions valued accordingly in oxen, ewes, lambs, wethers, rams, sheep, goats and sows and piglets.[4] The value of a cow was, of course, dependent on the state of the cow; first and foremost age and if it was capable of bearing calves and whether it was horned and free from defects, in other words in general good shape. Also horses are listed as standard value with valuations accordingly in cattle. And again there are a lot of considerations regarding a horse of standard value; age, good general health and it should be free from any defects. Stud-stallions were worth more for its qualities as a fighter etc.

The standard values on horses were given in cattle, and thus it was possible to calculate in any values given to a standard cow. Meaning that a standard horse – male older than four winters and younger than ten winters – equals the value of a standard cow, which again equals the value of a four year old ox that equals six standard ewes or goats that equals the value of a sow of two winters with nine piglets etc. (For a discussion on this matter, see Gelsinger, 1981, p. 36). In this way any commodity that was listed as legal or valid payment could be valued against each other. Other types of commodities would have to be assessed and valued accordingly. Some commodities would be taken up and given status as valid payments in the course of time, as stockfish that are recorded as being used for payment in (Árnessþing) around 1200 (Dipl. Isl. I, pp. 317, 319 and 320 (references in Jóhannesson, 1969, p. 265)). In the law provisions regarding payment of tithes (from 1096) commodities are listed as legal tender that was not part of the elaborate paragraph on standard values; wood, tar and incense (Dipl. Isl. I, pp. 19–20). The flexibility with which the medieval inhabitants accepted different commodities as money is well documented in contracts for Norwegian land transactions where the range of com-

4 The value of cattle is specified in exact terms in the Norwegian Landscape Laws as well (Gulathing's law §223, see Lunden, 1978, pp. 56–62).

modities used as money goes well beyond what was reckoned as legal tender (Gullbekk, 2009, pp. 343–353).

The key to this system of standard values and valid payments that was decided upon by the legal assembly in the 11th and 12th century was the ounce of silver as a standard unit. An ounce weighed 28,35 grams and it was valued in white silver that should stand the test of a nick and be more of silver than not. Then this silver ounce was made out in ells of homespun, accordingly one ounce of silver being valued at half a mark of homespun, or vice versa. In this way the two main units of value were silver and homespun, both measured according to the ounce as a common denominator unit.

This was, of course, a complicated system of value relations. The complexity factor was raised by the fact that every single commodity that was presented as payment had to be regarded within a framework of quality criterias. It is reasonable to assume that two parties engaged in a transaction would view the quality and value of their payment differently than the counterpart. This must, at times, have been time consuming and an obvious source of conflict. This was taken into consideration. In the same provision as defined standard values (§246) rules for assessment of payments was included. Each party was "to select his man as a lawful valuer and lawful viewer. And if they do not agree, then they are to draw lots and the one who draws the lot is to value it on oath" (Grágás §246). In the case of disagreement the valuation became a responsibility of honour.

The nature of using commodity money as means of exchange would imply a subject of bargaining over the quality of the commodities involved in the transaction. The value of a commodity would be defined by force of custom. This definition would, however, necessarily be set within narrow limits. In medieval Icelandic cattle should, according to the monetary definitions be older than three years, but younger than ten years, and with the ability to bear calves and give milk. In Norway if anyone would pay with cattle it should be younger than eight winters, and the cattle should without defects and generally in good condition (Gulatingslovi §223).

The laws give an insight into how the commodity money system was organized on Iceland, which the sagas provide accounts of how exchange was carried out. In the *Soga om røykdølane* Steingrim bought two extraordinary red oxen from Ørnolv. The oxen were valued at five hundred *vaðmál*. Steingrim paid with stud-stallions and half a mark of silver (Soga om røykdølane, ch. XI). This transaction provides a magnificent insight into the nature of how the commodity money system was applied in the saga society; Steingrim buys oxen valued in one commodity and then he makes the payment in another commodity together with silver, all valued in relationships to each other.

Legal sources provide evidence for set values on standard commodities, historical records show, however, that the value of standard commodities could vary, and sometimes vary considerably. The value of cattle raised from 75 alen to 120 alen during the 12th century. In the beginning of 12th century the price for wax was three alen *vaðmál* per mark, at the end of the same century the price had risen to eight alen *vaðmál* per mark. After 1200 it was down to 6 alen *vaðmál* per mark (Lárusson 1982, sp. 457–458).

The provisions on values and valid payments in Grágás are among the most comprehensive in the Viking world, and probably also for the medieval world not only on Iceland, but also for the Northern Lands. It demonstrates how a commodity money system worked and provide an excellent normative insight into a part of the economy that would be difficult to grasp from archaeological evidence.

THE ROLE OF COINS IN THE SAGA SOCIETY?

The question of how much coins there were in circulation in the Saga society is closely linked to the question of trade or exchange in medieval Iceland. Trade has traditionally been considered of secondary signification to self sufficiency, quite right so. The attempt to discuss the role of money in medieval Iceland, is not an attempt to quantify neither trade nor the use of money or how much money that was in circulation. However, money in medieval Iceland has always been considered a marginal phenomenon. Using the single finds of coins that has been discovered in recent years as a starting point, it could be argued that the single find material from the 11th century could be seen as shadows of a money-using society. At least, money might have been available at times in significant supply to have played a role in commerce alongside silver and commodities.

In a recent study Gareth Williams has argued that coinage was used in Viking Scotland on a wider scale than has traditionally been accepted. He does so, convincingly, on the basis of 21 single find coins from the Viking Age, of which nine coins were from the 11th century (Williams, 2000–2002, pp. 163–172). If we compare this to Iceland, the Icelanders are not doing bad, not at all, with twelve 11th century coins in single finds. If we move eastwards to Norway, the Norwegian single find material from the 11th century adds up to 60 coins. The majority of these single finds come from the urban excavations at Trondheim where one Anglo-Saxon, one German and 51 Norwegian coins from the 11th century were found (Risvaag, 2006, pp. 130–131). In fact, if we compare the Icelandic single finds with any parts of Norway, for example the Western part where towns did not develop until 12th century or the Oslofjord area (known as Viken), the Icelandic single coin find material from the 11th century are, in fact richer than that of two out of three main regions in Norway; Viken (Oslofjord area) three coins; Western Norway four coins; and Mid-Norway 52 coins (Skaare, 1976; Archive, University Coin Collection, Oslo). Of the single finds from Mid-Norway 45 were found during excavations of the Kjøpmannsgaten and Folkebibliotekstomten within the center of Trondheim (Risvaag, 2006, pp. 131–139). Trondheim is by far richest in single finds of 11th century coins in Norway. In the 11th century a royal mint was active in Trondheim and the coin finds reflects a society of merchants and town dwellers using coins in the market place.

In comparison the investigations of Kaupang in Vestfold yielded *c.*100 single finds of coins from the 9th and 10th century (Blackburn, 2008, p. 30). The site of Kaupang was, however, abandoned in the mid-10th century. As a result it has been possible to conduct investigations using metal detectors covering the Black earth area. In cases were productive sites or early urban settlements were abandoned and thus escaped urban development in the early modern and modern periods, evidence of coins from such places are found in much greater number than other more obvious places like London, Lincoln, York, Sigtuna, Lund, Oslo and Bergen. The highest number of medieval coins as stray finds from a town in Northern Europe comes from the abandon town Tårnborg in the Jutland peninsula in Denmark. The area of the town dwelling measures 900 meters x 200 meters including a church and a fortification. The number of stray finds add up to as many as 4,414 coins, of which 3,871 coins dates from the period 1240 to *c.*1341, all Danish (Grinder-Hansen, 2000, p. 228). These remarkable finds from Tårnborg present the problem of representativity as an obvious issue to take into consideration. There is every reason to use comparisons of coin finds from different sites to argue the case of monetization with care (Blackburn, 1989, pp. 16–20 and Blackburn, 2008, pp. 41–42).

The single finds of 11th century coins from Iceland provide evidence for coins being used and lost at different places. One striking aspect of these finds is that the composition is comparable to the general development of the coins in circulation in 11th century Norway. When a Norwegian coinage was established in the reign of Harald Hardrade (1047–1066) foreign coins are replaced by Norwegian coins. Also the Icelandic evidence suggests that the same change took place here. Again this must reflect a dynamic pool of currency rather than one of static nature. The number of single coin finds suggest that coins were used as widely in the saga society than the Scottish and Norwegian societies in the late Viking Age and early medieval period. Whether this was the case is difficult to determine. The number of single finds of coins from the 11th century in Icelandic sites during the last years, does, however, suggest that coins were used more widely than has been acknowledged before.

	Hoards	Single finds
Iceland	389	17
Viken (Oslofjord area)	*c*.817	3
Western Norway	*c*.4776	4
Mid-Norway (Trøndelag)	*c*.3722	52

Tab. 2. Coins in hoards and single finds from the 11th century in Iceland and the three largest regions in Norway: Viken (Østfold, Akershus, Oslo, Buskerud (southern part) and Vestfold); Western Norway (Rogaland, Hordaland, Sogn og Fjordane and Møre & Romsdal); Mid-Norway (Sør-Trøndelag and Nord-trøndelag).

THINGVELLIR AND SEASONAL USE OF MONEY

There is no place in the Old Norse literature that has been more often used as a scene for coin use than the Icelandic Things in general and the Althing at Thingvellir in particular. Saga references describe parties involved in payments of compensation money, payment of fines and disputes in payment of debts and other economic transactions during the thing assembly meetings. Trade was conducted and economic transactions settled in accordance with legal prescriptions. The thing meetings were ideal places for activities that needed the presence of witnesses. Assessment of value of payment would require witnesses. According to *Grágás* no-one was obliged to receive silver as payment without being able to test the quality of the silver first (Grágás Ia, 141, Grágás Ia, 248 and Grágás II, p. 214). This practice is well attested in the saga literature and it was often carried out in relation to weighing and counting silver and coins in financial transactions (Soga om Laksdølane, p. 172; Sagaen om Fosterbrødrene, ch. 8).

When five 11th century coins are found at Thingvellir, it seems reasonable to interpret these finds as numismatic evidence for commerce at the *Althing* by the use of money in 11th century. The coins are one German penny, one Anglo-Saxon penny issued by Cnut the Great (1018–1035) and three Norwegian pennies, of which two were struck during the reign of Harald Hardrade (1047–1066) and one for Olaf the Peaceful (1067–1093).[5] In addition there is a sixth coin found in a grave north of Thingvellir; a Norwegian bracteat from the reign of Sverre Sigurdsson (1177–1202). The grave was presumably Þorleifshaugur, the grave of Þorleifur Poet of Earls.[6]

5 The Anglo-Saxon penny Reykjavik museum no. 8186; Eldjárn, 1948, p. 41; the German phennig and the Norwegian pennies (communication from Anton Holt, The National Bank, Iceland).

6 Application for Inclusion in the World Heritage List, Þingvellir National Park, p. 25.

The archaeological investigations carried out at Thingvellir can, at best, be described as limited. The five coins that has been found does presumably represent only a few of the coins that are to be found if proper excavations were undertaken. A comparison with the Marketplace Kaupang in Norway suggests that there might be quite a few missing coins to be found as stray finds. When excavations were undertaken at Kaupang in the years 1956–1974 a total of 27 coins were found. During excavations in the years 1998–2003 additional 76 coins were found through excavations and metaldetecting (Blackburn, 2008, p. 30). The same experience has occurred at a number of similar sites in recent years. It is reasonable to assume that more coins will turn up at Thingvellir if the archaeologists were given permission to investigate the entire area.

Money means different things in different cultures, and in most societies money also means different things within the same culture. Thingvellir and other thingplaces, both in the Icelandic saga society and other places within the Northern world, were scenes for transactions where money meant different things; within the inner circle of the Assembly meeting compensations for manslaughter was decided upon side by side with fines being settled. These transactions had great social significance, and must be understood in that specific context. At the same time – just outside the core assembly area – beer and other goods was sold in ways resembling market principles, as testified in the sagas. The single finds of coins found at Thingvellir are presumably coin losses that reflect the activity of commerce in this setting of seasonal meetings where *flokks* of people would gather on regular basis. Commercial activity was following the footsteps of the thingmen not only on Iceland, but was a common feature also in Norway (Helle, 2001, p. 82), and presumably other places.

The Saga of Håkon Håkonsson, King of Norway 1217–1263, mention explicitly that flokks of farmers arrived at the assembly meeting at Øyrathing (Håkon Håkonssons saga, ch. 17). As in Iceland the travel to these assembly meetings were undertaken for several reasons. A fair share of medieval society was organized around seasonal meetings that occured on regular basis year after year; Assembly meetings, local thing meetings, church calendar, seasonal markets, harvest time or when foreign ships arrived with goods. This was also the time of year when people brought out their savings and used them for trade or display. The rest of the year savings was safeguarded at home. In some cases need for ready cash became a necessity as is described in the Fljotsdale saga where Groa went into her house and returned with money to pay for killing of a slave (The Fljotsdale Saga and The Droplaugarsons, ch. XII). The custom of hoarding coins and treasures in houses has been proven from archaeological evidence in Viking Age context on Gotland (Östergren, 1989). As is the case in all societies, situations occur and people respond to them in different ways, either by force or free enterprise. There were innumerable ways money could be spend, but the seasonal cycles of nature and human organization was presumably major factors for use of money in the Icelandic society.

CONCLUSION

In the Icelandic society silver was the main measure of value up until the turn of the 12th century. Silver also served as a main currency in the 11th century. According to the archaeological evidence silver almost disappear from the island after the 11th century. It is reasonable to assume that most of this silver was exported, or rather reexported, from the island in the late 11th and 12th century. The background for this was a general decrease in the availability of silver in Europe. The consequence was, however, that silver became less used as currency. Commodity money became more common. The commodity money system that was recorded in Grágás was certainly not a new invention. What was recorded was a system already in place, and a system of standard values that had been in use for a period of time, probably from the time of the first generations of colonizers. The Norwegians that arrived in Iceland brought with them the knowledge of a commodity money system that was adopted to local conditions. A commodity money system was in continuous development. When the church was established need for wax and tar in connection with the service and for ornamentation made these commodities part of the more general commodity money system.

One can always discuss how much trade was going on within the saga society, and indeed, barter was surely an important part of the commercial life, but when trade was carried out, it seems that the people in the saga society was more inclined to use commodities rather than silver. They were organizing their economy and living on the basis of a Commodity money system.

The coin finds in Iceland resembles the pattern of coin finds in Norway from the 11th century, but different from that found anywhere else in Scandinavia and Northern Europe. In Norway the foreign coins almost disappear from circulation in the second half of the 11th century being replaced by Norwegian issues. This shift is also apparent in the Icelandic single finds evidence. And, as there are no hoards from this period, we have to confine the analysis to the single finds. The single finds from second half of the 11th century strongly suggests that the Norwegians had taken over the Icelandic foreign trade. The dominance of Anglo-Saxon coins in the first half of the 11th century can be explained by the absence of Norwegian coinage in this period and the fact that Anglo-Saxon coins were more common than German in Norway at that time, especially in the Western parts of the country. The three Anglo-

Saxon coins from the 10th century in Icelandic single finds suggest a direct link between The British Isles and Iceland because such coins have, in fact, never been found in Norway.

The use of money in the saga society went down a rather different path. If we compare the use of money in the saga society in the 11th century with the situation in the 12th and 13th century, and even the 16th century, it becomes absolutely clear that Iceland did not adopt anything resembling money economy. In fact a shift from silver to *vaðmál* around the year 1100 and its continuation into the following centuries, makes it clear that the Icelandic economy was organized on the basis of a commodity money system rather than money economy that became increasingly more common in countries Iceland played contact with.

BIBLIOGRAPHY

Blackburn, M. (1989). What factors govern the number of coins found on an archaological site? In H. Clarke and E. Schia (Ed.), *Coins and Archaeology* (pp. 15–24). BAR International Series 556, Oxford.

Blackburn, M. (2008). The Coin-finds. In D. Skre (Ed.), *The Means of Exchange*, Kaupang Excavation Project Publication Series, vol. II. Århus: Århus University Press.

Byock, J. (2001). Viking Age Iceland. London: Penguin Books.

Eldjárn, K. (1948). Gaulverjabær-fundet og nogle mindre islandske møntfund fra vikingtiden. *Nordisk Numismatisk Årsskrift*, 39–62.

Eldjárn, K. (1953). Et nyt sölvfund på Island. *Nordisk Numismatisk Unions Medlemsblad*, 153–155.

The Fljotsdale Saga and The Droplaugarsons. (1990). Eleanor Haworth & Jean Young (Trans.). London: Everyman's Library.

Gelsinger, B. E. (1981). *Icelandic Enterprise. Commerce and Economy in the Middle Ages*. Columbia: University of South Carolina Press.

Grágás. (1980 and 2000). A. Dennis, P. Foote & R. Perkins (Trans.). In *Laws of Early Iceland. The Codex Regius of Grágás with material from other manuscripts*. Vol. I–II. Winnipeg: University of Manitoba Press.

Grinder-Hansen, K. (2000). *Kongemagtens krise. Det danske møntvæsen 1241–1340*. København: Museum Tusculanum Press.

Gulatingslovi. (1937). K. Robberstad (Trans.). Norrøne bokverk no. 33. Oslo.

Gullbekk, S.H. (2009). *Pengevesenets fremvekst og fall i Norge i middelalderen*. København: Museum Tusculanum Press.

Helle, K. (2001). *Gulatinget og Gulatingslova*. Leikanger: Skald.

Holt, A. (1998). Fynd av mynt från vikingatiden på Island. In Jens Christian Moesgaard & Preben Nielsen (Eds.). *Ord med mening*, festskrift til Jørgen Steen Jensen 1. November 1998 (pp. 45–47). København.

Håkon Håkonssons saga. (1964). A. Holtsmark (Trans.). Oslo.

Jóhannesson, J. (1969). *Islands historie i mellomalderen fristatstida.* Oslo-Bergen-Tromsø: Universitetsforlaget.

Jonsson, K. (1993). The routes for the importation of German and English coins to the Northern Lands in the Viking Age. In Bernd Kluge (Ed.). *Die Salier. Fernhandel und Geldwirtschaft. Beiträge zum deutschen Münzwesen in sächsischer und salischer Zeit* (pp. 207-208). Sigmarin: Jan Thorbecke Verlag.

Kristjánsdóttir, S. (1998). The Last Viking in Iceland, *Viking Heritage Newsletter,* no. 3, 4.

Lárusson, M. M. (1982). Priser (Island), *KLNM* XIII (2nd ed.), sp. 457–458.

Lunden, K. (1978). *Korn og kaup. Studiar over prisar og jordbruk på Vestlandet i mellomalderen.* Oslo-Bergen-Tromsø: Universitetsforlaget.

Ólafsson, G. (1990). The Excavations at Bessastaðir 1987. The Colonial Official's Residence in Iceland. *Acta Archaeologica,* LXI, 108–115.

Risvaag, J. A. (2006). *Mynt og by. Myntens rolle i Trondheim by i perioden ca. 1000–1630, belyst gjennom myntfunn og utmynting.* Trondheim: Doktoravhandlinger ved NTNU.

Skaare, K. (1969). "Olav Kyrres" myntreform. *Nordisk Numismatisk Årsskrift,* 21–36.

Skaare, K. (1976). *Coins and Coinage in Viking Age Norway,* Oslo-Bergen-Tromsø: Universitetsforlaget.

Soga om Fosterbrødrene. (1978). Jan Ragnar Hagland (Trans.). Norrøne bokverk 30, Oslo: Det norske samlaget.

Soga om Røykdølane. (1981). Leiv Dyrhaug (Trans.). Norrøne bokverk 48, Oslo: Det norske samlaget.

Soga om Laksdølane. (1994). Bjarne Fidjestøl (Trans.). Norrøne bokverk, Oslo: Det norske samlaget.

Williams, G. (2000–2002). Monetary Economy in Viking-Age Scotland in the light of single finds. *Nordisk Numismatisk Årskrift,* 163–172.

Östergren, Majvor (1989). *Mellan Stengrund och Stenhus: Gotlands vikingatida silverskatter som boplatsindikation,* Thesis and Papers in Archaeology 2, Visby.

Love in Early Iceland

GUNNAR KARLSSON

ABSTRACT

Many scholars have studied the occurrence of love in medieval Icelandic texts. Most of them have primarily been interested in love as a literary theme, and often the subject has been looked upon in relation to French troubadour poetry, which has sometimes been seen as the very invention of courtly love. The author of this paper is more interested in love as a feeling in real people in the Viking Age and Middle Ages. He reaches the conclusion that Icelandic literature is a valuable source of evidence about this subject. Especially the contemporary sagas, which are preserved in the Sturlunga Saga compilation, are extremely rich in evidence on different variants of relatively free love and badly controlled by society.

Keywords: Emotions, love, Iceland, Middle Ages, Eddic poetry, Sturlunga Saga.

"Every one has heard of courtly love, and every one knows that it appears quite suddenly at the end of the eleventh century in Languedoc." These are the words of the English scholar C.S. Lewis, written in the first chapter of his book, *The Allegory of Love,* published in 1936. The sentence has been quoted frequently in scholarly literature on the history of love, usually in order to contradict it. In this paper I shall also doubt Lewis's interpretation. Still, if his statement appears to be too absurd to spend time on it, it must be noticed that he was talking about *courtly* love, as it was expressed in the troubadour poetry, and that was love of quite a special kind. In the words of Lewis himself: "The sentiment, of course, is love, but love of a highly specialized sort, whose characteristics may be enumerated as Humility, Courtesy, Adultery, and the Religion of Love." (Lewis, 1936, p. 2).

I am not particularly looking for love in early Iceland as the origin of a literary tradition, as Lewis was doing. However, I choose his statement as a starting point because opinions similar to his have been popular in humanistic studies for the last decades. It has been assumed that feelings, which we tend to consider inherent to man, vary in different societies. Sometimes this is called social constructionism. It has been maintained, sometimes argued for and sometimes taken for granted without much reasoning, that feelings are not a constant element in people but constructed in different ways and different quantities according to the structure of different societies (Rosenwein, 2002, pp. 836–837). It must be mentioned, though, that an opposite view, sometimes called essentialism, has also had its adherents in this period. Thus, physical anthropologists in America have discovered the hormones which create and perpetuate passionate love in people as well as in other creatures (Fisher, 2004, pp. 47–76).

The subject of my paper is of course an immense one and has been discussed thoroughly in scholarly literature for decades. Jenny Jochens has dealt with different aspects of love, sex and marriage in a number of articles (e.g. Jochens, 1992; Jochens, 1994), besides important parts of her two books on women in Old Norse society and literature (Jochens, 1995; Jochens, 1996). In this century three major books have been published in Scandinavia dealing with important aspects of love. In 2001 the Icelandic scholar Auður Magnúsdóttir published her doctoral thesis on cohabitation, concubinage and matrimony, in medieval Iceland (Auður Magnúsdóttir, 2001). In the same year a monograph appeared on love, individual and society, in the West Nordic countries by the Norwegian Bjørn Bandlien (Bandlien, 2001). Later it was published in English with the title *Strategies of Passion: Love and marriage in medieval Iceland and Norway* (Bandlien, 2005). Finally, the Swedish scholar Daniel Sävborg has issued a book of 661 pages on sex, feelings and the art of narrative in medieval Nordic literature (Sävborg, 2007). All these authors have read through Icelandic source material extremely carefully and have, of course, much to say about the subject. None of them, though, has exactly the same approach as I have. Sävborg is primarily interested in love as a literary theme and literary tradition, whereas I try to use the literature as evidence about the feeling of love in medieval people. I come closer to the approach of Jochens, Auður Magnúsdóttir and Bandlien. However, they are all more interested in the connection of love and politics, in the relationship between love and power, than I am in this paper.

Returning to C.S. Lewis, he had some knowledge about the Icelandic sagas and used them to disprove that Germanic people knew the concept of courtly love. He wrote rather categorically (Lewis, 1936, p. 9):

> What is certain is that where a Germanic race reached its maturity untouched by the Latin spirit, as in Iceland, we find nothing at all like courtly love. The position of women in the Sagas is, indeed, higher than that which they enjoy in classical literature; but it is based on a purely commonsensible and unemphasized respect for the courage or prudence which some women, like some men, happen to possess. The Norsemen, in fact, treat their women not primarily as women but as people. It is an attitude which may lead in the fullness of time to an equal franchise or a Married Women's Property Act, but it has very little to do with romantic love.

One of Lewis's most prominent opponents was Peter Dronke who published his extensive study, *Medieval Latin and the Rise of European Love-Lyric* in the 1960s, first in 1965 and a revised edition in 1968. Although his book is mainly about love in Latin texts, as the title says, Dronke was interested in proving, with the help of many sources, that love lyric occurred much too early and in too many cultures to make possible that it had been invented in France in the eleventh century. Therefore his study starts in ancient Egypt, goes from there to the Islamic world, Arabic Spain and to Iceland. In the preface he thanks his wife Ursula Dronke for her specialist advice on Icelandic and Middle English (Dronke, 1968, p. ix, xx). In his chapter on Iceland, Dronke only discusses the two 10th-century poets, Kormákr and Hallfreðr, who, according to Dronke (1968, p. 39):

> show in a striking way the unity of 'popular' and 'courtly' love-poetry. On the one hand they were brought up in a highly professional kind of rhetoric. They cultivated a *trobar clus,* a poetry which has all the signs of having been composed for an esoteric court circle, with a taste for conceits and immense formal complexity and dexterity. On the other hand the skaldic poets would have composed in this manner to any woman, whatever her social position. Even their most highly wrought stanzas were composed 'for the people', that is, they became the property of the people, and were remembered and handed down orally for generations.

Dronke supports and illustrates this description with the help of four stanzas by these two poets, rather complicated, as skaldic poetry usually is. In order to give some minimal idea of them, I have chosen Dronke's retelling in English of the easiest stanza by Kormákr (Dronke, 1968, p. 40):

> The precious one who afflicts me I value at the whole of Iceland as far as farthest Tartary, and Denmark too. She is worth the ground of England and of Ireland, she the wise lady of the golden sun of the ocean.

The golden sun of the ocean is a *kenning* for gold.

Dronke of course knew, that the sagas where the stanzas are preserved and put into context were not written until some two to three centuries after the events of the sagas took place, or are said to have taken place. He also knew that a German scholar, F.R. Schröder, had suggested that the stanzas that were attributed to Kormákr were in fact composed and added to his saga in the 13th century under the influence of French troubadour poetry. "This conjucture", Dronke maintains (1968, p. 42n), "is supported by not a shred of evidence –

only by the prejudice that romantic love was invented by the troubadours." It has escaped Dronke's attention that four years before he published his book for the first time, the Icelandic scholar Bjarni Einarsson had argued thoroughly for the opinion that the stanzas of the Icelandic scalds were not original, and both they and the sagas were strongly influenced by French troubadour poetry (Bjarni Einarsson, 1961). Some discussion on Bjarni's thesis ensued (Einar Ól. Sveinsson, 1966; Andersson, 1969; Bjarni Einarsson, 1971; Bjarni Einarsson, 2003). One cannot say that either party has proved his case. However, it is obviously not possible to rely on the stanzas by Kormákr and Hallfreðr as evidence for courtly love, or any kind of love, in 10th-century Iceland.

Something similar applies to Eddic poetry. It is immensely rich in descriptions of love, both of gods and humans. Only a few examples must suffice here. In the highly masculine poem Hávamál, *The Sayings of Hár,* there is abundant wisdom about love. In the poem it is clearly assumed that a man can become infatuated by a woman, and that condition is justified by a stanza which sounds like this in Lee M. Hollander's translation (*The Poetic Edda,* 1986, pp. 27–28):

> At the loves of a man   to laugh is not meet
> for anyone ever;
> the wise oft fall,   when fools yield not,
> to the lure of a lovely maid.

This is a justification that would have been needed by the pagan god Freyr who became so enchanted by a girl whom he just caught a glimpse of in the land of giants that he sent his servant to fetch her. This is the subject of the poem Skírnismál, *The Lay of Skírnir* (*The Poetic Edda,* 1986, pp. 65–73). In Völundarkviða, *The Lay of Volund,* the wives of three brothers leave them. Two of them go to look for their wives, but the third, the artisan Völundr, remains at home and forges golden rings for his wife, "biding if back/his bride would come." (*The Poetic Edda,* 1986, p. 161). The heroic poems of Edda contain two long and complicated love stories. One is about Brynhildr, Sigurðr, Gunnarr and Guðrún. The other, about the hero Helgi, who was reborn twice, and his fiancé who was also reborn twice but with a different name each time. Contrary to the troubadour poetry, here the feelings of women towards men are described more vividly than the feelings of men towards women. For instance, the heroine Sigrún expresses herself vividly about her dead lover, Helgi Hundings-slayer, and since these are the words of a woman this time, I use the translation of Carolyne Larrington (*The Poetic Edda,* 1996, p. 139):

> So was Helgi beside the chieftains
> like the bright-growing ash beside the thorn-bush

and the young stag, drenched in dew,
who surpasses all other animals
and whose horns glow against the sky itself.

This is no doubt strong evidence of the existence of passionate love. The problem is that it is uncertain the feelings of which period and which society are expressed by this poetry. Firstly, it should be mentioned that we cannot be sure, of course, that the eddic poems are originally composed in Iceland by Icelanders, but that does not bother me at all. The title of the paper, Love in Early Iceland, was not to be taken that literally. A more genuine problem is the age of this poetry. It is of course generally assumed that the bulk of Eddic poetry was composed before the advent of French troubadours. But no manuscripts containing them are older than the 13th century. So, in a way, we end here in the same place as with the poetry of Kormákr and Hallfreðr.

On the other hand it seems extremely far fetched to assume that the rich and varied love poetry of Edda is in any considerable way inspired by troubadour poetry, as that poetry is described by scholars. C.S. Lewis would probably have responded that this was because Edda described entirely different kinds of love, but that, too could be doubted. Is there for instance a basic difference between the art of composing poetry praising an absent woman, as the troubadours did, and that of forging her golden rings in case she might return, as Völundr did?

Still, something else may be more important here. When we consider how much the Eddic poetry tells us about love, how rich and multifarious it is, there appears to be little reason to investigate it in the light of French troubadour poetry. Should Eddic poetry not be studied more in its own right?

The Icelandic family sagas, *Íslendingasögur,* are of course immensely rich in evidence about love, and not only the poet's sagas which Peter Dronke mentioned. Love is the driving force of a number of sagas like the two poet's sagas, apart from the ones that I have mentioned: *Bjarnar saga Hítdœlakappa,* The Saga of Bjorn, Champion of the Hitardal People, and *Gunnlaugs saga ormstungu,* The Saga of Gunnlaug Serpent-Tongue, not to mention *Laxdœla saga*, The Saga of the People of Laxardal. In a well known book, called *Chaos and Love* in the English translation, the Danish scholar Thomas Bredsdorff maintained that illegal love was the generating force behind the conflicts which put law and order in danger in the sagas (Bredsdorff, 2001). In a way perhaps Bredsdorff is right, but nevertheless, love and also illegal love, has its true place in the sagas. It is exactly the tension between the two kinds of demands, both of which are legitimate, the demand of passion and the demand of social order, that makes many of the sagas the works of art which they are.

This is exactly the weakness of *Íslendingasögur,* the Family Sagas which take place in the 10th and early 11th centuries, as historical sources about the feelings of real people. Since they are rather obviously composed as works of art the feelings of their characters are evidently often romanticized. They are portrayed as stronger, warmer and longer lasting than is the case among people. During the heydays of the free prose theory, while people believed that the family sagas were basically true, it was believed that people of saga age Iceland, tenth and early eleventh century, were generally greater than other people. A well known text book author wrote in 1915 (Jónas Jónsson, 1915, p. 57): "Never has Iceland fostered so many eminent people, both men and women, but far too rarely did fortune come with excellence." Nowadays, most of us believe that this eminence of saga age people was mostly created by good story tellers of later centuries, which makes the family sagas doubtful historical sources.

Great help here is offered by the so-called contemporary sagas which describe events from the 12th and 13th centuries. Earlier I have proposed that the oldest sagas of *Sturlunga saga,* the ones which take place before the extensive concentration of political power in Iceland and not always among the most prominent people, are our best sources about the working of the power system in Iceland in its original stage (Gunnar Karlsson, 1972, pp. 5–8; Gunnar Karlsson, 2004, pp. 21–22, 148). I believe that something similar applies to the sagas as sources about the feelings of people. The earliest contemporary sagas are the most promising ones.

As one would expect, love is a rare theme in the bishops' sagas. Still it can be found there. Thus one version of the saga of Bishop Þorlákr Þórhallsson contains a story of the attempts of the bishop to make one of the greatest chieftains of the country, Jón Loftsson at Oddi, abandon one of his concubines, Ragnheiðr Þórhallsdóttir, who happened to be the bishop's sister. Ragnheiðr had been brought up at Oddi together with Jón, and it is said in the saga that they had loved each other since their childhood (*Íslenzk fornrit* XVI, 2002, p. 166). When the bishop demanded their separation Jón made the following declaration (in my translation; *Íslenzk fornrit* XVI, 2002, p. 178):

> "I know," Jón said, "that your excommunication is righteous and my misdemeanour great enough. I will suffer your charge by moving into *Þórsmörk* [probably uninhabited at this time] or to some other place where people will not become guilty of intercourse with me, and stay there all the time I like with the woman that you are so preachy about. Your excommunication will not make me depart from my quandary, nor the pressure of any person, until God inspires me to depart from it willingly.

Of course this is a story of promiscuity. It can be added that Jón was married and had children with his wife and with three other women. The bishop's sister also had children with other men. That fact, however, does not make this particular story any less a story of true love, while it lasted.

The sagas of the Sturlunga saga compilation have many more episodes concerning my subject. One of them is also contained in one of the bishop's sagas, the saga of Bishop Guðmundr Arason (*Guðmundar sögur biskups* I, 1983, p. 20), but its oldest codification is thought to be conserved in the so-called Priest Saga of Bishop Guðmundr in Sturlunga Saga (*Sturlunga saga* I, 1946, p. 118; my translation): "Gunnarr and Rannveig had a daughter named Úlfheiðr. She was married against her will. Later Ari Þorgeirsson fell in love with her and had four children with her."

This story is told in the saga because among the four children of Úlfheiðr and Ari was the hero of the saga, Bishop Guðmundr Arason. This may not seem to be much of a love story. Nevertheless, something can be learned from it. Firstly, evidently it is seen as an excuse and justification for Úlfheiðr's extramarital affair that she was married against her will. Secondly, the relationship of Úlfheiðr and Ari seems to have been accepted and did not prevent their son from becoming a priest and even a bishop. It can be added that in the youngest version of the Saga of Bishop Guðmundr, the one which is attributed to Abbot Arngrímr Brandsson, this piece of information is left out. "Ari was the name of his father and Úlfeiðr mother" is all that is said about Guðmundr's parenthood (*Biskupa sögur* II, 1878, p. 6). Still, this version is considerably longer than the one which includes it (*Biskupa sögur* I, 1858, pp. 405–558; II, 1878, pp. 1–187). What makes the difference is that Arngrímr's saga was written for export; the preserved text was probably intended for translation into Latin in attempts to have the bishop canonized by the pope. Thus it can be said that the story was "cleaned" in accordance with the expected taste of the papacy, in a somewhat similar way as the episodes of the family sagas were cleaned according to popular taste for impressive stories. The great merit of the sagas of Sturlunga saga as historical sources is that they are preserved "unpure", in a more primitive form than the family sagas.

Among the most adventurous love stories of Sturlunga saga is the story of Yngvildr Þorgilsdóttir in the Saga of Hvamm-Sturla which takes place in Dalir in the Western Quarter. Yngvildr was the daughter of a major chieftain, Þorgils Oddason, and was married to a man named Halldór Bergsson just after the middle of the 12th century. It is said that she did not come to love her husband, she "varð ekki unnandi Halldóri, bónda sínum", and consequently it appeared, he went abroad and died on a pilgrimage to Rome. After that, Yngvildr moved to Sælingsdalstunga, sharing the farm with her brother-in-law. A little later a farmer's son living in the neighbourhood, Þorvarðr Þorgeirsson, fell from his horse and hurt himself so his foot bled, (which is apparently pointed out in the saga to indicate that his injuries were not very serious, for instance that his leg was not broken). Þorvarðr was brought home to Yngvildr who bandaged his foot. After that he stayed for quite a long time at her farm and some people said that they spoke together more than other people, as the saga puts it. But their friends denied that it was true, the saga says. This is obviously an insinuation of a sexual relationship, which was a serious thing because they, Yngvildr and Þorvarðr, were second cousins.

In the spring Þorvarðr went north to Eyjafjörðr, but Yngvildr moved to another farm in the Dalir district. There she had a separate bedroom made for her where she stayed during the summer, suffering from some ailment in her foot. In the autumn, a woman came to Yngvildr's farm from Eyjafjörðr, and after a short time that woman had a baby, a girl who was named Sigríðr and said to be the daughter of a certain Þorsteinn in the North. A little later mother and daughter moved back north to Eyjafjörðr.

Nevertheless, people suspected something, which the saga does not state clearly, but obviously it was believed that Yngvildr had in fact given birth to the baby. A man from the North carried a hot iron to prove that Þorvarðr had told the truth about the paternity of the girl. Bishop Klængr at Skálholt examined the hand of the man and testified that it was clear. It is not mentioned in the saga, what is known from other sources, that Bishop Klængr and Yngvildr were second cousins. In the summer Yngvildr rode to the North, dressed as a man, and a little later she and Þorvarðr sailed together to Norway (*Sturlunga saga* I, 1946, pp. 63, 69, 72–73).

Yngvildr and Þorvarðr did not live together permanently. She disappears from Sturlunga saga, although one episode can be added to her story. Somewhat later in Sturlunga saga, there appears a certain Jóra, who is said to be the daughter of Yngvildr and Bishop Klængr, her second cousin, who had testified about the hand, which had proved the innocence of Þorvarðr on the paternity of the baby Sigríðr (*Sturlunga saga* I, 1946, p. 230). It is for many reasons clear that Jóra must have been born after her mother's return from Norway, which means that Klængr had become a bishop when he begot Jóra (Björn Þórðarson, 1952, pp. 321–327). So, Yngvildr's love life does not seem to have ended when she and Þorvarðr parted.

Another interesting love story can be found in the Saga of Guðmundr dýri in Sturlunga saga. Its central character is Guðrún Þórðardóttir who at the same time was a young and beautiful woman and had inherited a farm from her father, Arnarnes in Eyjafjörðr. She was married to a certain Símon Þorvarðarson, a popular man, the saga says. However, during their first winter together Guðrún could not stay permanently with her husband. She "was sometimes away from the farm, sometimes at home", but Símon "took it quite gently". Their second winter she stayed at home, but then Símon drowned on a trip to fetch Lent food for the farm. In the following summer a man named Hrafn proposed to Guðrún. But she ran away on their wedding night when her new husband was accompanied to their bed. Still they lived together at Arnarnes until the following summer when she ran away to Skagafjörðr and from there to her former father-in-law, Símon's father, at Siglunes. There she declared that she loved everything connected with Símon. In the following summer she went with Þorvarðr to the trading centre of Gásir in Eyjafjörðr, where she became acquainted with Hákon Þórðarson from Laufás, and they spoke together daily. Þorvarðr took Guðrún to Arnarnes where he left her with her husband Hrafn. Now Hákon began to visit Arnarnes frequently until Guðrún asked him to stop doing so "while Hrafn is alive – but after that do what you want." Hákon took this for a request to kill Hrafn, which he consequently did. Hákon's father demanded that Guðrún paid Hrafn's relatives half of the compensation for him because she had planned his killing, but she denied that. Then the hero of the saga, Guðmundr dýri, who was Hákon's uncle, paid it all. Guðrún was married to Hákon who was tough on her and said that he did not want to be killed by her men. However, Guðrún seems to have had her revenge on Hákon. Some 30 pages and a decade later in the saga, enemies of Hákon's family attack Laufás, the farm of his father, where Hákon was staying. He was captured and one of the attackers, Sigurðr grikkr, volunteered to kill him. To that Hákon replied that Sigurðr was exactly the man whom he would choose as his killer, "because of all the men who are here I deserve it least of all from you. I housed you when you came absolutely moneyless to the country and allowed you to stay with me. But I caught you three times in the bed with my wife Guðrún." After this Sigurðr killed Hákon, and that is the end of the story (*Sturlunga saga* I, 1946, 168–171, 198–99).

Of course, the above-mentioned authors of major works on sex, love and different forms of cohabitation in medieval Iceland have referred to these, and more episodes in the contemporary sagas. Still, if we are looking for evidence of love in real life I do not find them used quite in the way or on the scale which they deserve. Daniel Sävborg is only interested in the literary aspect of the saga literature, and therefore he only examines whether the acts of saga characters which indicate love, are described in the same way in the contemporary sagas as in the family sagas (Sävborg, 2007, pp. 182–200). In the other works questions about rules, power, politics and accepted rights play a greater role than actual feelings. Jenny Jochens quotes the declaration of Jón Loftsson and retells the story of Yngvildr Þorgilsdóttir and uses them together to sustain her conclusion that a

> reading of *Sturlunga saga* leaves the impression that extramarital affairs were so common that if the sentence of lesser outlawry (*fjǫrbaugsgarðr*), which required all men who had fathered illegitimate children to be absent for three years, had been enforced, the island would have been cleared of grown males. (Jochens, 1995, p. 39).

Auður Magnúsdóttir admits, somewhat hesitantly though, that love has probably played a role in the relations of concubinage, marriage and companionship (*fylgilag*) in medieval Iceland, but she finds little of it in the contemporary sagas compared to the family sagas (Auður Magnúsdóttir, 2001, pp. 122–127). It is symptomatic of her approach that she makes no use of the story about Yngvildr Þorgilsdóttir, obviously because the most interesting part of it does not fall into any of her categories of relationships. Bjørn Bandlien is, in my opinion, on the right track when he uses these stories, and others, as evidence of an ancient concept of women's right to have something to say about their relationship with men (Bandlien, 2001, pp. 138–143; Bandlien, 2005, pp. 160–165). On the other hand, Bandlien's study does not do full justice to the source value of these narratives about feelings. To mention one example, Bandlien is absolutely sure that Guðrún Þórðardóttir had not chosen her second husband, Hrafn, although she had a legal right to do so as a widow, because she ran away from their bed on their wedding night (Bandlien, 2001, p. 139; Bandlien, 2005, p. 160). Here Bandlien does not take into consideration that Guðrún is obviously a psychopathic case and her feelings are extremely inconsistent. She is exactly the person who would be happy to marry a man one day, but run away from their bed that same night. Thus, I see in the oldest contemporary sagas, a valuable evidence of a society with a variable love life, relatively free, badly controlled while enjoying a high degree of tolerance.

This paper was of course not intended to do full justice to the love stories of the Sturlunga saga compilation. It was just meant to give some idea of the possibilities of discerning ideas of love and rights of feelings in medieval Icelandic literature. My conclusion is that it is a subject of study in its own right and does not gain much by being seen in relation to French troubadour poetry. Therefore, it is of little consequence whether the earliest Icelandic texts predate the troubadours or not. Still I cannot refrain from mentioning the one and only piece of text from Iceland which probably predates all troubadour poetry. That is a five cm long piece of wood with a runic inscription dug up in 1993 at the island of Viðey just offshore from Reykjavík. The inscription cannot be read apart from one single word, and that word is *ást:* love (Knirk, 1994, p. 20; Þórgunnur Snædal, 1998, pp. 17–18).

BIBLIOGRAPHY

Andersson, T. M. (1969). Skalds and Troubadours. *Medieval Scandinavia* 2, 7–41.

Auður Magnúsdóttir (2001). *Frillor och fruar. Politik och samlevnad på Island 1120–1400*. Göteborg: [S.n.].

Bandlien, B. (2001). *Å finne den rette. Kjærlighet, individ og samfunn i norrøn middelalder.* [S.l.]: Den Norske Historiske Forening.

Bandlien, B. (2005). *Strategies of Passion. Love and Marriage in Medieval Iceland and Norway* (trans. Betsy van der Hoek). *Medieval Texts and Cultures of Northern Europe* VI. Turnhout; Brepols.

Biskupa sögur I–II (1858–1878). Kaupmannahöfn: Hið íslenzka bókmentafélag.

Bjarni Einarsson (1961). *Skáldasögur. Um uppruna og eðli ástaskáldasagnanna fornu.* Reykjavík: Menningarsjóður.

Bjarni Einarsson (1971). The Lovesick Skald. A Reply to Theodore M. Andersson. *Medieval Scandinavia* 4, 21–41.

Bjarni Einarsson (2003). "Mansöngr" revisited. *Bibliotheca Arnamagnæana* XLII. *Opuscula* XI, 307–315.

Björn Þórðarson (1952). Móðir Jóru biskupsdóttur. *Saga* I(3), 289–346.

Bredsdorff, T. (2001). *Chaos and Love: the philosophy of the Icelandic family sagas.* Translated from Danish by John Tucker. København: Museum Tusculanum.

Dronke, P. (1968). *Medieval Latin and the Rise of European Love-Lyric* I. Oxford: Oxford University Press.

Einar Ól. Sveinsson (1966–1969). Kormakr the Poet and his Verses. *Saga-Book* 17, 18– 60.

Fisher, H. (2004). *Why We Love. The Nature and Chemistry of Romantic Love.* New York: Henry Holt and Company.

Guðmundar sögur biskups I (1983). *Ævi Guðmundar biskups. Guðmundar saga A*. Stefán Karlsson bjó til prentunar. *Editiones Arnamagnæanæ* Series B, vol. 6. København: C.A. Reitzels Forlag.

Gunnar Karlsson (1972). Goðar og bændur. *Saga* X, 5–57.

Gunnar Karlsson (2004). *Goðamenning. Staða og áhrif goðorðsmanna í þjóðveldi Íslendinga.* Reykjavík: Heimskringla.

Íslenzk fornrit XVI (2002). *Biskupa sögur* II. Ásdís Egilsdóttir gaf út. Reykjavík: Hið íslenzka fornritafélag.

Jochens, J. (1992). From libel to lament: male manifestations of love in Old Norse. *From Sagas to Society. Comparative Approaches to Early Iceland.* Ed. by Gísli Pálsson. Enfield Lock: Hisarlik Press, 247–264.

Jochens, J. (1994). Snorris Kvinder. *Samtíðarsögur. The Contemporary Sagas. Níunda alþjóðlega fornsagnaþingið. Akureyri 31.7.–6.8.1994.* Akureyri: Níunda alþjóðlega fornsagnaþingið, 380–394.

Jochens, J. (1995). *Women in Old Norse Society.* Ithaca: Cornell University Press.

Jochens, J. (1996). *Old Norse Images of Women.* Philadelphia: University of Pennsylvania Press.

Jónas Jónsson (1915). *Íslandssaga handa börnum* I. Reykjavík: Félagsprentsmiðjan.
Knirk, J. E. (1994). Runepinnen fra Viðey, Island. *Nytt om runer* 9, 20.
Lewis, C. S. (1936). *The Allegory of Love. A study in medieval tradition.* Oxford: Oxford University Press.
The Poetic Edda (1986). Translated with an Introduction and Explanatory Notes by Lee M. Hollander. Second Edition, revised. Austin: University of Texas Press.
The Poetic Edda (1996). Translated with an Introduction and Notes by Carolyne Larrington. Oxford: Oxford University Press.
Rosenwein, B. (2002, June). Worrying about Emotions in History. *The American Historical Review* 107(3), 821–845.
Sävborg, D. (2007). *Sagan om kärleken. Erotik, känslor och berättarkonst i norrön litteratur. Acta Universitatis Upsaliensis. Historia Litterarum* 27. Uppsala: Uppsala Universitet.
Sturlunga saga I (1946). Jón Jóhannesson, Magnús Finnbogason og Kristján Eldjárn (Eds). Reykjavík: Sturlunguútgáfan.
Þórgunnur Snædal (2000). Íslenskar rúnir í norrænu ljósi. *Árbók Hins íslenzka fornleifafélags* 1998, 5–33.

Protecting the Dead in Viking Age England

DAWN M. HADLEY

ABSTRACT

This paper examines the funerary practices of later Anglo-Saxon England, setting into their broader funerary context those burials that have been assigned to the Scandinavian settlers on the basis of evidence for cremation and inhumation accompanied by grave goods. The paper argues that it was not only the Scandinavians who employed burial strategies to make claims to status and to convey religious messages. Burial accompanied by a small array of artefacts is widespread, if not common, in later Anglo-Saxon England and, accordingly, it is suggested this practice cannot easily be used to identify Scandinavian burials. A rise in the deposition of artefacts that may have had amuletic properties in the tenth century is suggested as a possible response among the indigenous population to the turbulent circumstances engendered by the Scandinavian conquests and settlements.

Keywords: burial, grave goods, amulets, gender, masculinity, lordship.

The corpus of apparently Scandinavian burials in England is notoriously slender (Graham-Campbell, 2001; Richards, 2002). This has been attributed to various factors, including the tendency of the Scandinavians to bury their dead near to churches, where disturbance by subsequent generations of burial is thought to have limited the opportunities for excavating intact Scandinavian burials (Morris, 1981, p. 77; Hadley, 2008, p. 271). However, in recent decades thousands of undisturbed burials of the ninth and tenth centuries, many near to churches, have been excavated in those regions of northern and eastern England where Scandinavians mainly settled (Hadley, 2011), yet the number of furnished burials containing Scandinavian material culture has scarcely changed (for rare exceptions see Pitts, 2004; Speed & Walton Rogers, 2004). It has accordingly been suggested that we need to expand our focus to include this wealth of contemporary funerary evidence (Hadley, 2006, pp. 246–53). This paper considers what we might hope to learn about the Scandinavian impact by examining this broader funerary context, focusing on evidence for displays of social and family status and on ritual practices.

Encouragement to take this approach comes from the recent application of innovative scientific methods of analysis of human remains. The oxygen and strontium isotopes laid down in teeth during childhood can indicate place of residence in early life, as they are informed by drinking water and local food webs, which are regionally varied according to local geology and climate. These isotopes are incorporated into tooth enamel during tooth formation and they do not change subsequently (Budd, Millard, Chenery, Lucy & Roberts, 2004, pp. 127–8). Analysis of stable isotopes has confirmed that furnished burials excavated at Repton (Derbyshire) and at Adwick-le-Street (Yorkshire) were provided for individuals of almost certain Scandinavian origins (Budd, Millard, Chenery, Lucy & Roberts, 2004, pp. 137–8; Speed & Walton Rogers, 2004, pp. 61–3), but less well known is that similar results have also been produced among unfurnished burials at several cemeteries in northern England (Hadley, 2009a, p. 176; Buckberry, Montgomery, Neale & Towers, 2010). Stable isotope analysis does not, however, offer a panacea for the otherwise limited capacity of the funerary record to identify Scandinavian settlers. There is still much to refine about the methodology, while the evidence offered about place of origin is far from precise. In any case, much can happen in a person's life between childhood and death, such that geographical origins and cultural affiliations need not map precisely on to each other. At the very least, however, this technique is confirming that some individuals who spent their early years in Scandinavia were not afforded richly furnished burial, and it reinforces the importance of looking beyond those furnished burials that typically form the focus of analysis of the Scandinavian impact. Moreover, as we shall see, this broader focus reveals that although extensively furnished burials were distinctive in the range and numbers of grave goods that they contained, the messages they conveyed were not unfamiliar in funerary contexts in later Anglo-Saxon England (Hadley, 2009b; Hadley, 2011).

SCANDINAVIAN BURIALS IN ENGLAND: NEGOTIATING AUTHORITY

Many of the most richly furnished Scandinavian burials have been found near to churches, which suggests interment at an existing burial place (Richards, 2002, pp. 157–9), something that has been demonstrated conclusively at Repton (Biddle & Kjølbye-Biddle, 2001). While not underestimating the damage done to the Church by Viking armies, it is debatable whether this burial strategy should be regarded as representing purely an act of obliteration of the pre-existing social and religious order. Indeed, following its over-wintering at Repton in 873–4 the Viking 'great army' intervened in the political situation in the kingdom of Mercia and replaced the incumbent king with a local rival, while the army's dead were buried at Repton, which was the location of a major royal monastery (Biddle & Kjølbye-Biddle, 2001; Hadley, 2006, p. 12). In this context, it is plausible that the Scandinavian elite were seeking to legitimise their new regime by association with an existing centre of power (Richards, 2001, pp. 100–01). Such a scenario may also have occurred at other sites where the Scandinavian dead were buried near to churches. The processes of conversion cannot be readily inferred from this burial evidence, but it certainly conforms to a consistent pattern of the Church providing support, whether directly or indirectly, for the establishment of Scandinavian rulers in England as revealed by both the documentary and numismatic record (Hadley, 2006, pp. 192–227).

Barrows provided another striking landscape setting for Scandinavian burials. Unlike burial adjacent to churches, burial in barrows was widely practiced in Scandinavia, but not at this date in England. Yet barrows were certainly familiar components of the ninth- and tenth-century English landscape, and these symbols of ancient authority were often harnessed for various official functions. Barrows were, for example, focal points for both administrative assemblies and the execution and interment of felons (Semple, 1998; Reynolds, 2009), while many churches and manorial complexes were constructed on and around barrows (Semple, 1998, pp. 120–1). The Scandinavians similarly appear to have made use of existing barrows: for example, excavation of a Scandinavian burial in a barrow at Aspatria (Cumbria) also recovered two stones with cup and ring-marked decoration suggesting reuse of a Bronze-Age monument (Edwards, 1998, pp. 9–10). In their appropriation of both barrows and churches for burial the Scandinavians were arguably employing a symbolic language of lordship that was familiar to Anglo-Saxon society.

The statements of power made by place of burial were also arguably made within the grave, where the emphasis on masculine display is striking. Almost all of the known Scandinavian-type burials contain artefacts with strong masculine associations, including weapons, and equestrian equipment (Halsall, 2001, p. 270; Hadley, 2008). Weapons would have been directly associated with male violence, which was an integral component of masculine identity, but they were also symbolic of social status and lordship. Skaldic poetry and the sagas relate the ancestral associations that swords often possessed (Jesch, 2001), and they doubtless evoked associations with past adventures. Yet such masculine statements were articulated in only select male graves. This is made clear by the excavations at Repton, where contrasting funerary provision was accorded the burials of two adult males (aged *c.*35–45 years and *c.*17–20 years respectively), despite the fact that they were interred beneath the same stone setting and their joint grave was apparently marked with a single grave-marker.

The older male was provided with a wide array of grave goods (including a sword, knives, a key and a necklace with beads and a Thor's hammer), while the other male was interred with only a knife (Biddle & Kjølbye-Biddle, 2001, pp. 60–65). The former apparently died violently, struck on the head, with sword marks to the lower vertebrae and left femur, the latter possibly causing genital mutilation which may explain the placement of a boar's tusk with its known amuletic qualities between his thighs (Richards, 2003, p. 388; Hadley, 2008, p. 274). It can be suggested that a combination of his age-related status and manner of death necessitated a more elaborate burial than was accorded his comrade. In sum, these burials were arguably not simply a conservative reflection of Scandinavian practices, but were created with a view to making claims to land and status, and to emphasizing masculine lordship, in some, but certainly not all, male graves.

THE FUNERARY PRACTICES OF LATER ANGLO-SAXON ENGLAND

Understanding of the impact of the Scandinavians on England has been enhanced by consideration of the socio-political statements made through their burials, and it is equally important not to underestimate the diversity of later Anglo-Saxon burials. They included assorted types of coffin, stone settings, and grave linings (Hadley, 2002; Hadley, 2011; Thompson, 2002; Buckberry, 2007, pp. 117–21), and stone funerary monuments became increasingly common (Bailey, 1997). There is also widespread, if sporadic, evidence for the continuing inclusion of a restricted array of artefacts in burials after the conventional end of furnished burial *c.*700, especially dress-accessories and jewellery (Hadley, 2009b). There is a notable lack of explicit ecclesiastical condemnation of grave goods and little to suggest that the Church dictated the form that the burials of the laity should take (Thompson, 2004, p. 32). Contemporary comments suggest that lavish burial was not specifically condemned as un-Christian, although it was regarded as being of little value in securing the fate of the soul in the afterlife (Thompson, 2004, p. 111). Nonetheless, lavish burials can still periodically be identified. Most notably, at an earlier date, there is the unquestionably Christian and furnished burial of St Cuthbert (d. 687), to which items continued to be added over the following centuries, while according to the tenth-century *Regularis Concordia* monks were expected to be dressed for burial in shirt, cowl, stockings and shoes (Hadley, 2009b, p. 468). At least one eleventh-century bishop of Durham was interred with his crozier, and twelfth-century accounts of the opening of the tomb of King Edward the Confessor (d.1066) relate the jewels, rich fabrics and regalia with which he was interred

(Thompson, 2004, p. 34). Occasional evidence for clothed burial, including gold braid and silver dress-accessories, as well as items of jewellery, may have served as statements of elite status in the grave (Hadley, 2009b, pp. 469–74). We can, then, begin to see that the Christian grave was a place in which, at least for some, status was expected to be maintained.

Other grave deposits may have served an amuletic or apotropaic function. Crosses and scallop shells, given their association with pilgrimage, fall into this category (Hadley, 2009b, pp. 474–5, 482), as probably do the hazel and willow rods that survive in circumstances of good organic preservation. These have been interpreted as symbolic of pilgrimage or of the Resurrection, since these are long-lived trees if coppiced regularly. Equally as significant may have been the curative properties of these trees, which were certainly recognised in the later Middle Ages, at least, while a staff is invoked in an eleventh-century journeying charm (Gilchrist, 2008, pp. 126–8; Hadley, 2009b, p. 477). The placing of stones in the mouth or over the eyes has been identified at a few sites, and their associations with the parts of the body blessed by priests during the final moments of life suggests that they served some protective role (Hadley, 2009b, p. 477). It is also possible that coins served an amuletic function, a suggestion informed by their frequent positioning on or in contact with the body (Gilchrist, 2008, pp. 133–5; Hadley, 2009b, pp. 477–80). There appears to have been a long-standing medieval belief in the power of ancient artefacts, which may help to explain the appeal of Roman coins (Gilchrist, 2008, pp. 133–5). The circular quality of coins may have been another reason for their use as amulets; certainly in later periods the circle was regarded as possessing magical powers (Gilchrist, 2008, p. 135). Hoards of coins are normally interpreted as deposits made for safe-keeping, but when they occur in graves the possibility that they, too, had an amuletic quality seems at least as plausible as the suggestion that someone intended to retrieve them from beneath a putrefying corpse (Hadley, 2009b, pp. 481–2).

One of the most distinctive qualities of ninth- and tenth-century burials in England is the considerable evidence for the enclosing of the body in the grave, with various types of coffin and grave lining (Thompson, 2002). Victoria Thompson (2002) has suggested that this practice was influenced by ecclesiastical beliefs about the desirability of protection of the body from corruption, informed by the expectation that the most holy bodies – those of saints – lay incorrupt in their tombs. Nonetheless, such means of protecting the body were not evenly distributed within and between cemeteries, suggesting that wealth and access to resources were also factors, and that these grave forms were, in a sense, markers of status (Hadley, 2011). The silence of the written sources on arrangements for the preparation of the grave allows the possibility that the family and community played a part and this may begin to help explain the great diversity of burials (Thompson, 2004, pp. 57–88; Hadley, 2011). Recent studies have begun to reveal that incidences of diverse forms of grave furniture do not normally or consistently correlate with either the age or sex of the deceased, and the fact that more or less elaborate burial forms were as likely to have been accorded to adults as to infants suggests that family strategies and status informed decisions about appropriate burial (Buckberry, 2007; Hadley, 2010).

Yet when we look at the spatial distribution of burials we find a few exceptions to the basic lack of variation based on sex and age. Clusters of burials in prominent locations within churchyards – such as near to funerary monuments or close to the fabric of a church – include a preponderance of adult males in some cemeteries (Buckberry, 2007; Hadley, 2010). Conversely, it is also adult males that are most likely to be excluded from regular burial in consecrated ground, whether in execution cemeteries or in such locations as marshy ground, ditches, pits and river banks (Hadley, 2010). Young children were also sometimes buried in distinctive locations, in particular close to the fabric of churches, and in the vicinity of prominent male burials (Hadley, 2010). There are also frequent occurrences of multiple burials, both simultaneous and consecutive, among which the presence of young children within the graves of adult males is frequent (Hadley, 2010). This funerary strategy was arguably related to the aforementioned emphasis on family status, as successive burials referenced the graves of family members. In sum, the tendency to regard Christian Anglo-Saxon burials as egalitarian is no longer sustainable, as it is apparent that they were informed by a range of social and familial factors.

DISCUSSION

What, then, can we learn from this brief survey of the broader funerary landscape of Viking Age England? First, recent research suggests occasional deposition of artefacts – such as coins, jewellery, and dress-accessories – was a practice too widespread and long-lived to be a convincing marker of the burials of Scandinavians (Hadley, 2009b; Gilchrist, 2008). Stable isotope analysis might offer assistance but we are currently far from being able to rely on this technique. Second, the deposition of artefacts that we might define as amuletic seems to become increasingly common in the tenth century. Could the apparent rise of amulets in Christian Anglo-Saxon England somehow be a response to the uncertain times created by the Scandinavian raids and settlement? Third, it is clear that we can dispense with the notion that the pagan Scandinavians made statements about identity, status and belief in the grave while the Christian English, along with converted Scandinavians, did not. It is quite clear that there was plenty of latitude within Christian cemeteries to deposit a range of artefacts, while the grave itself was understood as a place in which the body needed to be protected and assisted on its way to the afterlife. We also need to remind ourselves that not all Scandinavians buried in England received lavish burial, which we might infer from their limited numbers and can prove in a handful of cases where stable isotope analysis has been undertaken. Finally, among furnished Scandinavian burials we can discern an emphasis on masculine lordship in a select number of graves, and this is something also reflected in the corpus of secular warrior imagery on the stone funerary monuments of tenth-century northern England (Hadley, 2008, pp. 275–8). Here, perhaps, in the interplay between gender and authority should we in future begin to interpret the small corpus of overtly Scandinavian burials in the broader funerary landscape.

BIBLIOGRAPHY

Bailey, R. N. (1997). *England's Earliest Sculptors*. Toronto: Pontifical Institute of Medieval Studies.

Biddle, M. & Kjølbye-Biddle, B. (2001). Repton and the 'great heathen army', 873–874. In J. Graham-Campbell, R. A. Hall, J. Jesch & D. N. Parsons (Eds.), *Vikings and the Danelaw: Select Papers from the Proceedings of the Thirteenth Viking Congress* (pp. 45–96). Oxford: Oxbow.

Buckberry, J. L. (2007). On Sacred Ground: social identity and churchyard burial in Lincolnshire and Yorkshire, c.700–1100. *Anglo-Saxon Studies in Archaeology and History* 14, 117–129.

Buckberry, J. L., Montgomery, J., Neale, N. & Towers, J. (2010). Finding Vikings in the Danelaw: an osteological and isotopic analysis of the Masham Anglo-Scandinavian cemetery. *American Journal of Physical Anthropology Supplement* 50, 74.

Budd, P., Millard, A., Chenery, C., Lucy, S. & Roberts, C. (2004). Investigating population movement by stable isotope analysis: a report from Britain. *Antiquity* 78, 127–141.

Gilchrist, R. (2008). Magic for the dead? The archaeology of magic in later medieval burials. *Medieval Archaeology* 52, 1–40.

Graham-Campbell, J. (2001). Pagan Scandinavian burial in the central and southern Danelaw. In J. Graham-Campbell, R. A. Hall, J. Jesch & D. N. Parsons (Eds.), *Vikings and the Danelaw. Select Papers from the Proceedings of the Thirteenth Viking Congress* (pp. 105–123). Oxford: Oxbow.

Hadley, D. M. (2006). *The Vikings in England: Settlement, Society and Culture*. Manchester: Manchester University Press.

Hadley, D. M. (2008). Warriors, heroes and companions: negotiating masculinity in Viking-Age England. *Anglo-Saxon Studies in Archaeology and History* 15, 270–284.

Hadley, D. M. (2009a). Ethnicity and identity in context: the material culture of Scandinavian settlement in England in the ninth and tenth centuries. In V. Gazeau & P. Badouin (Eds.), *Identité et ethnicité : concepts, débats historiographiques, exemples (Ve-XIIe siècles)* (pp. 167–183). Caen: CRAHM.

Hadley, D. M. (2009b). Burial, belief and identity in later Anglo-Saxon England. In R. Gilchrist & A. Reynolds (Eds.), *Reflections: 50 Years of Medieval Archaeology, 1957–2007* (pp. 466–488). Society for Medieval Archaeology Monograph, 30. Leeds: Maney.

Hadley, D. M. (2010). Burying the socially and physically distinctive in later Anglo-Saxon England. In J. L. Buckberry & A. K. Cherryson (Eds.), *Later Anglo-Saxon burial, c.650 to 1100AD* (pp. 103–115). Oxford: Oxbow.

Hadley, D. M. (2011). Later Anglo-Saxon burial. In S. Crawford, H. Hamerow & D. Hinton (Eds.), *Handbook to Anglo-Saxon Archaeology* (pp. 288-314). Oxford: Oxford University Press.

Morris, C. (1981). From sword to plough. In E. Roesdahl (Ed.), *The Vikings in England and in their Danish Homeland* (pp. 69–77). London: Anglo-Danish Viking Project.

Pitts, M. (2004). Cumbrian heritage. *British Archaeology* 79, 28–31.

Reynolds, A. (2009). *Anglo-Saxon Deviant Burial Customs.* Oxford: Oxford University Press.

Richards, J. D. (2001). Boundaries and cult centres: viking burial in Derbyshire. In J. Graham-Campbell, R. A. Hall, J. Jesch & D. N. Parsons (Eds.), *Vikings and the Danelaw. Select Papers from the Proceedings of the Thirteenth Viking Congress* (pp. 97–104). Oxford: Oxbow.

Richards, J. D. (2002). The case of the missing Vikings: Scandinavian burial in the Danelaw. In S. Lucy & A. Reynolds (Eds.), *Burial in Early Medieval England and Wales* (pp. 156–170). Society for Medieval Archaeology Monograph, 17. Leeds: Maney.

Richards, J. D. (2003). Pagans and Christians at the frontier: Viking burial in the Danelaw. In M. O. H. Carver (Ed.), *The Cross Goes North: processes of conversion in northern Europe AD 300–1300* (pp. 383–395). Woodbridge: Boydell.

Semple, S. (1998). A fear of the past: the place of the prehistoric burial mound in the ideology of middle and later Anglo-Saxon England. *World Archaeology* 30(1), 109–126.

Speed, G. & Walton Rogers, P. (2004). A burial of a viking woman at Adwick-le-Street, South Yorkshire. *Medieval Archaeology* 48, 51–90.

Thompson, V. (2002). Constructing salvation: a homiletic and penitential context for late Anglo-Saxon burial practice. In S. Lucy & A. Reynolds (Eds.), *Burial in Early Medieval England and Wales* (pp. 229–240). Society for Medieval Archaeology Monograph, 17. Leeds: Maney.

Thompson, V. (2004). *Dying and Death in later Anglo-Saxon England.* Woodbridge: Boydell.

A Seat of a Settler? – A Centre of a Magnate: Breiðabólstaðr and Reykholt

HELGI ÞORLÁKSSON

ABSTRACT

The author's main concern is to find the site of the first farm settled in the Reykholt-valley in the Borgarfjörður area of Iceland. The answer is that this most probably was Breiðabólstaðr with reference not only to the *Book of Settlements* but also to the meaning of the noun *breið*. Its meaning is 'a plain', often wet, and usually grown with sedge. The author points out that such plains must have been attractive for settlers in need of fodder for their cows and heifers during winter-time. Close to Breiðabólstaðr is the lake Breiðavatn and along the river, Reykjadalsá, *breið* is found in placenames. The land offered fine sedge as fodder for the more sensitive cattle. This would support what the *Book of Settlements* says about Breiðabólstaðr as the seat of a settler. The second concern is why the alleged seat of a chieftain for this area was moved from Breiðabólstaðr to Reykholt, near by. A possible answer is the hot spring and the pool in Reykholt. The author takes this into consideration and argues, this might well have been the main reason.

Keywords: Iceland, settlement, centre of power, *breið* as a well-grown wetland.

INTRODUCTION

Who was the first settler of the Reykholt-valley in Western-Iceland and where did he or she settle down? The different redactions of *The Book of Settlements* (*Landnámabók*) are not in harmony about this. Either Krömu-Oddr or Önundr breiðskeggr was the first settler:

> *Þórðarbók* (*Melabók*): Krömu-Oddr settled the piece of land between the rivers Hvítá and Reykjadalsá; his son was Önundr and the son of Önundr was Tungu-Oddr at Breiðabólstaðr. (*ÍF* I, p. 74, fn.).
>
> *Sturlubók*: Önundr breiðskeggr settled the piece of land between the rivers Hvítá and Reykjadalsá and lived at Breiðabólstaðr. His son was Tungu-Oddr. Krömu-Oddr is not mentioned. (*ÍF* I, p. 74–76).

My main concern here is to find the site of the first farm settled in the valley. We are left in doubt about the site where Krömu-Oddr settled but among scholars it seems to be taken for granted that he also lived at Breiðabólstaðr, like

Önundr breiðskeggr. This is the neighbouring farm to the east of Reykholt.[1] Not later than around 1185 or so, Breiðabólstaðr and Reykholt were two separate farms as shown by the contemporary chapter in the charter of the Reykholt-church.[2] According to *The Book of Settlements,* and other written sources, Reykholt only became the site for the main farm in this area after the settlement-period.

Historians do not take *The Book of Settlements* at its face value anymore and this invites questions like: Was Breiðabólstaðr in fact the original place of settlement in this area ? And, secondly, why was Reykholt settled at a later date since it turned out to become the more important of the two? Furthermore: Why did Reykholt become the residence for the big man or chief of the area? I will argue that Breiðabólstaðr must have been the original spot for the first inhabitants in this area. I will also try to explain why Reykholt became the main seat of the chieftains.

My work is a part of the Reykholt-project which started in 1999 and ended in 2007. Our publishing work is now extensive and at present we are working on the publication of a final book, containing all the main results, discussing new perspectives and suggesting work for the future.

The well known chieftain Snorri Sturluson and his political, literary and other activities during his period in Reykholt, from around 1206/1208 until 1241, has been our main interest in this project. However, generally speaking, Reykholt during the settlement period, the Viking times and the Middle Ages, is of great interest also.

Reykholt became one of the most important centres of power in Snorri's time. With the whole country taken into consideration and in terms of Iceland, the word *magnate* seems appropriate for Snorri. Before he settled down at this place, Reykholt was the seat of chieftains of this area, the so-called *goðar* (sing. *goði*), and it was a place of some considerable importance. The chieftains in Reykholt, prior to Snorri's time, were not only secular chieftains, they also, at the same time, were ordained, influential clergymen. The church in Reykholt was a self-owning institute, among the most important churches in Iceland. The technical term for such a self-owning institute among the churches was *staðr*. The church-building was of a considerable size for its time, the 13th century, according to recent excavations, led by Guðrún Sveinbjarnardóttir (2009, pp. 58–69). Communications must have played a part in making Reykholt a centre of ecclesiastical and secular power. It lies at crossroads, which is important (Tryggvi Már Ingvarsson, 2000, pp. 28–33).

1 Another form for its name was Reykjaholt.

2 The editor of the charter Reykjaholtsmáldagi, Guðvarður Már Gunnlaugsson, dates its oldest part to the second half of the 12th century and not later than 1208, *Reykjaholtsmáldagi*, p. 17 and see p. 14. The editor of the *Diplomatarium islandicum* I, Jón Sigurðsson, dated this part to *c.*1185 which is convenient; see the volume, pp. 279–280.

REYKHOLT BECOMES A CENTRE

A natural question is: Why did the neighbouring Breiðabólstaðr *not* function as the residential place of the chieftains and as the site of the important church in the 12th century? One possible reason is the hot spring in Reykholt and the pool, *c.*130 m away from the spring. According to the archaeological excavations, mentioned above, there was a church-building in Reykholt in the 11th century, lying *c.*70 m from the 13th century pool. In 13th century narratives it is taken for granted that the pool existed in the 10th century, even though people were not living at the site (*ÍF* I, p. 193). The pool, either natural or man-made, was possibly an attraction. Such pools could be very important, with people frequently gathering at some of the most popular in the 12th and 13th centuries.[3] A man with political ambition might have seen an opportunity in Reykholt and made use of the situation, politically speaking, by making the pool at the crossroads and building a church by the pool in order to secure as great a number as possible of tithe-paying farmers and peasants who might have found the pool attractive. He might also have had in mind to attract travellers who would otherwise have passed by.

A church by a pool, a residence moved		
Probably a settlement farm	**Pool and a church near by**	**12th century recident of chieftains**
Varmalækr*	Bær	Bær (close to important fords)
Kristnes*	Hrafnagil	Hrafnagil (centrally placed)
Hörgsholt	Hruni	Hruni (by a main road)
Breiðabólstaðr	Reykholt	Reykholt
*Suggested by Orri Vésteinsson		

A similar scenario has been suggested for some other sites, a church built at a pool and some new houses of habitation built at the same spot for the owner, an ambitious important man, who then moved to the place (Orri Vésteinsson, 2000a, pp. 50–53).

Guðrún Sveinbjarnardóttir concludes that the farm buildings in Reykholt might have been just a little older than the first church-building from the 11th century (Guðrún Sveinbjarnardóttir, 2009, p. 60; Guðrún Sveinbjarnardóttir et al., 2007, p. 202). However, the possible attraction of the pool might have been the main reason for someone politically ambitious to settle down in

3 For instance at Laugar in Sælingsdalr in Dalir, Vallalaug in Skagafjörðr and Hrafnagil in Eyjafjörðr; all were frequented and important meeting-places. On this see *Sturlunga saga* I–II.

Reykholt and he might have had a church-building in mind. It so appears that Breiðabólstaðr did not sustain an annex church or chapel in medieval times.

In 10th century Iceland if churches existed they probably were not so important and at that time a chieftain, like Tungu-Oddr, son of Önundr breiðskeggr, was fairly well placed at Breiðabólstaðr, as far as I can see.

THE MEANING OF *BREIÐ*

Why might Breiðabólstaðr have been chosen as the site for the first settler in the area? I suggest that the name itself can explain what the settler was after. *Breiða,* in compounds like this, is usually supposed to mean 'broad' but there is a better explanation.[4]

Above the farm there is a lake called Breiðavatn, *-vatn* meaning 'lake' or 'pond'. (See Map 1). The opinion has been aired that this name, Breiðavatn, is shortened from Breiðabólstaðarvatn. There is an interesting custom in this area to shorten the names of farms like this:

Breiðabólstaður becomes Breiði[5]
Steindórsstaðir becomes Steindi
Vilmundarstaðir becomes Vilmi
Kópareykir becomes Kópi
Snældubeinsstaðir becomes Snælda
Brennistaðir becomes Brenni.

It has therefore been suggested that Breiðavatn means the lake of the farm Breiði, i.e. of the farm Breiðabólstaður, shortened Breiði. There are at least two reasons to reject this:

1. The lake and its area does not belong to Breiðabólstaður alone, it also belongs to the neighbouring farm Úlfsstaðir.
2. We don't find the shortened names in placenames around. For instance:
   Steindórsstaðaöxl is never Steindaöxl
   Vilmundarstaðafljót is never Vilmafljót
   Brennistaðaháls is never Brennaháls.

4 On the name and earlier studies, see Svavar Sigmundsson, 2000, pp. 55–60. On -bólstaðr see Svavar Sigmundsson, 2009, pp. 330–342.

5 When referred to the usage of names after 1550 the modern spelling is used, thus Breiðabólstaður, not Breiðabólstaðr.

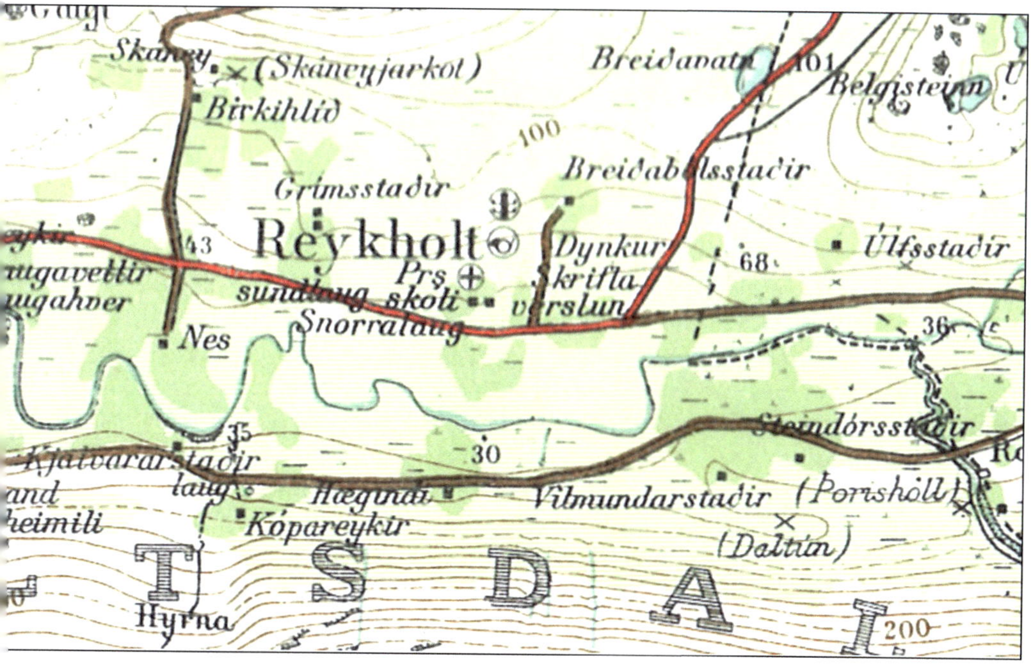

Map 1. Breiðavatn, Breiðabólstaður and Reykholt. (Detail of map 35, 1:100.000. © National Land Survey of Iceland. 1973).

We must find some other explanations for the origin of the names Breiðavatn and the surrounding area, called Breiðaflói, *flói* meaning 'wetland'. First of all we have to consider the meaning 'broad' in the adjective *breiðr.* Obviously the lake Breiðavatn is not broad in any sense and neither is the *flói* around it. Therefore this doesn't help to explain the name.

On the other hand, *breiða* in Breiðabólstaðr could have had something to do with fodder for the domestic livestock. The settlers most probably brought with them young cows or heifers and these were not able to survive during the winter-time without some shelter and fodder. Scientists seem to be in agreement about birch-wood in Iceland, around 870. According to them, the land was to a great extent covered with such wood. Land for hay-making was probably limited, in many low-lying places, and infields for making hay were not easily grown. However, in Iceland farmers in medieval and later times didn't only mow hay in cultivated, manured infields, to procure for fodder, they also cut sedge in outfields, in wetlands and meadows. This was often naturally grown sedge which had not been manured at all, in many instances not very inferior to grass or hay as fodder for the animals.

The noun *breið* occurs in Icelandic in meaning 'a plain', often wet, and usually grown with sedge. The noun is found in 19th century texts: For instance at the farm Knörr (Knör) there is a round pond called Breiðavatn. As mentioned, usually the adjective *breiðr* means 'broad' but this pond is not broad at all. Its water comes from the meadows which in 1839 were said to be fertile, excellent for mowing, and the noun used for them is *breiðar*, the plural feminine of the singular noun *breið* (Sýslu- og sóknalýsingar, p. 94, 91; DNS, 3705 a, Knörr).

There are more ponds and small lakes in Iceland which are called Breiðavatn or Breiðatjörn, *tjörn* meaning 'pond', but these can hardly be seen as broad. The most natural explanation for their names are often the wetlands at their sides, grown with sedge. An example is found at the farm Selá in Skagafjörður, there is the meadow called Breiðar which was mowed. It is by a small pond, called Breiðatjörn (DNS, 5701 b, Selá). The pond is obviously not broad, physically speaking. *Breiða* therefore most probably is the genitive plural of the noun *breið* (sing.)/ *breiðar* (plur.). There are more lakes and ponds in Iceland with the compound-names Breiða- which can not be seen as broad in any sense. By their sides there often are meadows which were mowed and turn out to be well grown; for instance the pond Breiðavatn in Mýrar and at its side a meadow which was mowed. The same goes for Breiðatjarnarengi in Arnarfjörður with the pond Breiðatjörn in its middle; the meadow (*engi*) was mowed.[6] Besides we have many examples of meadows being called *Breið* or *Breiðar*.

To conclude, *breið* in placenames often means flat or plain land, not necessarily broad but well grown and could be used as a meadow for mowing. Such meadows were important because they didn't need any fertilizing, were usually wet, without trees and suitable for mowing sedge or hay.

MOWING SEDGE AT BREIÐABÓLSTAÐR IN THE REYKHOLT-VALLEY

Let's turn back to Breiðabólstaðr in the Reykholt-valley. A possible explanation for the name of the farm is that the area around the lake Breiðavatn is *breið* or plural *breiðar*, i.e. flat land, wet and well grown. As mentioned earlier the area around Breiðavatn is called Breiðaflói, and *flói* means 'wetland', wetter than *mýrr* or *mýri*, which is mire or bog-land. (See Fig. 1).

6 For Breiðavatn in Mýrar see DNS 3608 d, Stóri Kálfalækur. For Breiðatjörn in Arnarfjörður se DNS 4701 a, Horn. There is also Breiðavatn among the lakes Veiðivötn; by its side is Breiðaver which was even mowed.

Fig. 1. Picture of Breiðavatn. The area is now partly drained, owing to the construction of a main road running through the area.

Could this area around the lake have been mowed? It seems, the most common type of sedge around the lake is *Carex nigra*, in Icelandic *mýrarstör*. The best type of sedge as fodder is *gulstör, Carex lyngbyei*. Secondly, concerning quality, is *Carex nigra*, good for grazing and good as fodder as well.

Sedge in order of quality

The best of the sedge as fodder is:
Gulstör, *Carex lyngbyei*
Mýrarstör, *Carex nigra* (is around Breiðavatn)
Blástör, *Carex rostrata*
Vetrarkvíðastör, *Carex chordorrhiza*
Hrafnastör, *Cares saxatilis*
Brok, *Eriophorum angustifolium*
Others

After Ásgeir L. Jónsson,1975, pp. 136–137.

According to Egill Erlendsson, who has recently studied the lake Breiðavatn and its surroundings, *Carex nigra* was also common around the lake in the 9th century.[7] The lake was of a similar size at that time, and the flat area around it was probably tree-less, while the encircling slopes sustained woody taxa.

7 For *Carex nigra* in the area Egill refers to Bending, s.a. The economy of the Norse settlement of the North Atlantic and its environmental impact.

I suggest that this wetland was most probably the main reason for the settlement at Breiðabólstaðr, just below the lake. The settlers with their small stock of animals were presumably busy the first year with cutting down trees and building shelter for the winter, both for themselves and their cows or heifers. The cows at this time were rather small and sturdy types. However, though they were robust they could not survive during the winter-time without shelters and needed some fodder. In cases like this it would have been the easiest way to make fodder out of sedge, like *Carex lyngbyei* and *Carex nigra*.

Several years ago Orri Vésteinsson pointed out that the settlers must have had a keen eye for what would be the best land for them. Considering the birch-wood he suggested that the settlers in the first place opted for flood plains at estuaries and secondly for flood-plains in the valleys, along the rivers. In other words chose flooded wetlands with fertile meadows (Orri Vésteinsson,1998, pp. 6–10; Orri Vésteinsson, 2000b, pp. 171–172; Orri Vésteinsson et al., 2002, pp. 118–121). There are no flood-plains in the Reykholt-valley in modern times and probably never were. However, these suggestions have inspired me.

The bottom of the valley was wetter than nowadays, according to Egill Erlendsson et al. (2008, p. 348 and map, p. 349). The valley was covered with trees although particularly on the higher slopes. There is a ford on the river, between Breiðabólstaðr and the farm on the other side of the valley, called Vilmundarstaðir, and this ford is called Breiðavað. On the banks close to it is another *breiða*-placename, Breiðamói, and in the river below is the hollow Breiðafljót. There is one spot in the land of Breiðabólstaðr, close to the ford Breiðavað, which seems to have been suitable for mowing sedge and might have been called *breið* in this sense. However it is rather narrow and is hardly the main reason for the name to the farm.[8] On the other hand we should take into consideration that the land of Reykholt also belonged to Breiðabólstaðr, originally, and around 1700 Reykholt had a meadow by the river (*Jarðabók ÁM/PV* IV, p. 213). Also it is not easy to figure out exactly what the situation might have been like around 870 when the valley bottom was wetter.

The area around the lake is most likely the main reason for the settlement and would explain the name Breiðabólstaðr. However there might have been stretches of wet meadows by the river around 870. These might also have occasioned the name.

We therefore have a reason to believe that *The Book of Settlements* might be right and Breiðabólstaðr was a settlement-farm. Its size is only average. However it is taken for granted as very plausible that the farms Breiðabólstaðr,

8 On these placenames at the river I gathered information from Vigfús Pétursson at Hægindi and Ragnhildur Þorsteinsdóttir at Úlfsstaðir. They confirm the record of these placenames, collected by Jón Þórisson. The record is preserved at DNS.

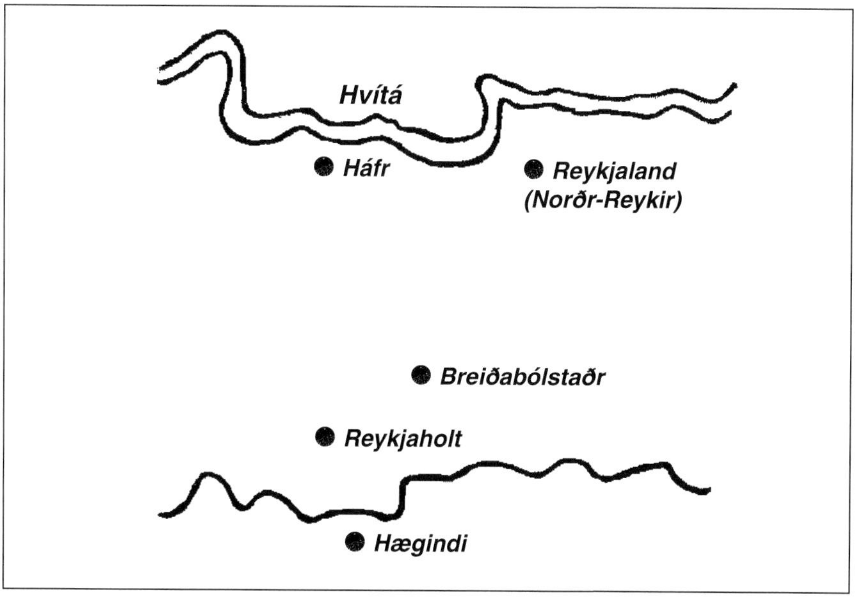

Map 2. *The possible original complex.* Hægindi as a part of the original complex is rather suspect since it is south of the river Reykjadalsá.

Reykholt, Norðr-Reykir (with Háfr) and Hægindi made an original complex between, and at the rivers Hvítá and Reykjadalsá. Around 1200 the whole complex was owned by the church in Reykholt. (See Map 2).

SLASHING AND BURNING

Now we can ask: What about slashing and burning? Would not that have been the easiest way to get rid of the wood and would not the ash have been excellent as fertilizer for cultivating infields? Placenames indicate that this was a method known to the settlers or at least known at an early stage of the habitation. At the 10th century farm Hrísbrú in Mosfellsdalr Egill Erlendsson has found indications of burning of this kind, he tells me, where microscopic charcoal fragments become prominent as the pollen of *Betula pubescens* decline drastically.[9] However, what is important here, is that he also tells me he has found no signs of such burning around Reykholt and Breiðabólstaðr in spite of thorough studies.

I suggest that the slash and burn method probably was not so inviting for the settlers in their first years. In Scandinavia this undertaking could be bur-

9 Another explanation is also possible, Egill tells me.

densome: Trees had to be cut down around the area to be burned. Twigs had to be cut off and the wood left for at least one year. This felling of trees and cutting of twigs could have been quite an effort. In the second year the burning could only be successful in dry weather. Only in the third year could the land be cultivated. This goes for the Scandinavian fir and I think the birch might have been similar. (On Scandinavian slashing and burning, see Sigurður Þórarinsson, 1944, pp. 173–203; Vilkuna,1972, col. 489–490; Bjørkvik, 1972, col. 495–497; Myhre & Øye, 2002, pp. 18–21).

BREIÐABÓLSTAÐRS

There are 15 Breiðabólstaðrs in Iceland and the mowing of sedge at the other 14 is of interest. Here is a list of all the Breiðabólstaðrs found in Iceland.[10]

1. Breiðabólstaðr in Reykholtsdalr. A settlement-farm (Landnámabók = Lnd.). 20c (=hundreds). Nearby are Breiðavatn and Breiðaflói.
2. Breiðabólstaðr in Skógarströnd. A settlement farm (Lnd.). 12c? A church. The lake Breiðabólstaðarvatn and Vatnsflói (wetland) are 2 km off the farm. Unknown whether used as meadows.
3. Breiðabólstaðr in Sökkólfsdalr. A settlement farm (Lnd.). 24c. Meadows mowed in Austurárdalur and there is Breiðakinn and Kotbreiðar.
4. Breiðabólstaðr in Fellsströnd. 24c. A part of the land is Blesamýri and at its side are Balabreiðurnar or Breiðurnar which were mowed.
5. Breiðabólstaðr (Staðr) in Reykjanes. A church, a *staðr* in the ecclesiastical meaning.
6. Breiðabólstaðr (Staðr) in Steingrímsfjörðr. An important church, a *staðr* in the ecclesiastical meaning. A residence of chieftains. In Farmannsdalshlíð are Breiður which were mowed and also Svartagilsbreiðar. Another part is Fýlubreiðar or Fífubreiðar which were mowed.
7. Breiðabólstaðr in Vestrhóp. A settlement farm (Sótastaðir, Lnd.). Possibly 60c. An important church. A residence of chieftains.
8. Breiðabólstaðr in Vatnsdalr. 40c. A church. Breiðiflói is at the brook, Breiðabólstaðarlækr.
9. Breiðabólstaðr in Svalbarðsströnd, Eyjafjörðr. 20c.
10. Breiðabólstaðr in Suðrsveit, Austur-Skaftafellssýsla. 30c. A settlement farm (Lnd.). Church.
11. Breiðabólstaðr in Pappýli. A settlement farm. Unknown whereabouts.
12. Breiðabólstaðr in Síða, Vestur-Skaftafellssýsla. Church. The area Flóð (wetland) at Breiðbalakvísl (river) was good for mowing.

10 The list is mainly based on placename records at DNS, *Jarðabók ÁM/PV* I–XI and the individual editions of *Sýslu- og sóknalýsingar Hins íslenska bókmenntafélags*.

13. Breiðabólstaðr in Fljótshlíð. An important church. A residence of chieftains. Good meadows for mowing.
14. Breiðabólstaðr in Ölfus. 40c. Church.
15. Breiðabólstaðr in Álftanes. A lake, Breiðabólstaðartjörn, and by it a place for mowing, called Samslægja.[11]

The Book of Settlements tells us that six of these were settlement farms (number 1, 2, 3, 7, 10 and 11). Other three (number 6, 8 and 13) probably also were because they were very important as church-sites and residences of chieftains. Churches are found in eight (number 5, 6, 7, 8, 10, 12, 13 and 14). The placename *breið* is found close to four of these (number 1, 3, 4 and 6) or possibly six (i.e. number 8 and 12 also). Other two are also excellent for mowing (number 7 and 13). Only two are somehow inferior, neither excellent nor settlement-farms, it seems. These are number 9 and 15.

OTHER WETLANDS

There are many more farm-names indicating that wetlands were important in Iceland at an early stage like those of the mýrr-type and others with the element *saur-*, meaning wetland and *kelda/keldur,* meaning bog-land.[12] Also *gaul* possibly means, swampy land.

1. Mýrr/Mýri or Mýrar (plural 8).
   Mýrr = bog-land. The better known compounds with -mýrr/-mýri are: Álftamýrr, Breiðamýrr (Lnd.), Flugumýrr (Lnd.), Langamýrr, Laxamýrr, Víðimýrr (Lnd.).
2. Saurar (8), Saurbær (16+3), other Saur- (4). Saurbær =„mýrlent mjög“ (= very swampy, Lnd.). Some of these are mentioned in Lnd. or were major farms.
3. Kelda (1) well, bog-land, swampy land.
   Keldur (4), Keldu- (3), Keldna- (1), -kelda (8). Keldugnúpr and Keldunes are mentioned in Lnd.
4. Gaul.[13]
   Gaul, Gaularás, Gaulverjabær (Lnd.).[14]

[11] For a map of the Breiðabólstaðrs, see Svavar Sigmundsson, 2009, p. 222; no 9 and 11 are left out.

[12] On the following list see Finnur Jónsson, 1907-1915, pp. 483, 484, 509, 571, 574. The numbers of instances are taken after Finnur and for the *saur*-placenames also after Barði Guðmundsson, 1959, pp. 129–130.

[13] On the meaning, see Þórhallur Vilmundarson, 1983, pp. 75–78.

[14] There are other placenames of interest too, like those ending in -leysa, Finnur Jónsson, op. cit., p. 570.

It is of course not easy to determine which of these farms were settlement-farms. However it is possible to conclude that some wetlands were coveted for farming at an early stage.

BREIÐABÓLSTAÐRS IN THE BRITISH ISLES

Strangely enough the farm-name Breiðabólstaðr is not to be found in Norway. On the other hand it is found in the Scottish Isles and Caithness. There the ending *-bólstaðr* is usually connected to good quality land, favourable land, although this is not necessarily so in Western-Norway. Gammeltoft published a special book, a monograph, on the *bólstaðr*-farms. Miklibólstaðr is the most common name of the *bólstaðr*-type in Norway; there are no less than 47 instances in all which constitute almost half of the Norwegian *bólstaðr*- material. However this placename is not found in other Norse settlements. At least it is not found in Iceland. Gammeltoft suggests some explanations for this and also why *bólstaðr*-names are not found in Norse settlements in Ireland and Greenland and only three unconfirmed in the Faroes (Gammeltoft, 2001, pp. 276–287). I won't go into that here.

There seem to be ten instances of Breiðabólstaðr-names in the Norse settlements in Scotland, two in Caithness, and eight more in the Scottish Isles, four of these in the Orkneys, two in Shetland and two in Skye. As there are no farms with such a name in Norway, the Icelandic names therefore must be modelled after the ones in Caithness and the Scottish Isles.

Here is a list of these (after Gammeltoft, 2000, pp. 103–104, and Marwick, 1952, pp. 6, 31, 76, 179):

Caithness:

1. Brabster (Brabastermyre 1538), Parish of Canisbay.
2. ⋆Brabster, Brabsterdorran (Brabisterdorane 1538), Parish of Bower.

Orkneys:

3. Brabustir (1500), Sanday, general meaning 'broad farm' (Marwick).
4. Braebuster (Brabustir 1492), Hoy.
5. Braebuster (Brabustare 1500), 'the largest farm in Deerness today', 18 d land (Marwick).
6. Brebuster (Brabustir 1492), Westray, only 1/2 d land (Marwick).

Shetland:

7. Brebister (Brabustare 1577), Parish of Northmaven (Stewart 1987, p. 55).
8 Breibister (Brabuster 1507/1513), Parish of Walls and Sandness.

Skye:
9. Breabost (Brebast 1776).
10. Prabost.

Example number 6 indicates that farms with these names were not necessarily large. Had the Norse in the Scottish lands and Iceland wanted to allude to the size of their lands they would probably sometimes have preferred Miklibólstaðr to Breiðibólstaðr. It therefore is hardly the size they are symbolizing with the placename Breiðabólstaðr.

In Shetland the placename Brae occurs, Stewart has some 20 instances. He suggests that these are often Norse in origin, rather than Scottish, and are derived from *breiðr*, meaning 'broad'. One of his examples is Braens which he thinks stems from *Breiðirnar* (Stewart, 1987, pp. 54–55, 59–60). That looks familiar. However he does not explain the topography. When it comes to what land looked like in these Braebost- and Brae-places in the Scottish lands I have so far very little to build on. Of course the first one, Brabstermyre in Caithness, is interesting; if myre is the Norse *mýrr* or *mýri* and means mire, wet ground, bog-land or marsh, as it seems.[15]

BACK TO BREIÐABÓLSTAÐRS IN ICELAND

The name-giving Breiðabólstaðr in Iceland does not seem to fit well with what Gammeltoft suggests for the element *bólstaðr* generally; that these were typically secondary settlements, on land which had been split up and parcelled out from main-farms, older ones on even larger land. However, when Iceland began to be settled to some extent around 890 the Norse settlements in the Scottish Isles had been developing for some 50 years or more. The stage of parcelling out might have been well under way there at the same time, i.e. around 890 when the settling in Iceland seems to have become lively. Chronologically, this fits in with what Gammeltoft thinks, that the *bólstaðr*-names began to be applied at that time in the Isles and somewhat later in Caithness (Gammeltoft, 2001, pp. 162–163). The adoption of the ending *bólstaðr* might therefore have been quite common around 890 in the Scottish Isles. In Iceland leaders among the early settlers, prior to 900 or therabouts, in all likelihood, took vast areas and probably split them up and parcelled out the best parts to their followers and themselves and also to likable newcomers. And *-bólstaðr* already prolific in the isles around 890, will have been found fitting among people coming from there as land was divided up in Iceland. The best land assigned for the leader naturally had the prefix, *breiða*.

15 See Gammeltoft (2001) on Mybster in Caithness, formerly Myrebestare, myre meaning *mýrr*, p. 137.

The nickname of the settler or the settler's son, Önundr breiðskeggr, does not necessarily have to mean broad-beard. Here is a suggestion for how to explain it, more for fun. Önundr breiðskeggr, was the alleged father of Tungu-Oddr at Breiðabólstaðr in Reykholts-valley. Skeggi/skegg/skeggr in compounds could mean a man generally or more specifically a male-inhabitant and *breiðskeggr* could therefore possibly have meant a male inhabitant at a *breið*. Comparable would, for instance, be Þórir Akraskeggr, living at the farm Akrar. The son of Önundr we are told was Tungu-Oddr, the Tunga or tongue being the area between the two rivers, Reykjadalsá and Hvítá; the name therefore would correspond *breiðskeggr*.

CONCLUSION

I suggest that the first part of the placename Breiðabólstaðr in Iceland is often derived from the noun *breið*, genitive plural, to denote well-grown wetland which could be easily mowed and yielded fairly good fodder for cows and heifers. At the early stage places with good *breiðar* were important. In the second part of the 10th century this was not of such a great concern anymore and other considerations were of more interest, like possibly the church in connection with the pool in Reykholt. The residence of chieftains in the Reykholt-valley therefore was moved from Breiðabólstaðr to a more favourable place.

BIBLIOGRAPHY

Ásgeir L. Jónsson (1975). Engjar og áveitur. *Votlendi.* (Rit Landverndar 4).

Barði Guðmundsson (1959). Uppruni íslenzkrar skáldmenntar. *Uppruni Íslendinga. Safn ritgerða.* (Eds.) Skúli Þórðarson & Stefán Pjetursson. Reykjavík, pp. 109–228.

Bending, J. M., s.a. The economy of the Norse settlement of the North Atlantic and its environmental impact. An archaeobotanical assessment. Unpublished PhD thesis, University of Sheffield.

Bjørkvik, Halvard (1972). Svedjebruk. *Norge. Kulturhistorisk leksikon for nordisk middelalder* XVII, 495–497.

Diplomatarium islandicum. Íslenzkt fornbréfasafn. I 834-1264. (Copenhagen 1857–76).

DNS = Department of Name Studies at The Árni Magnússon Institute for Icelandic Studies, Reykjavík.

Egill Erlendsson, Kevin J. Edwards, Ian Lawson & Orri Vésteinsson (2008). Can there be a correspondence between Icelandic palynological and settlement evidence? *Dynamics of Northern Societies. Proceedings of the SILA/NABO Conference on Arctic and North Atlantic Archaeology, Copenhagen, May 10th–14th 2004.* (Eds.) Jette Arneborg & Bjarne Grønnow (PNM Studies in Archaeology and History, 10. Copenhagen, pp. 347–353.

Finnur Jónsson (1907–1915). Bæjanöfn á Íslandi. *Safn til sögu Íslands og íslenzkra bókmenta* IV. Kaupmannahöfn & Reykjavík, pp. 412–584.

Gammeltoft, Peder (2001). *The Place-name Element* bólstaðr *in the North Atlantic Area.* Copenhagen.

Guðrún Sveinbjarnardóttir, Egill Erlendsson, Kim Vickers, Thomas H. McGovern, Karen B. Milek, Kevin J. Edwards, Ian Simpson & Gordon Cook (2007). The palaeoecology of a high status Icelandic farm. *Environmental Archaeology* 12/2, pp. 197–216.

Guðrún Sveinbjarnardóttir (2009). Kirkjur Reykholts – byggingasaga. *Endurfundir. Fornleifarannsóknir styrktar af Kristnihátíðarsjóði 2001–2005.* (Eds.) Guðmundur Ólafsson & Steinunn Kristjánsdóttir. Reykjavík, pp. 58–69.

Helgi Þorláksson (1998). Hruni. *Árnesingur* V, pp. 9–72.

ÍF I = *Íslendingabók, Landnámabók.* (Ed.) Jakob Benediktsson (Íslenzk fornrit I, Reykjavík 1968).

Jarðabók ÁM/PV = *Jarðabók Árna Magnússonar og Páls Vídalíns* I–XI (Kaupmannahöfn 1913–1943).

Marwick, Hugh (1952). *Orkney Farm-names.* Kirkwall.

Myhre, Bjørn & Ingvild Øye (2002). *Norges landbrukshistorie* I. *4000 f. Kr. – 1350 e. Kr. Jorda blir levevei.* Oslo.

Orri Vésteinsson (1998). Patterns of settlement in Iceland. A study in prehistory. *Saga-Book* 25 :1, pp. 1–29.

Orri Vésteinsson (2000a). *The Christianization of Iceland. Priests, Power and Social Change 1000–1300.* Oxford.

Orri Vésteinsson (2000b). The archaeology of *landnám.* Early settlement in Iceland. *Vikings. The North Atlantic Saga.* (Eds.) William W. Fitzhugh & Elisabeth I. Ward. Washington & London, pp. 164–174.

Orri Vésteinsson, Thomas H. McGovern & Christian Keller (2002). Enduring impacts: Social and environmental aspects of Viking age settlement in Iceland and Greenland. *Archaeologia islandica* 2, pp. 98–136.

Reykjaholtsmáldagi. (Ed.) Guðvarður Már Gunnlaugsson. Reykholt 2000.

Sigurður Þórarinsson (1944). *Tefrokronologiska studier på Island: Þjórsárdalur och dess förödelse.* Stockholm.

Stewart, John (1987). *Shetland Place-names.* Lerwick.

Sturlunga saga I–II. (Eds.) Jón Jóhannesson, Magnús Finnbogason & Kristján Eldjárn. Reykjavík 1946.

Svavar Sigmundsson (2000). Place-names in Reykholtsdalur. *Reykholt in Borgarfjörður. An Interdisciplinary Research Project. Workshop held 20–21 August 1999.* (Ed.) Guðrún Sveinbjarnardóttir (National Museum of Iceland. Divison of Monuments and Sites. Research Reports), pp. 55–60.

Svavar Sigmundsson (2009). Icelandic and Scottish place-names. *Proceedings of the XIXth International Congress of Onomastic Sciences. Perspectives and Methods of Onomastics.* (Ed.) W.F.H. Nicolaisen. Aberdeen, pp. 330–342. Reprinted in Svavar Sigmundsson, *Nefningar. Greinar eftir Svavar Sigmundsson gefnar út í tilefni af sjötugsafmæli hans 7. september 2009* (Reykjavík 2009), pp. 219–229.

Sýslu- og sóknalýsingar Hins íslenzka bókmenntafélags. (Eds.) Svavar Sigmundsson & Ólafur Halldórsson (Snæfellsnes III, Reykjavík 1970).

Tryggvi Már Ingvarsson (2000). Reykholt í Borgarfirði. Þjóðleiðir um Vesturland á Sturlungaöld. *Sagnir* 12, pp. 28–33.

Vilkuna, Kustaa (1972). Svedjebruk, *Kulturhistorisk leksikon for nordisk middelalder* XVII, 489–490.

Þórhallur Vilmundarson (1983). Safn til ÍSLENZKRAR ÖRNEFNABÓKAR 2. *Grímnir* 2, pp. 51–144.

Øye, Ingvild, see Myhre, Bjørn.

ABBREVIATIONS

Land. = Landnámabók, Book of Settlements, see *ÍF* I.

c = hundred, 120 ells or the equivalent of a legal cow.

The Beauty of *Bona Regalia* and the Growth of Supra-regional Powers in Scandinavia

FRODE IVERSEN

ABSTRACT

This article argues that the development of the so-called *bona regalia* represent a key to understanding the growth of supra-regional power in Northern Europe. *Bona regalia* were royal property and farms belonging to royal office – to the crown, and not the king in person. *Bona patrimonialia* was on the other hand, the kings dynastic property. I will also highlight the fact that these two types of royal manors/estates/ rights had uneven distribution within the states of northern Europe. The hypothesis is that *bona regalia* were closely associated with the establishment of the supra-regional royal power in submitted regions.

Keywords: Bona regalia, Huseby, state formation, royal lands, Scandinavia, Viking Age, Middle Ages.

In his autobiography Emperor Charles IV wrote: "When the community of upright men in Bohemia saw that we were of the ancient lineage of the kings of Bohemia, they held us in affection and gave us aid …" (Charles IV, 70f). In the 1330s Charles had been installed as Margrave of Moravia by his father. The Holy Roman Empire had nearly lost control of its margravate. The barons of Moravia had divided this kingdom among themselves. The upright men of Bohemia – *communitas de Boemia* – accepted Charles as king, and helped him identify the crown estates of Moravia – the *bona regalia*. A number of properties were identified, and Charles named 16 of these castles (*castra*). He spent considerable resources to restore the most important ones and revitalize the crown's grip on Moravia (Charles IV, 70–72).

Although there are differences, this example seems relevant for the political situation in Scandinavia prior to the 14th century. The story highlights important factors and institutions in the maintaining of supremacy in a given province in a political "in-between zone". The major players were; (1) the margrave (the supra-regional king's son), considered a king in a regional perspective and a margrave in a supra-regional perspective, (2) the supra-regional king and the (3) local lords and barons, and (4) the community of upright men – most likely the "parliament" and the thing-men. The "parliaments" interactions with the crown seem to have been important and institutionalised, and relevant to the Scandinavian case, albeit on a different scale. In practice "the upright men" controlled the land of the crown in the province – the *bona regalia*. After the act of acceptance, legitimized by kinship to the old rulers of the region, the new king was given access to this land. In this article, I will discuss similar aspects of royal land in Scandinavia based on the concepts of *bona regalia* and *bona patrimonalia*, and emphasize the importance of *bona regalia* in the very beginning of the process of state-formation.

Bona regalia is defined as the crown's institutional property, as opposed to the personal lands of kings – the *bona patrimonalia*. *Bona regalia* – *kungalev* in Scandinavian sources – differ from ordinary crown lands (*fiscus*) as they probably had centralised functions of the early state. Farms with such functions could most likely not be alienated as easily as ordinary crown land. I will try to explain the *bona regalia* in spatial terms, and compare its spread in Scandinavia with the dynastic core areas, which seem to have different geographical locations. A dynastic core area is controlled by a powerful family or dynasty through their private property (*patrimonium*).

In recent works on state formation, spatial terms such as *core*, *semi-peripheries* and *peripheries* have won popularity as analytic tools (Schneider, 1977; Peregrine, 2007), inspired by the world system theory of Immanuel Wallerstein. These terms also seem relevant to this study, but must be linked to the historical content. The growth of supra-regional powers in Europe was a complex process. Asymmetric regions with different economic bases and political organization level were tied together by various types of interactions, use of military force, diplomacy and treaties. There were core areas in these processes and there were peripheries, depending on where the leading power was geographically located at different times.

In earlier work I have argued for a model with dynastic core areas (Iversen, 2007; 2008; 2009). These I have tried to demonstrate through studies of royal property. Such areas have been suggested in various works, but little has been demonstrated conclusively. For the German regions in the 10th and 11th century it has been discussed for instance by John W. Bernhardt (1993) and Eckhard Müller-Mertens (1980). I have used analogies from Sussex and Kent, where it is possible to identify concentrations of the royal villas prior to mid 11th century within relatively small geographic areas (Iversen, 2007). I have also identified such areas in the Carolingian period in the German regions based on clusters of the royal villas referred to as palaces (*palatia*) in written sources (Iversen, 2009, 102f.). In this article, I will focus on royal lands in *semi-peripheries* and *peripheries* in a Scandinavian context, and the growth of supra-regional power.

Long term supra-regional kings depended on the establishment of physical systems and institutions to consolidate their domination. My hypothesis is that *bona regalia* is primarily a provincial phenomenon. I will differentiate between two kinds of *bona regalia*-farms; those *with uniformed* names and those *without* such names. The *Kingston-farms* in England, *Köningshöfen* in medieval Germany, and *Husebyar* in Scandinavia represent groups of farms with uniformed names. Several of the *Kingston-farms* had "double names" e.g. *Keinton Mandeville*, *Kingston Seymour* (Probert, 2008), and this is also the case for a handful of the Nordic *Huseby*-farms (Brink, 2000a; 2000b). It is not unlikely such farms were named or renamed when they were given responsibilities for the kingdom. The *bo-farms* in Västergötland (Westerdahl, 1978) and the *Uppsala öd* in Norrland, sometimes called *Huseby* and sometimes *Hög* (Grundberg, 2000), have elements of such similarities as well.

On the other hand, the so-called *farm of one night* in England (Lavelle, 2007) and the *kungalev*-farms in Denmark did not have uniformed names. Neither did the *Utskyld*-farms, which Asgaut Steinnes (1953) has suggested were part of an *itinerant kingship* in 10th and 11th century in South-West Norway.[1] Then again, several Huseby-farms belonged to monasteries and bishops prior to mid 13th century, e. g. Husby, Vansjö to *Vårfruberga* monastery (Södermanland) in 1233, which also seems to have been part of the foundation grant (Rosèn, 1949, 74, 76; 1962, 94). According to Snorre (*c.*1230), powerful magnates also possessed Huseby-farms, e.g. the pagan chieftain Tore Skjegge (mid 10th century) at Husabø, Inderøya (Trøndelag) (Hkr, Håkon den godes saga, chapter 18) and the famous Einar Tambarskjelve (*c.*980–1050) at Huseby, Skaun (Trøndelag) (Hkr, Olav den helliges saga, chapter 39).

Obviously, this is a complex matter with both chronological and regional variations, and different ownerships. However, in my view, it does not seem unreasonable that *bona regalia* farms in general were part of the *servitum regis* and *itinerant kingship* in *semi-peripheries* in the 10th century, and even earlier. Those with uniformed names seem somewhat younger, and might have served as collection units in the *peripheries* for royal fees and tributes.

The transformation from petty to supra-regional kingdoms in northern Europe has previously been seen as a teleological process that resulted in "nature-given" planned national states (Bagge, 2003). Moving away from this, I will also show how the *bona regalia* as strategic local communities in *semi-peripheries* and *peripheries,* had to meet the demands of shifting supra-regional rulers.

1 These were farms paying the *utskyld*-tax in the 14th century onwards. J. A. Gjerløw (1988; 1990) has shown that the *utskyld* was a fee to the church, and it is unclear how this functioned towards the kingdom.

BONA REGALIA

The division of royal lands between *bona regalia* and *bona patrimonalia* is recognised in the 11th century in Northern Europe. The phenomenon has, among others, been discussed by F. Maitland (1897) for England, by Jerker Rosén (1949) for Sweden, by Halvard Bjørkvik (1968a) for Norway, and Anders Andrén (1983) for Denmark. The distribution of *bona regalias* and their role in the process of the development of supra-regional power is poorly understood. In Sweden, *bona regalia* may have included royal villas and administrative farms such as the Huseby-farms and the complex of *Uppsala öd*, as well as the crown rights (*Iura regni*) to commons, farms cleared in commons and different kinds of resources without owners or of weak ownership (Schück, 1914, 4; Rosén, 1949, 71; Hamre, 1962; Bjørkvik, 1968, 43ff; Andrén, 1983; Brink, 2000b, 70).

Unlike legal historians such as Absalon Taranger (1904) and Fredrik Brandt, Halvard Bjørkvik (1968) rejected a division in the royal lands in Norway prior to the 13th century. In his view the distinction was unnecessary; to inherit the kingdom, the king had to be a successor of the *Fairhair*-dynasty, and could not be elected from other dynasties. This was different from the situation in Sweden and Denmark where there were several rival dynasties (Bjørkvik, 1968, 45). Bjørkvik's argument seems slightly too close to the Norwegian national narrative, under-communicating e.g. the Danish influence. As Bjørkvik himself pointed out the distinction appears in the *rural law of Magnus the lawmender*, 1274 (L II 7).

On the other hand, in Norway the division between the king's own property and the *veitsle*-land seems to be fundamental in this context. The word *Veizla*, f. has several meanings, and refers to land ceded to retainers for royal service. Veitsle-land is closely associated with the *lendr maðr*, m. appearing in the early 11th century (Iversen, 1999). *Lendmenn* were military leaders from leading families, more or less equivalent to the English baron – the trusted men of the king with delegated royal authority within their areas (Storm, 1882; Iversen, 1999). The manors of the *lendmenn* were the leading aristocratic and royal centres in the regions. According to the *Hirðskrá c.*1273–1277, land paying of 15 mark silver annually was the minimum value for a such a baron (chapter 13 (18)), and before being hailed by the *Hird*, (*hirð*, f.) new kings had to renew these privileges (chapter 2 (5)). The veitsle-land was probably a kind of *bona regalia*, and by analysing the prevalence of lendmenn in a geographical context some aspects of it can be revealed prior to the 14th century.

In Sweden, royal lands were often referred to as *bona regalia, bona coronae* or *bona acquisita* (Rosén, 1949, 22). *Bona corona* and *bona regalia* denote crown lands, and *bona acquisita* the *king*'s family property (Line, 2007, 284). *Bona vacanti* denotes, on the other hand, waste land or empty regions where the kingdom claimed rights (ibid). Still, in the reign of Knut Eriksson in the second half of the 12th century, it was differentiated between the king's personal property – *ex paterna successione* – and property he held by virtue of royal duties – *ex regio iure* (DS 67/SDHK 218). The earliest existing systematic inventory of the Swedish royal land is from the late Middle Ages (Larsson, 1985). Then there was no longer a distinction between these different forms of royal lands.

In England there were at least three types of royal land by the mid 11th century (Maitland, 1897, 255). *Regales terrae*, were lands "which pass from king to king" (ibid), and correspond to *bona regalia. Regii pueri* was land belonging to the king's family and *propria hereditas* was the king's own heritage. The distinction between the land of the *crown* and the land of the *king* appears in a charter issued by king Æthelred 1014–1016 (K 1312 (vi. 172)). In Germany the king's *patrimonium* is referred to as *ad regnum non pertinens* – which does not belong to the kingdom. The legal distinction between *patrimonalia* and *regalia* appears in 1020 in the reign of the Salian king Henry II (976–1024). In 1065 (under Henry IV) the king's private manors are named as *propria hereditates* and the crown's estate as *res ad regni fiscum pertinens* (LexMa; Andrén, 1983; Brink, 2000b; Stylegar & Westerdahl, 2004).

The analytical challenge is to connect the phenomenon of *bona regalia* with actual property, and then study this in spatial terms. In Denmark, the cadastre of King Valdemar, 1231 AD fortunately enables us to find clues to these complex matters, as it actually registers and differentiates between the king's *patrimonium* and the *kungalev* (*regalia*). I will revisit the Huseby farms and discuss their role prior to the 13th century, hopefully with some new perspectives. In Sweden, in particular, I will try to relate them to different kinds of taxation systems discussed by the historian Thomas Lindkvist (1989), and I will also draw on the newest work in the field, by Frans-Arne Stylegar & Christer Westerdahl (2004). I will consider whether the Huseby-farms can be linked to fiefs. I will also investigate whether there are grounds for a hypothesis of a dual tax collection system prior to 1200, and I will draw a distinction between core areas controlled directly by the king, and *semi-peripheries* and *peripheries* controlled indirectly through alliance and delegated royal power. It is hardly meaningful to use the terms *regalia* and *patrimonalia* as analytical tools for the situation prior to the 11th century. The terms are dependent on each other, and are probably also historically linked to the rise of supra-regional kingdoms. It can, however, be fruitful to use the term *dynastic core areas* describing areas where powerful families of royal rank had their power bases in earlier times.

FIEFS AND VASSALS

We do not know how much revenue different regions in Scandinavia during the Viking Age could bring supra-regional kings. The *Tribal Hidage* (*c.*650–850) provides detailed information on what is believed to be the tribute value to a number of kingdoms and provinces south of the Humber, England (Kirby, 2000, 9–11). There is no reason to believe that such ideas would be strange to powerful people in Scandinavia. The so-called *Alfiva-law* mentions Christmas gifts (*julegafor*) to the king, and this is interpreted as the tribute from Norway based on taxes introduced by Canute's conquest in 1028 (Andersen, 1977, 145). His son Svein and Svein's mother Alfiva (Ælgifu) of Northampton served as Canute's vassals for a brief period (1029–1035). These unpopular taxes were first abolished a century later, at least in northern Norway (Ágr, chapter 52; F XVI, 1–3). Landowners in the provinces of Hålogaland and Namdalen regained *c.*1103–1107 full rights to commons, and were exempt from building and repairing houses at royal villas. Still every fisherman in Vågan had to pay five fish to the king for the right to fishing (NgL I, p. 257f; RN I, nr. 56).

Supra-regional power sought rights where it hardly existed, or where they were weak and could be challenged. An account of *Knýtlinga saga* (*c.*1260) sheds light on the relationship between central power and the periphery in the 11th century. The supra-regional King Canute "the holy" (*c.*1043–1086) threatened to take away from the inhabitants in the province of Halland their rights to keep cattle and swine in the forests. He also threatened to take away the (free) fishing in Öresund from the inhabitants of Skåne. Canute claimed rights on behalf of the kingdom to resources in the sea and the forest (Ulsig, 2001, 29f).

Pre-emption, called *konungs kaup*, was an important right of the crown (L VIII, 9). In Norway, the king had exclusive rights to the purchase of furs north of *Umeyiarsund*, identified as either Vennesund in the province of Helgeland or Strimasund-Vilasund in Överuman near the present border between Norway and Sweden (F XVI, 2; RN I, nr. 56). The privilege to delegate such rights was a powerful tool for supra-regional kings in building alliances and developing new taxable objects in subordinated provinces (Blom, 1967). The Crown also had preemption to hunting-hawks and falcons in Norway (L VII, 52). It is a clear symbol of subordination when earl *Håkon Jarl* of Lade (province of Trøndelag) supposedly sent annually, twenty hunting-hawks to the supra-regional King Harold Bluetooth in 970/80th, according to Theodoric the monk (*c.*1180) (*Historia de antiquitate regum norwagiensium*, chapter 5). Norway is also referred to as *Harold's hawk island* (*Haralds Haukøy*) in a somewhat older source (*Bersöglisvísur* (*c.*1040) (verse 18, Msk, p. 32).

Ebbe Hertzberg (1893) has discussed the role of the fief (*lén*) in the Viking

Age. In-between areas and fringes were often given as fiefs. Hertzberg presents 13 examples from the sagas, over a period for nearly 450 years (Hertzberg, 1893, 285). The provinces of Sogn, half the Faroe Islands, Orkney, Shetland, half-Rogaland and Borgarsyssel are mentioned as fiefs (*lén*). Royal power was probably weak in these areas at the time. Recently, the situation for the North Atlantic islands, the so-called *Skattland* (*skattlond*) has been discussed in more depth (Wærdahl, 2006). Also *Hirdskråen* (Chapter 14) and the *rural law of Magnus the lawmender* (L II, 9) have provisions for this. Large fiefs were accompanied with an earl's title. The powerful magnate Erling "Skakke" Ormsson (1115–1179) with a base in Etne in the province of Sunnhordland, Western Norway gained an earl's title around 1170. He then got the province of Viken, Eastern Norway to *léns ok yfirsóknar* of King Valdemar of Denmark (Hkr, Magnus Erlingssons saga, chapter 30). At the time Viken was a political *periphery* with strong Danish and Western Norwegian interests.

Ebbe Hertzberg (1893, 309) believed the income of the fief, as a general rule, was shared; with 2/3 going to the king and 1/3 to the vassal, referring to an ordinance from 1320 (NgL III, 1 nr 64, p. 150) and the sagas. However, the ordinance clearly deals with the *sýslumaðr* in an urban context, and is hardly relevant to this question. More likely, this was the subject of negotiations between the parties. According to Grethe Authén Blom, who has studied the early policies in this field (until 1387), kings in the 10th and 11th century gave their foremost allies up to half of the fiefs' income (Blom, 1967, 45, 53–60). The main point is, however, that a significant portion of the income fell to the king. The bulk of the income must have been taxes and fines (*sakøre*). These categories accounted later (15th and 16th century) for close to 80% of the crown's total income of Norway. Taxes alone accounted for 50% and fines over 30%. Revenues (*landskyld*) from crown land accounted for 12% and taxes on fishing (especially salmon) and hunting around 8% (Bjørkvik, 1968, 179). Prior to the mid 14th century, Halvard Bjørkvik estimates tax and fines to be lower; 65% of the total income (Bjørkvik, 1996, 62).

DENMARK

I will now briefly discuss the situation in Denmark. The cadastre of King Valdemar bears witness to an extensive system of royal villas in Denmark (Aakjær, 1926–1942; Andrén, 1983). The cadastre is special in a European context as it draws a clear distinction between *bona regalia* and *bona patrimonalia*. It is possible to identify and map 93 regalia-manors and 56 dynastic manors, in addition to a number of unidentifiable properties. Over a quarter of the *kungalev*, 26 properties, are also mentioned in earlier sources (Andrén, 1983, 37f.

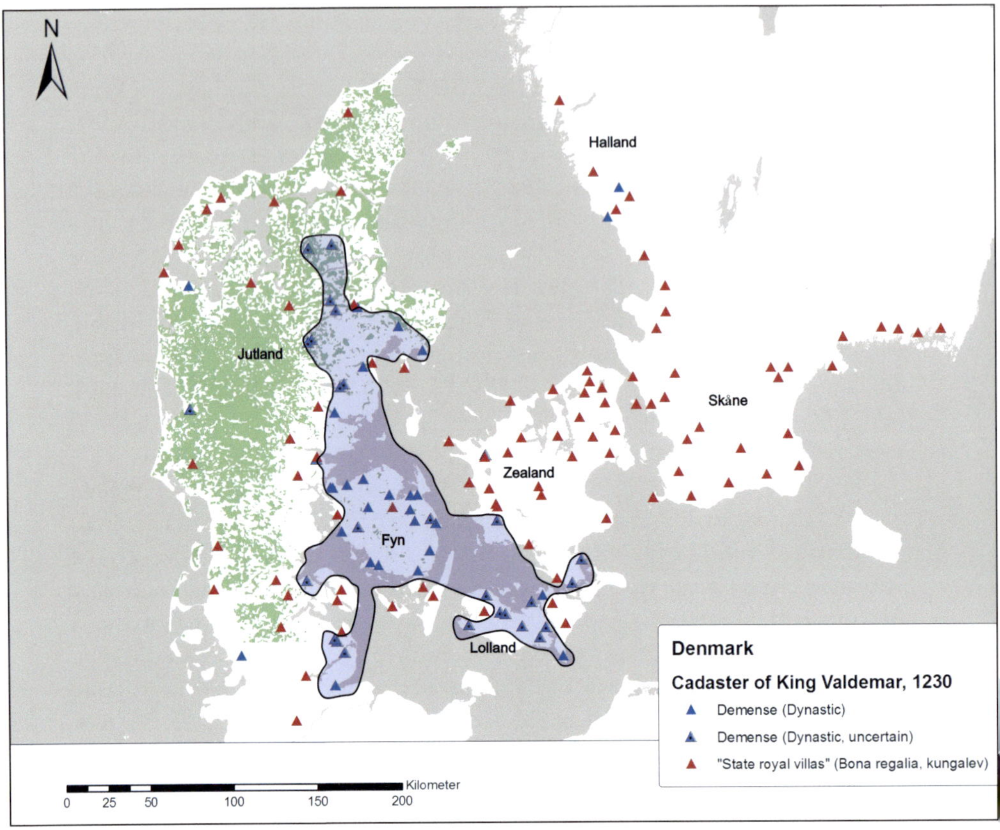

Fig.1. Bona regalia and bona patrimonalia in Denmark, according to the cadastre of King Valdemar *c.*1230 AD.

and note 36) (Figure 1). The king's *patrimonium* in the 1230s in Denmark lay in Lolland and Fyn, in parts of Eastern Jutland and eastern Schleswig. 50 out of 56 of the *patrimonium* manors (demesne) lay within the area I have marked out in Figure 1. This area was essential in controlling traffic between the North Sea and Baltic Sea.

The *bona regalia* and the *patrimonium* of King Valdemar clearly had different geographical locations in Denmark around 1230. The *kungalev* were located in the eastern and western parts of the country (Skåne and Halland, Jutland), and in the northern part of the island Zealand. There were hardly any *bona regalia* in the middle of Denmark, neither on the islands of Fyn and Lolland, nor in south Zealand. We do not know how far back in time this pattern goes. In several works, Anne Pedersen (1997; 1999) has discussed equestrian graves from the late Iron Age in Denmark. At least 60–70 of the equestrian graves can be

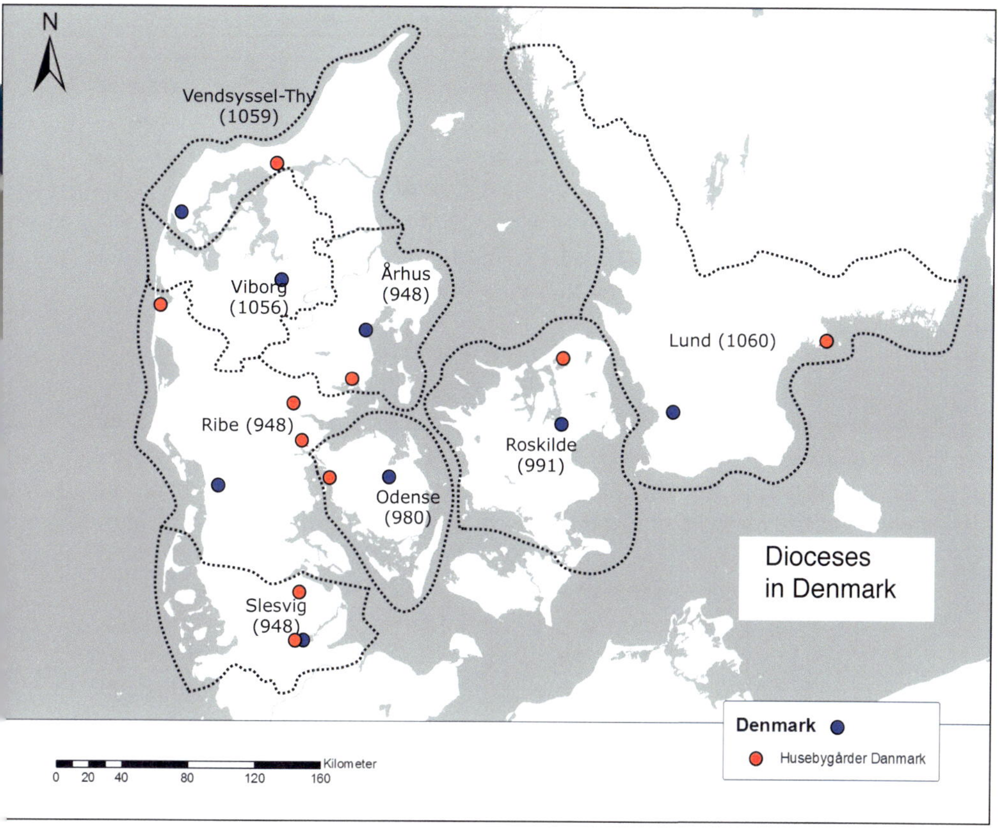

Fig. 2. Huseby-farms and dioceses in Denmark.

mapped more precisely, and are found in North Jutland, in Schlesvig-Holstein to the south, and on Langeland, south of Fyn. These were areas where Valdemar had little land *c.*1230. Only a few equestrian graves are known in Fyn, where Valdemar's *patrimonium* dominated later. There is a significant time span between the two source categories, and there is not a 1 to 1 pattern in terms of mutual geographic exclusion. Nevertheless, this suggests that the equestrian graves may represent some form of alliance with partners on a lower level, located in areas outside direct dynastic control. On Zealand, around Lejre, where there are few equestrian graves as well, one can also imagine such dynastic core areas.

Only ten Huseby-farms are known in Denmark in the Middle Ages (Stylegar & Westerdahl, 2004) (Figure 2). None of them are mentioned in the Cadastre of King Valdemar, neither as *bona regalia* nor *patrimonium*. However, they lie on strategic long sea-routes and correspond to some degree with the earliest dioceses in Denmark. There were two Huseby-farms in Schlesvig and three in Ribe, one of them was the farm next to the important royal site of Jelling. It is possible that Husby in Hardsyssel close to the northern border of Ribe was connected with the Viborg diocese, which did not have a Huseby-farm. There was only one Huseby each in the other dioceses of Denmark. It is uncertain how to interpret this. It might make sense if we see the Huseby-farms in Denmark as storage facilities for the king's income from these regions, and where the bishops played a major role collecting taxes and revenues on behalf of the king. We shall now examine the conditions in Norway and Sweden.

NORWAY AND SWEDEN

In Norway and Sweden, we do not have any cadastres differentiating between *bona regalia* and *bona patrimonium*. The provincial laws nevertheless give us some clues, especially in Sweden. In some of these laws, and also in the Icelandic sagas, there are references to the so-called *Uppsala öd* (Brink, 2000b; Stylegar & Westerdahl, 2004 with references). It has been suggested that this complex is connected with the Huseby-farms.

There are all together nearly 140 Huseby-farms in the Nordic countries, Schleswig and the Orkneys (Steinnes, 1955; 1959; Stylegar & Westerdahl, 2004). Since Henrik Schück's (1914) classic work on *Uppsala öd* they have been central to the academic discussion on early royal power, in particular in Sweden and Norway (Stylegar & Westerdahl, 2004 with references; Berend, 2007, 175). It has been pointed out many times that *Uppsala öd* and the Huseby-farms seem to represent *bona regalia* (Brink, 2000a, 274–278). Recently, Barbara Crawford also discussed the four Huseby-farms (*Houseby*) in Orkney in more detail (Crawford, 2006). There are no Huseby-farms on the Faeroes or Iceland. In Norway, most of the 54 Huseby-farms are located in the grain-producing areas in Trøndelag and in the eastern part of Norway. The same applies to Sweden, where there are many Huseby-farms in Uppland in the east (Brink, 2000b). In Västgötland another group of *Uppsala öd* appear in the later *Vestgötalagen* from around 1300 AD, – where the eight so-called bo-farms are referred to as *Uppsala öd*. I will not discuss them in this context, but focus on the Huseby-farms, and the same applies to the *Uppsala öd* in Norrland.

SWEDEN

Thomas Lindkvist (1989) has argued that Sweden in the early Middle Ages can be divided into various "fiscal regions". These he defines by types of taxes and their historical origins. He distinguishes between individual and collective taxes. Collective taxes are assessed per area (e.g. hundred) and individual taxes

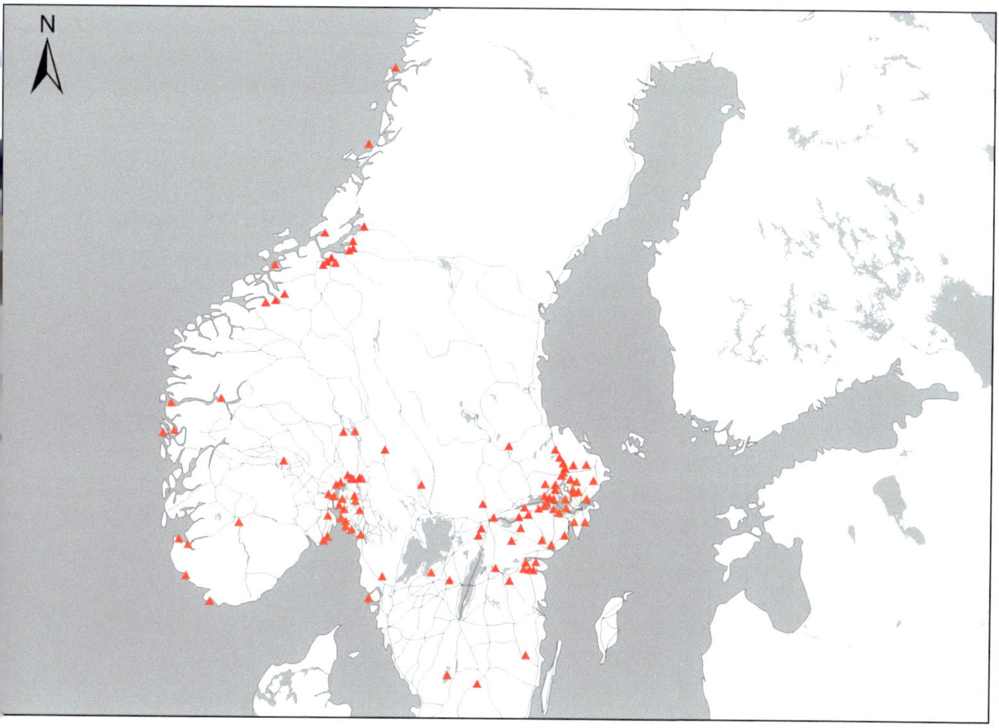

Fig. 3. Huseby-farms in Norway and Sweden.

per household and/or register (*mantall*) (Lindkvist, 1989, 173). Individual taxes require a high degree of direct control over the producers, and Lindkvist perceives them as "feudal" in character. At the same time he argues that collective taxes are more "primitive" because the individual's contribution was beyond the king's direct control. Consequently the king only dealt with the thing or the vassals in these areas.

Especially interesting in our context is the clear geographic distribution of individual and collective taxes in Sweden. There seems to be a pattern of individual taxes in the west (Västergötland, parts of Närke, northern Småland), collective taxes in the east (Uppland, eastern Västmanland and Södermanland), and a middle zone with both types represented (Östergötland). In Västergötland individual taxes dominated completely. They had their origin in the *servitium regis*, the king's right to provision (*gjesting*) (*gengärden*) and the "all men" tax (*allmänningsöret*). In Östergötland there were additional taxes based on the king's right to commons, and collective taxes were also known in coastal areas in the east (*leidangsskatt*). On the other hand, the areas around Mälaren dominated collective taxes completely in the 13th and 14th century (*leidangsskatt*).

An implication of Lindkvist's hypothesis is that we might have to imagine that supra-regional power in Sweden originally was weaker in the areas with a high proportion of collective taxes. There is an interesting correlation between the prevalence of Huseby-farms and such areas, as pointed out by Stylegar & Westerdahl (2004). The Huseby-farms seem to have been located in areas with weak supra-regional power.

Except for a manor here and there, it is hard to point out the *bona patrimonalia* in Sweden. However, a combined analysis of royal itineraries and a more thorough review of the rural places where the king issued charters could put us on track. Figure 4 shows Sweden in the 13th and mid 14th century. The dots on the map are based on the locations where the king issued charters prior to the mid 14th century, in total at 62 rural and 19 urban sites. The urban ones are located along the so-called *Eriksgatan*. This was the most important

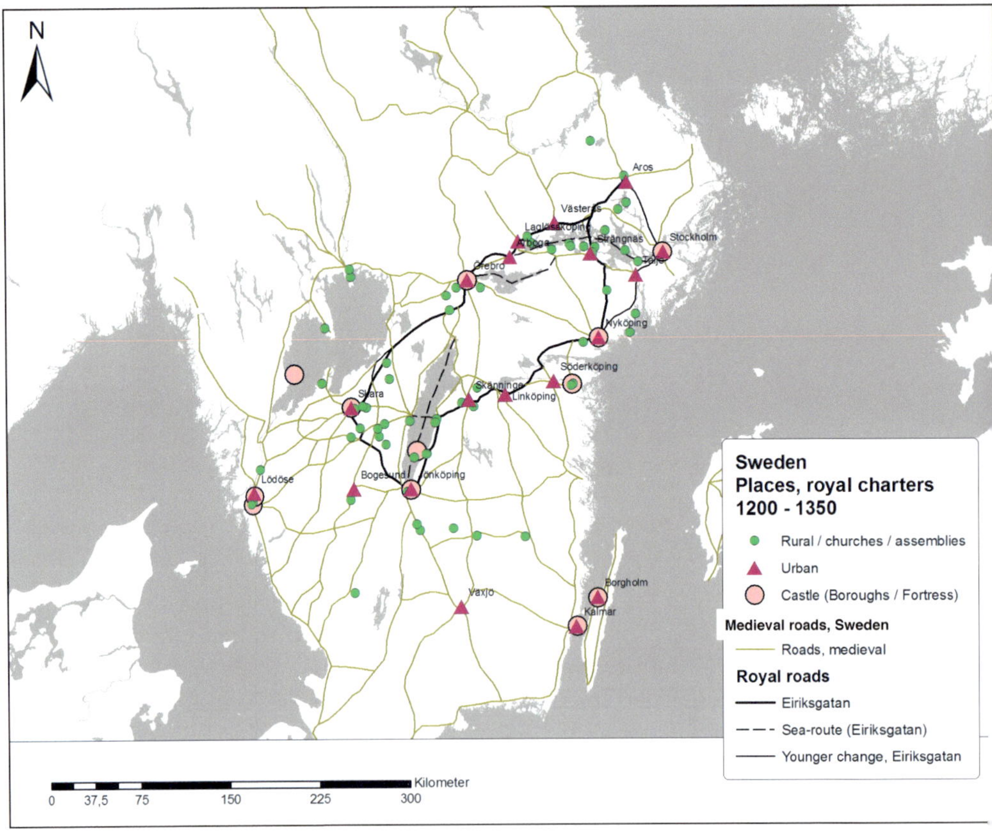

Fig. 4. Sweden mid 14th century.

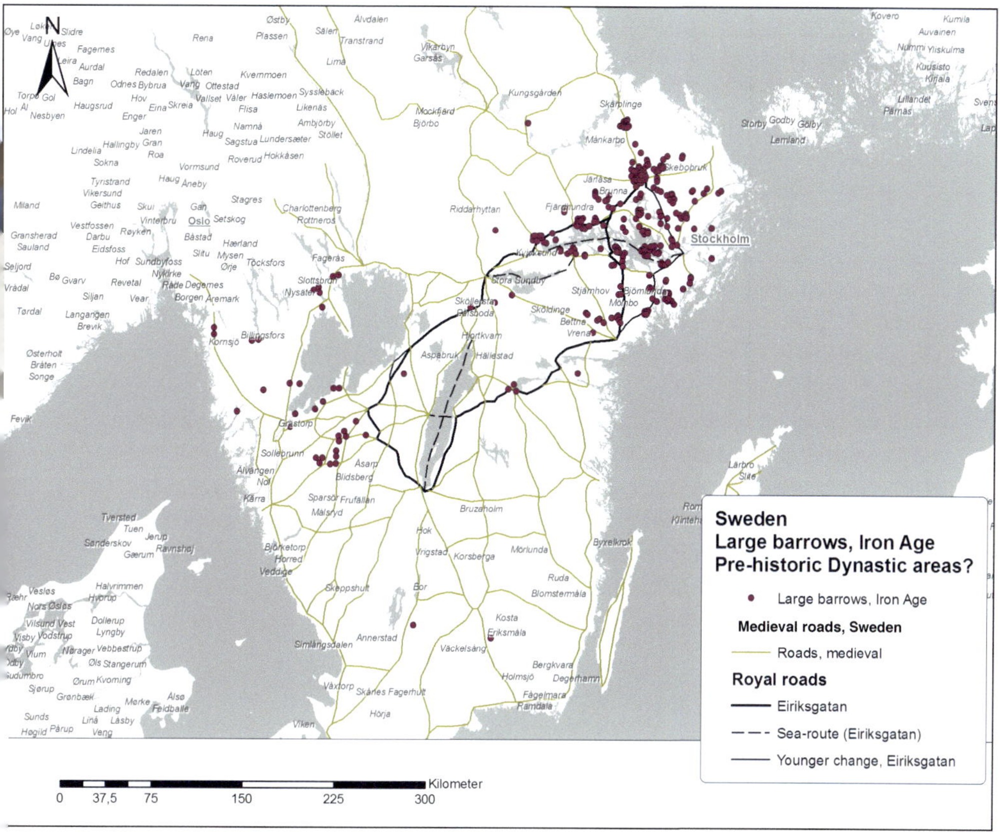

Fig. 5. Great mounds in Sweden, prior to the 11th century.

medieval royal road in Sweden. *Eriksgatan* was the "coronation road" until the reign of King Gustav Wasa in the 16th century. The pretender had to do the 'circuit', to be accepted in all of the ancient (law) provinces, to become the king of Sweden. We have less knowledge of the earlier situation.

The prevalence of the nearly 320 great mounds (*storhauger*) in Sweden prior to the 11th century (Hyenstrand, 1980, 34; Bratt, 2008) indicates at least two main areas standing out as potential dynastic core areas; Västergötland and the area of the Mälar valley (Figure 5). Traditionally, great mounds have been interpreted as an expression of power in a fairly direct one to one ratio. I will not go into the full discussion here, but note that maybe it is in these areas we should expect dynastic power from an early phase with petty kingdoms. Evaluated by the distribution of great mounds, there seem to have been many powerful elites in the eastern parts of Sweden before the rise of a wider supra-regional power.

The name *Uppsala öd* meaning "the wealth of Uppsala" may indicate that the Uppsala area, and a royal dynasty here, were subjected to a dynasty from the west. The Uppland province is extremely well organized, or reorganized. This is clearly seen in the medieval administrative names: *Tiundaland* (the land of ten hundreds), *Åttungaland* (the land of eight hundreds), and *Fjärdrundaland* (the land of four hundreds). The names *af Tindæ Landi* and *Fiærðundæ landi* are known in a document from the 14th century describing a border-agreement between Denmark and Sweden from the mid 11th century (KLNM 18, 402). The so-called Florentine document from 1120 is the oldest source using the names – *Tindia*, *Fedundria* and *Atanth* (ibid). There is no reason to doubt that these units existed under these names, at least in the 11th century, if not earlier.

This may indicate an administrative reorganization of the landscape in eastern Sweden, and fits in well with the idea of the establishment of supra-regional power in Sweden, and the rise of the *bona regalia* called *Uppsala öd*. It also fits well with the prevalence of Huseby farms, which has its most systematic distribution in Uppland with a good correlation using 'hundreds', and this also gives support to Lindkvist's hypothesis about the taxes.

NORWAY

There were several petty kingdoms in Scandinavia prior the 11th century. In Norway, they tend to have followed the areas of the earliest known provincial laws. This applied particularly to Trøndelag (The law of Frostathing) and in the Western part of Norway (The law of Gulathing). These provinces had strong competing elites. Western Norway is today considered as the geographical starting point for the rise of supra-regional power in the 9th and 10th centuries. Historians such as Claus Krag (1990; 1993; 1995), Knut Helle (1982; 2001) and Jón Viðar Sigurðsson (2008) have pointed out that Trøndelag was the first province to be submitted to an expanding supra-regional kingdom, and that the eastern parts of Norway were gradually integrated from the 11th century onwards. Norway was an unstable political unit with alternating domination and rival elites. The royal power in Trøndelag was gathered around the so-called Earls of Lade (*Ladejarlene*), searching for alliances with kings in Denmark.

We know of nearly 40 potential dynastic royal manors in Norway prior to the mid 12th century. They are mainly identified in the sagas from the 13th century (Storm, 1882; Iversen, 1999; 2008). It is interesting to note that the Huseby-farms in Norway, the assumed *bona regalia,* are in general located in the submitted provinces, in Trøndelag and the Viken-area in eastern Norway.

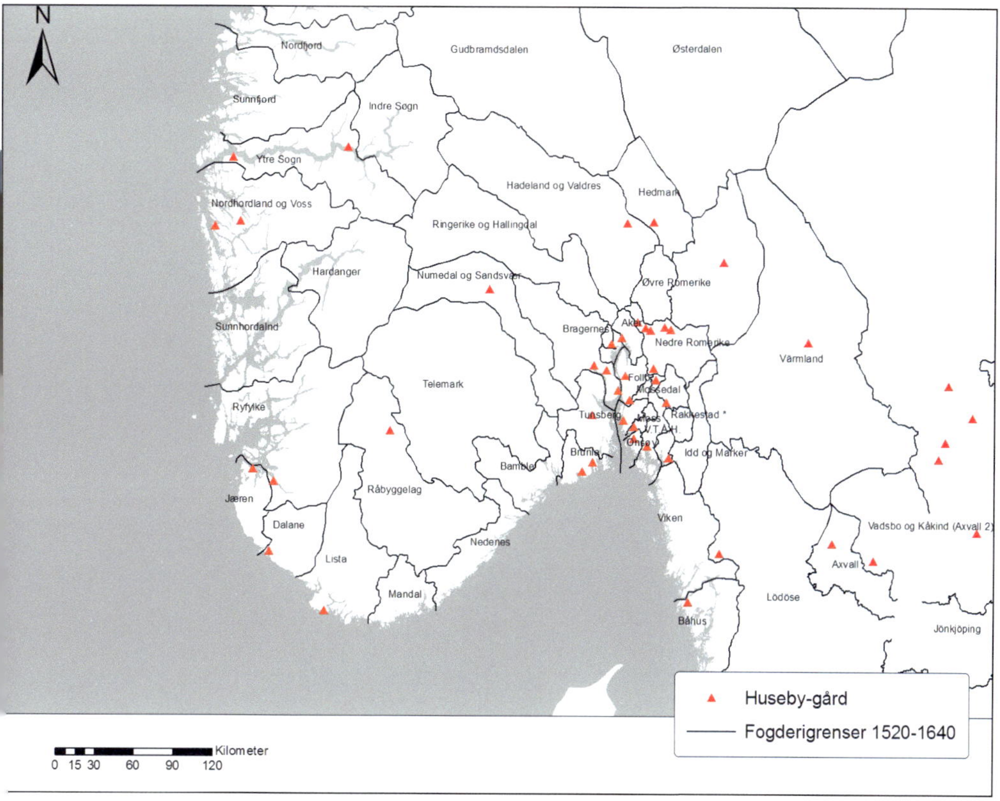

Fig. 6. Huseby-farms and taxation regions (fogderier) in the late Middle Ages.

On the other hand, there is some correspondence between the distribution of Huseby-farms and taxation regions documented in the late Middle Ages (*fogderi*), at least in the southern and northern parts of Norway (Figure 6). This is somewhat more dubious in Trøndelag were they tend to relate to the old fylkes-division instead.

Let us take a closer look at Viken, as our last example. In the Viking and Middle Ages this area was a cultural and political melting pot squeezed in between Sweden, Denmark and Norway, and had switched political affiliation over time. Viken was often subjected to the kings of Denmark at least from the 9th century to the fall of the Danish vassals, the Earls of Lade in Trøndelag, in the beginning of the 11th century. First, in the 13th century stable political structures were established here, as seen from a Norwegian perspective. In the sagas it is possible to identify at least 5 or 6 dynastic royal manors in this area, in addition to 20 baron-seats (*lendmenn*) – shown as black dots in Figure 7.

The barons in eastern Norway controlled the traffic routes from the moun-

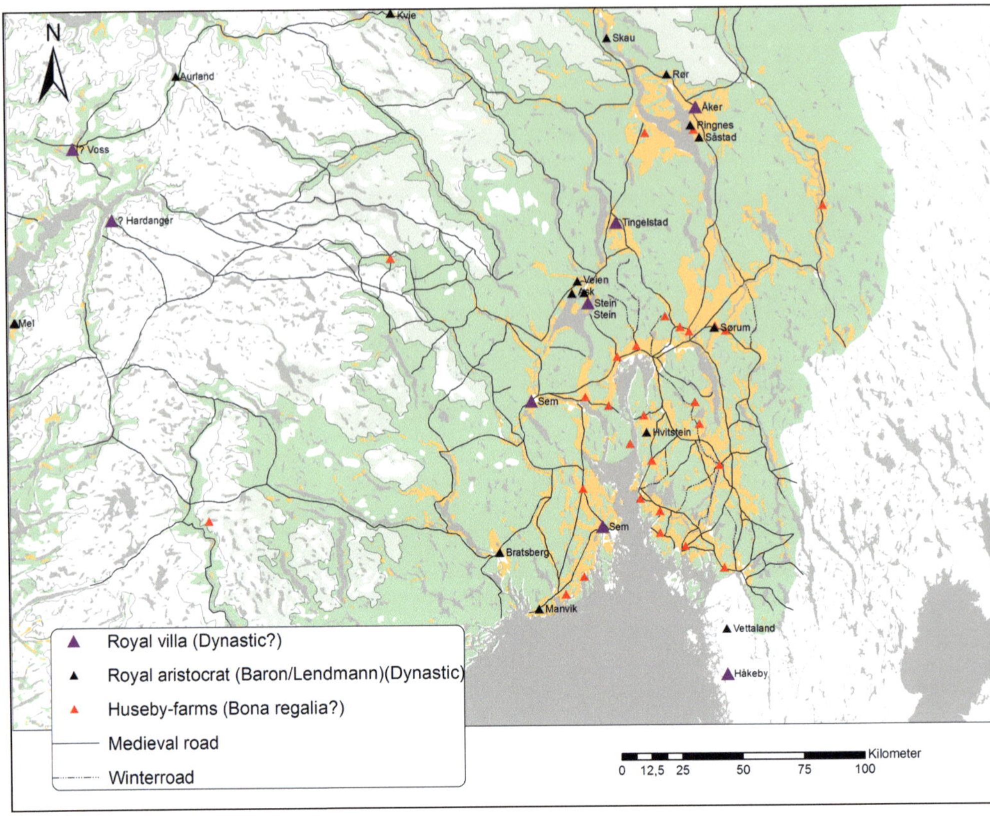

Fig. 7. The spatial organisation of Royal land in eastern Norway, prior to 14th century.

tains down to the coast. In the commons of the Highlands, large amounts of iron were produced (Larsen et al., 2008), adding to the fact that this was the most important hunting area in Norway. In particular, it was reindeer that was hunted. The goods had to be transported down to the coast, passing the major power centres along the routes. Also the Huseby-farms lay along important routes in the lowlands, and in the coastal areas in Viken. There was only one single Huseby-farm in each so-called *skipreide*, which is equivalent to the hundred, but not all of the skipreids in the Viken-area had Huseby-farms. There is a possible connection with the younger taxation regions (*fogderi*) which could have comprised of several skipreider. A thoughtful geographical organization seems to be an element of the *bona regalia* in Norway, and Sweden.

THE BEAUTY OF BONA REGALIA – SOME PERSPECTIVES

Terms such as *conglomerate state* or *composite states* (Gustafsson, 1998 with references) have been used to describe fragile states and supra-regional kingdoms in the Middle Ages. However, in the debate *bona regalia* have in a small degree been recognized as a mechanism of early state-formation in northern Europe. Neither in the standard-works of the 19th century, e.g. by Henry Lewis Morgan (1877) and Friedrich Engels (1884), nor in later work when discussing chiefdoms and states in evolutionary perspectives (e.g. Elman Service, 1962; 1975), have *bona regalia* been given their rightful place. I have somewhat simplified the argument that we should at least distinguish between three kinds of geographical zones in the development of supra-regional royal powers in Scandinavia. *Dynastic core areas* with deep roots as power centres, also characterising petty kingdoms, had direct lordship and were controlled through dynastic property. In the nearby *semi-peripheries* minor travelling kings had rights to *veitsler*, and provisions at specific farms which later were regarded as part of the *bona regalia*. Such farms are probably equivalent with the English *farm of one night*.

During 9th and 10th centuries some of these royal dynasties gained ground. They experienced a need to develop more permanent structures in submitted and disputed regions. *Bona regalia* developed in a more systematic form, especially in the *peripheries*. In these regions supra-regional kings depended on existing powerful dynasties and the church. Fringe areas were defined as fiefs and earldoms, and became increasingly important. A system for taking care of the king's income from fiefs developed, and was closely associated with the Huseby-farms in Scandinavia and Kingston-farms in England. It was indirectly controlled both by local magnates perhaps in cooperation with the Thing-institution. A variety of revenues and goods to the king were stored at farms with good housing-facilities. In such areas supra-regional kings also needed the acceptance of the Thing-institution to get access to the *bona regalia*. The local communities themselves were driving forces in such processes, benefiting from the king's authority and power to sanction the law. By interactions between the kings, earls, magnates and the Thing-institution, supra-regional powers in Scandinavia developed from the 9th to 12th century, and the creation of *bona regalia* seem to be of great importance in this process.

BIBLIOGRAPHY

Aakjær, Svend (1926–1942). *Kong Valdemars jordebog, udgivet af Samfund til udgivelse af gammel nordisk litteratur.* Copenhagen.

Ágr = *Ágrip af Nóregs konunga sögum*, Finnur Jónsson (1929). *Altnordische Saga-Bibliothek* 18. Halle.

Andersen, Per Sveaas (1977). *Samlingen av Norge og kristningen av landet – 800–1130. Handbok i Norges historie* 2. Oslo.

Andrén, Anders (1983). Städer och kungamakt – en studie i Danmarks politiska geografi före 1230. *Scandia* 49: 1, 31–76. Lund.

Bagge, Sverre (2003). *Fra knyttneve til scepter : makt i middelalderens Norge. Makt- og demokratiutredningen 1998–2003*, no. 67. Oslo.

Berend, Nora (Ed.) (2007). *Christianization and the rise of Christian monarchy: Scandinavia, Central Europa and Rus c. 900–1200.* Cambridge.

Bernhardt, John W. (1993). *Itinerant kingship and royal monasteries in early medieval Germany, c. 936–1075. Cambridge studies in medieval life and thought.* 4th series no 21. Cambridge.

Bjørkvik, Halvard (1968a). Bona regalia, patrimonium og kongeleg donasjonspolitikk i mellomalderen. *Nordiska historikermötet Helsingfors 1967, Historiallinen Arkisto* 63, 43–55. Helsingfors.

Bjørkvik, Halvard (1968). *Krongodset i mellomalderen.* Unpublished manuscript.

Bjørkvik, Halvard (1996). *Folketap og sammenbrudd, 1350–1520. Aschehougs Norgeshistorie* no. 4. Oslo.

Blom, Grethe Authén (1967). *Kongemakt og privilegier i Norge inntil 1387.* Oslo.

Bratt, Peter (2008). *Makt uttryckt i jord och sten. Stora högar och maktstrukturer i Mälardalen under järnåldern. Stockholm Studies in Archaeology* 46. Stockholm.

Brink, Stefan (2000a). Husby. *Reallexikon der germanischen Altertumskunde*, bd. 15, pp. 274–278, Göttingen.

Brink, Stefan (2000b). Nordens husabyar – unga eller gamla? *En bok om husabyar* (Ed. Michael Olausson), 65–73. Uppsala.

Charles IV. *Autobiography of emperor Charles IV and his Legend of St. Wenceslas / Karoli IV imperatoris Romanorum vita ab eo ipso conscriptaet Hysteria nova de sancto Wenceslao martyre* (Eds. Balázs Nagy & Frank Schaer, 2001). Budapest.

Crawford, Barbara (2006). Kongemakt og jarlemakt, stedsnavn som bevis? *Viking* 2006, 195–214. Oslo.

DS = *Svenskt diplomatarium. Åren 817–1285*, no. 1 (Ed. Joh. Gust. Liljegren, 1829), http://www.riksarkivet.se/default.aspx?id=2453&refid=8005

Engels, Friedrich (1884). *The origin of the family, private property, and the state.* Penguin classics 1985. Harmondsworth.

F = *Frostatingslova* (Eds. Jan Ragnar Hagland & Jørn Sandnes, 1994).

Fritzner, Johan (1891). *Ordbog over Det gamle norske Sprog*, second edition, 1954. Oslo.

Gjerløw, J. A. (1988). Utskylden. Funksjon – opprinnelse – avvikling. *Historisk Tidsskrift* 67, pp. 361–398. Oslo.

Gjerløw, J. A. (1990). Litt mer om utskylden. *Historisk Tidsskrift* 69, pp. 214–215. Oslo.

Grundberg, Leif (2000). Husabyar i Norrland? Undersökningar kring Hälsingelagens Uppsala öd. *En bok om husabyar* (Ed. Michael Olausson), 75–91. Uppsala.

Gustafsson, Harald (1998). The Conglomerate State: A Perspective on State Formation in Early Modern Europe. *Scandinavian Journal of History*, Vol. 23, Nos. 3–4, pp. 189–213.

Hamre, Lars (1962. Iura regni. *KLNM* VII, 524–525.

Hertzberg, Ebbe (1893). *Len og veizla i Norges sagatid. Germanistische Abhandlungen zum LXX. Geburtstag Konrad von Maurers*, 285–331. Göttingen.

Hirðskrá = Hirdskråen. *Hirdloven til Norges konge og hans håndgangne menn – etter AM 322 fol*, utgave ved Steinar Imsen (2000). Oslo.

Hkr = *Snorri Sturluson. Heimskringla* I–II, Bjarni Aðalbjarnarson, *Íslenzk fornrit*, 1941 (new edition, 1979). Reykjavík.

Hyenstrand, Åke (1980). Mälarområdets centralortsbildning i tids- och rumsperspektiv. *Handelsplats – Stad – Omland. Symposium om det medeltida stadsväsendet i Mellansverige. Medeltidsstaden 18*. Stockholm.

Iversen, Frode (1999). *Var middelalderens lendmannsgårder kjerner i eldre godssamlinger? En analyse av romlig organisering av graver og eiendomsstruktur i Hordaland og Sogn og Fjordane. Arkeologiske avhandlinger og rapporter fra Universitetet i Bergen* 4. Bergen.

Iversen, Frode (2007). Könige an der Küste und Bauern im Binnenland – Regionale Unterschiede in Westnorwegen in der jüngeren Eisenzeit (800–1050 n. Chr.). *Bauern zwischen Herrschaft und Genossenschaft / Peasant relations to lords and government* (Eds.) Getrud Thoma, Tore Iversen & John Ragnar Myking. Tapir Academic Press 2007, 149–165. Trondheim.

Iversen, Frode (2008). *Eiendom, makt og statsdannelse: kongsgårder og gods i Hordaland i yngre jernalder og middelalder. Universitetet i Bergen Arkeologiske skrifter, UBAS, Nordisk* 6. Bergen.

Iversen, Frode (2009). Royal villas in Northern Europe. *The archaeology of early medieval villages in Europe* (Ed. Julio A. Q. Castillo), pp. 99–112. Euskal Herriko Unibertsitatea.

Kirby, D. P. (2000). *The earliest English kings*. New York.

KLNM = *Kulturhistorisk Leksikon for Nordisk Middelalder – fra vikingtid til reformasjonstid* I–XXII, 1956–1978. København.

L = *Den nyere Lands-Lov, utgiven av Kong Magnus Haakonsson. NgL* II, 1–178.

Larsen, J. H, Rundeberget, B, Stylegar, F. A. (2008). *Jernvinna på Agder. Jernvinneseminaret i Sirdal 25.–26. oktober 2007. Artikler utgitt i anledning Jan Henning Larsens 60-årsdag. Rapport no 5*. Kristiansand, Oslo.

Larsson, Lars Olof (1985). *Jordägofördelningen i Sverige under Gustav Vasas regering, Scandia 51*.

LexMA = Lexikon des Mittelalters bd. 1–9, 1980–1998. Stuttgart/Metzler.

Lindkvist, Thomas (1989). Skatter och stat i den tidiga medeltidens Sverige. *Medeltidens födelse*, pp. 171–184. Lund.

Line, Philip (2007) *Kingship and state formation in Sweden, 1130–1290. The Northern world* vol. 27. Leiden, Brill.

Maitland, F. (1897) *Domesday book and beyond: three essays in the early history of England*. Cambridge Boston.

Morgan, Henry Lewis (1877). *Ancient society : or researches in the lines of human progress from savagery through barbarism to civilization*, 1963, Cleveland.

Müller-Mertens, Eckhard (1980). *Die Reichsstruktur im Spiegel der Herrschaftspraxis Ottos des Grossen, mit historiographischen Prolegomena zur Frage Feudalstaat auf deutschem Boden, seit wann deutscher Feudalstaat? Forschungen zur mittelalterlichen Geschichte* Bd. 25. Berlin.

Pedersen, Anne (1997). Weapons and riding gear in burials – evidence of military and social rank in 10th Denmark? *Military Aspects of Scandinavian Society in a European Perspective AD 1–1300* (Eds.) A. Nørgård Jørgensen & B. Clausen, *Publications of the National Museum. Studies in Archaeology & History* 2, pp. 123–135. Copenhagen.

Pedersen, Anne (1999). Riding gear from late Viking-Age Denmark. *Journal of Danish Archaelogy* 13.

Peregrine, Peter N. (2007) Archaeology and World-Systems Theory. *Sociological Inquiry* 60, 1, pp. 486–495.

Rosén, Jerker (1949). *Kronoavsöndringar under äldre medeltid. Skrifter /Kungl. Humanistiska Vetenskapssamfundet i Lund* 46. Lund.

Schneider, Jane (1977). Was There a Pre-Capitalist World System? *Peasant Studies* 6, 1, 20–29.

Schück, Henrik (1914). *Uppsala öd. Uppsala universitetes årsskrift. Program* 2, pp. 3–36. Uppsala.

Service, Elman R. (1962). *Primitive social organization, an evolutionary perspective / Studies in anthropology*. New York.

Service, Elman R. (1975). *Origins of the State and Civilization: The Processes of Cultural Evolution*. New York.

Sigurðsson, Jón Viðar (1998). *Det norrøne samfunnet, vikingen, kongen, erkebiskopen og bonden*. Oslo.

Steinnes, Asgaut (1953). Utskyld. *Historisk Tidsskrift* 36, pp. 301–303, 370–383, 410–411. Oslo.

Steinnes, Asgaut (1955). *Husebyar. Den norske historiske forening. Skrifter* 32. Oslo.

Steinnes, Asgaut (1959). The Huseby System in Orkney. *Scottish Historical Review* 38, pp. 36–46. Edinburgh.

Storm, Gustav (1882). Om Lendermandsklassens Talrighed i 12. og 13. Aarhundrede. *Historisk Tidsskrift* 2: 4. Kristiania.

Stylegar, Frans-Arne & Westerdahl, Christer (2004). Husebyene i Norden. *Viking* 2004, pp. 101–138. Oslo.

Taranger, Absalon (1904). *Udsigt over den norske rets historie* 2. Kristiania.

Ulsig, Erik (2001). Højmiddelalder (1050–1350). Middelalderens Danmark, pp. 28–39. Copenhagen.

The Harbour of Hedeby

SVEN KALMRING

ABSTRACT

The proto-urban emporium of Hedeby was one of the most important trading centres of the Viking world. Because of its position in the borderland between the Carolingian Realm (respectively later German Empire), and Scandinavia, two traffic routes could be controlled from here: The north-south directed overland traffic route and – even more important – a portage between the North Sea and the Baltic. The harbour of Hedeby in its double function as the area for mooring ships and stock turnover, as well as the market place to the settlement, inheres a central significance for the comprehension of the site. By an enduring adaptation to the changing demands of professional seafaring, it safeguarded the economic basis of the emporium itself. Even though the harbour at first glance has to be considered as a maritime phenomenon, the overall development of Hedeby was directly subjected to the usability of it.

Keywords: Hedeby, harbour, harbour facilities, professional seafaring, stock turnover, far distant trade, market places, urbanisation.

The research excavation in the harbour of Hedeby carried out by K. Schietzel (1980, pp. 100; 1981, pp. 94 note 21; 1984a, pp. 188; Schietzel & Crumlin-Pedersen, 1980, p. 6) in the year 1979/80 provided the rare opportunity to get a detailed insight into one of the most important early medieval ports of northern Europe within a large-scale section (Fig. 1 & 2). Furthermore, the various artifacts – of which the organic material is especially well preserved due to transgression – allow comprehensive studies, which not only reflect the far-reaching trade connections, but also highlight the Viking Age harbour operations in an extraordinarily rich diversity.

HARBOUR EXCAVATION AND SURVEYS

Hedebys outstanding function as a "hub of the North Sea- and Baltic trade" (Jöns & Müller-Wille, 2002, p. 347) is due to its special topographical situation which encompasses many location factors (Jankuhn, 1986, p. 55; Schietzel, 1984b; Radtke, 1999, p. 363; Crumlin-Pedersen, 1997, p. 30; Brandt, 2006; 2005; Sindbæk, 2005, p. 110). It led to the development – possibly because of the increasing importance of the Baltic trade with gradual replacement of Ribe

Fig. 1. Hedeby. Settlement area and cofferdam of the harbour excavation in 1979.

(Feveile, 2006, p. 52; von Carnap-Bornheim & Hilberg, 2005, p. 469; 2007, p. 201) – of the site becoming one of the nodal points in Viking Age long-distance trade. The reference to Hedeby within the written sources confirm its role as a high-sea port, international maritime trading place and naval base. Additionally, the connections mentioned in the historical sources concerning the harbour offer a valuable addition on the trade connections. These can be reconstructed by the imported artifacts (cf. Kalmring, 2010, pp. 37). The function that Hedeby was able to take within the Viking Age trading network was strongly dependent on the surrounding waterways, above all the Haddebyer Noor and the Schlei fjord (Gripp, 1941, p. 55; Köster & Bonsen, 1970).

After the discovery of a Viking Age shipwreck in 1953 in the Haddebyer Noor (Kersten, 1954; Hingst & Kersten, 1955; Hingst, 1958), a long period of developing suitable concepts for excavation followed, until the vessel could finally be excavated in 1979 within a cofferdam. Due to the scientific success of the recovery of the wreck, the excavation area was enlarged. By the end of the excavation 2236 m^2 of the Viking Age harbour, as well as the adjacent shore areas were archaeologically examined. Apart from the excavated area from 1979/80 itself there was another 97% of the Viking Age harbour area which could only be surveyed by the help of divers, sonar and seismic exploration methods (Stümpel & Borth-Hoffmann, 1983; Grøn et al., 1998, p.155;

Fig. 2. Hedeby harbour. Substructures of harbour facilities during the excavation in July 1980.

Kramer, 1998/99). Unfortunately, this led only to a partially documented, and in itself, very controversial picture. The research desideratum has yet to be concluded by future surveys and is eagerly awaited. Apart from the burial ship from the boat-chambergrave, two logboats and several ship building elements, in total four shipwrecks are known from Hedeby (Crumlin-Pedersen, 1976; 1997; Hirte, 1997; Kühn, 2004).

In the course of the excavation from 1979/80 a total of 2044 timbers and 1641 post holes were uncovered and documented by 69 partial plana and 51 profiles of nearly 520 m in length. Additionally, samples from 791 timbers were taken for a later dendrochronological analysis, of which only 264 turned out to be datable. In order to analyse the extraordinarily complex system of the harbour methodology appropriately and exhaustively, the amount of accessible data made it necessary to build up a geographical information system (GIS).

DEVELOPMENT OF THE SHORE

Within the area of excavation, the first archaeologically comprehensible activities of undetermined age before the last quarter of the 8th century, can be found on the southern edge of the subaqueous terrace in the form of pit-like hollows in the natural ground. Moreover, there is reason to believe that some poles – as those that were pushed through the ship's side of Hedeby wreck 1 – are not from the Viking Age, but of much older origin. The so-called "Nydam-plank" (cf. Crumlin-Pedersen, 1997, p. 114, fig. 5.10) embedded in the layer of the former ground level in the southern shore area, testifies to an earlier but still extensive activity in the time around or after 749. A distinct development can be observed in the Viking Age long before the emergence of the first harbour constructions, that points to the use of the shoreline as a simple landing place.

The first Viking Age settlement activities on the shore of the Haddebyer Noor can be recognised in the northern shore area. Here, immediately behind the barrier beach, the surface was braced by a layer of brushwood earlier than the year 817, and a ditch was dug vertical to the waterline that might have been accompanied by a wattle fence on its southern side. As this reminds of the systematic plot division of the market place in Ribe (cf. Jensen, 1991, p. 5; Feveille, 2006, p. 27), it is possible to speak, with reservation, of an initial "Ribe phase" in Hedeby. Due to the minor extension of the excavation area towards the west of the southern shore area, the earliest phase could not be traced, but here as well the pre-Viking ground level initially was braced by a layer of brushwood on its bankside floodplains. In the following period the ground level of the waterside was raised with dung, fine turf and sand in several phases and expanded towards the Haddebyer Noor. The offsetting of the surface generated by the artificial accumulation of soil in the direction to the embankment, was screened by a shoreline stabilised against soil erosion caused by floodwater. It was accompanied by the dividing of the area with palisade, or wattle fences, which also had to be expanded towards the Noor with each phase of construction. The phases of expanding the terrain, found in the northern shore area, took place in the years 817, 836, around 844, around 857 as well as around 885 and stretched out over an area of about 18 m in total. Between the excavated central plot and the edge-gated neighbouring plot south of it, a road was found – which in comparison to the accumulated plots, was placed a little lower. This led towards the Haddebyer Noor and also served as drainage for rainwater from the settlement (cf. also Schultze, 2008, p. 119). In the southern shore area four construction phases of artificial accumulation of soil were determined, of which the first two were carried out around or after 823, the third around 874 and the fourth around 890. These expansions shifted the settlement area about 11 m towards the shore of the Haddebyer Noor. In connection with the construction, the northern of the two plots was expanded by relocating the plot boundary towards the south. Between the two plots a road ran in east-southeast west-northwest direction, which – in comparison to the level of the plots – again was placed a little lower.

EMERGENCE OF HARBOUR FACILITIES

The construction of harbour facilities begins at the end of the first third of the 9th century. All structures were erected as multiple-row piling bridges (cf. Schou Jørgensen, 1998, p. 9; Spichal, 2005). On top of the piles, crossbeams were placed with a mortise and tenon joist diagonally to the lengthwise piling construction. It is probable that the superstructure consisted of bearers in the form of narrow stakes that were laid irregular upon the crossbeams without any stable assembly. The boards of the coating, which were aligned in a right angle towards the structure, formed the completion of the superstructure and constituted the pathway. Since the narrow stakes of the bearers were not connected with the boards, the latter were connected by so-called *Rödelleisten* (cf. Unverzagt & Schuldt, 1963, p. 49, fig. 23), small battens nailed along the outer edges of the coating.

At first a solid access to a landing place at the shore of the Haddebyer Noor was created (Fig. 3). For the time being it only allowed the approach of vessels with their bow pulled up onto the soft beach. Around 865 an east-southeast orientated first long, slender jetty developed south of this first structure, which led further out on the Noor and offered personnel carriers and small coastal vessels already a swimming berth (Kalmring, 2010, p. 206). However, since the jetty was not very wide, the vessels seem to have moored with the stem ahead. The stern was secured against drifting by a pile mooring – demonstrated by three major postholes in the field observation. Between around 865 and 884

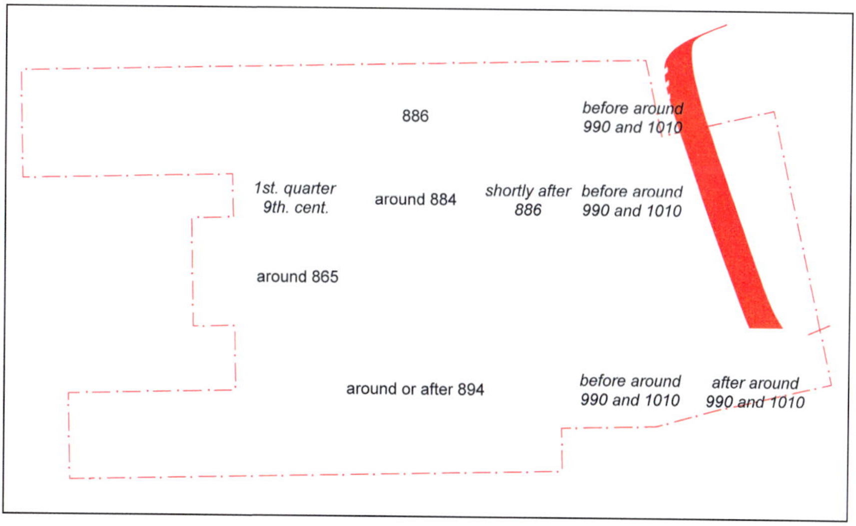

Fig. 3. Hedeby harbour. Overview and dating of the excavated harbour facilities.

the two harbour facilities were connected by a structure turning them into one single platform. Around 884 the part of the solid access to the landing place was expanded into deeper waters to be used as a jetty as well. Because of the special terrain morphology in context with the underwater terrace, the extension had to be much longer than the southern jetty to reach a comparable water depth in order to allow a floating berth. Due to its trapezoid shape the area of the southern jetty from around 865 was integrated into the platform as well. In contrast to the southern jetty the beachhead of the extension was so broad that in this phase of harbour development, the vessels could moor alongside the facility. Accompanied by the last extension of an artificial accumulation of soil towards the shoreline in the northern shore area, in the year 886, directly at the northern side of the existing platform, the first large and solid jetty was built systematically, reaching out far into the Haddebyer Noor.

Since the plot boundary of the northern shore area coincided with the border between the jetty and the existing platform a private enterprise has to be considered for the harbour structures (cf. note 117; 156) – even though they were directly attached to one another. As the jetty from 886 reached out much further than the beachhead of the platform itself, the use of the latter was strongly constrained, and quickly had to be expanded by an extension to the level of the beachhead of the jetty from 886. It was not until a few years after the last phases of extensions on the southern shore area – with a final artificial accumulation of soil around 890 – that a first harbour facility was erected around or after 894: a jetty of similar size and length as the northern one from 886. Hence, in this phase of harbour development all three jetties ended up at the same height. Shortly after 894, the southern jetty was connected by a structure to the first small jetty from 865. Thus, an impressive U-shaped platform developed with a central long and slender open area of water.

According to the reconstructed water depth in front of each of the three large jetties, personnel carriers as well as small coastal vessels and medium-sized cargo carriers (cf. Crumlin-Pedersen, 1999, p. 18, fig. 6) were able to moor alongside. The construction and the expansion of the harbour facilities was in accordance with the requirements of sea trade and the demands of the biggest cargo ships operating at any one time. They only found a sufficient water depth at the beachheads themselves. However, the adjacent long sides were used for mooring vessels of local sea traffic.

Due to the gradual decrease of water depth as a consequence of disposal of settlement waste in the harbour basin, as well as to the increase of the cargo ships in size, consequently leading to a bigger draught of the vessels, the harbour needed another extension in the time before around 990 and 1010. This was essential for the survival as a maritime trading place, and in order to be able to continue to participate of trading. In this phase of harbour development,

Fig. 4. Hedeby harbour. Overbuilt bow area of Hedeby wreck 1 in August 1979.

once again all of the three beachheads ended up almost at the same height into the Haddebyer Noor. It was not until then that the jetty had sufficient water depth for mooring high-sea cargo carriers such as Hedeby wreck 3 (Crumlin-Pedersen, 1997, p. 99, fig. 4.36), which had a draught of 1.51 m.

The reaction to the sinking of Hedeby wreck 1 right in front of the jetties in the area of the northern two constructions, was the systematic wrecking of the vessel lying on the sea-bottom by means of levers (Kalmring, 2010, p. 329). The preservation condition of wreck 1 at the time of excavation gives impressive evidence of the success of this action. The stem of the vessel was too far away from the beachhead of the southern facility to be able to proceed here accordingly. In order to re-establish the availability of the jetty in this area another extension had to be built reaching out over the wreck (Fig. 4), which sunk between 990 and 1010. With this last addition, which proves the continuous use of the harbour into the 11th century, and draws it nearer to the harbour of Schleswig (Vogel, 1997, p. 96, fig. 4) again, the wooden platform composed of the separate harbour facilities, possessed an impressive area of more than 1,475 m^2.

As harbour facilities never fulfilled an end in itself, but always responded to the changing demands of merchant shipping, only the definition of the latter – in addition to the mere knowledge of the constructional solution found – allows a better comprehension of the specific functionality of a harbour. For this reason, the results of the stratigraphical development, as well as the data of the height of the Viking Age average water level, have to be seen in relation to the draught of those vessels, which can be assumed to have called at Hedeby harbour. However, a classification of the Hedeby harbour in terms of cultural history, based on selected examples on the present state of research on the Early and High Middle Ages in North and Central Europe (cf. Bill & Clausen, 1999) has to be regarded as decidedly unsatisfactory.

The harbour facilities that have been uncovered with the excavation, are not viable with operating as an experienced harbour at an international maritime trading place such as Hedeby, without miscellaneous infrastructural installations. They include facilities for embarkation and disembarkation, possibilities for delivery and evacuation, stocking of trade goods as well as accommodations for long distance tradesmen and their ship's crews.

FINDS AND ARTIFACT DISTRIBUTION

Because of their find spots in reference to the harbour constructions, artifacts from the excavation (cf. Schietzel, 1983 pp.), apart from offering information on the reasons for certain distribution patterns, permit chronological considerations for some object groups, since the extensions of the constructions gradually "sealed" the previously open water surface. Objects of the ship's gear and ballast stones not only reveal intense harbour operations, but textile remains

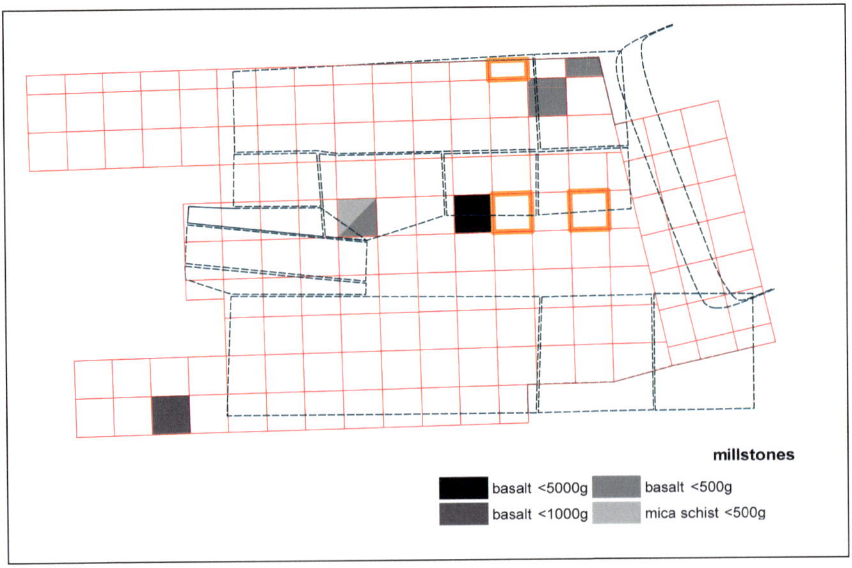

Fig. 5. Hedeby harbour. Distribution map of found millstones.

and rivets accumulated in the open water area, give evidence of the maintenance and repair of vessels. The high frequency and specific distribution of carpenter axes, adzes and wooden spikes underneath the harbour facilities, seem to testify to the continuous building activity and repair work that – because of the damages caused by ice drift in wintertime – became necessary every spring.

The trading goods that dropped between ship and harbour facilities and into the harbour basin during stock turnover often show a very characteristic distribution, and were found – as long as they were heavier than water – at the front and long sides of the constructions. These losses, which resulted from embarking and disembarking, include artifact groups like iron bars (Westphalen, 2002, p. 110) and millstones (Fig. 5; Schön, 1995). A comprehensive analysis of other important and extensive find groups, such as whet- and grindstones or soapstone (cf. Resi, 1979; 1990), which in this context would be interesting as import merchandise, is still expected. Nevertheless, it is already apparent that the proportion of the raw material among the whet- and grindstones from the harbour excavation is considerably higher than from the settlement excavations and systematic surveys. Also among the soapstone finds, vessels without any signs of usage were found more often than vessels with wear marks. Artifact groups such as iron slags (Westphalen, 1989) and the vast amount of animal bones (Hüster Plogmann, 2006; Heinrich, 2006) represent the settlement waste that was disposed in the Haddebyer Noor. Objects from daily use and dress

Fig. 6. Hedeby harbour. Sword 12. Blade with inhered remains of the scabbard (after Geibig, 1999, pl. 16).

equipment, that fell between the gaps among the boards of the coating, should be substituted among the group of single finds – such as the Gotland penannular fibula, the box brooch (Müller-Wille, 1988, p. 741) or the tongue-shaped brooch (Wamers, 1984). Figurines and model boats (Crumlin-Pedersen, 1997, p. 169; Westphal, 2006, p. 84) seem to represent losses from children's play.

On the other hand, different artifact groups provide indications about the use of the shore areas subdivided into plots, in which housing constructions – framework wall constructions, post-and-beam constructions and multi-phased houses without any wooden preservation – were merely found in the outermost eastern part of the excavated area: The noticeable cluster of 94 glass beads within grid square 17 and 18 (Steppuhn, 1998) in the northern shore area in combination with three pieces of process waste in grid square 17, 18 and 32/33 for example, might indicate the workshop of a bead-maker. Since all of the ten swords from the harbour excavation (Geibig, 1999) had remains of their scabbard ingrained in the blade (Fig. 6; Hägg, 1991, p. 248) a loss during combat can be excluded. Because of their reference to the harbour constructions, only two swords might have fallen into the water while embarking or disembarking, which means that for the majority, weapon sacrifices have to be considered.

It was observed that nearly every artifact group had an increased concentration of finds in the seaward part of the two northern jetties, which might – in contrast to the southern jetty – indicate a more frequent use of this area, and possibly suggest a financially strong operator, with considerably more commercial ties.

CONCLUSION

The U-shaped wooden platform composed of individual harbour facilities and their connecting structures, with an impressive area of almost 1500 m^2, calls for an interpretation that cannot be restricted to the demands of merchant shipping, or an intentional facilitation to stock turnover between ships and land (Kalmring 2010, p. 444). In this regard, the geomagnetic survey of Hedeby from 2002 (Hilberg, 2003; 2007, Fig. 3) seems to be particularly relevant, as it does not reveal any central place in the settlement area where goods reaching Hedeby could have been sold, but rather a densely build settlement. On a closer examination of some selected, well-documented excavations of market places, it becomes apparent, that – in contrast to continental Europe, where market places can be accounted for since the second half of the 10th century – in the western Baltic they did not appear before the 13th century (Hybel & Poulsen, 2007, p. 241). Therefore, the existence of an open space for market transactions within the settlement area of Hedeby is unlikely. Corresponding to the conclusions resulting from the high medieval features of Schleswig (Lüdtke,

1984; 1997; Vogel, 2002, p. 375f) and Lübeck (Ellmers, 1990; Mührenberg, 1993), it rather has to be assumed that the harbour of Hedeby, with its constructions, did not only meet the demands of merchant shipping, but contemporaneously served as the market place of the settlement. The various artifacts from the harbour excavation as a reflection of the market transactions seem to confirm this assumption. However, the use of the harbour facilities was not an independent development, but – as a few charters from the reign of Charles the Bald suggest (cf. Adam, 1996, p. 190 note 321) – seem to follow models from the Frankish realm.

According to the development of the shore areas, initially long before the erection of the first harbour facilities, a beach market in the range of a simple landing place has to be expected in Hedeby. The following gradual construction of the harbour – with a solid access to a landing place, the appearance of first jetties culminating in the assembly of facilities, by connecting structures to one single platform – makes each step of development based on a beach market in Hedeby comprehensible. Thus, the platforms can be conceived as the shift of a beach market moving up to the harbour facilities.

Consequently, the harbour of Hedeby is of prime importance in the understanding of the maritime trading place itself. By its continuous adjustment to the changing demands of long distance trade – that is professional merchant shipping and the development of specialised cargo carriers regarding the process of urbanisation, and formation of larger power structures – it guaranteed the enduring participation of maritime trade. Thus, this was the economic basis for the existence of the settlement itself, and at the same time the market place of the early town, as its central place for the exchange of goods.

Hedeby harbour reveals itself as a complex system consisting of various subsystems that are to some extent mutually dependent and overlap themselves. Thus, apart from its attribute as a complex archaeological subsystem, the harbour can be seen as an ecological, logistical and economical system. Furthermore, it enables primary conclusions of its function as a social, legal and military system. The evidence of the harbour of Hedeby forming a cultic system (Steuer, 2006, p. 42; Kalmring, 2010, p. 407; cf. also Lund, 2004, p. 209) seems to be striking in particular in this context.

Even if the harbour initially has to be regarded as a maritime phenomenon, the overall settlement development of Hedeby is directly subjected to the usefulness of the harbour basin, as well as the construction and extension of the harbour facilities. The identification of the platform that developed in this manner as the market place of Hedeby and thus, as a stage of goods exchange, allows the identification of the economical centre of the settlement. Consequently, the analysis of the harbour excavation decisively contributes to the understanding of the settlement development in Hedeby itself.

BIBLIOGRAPHY

Adam, H. (1996). *Das Zollwesen im fränkischen Reich und das spätkarolingische Wirtschaftsleben. Ein Überblick über Zoll, Handel und Verkehr im 9. Jahrhundert.* Vierteljahresschr. Sozial-u. Wirtschaftsgesch. Beih. 126. Stuttgart: Steiner.

Bill, J. & Clausen, L. (1999). *Maritime Topography and the Medieval Town.* Publ. Natmus. Stud. Arch. and Hist. 4. Copenhagen: National Museum.

Brandt, K. (2005). Die Schleswiger Landenge in der Wikingerzeit und im Mittelalter. In C. von Carnap-Bornheim & H. Friesinger (Eds.), *Wasserwege: Lebensadern – Trennungslinien. Grundprobleme der frühgeschichtlichen Entwicklung im mittleren Donauraum.* Schr. Arch. Landesmus. Ergr. 3 (pp. 269–288). Neumünster: Wachholtz.

Brandt, K. (2006). Portage at the base of Jutland during the Viking Period and the Middle Ages. In Chr. Westerdahl (Ed.), *The Significance of Portages.* BAR Internat. Ser. 1499 (pp. 53–63). Oxford: Archaeopress.

von Carnap-Bornheim, C. & Hilberg, V. (2005). Haithabu – ein frühstädtisches Zentrum in neuem Licht. *Arch. Nachrbl.*, 10, 465–471.

von Carnap-Bornheim, C. & Hilberg, V. (2007). Recent archaeological research in Haithabu. In J. Henning (Ed.), *Post-Roman Towns, Trade and Settlement in Europe and Byzantium 1. The Heirs of the Roman West.* Millennium studies in the culture and history of the first millennium C.E. 5/1 (pp. 199–218). Berlin & New York: de Gruyter.

Crumlin-Pedersen, O. (1976). Boot. In M. Müller-Wille, *Das Bootkammergrab von Haithabu.* Ber. Ausgr. Haithabu 8 (20–28). Neumünster: Wachholtz.

Crumlin-Pedersen, O. (1997). *Viking-Age Ships and Shipbuilding in Hedeby/Haithabu and Schleswig.* Ships & Boats of the North 1. Schleswig & Roskilde.

Crumlin-Pedersen, O. (1999). Ships as indicators of trade in Northern Europe 600–1200. In Bill & Clausen, 1999, pp. 11–20.

Ellmers, D. (1990). Die Verlagerung des Fernhandels vom öffentlichen Ufermarkt in die privaten Häuser der Kaufleute. *Lübecker Schr. Arch. u. Kulturgesch.* 20, 101–118.

Feveille, C. (2006). Ribe på nordsiden af åen, 8.–12. århundrede. In C. Feveille (Ed.), *Ribe Studier. Det ældste Ribe. Udgravninger på nordsiden af Ribe Å 1984–2000 1.1.* Jysk Ark. Selskabs skrifter 51 (pp. 13–63). Århus: Aarhus Universitetsforlag.

Geibig, A. (1999). Die Schwerter aus dem Hafen von Haithabu. *Ber. Ausgr. Haithabu 33* (pp. 9–91). Neumünster: Wachholtz.

Gripp, K. (1941). Die Entstehung der Landschaft um Haithabu. *Offa* 5, 37–64.

Grøn, O., et al. (1998). The Use of High Resolution Sub-Bottom Profilers for Geo-Archaeological Survey. Results from Jungshoved, Kerteminde Firth and Haithabu/Hedeby. In A. Wesse (Ed.), *Studien zur Archäologie des Ostseeraumes. Von der Eisenzeit zum Mittelalter* (pp. 151–160). Neumünster: Wachholtz.

Heinrich, D. (2006). Die Fischreste aus dem Hafen von Haithabu – Handaufgelesene Funde. *Ber. Ausgr. Haithabu 35* (pp. 157–239). Neumünster: Wachholtz.

Hilberg, V. (2003). Geophysikalische Prospektion des Jahres 2002 in Haithabu. *Arch. Schleswig/Ark. Slesvig* 10, 157–173.

Hilberg, V. (2007). Haithabu im 11. Jahrhundert. Auf der Suche nach dem Niedergang eines dänischen *emporiums* der Wikingerzeit. In M. Posselt, B. Zickgraf & C. Dobiat (Eds.), *Geophysik und Ausgrabung. Einsatz und Auswertung zerstörungsfreier Prospektion in der Archäologie.* Internat. Arch. Naturwiss. u. Technologie 6 (pp. 187–203). Rahden: Leidorf.

Hingst, H. (1958). Dykkerundersøgelser i havnen ved Hedeby. *Sønderjysk Månedsskr.* 1, 8–13.

Hingst, H. & Kersten, K. (1955). Die Tauchaktion vor Haithabu im Jahre 1953. *Germania* 33, 265–271.

Hirte, Chr. (1997). Logboat. In O. Crumlin-Pedersen, *Viking-Age Ships and Shipbuilding in Hedeby/Haithabu and Schleswig.* Ships & Boats of the North 1 (pp. 148–168). Schleswig & Roskilde.

Hüster Plogmann, H. (2006). Untersuchungen an Skelettresten von Säugetieren und Vögeln aus dem Hafen von Haithabu. *Ber. Ausgr. Haithabu 35* (pp. 25–156). Neumünster: Wachholtz.

Hybel, N. & Poulsen, B. (2007). *The Danish Resources c. 1000–1550. Growth and Recession.* Northern World 34. Leiden & Boston: Brill.

Hägg, I. (1991). *Die Textilfunde aus der Siedlung und aus den Gräbern von Haithabu. Beschreibung und Gliederung.* Ber. Ausgr. Haithabu 29. Neumünster: Wachholtz.

Jankuhn, H. (1986[8]). *Haithabu. Ein Handelsplatz der Wikingerzeit.* Neumünster: Wachholtz.

Jensen, S. (1991). *Ribe zur Wikingerzeit.* Ribe: Den Antikvariske Samling.

Jöns, H. & Müller-Wille, M. (2002). Der Ostseehandel. Schiffsverkehr und Warenströme. In W. Menghin & D. Planck (Eds.), *Menschen – Zeiten – Räume. Archäologie in Deutschland* (pp. 346–351). Stuttgart: Theiss.

Kalmring, S. (2010). *Der Hafen von Haithabu.* Ausgr. Haithabu 14. Neumünster: Wachholtz.

Kersten, K. (1954). Die Taucharbeiten im Hafen von Haithabu im Jahre 1953. *Stader Jahrb. N.F.* 44, 49–53.

Kramer, W. (1998/99). Neue Untersuchungen im Hafen von Haithabu. *Arch. Nachr. Schleswig-Holstein* 9/10, 90–118.

Kühn, H. J. (2004). Ein hochmittelalterlicher Fährprahm im Haddebyer Noor (Haithabu Wrack IV). In K. Brandt & H. J. Kühn (Eds.), *Der Prahm aus dem Hafen von Haithabu. Beiträge zu antiken und mittelalterlichen Flachbodenschiffen.* Schr. Arch. Landesmus. Erg. 2 (pp. 9–16). Neumünster: Wachholtz.

Köster, R. & Bonsen, U. (1970[2]). Die Schlei und ihre Anrainerlandschaften. In H. Schlenger, K. H. Paffen & R. Stewig (Eds.), *Schleswig-Holstein. Ein geographisch-landeskundlicher Exkursionsführer* (pp. 230–240). Kiel: Hirt.

Lüdtke, H. (1984). Die Entdeckung einer mittelalterlichen Kirche unter dem Marktplatz von Schleswig. *Arch. Korrbl.* 14, 111–117.

Lüdtke, H. (1997). Die archäologischen Untersuchungen unter dem Schleswiger Rathausmarkt. *Ausgr. Schleswig. Ber. u. Stud. 12* (pp. 9–84). Neumünster: Wachholtz.

Lund, J. (2004). Våben i vand. Om deponeringer i vikingetiden. *KUML*, 197–220.

Mührenberg, D. (1993). Der Markt zu Lübeck. Ergebnisse archäologischer Untersuchungen. *Lübecker Schr. Arch. u. Kulturgesch.* 23, 83–154.

Müller-Wille, M. (1988). Fremdgut und Import östlicher Provenienz in Schleswig-Holstein (9.–12. Jahrhundert). *Ber. RGK* 69, 740–783.

Radtke, Chr. (1999²). Haiðaby. In H. Beck et al. (Eds.), *Reallexikon der Germanischen Altertumskunde* (Vol. 13, pp. 363–381). Berlin & NewYork: de Gruyter.

Resi, H. G. (1979). *Die Specksteinfunde aus Haithabu.* Ber. Ausgr. Haithabu 14. Neumünster: Wachholtz.

Resi, H. G. (1990). *Die Wetz- und Schleifsteine aus Haithabu.* Ber. Ausgr. Haithabu 28. Neumünster: Wachholtz.

Schietzel, K. (1980). Untersuchung im Hafen von Haithabu und Bergung eines wikingerzeitlichen Schiffswracks. *Arch. Advertiser*, 94–103.

Schietzel, K. (1981). Stand der siedlungsarchäologischen Forschung in Haithabu – Ergebnisse und Probleme. *Ber. Ausgr. Haithabu 16.* Neumünster: Wachholtz.

Schietzel, K. (1983 pp.). *Berichte über die Ausgrabungen in Haithabu* (Vol. 1–36). Neumünster: Wachholtz.

Schietzel, K. (1984a). Hafenanlagen von Haithabu. In H. Jankuhn, K. Schietzel & H. Reichstein (Eds.), *Archäologische und naturwissenschaftliche Untersuchungen an ländlichen und frühstädtischen Siedlungen im deutschen Küstengebiet vom 5. Jahrhundert v.Chr. bis zum 11. Jahrhundert n.Chr. 2. Handelsplätze des frühen und hohen Mittelalters* (pp. 184–191). Weinheim: Acta Humanoria.

Schietzel, K. (1984b). Land- und Seewege im Bereich der Schleswiger Landenge. In H. Jankuhn, K. Schietzel & H. Reichstein (Eds.), *Archäologische und naturwissenschaftliche Untersuchungen an ländlichen und frühstädtischen Siedlungen im deutschen Küstengebiet vom 5. Jahrhundert v.Chr. bis zum 11. Jahrhundert n.Chr. 2. Handelsplätze des frühen und hohen Mittelalters* (pp. 97–99). Weinheim: Acta Humanoria.

Schietzel, K. & Crumlin-Pedersen, O. (1980), Havnen i Hedeby. *Skalk* 3, 3–10.

Schou Jørgensen, M. (1998). Den berømte bro. *Skalk* 5, 5–11.

Schultze, J. (2008). *Haithabu – Die Siedlungsgrabungen I. Methoden und Möglichkeiten der Auswertung.* Ausgr. Haithabu 13. Neumünster: Wachholtz.

Schön, V. (1995). *Die Mühlsteine von Haithabu und Schleswig. Ein Beitrag zur Entwicklungsgeschichte des mittelalterlichen Mühlenwesens in Nordeuropa.* Ber. Ausgr. Haithabu 31. Neumünster: Wachholtz.

Sindbæk, S. M. (2005). *Ruter og Rutinisering. Vikingetidens Fjernhandel i Nordeuropa.* København: Multivers Academic.

Spichal, U. (2005). Wege übers Wasser. Hölzerne Fluss- und Sumpfbrücken in der Vor- und Frühgeschichte. In H. Eilbracht, V. Brieske & B. Grodde (Eds.), *Itinera Archaeologica. Vom Neolithikum bis in die frühe Neuzeit.* Internat. Arch. Stud. honoraria 22 (pp. 271–280). Rahden: Verlag Marie Leidorf.

Steppuhn, P. (1998). *Die Glasfunde von Haithabu.* Ber. Ausgr. Haithabu 32. Neumünster: Wachholtz.

Steuer, H. (2006). Waffenopfer. In H. Beck et al. (Eds.), *Reallexikon der Germanischen Altertumskunde* (Vol. 33, pp. 21–46). Berlin & NewYork: de Gruyter.

Stümpel, H. & Borth-Hoffmann, B. (1983). Seismische Untersuchungen im Hafen von Haithabu. *Ber. Ausgr. Haithabu 18* (pp. 9–28). Neumünster: Wachholtz.

Unverzagt, W. & Schuldt, E. (1963). *Teterow. Ein slawischer Burgwall in Mecklenburg.* Deutsche Akad. Wiss. Berlin. Schr. Sektion Vor- u. Frühgesch. 13. Berlin: Akademie Verlag.

Vogel, V. (1997). Schleswig – Stadt und Hafen im 11./12. Jahrhundert. In G. de Boe & F. Verhaeghe (Eds.), *Travel Technology & Organisation in Medieval Europe. Papers of the 'Medieval Europe Brugge 1997' Conference 8* . I.A.P. Rapporten 8 (pp. 91–99). Zellik: IAP.

Vogel, V. (2002). Archäologische Belege für Fernkontakte der Stadt Schleswig im 11. – 13. Jahrhundert. In K. Brandt, M. Müller-Wille & Chr. Radtke (Eds.), *Haithabu und die frühe Stadtentwicklung im nördlichen Europa.* Schr. Arch. Landesmus. 8 (pp. 367–378). Neumünster: Wachholtz.

Wamers, E. (1984). Eine Zungenfibel aus dem Hafen von Haithabu. *Ber. Ausgr. Haithabu 19* (pp. 63–127). Neumünster: Wachholtz.

Westphal, F. (2006). *Holzfunde von Haithabu.* Ausgr. Haithabu 11. Neumünster: Wachholtz.

Westphalen, P. (1989). *Die Eisenschlacken von Haithabu. Ein Beitrag zur Geschichte des Schmiedehandwerks in Nordeuropa.* Ber. Ausgr. Haithabu 26. Neumünster: Wachholtz.

Westphalen, P. (2002). *Die Eisenfunde von Haithabu.* Ausgr. Haithabu 10. Neumünster: Wachholtz.

The Viðey Rune-stick: Iceland's Earliest Runic Inscription

JAMES E. KNIRK

ABSTRACT

In 1993 a rune-stick probably dating to the 1000s or (early) 1100s was found during archaeological excavations on Viðey. The inscription was published concisely in 1994 by the author of this article, and his partially free-hand drawings in that presentation have served as documentation ever since. In 2003 new readings, in particular of the B side, were published by Þórgunnur Snædal. In the present article the author documents with photographs that those new readings have no empirical basis and that the reading must be: **–ab:fer:kui:?–** / –**(u)el(þi):f(uþ)**– / **???ate:ast:**. Although there are various possibilities for understanding individual words, there is as yet no satisfactory interpretation of this decimated text. The last word is probably *ást*, "love", a not infrequent topic in runic inscriptions. In addition, nicks observed in the upper edges of the A and C sides show that also the D side, chipped off in medieval times, originally had runes.

Keywords: Runic inscription, rune-stick, Iceland, Viðey monastery, late Viking Age, love.

Archaeological excavations were carried out from 1987 until 1995 on the island of Viðey in the bay just north of Reykjavík in an attempt to localize and examine the remains of a monastery well known from medieval written sources (see Steinunn Kristjánsdóttir, 1995; Margrét Hallgrímsdóttir, 1998; cf. 1991, pp. 92-101, 132). Founded by the chieftain Þorvaldr Gizurarson in 1226, the Augustinian cloister quickly became one of the wealthiest monastic establishments in Iceland. In 1539, during the turmoil of the Reformation, the order was dissolved, its wealth confiscated and the properties claimed as royal holdings. At least some buildings were demolished that year, but others may have been left standing, since the monastery (as it was still called) was in use as a hospice from around 1600 until the mid-1700s. In 1751 the fiscal governor of Iceland, Skúli Magnússon, moved to Viðey and soon built a large stone house there, Viðeyjarstofa, just east of the remains of the medieval church and graveyard.

The dig, begun by Mjöll Snæsdóttir and Sigurður Bergsteinsson in 1987, was taken over by Margrét Hallgrímsdóttir in 1988, and she was joined by Steinunn Kristjánsdóttir in 1994. The excavation concentrated for some years on the remains of a large farm building of passage type north of Viðeyjarstofa. Among other finds, rosary beads and also wax tablets from the 1400s with religious texts in Icelandic, Latin and Dutch (cf. Margrét Hallgrímsdóttir, 1991, pp. 102-132) associated the building with the cloister. In 1994 remains of medieval walls with approximately the same east-west orientation as the medieval church were found beneath the walls of the passage in the farm building; these were identified by Steinunn (1995, pp. 34-36, 45-46) as contemporary with the medieval church and most likely walls of part of the monastery, whereas the farm building of passage type could for the most part have been a post-Reformation structure. About this, however, there is disagreement. Margrét considered all the excavated buildings, and the church, to be parts of the monastery. Based on aerial photographs and georadar data, she identified, in addition, a structure situated south of Viðeyjarstofa, in an area which has not yet been excavated, as a further building belonging to the monastery.

In 1993, levels beneath the farm building of passage type were excavated. Remains of a large hall with a long central fireplace were found (Steinunn Kristjánsdóttir, 1995, pp. 41-45, 51-52), and on 29 July a fragmentary rune-stick was unearthed on a floor of the hall by an American archaeologist named Skía; in spite of diligent efforts, no further fragments of the stick were found. The hall, typical of the Viking Age, surely predates the 13th-century monastery, thus making this piece most likely the earliest runic find yet made in Iceland.

In August 1994, I examined the stick and its inscription during a few hours in Reykjavík. Although I did not have a binocular microscope, a good source of light, or a macro lens for the camera, the results of the examination were sufficient for a first scholarly reading, which was formulated in my report of 22 August 1994. There, based on Margrét's preliminary estimation, the find was dated to the 1100s or 1200s. Later that year a one-page simplification of the report appeared in *Nytt om runer*. My more or less free-hand drawings have for fifteen years been the documentation used in all treatments of the inscription (see Fig. 1).

The stick (find no. V93-372) is only a modest fragment, 53 mm. long, 17 mm. wide and 7 mm. thick (maximum measurements). It is apparently broken in both ends and has runes preserved on three sides; a splinter has removed the lower part of all runes on the one narrow side, and the surface of the fourth side, also a narrow side, is entirely chipped away. Most damage is not new but medieval. Line A is on a broad side and is best preserved; line B is directly "under" A and runs in the same direction. Line C, which has an open space at the end, is on the other broad side and runs in the opposite direction, so the stick has to be flipped end for end. The runes are cut from edge to edge on each side.

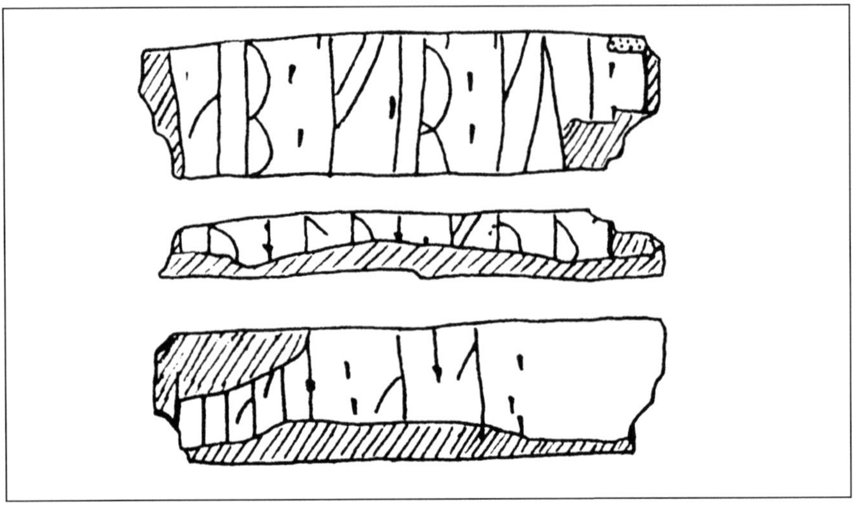

Fig. 1. Free-hand drawing of the Viðey rune-stick in Knirk's report from 1994.

My reading of the fragmentary text with suggestions for possible interpretations was as follows. Here a question mark indicates remains of an unidentifiable rune, parentheses indicate that the reading of the enclosed rune is uncertain, and a dash represents a probable lacuna; the final punctuation mark in line C (read with the stick turned end for end) consists actually of three dots.

A. –**ab:fer:kui:?**–

B. –(**u**)**el**(**þe:**)**f**(**uþ?**)–

C. –**???at**(**e**)**:ast:**

Line A might possibly be in Latin: *fer qui/cui,* "Bring! He/to him who", or *aufer/abfer* ..., "Take away! ...", whereas line B may end with **fuþ** and thus be the beginning of the rune-row, *fuþ[ork ...]*; line C ends with the word *ást,* "love".

The rune-stick from Viðey has been mentioned or discussed several times during the past fifteen years. It was presented in passing by Steinunn Kristjánsdóttir (1995, pp. 38-39), and there the dating was pushed back 100 years, to the "11th or 12th century". François-Xavier Dillmann (1996, pp. 51-55) also discussed the inscription, dating it to the 10th or 11th century with reference to Margrét Hallgrímsdóttir's published report for the 1993 excavation (1994, pp. 8-11). Margrét presented the rune-stick in an article about the Viðey excavation (1998, pp. 644-646), dating it as in her excavation report, describing it and its text as fragmentary, and stating that the text ends with the word *ást,* "love". With reference to letters written to her by Þórgunnur Snædal on 8 and 9 December 1997, she assumed that love was the topic of the entire text, which was perhaps in poetic form, and mentioned speculation as to whether it might have been a confession of love, a proposal, or even a love-charm.

In an overview from 2000 of Icelandic runic inscriptions, Þórgunnur Snædal mentioned the Viðey stick (pp. 17-18), and three years later published preliminarily her complete corpus of Icelandic runic inscriptions (2003; discussion of the Viðey find on pp. 34-35). The layer in which the stick was found is dated to the 10th or 11th century, while the characters are said to be typical Viking Age runes that indicate an 11th-century date (probably due to the dotted *e*-rune). She agrees basically with my reading of the two broad sides (reading **ab:fer:kui:** and **??ati:ast**) but has a new reading of the narrow B side: **iiluek??**. Although she calls the piece a fragment, no lacunae are indicated, and she claims that the beginning of the inscription is preserved on side A. She doubts my interpretation of this line as possibly a Latin text due to the dating of the find layer. Runic inscriptions in Latin are known from the 12th century at the earliest, and then are as a rule found in churches or on ecclesiastical items.

The Viðey rune-stick was apparently found under, not in, an ecclesiastical setting. Although the monastery was founded in 1226, there was, according to Bishop Páll Jónsson's list of churches in Skálholt's bishopric, a church on the island from around 1200 (Margrét Hallgrímsdóttir, 1991, pp. 91-93; cf. 1998, p. 649). The church may have been built at this particular site because those living there at the time were devout Christians. There may then be some "continuity" between what one finds under and what one finds in the monastery layers. There is thus no real problem with finding a runic text containing Latin in this setting, near a church and a monastery. It can be noted, in addition, that many of the runic inscriptions with Latin text found on the Wharf (Bryggen) in Bergen, definitely a secular setting, date to the late 12th century.

The problem is the dating, which has been pushed back 100 to 200 years in relation to Margrét's preliminary estimate in a letter to me of 24 January 1994, on which my interpretation was based. Pollen analysis of samples taken in 1992 indicated habitation on Viðey as early as 900, and the dating of the initial construction of the hall was subsequently revised to the 10th century apparently to accord better with the results of the pollen analysis. At any rate, although there does not seem to be much general agreement between the main archaeologists who participated in the excavation concerning the dating of the various buildings in the farm complex of passage type and their relationship to one another, there is total agreement that the large hall with a long central fireplace is to be dated to the time before the monastery.

According to the excavation report and the original documentation, there were a total of four layers of floor in the large hall, and the stick was found slightly above a thin floor layer, number three counting from the top down-

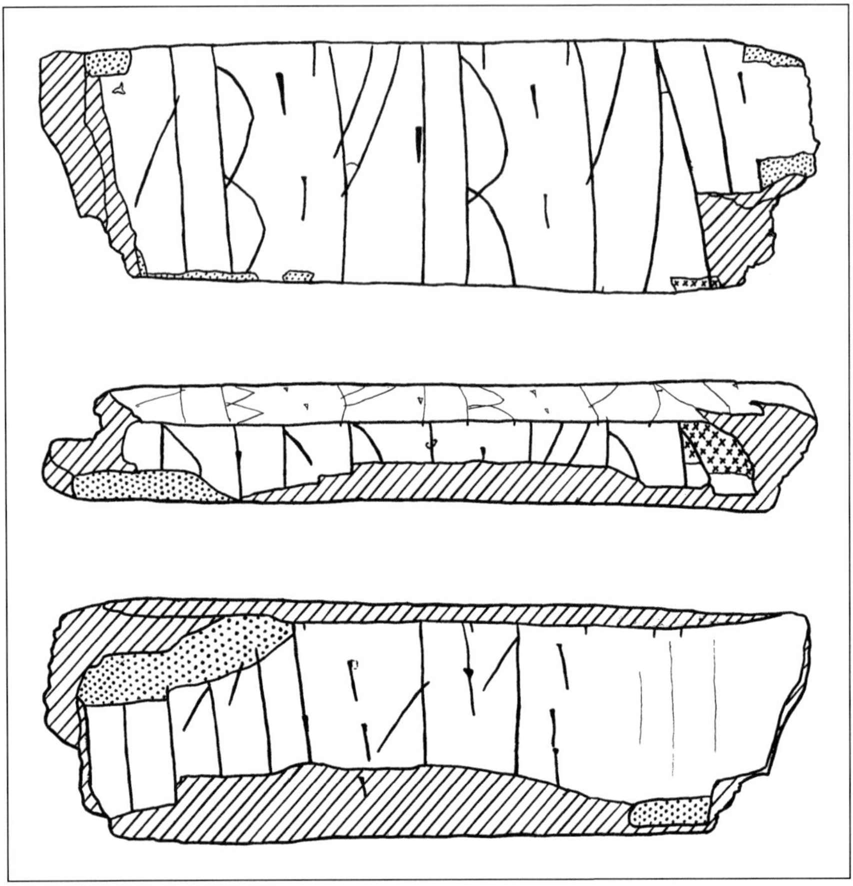

Fig. 2. Documentation drawing from 2009/2010 of the three inscription-bearing sides of the Viðey rune-stick (× 2/1). Medieval damage is indicated by parallel hatching, damage in connection with the excavation by dots, and post-1994 damage by small *x*s. Draftsman: J. E. Knirk.

ward, at the bottom of a fill layer. It might be part of the fill layer and belong to the construction of the second, next uppermost floor. Until possible further publications clear up the archaeological and dating problems, it is prudent to accept Steinunn's broad dating of the hall to the 10th to12th centuries (1995, p. 42). The rune-stick may date to somewhat late in the period.

In 2009, I again inspected the rune-stick from Viðey, this time with my own technical equipment (binocular microscope, fiber optic light source, digital camera with macro lens). The purpose of this paper is to present new drawings (Fig. 2) of the inscription based on my photographs from 2009 (and

Fig. 3. Viðey rune-stick, side A (× 2/1). © Museum of Cultural History, University of Oslo; photographer: J. E. Knirk.

1994) and to document the reading with the photographs themselves. In the following, observations from Þórgunnur's report concerning her reading of the inscription, sent by letter to Margrét on 8 January 1998 (now in the archives at Árbær Open Air Museum), are sometimes referred to.

There are only minor changes in the new documentation drawing concerning the exact form of runes, e.g., the twig on the *a*-rune is straight, not curved as it was in my free-hand drawing, for instance on rune 1 on side A (runes are hereafter designated as, e.g., A:1). Knife cuts representing remains of a stave are clearly visible along or rather in the very edge of the vertical break at the end of the line A and at the beginning of line C; the stick broke precisely here because the surface fibers had been severed by the carving of the stave and the wood weakened. Remains of unidentifiable runes must be indicated here (A:9, C:1), as well as probable lacunae, in any transliteration. Although the edge at the left end of side A is fairly smooth, not rough like the break in the other end, it is not likely – due to the irregular shape – that this is an original end; it may have been a medieval break that was worn smooth before the stick came into the ground. Thus the reading of side A is still (see Fig. 3): **–ab:fer:kui:?–**. The dot on A:4, which slightly missed the stave, as well as the dots in punctuation marks illustrate the somewhat triangular shape, wider at the top, of the

Fig. 4. Viðey rune-stick, side B (× 2/1). © Museum of Cultural History, University of Oslo; photographer: J. E. Knirk.

impression of the point of the knife. This same shape is seen as a dot on B:2 and C:6, which thus are confirmed as definite *e*-runes.

Side B, which is only 6 mm. wide, is still the most difficult to read (see Fig. 4). B:2 **e** is 5 mm. tall and is thus preserved in almost full height; all of the runes here lack 1-3 mm. at the base. On B:1, the branch from the top of the stave at an angle downward to the right and then vertical is indeed thin, but nonetheless clear (Þórgunnur's report mentions the relatively long distance from this stave to the next rune). The general shape indicates a **u**, but this reading is not entirely certain (**b**, **r**, or **þ** are other less likely possibilities). The form of the probable *u*-rune would, however, not correspond to the somewhat exceptional upside-down V-shape of the *u*-rune on side A; the same is true for B:7 (**u**). A reading of B:3 as **þ**, with a pocket that goes from top to bottom of the stave, appears likely, but again here, the alternatives are **u** and less likely **b** or **r**. That the pocket extends over the entire length of the stave might be due to the tiny vertical space available on this side (6 mm.). B:5, which high up has small holes (damage?) adjacent to either side of the stave, must be considered a slightly uncertain **i** since so little of the rune is preserved. The following upper dot of a word-separator (considered possible in Þórgunnur's report) has the shape of the imprint of a knife point. In her report, Þórgunnur states that there appear to be two branches on B:6, but that the lower one would not reach the stave before its base; therefore she disregards the lower branch as "an additional stroke and not part of the rune", reading **k**. B:6 is, however, a definite **f** (see Fig. 5, *left*), whose somewhat unusual form, with the lower branch probably extending almost to the base, is surely dictated by the minimal vertical space available.

There is post-1994 damage at the end of side B (also visible at the very bottom of A:7 **u**). Much of the surface from the stave of B:8 to the edge has flaked off, removing the upper three-fourths of the remains of the rune. On the photograph from 1994 (Fig. 5, *right*), a bow is clear, and there and in what still

Fig. 5. Viðey rune-stick, side B: *Left,* the last runes, **f(uþ)**, on a photograph from 2009 (after damage); *right,* the last runes on a photograph from 1994 (before damage, and with some color distortion). © Museum of Cultural History, University of Oslo; photographer: J. E. Knirk.

Fig. 6. Viðey rune-stick, side C (× 2/1). © Museum of Cultural History, University of Oslo; photographer: J. E. Knirk.

now exists of the bottom of the bow, a cut back toward the stave is visible (cf. Fig. 2), indicating most likely the pocket of a **þ**. Any remains of a stave along or in the edge of the medieval break at the end of the line were lost in connection with the post-1994 damage. The reading is then: –(**u**)**el**(**þi:**)**f**(**uþ**)–.

On side C, in the area broken off along the bottom of the runes, a third knife impression in the word-separator is visible, and thus both punctuation marks on this side have three dots (simplified in the transliteration here, however, to a colon). The reading is then (see Fig. 6): –**???ate:ast:**. It should be mentioned that extremely faint traces of three vertical lines, not necessarily cuts, were found in the blank area after line C. They are, however, so faint and the surface there so well preserved that they cannot represent damaged remains of the present inscription.

There are five short cuts or nicks at the upper edge of side A, each 2-2.5 mm. long (see Fig. 2; the last one is at the edge of the modern break above the final word-separator). I had observed the first three in 1994 (see Fig. 1), whereas Þórgunnur in her report mentioned only the third one. At the upper edge of side B there were six nicks each less than 1 mm. in length, and on side C, five similar ones (see Fig. 2). The explanation of the nicks on side B is obvious: the base of the staves of the runes A:3-7 **f**, **e**, **r** (and its lower branch too), **k** and **u** all continue over the edge. This is the natural result of carving runes up to the very edge of a wooden surface. The only explanation for the nicks at the top edge of sides A and C is that the D side between them also had runes, even though none are now visible (see Fig. 7).

In general, it seems that cuts over the edge at the base of runes naturally are somewhat longer than those at the top. The longer cuts occur on side A, indicating perhaps that they represent the bottom of runes on side D, in which case the runes there ran in the same direction as those on sides A and B. This possible arrangement, however, causes problems for determining the order in which

Fig. 7. Viðey rune-stick, side D (× 2/1). © Museum of Cultural History, University of Oslo; photographer: J. E. Knirk.

to read the lines. Lines D, A (in between), and B run in the same direction, but sides D and B are narrow and therefore not well suited for the first line of an inscription. An explanation might be that line C was carved first and that the other three lines were then added, running in the opposite direction and in an order which cannot now be determined. Line C may in addition have been carved by a different hand, since both punctuation marks consist of three dots; the runic forms, however, do not otherwise suggest a different carver.

It is almost impossible to find a cohesive Old Norse interpretation of side A. For instance: the runes –**ab** could be the end of several words, among others *kamb* (accusative of "comb", with the standard dropping of nasals before certain consonants in runic orthography) or even *lamb*, "lamb" (but for both of these one would expect to find remains of a branch of the *k*- or *l*-rune at the beginning of the line), **fer** could be the verb form *fer* or *ferr*, "travel/go" in the 1st, 2nd, or 3rd person, and **kui** could be the word *kví*, "pen, fold (for sheep)"; but there is no obvious relationship between these words, other than the syntactically strange "lamb goes pen". Þórgunnur's suggestion in a letter from December 1997 referred to by Margrét (see above) that the text might be in verse, maybe even a love-charm, would perhaps allow for poetic syntax of this type. Complicating factors are for instance that –**ab** could in addition stand for *-af*, that **kui** could represent the female name *Gói*, that the runic sequences may be parts of compounds, and even that interpunction does not necessarily indicate word division.

A possible interpretation of side A as a text in Latin was presented in 1994. That interpretation is, however, somewhat suspect, since the text does not consist of a Christian liturgical quotation, which is the usual theme of such inscriptions. Furthermore, since the dating of the stick has apparently been pushed back to probably the 11th or (early) 12th century, the inscription would most likely be too early for it to contain a Latin text.

Alternatives are myriad for readings of the runic remains on side B, but there is no obvious Old Norse interpretation. Still, the possibility of reading the runes after the word-separator as **fuþ** seems strong. This does not mean, however, that we have a *fuþork* or rune-row here. As is well known, Old

Norse *fuð* was a designation for "vagina" or "anus", so there may be ways to connect the reading of side B with the identifiable word on side C. The linguistic content of the badly preserved runes at the beginning of side C cannot even be guessed at, whereas the last word on this side, **ast**, can with great certainty be interpreted as *ást,* "love".

In summary: New inspections in 2009 of the rune-stick from Viðey confirmed in almost all respects the reading from 1994, although some minor points had to be revised. Þórgunnur's new reading of side B was rejected; among other things, the **f** is certain and cannot be read as a **k** by arbitrarily disregarding the second branch. In addition, it was established that there were runes on the fourth side, but that they have been lost. Additional runes were definitely lost in at least two and probably five lacunae. New documentation drawings were prepared, and various difficult readings were documented photographically. The importance of good technical equipment and repeated examinations was demonstrated. The reading is:

A. **–ab:fer:kui:?–**

B. **–(u)el(þi:)f(uþ)–**

C. **–???ate:ast:** [Both punctuation marks consist of three dots.]

D. [Nicks in the upper edge of sides A and C representing remains of staves and perhaps branches of runes that have been lost.]

The runes in lines A (on a broad side), B, and perhaps D run in the same direction, but the order in which the lines are to be read is uncertain; the runes in line C (also on a broad side) run in the opposite direction.

Even though the inscription on the rune-stick from Viðey still has not been interpreted satisfactorily and the archaeological dating has not yet been firmly established, the new photographs and drawings published here should provide a firm foundation for further interpretive work. The only part that must be considered almost certain is the interpretation of the last word as *ást*, "love".

BIBLIOGRAPHY

Archival documentation of the Viðey excavation and finds in the City Museum of Reykjavík, division Árbær Open Air Museum (Árbæjarsafn).

Archival documentation of the Viðey rune-stick in the Runic Archives, Museum of Cultural History, University of Oslo.

Dillmann, F.-X. (1996). Les runes dans la littérature norroise: À propos d'une découverte archéologique en Islande. *Proxima Thulé*, 2, 51-89.

Knirk, J. E. (1994). Runepinnen fra Viðey, Island. *Nytt om runer*, 9, 20.

Margrét Hallgrímsdóttir (1991). Rannsóknir í Viðey: Vaxspjöld frá 15. öld finnast við uppgröft rústa Viðeyjarklausturs. *Árbók hins íslenzka fornleifafélags*, 1990, 91-132.

Margrét Hallgrímsdóttir (1994). *Viðey: Fornleifarannsókn 1993: Áfangaskýrsla*. Skýrslur Árbæjarsafns, 38. Reykjavík: Árbæjarsafn.

Margrét Hallgrímsdóttir (1998). Trú, von og kærleikur forfeðranna í Viðey: Um fornleifarannsóknina í Viðey. *Afmælisrit: Davíð Oddsson fimmtugur 17. janúar 1998* (pp. 639-668). Reykjavík: Bókafélagið.

Steinunn Kristjánsdóttir (1995). Klaustureyjan á Sundum: Yfirlit Viðeyjarrannsókna. *Árbók hins íslenzka fornleifafélags*, 1994, 29-52.

Þórgunnur Snædal (2000). Íslenskar rúnir í norrænu ljósi. *Árbók hins íslenzka fornleifafélags*, 1998, 5-33.

Þórgunnur Snædal (2003). Rúnaristur á Íslandi. *Árbók hins íslenzka fornleifafélags*, 2000-2001, 5-68.

Excavations at the Viking Age Settlement of Hofstaðir in North-Eastern Iceland

GAVIN LUCAS

ABSTRACT

This paper discusses the recent excavations at the Viking settlement of Hofstaðir in the north-east of Iceland. The site was originally excavated in the early twentieth century and became renowned as a type site for pagan temples. Between 1991 and 2002 the site was re-investigated, resulting in a much richer understanding of its history and development. Its occupation spanned about 90 years between the mid 10th and early 11th century and within that time, various structures were built, repaired and abandoned; at the centre of the settlement is a large aisled hall, nearly 40 m long and represents one of only a few monumental halls known from Iceland. The building is interpreted as a specialized feasting hall used seasonally during the summer months based on various unusual architectural features as well as the presence of numerous cattle skulls exhibiting characteristics indicative of ritualized slaughter and display.

Keywords: Hofstaðir, Iceland, temple, ritual, feasting, chieftain.

INTRODUCTION

The site of Hofstaðir first entered the archaeological literature at the turn of the 20th century, through one of the first antiquarian surveys of Northern Iceland (Friðriksson, 1994). The remains of an oblong turf structure in the homefield of the modern farm, were known as a "temple ruin", and caught special attention for its sheer size as well as its place name. Soon after, Hofstaðir became the scene of the first large-scale excavation in Iceland in 1908 – the results "confirming" the nature of the site as a Viking temple, the first to be identified in Northern Europe (Bruun & Jónsson, 1909, 1911; Bruun, 1928). The 1908 excavation revealed two principal structures at Hofstaðir (Fig.1). One was the "temple-ruin" itself, a huge hall-like building which was divided in two: a huge "banqueting-hall" (marked AB on his plan) and, abutting it on the northern end, a much smaller room, which the excavators believed to have been the inner sanctuary where the idols were kept (C). The building

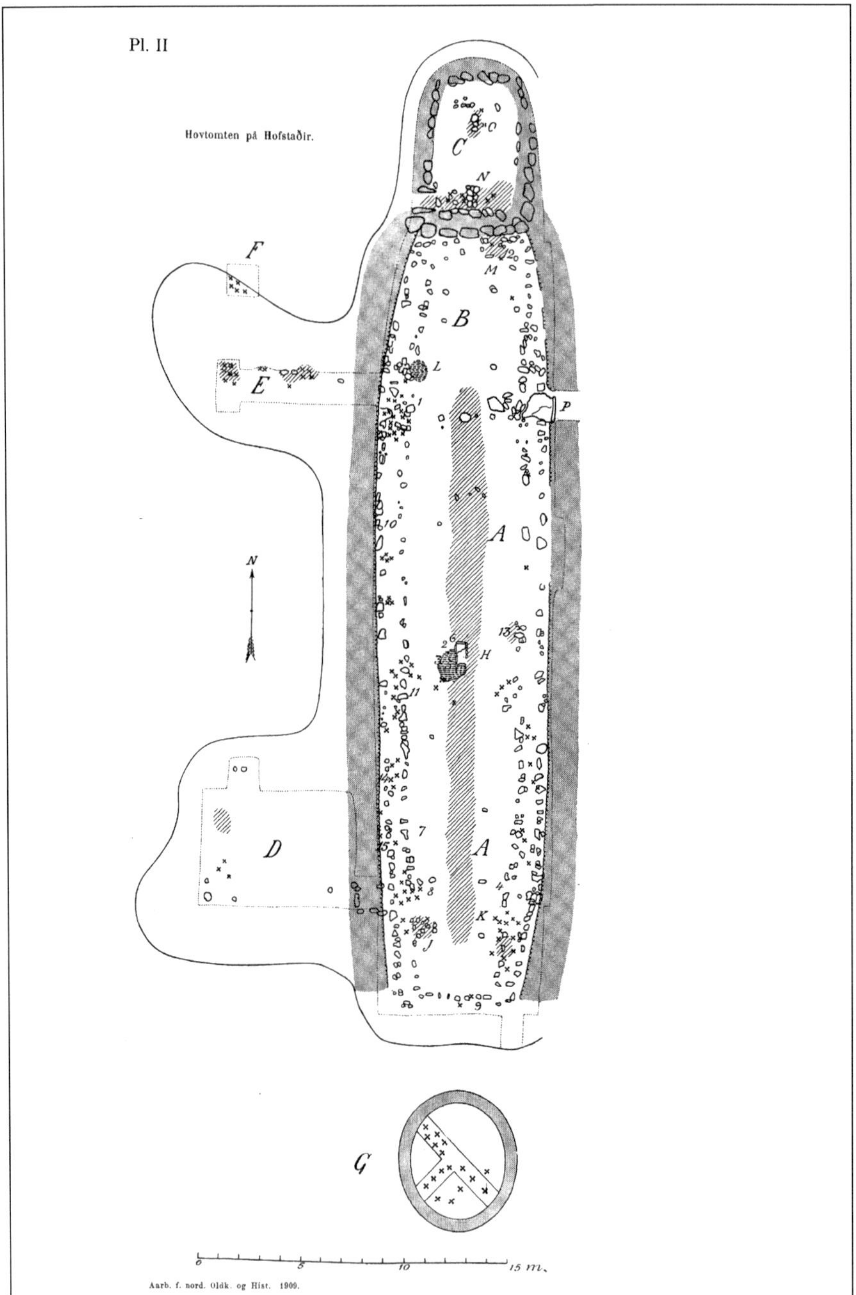

Fig. 1. Plan of Hofstaðir, 1908 (source: Bruun & Jónsson, 1909, Plate II; Bruun, 1928,40).

was oriented from north to south but on its western side there were cultural layers that were not clearly identified by the excavators, but were thought possibly to be the remains of two further rooms (marked E and D). The other principal structure was a small circular or orbital ruin (G), situated about 9 m south of the gable end of the great hall. Two diagonal test trenches were dug inside this ruin and they revealed that it was a hole full of ash, fire-cracked stones and animal bones. The excavators were perplexed by this feature, but suggested that it could have served for dumping rubbish, although they found the form of the hole to be surprisingly regular. They concluded that the most plausible explanation was that this strange hole had been used for rubbish after great feasts in the temple.

Since the publication of the 1908 excavation, the Hofstaðir hall was widely referred to as remains of a Viking Age temple in important works of synthesis in Nordic archaeology and history (e.g. Arbman & Stenberger, 1935, 207-8; Shetelig & Falk, 1937, 422). Its impact on Nordic culture historical literature was significant during the first half of the twentieth century, a theme which certainly warrants retrospection, although this is a topic that will not be pursued in this paper. Indeed, the importance of the site was soon to be questioned; decades later (in 1939), the first farm sites from the Viking and medieval periods in Iceland were excavated with more modern methods (Stenberger, 1943; also see Vésteinsson, 2004). This was not only a breakthrough regarding the establishment of new archaeological evidence for ancient Nordic architecture and its development, but also, one of the surprising results were the striking similarities between the temple at Hofstaðir and the newly uncovered ordinary farm dwelling remains. Another breaking point in Icelandic archaeology was the thorough revision of the previous approach to pagan religion in the Viking Age. The various alleged evidence for ritual sites were refuted – except for Hofstaðir. The sheer size of the hall was considered exceptional and demanding explanation, as well as a strange pit associated with the hall, full of ash and bone. After being partially re-excavated it was suggested to have served for ceremonial cooking at the temple-farm of Hofstaðir (Olsen, 1965).

Towards the end of the 20th century, a new generation of archaeologists in Iceland was engaged in a lively debate on the role of the sagas in archaeology. This topic became the subject of research, and the scene of a new theoretical dimension, where not only sagas, but also popular explanations, place-names and legends were regarded as having been important agents in the dating and identification of archaeological evidence (Friðriksson, 1994). During this period, earlier methods and results were questioned and some sites re-excavated or re-interpreted. Eventually, attention turned towards Hofstaðir and its alleged role as a place for ritual gathering and feasting. Hofstaðir was in fact a type-site for all the problems inherited from the research tradition of the last century:

the site was first "known" as a temple site, the farm name appears to refer to a temple, and the structures had first been thought to fit temple descriptions in the sagas. On the other hand, the archaeological record of the site was weak. For example, the site had simply been presumed to date to the heathen period in Iceland. It was also assumed that the pit and the hall were contemporary. Earlier excavations were carried out before scientific methods of dating were introduced or had become standard. Traditional dating methods such as finds typology were only of limited use as the objects found were both few and non-descript. In addition, as the digging was concentrated on the inside of the buildings, the general stratigraphy of the site was not examined. In 1990, preparations for a re-excavation of Hofstaðir were started.

In 1991 a research programme was initiated with the aim of shedding light on these and other un-answered questions of Icelandic temple-archaeology. A large number of alleged temple sites in the north of Iceland were surveyed and the Hofstaðir site was mapped in detail. The following year a limited excavation was carried out at Hofstaðir with the primary aim to date the ruin and examine the evidence for its function. It was confirmed that the site was indeed from the 9th–11th century. Subsequently, attention was turned to the cooking pit. In 1995 the trenches from 1908 – which had been also re-excavated in 1965 – were emptied and it was discovered that the feature was not a cooking pit but in fact a sunken hut or pithouse, which had later been filled with midden deposits (Friðriksson & Vésteinsson, 1997). Although the ritual question has never been abandoned, it became clear that Hofstaðir was ideal for further research into the settlement period, including not just the habitation remains, but also their environmental context. What was the settlement process? How did the first generations of Icelanders survive? What was their impact on their environment? With these questions in mind, a new large-scale multi-disciplinary, and multi-national project was launched which conducted an annual season of excavation at the site for the next seven years (1996–2002).

Now, after a decade of excavation and off-site environmental work, the site has renewed its role in Icelandic archaeology along multiple paths: as the largest known settlement from the Viking period in Iceland; becoming the first total excavation of a farm from the settlement period using high resolution excavation and recording methods; part of the first regional landscape project; and hosting the first archaeological fieldschool in the country. The results of this project are presented in detail in the site monograph (see Lucas, 2009), so only a review of selected aspects will be presented here. In the next section, a brief summary of the occupational sequence will be given, followed by a recapitulation of the more unusual and in some ways, unique aspects to the site and the interpretations they suggest.

Period	Phase	Date*	Structures/Activity
Viking	I	c. AD 940[t/r]	AB, G, A5
	II	c. AD 980[r]	AB (incl. E1 & D2) A2, A4, C2, E2, D1
	III	c. AD 1030[t]	Collapse, some re-use as hay storage
Medieval	IV	c. AD 1070[t]	Aeolian accumulation
	V	c. AD 1300[t]	C1
Post-medieval	VI	c. AD 1477[t]	Aeolian accumulation
	VII	c. AD 1850[a d]	A1, A3, C3, Bruun excavation
*Source: t = tephra, r = radiocarbon, d = documents, a = artefacts			

Table 1. Summary of site phasing, with dates showing the start of each phase.

OUTLINE OF THE OCCUPATIONAL SEQUENCE

The archaeological remains within the excavation area have been broadly divided into three periods, and within those seven sub-periods or phases based on stratigraphy, tephrachronology and radiocarbon dates (Table 1). As is evident from the table, the Viking period (Phases I-III) covers a short time span, but it is also the most intensive in terms of archaeological activity. It is unlikely that the division presented here (particularly of Phase I and II) represents a major, synchronized period of building activity, but rather the structures may have all been added piecemeal – and in many cases abandoned piecemeal. In short, the phasing may be misleading as to the chronological development of the site (i.e. over-emphasizing the split between an 'early' and 'late' phase), but the alternative (subsuming all change into one phase) is equally if not more misleading. Ideally, more phase divisions would have been preferable, but methodologically this was impossible to do with any confidence. The medieval and later periods (Phases IV-VII) see much less activity and are dominated by periods of aeolian accumulation (Phases IV & VI) interrupted by a minor re-use of the ruin in the 14th century (Phase V) and then farm outbuildings in the 19th and 20th century as well as Bruun's excavation of 1908 (Phase VII). These later phases will not be discussed further in this paper, whose focus lies with the Viking Age remains. It is clear from the sequence that the duration of Viking Age occupation at the site (Phases I-II) was relatively short-lived – *c.* 90 years or a century at most. Both radiocarbon and especially dated volcanic tephras provide these very tight chronological brackets. Within that time however, the site underwent various transformations which are outlined below (see Fig. 2).

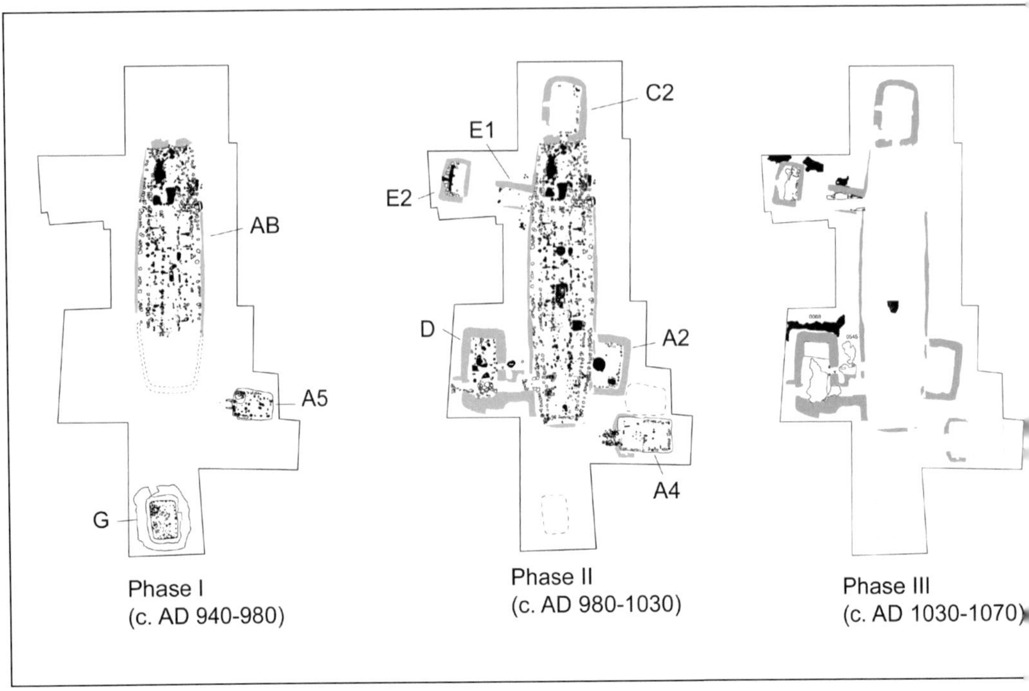

Fig. 2. Three phases of the Viking period site (drawing: G. Lucas).

Phase I (c.940–980 AD)

The settlement started relatively small with the construction of an aisled hall (AB[1]), pithouse (G) and smithy (A5) on previously created pasture. One could argue over the primacy of the first structures, i.e. whether they are all built together or, for example that the sunken featured building G was the first structure, but the evidence is too tenuous. The first smithy (A5) may have been a slightly later construction based on a lack of associated middens, but this too can only be a tentative suggestion. Most contentious is the original size of the aisled hall (AB). Based on various lines of evidence, it seems quite plausible that it was initially a much smaller building (*c.*28 m long) but still larger than most ordinary aisled halls from Iceland. The construction of the hall also seems to have been marked by a number of acts which are typically described as foundation deposits. In particular, two plausible, primary foundation deposits are 17 probable stone gaming pieces in a posthole in the northwest corner of the central part of the hall and the fragment of crucible and human tooth occuring in the posthole, opposite the primary hearth. The location of these deposits may not be coincidental either as comparative studies indicate that corner posts

1 The labelling of the various structures follows Bruun's 1908 system.

and hearths are common places for such deposits in the Scandinavian Iron Age (Carlie, 2006). Such deposits may have acted as apotropaic acts to help ensure future good fortune for the building and its occupants. However, it may also be worth noting that the placement of special deposits in the posts by the hearth at Borg were interpreted as having possible connections to the high seat (Munch, 2003, 261) and the same may apply here. The fact these are structural posts is not significant as high seats were often integrated into the structural posts. No known examples of foundation deposits exist for other halls in Iceland, but structural postholes have rarely been found or recognized. However, gaming pieces and other objects were retreived from the postholes of a structure at nearby Sveigakot (Vésteinsson, pers. comm.). Besides these deposits, a range of more general activities appear in the primary phase of settlement – textile production in the sunken featured building G and metalworking in A5. It appears as if iron smelting (as well as iron smithing) was a major element of metalworking in this phase, based on the proportions of tap slag recoved from the site in this phase. The faunal evidence points to a full livestock package present from the start (i.e. cow, sheep, goat, pig), as well as strong coastal connections in terms of fish, birds, sea mammals and shellfish.

Phase II (c.980–1030 AD)

This phase marks the floruit of the settlement and its substantial enlargement. It is quite clear that the various structural changes which occur in this phase are not contemporary and may have even been rather piecemeal but the chronological resolution does not permit us to see this. One can however tentatively divide this phase into two sub-phases. The first, which may even overlap with the latter part of phase I, entials the construction of a new smithy (A4), a small hall (D) and a latrine (E2). The aisled hall may also have been dramatically enlarged but at the very least, the central area was re-organized to create a larger open space, with a new hearth and associated ember pit constructed. Possibly contemporary with this structural re-organization of the central part of the hall is a foundation deposit from a posthole opposite the new hearth. This posthole contained a spindle whorl and a knife and its location opposite the secondary hearth is unlikely to be coincidental and might suggest that relocating the hearth required a new ritual act. This posthole is also not a primary post but replaces an earlier one, indicating it cannot be one of the original foundation deposits. Sometime around AD 1000, the annexes C2 and A2 were added to the hall, the latter a food storage and preparation room. The long porch E1 would also be put in this phase.

What is striking about this phase are both the continuities and the differences with the preceding period. Much the same range of activities were occurring – metalworking as well as the usual range of farming activities.

There is some indication that the emphasis on smelting decreased in this phase, and perhaps was practised only minimally on site, with primary smelting now occurring further away (perhaps in more specialized locations in the landscape; see McDonnell in Lucas, 2009). Moreover, it also appears that textile production had possibly ceased – very few related finds (loomweights and spindle whorls) occur in later phases and they may even be residual. Certainly there was no evidence of an *in situ* loom in any of the structures replacing that in the sunken featured building G. This might suggest that some of the activities (smelting and weaving) were moving out from the settlement and occuring elsewhere. The faunal record however shows almost no difference in the species composition or husbandry practices between phases but is remarkably stable and it is likely the settlement continued to host large seasonal gatherings where feasting was a major component. The difference lies in the scale and emphasis on these seasonal gatherings. This is most clearly marked in the increase of the central space of hall – regardless of whether the whole building was enlarged, the central area for housing people increased by *c*.50% of its original size which implies that if it could accomodate *c*.30 people in phase I, this figure is now *c*.45. Irrespective of the accuracy of these population estimates, the increased size is probably reflecting an increase in the number of people attending the seasonal gatherings. The central hearth is still small compared with the size of the living area – in fact now proportionately even smaller, the significance of which will be taken up further below. In addition, the purpose built latrine is highly unusual and unprecedented on other contemporary sites in Iceland – although examples occur on later sites and literary references suggest they may have been common (Sigurðardóttir, 1998,71). Nonetheless, it seems that a great deal of effort has gone into attending to the requirements of housing large numbers of people and a purpose built latrine may not be such an important structure on an ordinary, small farmstead.

One other aspect is also worth remarking on though and that is the clustering of the structures. If in phase I the buildings are fairly spread out, in the earlier part of phase II they come closer together and by the latter part of phase II, the new buildings are simply added onto the aisled hall rather than free-standing. This development of settlement closure at Hofstaðir could conventionally be seen as part of a longer term process of farmhouse development in Iceland, whereby the aisled hall gradually attracts buildings onto it as annexes and develops into the medieval passage house (Ólafsson, 2004; Ágústsson, 1987). Whether this is a uniform or real process over the long term throughout Iceland is debatable, but regardless of that, the case at Hofstaðir needs some consideration. Climatic factors can hardly be cited as the cause, for the onset of the Little Ice Age is still centuries away, though fuel shortages through deforestation may have stimulated a desire to improve heat retention in buildings and this could be one explanation. However, the changes may be equally about ideologies connected to settlement space and to create the feeling of being in a single large building. In short to emphasize the continuities between buildings as part of a single space, whereas multiple, detached structures reinforce spatial distinctions. This is not to argue that the settlement space becomes homogenized – there were clearly still differences in rooms in terms of activities etc., but enhancing the connectivity between rooms might have served to enhance the connectivity of people living and visiting the site, enhancing a sense of a connected community. This is particularly interesting in the context of the seasonal gatherings where increased numbers and indeed, potentially increased social friction may have needed to be mollified and checked, and one effective way of doing this was through the spatial environment in which people came together.

Phase III (c.1030–1070 AD)

Sometime around the middle of the first half of the 11th century, all the structures appear to have been abandoned, at least as habitations. Continuity of activity on site is represented by the re-use of the structures on the western side (D and E2) as well as probably the aisled hall (AB) for storing hay and there are also turf-/peat ash dumps against the ruins. Both of these activities indicate that the land was still farmed and occupied and in all likelihood, a new settlement was built *c.*100 m to the southwest where the medieval church and farm mound lie. Whether this re-location represents a change in land ownership/tenancy is impossible to tell, but it may be significant that re-location of settlement appears to be a common phenomenon in Iceland during the 11th century. Most examples of known and excavated Viking settlements in Iceland have little or no later structural activity over them; however, too few farm mounds have been excavated to see if they have Viking Age or later origins so this may not be universal, even if present and of those that have, the earliest remains tend to be very fragmentary and the dating imprecise (e.g. Bergþórshvoll, Bessastaðir, Viðey, Nes and Stóraborg).

The date spans of settlement period halls are not always well defined, but Hofstaðir does present us with quite a tight chronology: the settlement as a whole lasted for *c.*90 years or a century at most. This is obviously more than one person's lifetime and probably covers at least three if not four generations of a lineage. Indeed, the changes which are marked in phase II could easily be associated with generational change, and might denote the attempt to consolidate a family dynasty. The re-location is therefore unlikely to be related to the life cycle of the household as has been argued in later prehistoric contexts (Gerritsen, 1999). Indeed, the structural changes and additions at Hofstaðir give every indication that a farm mound could have developed on this location if other circumstances had not intervened. The ideology of permanence of location and re-building on the same spot as one's ancestors is probably already present at the time of settlement and the shifting of house plots had probably stopped well before the 9th century in the North Atlantic region where farm mounds are a characteristic feature of settlements (Bertelsen, 1979; Bertelsen, 1989). We are thus still left with the question of what happened in the 11th century: why was the settlement abandoned and re-located?

Climatic reasons are (or were) always popular explanations in Icelandic archaeology; the location of the settlement so close to a break of slope may have created problems particularly in periods of heavy snow fall or rain. There was clearly some attempt to control water seepage into the aisled hall with the sump and flagged pavement in the north-eastern entrance. However, it is doubtful the first settlers lacked such foresight if the problems were severe enough to force a re-location; moreover, major environmental change which could have disproved such foresight does not occur until long after the re-location. Nonetheless, other factors beside climatic change could alter the affects of snow and rain, particularly de-forestation may have exacerbated snowdrift (Smith, 1995, 338). De-forestation was certainly a prominent element in the first swathe of settlement, although nowhere near as dramatic and ubiquitous as originally believed – rather after an initial period of clearance, there appears to have been a rather longer phase of woodland management with gradual tree loss (see Lawson, in Lucas, 2009). Since Hofstaðir is a later settlement, it is quite likely by the time of its founding, such woodland management practices had already been instigated and this is indeed suggested by the analysis of birch charcoal from the middens on the site (*ibid.*). If so, we can hardly call on localised hydrological effects to explain the re-location.

It is more fruitful to turn to the archaeological evidence itself in trying to understand the abandonment of the site – in particular, the ritualized nature of abandonment seen in annexe A2. There are three aspects to the abandonment of the annexe A2 which appear out of the ordinary: the backfilling of the barrel pit with metalworking waste, the slaughter and deposition of a whole sheep and finally the collection of 14 cattle skulls which appear to have previously been mounted outside the aisled hall, possibly on the walls/roof. The latter two occur in turf wall/roof collapse deposits inside the room; these deposits probably represent deliberate demolition rather than gradual decay as they are fairly extensive and homogeneous layers. The metalworking waste as backfill of the barrel pit is unlikely to have come from the room but rather introduced from a smithy elsewhere (probably structure A4). It is an extremely pointless act from a practical perspective, if one defines practicalities by our own standards, but may have had a deeply practical symbolic significance to the people at the time. Iron working is certainly one of those activities which has received substantial attention in connection to ritual, and there is a great deal of Scandinavian folklore which links iron working to elves and dwarfs as well as various medieval literary references to the magical skills involved in iron working (e.g. Espelund, 2007; 2004). The Icelandic literature is replete with references to blacksmiths as mythical heros, most famously Völund in the poetic Edda. In the absence of any sustained research on the ideology of Viking Age iron working (which rather tends to be dominated by technological studies; e.g. see Stenvik, 2003), one can only tentatively posit that iron working may have been connected with 'magical' powers of transformation and that the waste of metalworking was correspondingly charged with associated symbolism. The magical properties of slag could have been intentionally invoked as part of the demolition and abandonment process.

As the building was being demolished, a slaughtered sheep was thrown into the room (Fig. 3). This sheep was unusual because it was naturally polled (hornless) and was probably killed by a blow to the forehead – both features are not commonly seen on other sheep skulls from the site (see McGovern, in Lucas, 2009). The skeleton was only semi-articulated as not all the parts were in the same place and the skeleton had either been disturbed or partially dismembered. This appears to represent a deliberate act of slaughter during abandonment. In contrast however, are the 14 cattle skulls also found in the demolition layers; like the sheep, some of these cattle appear to have been hornless and also killed/stunned by a blow between the eyes but also decapitated (*ibid.*, Fig. 4). These skulls display clear signs of weathering on the front side, indicating they had been exposed to the outside for a period of time. A probable interpretation is

Fig. 3. Photograph of sheep carcass in A2 (photo: G. Lucas).

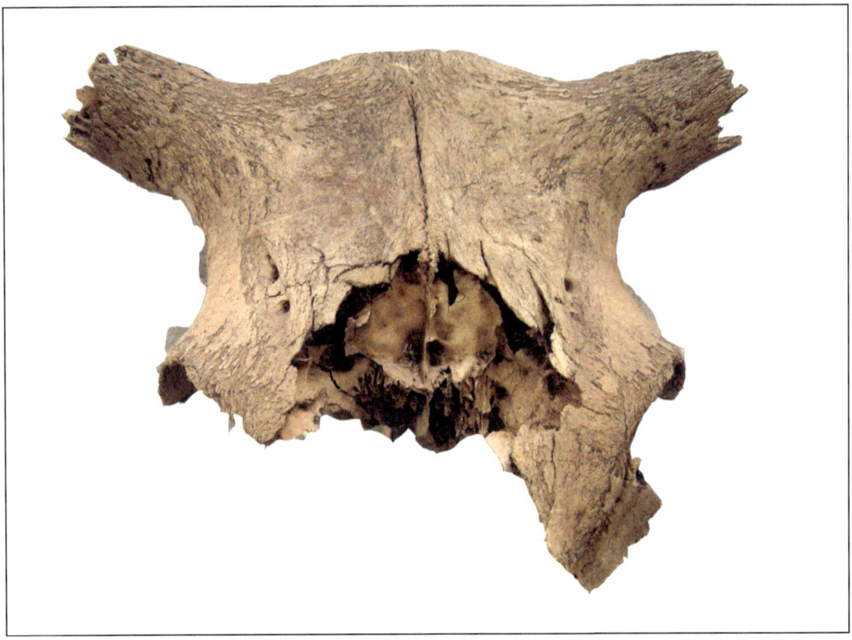

Fig. 4. Photograph of skull specimen 4 showing depressed fracture caused by blow to the forehead (photo: T.H. McGovern).

that they were hung for display – possibly on the outside walls or roof of the aisled hall and collected and dumped into the annexe A2 at the abandonment of the settlement. What makes this even more likely is that they are not the only skulls found at the site; a smaller cluster of 8 cattle skulls, in similar condition was found in the small space between the small hall D and the aisled hall AB in similar turf collapse layers and a further single skull by the northwestern entrance behind the porch E1. These skulls – or at least the two larger groups associated with D and A2 – are clearly the result of deliberate collection and possible deposition associated with the abandonment of the settlement.

These three elements to the abandonment of the annexe A2 all suggest intentional acts which have a ritualized or symbolic significance, possibly relating to the need to ensure a proper 'ending', just as the foundation deposits in the postholes of the hall were intended to ensure a good beginning. One can only guess at the specific beliefs surrounding these acts, but it would certainly seem that the adandonment of the settlement was perhaps regarded as a more charged event that the foundation if one only compares the material practices associated with these two points in its biography. Perhaps this is not surprising as the accumulated history of the site over its 90 years of occupation will have given it a much greater sense of place than when the site was first settled.

Fig. 5. Photograph of secondary hearth with robber cut of ember pit in the foreground (photo: R. Edvardsson).

Why these acts should be largely focused on the annexe however is somewhat obscure; it is unfortunate that Bruun excavated almost all the internal abandonment phase deposits of the aisled hall AB and small hall D, while the other annexe C2 has been largely truncated by later building activity. Lacking such information, it is difficult to know how unique the annexe A2 was in receiving this ritualized attention. The only clue to possible comparable activity in the hall is the robbing of the stone-lined ember pit next to the hearth (Fig. 5); if this was solely to retrieve useful stones, it is unclear why the hearth itself was spared. It is possible therefore that this pit had symbolic significance and the robbing is in fact another deliberate act of closure. Given the function of the ember pit to keep coals burning, to keep the hearth alive, it is not difficult to see it as metonym for the continuity of the building; its removal would then be like removing the heart from a living body. Unfortunately, the date of this robbing cannot be as clearly tied in to the chronology of abandonment as the events associated with A2, so this must only remain a tentative interpretation.

A VIKING AGE FEASTING HALL?

The summary outline given above of the occupational sequence at Hofstaðir during the Viking Age throws up many questions about the precise nature of this site; in particular, it is worth re-iterating the key aspects which make the site unusual and/or unique. First concerns the size of the aisled hall; at nearly 40 m long, it exceeds threefold the normal length of such halls found in Iceland and is almost double the size of larger halls such as that recently excavated at Hrísbrú in Mosfell (Byock et al., 2005). The hall at Hofstaðir is thus comparable to other monumental halls in Scandinavia such as Lejre or Borg, which even if larger, are so only relative to the settlement norm in their countries (Munch et al., 2003; Christensen, 1993). However, there does not appear to be any evidence of partitioning in the central hall at either Lejre or Borg, so Hofstaðir becomes doubly special; this partitioning, alongside the presence of a specialized latrine and the relatively diminutive hearth in the hall, can actually be used to suggest a specific interpretation of the hall as a place for hosting seasonal large gatherings. First consider the hearth; by comparative standards, it is very small (Fig.6) and in the winter (where temperatures can drop to -30

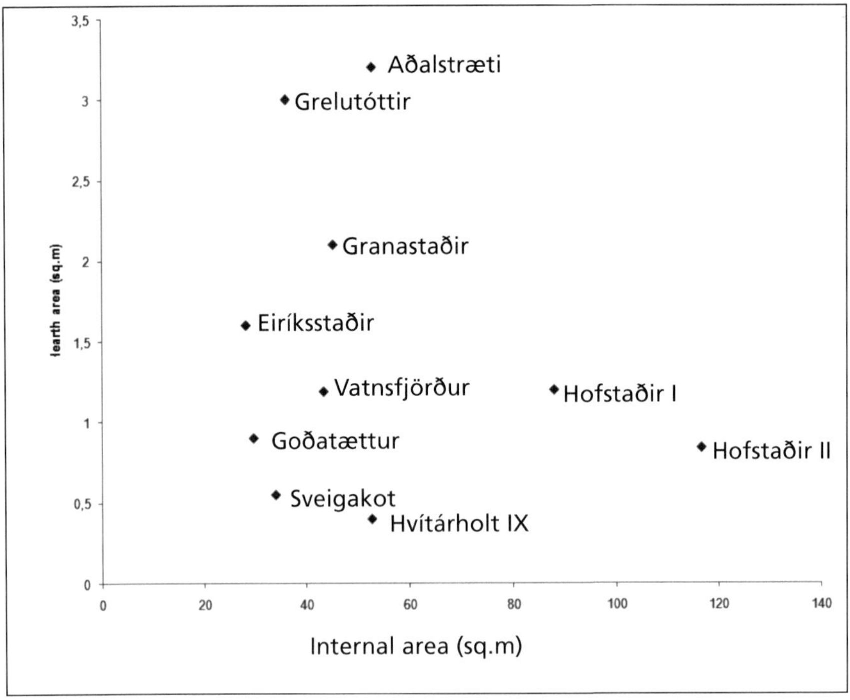

Fig. 6. Ratio of hearth to internal area of several excavated halls from Iceland.

°C), not particularly effective for those in the more distant parts of the hall, which might point to summer-only occupation. Second, the presence of partitions in the side aisles is, as pointed out before, very unusual; although it has been claimed to exist on other sites in Iceland, the evidence is by no means clear given the excavation techniques often deployed. If their presence at Hofstaðir is really unusual, it may be because it would have been considered unnecessary on an ordinary farm where the household members all considered each other kin with no need for such privacy or distinctions. The presence of such partitions at Hofstaðir may strengthen the idea that the hall was mainly used to accomodate non-kin, where segregated berths acted to underline this difference. Finally there is the latrine, which again would have perhaps been un-necessary on an ordinary farm (and indeed where none have been found of this date in Iceland), but played a more important role in a communal building. The fact that there was clearly seating for at least three people at a time in this latrine is highly suggestive and as a smaller and detached communal space, it may have also provided a significant locale for more private meetings that were not possible in the aisled hall. The final major feature to the site concerns its faunal assemblage, specifically evidence for periodic feasting as exemplified by a superimposed meat profile on a baseline subsistence pattern; and also periodic sacrifice of cattle as evidenced through decapitation of prime bulls and the display of their heads (see McGovern in Lucas, 2009; also Lucas & McGovern, 2008).

Drawing all these strands together, it can be argued that Hofstaðir represents a specialized feasting hall, which while it certainly was occupied by a year-round household conducting basic subsistence activities, seasonally – i.e. in the summer – it also acted as a host for larger gatherings of people from the region. It serves no purpose to ask whether such gatherings were religious or political; clearly they could be, and probably were both. A more interesting question rather concerns the status of the resident household: is this a chieftain's farm? One answer would suggest it was; that the settlement, for example, represents an ultimately failed attempt to create a power centre on the western side of lake Mývatn to counter that of Reykjahlíð on the east. The western and southern side of the lake has many smaller settlements and each may have been vying for ascendancy; for a bried period of a century, Hofstaðir may have acquired such status but then collapsed, to be eventually replaced by Skútustaðir (Fig. 7; Friðriksson et al., 2004; McGovern et al., 2007, 38). Certainly the evidence of feasting and hosting large gatherings bespeaks of status – and more particularly, attempts to create and maintain such status through the social networking that hosting such gatherings entailed. An alternative scenario would make Hofstaðir a tenant farm of another chiefly or aspiring settlement (such as Geirastaðir), which could have used Hofstaðir as an indirect means of enhancing and assert-

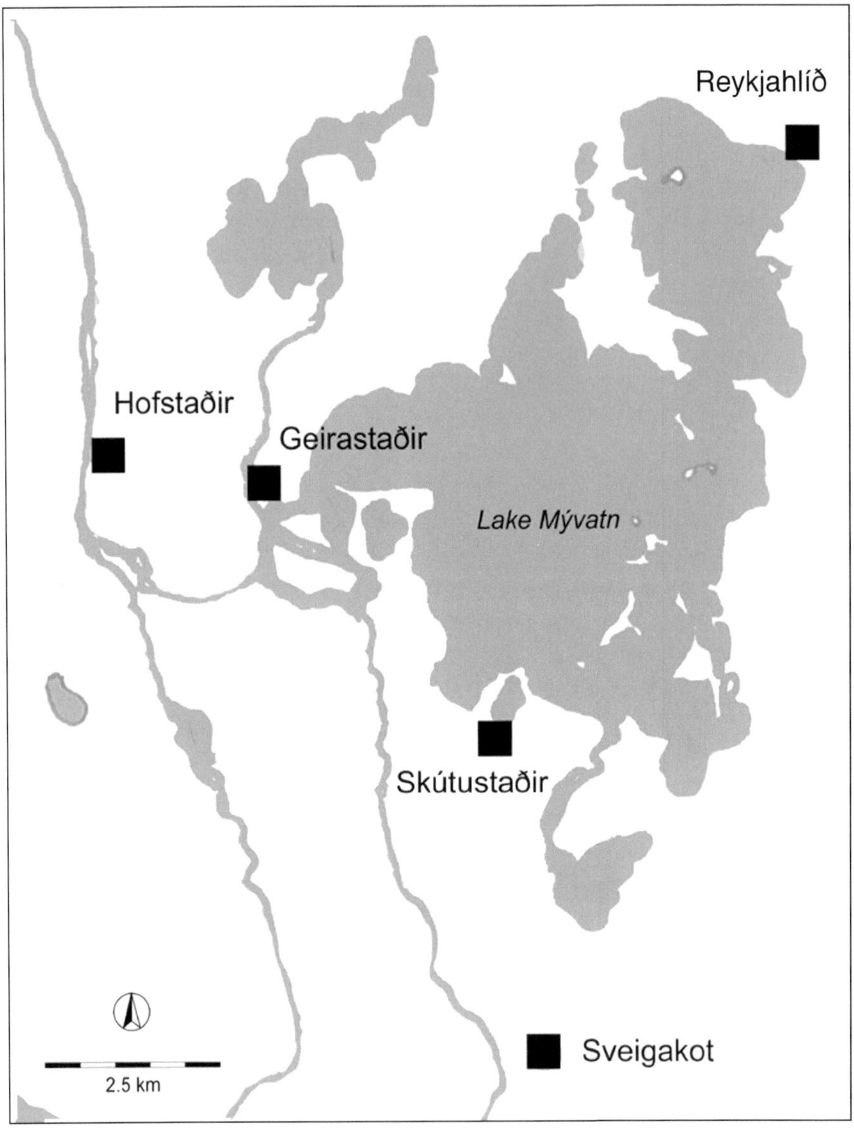

Fig. 7. Hofstaðir in relation to known contemporary Settlement period sites around Lake Mývatn (drawing: G. Lucas).

ing status by planting a token 'caretaker' household on the site. Hofstaðir thus may have appeared on the surface to be a politically neutral place to hold large regional gatherings precisely because it was *not* the residence of an elite farmstead (Lucas, 2007).

Whatever the status of its inhabitants, the reasons for its demise remain equally enigmatic. The persistence of pagan rites in the way the site was abandoned more than quarter of a century *after* the formal adoption of Christianity by the *alþingi* in 1000 AD, may suggest this was a site of pagan resistance to Christianity which ultimately failed by backing the wrong horse, so to speak. However, excavations at the chapel at Hofstaðir point to an early date in the first half of the 11th century for its foundation (Hildur Gestsdóttir, pers.comm.) and it remains unclear if the first chapel was built before or after the abandonment of the hall. The answer to this will clearly have vital implications for how one interprets that abandonment. There is no doubt that the rise and fall of Hofstaðir are entwined in complex processes of a political and religious nature and the only way to better understand its history, is to dig deeper outside the site itself – both the chapel and farm mound of Hofstaðir itself and other contemporary sites in the Mývatn region. In that sense, even if the excavations at the Viking Age settlement have now been completed, the interpretation of this settlement will remain open, which is perhaps only fitting for a site of this importance to Icelandic archaeology.

ACKNOWLEDGEMENTS

This paper summarizes the work of a large number of people and although sole author, my role here is more of a spokesperson; while I cannot credit all those involved in such a short note, I would particularly like to acknowledge the following: Adolf Friðriksson, Orri Vésteinsson, Ian Lawson, Thomas McGovern, Colleen Batey, Garðar Guðmundsson, Ian Simpson and Gerry McDonnell, and more generally the Institute of Archaeology (Reykjavík) and NABO. Nonetheless, the interpretations offered here should not necessarily be seen to reflect the views of others on this project. In addition, I would like to thank all those who commented on the presented version of this paper at the Viking Congress and two anonymous referees for their helpful comments on the subsequent written draft.

BIBLIOGRAPHY

Ágústsson, H. (1987). Íslenski torfbærinn. In F. F. Jóhannsson (Ed.), *Íslensk þjóðmenning* (I), pp. 227–344. Reykjavík: Bókaútgáfan Þjóðsaga.

Arbman, H., & Stenberger, M. (1935). *Vikingar i västerled*. Stockholm: Albert Bonniers Förlag.

Bertelsen, A. R. (1979). Farm mounds in north Norway: a review of recent research. *Norwegian Archaeological Review* 12(1), 48–56.

Bertelsen, A. R. (1989). Gårdshaugene in Nord-Norge. Eksempler på nordatlantiske teller. *Hikuin* 15, 171–181.

Bruun, D., & Finnur Jónsson (1909). Om hove og hovudgravninger paa Island. *Aarbøger for nordisk Oldkyndighed og Historie* 1909, 245–316.

Bruun, D., & Finnur Jónsson (1911). Finds and excavations of Heathen Temples in Iceland. *Saga Book of the Viking Club* 7, 25–37.

Bruun, D. (1928). *Fortidsminder og Nutidshjem paa Island*. Copenhagen: Gyldendalske Boghandel.

Byock, J., Walker, P., Erlandson, J., Holck, P., Zori, D., Guðmundsson, M., & Tveskov, M. (2005). A Viking Age valley in Iceland: the Mosfell archaeological project. *Medieval Archaeology* XLIX, 195–218.

Carlie, A. (2006). Ancient building cults. Aspects of ritual traditions in southern Scandinavia. In A. Andrén, K. Jennbert & C. Raudvere (Eds.), *Old Norse Religion in long-term perspectives. Origins, changes and interactions*. Lund: Nordic Academic Press, pp. 206–211.

Christensen, T. (1993). Lejre Beyond Legend – The Archaeological Evidence. *Journal of Danish Archaeology* 10, 163–185.

Espelund, A. (2007). Ancient ironmaking in Iceland, Greenland and Newfoundland *Archaeologia Islandica* 6, 48–73.

Espelund, A. (2004). *Jernet i Vest-Telemark*. Trondheim: Arketype Forlag.

Fridriksson, A., & Vésteinsson, O. (1997). 'Hofstaðir revisited', in *Norwegian Archaeological Review* 30(2), 103–112.

Fridriksson, A., Vésteinsson, O., & McGovern, Thomas H. (2004). Recent Investigations at Hofstaðir, Northern Iceland. In R. A. Hously & G. Coles (Eds.), *Atlantic Connections and Adaptations; economies, environments and subsistence in lands bordering the North Atlantic*, AEA/NABO Environmental Archaeology Monographs 21, Oxbow Books, pp. 191–203.

Friðriksson, A. (1994). *Sagas and popular Antiquarianism in Icelandic Archaeology*. Avebury: Aldershot.

Gerritsen, F. (1999). To build and to abandon. The cultural biography of late prehistoric houses and farmsteads in the southern Netherlands, *Archaeological Dialogues* 6, 78–97.

Lucas, G. (Ed.) (2009). *Hofstaðir. Excavations of a Viking Age Feasting Hall in North-Eastern Iceland*. Reykjavík: Institute of Archaeology.

Lucas, G., & McGovern, T. H. (2008). Bloody slaughter: ritual decapitation and display at Viking age Hofstaðir N Iceland, *Journal of European Archaeology* 10(1), 7–30.

Lucas, G. (2007). The Viking Settlement at Hofstaðir in Mývatnssveit. In B. Eyþórsson & H. Lárusson (Eds.) *Þriðja íslenska söguþingið 18. – 21. maí 2006.* Reykjavík: Aðstandendur þriðja íslenska söguþingsins, pp. 198–204.

McGovern, T. H., Vésteinsson, O., Fridriksson, A., Church, M. J., Lawson, I., Simpson, I. A., Einarsson, Á., Dugmore, A., Cook, G., Perdikaris, S., Edwards, K., Thomson, A. M., Adderley, W. P., Newton, A., Lucas, G., & Aldred, O. (2007). Landscapes of Settlement in Northern Iceland: Historical Ecology of Human Impact & Climate Fluctuation on the Millennial Scale, *American Anthropologist* 109(1), 27–51.

Munch, G. S. (2003). Borg as a pagan centre. In Munch et al. (Eds.), *Borg in Lofoten. A chieftan's farm in North Norway*. Trondheim: Tapir Academic Press, pp. 253–263.

Munch, G. S., Johansen, O. S., & Roesdahl, E. (Eds.) (2003). *Borg in Lofoten. A chieftan's farm in North Norway*. Trondheim: Tapir Academic Press.

Ólafsson, G. (2004). Frá skála til gangabæjar. In Á. Björnsson & H. Róbertsdóttir (Eds.), *Hlutavelta tímans*. Reykjavík: Þjóðminjasafn Íslands, pp. 130–139.

Olsen, O. (1965). Hørg, hov og kirke. Historiske og arkæologiske vikingetidsstudier. *Aarbøger for nordisk Oldkyndighed og Historie* 1965, 5–307.

Shetelig, H., & Falk, H. (1937). *Scandinavian Archaeology*. Oxford: Clarendon Press.

Sigurðardóttir, S. (1998). Um náðhús. *Árbók Hins íslenzka fornleifafélags* 1996–97, 69–94.

Smith, K. (1995). Landnám: the settlement of Iceland in archaeological and historical perspective. *World Archaeology* 26, 319–347.

Stenberger, M. (Ed.) (1943). *Forntida gårdar i Island. Nordiska arkeologiska undersökningen i Island 1939*. Copenhagen: Ejnar Munksgaard.

Stenvik, L. F. (2003). Iron Production in Scandinavian Archaeology. *Norwegian Archaeological Review* 36(2), 119–134.

Vésteinsson, O. (2004). Icelandic farmhouse excavations: field methods and site choices. *Archaeologia Islandica* 3, 71–100.

Vikings in the International Polar Year 2007–09: Still bloodthirsty, but also ecodynamic and educational

THOMAS H. McGOVERN

ABSTRACT

The International Polar Year of 2007-09 (http://www.ipy.org/) was the first IPY to fully integrate northern humans into the international interdisciplinary surge of scientific and educational activities aimed at the north. Many historians, archaeologists, and social scientists have participated in the latest IPY, many of them also active in the NABO cooperative (North Atlantic Biocultural Organization,www.nabo.org). Grant support to NABO from the IPY (Iceland, US, Denmark, Canada, Greenland) has provided some fresh perspectives on Viking Age ritual activity in Iceland, and a new look at Viking-medieval human ecodynamics (providing some important revisions to the account provided by Jared Diamond's 2005 book *Collapse* of heedless Norse environmental impacts). IPY support for the more active involvement of northern communities in global science and the promotion of education at all levels has also resulted in a successful collaboration in the *Fornleifaskóli barnanna/ Kid's Archaeology* project has now developed in northern Iceland and is spreading to Greenland, Orkney and (through the international *Islands of Change* project) to Barbuda in the West Indies. Vikings continue to play many roles in the modern world beyond their 19th c. function as icons of Nordic national identity, and the 2007-09 IPY has aided both a better understanding of the actual Viking world of the 9th –11th c. and provided new roles for the Viking heritage in the 21st century.

Keywords: Vikings, North Atlantic, NABO, IPY, Hofstaðir, sacrificial deposit, Northern education, stable isotopes, human ecodynamics.

VIKINGS AND THE TWENTY FIRST CENTURY

Vikings have always made a strong impression, and their place in European history and culture has been controversial since they forcefully attracted literate notice in the 9th century. As many have noted (Lucas, 2001), each generation reshapes and refashions its past, and the Nordic traders, raiders, and settlers of the 8th–11th centuries have long provided rich material for such image management. The Viking heritage shared by the Nordic countries has been repeatedly invoked since the 19th century as both a source of national identity and independence and (especially in the late 20th century) as source of international solidarity connecting Scandinavian nations with a wider Europe. "Viking" is still the single most popular name for sports clubs worldwide from Scandinavia to North America to Brazil (Ward, 2000) and Icelandic financial speculators of the early 21st century were pleased to be described as "economic Vikings" by their many promoters prior to the 2008 shock. Another 21st century reshaping of the heritage of the Viking Age has resulted from a growing movement within archaeology, paleoecology, and environmental history variously termed *Historical Ecology* (Crumley, 1994, 2006), *Socionatural Complex Systems* (Redman, 1999; Redman et al., 2004; Kohler T. & Sander van der Leeuw (Eds.), 2007), *Complex Adaptive Systems* (Dean, 2000; Gunderson et al., 2008) and *Long Term Human Ecodynamics* (Kirch, 2007; McGovern et al., 2007) which seeks to combine disciplinary strengths, new analytical approaches, enhanced digital resources, and new data from archive, field site, and laboratory in order to make the past record of human interaction with landscape, seascape, resources, weather, time, and fate more useful to modern peoples attempting to cope with rapid social, economic, and environmental change. Viking Age North Atlantic settlers and their medieval descendants have become actors and case studies in a new set of controversies about the complex dynamic of human intention, variability in the natural world, and often unexpected intersections between short term events and the grand processes of the *longue durée*.

Nearly a decade ago, Dr. Jared Diamond began researching his global scale investigation of "how human societies choose to succeed or fail" which made extensive reference to dramatic North Atlantic cases of complete social extinction (Norse Greenland) and large scale environmental degradation (Medieval to Early Modern Iceland). These accounts presented in *Collapse* (Diamond, 2005) depicted the Viking Age settlers as establishing essentially unsustainable European-derived economies in the arctic, drawing down natural resources (animals, plants, soil), and creating potentially fatal vulnerabilities for their medieval descendants confronting the climatic impacts of the Little Ice Age. Diamond based this vision of ecocidal Vikings on what was then current research and certainly consulted widely with many active regional scholars and while it is a popularized summary, his account in *Collapse* is not out of line with contemporary late 20th c. scholarship (e.g. Amorosi, Buckland et al., 1997; McGovern, 1981; McGovern et al., 1988; McGovern, 1994; Ogilvie & McGovern, 2001). However, support from multiple sources (Icelandic Millennium Fund, IPY, RANNÍS, US National Science Foundation, UK Leverhulme Trust, Danish National Museum, Greenland Museum and Archives, & The Commission for Research in Greenland) to North Atlantic research since 2000 has transformed our scientific understanding of the processes of the Viking Age colonization of the North Atlantic and the long term human ecodynamics that ensued after Landnám. Daimond's account now appears not so much wrong as overly simple, and in need of just the sort of revision and correction that he himself would expect from an active interdisciplinary research community.

VIKINGS AND HUMAN ECODYNAMICS: SOME UPDATES TO *COLLAPSE*

Did the Viking Age colonization of the North Atlantic prefigure modern environmental management disasters? Did the original colonists place unsustainable demands upon island ecosystems, running up a long term bill to be paid by their own descendants? Were Vikings as destructive to North Atlantic environments as they were to monastic settlements? Multiple lines of evidence (derived from archaeology, zooarchaeology, geoarchaeology, archaeobotany, history, and natural science) suggest that Viking Age North Atlantic settlements certainly transformed island ecology and forever changed the biogeography and landscapes of these northern islands (Dugmore, Church et al., 2004). However, the human managers of this rapid change were far from heedless, and we now recognize that the long term record includes multiple cases of successful long term resource management, well managed use of common resources, skillful coordination of community labor, and sensible codified land management strategies enforced both from community level and top-down via legal codes and aristocratic managers. Thanks to sustained funding support and sustained international collaboration we are now in a position to better identify common patterns and local variability in a surprisingly flexible and adaptable set of Norse Atlantic island economies, and to look at the multiple outcomes of the Viking Age North Atlantic *Landnám* from a genuinely pan-Atlantic viewpoint.

This long term record still features ultimately unhappy outcomes, despite what now looks like some fairly successful and well managed long term economic planning. However well adapted they may now appear, the Norse Greenlanders still became extinct and in Iceland a heavy price has been paid in terms of soil and vegetation loss. The environmental lessons of the Viking to Medieval North Atlantic remain cautionary tales for present and future managers of an island earth, if anything made more ominous by our new and more positive view of Vikings as good land managers who still sometimes failed to sustain their societies or ecosystems despite doing a great many things right.

SUSTAINABLE PUFFINS, PIGS, AND BARLEY IN THE FAROE ISLANDS

Thanks to major support from the Leverhulme Trust and NSF, international investigations on the Faroe Islands (continuing as the Heart of the Atlantic Project centered on the island of Sandoy) since 2002 have provided fresh perspectives on the Viking Age and Medieval Faroes. Pollen evidence suggests that the Faroes were never heavily wooded and thus deforestation was not a major human impact (Lawson et al., 2005; Arge et al., 2005). Geomorphological studies suggest only limited geomorphological impacts associated with settlement with good control of slope wash despite steep slopes and high rainfall (Edwards et al., 2005). Combinations of soil science and agro-ecological modeling indicate that the Faroese were steadily enhancing the fertility of their soils and controlling soil erosion from Viking Age well into early modern times (Adderly et al., 2005; Thomson et al., 2005). Zooarchaeology indicates that the Viking Age Faroese imported significant numbers of pigs as well as sheep and cattle, and that they made major use of sea bird colonies (especially puffins) while successfully growing barley on their increasingly well fertilized and well drained fields (Church et al., 2005). Pigs are very capable of destroying both puffin colonies and barley fields if not closely managed, and a combination of place name evidence, locational analysis, and zooarchaeology has indicated just such a careful and controlled movement of well managed herds of pigs around the cultural landscape of Viking Age and early medieval Sandoy (Arge et al., 2009). Pigs became extinct in the Faroes in the later Middle Ages, and the 13th century seems to have seen a reorganization of land use that also devalued *sel*/sæter use (Mahler, 2007), but (highly regulated) exploitation of sea bird colonies remained a central feature of Faroese society and economy to the present. The Faroes will certainly repay more sustained international interdisciplinary investigation, but at present the story of Faroese resource management seems to be full of successful long term sustainability and effective management of potentially fragile island resources. Certainly no Viking Age ecocide or medieval collapse is visible here.

LONG TERM SUSTAINABLE RESOURCE USE IN ICELAND AND GREENLAND?

The *Landnám* in Iceland is still temporally defined by association with the "Landnám tephra" dated by connection to the Greenland Ice Sheets to AD 871+/-2, and there is growing evidence from many parts of Iceland suggesting that the initial settlement involved many more colonizers and much more rapid filling of Icelandic landscapes both inland and coastal than we had previously imagined (contrast Vésteinsson, McGovern & Keller, 2002 with McGovern, Vésteinsson et al., 2007) with multiple nearby sites showing significant human occupation evidence directly upon the Landnám tephra (Vésteinsson (Ed.), 2007). This rapid large scale colonization event may make more comprehensible some indicators of rapid environmental impact including at least locally complete deforestation (Hallsdóttir, 1987) and the local extinction of resident walrus colonies (Vésteinsson et al., 2006). However, other pollen sequences suggest a far more gradual draw down of Icelandic forest resources (Lawson et al., 2006, 2007, 2008), and well dated sequences of charcoal production pits suggest a successive series of management strategies rather than a simple pattern of rapid and widespread destruction of forest resources (Church et al., 2007; Dugmore et al., 2007). While much work remains to be done on the nature and timing of deforestation in Iceland, it is clear that early visions of heedless and rapid destruction are incorrect, despite our new recognition of the scale and rapidity of the Icelandic Landnám event.

Mývatn is recognized as a wetland of international importance as bird habitat. It harbours large populations of migratory waterfowl who come to the lake basin each spring from north-western Europe, primarily from the British Isles, to lay eggs and raise their young. Residents of the district gather tens of thousands of eggs each year, but respect rules limiting the number of eggs taken per nest and discouraging the killing of adult waterfowl. Records maintained since the mid-19th century indicate that this local practice has maintained a sustainable yield of eggs with no long term adverse impact on the waterfowl populations (Einarsson et al., 2004). Multiple archaeological excavations in the Mývatn area datable by both tephra and AMS radiocarbon chronology to the late 9th century have produced masses of bird egg shell and very few bird bones. The eggshells identified included sea bird and ptarmigan (grouse, *Lagopus mutus*), but were mainly from waterfowl eggs; the few adult bird bones were overwhelmingly from ptarmigan rather than waterfowl (McGovern et al., 2006). It would appear that the residents of the Mývatn district have been successfully managing this fragile living resource for over 1,200 years. Cases of well-documented community genuinely long term sustainable resource management are rare worldwide, and it is surely significant that Viking Age Iceland has contributed such a strong evidence of the effective application of TEK ("Traditional Ecological Knowledge", Norberg & Cumming, 2008; Peloquin & Berkes, 2009; Roba & Oba, 2009) on the millennial scale.

The Viking Age Landnám in Iceland thus presents evidence for much environmental change some of which involved a significant expansion in biological diversity as well as local extinctions. Some of these changes are hard to identify as degradation of landscape (reduced primary productivity, loss of biodiversity, reduced food web complexity) and as Hill (2009,161) argues, we need to be careful in defining "degradation" vs. "change" in human ecodynamics research (see also Fisher et al., 2009; Hornberg & Crumley, 2006; McIntosh et al., 2000; Norberg & Cumming, 2008).

Modeling work (BuModel) by Amanda Thomson (2003, 2005) suggests that no plausible past stocking level of sheep would have been likely to radically exceed basic biomass productivity in the highlands, and that the critical stocking issue is the length of summer grazing – a few weeks of grazing past the end of the growing season of the grass-sedge communities in the higher elevation could begin a cycle of soil exposure and deflation that would be hard to control given the highly erosion-prone andisols of Iceland. If there were successive rangeland management failures, these seem to be much more likely to involve slightly mis-scheduling the optimal timing of the end of highland grazing ("missing sustainability by a week") rather than a simple overstocking problem (Simpson et al., 1999, 2001, 2003, 2004). Periods of later medieval cooling (shortening growing season first in the highlands) would complicate the effective application of range management TEK accumulated during the Viking Age, and periods of high medieval and early modern inter-annual variability documented in the Greenland Ice Sheet proxy records (Dugmore et al., 2007) might pose scheduling challenges no farming strategy (traditional or neo-technical) would be likely to successfully overcome. The starting dates for the major destabilization of vegetation cover and the widespread erosion of soils in central and northern Iceland are major research concerns at present, but it seems clear that some major erosion events in the well studied Mývatn district post-date the medieval period and may reflect loss of human labor and management capability following the population losses of the early 18th c. small pox epidemics. The Icelandic erosion story may be as much about the loss of human labor inputs as about climate fluctuation and the resulting range management dilemma (cf. Fisher, 2009). The eventual massive loss of vegetation, soil, and productive capacity that has deprived Iceland of up to 40% of the soil present at Landnám – degradation by any standard – is still certainly a reality, but its causes are far more complex than a simple "Viking ecocide" model would suggest.

Norse Greenland also appears to have had some successes in long term environmental management (Arneborg, 2002, 2003a, 2003b, 2005; Dugmore et al., 2007; Berglund, 2010; Ogilvie et al., 2010). Recent work in the geomorphology of the Eastern Settlement area indicates that most evidence for large scale soil erosion are restricted to zones affected by natural katabatic wind scouring, and that most highland districts settled by the Norse farmers and used seasonally by their mixed flocks of sheep and goats retain most of their soil accumulated in the Holocene: there was never the same massive soil erosion impact in SW Greenland as in Iceland (Dugmore et al., 2007). New stratigraphic excavations in several parts of the Eastern Settlement now confirm patterns seen earlier in the smaller Western Settlement in finding caribou bone in all layers from Viking Age Landnám in the early 11th c. extending down to the end of Norse Greenland *c.*1450 (Arneborg et al., 2008; Edvardsson et al., 2007; Madsen et al., 2009; Smiarowski, 2007, 2008). Caribou are still present today in the former Western Settlement, but they were driven to extinction in the former Eastern Settlement by the early 19th c. when Inuit hunters using firearms killed the last of them. Caribou in SW Greenland are vulnerable to such local extinctions from changing climate (especially range icing events) as well as human predation. Greenland caribou would presumably have been under heavy pressure during the Norse occupation from climate fluctuations, Norse hunting (probably using both drive systems and large deer hounds, McGovern and Jordan, 1982), and range competition from domestic stock. However, no extinction of caribou occurred in either settlement area during the Norse period as the hunt was under stringent top down as well as community level social control. In the Eastern Settlement the caribou hunt was directly under the control of the bishops, according to Ívar Bárðarson's account from the mid-14th century (Gad, 1970,141), and the role of secular and ecclesiastical aristocracy in game management in medieval Europe is abundantly documented. In light of the new data from the Faroes and the strong example of millennial scale sustainability in Mývatnssveit it may be time to re-assess this "non-extinction" as another positive example of successful Norse resource management by Viking Age settlers maintained by their medieval descendants (Berglund, 2010). Given the post-medieval record of caribou extinctions in West Greenland, it seems likely that medieval caribou population survival in the face of apparently regular human hunting pressure was no accident, and that aristocratic Greenlandic managers were far from incompetent.

The evidence for fully intentional and well designed long term resource management in the Nordic North Atlantic comes not only from zooarchaeology and soil science but also from surviving documents – particularly the medieval legal codes best preserved in Iceland (*Grágás*, transl. Dennis et al., 2000). Problem animals (as pigs had become in Iceland by *c.*1100) were particularly heavily regulated, with fines and penalties prescribed for inattentive management that could damage landscape and grazing. As Simpson et al. (2004) have pointed out, the Grágás legal code precludes most of the "tragedy of the commons" effects of unregulated use of upland grazing (and other common resources) with clear specification of over-use indicators and enforcement structures at different levels well articulated. Much land management language in Grágás in fact shows considerable similarity to modern "best practice" rangeland management strategies now circulated by international aid agencies. We lack comparable surviving Greenlandic legal documents, but we do know from Icelandic references that these existed and that they were similar to Icelandic codes but with distinct provisions covering the very different Greenlandic economy (Gad, 1970). It seems likely that these lost codes covered communal labor obligations and resource use as in Iceland, and the archaeological evidence suggests that rangeland management, caribou hunting, and the vital annual seal hunt were probably heavily regulated.

NORSE SEAL HUNTERS: A BIT TOO SUCCESSFUL?

Past assessments of Norse sealing (as passed on by Diamond's *Collapse*) have tended to focus on the absence of harpoons and other Inuit-derived seal hunting artifacts in Norse Greenlandic finds and a corresponding shortage of the bones of the ringed (*Phoca hispida*) and bearded (*Erignatus barbatus)* seals normally taken by Inuit hunters with this specialized gear in the Norse archaeofauna (McGovern, 1981, 1985). Norse sealing was seen as poorly suited to Greenlandic conditions, and its lack of Inuit-style marine hunting gear was seen as a major adaptive failure that contributed directly to the eventual Norse extinction (McGovern, 1994).

More recent work with new stratified archaeofauna from Greenland and the results of the major stable isotopes project on human and animal bone from the North Atlantic carried out by Jette Arneborg and her associates (Arneborg et al., 1999, in press) has produced a major re-assessment of the success of Norse sealing and its role in the eventual extinction of the community (Berglund, 2010; Dugmore et al., 2007; Ogilvie et al., 2010). Both the zooarchaeological and stable isotopic evidence serve to emphasize that the Norse Greenlanders were provisioning themselves very successfully on seals, with both inland and coastal farms showing up to 80% seal bone and human isotopic evidence indicating progressively more marine contribution to the diet. Norse Greenlandic seal hunting focused upon hunting the harbor seals (*Phoca vitulina*) familiar from Iceland and the British Isles but especially focused upon taking the hugely abundant migratory harp (*Phoca groenlandica*) and hooded (*Cystophora cristata*) arctic seals encountered for the first time by the Viking Age settlers in SW Greenland. Current evidence suggests that Norse sealing in Greenland was strongly targeted upon the spring seal migration and made full use of communal labor and probably all available boats to carry out mass seal drives (probably using nets strung across narrows) that took many migratory seals at once. While Norse exploitation of non-migratory harbor seals in Iceland (and perhaps in Greenland) was not managed communally (harbor seal colonies are vulnerable to over-hunting and disturbance and were owned and managed as fragile resources in Iceland), quantitative models suggest that the Norse Greenlanders needed to mobilize most of their active adults and all available boats to take enough migratory seals during their brief window of opportunity to provision the whole settlement for the rest of the year (Ogilvie et al., 2010). The nearest surviving analog is probably the Faroese pilot whale hunt, a highly regulated communal activity extending at least to the early Middle Ages. The modern pilot whale hunt is bound up in law and tradition and historically linked to many other parts of the subsistence system requiring pooled labor, and now still seen as a key element in the Faroese national identity. Norse sealing in Greenland was probably equally embedded in a web of social contacts and obligations, and individual households would certainly lower their adaptive potential (and social status) by attempting to substitute individualized Inuit seal hunting styles for the proven communal hunt focused on the specialized migratory seal hunt. Norse Greenlanders were thus quite capable seal hunters, but their approach to harvesting seals was communal and tightly scheduled rather than based upon individual hunters taking seals year round in a range of environments (open water, ice edge, breathing hole). While Norse hunting strategies were indeed ineffective in taking the full range of Greenlandic seals available, they were clearly highly efficient in their more specialized niche and great skill was certainly shown in coordinating community labor (including inland farmers) to target the variable but brief period of peak availability of the migratory seals in the outer fjord zone.

Multiple climate proxy data sets indicate that a major climatic threshold was crossed in SW Greenland *c.*AD 1250–1300, when drift ice from East Greenland first began to appear in the fjords of the Eastern Settlement in summer (Jennings & Weiner, 1996; Jennings et al., 2001a, 2001b; Jensen, 2004). As discussed more fully in Ogilvie et al. (2010), the advent of summer drift ice certainly adversely affected navigation conditions, shore side pasture productivity, and the viability of the non-migratory harbor seal colonies. This mid-13th century climate threshold-crossing thus posed an immediate threat to multiple portions of the Greenlandic Norse economy at once. If the Norse Greenlanders had been seriously maladapted as marine hunters or were simply incapable managers we might have expected an extinction event 200 years before 1450. Instead the Greenlandic community was capable of mounting a successful adaptive response – the intensification of the communal migratory seal hunt. As the proportion of marine food increases in the human bone after 1250, so the proportion of migratory to non-migratory seals increases as does the absolute percentage of seal bones relative to all other species in the Norse middens. More intensive hunting of a more restricted range of seals clearly paid off and allowed the Norse Greenlanders at least two more centuries as a functioning society. Survival of the mid-13th century climate impact thus is plausibly tied to an effective and uniquely Norse maritime adaptation to migratory seal hunting in Greenland that could be further intensified to make up for shortfalls in domestic mammal herding, caribou hunting, or the hunting of the non-migratory harbor seals.

Was this specialized maritime adaptation actually a bit too good? Did the intensification of this highly specialized and demonstrably effective Norse approach to migratory seal hunting represent a trade off of improved adaptation for increased vulnerability? Arctic maritime hunting is dangerous work for any society (in the late 19th c. 90% of male Inuit hunters in Greenland died at sea – Vibe, 1967) and the sea continues to claim its toll from North Atlantic seafaring communities to this day. At the same time the Norse Greenlanders were putting more effort (and more of their scarce boats and active community members) into hunting seals and ferrying the carcasses back to the inner fjords in the early spring, the proxy indicators for storminess in the GISP ice core records show a dramatic increase in storms severe enough to deposit sea salt atop the ice sheet, with a major transition to increasing frequency and severity of storms taking place in the early 15th century (Dugmore et al., 2007). Did catastrophic loss of life and boats sometime in the middle of the 15th century push this small community over the edge of viability? New work in Norse Greenland will surely raise new and intriguing questions about the lost settlements, but we can now be clear that lack of maritime hunting capability was not a cause for the eventual extinction. Norse Greenlanders may in fact have generally managed natural resources well, developed a highly integrated and effective economy that balanced marine and terrestrial resource use, showed notable flexibility in adapting seal hunting strategy to cope with the challenges of the mid-13th century climate impact, and yet ultimately failed to survive the accumulating stresses of the 15th century: perhaps a paradoxical victim of successful economic adaptation and specialization in communal maritime hunting.

This vision of an adaptable but still extinct Norse Greenland is certainly as relevant to the modern world as the simpler version provided to Diamond for *Collapse,* but perhaps it is actually more frightening in its implications. It is surely harder now to distance ourselves from "ecocidal and poorly adapted" descendants of the Viking settlers or to comfortably regard ourselves as better and wiser stewards of resources, labor, and knowledge in a rapidly changing planet. Vikings have played many controversial roles since the 9th century, and the 21st century will surely see more debate and controversy surrounding Vikings as agents in a complex and ecodynamic story linking past, present and future.

BLOODY DEEDS AT HOFSTAÐIR, STABLE ISOTOPES, AND PAGAN RITUAL ACTIVITY

Sustained excavations at the Viking Age site of Hofstaðir in Mývatnssveit by the Archaeological Institute of Iceland (FSI) has now seen publication in monograph form (Lucas, 2009; Lucas, this volume; Batey, this volume). This site, with its exceptionally large hall structure and provocative place name has featured in discussions of Viking pre-christian religion and ritual for well over a century (Friðriksson et al., 2004), and the FSI multi-disciplinary excavations have added new dimensions to this ongoing story (as well as 109,373 analyzed fragments of animal bone). As discussed in detail elsewhere (Lucas & McGovern, 2008; McGovern in Lucas, 2009) the unexpected discovery of at least 23 cattle skulls in pits and other deposits associated with the demolition of the Viking Age great hall c.AD 1000–1050 provided an unusual opportunity to combine zooarchaeology, forensic analysis, and the archaeology of ritual. The cattle skulls are heavily weathered on the frontal (face) side, but typically unweathered on the dorsal (bottom) side, suggesting that they were exposed to the elements for some time, probably on the outside of the great hall. The five available AMS radiocarbon assays on the skulls indicate that the animals died at different times (the last dying c.AD 1000), and thus seem to reflect a recurring (perhaps annual?) event rather than a single mass killing. Butchery marks include depressed fracture of the frontals caused by a heavy and immediately fatal crushing blow between the eyes, and (where the base of the skull is preserved) a powerful shearing blow which would have beheaded the animal. Horn cores were left attached, and not removed for horn craft working (an otherwise universal use of horn and horn cores). At least two different styles of presentation are represented by these specimens; one comprising the "full face" of a skull with only the lower jaw removed, the other comprising a "horn rack" with only the frontal bones and attached horn cores present, and the lower face cut away prior to mounting. The horn core diameters indicate that the majority (if not all) of these skulls in fact came from bulls rather than cows, and from fairly large animals by the standards of the Viking Age North Atlantic. Where tooth rows are preserved and allow age reconstruction, the animals are all young adults – fully grown but not aged animals. This 'prime beef' culling profile is in strong contrast to the normal North Atlantic 'dairy profile' in which most cattle were culled either as very young calves or as old adults (probably worn out milk cows). Many of the skulls were fragmentary when recovered, and the count of 23 such preparations represents a conservative minimum; many additional fragments could have come from additional skull preparations too fragmented to securely identify. In addition, several neck vertebrae were recovered from the midden deposit nearby showing massive shearing blows by a sword, axe, or similarly broad bladed instrument that would have beheaded the animal. Such powerful full-force blows cutting into bone and through major muscle groups would certainly have put the weapon at risk, just as in actual combat, and this is by no means the usual pattern of careful tool use and rational and systematic butchery seen in other Viking Age and medieval archaeofauna in Iceland. These patterns appear to reflect not simple butchery but some fairly theatrical ritual activity. A plausible reconstruction of the event (perhaps somewhat similar to cattle sacrifices still carried out in Nepal with specialized kukri swords in late November) would have at least two participants - one standing in front of the bull and striking it with a blunt object (hammer or poll of an axe) between the eyes, and the other standing to the animals right side (shearing cuts consistently come from this orientation) immediately striking full force with sword or axe in an effort to detach the bull's head while it was still upright. If the team got their timing right, the result would be a dramatic fountain of blood as the animal's heart would still be beating when decapitated. Such a dramatic demonstration of warrior skills (and high quality weaponry), dramatic expenditure of blood (normally retained for a multitude of dishes), and the slaughter of what would certainly have been an extremely expensive young adult bull seems to have been a regular event at Hofstaðir, repeated two dozen times or so in the fairly brief period of occupation (mid-10th to early 11th century on radiocarbon and tephra evidence). We now have a suite of new questions to ask about Viking Age sacrifice, impact of ritual on landscape and chieftainship, and size and scale of community interactions in Viking Age north Iceland. International interdisciplinary collaboration of this sort is not only changing our 21st century view of Vikings as environmental managers, it is also providing some surprising new insights into what ritual acts the Vikings may have actually done before Snorri began writing about them. Thanks to IPY support, we can now see Vikings as properly ecodynamic and rather less ecocidal, but we can also confirm their still legendary thirst for blood.

EDUCATION AND COMMUNITY INVOLVEMENT IN SCIENCE AND HERITAGE

If Vikings are still bloodthirsty and now perhaps more eco-positive, they are also very educational. Thanks to an initiative begun in 2007 by Baldur Daníelsson headmaster of Litlulaugaskóli in Laugar and Unnsteinn Ingason of nearby Narfastaðir Farm Hotel, a new international program to use archaeology and paleoecology as a tool for getting rural students engaged in science and involved in local heritage conservation is now spreading more widely in Iceland and is now beginning to involve schools and students in

Greenland, Orkney, and Barbuda (West Indies). This Kids' Archaeology Program (*Fornleifaskóli barnanna*) initiative has been aided by generous support from *Fornleifastofnun Íslands* (Archaeological Institute Iceland), *Hið þingeyska fornleifafélag* (Thingeyjarsveit Archaeological Association), *Þingeyskur sagnagarður, Þingeyjarsveit municipality,* City University of New York (CUNY) and the NABO cooperative (details of this rapidly evolving program are available at www.nabohome.org). Kid's Archaeology has partnered with a new science and education program *Islands of Change* directed by Sophia Perdikaris (CUNY) which connects schools, students, faculty and communities in diverse rural and urban island communities (Barbuda, Iceland, NYC). The Islands of Change project will carry forward (using some of the Obama administrations stimulus funding to NSF) an initiative started by the IPY project called "GPS + Camera= Empowerment". This initiative seeks to enhance active local participation in global science and heritage conservation by providing kits of hand held GPS units and digital cameras that can allow student groups supervised by their teachers and other professionals to systematically collect place-based information about environment, heritage, and archaeology and geo-reference photos and other information collected. Garmin GPS units are used for collection of the locational information, with mapping software kindly donated to the project by Ríkarður Sigmundsson of Garmin Iceland. Improved place name locations and additional place name information collected by the Kids' Archaeology project will be used to update and improve the Garmin base maps for Iceland, providing a better long term resource for all. The information collected will be uploaded to the NABO projects reporting system based on *Google Maps/Google Earth* via a user friendly interface developed by the NABO webmaster Dr. Anthony Newton of U Edinburgh School of GeoSciences for reporting the other science data collected as part of the IPY effort. Classes will be able to see and access their information as it is posted and also see information posted by their friends in Barbuda and in other North Atlantic areas participating in the initiative. A wide range of digital materials (photos, interviews with elders, place based school projects, significant landscape points) can be shared and disseminated through this map based interface system (already familiar to most Icelanders through their use of *Google Earth*). International cooperation and shared expertise provide a good basis for partnership in both science and education, and by combining the Islands of Change project with the Kids' Archaeology program we plan to work together to go beyond community outreach to have genuine community involvement in real cutting edge global change science. The Kid's Archaeology project will be contributing valuable information in the same format and location as the professional science projects. Kids and their teachers will be making a real contribution to international science and local heritage while also learning new skills and making new friends. Vikings will continue to stimulate and fascinate both their own descendants and children across the world. Still bloodthirsty, now ecodynamic, and forever educational, the Viking Age continues to enrich and instruct our own.

ACKNOWLEDGEMENTS

Thanks to Símun V. Arge, Jette Arneborg, Philippa Ascough, Andrew Casely, Mike Church, Gordon Cook, Andrew Dugmore, Ragnar Edvardsson, Árni Einarsson, Adolf Fridriksson, George Hambrecht, Ramona Harrison, Unnsteinn Ingason, Sif Jóhannesdóttir, Christian Keller, Ian Lawson, Gavin Lucas, Christian Koch Madsen, Anthony Newton, Astrid Ogilvie, Sophia Perdikaris, Howell Roberts, Ian Simpson, Konrad Smiarowski, Amanda Thomson, and Orri Vésteinsson.

The research reported here was made possible by generous grants from the US National Science Foundation (0732327, 0352596, 0527732, 0851727), National Geographic Society, RANNÍS, CUNY PSC Grants Program, and the Leverhulme Trust.

BIBLIOGRAPHY

Adderley, W. P. & Simpson, Ian (2005). Early Norse Home-field productivity in the Faroe Islands, *Human Ecology* 33(5),711–736.

Amorosi T., Buckland P., Dugmore A., Ingimundarson J. & McGovern T.H. (1997). Raiding the Landscape: Human impact in the North Atlantic. In: B. Fitzhugh & T. Hunt (Eds.) *Island Archaeology, Human Ecology* 25(3), 491–518.

Arge, Símun V., Guðrún Sveinbjarnardóttir, Kevin J. Edwards & Paul C. Buckland (2005). Viking and Medieval Settlement in the Faroes: People, Place and Environment. *Human Ecology,* Vol. 33, No. 5, October 2005; pp. 597–620.

Arge, Símun V., Mike J. Church, & Seth D. Brewington Pigs in the Faroe Islands: An Ancient Facet of the Islands' Paleoeconomy, *Journal of the North Atlantic* 2 (1), 19–32.

Arneborg, J. (2005). Greenland irrigation systems on a West Nordic background. An overview of the evidence of irrigation systems in Norse Greenland c. 980 – 1450 AD. *Water management in medieval rural economy.* Památky Archaeologické – Supplementum 17, Ruralia V. Prague, pp. 137–145.

Arneborg, J. (2003). Norse Greenland Archaeology: The Dialogue between the Written and the Archaeological Record. In S. M. Lewis: *Vinland Revisited: The Norse World at the Turn of the First Millennium. Selected papers from the Viking*

Millennium International Symposium 15 – 24 September, Newfoundland and Labrador. St. John's. Newfoundland Historic Sites Association.

Arneborg, J. (2003). Norse Greenland – Reflections on the Discussion of Depopulation. In Barrett H.J. (Ed.) *Contact, Continuity and Collapse: The Norse Colonization of the North Atlantic.* Turnhout: Brepols, York Studies in the Early Middle Ages, pp. 163–181.

Arneborg, J. (2002). Inhospitable Regions and Marginality – Settlement at the End of the World. Helmig, G., B. Scholkmann & M. Untermann (Eds.): *Centre – Region – Periphery Medieval Europe.* Basel. Hertigen 2002, vol. 3, pp. 15–24.

Arneborg, Jette, Jan Heinemeier, Niels Lynnerup, Henrik L. Nielsen, Niels Rud & Árný E. Sveinbjörnsdóttir (1999). Change of diet of the Greenland Vikings determined from stable carbon isotope analysis and C14 dating of their bones. *Radiocarbon,* 41, 157–168.

Arneborg, Jette, Martin Hebsgaard, Niels Lynnerup, Christian Koch Madsen, Caroline Polke Paulsen & Konrad Smiarowski (2008). RESOURCES, MOBILITY, AND CULTURAL IDENTITY IN NORSE GREENLAND, VATNAHVERFI PROJECT – REPORT FROM THE FIELD WORK 2008, IPY and Danish National Museum Field Report accessed on line Dec. 22nd 2009 at http://www.nabohome.org/publications/fieldreports/Vatnahverfi2008Rapport.pdf

Ascough, P., Cook, G. T., Dugmore, A. J., and Scott, E. M. (2007a). The North Atlantic Marine Reservoir Effect in the Early Holocene: Implications for Defining and Understanding MRE Values. *Nuclear Instruments and Methods in Physics B* vol 259 (1), 438–447.

Ascough, P. L., Gordon Cook, Mike Church, Andrew Dugmore, Thomas H. McGovern, Elaine Dunbar, Árni Einarsson, Adolf Friðriksson, Hildur Gestsdóttir (2007b). Reservoirs and Radiocarbon; 14C dating problems in Mývatnssveit Northern Iceland. *Radiocarbon* 49(2), 1–15.

Berglund, J. (2010). Did the Medieval Norse Society in Greenland Really Fail? In P. A. McAnany & N. Yoffee (Eds.) *Questioning Collapse.* Cambridge University Press, 45–70.

Church, Mike, Símun Arge, S. Brewington, T. H. McGovern, J. Woollett, Sophia Perdikaris, Ian T. Lawson, Gordon C. Cook, Colin Amundsen, Ramona Harrison, Yekaterina Krivogorskaya (2005). Puffins, pigs, cod and barley: paleoeconomy at Undir Junkarinsfløtti, Sandoy, Faroe Islands. *Environmental Archaeology* 10, 2, 198–221.

Church, M. et al. (2007). Charcoal production during the Norse and early medieval periods in Eyjafjallahreppur, southern Iceland. *Radiocarbon,* 49 (2), pp. 659–672.

Crumley, Carole L. (1994). *Historical Ecology: Cultural Knowledge and Changing Landscapes.* Santa Fe New Mexico, School of American Research Press.

Crumley, Carole L. (2006). Historical Ecology: Integrated Thinking at Multiple Temporal and Spatial Scales. In Alf Hornberg and Carole Crumley (Eds.) *The*

World System and the Earth System, Global Socioenvironmental Change Since the Neolithic. Left Coast Press, Walnut Creek California, pp. 15–29.

Dean, Jeffery S. (2000). Complexity Theory and Socionatural Change in the American Southwest. In Roderick J. McIntosh, J. A. Tainter, & S. K. McIntosh (Eds.) *The Way the Wind Blows: Climate, History, and Human Action*. Columbia U Press, pp. 89–121.

Dennis, Andrew, Peter Foote, Richard Perkins (trans.) (2000). *Laws of Early Iceland, Grágás II*. Univ. of Manitoba Press, Manitoba.

Diamond, Jared (2005). *Collapse: How Societies Choose to Succeed or Fail*. Plenum NY.

Dugmore, A. J., Church, M. J., Buckland, P. C., Edwards, K. J., Lawson, I., McGovern, T. H., Panagiotakopulu, E., Simpson, I. A., Skidmore, P. & Sveinbjarnardóttir, G. (2004). The Norse *Landnám* on the North Atlantic islands: an environmental impact assessment, *Polar Record* 41, 1–17.

Dugmore, Andrew J., Mike J. Church, Kerry-Anne Mairs, T.H. McGovern, Sophia Perdikaris, and Orri Vésteinsson (2007a). Abandoned farms, volcanic impacts, and woodland management: revisiting Thjórsárdalur, the "Pompeii of Iceland". *Arctic Anthropology* 44(1), 1–12.

Dugmore, Andrew J., Douglas M. Borthwick, Mike J. Church, Alastair Dawson, Kevin J. Edwards, Christian Keller, Paul Mayewski, Thomas H. McGovern, Kerry-Anne Mairs & Guðrún Sveinbjarnardóttir (2007b). The Role of Climate in Settlement and Landscape Change in the North Atlantic Islands: An Assessment of Cumulative Deviations in High-Resolution Proxy Climate Records. *Human Ecology* (2007) 35,169–178.

Dugmore, Andrew J., Christian Keller & Thomas H. McGovern (2007c). Reflections on climate change, trade, and the contrasting fates of human settlements in the North Atlantic islands. *Arctic Anthropology* 44(1), 12–37.

Edwards, K. J., Borthwick, D., Cook, G. T., Dugmore, A. J., Mairs, K.-A., Church, M. J., Simpson, I. A. & Adderley, P. A. (2005). Landscape change in eastern Suðuroy, Faroe Islands: a hypothesis-based approach to the determination of natural processes and human artifice. *Human Ecology* 33, 621–651.

Edvardsson, Ragnar (Ed.) (2007). Archaeological Excavations at Qassiarsuk 2005–2006 Field report, Náttúrustofa Vestfjarða, NABO, and Grønlands Nationalmuseum & Arkiv field report accessed on line Dec. 22nd 2009 at http://www.nabohome.org/publications/fieldreports/BrattahlidE29NFieldReport07.pdf

Einarsson, Á., Stefánsdóttir, G., Jóhannesson, H., Ólafsson, J. S., Gíslason, G. M., Wakana, I., Guðbergsson, G. & Garðarsson, A. (2004). The ecology of Lake Mývatn and the river Laxá: variation in space and time. *Aquatic Ecology* 38, 317–348.

Fisher, C. T., J. B. Hill & Gary Feinman (Eds.) (2009). *The Archaeology of Environmental Change: Socionatural Legacies of Degradation and Resilience*. U Arizona Press, Tucson.

Fisher, C.T. (2009). Abandoning the Garden: the population/land degradation fallacy as applied to the Lake Patzcuaro Basin in Mexico. In J. B. Hill & Gary Feinman (Eds.) (2009). *The Archaeology of Environmental Change: Socionatural Legacies of Degradation and Resilience.* U Arizona Press, Tucson, pp. 209–323.

Friðriksson, Adolf, Orri Vésteinsson, T. H. McGovern (2004). Recent investigations at Hofstaðir, northern Iceland. In R. A. Hously & G. Coles (Eds.) *Atlantic Connections and Adaptations: Economies, environments and subsistence in lands bordering the North Atlantic,* AEA/NABO Environmental Archaeology Monographs 21, Oxbow Books. Pp. 191–202.

Gad, Finn (1970). *The History of Greenland Vol 1.* London C. Hurst and Company.

Gunderson, Lance, Garry Peterson, C. S. Holling (2008). Practicing adaptive management in complex social-ecological systems. In Jon Norberg & Graeme S. Cumming, *Complexity Theory for a Sustainable Future.* Columbia U Press NYC, pp. 223–246.

Hallsdóttir, Margrét (1987). *Pollen analytical studies of human influence in relation to the Landnam tephra layer in Southwest Iceland.* Lund: Univ. Lund.

Hill, J. Brett (2009). What difference does environmental degradation make? In Fisher, C. T., J. B. Hill & Gary Feinman (Eds.) (2009). *The Archaeology of Environmental Change: Socionatural Legacies of Degradation and Resilience.* U Arizona Press Tucson, pp. 160–177.

Hornberg, Alf, J. R. McNeill, & Joan Martinez-Alier (Eds.) (2007). *Rethinking Environmental History: World System History and Global Environmental Change.* Altamira Press.

Jennings, A. E. & Nancy J. Weiner (1996). Environmental change in eastern Greenland during the last 1300 years; evidence from foraminifera and lithofacies in Nansen Fjord, 68 degrees N. *The Holocene,* 8(3), 434–441.

Jennings, A. E., Hagen, S., Harðardóttir, J., Stein, R., Ogilvie, A. E. J. and Jónsdóttir, I. (2001a). Oceanographic change and terrestrial human impacts in a post A.D. 1400 sediment record on the southwest Iceland shelf. *Climatic Change* 48, 83–100.

Jennings, A. E., Hagen, S., Harðardóttir, J., Stein, R., Ogilvie, A. E. J. and Jónsdóttir, I. (2001b). Oceanographic Change and Terrestrial Human Impacts in a Post A.D. 1400 Sediment Record from the Southwest Iceland Shelf. In *The Iceberg in the Mist: Northern Research in Pursuit of a "Little Ice Age".* (Eds.) A. E. J. Ogilvie & T. Jónsson. London: Kluwer Academic Publishers.

Jensen et al. (2004). Diatom evidence of hydrographic changes and ice conditions in Igaliku Fjord, South Greenland, during the past 1500 years. *The Holocene* 14,2, 152–164.

Kirch, P. V. (2007). Hawaii as a Model System for Human Ecodynamics. *American Anthropologist* Volume 109, Issue 1, pp. 8–26.

Kohler,T. & Sander van der Leeuw (Ed.) (2007). *The Model-Based Archaeology of Socionatural Systems.* SAR press Santa Fe.

Lawson, Ian T., Church, M. J., McGovern, T. H., Arge, S. V., Edwards, K.

J., Gathorne-Hardy, F. J., Dugmore, A. J., Mairs, K.-A., Thomson, A. M., Woollett, J. & Sveinbjarnardóttir, G. (2005). Historical ecology on Sandoy, Faroe Islands: paleoenvironmental and archaeological perspectives. *Human Ecology* 33, 651–685.

Lawson, I.T., Gathorne-Hardy, F. J., Church, M., Einarsson, Á., Edwards, K. J., Perdikaris, S., McGovern, T. H., Amundsen, C. & Sveinbjarnardóttir, G. (2006). Human impact on freshwater environments in Norse and early medieval Mývatnssveit, Iceland. In Arneborg, J., Grønnow, B. (Ed.*) Dynamics of Northern Societies, Proceedings of the SILA/NABO Conference on Arctic and North Atlantic Archaeology*, Copenhagen, May 10th–14th, 2004. National Museum of Denmark, pp. 375–382.

Lawson, I. T., Gathorne-Hardy, F. J., Church, M. J., Newton, A. J., Edwards, K. J., Dugmore, A. J., Einarsson, Á. (2007). Environmental impacts of the Norse settlement: palaeoenvironmental data from Mývatnssveit, northern Iceland. *Boreas* 36(1), pp.1–19.

Lawson, I. T., Edwards, K. J., Church, M. J. et al. (2008). Human impact on an island ecosystem: pollen data from Sandoy, Faroe Islands. *Journal of Biogeography* 35 (6), 1130–1152.

Lucas, Gavin (2001). *Critical Approaches to Fieldwork; Contemporary and Historical Archaeological Practice.* Routledge Inc, NYC.

Lucas, Gavin (2009). *Hofstaðir; Excavations of a Viking Age Feasting Hall in North-Eastern Iceland*, Institute of Archaeology Monograph Series 1, Reykjavík.

Lucas, Gavin & Thomas H. McGovern (2008). Bloody slaughter: ritual decapitation and display at Viking age Hofstaðir N Iceland. *Journal of European Archaeology* 10(1), 7–30.

Madsen, Christian Koch with Jette Arneborg, Poul Baltzer Heide & Konrad Smiarowski (2009). Norse Coastal Farms Field Report of a Survey in the Southwest "Vatnahverfi Peninsula" Summer 2009, IPY and National Museum of Denmark Field Report accessed Dec. 22nd 2009 at http://www.nabohome.org/publications/fieldreports/VatnahverfiFieldReport2009.pdf

Mahler, D. (2007). *Sæteren ved Argisbrekka.* Fróðskapur. Tórshavn: Faroe University Press.

McGovern, Thomas H. (1981). The economics of extinction in Norse Greenland. In T. M. L. Wigley et al. (Eds.) *Climate and History*, Cambridge Univ. Press.

McGovern, T. H. & R. H. Jordan (1982). Settlement and land use in the inner fjords of Godthaab District, West Greenland, *Arctic Anthropology* 19(1), 63–80.

McGovern, T. H. (1985). Contributions to the Paleoeconomy of Norse Greenland, *Acta Archaeologica,* Vol 54, 73–122.

McGovern, T. H., G. F. Bigelow, T. Amorosi, & D. Russell (1988). Northern Islands, Human Error, & Environmental Degradation: a Preliminary Model for Social and Ecological Change in the Medieval North Atlantic. *Human Ecology* 16(3), 45–105.

McGovern, T. H. (1994). Management for extinction in Norse Greenland. In C. Crumley (Ed.) *Historical Ecology: Cultural Knowledge and Changing Landscapes.* School of American Research Monograph, Santa Fe NM, pp. 127–154.

McGovern, T. H., Sophia Perdikaris, Árni Einarsson, Jane Sidell (2006). Coastal Connections, Local Fishing, and Sustainable egg harvesting, patterns of Viking age inland wild resource use in Mývatn District, Northern Iceland. *Environmental Archaeology* 11.1, 102–128.

McGovern, Thomas H., Orri Vésteinsson, Adolf Friðriksson, Mike Church, Ian Lawson, Ian A. Simpson, Árni Einarsson, Andy Dugmore, Gordon Cook, Sophia Perdikaris, Kevin Edwards, Amanda M. Thomson, W. Paul Adderley, Anthony Newton, Gavin Lucas, Oscar Aldred (2007). Landscapes of Settlement in Northern Iceland: Historical Ecology of Human Impact & Climate Fluctuation on the Millennial Scale. *American Anthropologist* 109(1), 27–51.

Norberg, Jon, James Wilson, Brian Walker & Elinor Ostrom (2008). Diversity and Resilience of Social-Ecological Systems. In Jon Norberg & Graeme S. Cumming, *Complexity Theory for a Sustainable Future.* Columbia U Press NYC, pp. 46–81.

Ogilvie, Astrid & T. H. McGovern (2000). Sagas & Science: Climate and Human Impacts in the North Atlantic. In W. W. Fitzhugh (Ed.), *Viking Voyagers.* Smithsonian Inst Press, pp. 385–394.

Ogilvie, A. E. J., Woollett, J. M., Smiarowski, K., Arneborg, J., Troelstra, S., Pálsdóttir, A. and McGovern, T. H. (2010). Seals and sea ice in medieval Greenland. In press, *Journal of the North Atlantic.*

Peloquin, C. & F. Berkes (2009). Local knowledge, subsistence harvests and social-ecological complexity in James Bay. *Human Ecology* 37(5), 533–547.

Redman, C. (1999). *Human Impact on Ancient Environments.* Tucson U Arizona Press.

Redman, C., P. R. Fish, J. D. Rogers, S. R. James (Eds.) (2004). *Introduction to the Archaeology of Global Change: the Impact of Humans on their Environment.* Smithsonian Inst. Press, Washington DC.

Roba, H. G. & G. Oba (2009). Efficacy of integrating herder knowledge and ecological methods for monitoring rangeland degradation. *Human Ecology* 37(5), 533–547.

Simpson, I. A., Milek, K. B. & Guðmundsson, G. (1999). A re-interpretation of the great pit at Hofstaðir, Iceland, using sediment thin section micromorphology. *Geoarchaeology* 14, 511–530.

Simpson, I. A., Dugmore, A. J., Thomson, A. M. & Vésteinsson, O. (2001). Crossing the thresholds: human ecology and historical patterns of landscape degradation. *Catena* 42, 175–192.

Simpson, I. A., Vésteinsson, O., Adderley, W. P. & McGovern T. H. (2003). Fuel resources in landscapes of settlement. *Journal of Archaeological Science* 30, 1401–1420.

Simpson, I. A., Guðmundsson, G., Thomson, A. M. & Cluett, J. (2004). Assessing the role of winter grazing in historic land degradation, Mývatnssveit, north-east Iceland. *Geoarchaeology* 19, 471–503.

Śmiarowski, Konrad (2007). Greenland 2007 Field Season Preliminary Report, IPY field report accessed Dec. 22, 2009 at http://www.nabohome.org/publications/fieldreports/Greenland2007FieldReportKS05-23-09.pdf

Śmiarowski, Konrad (2008). Archaeological Investigations in Vatnahverfi, Greenland 2008 Season Preliminary Report, IPY field report accessed on line Dec. 22 2009 at http://www.nabohome.org/publications/fieldreports/Greenland2008Field%20ReportKS05-23-09.pdf

Śmiarowski, Konrad, Albína Pálsdóttir, Thomas H. McGovern (2007). Preliminary Assessment Report of the Archaeofauna from KNK 203 (E 74), a Norse Farm in the Eastern Settlement, Greenland. CUNY Northern Science and Education Center Zooarchaeology Laboratory Report No.39, accessed on line Dec. 22nd 2009 at http://www.abohome.org/publications/labreports/Norsec39E74PrelimZooarchAssessment.pdf

Thomson, Amanda (2003). *Human Impacts and Herding Ecology in N Iceland: Búmodel and its implications.* PhD thesis. School of Environmental Sciences U Stirling, Scotland.

Thomson, Amanda, I. A. Simpson, J. L. Brown (2005). Sustainable rangeland grazing in Norse Faroe. *Human Ecology* 33 (5), 737–761.

Vésteinsson, Orri, T. H. McGovern & Christian Keller (2002). Enduring Impacts: social and environmental aspects of Viking Age Settlement in Iceland and Greenland. *Archaeologica islandica* 2, 98–136.

Vésteinsson, Orri, Helgi Þorláksson, Árni Einarsson (2006). *Reykjavik AD 871+/-2*, Reykjavík: Reykjavík City Museum.

Vésteinsson, Orri (Ed.) (2007). *Archaeological Investigations in Mývatnssveit 2007.* Field report of Fornleifastofnun Íslands FS386-02263, Reykjavík 2008, accessed on line Dec. 22 2009 from http://www.nabohome.org/publications/fieldreports/ArchaeologicalinvestigationsinMyvatnssveit2007.pdf

Vibe, Christian (1967). Arctic animals in relation to climatic fluctuations. *Meddelelser om Grønland* 170(5).

Ward, Elisabeth I. (2000). Reflections on an Icon: Vikings in American Culture. In W. W. Fitzhugh & E. I. Ward (Eds.) *Vikings, the North Atlantic Saga.* Smithsonian Inst. Press, Washington DC, pp. 365–374.

Death as an Omen

ELSE MUNDAL

ABSTRACT

This article discusses omens connected to a man's death. In *Egils saga Skalla-Grímssonar,* it is mentioned that Þórólfr, Egill's brother, was killed by the king, Haraldr hárfagri, and fell forwards onto the king's feet. Kveld-Úlfr, Þórólfr's old father, interpreted the incident, saying that a man who fell forwards would be avenged. In spite of the fact that we have a saga which offers an interpretation of falling forwards when killed, omens of this type have been overlooked in analyses of saga literature. This article examines other scenes in sagas of Icelanders that seem to contain omens of the same type. Finally, the question is raised whether some descriptions in *Sturlunga saga* of men leaning backwards, or in some cases forward when killed, could be based on the old omen, but given a new meaning in a Christian context.

Keywords: Omen, death, falling forwards/backwards, revenge, Old Norse culture, Old Norse literature.

In Old Norse literature, especially in the sagas of Icelanders, the death of a saga hero is often prophesied or foreseen. However, death in the sagas, or rather the circumstances surrounding a death, can also function as an omen in itself which reveals what will happen in the future. There are some well-known examples of this type of omen to be found in saga literature. To die in the high seat, for example, seems to signal that the newly dead man is unwilling to leave his position of power in this world and therefore is likely to remain as a ghost. The death of Þórólfr bægifótr as described in chapter 33 of *Eyrbyggja saga* is a good example of such an omen.[1] Additionally, if dead people became so heavy that it was difficult or impossible to carry them to their grave, that was another omen which signalled that the dead person was likely to return as a revenant to disturb the living. A good example of this is found in chapter 6 of *Grœnlendinga saga*, when Grímhildr dies during a plague. Her corpse is so heavy that it is dif-

1 Þórólfr bægifótr's death in the high seat frightened everyone, and it is obvious from the text that people took it as a sign that Þórólfr would become a ghost. His son, Arnkell, took steps to prevent his father from returning from the dead by taking him out through a hole in the wall rather than through the door; a precaution also found in folk beliefs from later times. By removing the body in this fashion, the hope was that the dead person should not find his way back to his old house. In *Eyrbyggja saga* this precaution was futile, and Þórólfr returned as a dangerous and troublesome ghost.

ficult for her husband to remove it from the house.[2] Furthermore, while the deaths of people such as Þórólfr and Grímhildr indicate that they will remain with the living, it is often the case that ghosts of this type also want to bring living people over to the realm of the dead. Consequently, dead people who rise up and start walking around, in most cases immediately after their death, can strike fear into those who encounter them, and they are often spoken of as the "living dead". In sagas such as *Eyrbyggja saga*, *Grœnlendinga saga* and *Svarfdœla* saga, many such ghosts feature in the texts. In general, such figures indicate that the society is in trouble, and more people will die.

It seems, however, that the significance of such prophetic deaths and the circumstances surrounding them could alter along with the change of religion from paganism to Christianity. Such a shift of perspective is logical, since in the Christian culture, the most important information revealed by the circumstances surrounding a person's death was whether their soul would go to Heaven or Hell. Therefore death omens which, in the heathen culture, might reveal what was going to happen in the future, could now be reinterpreted in light of the dead person's Christian identity.

Consequently, it seems that a death in the high seat is really dangerous only in a "heathen" context. Such a death is also described in chapter 22 of *Vatnsdœla saga*, where Ingimundr dies in the high seat having been fatally wounded. However, the difference between Ingimundr and Þórólfr bægifótr is that Ingimundr is a very good man, a heathen who behaves like a Christian. The last thing he does before he dies is to send a message to his killer warning him to run away before Ingimundr's sons kill him in revenge. Thus, in such a "Christian" context, the old bad omen has ceased to function. Similarly, the motif of the heavy corpse or coffin is also found in Christian literature. In this context the meaning of the motif has changed, so that it is no longer a bad omen that predicts future problems. Instead, it only means that there is something the dead person wants to be done before he or she can go to his or her rest. Even those who can be referred to as the "living dead" are less frightening in a Christian context. For example, Þórgunna in *Eyrbyggja saga* is described as one of the "living dead", but she is also a Christian woman, and after her death she rises from her coffin to cook for the men who are taking her body all the way from Snæfellsnes to Skálholt to entomb her there. Elsewhere, for example in *Grœnlendinga saga*, the living dead are described in a very terrifying way. But in addition to the frightening stories describing events such as dead people

2 Þórólfr bægifótr's corpse also became so heavy that he was difficult to move, and his son Arnkell had some difficulty in removing him from his high seat. This may have been because the dead man was strong, and not necessarily because he was supernaturally heavy. However, when Arnkell together with others tried to transfer Þórólfr from his first grave mound to another after he had begun walking around as a ghost, he had become so heavy that it was very difficult to move him, even with the help of oxen.

trying to climb into the beds of the living, we recognize motifs or elements of motifs borrowed from Christian texts. For instance, Þorsteinn Eiríksson walks around after his death and wants to speak to his wife, and although people are afraid, he represents no danger to her. He wants to tell her about her future, and reassure her that he has come to a good place. In this scene, we recognize a motif known from legends and visions in which dead people return, most often in a dream, to give good advice or important information to the living.[3] Such a blend of the terrifying Old Norse "living dead" tradition and the Christian motif is strange, but demonstrates the great ability of folk belief to adapt to changes in its surrounding culture and religion.

The examples mentioned above are well-known omens in Old Norse literary sources, and it is usually easy to understand how they function. Much has been written about these striking and exciting motifs.[4] There are, however, also motifs connected to a man's death that serve as important omens, but which nevertheless have not attracted attention.

In this article I want to focus on omens connected to the circumstances surrounding a death which have been overlooked in previous research. These particular cases indicate whether there will be revenge after a killing based on how, or in what direction, the man who was killed fell. Despite the fact that one saga offers an interpretation of such a death, it seems that, in general, they are no longer properly recognized and understood when we meet them in the Old Norse texts. I will draw attention to a few episodes in saga literature which include omens of this type, starting with the episode in *Egils saga Skalla-Grímssonar* that offers an explanation of the death's prophetic significance. I will then address the question of whether these omens – like those connected to deaths in the high seat, heavy corpses and the visitations of dead people – were also given new meanings in a Christian context.

In the Old Norse heathen culture, and also for a long time after its Christianization, the question of revenge was very important. Consequently, when a person had been killed, it was only reasonable that the circumstances of the killing might be interpreted as omens regarding the course that vengeance would take. In the saga texts there are not very many warnings of this type, probably because the killings and revenge killings were constructed as the climax of the story, and were foreshadowed in many ways, ever more clearly as the dramatic finale approached. As a result, it would not have been necessary to introduce predictions of revenge by revealing additional details about the original killing.

3 In the Old Norse material the miracles connected to the legends about St Óláfr offer several good examples of this motif.

4 See for instance Sayers (1986), Vésteinn Ólason (2003), and Martin (2005) with references.

Despite this, there are, however, some interesting examples of this type of omen, which build on how and in what direction a man fell when he was killed.

In chapter 22 of *Egils saga Skalla-Grímssonar*, it is told how Þórólfr Kveld-Úlfsson is killed by King Haraldr hárfagri himself, and the saga states: *sjálfr konungr veitti honum banasár, ok fell Þórólfr fram á fœtr konungi* (the king himself gave him his mortal wound, and Þórólfr fell forwards onto the king's feet). These details are emphasised in the text, and their significance is made clearer later in the saga, for they are repeated when the story about Þórólfr's death is told to his old father, Kveld-Úlfr (chapter 24). Kveld-Úlfr asks carefully about any details connected to his son's death, and the saga says:

> Ǫlvir sagði allt þat, er hann spurði, svá þat, at Haraldr konungr veitti honum sár þat, er œrit myndi eitt til bana, ok Þórólfr fell nær á fœtr konungi á grúfu.
>
> Ǫlvir told him everything he asked about, also that King Haraldr gave him the wound which alone was enough to kill him and that Þórólfr fell forwards, almost onto the king's feet.

In this particular case the meaning of falling forwards onto somebody's feet is explained in the text. The saga continues with Kveld-Úlfr's remarks to Ǫlvir:

> "Vel hefir þú sagt, því at þat hafa gamlir menn mælt, at þess manns myndi hefnt verða, ef hann felli á grúfu, ok þeim nær koma hefndin er fyrir yrði, er hinn felli; [...]."
>
> "Well have you told the story, because old people have said that the man who fell forwards will be avenged, and the revenge will strike close to the man before whom he falls; [...]."

Kveld-Úlfr continues by saying that he doubts that they [his family] will experience the luck to see Þórólfr avenged. However, it would be against the rules of saga composition to signal an omen that was not later developed, and – as we know – in the next generation Þórólfr's nephew, Egill Skalla-Grímsson, drives King Eiríkr blóðøx (King Haraldr's son) from his kingdom with the help of his skill in magic, and kills one of Eiríkr's sons (King Haraldr's grandson).

A similar description of a killing which seems to contain an omen signalling revenge is found in chapter 45 of *Grettis saga Ásmundarsonar*, which tells how Atli, Grettir's brother, is killed. The killer arrives at Atli's farm and knocks at the door. A woman goes out, but does not see the newcomer who is hiding, and so she goes back inside. There is another knock at the door, and Atli goes out himself:

> […] hann sá engan úti. Væta var úti mikil, ok því gekk hann eigi út ok helt sinni hendi í hvárn dyrustafinn ok litask svá um. Í því bili snaraði Þorbjǫrn fram fyrir dyrrnar ok lagði tveim hǫndum til Atla með spjótinu á honum miðjum, svá at stóð í gegnum hann. Atli mælti við, er hann fekk lagit: "Þau tíðkast nú in breiðu spjótin," segir hann. Síðan fell hann fram á þreskǫldinn. Þá kómu fram konur, er í stofunni hǫfðu verit; þær sá, at Atli var dauðr.

> […] he saw nobody out there. It was very wet outside, and so he did not go out, but held onto the doorposts with each hand and looked around. At that moment Þorbjǫrn rushed in front of the door and with both his hands he stabbed Atli in the middle of his body with his spear, so that it stood through him. When he was stabbed, Atli spoke: "The broad spears are in fashion these days," he said. Thereafter he fell forwards onto the door-sill. Then the women who had been in the house came out; they saw that Atli was dead.

If we examine this scene, it is not very likely that Atli should fall forwards. He is standing in the doorway looking out, and the killer jumps at him from the outside. Consequently, we might expect Atli to fall backwards into the house. However, the author probably wants to foreshadow Atli's revenge, and sure enough, later in chapter 48, Grettir avenges his brother.

In *Brennu-Njáls saga*, chapter 146, there is a description of the killing of a man who falls forwards when dying, which initially does not seem to fit in with previous examples of this motif. Kári, having escaped from the burning at Njáll's house, is attacked by Mǫrðr Sigfússson, Sigurðr Lambason and Lambi Sigurðarson. He defends himself bravely with weapons in both hands, attacking Sigurðr Lambason with his right hand so that, as the saga says: *fell hann þegar dauðr* (he fell and was dead at once). At the same time, Kári brandishes his sword in his left hand at Mǫrðr Sigfússon, and in this case the saga reports: *fell hann áfram ok þegar dauðr* (he fell forwards and was dead at once). In total, four men are killed in this battle, and it is said of three of them that they fell and were dead at once. Only in the case of Mǫrðr Sigfússon is it mentioned that he fell forwards. It could, of course, be a coincidence that the direction of the fall is mentioned only in connection with Mǫrðr Sigfússon, but if we look at what happens later in the saga, it turns out that the surviving sons of Sigfúss, the brothers of Mǫrðr, take the leadership in a failed attempt to take revenge on Kári. Consequently, the earlier mention of Mǫrðr falling forwards may have been meant to signal that an attempted revenge would come as a consequence of the killing of him.

Since it is said that to fall forwards forebodes revenge, to fall backwards into the hands of one's own people rather than in the direction of the enemy might be expected to mean the opposite, namely that the man who had been killed would not be avenged. One description of a killing which seems to predict just such an outcome can be found in chapter 3 of *Fóstbrœðra saga* in the scene describing how Þorgeirr Hávarsson, one of the heroes of the tale, takes revenge for the murder of his father. Þorgeirr, who is 15 years old at the time, is staying with his foster-brother Þormóðr in Ísafjǫrðr when he hears that his father has been killed in Borgarfjǫrðr. He goes south at once, and arrives at the killer's farm late in the evening after dark. He asks his father's killer to come out, and demands compensation, but the man answers that he never pays fines. Þorgeirr is standing outside in the dark, his father's killer is standing in the doorway of his house with his men behind him, and both are armed. The saga continues:

> [...] þá gengr Þorgeirr at durunum ok lagði spjóti á honum miðjum ok þegar í gegnum hann, svá at hann fell í dyrrnar inn í fang þeim fylgðarmǫnnum sínum.

> [...] then Þorgeirr went to the door and drove his spear against him in the middle of his body, and it pierced him at once so that he fell into the doorway and into the arms of his companions.

Þorgeirr at once disappears in the dark and rides on to his mother's farm where he arrives in the middle of the night. He tells his mother the news, and ends his story by saying: [...] *ok fell hann á bak aptr í fang fylgðarmǫnnum sínum* ([...] and he fell backwards into the laps of his companions). This detail is here emphasised by first being mentioned in the description of the killing and then repeated by Þorgeirr when telling the story to his mother. In this case, the reason that such an omen is used in *Fóstbrœðra saga* is likely to be that the author wanted to emphasise that there was no causal connection between Þorgeirr's first killing and his own death later on. Þorgeirr is in many ways a negative character from the very beginning of the saga, but by avenging his father as a fifteen-year-old boy he proves his worth as a real saga hero. Furthermore, by indicating that there will be no retribution for this killing, this omen has a calming effect, since it becomes clear that Þorgeirr is in no immediate danger as a result of his actions.

In chapter 13 of *Fóstbrœðra saga* Þorgeirr kills again, this time at the request of King Óláfr the saint. His target is a man named Þórir who has attacked a member of the king's bodyguard, and there follows descriptions of a scene very similar to that in chapter 3. Þorgeirr arrives at the farm of the man he plans to kill late in the evening, asks the man to come to the door, and demands compensation. When the man is unwilling to give any compensation Þorgeirr suddenly kills him with his spear. The saga rounds off the scene by saying: *fell Þórir inn í dyrrnar ok dauðr* (Þórir fell into the doorway and was dead). In this case too, Þorgeirr kills with good reason, and as the story is told in *Fóstbrœðra saga*, the killing of Þórir does not result in revenge being taken on Þorgeirr.[5]

With the exception of *Egils saga Skalla-Grímssonar*, there is no other explanation in any saga text of the meaning of falling forwards or backwards when killed. However, if it were a common folk belief that the way in which a man fell could predict whether or not he would be avenged, an explanation would not have been necessary, since the saga audience would have understood its significance. Omens of this type may not be very frequent, but there seems to be an underlying folk belief which can be applied when needed. This same belief is probably reflected in an Old Norse saying found in *Sturlunga saga* (chapter 311 – *Þórðar saga kakala*): *falla á fœtr frændum sínum*. It can be literally translated as 'to fall onto the feet of one's relatives' but more loosely means something like 'not to obtain anything'.

The examples and arguments outlined above should not be extended to suggest that any description of how or in what direction a slain man falls has a deeper meaning or is to be seen as an omen. There are some cases in which describing how a man fell may have been included in order to explain the damage on the dead body,[6] and there are cases in which the direction of the fall is described so imprecisely that it can hardly be meant as an omen.[7]

An omen of revenge is of course closely connected to literature dealing with killings and feuds, and it is perhaps not obvious that such a motif could be influenced by Christianity and given a new meaning in a Christian context. There are, however, a few very interesting descriptions of killings in *Sturlunga saga*, which, as opposed to the sagas of Icelanders, describe warfare and kill-

5 According to *Þórarins þáttr* Þorgeirr was outlawed because of the killing of two men, one of whom was Þórir.

6 *Kjalnesinga saga*, chapter 18, contains a description of the fight between Búi and his son Jǫkull, Búi's son with a troll woman. Here it is stated that Búi fell forwards, but it is hardly meant as an omen of revenge (and indeed no revenge takes place). Búi is not killed when falling forwards, but dies three nights later, and when it is mentioned that he fell forwards it is probably to explain the fatal chest wound caused by a stone that he lands upon.

7 In *Þorsteins saga hvíta*, chapter 6, we have a description of a scene that has very much in common with the aforementioned scenes in *Grettis saga Ásmundarsonar*, chapter 45, and in *Fóstbrœðra saga*, chapters 3 and 13. Þorsteinn arrives at the farm of Einarr whom he plans to kill. When Einarr comes to the door and sees who has arrived, he tries to escape by running into the house. Þorsteinn kills Einarr, and the saga states that he fell into the *skemma* (a small house/room). Einarr's family later took revenge on Þorsteinn by killing his brothers. However, in this case the direction in which the dead men fell can hardly be understood as a prophecy of revenge. Einarr probably fell forwards since he turned around in the doorway and ran into the house, but he does not fall in the direction of Þorsteinn – which would have been a foreboding of revenge – but rather away from him.

ings in a society that had been Christian for a long time, and where it should be expected that a Christian way of thinking had taken root. In *Sturlunga saga* (chapter 328 – *Þórðar saga kakala*) in the description of the killing of Þórðr Bjarnarson, it is told that after having asked for permission to go to confession he leans backwards and lies down on his back, waiting for his enemies to kill him. The same is said about Tumi a few chapters later (chapter 332). The description of the killing of Kálfr and his son Guttormr (chapter 248 – *Íslendinga saga*) follows the same pattern. The two men know that they will be killed and go to a priest to make their confession. In this case they also bring a cross from the church with them out into the churchyard, and lie down beside the cross to receive the deadly blow. The description of the killing of Sturla Sighvatsson (chapter 288 – *Íslendinga saga*) follows more or less the same structure. Sturla confesses his sins to a priest before lying down to be killed. In some of these killings the men who lie down are already fatally wounded, in other cases they are not. In most of the cases we can see from the context that they are leaning back (from descriptions of where they are wounded, from the fact that they look at their killers, and so on). In the case of Þórðr Bjarnarson it is emphasised in the text, which states: *Lagðist Þórður þá niður opinn* (Þórðr lay down with his face up).

The confessions of the men who are about to be killed, their proximity to the church, churchyard and holy objects, and the brutal nature of their deaths, mean that these killings can often resonate with descriptions of the executions of martyrs. It is difficult to know how much significance should be placed upon descriptions of dying men leaning backwards, as to lean backwards is a natural position for a wounded man to adopt. For example, when St Óláfr in the different descriptions of his death leaned against a stone before he was killed by his enemies, it is difficult to say that there is a deeper meaning to be read from the position in which he died. It is, however, tempting to ask whether the descriptions of men who first asked for permission to confess and then leaned backwards waiting passively for the deadly blow should be seen to be connected with the aforementioned omen that predicted that if a man fell forwards he would be avenged, and if he fell backwards he would not. Leaning backwards could perhaps signal that no retaliation was desired, as these men died as Christians without any thoughts of revenge. Thus, the old omen is then turned into a symbol of a non-aggressive and forgiving Christian disposition in this new religious context.

There are also cases where it is emphasised that dying men lean forwards. About Markús Sighvatsson (chapter 288 – *Íslendinga saga*), it is said that he *lagðist á grúfu*, which means that he bent forwards with his face down. This is the position of praying. However, when seen in connection with the old belief that falling forwards when dying signalled that there would be future revenge, the question is whether this position could indicate a hateful attitude towards one's enemies and hopes for vengeance?

The motifs discussed in this article are only examples of descriptions of killings which at the same time might function as omens, and in no way do I claim to have provided a complete list. My purpose has been to call attention to a type of omen connected with death which I think has been overlooked by modern saga readers, but which probably gave useful hints to the medieval audience. If the motifs as they appear in the aforementioned episodes in *Sturlunga saga* did indeed develop from the motifs that functioned as omens of revenge in the heathen context, they demonstrate the remarkable ability of these cultural elements to adapt to new circumstances. Subsequently, in the Christian context they seem to have stopped functioning as prophetic omens, and started functioning as motifs that underline and support new Christian themes.

BIBLIOGRAPHY

Brennu-Njáls saga. (1954). Einar Ól. Sveinsson (Ed.), Íslenzk fornrit XII. Reykjavík: Hið íslenzka fornritafélag.

Egils saga Skalla-Grímssonar. (1933). Sigurður Nordal (Ed.), Íslenzk fornrit II. Reykjavík: Hið íslenzka fornritafélag.

Eyrbyggja saga. (1935). Einar Ól. Sveinsson & Matthías Þórðarson (Eds.), Íslenzk fornrit IV. Reykjavík: Hið íslenzka fornritafélag.

Fóstbrœðra saga. (1943). Björn K. Þórólfsson & Guðni Jónsson (Eds.), Íslenzk fornrit VI. Reykjavík: Hið íslenzka fornritafélag.

Grettis saga Ásmundarsonar. (1936). Guðni Jónsson (Ed.), Íslenzk fornrit XII. Reykjavík: Hið íslenzka fornritafélag.

Grœnlendinga saga. (1935). Einar Ól. Sveinsson & Matthías Þórðarson (Eds.), Íslenzk fornrit IV. Reykjavík: Hið íslenzka fornritafélag.

Kjalnesinga saga. (1959). Jóhannes Halldórsson (Ed.), Íslenzk fornrit XIV. Reykjavík: Hið íslenzka fornritafélag.

Martin, J. D. (2005). Law and the (Un)dead: medieval models for understanding the hauntings in *Eyrbyggja saga*. *Saga Book 29*, 67–82.

Sayers, W. (1996). The Alien and Alienated as Unquiet Dead in the Sagas of the Icelanders. In Cohen, J. J. (Ed.), *Monster Theory: Reading Culture* (pp. 242–263). Minneapolis: University of Minnesota Press.

Sturlunga saga. (1988). Örnólfur Thorsson (Ed.), Reykjavík: Svart á hvítu.

Svarfdœla saga. (1956). Jónas Kristjánsson (Ed.), Íslenzk fornrit IX. Reykjavík: Hið íslenzka fornritafélag.

Vatnsdœla saga. (1939). Einar Ól. Sveinsson (Ed.), Íslenzk fornrit VIII. Reykjavík: Hið íslenzka fornritafélag.

Vésteinn Ólason. (2003). The Un/Grateful Dead – From Baldr to Bægifótr. In M. Clunies Ross (Ed.), *Old Norse Myths, Literature and Society* (pp. 153–171). Cambridge: Cambridge University Press.

Þórarins þáttr. (1940). Björn Sigfússon (Ed.), Íslenzk fornrit X. Reykjavík: Hið íslenzka fornritafélag.

Þorsteins saga hvíta. (1950). Jón Jóhannesson (Ed.), Íslenzk fornrit XI. Reykjavík: Hið íslenzka fornritafélag.

Where did All the People Go? Looking for Eleventh-Century Graves in Southern Norway

SÆBJØRG WALAKER NORDEIDE

ABSTRACT

Old Norse burial rituals generally continued until the middle of the tenth or the eleventh century in Norway. The disappearance of Norse graves is generally explained by the introduction of Christianity: The people had converted, and Christian cult took over from the Norse rituals. However, the earliest Christian churches and burials generally do not appear before well into the twelfth century. Although in some areas there may be an overlap in time when both Christians and non-Christians existed, there is a considerable time gap when neither Old Norse nor Christian graves are found in most areas of Norway. This article discusses the missing graves in this period. It is suggested that the first converts were the landowners, who had to concentrate on central grave fields. The poorer people's graves are missing for this period.

Keywords: Late Iron Age graves, Christian graves, Christianization, archaeology, Norway, urbanization.

INTRODUCTION

Old Norse[1] burial rituals generally continued until the middle of the tenth/beginning of the eleventh century in Norway. Thus far, the latest certain case identified in southern Norway has been dated to the end of the eleventh century. The disappearance of Norse graves is generally assumed to be linked to the introduction of Christianity, with Christian burials replacing Norse rituals (Brendalsmo, 2002, p. 262; Solberg, 2000, p. 313). However, it is not as simple as this; with a few exceptions, the earliest securely dated Christian churches and burials do not appear until well into the twelfth century, and most medieval churches still standing were not built before the Nidaros archbishopric was founded in 1152/53. Even if many church excavations have revealed earlier churches, as well as even earlier Christian graves, the evidence for churches prior to the late-eleventh century and up to 1100/1150 is poor. In most areas of Norway there seems to be a considerable time gap when neither Old Norse

[1] Throughout this article, I will use the term 'Old Norse' to mean 'non-Christian' but excluding the Saami. There may be Saami graves in the south as well, but these are yet to be identified.

nor Christian graves are found.[2] The main questions that I will seek to answer in this paper are: Where are the people's graves in this period when neither Christian nor non-Christian graves are found? Was the time gap dominated by Christian or non-Christian cults?

THE END OF OLD NORSE RELIGIOUS CULTS – THE LACK OF OLD NORSE GRAVES

There are an estimated 6000 graves surviving in Norway from the Viking Age, around AD 800–1030 (Solberg, 2000, p. 222), but this number of graves is much too low to account for any estimation of the population in the area during these years. Many graves and other traces of the religious cults from the time before around 1150/1200 have obviously not been traced archaeologically. The tumuli, obvious as they are in the landscape, are easiest to detect and thus well represented in the records. Furnished graves are also easier to find than those with no grave goods, while very few totally unfurnished graves without tumuli are found. The buried persons in many of the furnished graves, particularly in barrows, were probably rich people, members of the landowning classes (Brøgger, 1937; Solberg, 2000, p. 268; Thäte, 2007). If this is the case, then it would explain why the graves of average and poor people are underrepresented or generally missing in the records of late Iron Age graves. Nevertheless, we have to presume that every person, rich or poor, was buried. Consequently, the question of where the missing graves or cult places are most likely to be located is an important one.

Part of this problem could probably be explained by the fact that almost no cemeteries in Norway have been excavated in their entirety. Many barrows were excavated more than a century ago, and often the main goal was to discover what was at the centre of a barrow and not whether there could be anything of interest in the mound itself – in the stratigraphy or outside or around the tumulus (Gansum, 2004, pp. 310–312). However, there are several indications in old records that more graves existed on a site where one or more graves are recorded, as in the annual publication from *Foreningen til Norske Fortidsminnesmerkers Bevaring*. For instance, in Rauma in Romsdal, five burial mounds were recorded at Høgreiten in 1878, but at the same time there was information suggesting that many more once existed but had disappeared (Bendixen, 1879). Similarly at Hen there were reports of a rich cemetery with tumuli at the site of the later church by the end of nineteenth century, but by that time most of it had been lost (Ziegler, 1892).

2 The discussions in this article are based on analyses of archaeological data discussed and presented in greater details elsewhere (Nordeide, in press).

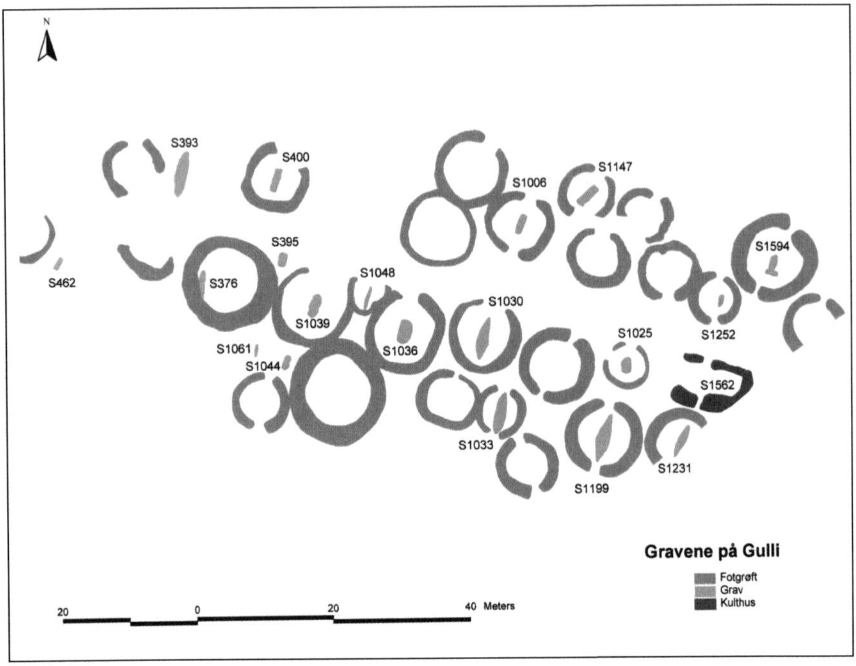

Fig. 1. A Viking Age cemetery at Gulli, Vestfold (Gjerpe, 2005, p. 25).

More often than not, graves are found close to previously recorded graves rather than on new sites, and new discoveries of big cemeteries at modern large-scale excavation projects are rare. One exception is Gulli in Vestfold (Fig. 1), where a late Iron Age cemetery with many graves – originally with tumuli – was discovered during a motorway rescue project (Gjerpe, 2005). On this basis, it is reasonable to assume that some of the missing graves from the late Iron Age would be more likely to be located close to those already recorded rather than as big cemeteries at unknown sites.

Old Norse graves generally seem to have disappeared around the middle of the tenth/early eleventh century. But the chronology of the archaeological material is mostly based on typology developed a century ago by scholars such as Oluf Rygh and Jan Petersen (J. Petersen, 1919, 1928, 1951; Rygh, 1885). Although this chronology has proved to be reliable, it also has its problems and is not very precise. Besides, over the years curators have automatically dated barrows based on the presumption that a barrow is pre-Christian, and should accordingly be given a pre-1030 date, which is the year of the 'official' conversion of Norway when King Olav, the later St. Olav, was killed in the battle at Stiklestad. Any find that has not suited this model has been dismissed or explained as some kind of error or anomaly. Poor methods may thus account for some of the missing graves, and some of the time gap regarding grave finds, may be explained by problems in chronology, but this does not provide a sufficiently complete answer to my questions.

Although written sources from this period are scarce and their chronology and reliability uncertain, it looks as though there is a strong link between Christianity, early kings and the first legislation made in Norway. One of the earliest aspects of legislation was to pave the way for a Christian way of life, through measures such as forbidding alternative religions. Burials in tumuli, cult activity at barrows and Old Norse sacrificial meals were forbidden, and the penalty was harsh: those who did not respect the law were to be expelled from the country (see for instance Gulating Codex Chap. 1/29, Robberstad, 1969). This would most likely contribute to the disappearance of a public Old Norse cult, but the disappearance of Old Norse graves linked to public cults was not necessarily synonymous with the end of belief in an Old Norse religion.

In sum, the recorded graves partly reflect the social profile and the character of the cult, which could affect both the visibility of a grave and thus the chance for it to be recovered. In addition, preservation conditions, excavation methods, early medieval legislation and modern cultivation have influenced the number of burial sites that have been recorded. We may assume that very many graves are yet missing.

THE INTRODUCTION OF CHRISTIANITY – THE OLDEST CHURCHES

There is no general view of all excavations in churches and at church sites in Norway, but after discussions with various colleagues at Universities, NIKU and Riksantikvaren,[3] I have studied the most relevant excavation reports, paying close attention to securely dated contexts. Based on this, the very earliest, most securely dated Christian churches and graves have been filtered (Table 1). The chronology of the standing churches is often more precise than of non-Christian graves, particularly when we are able to rely on dendrochronology. However, this evidence proves that extremely few churches still standing in Norway can be dated to earlier than the middle of the twelfth century (Table 2). Graves and traces from one or more churches preceding the standing constructions are often discovered during excavations on church sites (Müller, 1991), but potential dating evidence is often not observed in a secure context and may sometimes be confused with non-Christian graves at the same site.

3 Riksantikvaren (Directorate for Cultural Heritage Management) is responsible for the management of churches, including restoration and excavations.

Place	**Chronological basis**	**Earliest date for traces of Christian cult**
Trondheim	C14, graves; coin	981–1025; 1029/35
Veøy	C14, graves	780–961, 772–965
Borgund	Coin in grave	1003/9
Bø	C14, grave	950–1080
Skien	(C14, Christian grave?); church	(890–990); 990–1030
Tønsberg	C14, graves, St. Peters church	950–1080
Oslo	C14, graves, St. Clement's	980–1020

Table 1. The earliest dated traces of Christian cult. All radiocarbon dates are calibrated, 68% (Nordeide, in press).

Hence interpretation is not clear.[4] Places where Christian graves preceded a church or have been found where no church is recorded at all, are for instance at Mære in Nord-Trøndelag (Lidén, 1969), Villa in Romsdal (T. Petersen, 1959), Kaupanger in Sogn (Lidén, Bjerknes, Anker, Buvarp, & Skaare, 1969) and St. Clement's in Oslo (Eide, 1974; Nordeide, & Gulliksen, 2007). A few places can be added to the list in Table 1 for slightly later Christian graves and churches compared to those listed, but which can still be dated to the 11th century. These places are, however, not as many or as old in order to explain the time gap between the Old Norse and Christian cult as indicated by the dates of the recorded sites.

4 One site should be particularly mentioned: after mass was removed for an underground storage in a church at Liknes, Vest-Agder, only profiles were left to study. It has been argued that this is an example of an exceptionally early Christian church and graves. The identification of the graves as Christian is based on the fact that there has been a church on the site from the thirteenth century, the bodies were E–W oriented and the graves were around 1m deep (Brendalsmo & Stylegar, 2001). However there is no evidence to suggest that the graves were Christian or that there was an earlier church: The location is situated on an E–W oriented peninsula, and as graves normally follow topography (Nilsen, 1997, p. 80; Nordeide, in press; Næss, 1970), this would in this case be E–W. The place was already being used as cemetery in early Iron Age, a rich burial mound from the fifth-to-sixth centuries is located very close by, and even late Iron Age graves can be around 1m deep. Besides, it looks as though the excavators have misinterpreted the profile when they argue that a fire layer is later than intrusions that clearly cut the fire layer (west profile), hence wrongly interpreting graves earlier than the fire layer as being dated to AD 980–1060, when they in fact should be later. As a final point, there is no evidence that the fire layer could be associated with a (church) building: the basis for this interpretation is the 'character' of a layer only observed in a profile. In their interpretation of the layer, the excavators indicate the size of the church on the basis of the thickness of the layer in the profile, which is a highly speculative analysis. This site needs further investigation in order to reach any reasonable conclusion.

Building	Part of building	Earliest year (AD) Outermost ring	Bark/last ring preserved?
Urnes Stave Church	North portal	1050	No
Urnes Stave Church	Sill beam, nave	1131	Yes
Urnes Stave Church	?	1129/1130	Yes
Alstadhaug Church	Roof	1166–1167	Yes
Ål Stave Church	Phase 1	1143	No. Some rings missing.
Ål Stave Church	Phase 2, latest sample	1247	No
Lom Stave Church	?	1157–1158	No
Uvdal Stave Church	'Original logs'	1167–1168	Yes
Heddal Stave Church	Portal, carvings	1196	No

Table 2. Earliest dendrochronological dates of churches in Norway, based on Terje Thun's results (Thun, 2002).

It is reasonable to suggest that it would take some time from the date when some persons were Christianised until several churches were built and staffed, but as soon as Christian congregations were founded, the establishment of cemeteries was among the urgent matters to solve. As demonstrated above, Christian graves were established several places before any church was constructed. However, as with a church, a cemetery required consecration by a bishop (Gittos, 2002; Hagland & Sandnes, 1994, p. 20; Robberstad, 1969, p. 25). In the earliest phase of Christianisation it is likely that people had to focus their religious activities on a few places, and Christian rituals would probably have had to take place in the open until a church was provided. Until Christian congregations and churches were established locally, these people would have had to travel to visit a Christian cult site. It has previously been suggested that in the case of inland eastern Norway, the Church built up a network with a hierarchy of churches with associated priests who could serve a larger religious community, probably preceded by some provisional systems (Skre, 1995). It has also been argued that the cemetery preceding the Trinitatis stone church in Lund was a central cemetery for the Christians in the whole of Scania during the years from 994 to around 1050 (Carelli, 2004), and a similar function has been suggested for the cemetery at St. Clement's in Oslo (Nordeide & Gulliksen, 2007). From the beginning, the people buried in the big Christian cemeteries at Lund and Oslo could have been the newly converted people from the surrounding region.

THE EARLIEST CHRISTIAN GRAVES – IN TOWNS

From the earliest stages of its development, the Church was organised according to bases in the towns, with the bishops in a *civitas* (Culleton, 1999, p. 66; Tveito, 2005, p. 38). Many ex-Roman towns became bishops' seats and burial places for the elite in particular (Schofield & Vince, 1994; Schofield & Steuer, 2008). The town may even have been planned and functioned in accordance with Biblical ideas (Lilley, 2009, passim). Based on this, the early Christian Church in Norway may not have been very different from its continental relatives: most of the names on the list of earliest Christian cult places are the same as the majority of the rather few, early, Norwegian towns (Nordeide, 2010). Some of the dated Christian cemeteries may be contemporary or may even precede the urban settlement, for instance in Oslo, Tønsberg, Veøy and Borgund (Fig. 2).

The argument for a connection between king and urbanisation has been made, based mainly on later written sources (Helle & Nedkvitne, 1982, pp. 68–69; Bagge, 2010, pp. 121–125). Several kings are honoured in the sagas for various town foundations and church donations. By the end of the tenth/start of the eleventh century, their presence in the towns is later witnessed through their fortified residences which they built in, or close to, medieval towns (Snorri & Hollander, 1967, passim). As royal residences were most probably timber buildings during the eleventh century, there is not much in the way of archaeological evidence to testify to a royal presence at this time, although royal activities such as minting are evidenced by numismatic evidence. The only minting sites articulated on coins being the two towns of Hamar and Nidaros (Skaare, 1976). In this way, testimonies tie urbanisation to royal initiative and the establishment of the church, but according to archaeological sources, the Christian cult seems to appear first and / or be contemporary with the first urban settlement. This observation cannot be explained as biased by excavation strategies. Although more excavations have been performed in towns than in rural areas, urban excavations have concentrated on ordinary plots, while relevant excavations in rural areas have mostly concentrated on churches. The reason for this is that standing urban churches generally are stone buildings, while rural, churches are wooden. The wooden churches have been in need of restoration and are excavated as part of a national restoration plan.

DISCUSSION

The necessity for the king to decide specific laws preventing people from performing their old rituals indicate that, in general, the ordinary and poorer

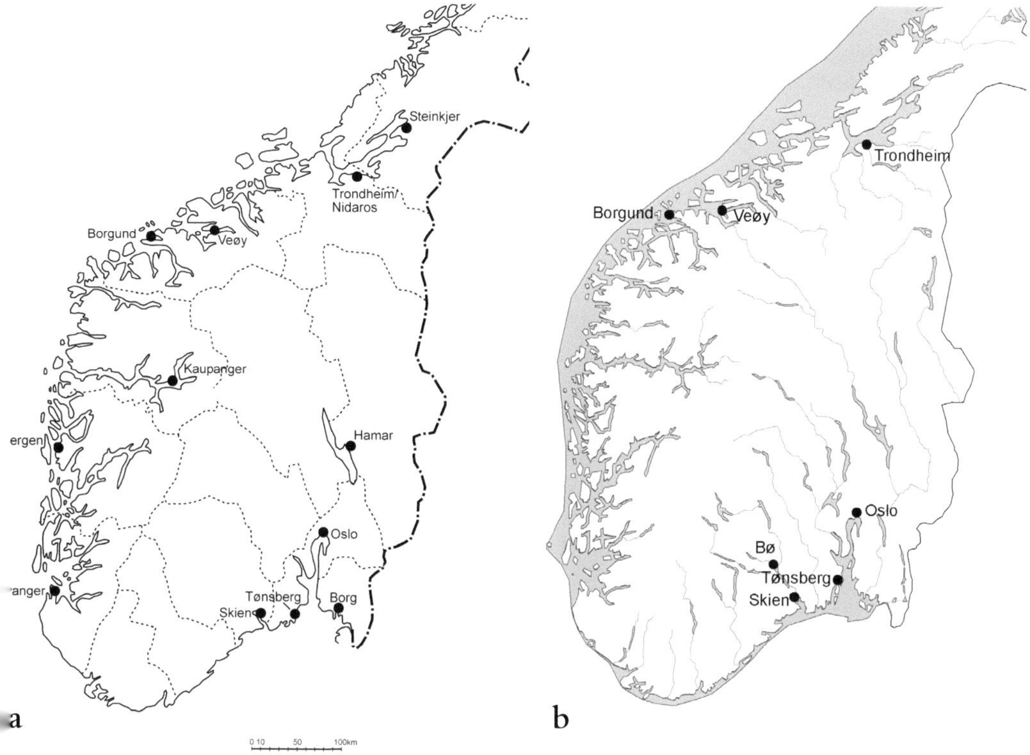

Fig. 2. Medieval towns and central places in modern, south Norway (a) compared to the earliest known Christian cult sites (b).

people in Norway did not ask for a new religion around 1000 AD. On the contrary, we get the impression that, were it not for the laws, they would have preferred to go on with their traditions – their 'siðr'. The rich, Old Norse burial cult and its seemingly abrupt cessation confirm that there was no crisis in the old religion, rather the contrary (Gellein, 1997, p. 97; Nordeide, in press). It was the new leadership – the king and his allies among the loyal landowners – who needed Christianity and the Church to provide a strong ideological foundation for the monarchy, as well as bringing technological innovations and developments in social and political organisations. That the Christianisation of Norway was a top-down process has been argued for before (Bagge & Nordeide, 2007). It is also likely that both the king and the Church first appealed to the social elite who saw the benefit of raising a Christian monarchy. Consequently, it is probable that the people from the upper classes were converted first. This is a pattern observed in several countries at this time (Slupecki & Valor, 2007).

If the wealthier people in Norway were the first converts, then the earliest Christian graves probably belonged to the wealthier people too. It is possible, therefore, that the earliest Christian cemeteries in towns could be composed of the king's alliance of wealthy landowners. Such individuals belonged to the same social class that in earlier periods was likely to have been buried in the type of graves dominating the archaeological records. As alluded to above, it is assumed that most of the recorded graves belonged to the landowners.

This type of grave would thus disappear, while other types of graves are still missing.

The towns were a new type of settlement in Norway at this time. Viking Age Kaupang seems to be the only earlier central place of some size until Trondheim was founded at the end of the Viking period. Elsewhere in Europe, however, large areas were urbanised, well known to the Church and people who travelled widely, such as the kings. Besides, one of the 'missionary kings', King Olav Tryggvason (who reigned from 995 to 1000) grew up in Novgorod in Russia. There is no reason to think that the kings-to-be did not know about the logistic advantages represented by a town, as well as the potential for power, cultural influence and the encounters that could follow from such a centre. Any king with aspirations to national and international influence would also have to consider the fact that major parts of Europe were Christian. If any cooperation between the new monarchy and these parts of Europe was to be expected, then the Norse counterpart of the elite in other parts of Europe would have to be Christian too. Additionally, those who visited the polity should be offered the opportunity to participate in Christian cult rituals, such as the mass; if the ruler wished to attract skilled foreign Christians – such as masons – to his towns, a lack of churches could be a hindrance (Olsen, 1999). An early Christian church and cemetery therefore had the power to attract a multitude of people, both dead and living.

Similar social, ritual and organisational patterns can be observed in the case of the Christianisation process in Denmark. Although burials of aristocrats in barrows continued in Denmark until the end of the tenth century, the kings were buried as Christians after the official conversion in around 965. Rune-stones continued to be raised as memorials until the 1020s, but church-building on a large scale did not start until the second half of the eleventh century, and it has been suggested that until then, churches only existed in important towns and market-places. In general, it is thought that Denmark at that time was served by the urban churches and a certain number of minsters or main churches where major rituals could be performed. However, as Else Roesdahl has noted, 'there seems, then, to be a 'memorial gap' in Denmark from the 1020s until the construction of churches started in earnest around 1060–70.' (Roesdahl, 2006, p. 178).

Taking comparative examples of the Christianisation process elsewhere in Europe, it is worth bearing in mind that the Church of Ireland may not have taken responsibility for burying common people at first, concentrating rather on ecclesiastical staff and lay members (Petts, 2002). It has also been argued that the Christian conversion in northwest Europe between 800–1200 generally started with rulers and elites, working its way downwards to ordinary people (Slupecki & Valor, 2007; Berend, 2007, p. 19). Consequently, based on comparative, European examples, the first Christian burials in Norway could be expected to be upper-class burials in towns, exactly as has been suggested above: To judge from dating evidence in Norway, the earliest Christian rituals took place at strategic places, identified as towns or towns-to-be, and the social elite seem to have been the first Christians. It follows from this that the landowners' previous conspicuous funerals would be moved from the village to central places. Consequently, the more powerful converts and the poorer subjects would have staged their rituals in different arenas, with the burial rituals associated with the social elite becoming more exclusive and elitist in the process.

If this observation is correct, it is no wonder that towns from this period in medieval Norway were spread evenly, providing a reasonable way for people to travel in each region for the purpose of performing Christian rituals as well as for other activities. However, such local religious arenas, the cult of the ordinary people, are still to be discovered. The rural cemeteries from the period around AD 950/1050–1100[5] are mostly absent from our records, and since the written sources are comparatively late and concern the upper strata of society, there is little evidence, if any at all, to judge whether the remaining people were Christian or not.

CONCLUSION

Returning to my opening questions: powerful people previously found buried in furnished graves were probably the first converts to Christianity. After their conversion they were likely to be buried at central cemeteries, at places that eventually became central places and/or towns. At these places the converts could practice their beliefs and also communicate with Christian foreign visitors. The towns became the first, important Christian cult places, and *vice versa.* By contrast, ordinary people would likely continue to bury their dead locally as before. These graves are still difficult to find and identify, and due to a lack of sources, my latter question cannot be answered at the present time; it is not possible to decide whether these people were predominantly Christians or otherwise during this period.

5 The date varies from place to place.

BIBLIOGRAPHY

Bagge, S. (2010). *From Viking Stronghold to Christian Kingdom. State Formation in Norway, c. 900–1350* Copenhagen: Museum Tusculanum Press.

Bagge, S., & Nordeide, S. W. (2007). The kingdom of Norway. I N. Berend (Ed.), *Christianization and the Rise of Christian Monarchy* (pp. 121–166). Cambridge: Cambridge University Press.

Bendixen, B. E. (1879). Fornlevninger i Nordmøre og Romsdal. *Foreningen til norske Fortidsmindesmerkers Bevaring Aarsberetning 1872*, pp. 63–160.

Berend, N. (2007). Introduction. I. N. Berend (Ed.), *Christianization and the Rise of Christian Monarchy. Scandinavia, Central Europe and Rus' c. 900–1200* (pp. 1–46). Cambridge: Cambridge University Press.

Brendalsmo, A. J. (2002). *Kirkebygg og kirkebyggere. Byggherrer i Trøndelag ca1000–1600*. Unpublished doctoral thesis, University of Tromsø, Tromsø.

Brendalsmo, A. J., & Stylegar, F.-A. (2001). *Kirkested i 1000 år. Grend, gård og grav i Liknes* (Vol. 111). Oslo: NIKU.

Brøgger, A. W. (1937). Gullalder *Viking, 1*, pp. 137–195.

Carelli, P. (2004). Lunds äldsta kyrkogård och förekomsten av ett senvikingatida danskt parochialsystem. I. N. Lund (Ed.), *Kristendommen i Danmark før 1050* (pp. 253–258). Roskilde: Roskilde Museums Forlag.

Culleton, E. (1999). *Celtic and Early Christian Wexford. AD 400 to 1166*. Wexford: Four Courts Press.

Eide, O. E. (1974). *De toskipede kirker i Oslo. Et forsøk på redatering og opphavsbestemmelse med utgangspunkt i de siste utgravningene i Clemenskirken*. Unpublished final thesis. Stencil. Authors publication. University of Bergen. Bergen.

Gansum, T. (2004). *Hauger som konstruksjoner: arkeologiske forventninger gjennom 200 år* (Vol. 33). Sollentuna: Göteborgs Universitet/Riksantikvarieämbetet.

Gellein, K. (1997). *Kristen innflytelse i hedensk tid? En analyse med utgangspunkt i graver fra yngre jernalder i Hordaland*. Unpublished final thesis, University of Bergen, Bergen.

Gittos, H. (2002). Creating the Sacred: Anglo-Saxon Rites for Consecrating Cemeteries. I S. Lucy & A. Reynolds (Eds.), *Burial in Early Medieval England and Wales* (Vol. 17, pp. 195–208). London: The Society for Medieval Archaeology.

Gjerpe, L. E. (Ed.). (2005). *Gravfeltet på Gulli. E 18-prosjektet Vestfold* (Vol. 1). Oslo: Kulturhistorisk museum Fornminneseksjonen.

Hagland, J. R., & Sandnes, J. (1994). *Frostatingslova*. Oslo: Det Norske Samlaget.

Helle, K., & Nedkvitne, A. (1982). Norge. Sentrumsdannelser og byutvikling i norsk middelalder. In G. A. Blom (Ed.), *Urbaniseringsprosessen i Norden. Del 1: Middelaldersteder. Bidragene fra Island og Norge* (Vol. 1, pp. 37–126). Oslo-Bergen-Tromsø: Universitetsforlaget.

Lidén, H. E. (1969). From Pagan Sanctuary to Christian Church. The Excavation of Mære Church in Trøndelag. *Norwegian Archaeological Review* (2), pp. 3–21.

Lidén, H. E., Bjerknes, K., Anker, A., Buvarp, H., & Skaare, K. (1969). Kaupanger stavkirke. *Foreningen til norske fortidsminnesmerkers bevaring, Årbok 1968*, pp. 59–124.

Lilley, K. D. (2009). *City and Cosmos: The Medieval World in Urban Form*. London: Reaktion Books.

Müller, I. H. V. (1991). Fra ættefellesskap til sognefellesskap. Om overgangen fra hedensk til kristen gravskikk. I. G. Steinsland, J. Pentikäinen & P. M. Sørensen (Eds.), *Nordisk hedendom: et symposium* (pp. 359–372). Odense: Odense Universitetsforlag.

Nilsen, R. H. L. (1997). *Båtgravskikk? Om berettigelsen av å opprettholde begrepet "Båtgravskikk" som analytisk kildekategori i arkeologien*. Unpublished final thesis, Norwegian University of Science and Technology, Trondheim.

Nordeide, S. W. (2010). Urbanism and Christianity in Norway. I. J. Sheehan & D. Ó. Corráin (Eds.), *The Viking Age: Ireland and the West. Proceedings of the XVth Viking Congress, Cork, 18–27 August 2005* (pp. 248–257). Dublin: Four Courts Press.

Nordeide, S. W. (in press). *The Viking Age as a Period of Religious Transformation: The Christianization of Norway from AD 560 – 1150/1200* (Vol. 2): Brepols.

Nordeide, S. W., & Gulliksen, S. (2007). First Generation Christians, Second Generation Radiocarbon Dates: The Cemetery at St. Clement's in Oslo. *Norwegian Archaeological Review, 40*(1), pp. 1–25.

Næss, J.-R. (1970). The Significance of Orientation Elements in Iron Age Burial Customs at Voss: a Tentative Interpretation. *Norwegian Archaeological Review, 3*, pp. 73–83.

Olsen, O. (1999). *Da Danmark blev til, Seks radioforedrag*. Copenhagen: Fremad.

Petersen, J. (1919). *De norske vikingesverd: en typologisk-kronologisk studie over vikingetidens vaaben*. Kristiania: Videnskabsselskapet i Kristiania.

Petersen, J. (1928). *Vikingetidens smykker*. Stavanger: Stavanger Museum.

Petersen, J. (1951). *Vikingetidens redskaper* (Vol. 1951/4). Oslo: Det Norske Videnskaps-Akademi i Oslo.

Petersen, T. (1959). Tresfjord i oldtiden. I. A. Skeidsvoll (Ed.), *Bygdebok for Tresfjord* (pp. 28–57). Bergen.

Petts, D. (2002). Cemeteries and Boundaries in Western Britain. I. S. Lucy & A. Reynolds (Eds.), *Burial in Early Medieval England and Wales* (Vol. 17, pp. 24–46). London: The Society for Medieval Archaeology.

Robberstad, K. (1969). *Gulatingslovi* (3 ed. Vol. 33). Oslo: Det Norske Samlaget.

Roesdahl, E. (2006). Aristocratic Burial in Late Viking Age Denmark. Custom, Regionality, Conversion. I. C. v. Carnap-Borheim, D. Krausse & A. Wesse (Eds.), *Herrschaft – Tod – Bestattung. Zu den vor- und frühgeschichtlichen Prunkgräbern als archäologisch-historische Quelle* (Vol. 139, pp. 169–183). Bonn: Institut für Ur- und Frühgeschichte der Universität Kiel / Verlag Dr. Rudolf Habelt GMBH.

Rygh, O. (1885). *Norske Oldsager. Ordnede og forklarede*. Christiania: Cammermeyer.

Schofield, J., & Steuer, H. (2008). Urban Settlement. I. G. Graham-Campbell & M. Valor (Eds.), *The Archaeology of Medieval Europe* (Vol. 1, pp. 111–153). Aarhus: Aarhus University Press.

Schofield, J., & Vince, A. (1994). *Medieval Towns*. London.

Skaare, K. (1976). *Coins and coinage in Viking-Age Norway: the establishment of a national coinage in Norway in the XI century, with a survey of the preceding currency history*. Oslo, Bergen, Tromsø: Universitetsforlaget.

Skre, D. (1995). Kirken før sognet. Den tidligste kirkeordningen i Norge. I. H. E. Lidén (Ed.), *Møtet mellom hedendom og kristendom i Norge* (pp. 170–233). Oslo: Universitetsforlaget.

Slupecki, L., & Valor, M. (2007). Religions. I. G. Graham-Campbell & M. Valor (Eds.), *The Archaeology of Medieval Europe. Eighth to Twelfth Centuries AD* (pp. 366–397). Aarhus: Aarhus University Press.

Snorri, S., & Hollander, L. M. (1967). *Heimskringla. History of the Kings of Norway*. Austin: The American-Scandinavian foundation.

Solberg, B. (2000). *Jernalderen i Norge. Ca. 500 f.Kr.–1030 e.Kr.* Oslo: J. W. Cappelens Forlag a.s.

Thun, T. (2002). *Dendrochronological constructions of Norwegian conifer chronologies providing dating of historical material*. Unpublished doctoral thesis, Norwegian University of Science and Technology, Trondheim.

Thäte, E. S. (2007). *Monuments and minds: monument re-use in Scandinavia in the second half of the first millennium AD* (Vol. 27). Lund: Institute of Archaeology, University of Lund/Wallin & Dalholm.

Tveito, O. (2005). *Ad fines orbis terrae – like til jordens ender. En studie i primær trosformidling i nordisk kristningskontekst* (Vol. 209). Oslo: Det historisk filosofiske fakultet, University of Oslo.

Ziegler, R. (1892). Undersøgelser i Romsdal i 1891. *Foreningen til norske Fortidsmindesmerkers Bevaring Aarsberetning 1891*, pp. 60–75.

Norse Influence at Govan on the Firth of Clyde, Scotland

OLWYN A. OWEN & STEPHEN T. DRISCOLL

ABSTRACT

This paper summarises the evidence for Norse influence at Govan. Govan is now part of the city of Glasgow and is perhaps best known for its world-famous shipyards. At its heart survives a fine 19th-century church within a pear-shaped graveyard, which has produced a rich collection of carved stones from the 10th and 11th centuries. These include five hogback tombstones, strongly suggesting Norse influence at this early medieval ecclesiastical, royal and administrative centre. Recent analysis of cartographic and historical sources, together with trial excavations, has begun to shed further light on the place of Govan in Norse Scotland.

Keywords: Govan, Strathclyde, Scotland, carved stones, hogback, thing place, church, royal centre.

Think of Viking Scotland. The chances are that the image that springs to mind is a beautiful island in the far north or west, studded with Scandinavian place-names and the remains of Norse settlement. Govan does not fit this picture in any respect. Govan lies on the south bank of the Firth of Clyde and was formally absorbed into the city of Glasgow in 1912. Today it appears a bruised and battered post-industrial landscape, and is sadly an area of considerable social deprivation.

Appearances can be deceptive, though, for Govan is a truly remarkable place, with two periods of greatness to its name. Its most recent heyday came in the 19th century with the arrival of shipbuilding and associated industries, which led to the colossal transformation of Govan from rural village to industrial heartland. Indeed, its once world-famous shipyards are still synonymous with the name of Govan: ('shipbuilding made Govan and Govan made shipbuilding': Brotchie, 1905, 243; Dalglish & Driscoll, 2009, 80–95).

But Govan's first period of greatness was a thousand years earlier, in the 10th and 11th centuries. A closer look at the aerial photograph of Govan (Fig. 1) reveals a church, hemmed in by modern development but still standing within a pear-shaped graveyard – and in Scotland, curvilinear churchyards are a tell-tale sign of an early religious site. The present church is a fine mid-19th century building, the work of the renowned Scottish architect, Rowand

Fig. 1. A modern aerial photograph of Govan Old and its graveyard. © Steven Driscoll.

Anderson. However, historical and archaeological evidence shows that this is only the latest in a long line of ecclesiastical buildings stretching back to early historic times (Dalglish & Driscoll, 2009, 38, Fig. 3.13). The earliest dating evidence comes from two Christian burials found beneath the remains of an early church, which have produced radiocarbon dates spanning the 5th–6th centuries (Driscoll, 2004, 8). Intriguingly, though, there is no evidence at all that this was ever a monastic site.

Govan has attracted antiquarian interest since the mid 19th century (Stuart, 1856; Stirling Maxwell, 1899), when carved stones began to be recovered from the churchyard. A total of 46 stones is known, of which 30 survive today, most displayed within the present church. The original total was probably higher, and of course there may be more still buried in the graveyard. Altogether, early medieval Govan has produced an outstanding corpus of sculpture. It rivals that of Iona or St Andrews, and is probably the largest collection in Scotland from the 10th and 11th centuries. There is a distinctive style to these carvings and others from the local area, so much so that the notion of a 'Govan School' has grown over the years (Macquarrie, 1990; Driscoll et al., 2005; Macquarrie, 2006), typified by Govan's signature monument, the recumbent cross-slab.

Fig. 2. The Govan sarcophagus. © Crown copyright: Royal Commission on the Ancient and Historical Monuments of Scotland. Licensor www.rcahams.gov.uk.

Forty-two of the 46 stones are recumbent burial monuments, and the remaining four are upright crosses. Though many of these carved stones are similar in type and design, they are not the same. This implies that they were commissioned individually, rather than mass-produced, which in turn suggests they were carved probably at the behest of a secular elite. Whether there was a single workshop supplying sculpture for the region, or several related workshops employing craftsmen trained in a common tradition, such a rich haul of sculpture from a single location is ample testament to the significance of Govan in the early medieval period.

The finest is undoubtedly a magnificent sarcophagus (Fig. 2), carved from a single block of stone and elaborately decorated with interlace and figurative scenes. The iconography of the warrior hunting a deer hints at royal associations, which – combined with the quality of the carving and the unique form of the monument – suggests it may once have held the remains of one of the Strathclyde kings. The church at Govan has an unusual dedication to St Constantine. Macquarrie (1994, 32) has argued that the founder of Govan was either the Scottish King Constantine, who reigned from 862–878, or his son Donald; but, given the archaeological evidence for an earlier foundation from

Fig. 3. Two of the Govan hogbacks. © Crown copyright: Royal Commission on the Ancient and Historical Monuments of Scotland. Licensor www.rcahams.gov.uk.

around the 6th century, these kings (and the church) are most likely named after an earlier saint Constantine – for which there are several candidates (Thomas, 1994, 20–21). What is clear is that this sarcophagus was meant to be seen, and it is reasonable to suppose it was displayed in an early church.

Other notable stones include the Jordanhill cross, which stood up to 2.5 m high and is completely covered with interlace, save for a rather worn image of a man on horseback (Ritchie, 1999, 11, Fig. 10); and the so-called 'Sun Stone', a freestanding cross-slab named because of its great boss and swirling rays (Ritchie, 1999, 13, Fig. 14). Most of the stones, though, are recumbent cross-slabs, many of them re-carved and re-used for burials in the 17th and 18th centuries (Cramp, 1994). The sheer quantity of monuments implies this was an important cemetery for the elite of the time, with the sarcophagus at least denoting royal patronage.

The most tangible evidence of Norse influence at Govan is five hogback tombstones (Fig. 3), characterised by Jim Lang (1984) as Viking colonial monuments. These massive house-shaped sandstone blocks, typified by their pronounced curving roof ridge and shingles, were an invention of the Viking kingdom of York in the 10th century, from where the fashion spread to other areas of northern England settled by Vikings, and to parts of southern Scotland where there was a significant Norse presence (Lang, 1974; 1984; 1994). Together, the five Govan hogbacks form the largest known group in Scotland, and 'apart from Govan 1, they are quite the largest and heaviest of all hogbacks' (Lang, 1974, 212); one is the largest in Britain. Govan 1 is the earliest in the group according to Lang's typology, and it is so similar to Cumbrian hogbacks – with its slim dimensions and steeply pitched roof – that Lang suggested it might have been imported to Govan from Cumbria, though there is no evidence for this.

On art-historical grounds, these hogbacks are all 10th century in date, although, interestingly, three were subsequently modified suggesting that they were valued and remained active monuments for more than a single generation (Ritchie, 2004, 4). These are among the earliest of the Scottish hogbacks: they are also among the earliest elements of the Govan collection.

Of course the hogbacks are not in themselves proof of Scandinavian settlement in this locality, though they are unambiguous evidence of a maritime connection between the Cumbrian settlements and the Clyde Estuary (Crawford, 1994, 104–5). The western waterways were of undoubted impor-

Fig. 4. Dumbarton Rock – the citadel of the Strathclyde Britons until its sacking by the Vikings in AD 870. © Crown copyright reproduced courtesy of Historic Scotland. www.historicscotlandimages.gov.uk

tance to the Norse, and yet the place-name evidence for Norse Scotland shows Govan lying just east of and outside the main areas of Scandinavian influence. As Lang (1994, 131) wrote: 'It would be unsafe to use [the hogbacks] as indicators of a protracted Viking colonial presence. As stone, the Govan hogbacks are indeed substantial; as evidence for settlement and communications, they will always be flimsy'. But the question inevitably rises: What *do* these hogbacks represent? What do they tell us about the relationship between the Norse in the Irish Sea province and the early historic kings of the north Britons? What *precisely* was the nature and extent of Norse influence at Govan?

The Firth of Clyde was clearly an important waterway to the Norse incomers, including the Dublin Norse. Indeed, it has been suggested that they may have utilised the Firths of Clyde and Forth as a through-route across lowland Scotland for commercial and political purposes (Crawford, 1994, 109–10; Crawford, 2000, 125–6, Fig. 1). At the start of the Viking Age, control of the Clyde was exercised from a citadel on Dumbarton Rock, the principal stronghold of the British kingdom of Strathclyde, which lies only some 12 miles downstream from Govan (Fig. 4). In AD 870, the Annals of Ulster record that 'two kings of the northmen', Olaf and Ivar, besieged Dumbarton for four months – showing it was clearly a prize worth the taking (AU 870.6, 871.2: MacAirt & MacNiocaill, 1983). They scored a famous victory, sacking and destroying the fortress, and the following year carried a great booty of slaves on 200 ships from northern Britain back to Dublin. Dumbarton never recovered. The obvious inference is that the centre of power moved to Govan around AD 900, where there was already a church and a royal estate. Like Dumbarton Rock, Govan was also well located strategically – at a fording point across the Clyde and at its confluence with the River Kelvin.

Govan has seen a spate of detailed research and excavation over the last 15 years. A seminal conference and publication in the early 1990s (Ritchie, 1994) was followed by a series of trial trenches dug inside and outside the churchyard (Fig. 5) (Cullen & Driscoll, 1995; Driscoll & Will, 1996; Driscoll & Will, 1997; Driscoll et al., 2008), culminating most recently in a Burgh Survey of Govan, a project sponsored by Historic Scotland, which aims to identify areas of archaeological potential in Scotland's historic towns (Dalglish & Driscoll, 2009). Most of this work was carried out by Professor Stephen Driscoll of Glasgow University, who has argued that Govan was an early medieval royal centre – a complex of church, royal estate and administrative centre (Driscoll, 1998; 2003; 2004).

The earliest map source for Govan is by Timothy Pont in the late 16th century, which shows the village stretching east from the church and the Clyde still with its small islands before it was deepened to accommodate large ships (Dalglish & Driscoll, 2009, 22, Fig. 2.4). The most accurate and detailed

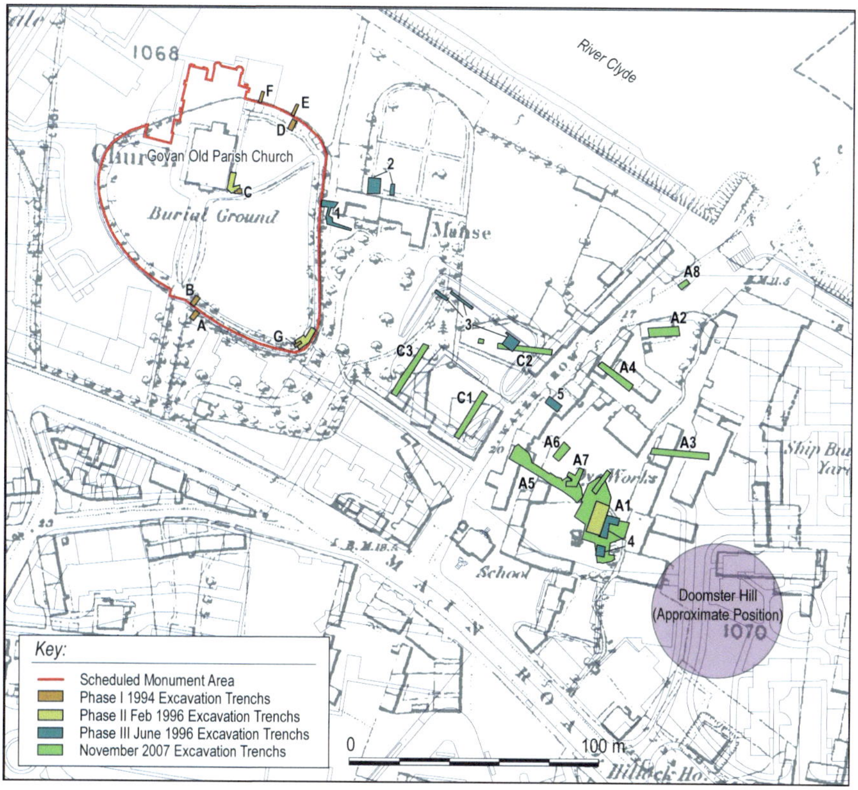

Fig. 5. Map showing the locations of the archaeological excavations, conducted 1994-2007, and the approximate location of Doomster Hill, plotted against the 1st edition of the Ordnance Survey map (based on OS mapping © Crown Copyright. All rights reserved Historic Scotland Licence No. 100017509[2009]).

early map is by William Roy, part of the *Military Survey of Scotland*, undertaken shortly after 1745 (Fig. 6). It shows the church, and Partick just across the river, which historical evidence suggests was the site of an early medieval royal estate (Dalglish & Driscoll, 2009, 18).

But it also shows another major feature of Govan's early topography. Adjacent to the river, some 150 m east of the churchyard, was a massive flat-topped mound, known as the Hillock or Doomster Hill. The very name 'Govan' is likely to refer to the Doomster Hill. Clancy (1996, 2–3) suggests that Govan was named when local people still spoke a north British dialect akin to old Welsh, and that the name comes from 'gwo/ go', meaning 'small', and

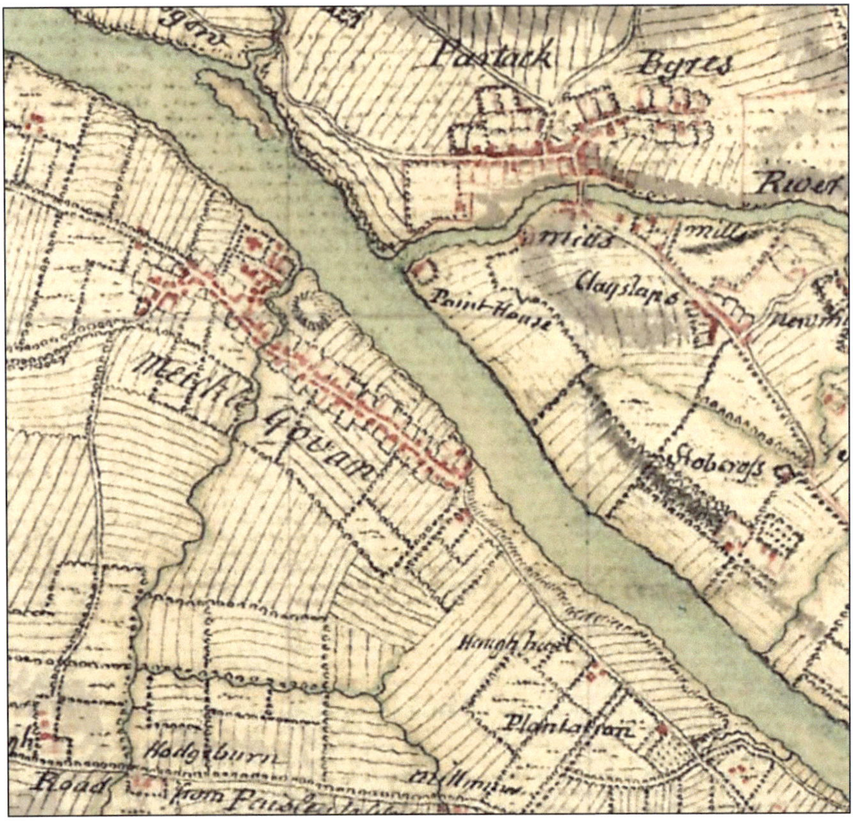

Fig. 6. Part of the 'Military Survey of Scotland' by William Roy, undertaken shortly after 1745.

'ban', meaning 'hill'. Govan is relatively flat and it would not be surprising if it was named after its only prominent topographic feature. This would imply that this artificial mound existed not much later than the 10th century.

Unfortunately the hill was levelled during the mid 19th-century industrialisation to make way for a shipyard. However, on the basis of detailed analysis of antiquarian and historical records, early cartographic sources, the etymological evidence, and trial excavations, by far the most likely interpretation of this massive artificial mound is that it was an open-air court site and assembly place. The name of the hill itself refers to the Doomster or Dempster, the legal officer who pronounced sentence, and this function is substantiated by several post-medieval accounts (Davidson-Kelly, 1994, 1–3). However, the date of its foundation is probably much earlier. The recent excavations unearthed an early metalled roadway in the south-east of the churchyard which led directly

Fig. 7. Detail from Robert Paul's 1758 *View of the Banks of the Clyde*. (The Doomster Hill is towards the bottom left). © Glasgow City Libraries. Licensor www.scran.ac.uk.

towards the Doomster Hill, and a deposit of charcoal incorporated in the road produced a calibrated radiocarbon date of AD 734–892 (Driscoll, 1998, 103-4; Driscoll, 2004, 17). This strongly suggests that a ceremonial route directly linked the early medieval church to the Doomster Hill.

The Doomster Hill is also represented on other early maps, such as John Ainslie's *Map of the County of Renfrew* from 1800 (Dalglish & Driscoll, 2009, 24, Fig. 2.8), but the best visual record of it is found in Robert Paul's 1758 *View of the Banks of the Clyde* (Fig. 7). This provides some crucial information about its form. It shows the enormous mound with a distinctly stepped profile, with two clear levels, and surrounded by a large ditch. The ferry area and medieval settlement of Water Row are also clearly shown, with the church visible among the trees. On the basis of analysis of all the antiquarian accounts and cartographic evidence, the mound was possibly up to 45 m in diameter, about 30 m across on top, and stood about 5 m high.

It would be immensely difficult to locate the Doomster Hill on the ground in modern-day Govan, given the extent of 19th-century industrialisation. Moreover, the subsequent levelling of industrial sites has resulted in up to two metres of rubble overlying parts of the area. A trial trench in 1996 located a massive cut feature, initially interpreted as the ditch of the Doomster Hill (Driscoll & Will, 1996, 15–17; Driscoll & Will, 1997, 23–7). However, further work in 2007 found that the 'ditch' did not continue and its basal fill produced

Fig. 8. Tynwald Hill on the Isle of Man, photographed c 1900. © Manx Heritage.

later material, indicating it was a large post-medieval sand pit (Driscoll et al., 2008). Nonetheless, this work has helped to refine further the likely location of the hill, which is now thought to lie around modern Napier Street (the detailed evidence for the site of the Doomster Hill is set out in the Burgh Survey: Dalglish & Driscoll 2009, 40–45).

Court hills are well known in medieval Scotland, as elsewhere, but the distinctive stepped form of the Doomster Hill shown in Paul's *View* recalls nothing so much as famous Norse assembly places in the Irish Sea area, notably Tynwald Hill on the Isle of Man (Fig. 8). This mound was also stepped, at least from the time of the earliest illustrations in the 17th century, and has had four terraces since its 19th-century restoration. The site was re-surveyed in 1993 for Manx National Heritage and it was concluded: 'there is good reason to believe that its stepped profile is ancient' (Darvill, 2004, 222). Like the Doomster Hill, a ceremonial route links Tynwald Hill to St John's Church (Darvill, 2004, 220, Fig. 10.2).

The Thingmote in Dublin has recently been recognised as a royal inauguration site and meeting place from at least the 12th century, and was still in use as an assembly place in the 17th century. In a survey of 1682 this, too, was shown as a substantial mound with a stepped profile, perhaps around 8 metres high and 15 metres in diameter (FitzPatrick, 1997, i, 76). Both Tynwald Hill and the Thingmote appear to have been high status sites with royal associations.

Other examples closer to hand include the stepped mound at Thingmount in Langdale, Cumbria, with its four terraces on a mound 2 metres high and about 30 metres across (Higham, 1985, 36, Plate IV; Quartermaine & Krupa, 1994); Lincluden Mote in Galloway, which also has four terraces, on a mound standing up to 8 metres high (Piggott & Simpson, 1970, 65); and the so-called 'motte' at Tinwald, Dumfriesshire, where aerial photography hints there may once have been a step in the sides of this ploughed and degraded mound (RCAHMS 1997, 187–8).

The existence of thing places in Norse Scotland is well attested elsewhere through place-names, such as Tingwall in Orkney and Dingwall in Sutherland, and occasionally on the ground, as at Law Ting Holm in Shetland (Crawford, 1987, 206–10). However, the Doomster Hill appears to belong to a group of distinctive stepped mounds scattered around the Irish Sea area – in Dublin, the Isle of Man, Cumbria, south-west Scotland and Strathclyde (Darvill, 2002, 229, Fig. 10.6).

What are we to make of all this? The history of Strathclyde in this period is shrouded in mystery, and the centuries after the destruction of Dumbarton by Vikings in 870 are particularly obscure. This was an era of ever-shifting allegiances and alliances, reflecting the competing interests of Britons, Gaels, Picts, Angles, Norwegians and Danes. One of the most telling facts about the Govan sculpture, though, is its restricted date span. The strong consensus on art-historical grounds (Ritchie, 1994) is that this great flowering of stone carving at Govan took place roughly between 900 and 1100, with the hogbacks dating from the earlier part of this period. The fact that this was clearly the burial place of the secular elite is compelling evidence that Govan in the 10th and 11th centuries remained a flourishing royal and administrative centre – testifying to the expedience and political fleet-footedness of its rulers even in the face of the encroachment of the kingdom of Alba westwards (Driscoll, 2002).

Norse influence is a consistent strand in the story of 10th- and 11th-century Govan and Strathclyde. With the hogbacks, and the evidence for a high status Norse-style thing place, perhaps it is time to accept that there was not only Norse influence at Govan, but in the 10th century at least, Norse involvement at Govan – probably a political accommodation, based around trading along the Clyde. Indeed, given the coherence of the structures at Govan, it must be at least possible that Govan was a planned replacement for Dumbarton, with the 10th- and 11th-century Strathclyde kingdom re-defining itself in Norse terms (Fig. 9).

As Driscoll has proposed elsewhere: 'Norse aspects are so abundant that we

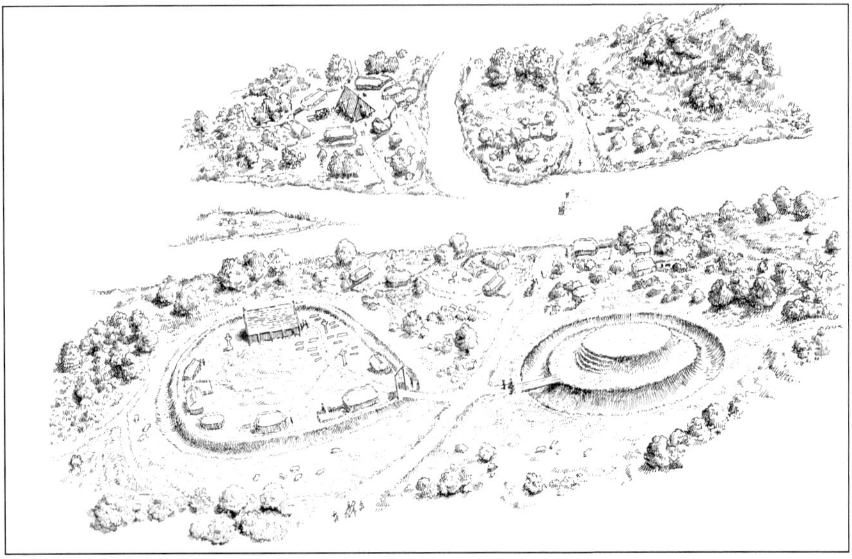

Fig. 9. Reconstruction of Govan and Partick c AD 1000, showing the Church and the Doomster Hill, and the roadway linking the two. The royal estate of Partick lay on the north shore. © Chris Brown.

must at least entertain the notion that, from the late 9th century, there was a significant Norse component in the rulership of the kingdom of Strathclyde ... Certainly Strathclyde of the late 9th and early 10th centuries was alive with Vikings from Dublin and York, but then so was Alba. Custatin mac Aeda, who dominated northern affairs for the first half of the 10th century, married his daughter into the Dublin Viking dynasty and had descendants with Norse names. Given that context it would hardly be surprising to see a hybrid Norse and Celtic aristocracy ruling in Strathclyde, as elsewhere around the Irish Sea' (Driscoll, 1998, 112–13).

By the early 12th century, the centre of power had shifted again. The kingdom of Strathclyde had been subsumed into the kingdom of the Scots, and Govan had effectively been replaced in eminence by Glasgow (Driscoll, 1998). Govan's first period of greatness was over.

ACKNOWLEDGEMENTS

The authors wish especially to acknowledge the contribution and encouragement of Reverend Tom Davidson-Kelly, who has worked tirelessly over many years to raise awareness of the significance of the early historic site and carved stones at Govan. Olwyn Owen is grateful to Historic Scotland which funded her attendance at the Congress in Iceland.

BIBLIOGRAPHY

Brotchie, T. C. F. (1905). *The history of Govan.* Glasgow: The Old Govan Club (reprinted 1938).

Clancy, T. O. (1996). Govan: The name. *Eighth Annual Report of the Society of Friends of Govan Old*, 2–3.

Cramp, R. (1994). The Govan recumbent cross-slabs. In A. Ritchie (Ed.), *Govan and its early medieval sculpture*, 55–61. Stroud: Alan Sutton Publishing Ltd.

Crawford, B. E. (1987). *Scandinavian Scotland.* Leicester: Leicester University Press.

Crawford, B. E. (1994). The 'Norse Background' to the Govan hogbacks. In A. Ritchie (Ed.), *Govan and its early medieval sculpture*, 103–12. Stroud: Alan Sutton Publishing Ltd.

Crawford, B. E. (2000). The Scandinavian contribution to the development of the kingdom of Scotland. *Acta Archaeologica*, 71, 123–34.

Cullen, I. & Driscoll, S. T. (1995). *Excavations at Govan Old Parish Church 1994.* Glasgow: GUARD Report 175.1.

Dalglish, C. & Driscoll, S. T. (2009). *Historic Govan: Archaeology and development.* York & Edinburgh: Council for British Archaeology & Historic Scotland. (= The Scottish Burgh Survey).

Darvill, T. (2004). Tynwald Hill and the 'things' of power. In A. Pantos & S. Semple (Eds.), *Early medieval assembly places*, 217–32. Dublin: Four Courts Press.

Davidson-Kelly, T. (1994). The Govan collection in the context of local history. In A. Ritchie (Ed.), *Govan and its early medieval sculpture*, 1–17. Stroud: Alan Sutton Publishing Ltd.

Driscoll, S. T. (1998). Church archaeology in Glasgow and the kingdom of Strathclyde. *The Innes Review*, 49, no. 2, 95–114.

Driscoll, S. T. (2002). *Alba: The Gaelic kingdom of Scotland AD 800–1124.* Edinburgh: Birlinn Ltd.

Driscoll, S. T. (2003). Govan: An early medieval royal centre on the Clyde. In R. Welander, D. Breeze & T. O. Clancy (Eds.), *The Stone of Destiny: Artefact and icon (77–83). Edinburgh:* Society of Antiquaries of Scotland Monograph, no. 22.

Driscoll, S. T. (2004). *Govan from cradle to grave.* Glasgow: The Society of Friends of Govan Old.

Driscoll, S. T. & Will, R. S. (1996). *Water Row, Govan.* Glasgow: GUARD Report 175.2.

Driscoll, S. T. & Will, R. S. (1997). *Govan Old Parish Church and Water Row.* Glasgow: GUARD Report 175.3.

Driscoll, S. T., O'Grady, O. & Forsyth, K. (2005). The Govan School revisited:

Searching for meaning in the early medieval sculpture of Strathclyde. In S. Foster & M. Cross (Eds.), *Able minds and practiced hands*, 135–58. Leeds: Society for Medieval Archaeology.

Driscoll, S. T., Will, R. S. & Shearer, I. (2008). *Water Row, Govan: Archaeological evaluation 2007*. Glasgow: GUARD Report 2497.

FitzPatrick, E. (1997). *The practice and siting of royal inauguration in medieval Ireland*. Unpublished Ph.D. thesis, 2 vols: Trinity College, Dublin.

Higham, N. (1985). The Scandinavians in north Cumbria: Raids and settlement in the later ninth to mid tenth centuries. In Baldwin, J. R. & Whyte, I. D. (Eds.), *The Scandinavians in Cumbria*, 36–51. Edinburgh: The Scottish Society for Northern Studies.

Lang, J. T. (1974). Hogback monuments in Scotland. *Proceedings of the Society of Antiquaries of Scotland*, 105 (1972–4), 206–35.

Lang, J. T. (1984). The hogback – A Viking colonial monument. *Anglo-Saxon Studies in Archaeology and History*, 3, 85–176.

Lang, J. T. (1994). The Govan hogbacks: A reappraisal. In A. Ritchie (Ed.), *Govan and its early medieval sculpture*, 113–22. Stroud: Alan Sutton Publishing Ltd.

MacAirt, S. & McNiocaill, G. (Eds.) (1983). *The Annals of Ulster to AD 1131*. Dublin: Dublin Institute for Advanced Studies.

Macquarrie, A. (1990). Early Christian Govan: The historical context, *Records of the Scottish Church History Society*, 24, 1–17.

Macquarrie, A. (1994). The historical context of the Govan stones. In A. Ritchie (Ed.), *Govan and its early medieval sculpture*, 27–32. Stroud: Alan Sutton Publishing Ltd.

Macquarrie, A. (2006). *Crosses and upright monuments in Strathclyde: Typology, dating and purpose*. Glasgow: The Society of Friends of Govan Old.

Piggott, S. & Simpson, W. D. (1970). *Illustrated guide to ancient monuments*, vol vi. Edinburgh: HMSO.

Quartermaine, J. & Krupa, M. (1994). *Thingmount, Little Langdale, Cumbria: Archaeological survey*. Lancaster: Lancaster University Archaeological Unit (for the National Trust). (Limited circulation printed report).

Ritchie, A. (Ed.) (1994). *Govan and its early medieval sculpture*. Stroud: Alan Sutton Publishing Ltd.

Ritchie, A. (2004). *Hogback gravestones at Govan and beyond*. Glasgow: The Society of Friends of Govan Old.

Ritchie, A. (1999). *Govan and its carved stones*. Balgavies, Angus: The Pinkfoot Press.

Royal Commission on the Ancient and Historical Monuments of Scotland (1997). *Eastern Dumfriesshire: An archaeological landscape*. Edinburgh: RCAHMS.

Stirling Maxwell, J. (1899). *Sculptured stones in the kirkyard of Govan*. Glasgow.

Stuart, J. (1856). *The sculptured stones of Scotland*. Aberdeen: Spalding Club.

Thomas, C. (1994). Christianity at Govan: But when? In A. Ritchie (Ed.), *Govan and its early medieval sculpture*, 19–26. Stroud: Alan Sutton Publishing Ltd.

Scandinavia in the Melting-pot, 950–1000

ELSE ROESDAHL

ABSTRACT

During the second half of the tenth century Scandinavian societies underwent rapid and crucial changes. The coming of Christianity is often seen as the totally dominant factor, but it was only part of a story. It also comprised new views of kingship, new types of settlement, new interests in traditional culture as inspiration for memorials and identity, innovative building enterprises, new transport technologies, economic initiatives, an innovative art style, the militarisation of society and much more. The discovery of Greenland and 'America' promised endless space and possibilities. At the same time European influences (particularly from Germany and England) challenged many traditional Scandinavian cultural traits, while until 983 the Ottonian Empire confronted Denmark politically and militarily. All this gave rise to different outlooks. Around the turn of the millennium, a new Scandinavian focus on rich opportunities in England was to dominate the next half-century. Scandinavia was emerging from a melting-pot. These ideas are investigated with a focus on Denmark, at that time the leading political and cultural unit in the North. Because of the proximity to Germany, the challenges met, and the answers given, were often stronger in Denmark than elsewhere in Scandinavia. Another purpose of this study is to present an overview and synthesis of a period within the Viking Age, thereby challenging the increasing atomization and specialisation of our subject – not just between, but now also within, disciplines. In order to advance Viking studies and better understand the Viking Age we still need broad interpretations and discussions, preferably on an interdisciplinary basis.

Keywords: Tenth-century Denmark, tenth-century Scandinavia, Viking Age, Conversion, royal power, Viking Age monuments, cultural change, economic changes, identity, Jelling.

There are times in history when important things move particularly quickly, and consequently, new societies and ideas emerge. The second half of the tenth century in Scandinavia was just such a time. Here, I will survey this period, pointing out the major changes and discussing the reasons for them – sometimes against a European background – and contrast this with features and trends in Scandinavia around the year 1000.

Our view of the period is dominated by the series of conversions to Christianity, which swept through much of western Scandinavia. Following the conversion of Denmark, *c.*965, Iceland and Greenland and probably the Faeroes accepted Christianity in or around the year 1000. At this time Norway was also deeply influenced by the new religion, as were the Swedish lands, where the king, Olof Skötkonung, was a Christian. But conversion was only one of the changes affecting society during this period – although it was a major one. The conversions must be seen in the context of all the other events which happened at more or less the same time, and which together heralded the beginning of a new era.

During the second half of the tenth century the greater part of Scandinavia changed – or was on a fast track to change – from lands which were basically pagan and had strong and specific Scandinavian cultural traits, to Christian (or partly Christian) countries. There were strong influences from Europe, with new or changing societies and material culture. However, as is the rule, almost everywhere at times of rapid change and cultural challenge (for example Carver, 2001; Pedersen & Otto, 2005), Scandinavia developed during this period interests focused on old traditions and 'invented' new ones. Thus interesting experiments and great achievements were initiated, often based on traditional Scandinavian culture. It was also a period of much military turbulence, a time in which many of the most celebrated Viking characters and heroes known from the sagas lived – such figures as Egil Skallagrimsson, Harald Bluetooth, Hákon Jarl, Styrbjørn, Eric the Victorious, the 'Jomsvikingar', and many more. Society was in a melting-pot.

Why and how did it all happen, and what did in fact happen? Today we can illuminate such questions more clearly than before, partly because archaeology has provided us with much new evidence, and natural sciences with many precise dates. Furthermore, the application of analogies and anthropological theory has initiated new ideas, as has a more rigorous approach to interdisciplinary and synthetic works.

BACKGROUND

Before embarking on a discussion of these influences, achievements, changes and challenges, I would like to present a sketch of the contemporary European and Scandinavian scenes.

The major European power at the time was the German realm, which under the emperors Otto I and Otto II had a continuing interest in Denmark and the Slavic lands. Their interest constituted a major threat to Danish independence and the pagan religion, and thus to Scandinavian culture in general. The Ottos were crowned emperors and were zealous Christians, who built magnificent churches and residences for a court that was probably the most splendid in Europe. Importantly, Germany was Denmark's neighbour to the south (Müller-Mertens, 1999; see also Althoff, 1999; Nelson, 1999).

The largest Scandinavian town at the time, Hedeby, was situated near the border with the Empire, and there were many strong links between Danes and Germans, links which included political, mercantile and military encounters. The physical border, the Danevirke, was re-fortified against German threats in the 960s, and the rampart around Hedeby was probably strengthened at the same time. In 974, however, the Danes lost a battle at the Danevirke. According to the skaldic poem *Vellekla,* the Norwegian Hákon Jarl and his followers fought bravely on the Danish side, but it has been argued that this was in a later battle, in 983 (Sawyer 1988/2002, pp. 231–232). Following this defeat the Germans built and garrisoned a fortress somewhere in the border area. But eight years later, in 982, the scene changed completely. Otto II was defeated in the important battle at Cotrone in Italy and in the following year died in Rome; while the above-mentioned fortress was destroyed and Hamburg burned by Danes and Slavs. For a long time to come the North was of minimal interest to the Empire and Scandinavians could draw breath and look elsewhere (for example Skovgaard-Petersen, 1977, pp. 170–182; H. H. Andersen, 1984; Albrectsen, 1994).

So, until 983, Germany was probably the most important single factor in the history and development of tenth-century Denmark. Many of the changes, developments, achievements and inspirations in Denmark at this time should almost certainly be seen as responses to challenges from Germany, and much of this energy seems to have spilled over into the rest of Scandinavia.

Another important European power was England (Keynes, 1999). Many Scandinavians had lived there since the conquests of the late ninth century, and continuing links with Scandinavia must have played an important part in the Christianisation of their homelands, particularly in Norway where many English missionaries came to preach. The Norwegian king Hákon Athelstansfostre (died *c.*960) had been brought up in England at the court of king Athelstan, while Icelanders, like Egil Skallagrimsson, also went to England (where he composed some of his most famous poems). From the mid-tenth century the whole of what is now England was united under one king. England, however, never threatened Scandinavia militarily. On the contrary, from the 990s onwards, when pressure from Germany had ceased and new young blood had taken the Danish throne after a revolt, England became the target for Scandinavian raids, adventures and conquest on a hitherto unknown scale. This was indeed a new era.

Scotland and Ireland, and the Slav, Baltic and Finnish lands around the Baltic Sea, together with Russia, were other 'neighbours' of Scandinavia. These lands had influential Scandinavian populations, and each had their particular links to their original homelands. Foreigners from exotic lands also came to Scandinavia. Such a person was the Spanish-Arab At-Tartuchi, who visited

Hedeby *c.*970, whilst Vikings (or at least some of them) famously travelled far and wide, for many reasons and in many capacities; such as the Danish embassy which appeared at the imperial court in Quedlinburg in eastern Germany in 973.

The Viking world was huge and became even bigger during this period. Greenland was explored and then settled from Iceland from around 985; while the first Scandinavian voyages to America occurred around the year 1000. The widely-travelled Guðríður, who was born in Iceland and died there, was one of the first Scandinavian women in America (as recorded by sagas). She also went on a pilgrimage to the Holy Land. It was probably also at this time that trade-routes between North Norway and North Russia became more clearly established – routes which have existed ever since. A century earlier, *c.*890, the Norwegian Ohthere would have been one of the first to investigate the possibilities (survey in, for example, Brink (ed.) with Price, 2008, pp. 341–617).

All this implies a dissemination of ideas and knowledge, and explains why important influences spread so quickly through most of the huge area that was Scandinavia, and why they also sometimes appeared simultaneously in different lands. It was clearly a time of great optimism and of a desire for new experiences.

A CHALLENGED SCANDINAVIA

In the following, I shall discuss specific examples of achievement, challenge and change in Scandinavia in the second half of the tenth century. As an archaeologist I shall naturally concentrate on my own discipline, but I shall use elements of other disciplines, which can provide much further evidence to broaden the picture. My survey will begin in Denmark, not just because I am Danish, but because Denmark at the time was the leading political and cultural unit in the North. Moreover, Denmark was close to Germany and the mighty Ottonian Empire. New European trends and ideas, therefore, were often adopted in Denmark before being introduced into other Scandinavian lands. Furthermore, the challenges encountered and the answers given were often stronger in Denmark than elsewhere in Scandinavia. Many diagnostic examples of the rapidly changing times are therefore clearly seen in Denmark. But the other Scandinavian lands will of course appear in the picture.

The 'Trelleborg' fortresses

The Danish geometrically-formed fortresses of the Trelleborg type are perhaps the most enigmatic structures of the Viking Age (Fig. 1) and are symbolic of this time of change and of the politics of their builder, Harald Bluetooth. They were built *c.*980 and give an insight into the power structures and concepts, and

Fig.1. Trelleborg seen from the north-east. The fortress was situated at the confluence of two rivers, at some distance from the sea. The outer ward was protected by a low rampart which enclosed 15 buildings and a cemetery. In the foreground to the left is the reconstructed Trelleborg house. Photo: Torkild Balslev (Dept. of Medieval and Renaissance Archaeology, Aarhus University).

into the technological and organisational skills of the time. When they were first identified in the 1930–50s, they caused a major revision of the general concept of Vikings and of the Viking Age.

Four or five fortresses are known. They are of varying size and are distributed widely throughout the country: Trelleborg in West Sjælland, Nonnebakken in Fyn, Fyrkat in north-east Jutland, and Aggersborg in North Jutland, while Borgeby in Skåne, near Malmö, may also belong to the group (Nørlund, 1948; Olsen & Schmidt, 1977; Roesdahl, 1977; idem, 1981; idem, 1987; Svanberg & Söderberg, 1999). All are situated near important roads, while Aggersborg, on the shore of the Limfjord, also had important access to the sea. There was probably no maritime access from the others. They are unique structures built of timber, turf and earth, with precisely circular ramparts, concentric ditches and gates at the four points of the compass connected by streets. They contained huge regularly-placed timber houses, each about 30 m in length, arranged in quadrants.

They are the oldest royal fortresses known in Denmark, but lasted for very few (perhaps only around 10) years. Their layout has no known predecessor, nor apparently any successor, in Denmark. They were probably influenced by slightly older fortresses in the Netherlands and northern France, with the addition of details drawn from German imperial architecture. But many important elements, like the houses and the building materials, are of Danish origin and may simply draw on ideas expressed in traditional magnates' or royal complexes – Tissø, for example, with its heavy palisade and many buildings (Jørgensen, 2008). But the plan of the fortresses had been totally re-shaped, in that an aristocratic centre had been converted into a proper fortification of innovative form, designed as the prestige architecture of, as I believe, a national identity. This nation-wide project of constructing circular fortresses would have been both extremely impressive and very costly.

The purpose and function of the fortresses have been a matter of much discussion (a number of theories are summarized in Roesdahl, 1996; cf. Olsen, 1999). With its extraordinary size, Aggersborg is perhaps the most puzzling of the group. The rampart was ¾ km in circumference; inside were 48 regularly-placed timber houses, each 32 m long. The other fortresses each enclosed sixteen houses, set within circular ramparts and arranged according to the same strict geometric principles, although Trelleborg had an additional 15 houses outside the circle, protected by a secondary rampart. Thus there were, altogether, 31 long houses at Trelleborg.

It helps our understanding of the fortresses if we consider them in the context of their time – particularly in relation to the continuing difficult relations with Germany , which led up to the Danish defeat of 974 and the consequent loss of Norway. These events should be placed alongside the joint Danish-Slav raids in northern Germany in 983 and the faltering German interest in the North from 983, as well as the Danish revolt against Harald Bluetooth *c.*987, in which he lost his life and his son Sven took over the kingdom (for example Roesdahl, 2002).

As fortresses they would accord well with the many fortifications which sprang up at this time in the Slav and German lands as a consequence of the German expansion eastwards (Dulinicz, 2002; Henning, 2002). The Danish examples could well have been in part conceived as a potential systematic defence against German intrusion, as may also be the case with the ramparts which protected the towns of Hedeby, Ribe and Aarhus. Furthermore, Aggersborg had easy access to Norway through a now lost northerly water-route from the Limfjord, which started at the very point where Aggersborg was situated. This fortress may well have been intended to play a part in a re-establishment of Danish power in that country.

The fortresses which were situated near important land-routes, and Aggersborg's position on the shore of the Limfjord – the all-important sailing-route between the North Sea and the Baltic – would provide bases to control traffic and perhaps even to exact tolls. Importantly, the fortresses were also royal strongholds within Denmark, which at the time was hardly entirely peaceful. They would surely have had administrative and fiscal functions, such as the collection of taxes, the storage of gifts and dues to the king and places for meetings. Evidence of the presence of craftsmen such as blacksmiths and goldsmiths on these sites, imply the production of important goods such as weapons and jewellery under royal control.

It is interesting that at the same time, *c.*980, the Swedish king, Erik the Victorious, founded Sigtuna as a new systematically-planned settlement (Tesch, 2008). But here the circumstances were different. This was not a fortress, rather it was the beginnings of a town, probably meant as a substitute for Birka. The general urban plan with long plots aligned along a street is paralleled in many other towns in contemporary northern Europe. In contrast to the fortresses of the Trelleborg type, which almost certainly went out of use around the time of the death of Harald Bluetooth, Sigtuna succeeded as an important centre. But both signal a time of challenges and new achievements.

Jelling

This period of change is even more clearly to be seen at Jelling – the site of Danish dynastic monuments from the period of the Conversion, most of which were also built by Harald Bluetooth, probably between *c.*958 and the 970s. The Jelling monuments (Fig. 2) have been much described and discussed and are currently the focus of a major National Museum research project which will reconsider data as well as all current theories. Information concerning the project, directed by Anne Pedersen, may be found via the Danish National Museum home page or at http://Jelling.natmus.dk/, which has a link to a comprehensive bibliography on all matters relating to Jelling. Here I wish to briefly discuss Jelling in the context of change.

Let us review the main features of the site (Figs. 2–3). First, there is the small rune-stone erected by king Gorm in memory of his wife, Thyre, the original position of which is unknown. Second, there was a huge stone-setting, almost certainly a ship-setting, which was at least 170 m long and, according to recent excavations possibly, though I doubt it, some 350 m long; only portions of the setting are preserved, and it is feasible that the stones found belong to more than one setting. Third, there is the huge North Mound with remains of fine male grave-goods found in and around a burial chamber; the mound was almost certainly built for Harald's father, Gorm, although alternative theories have of course been proposed. Then, to the south, is a slightly later and even bigger mound without a grave; its function is much discussed – it may well have been

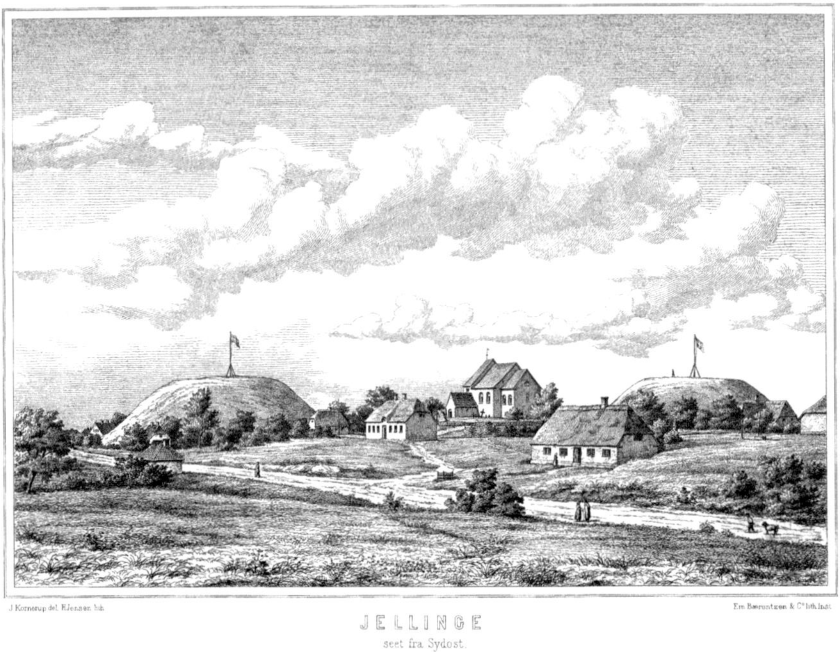

Fig. 2. Jelling seen from the south-east in the late nineteenth century. The stone church, between the two mounds, was built *c.*1100 and succeeded earlier stave-churches. Harald Bluetooth's rune-stone, just south of the church porch, was placed exactly between the centres of the mounds. The North Mound to the right presumably contained the burial of king Gorm, who was probably moved to the grave underneath the earliest church after the official introduction of Christianity in *c.*965. The South Mound, which had no grave, was erected a few years after the Conversion; it was probably both a memorial and a thing mound. After Kornerup 1875.

a memorial to Harald's mother, Thyre, and at the same time may have served as an assembly or thing mound, (see below). Furthermore, there is king Harald's splendid rune-stone memorialising his parents and glorifying himself, which is placed exactly between the centres of the two mounds, on the axis created by the ship-setting. Finally, there are traces, under the present medieval church, of a large timbered building which in my opinion was probably a church; under this was a grave which held male bones moved from elsewhere and wrapped in fine cloth, together with two splendid strap-ends. It still makes sense to interpret these bones as those of Gorm, who would have been moved from the pagan burial mound into the Christian church. The whole complex was surrounded by a recently-identified substantial palisade, some 360 m in length (Fig. 3). The

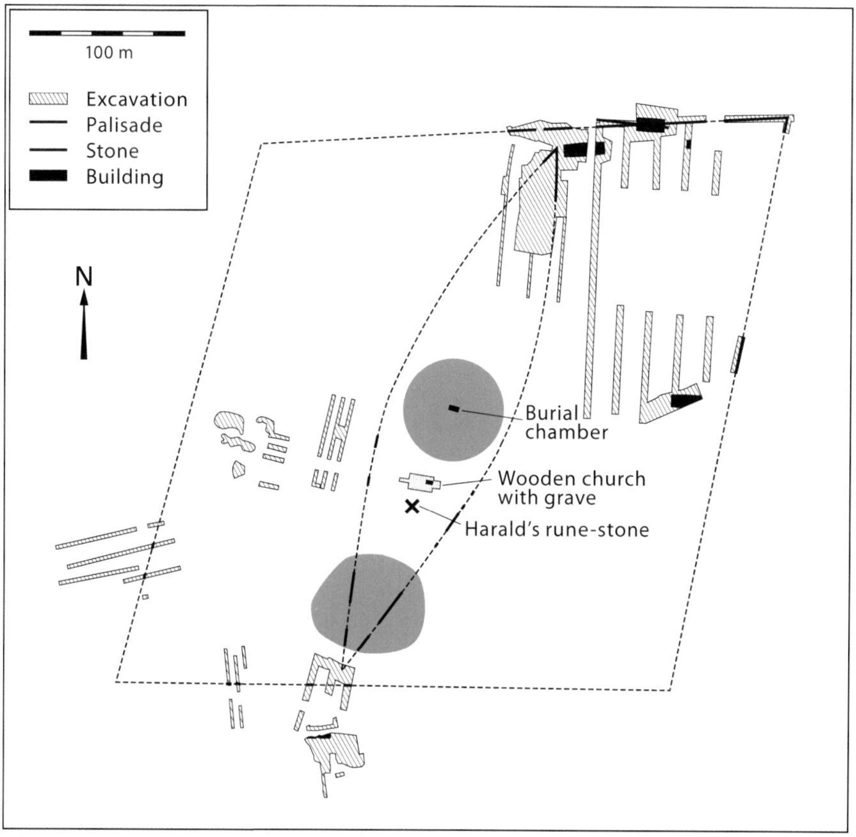

Fig. 3. Jelling. Schematic drawing of monuments, the recently identified palisade, other structures and excavated areas. The huge ship-setting is shown according to the excavator's interpretation; further investigation should reveal if the stones found are part of more than one structure. Drawing: Julie Lolk 2010, based on illustration in Andersen, 2009.

North Mound is in the centre of this four-sided enclosure (Kornerup, 1875; Krogh, 1982; Krogh, 1993; Pedersen, 2006; Krogh & Leth-Larsen, 2007; S.W. Andersen, 2009; Andersen, Jessen & Holst, 2011).

Every element of the monument, with the exception of Gorm's rune-stone, is the largest of its kind in Denmark. The ship-setting, regardless of whether it was 170 or 350 m long, is also by far the biggest in the whole of Scandinavia, and the rune-stone is the finest of all rune-stones. Together, the whole forms a splendid, complicated and carefully planned monument.

Like the fortresses, it was also 'new', in the sense that Jelling was, as far as we know after many years of systematic investigation, a place of no importance

Fig. 4. The figure of Christ on king Harald's rune-stone in Jelling. The text on the stone reads: 'King Harald ordered these monuments to be made after Gorm his father and after Thyre his mother. That Harald who won for himself all Denmark, and Norway, and made the Danes Christian'. Photo: Else Roesdahl 2009.

until it was decided around the mid-tenth century to establish a major royal centre here. This must have happened during the lifetime of Harald Bluetooth's father, Gorm, who was one of the first kings of a new dynasty. His son, Harald, then expanded it on a grand scale into what we more-or less know today. It is probably also associated with the massive 760 m long bridge south of Jelling at Ravning Enge (Schou Jørgensen, 1997). Built *c.*980, it is the earliest known bridge in Scandinavia.

All monuments at Jelling, save the church and the Ravning bridge, were based on traditional Scandinavian models, and the church may have been decorated in Scandinavian style. Some of the monuments – the ship-setting(s), the mounds and the rune-stones – were traditional forms now re-used and surely intended as a sign of respect for the past (Roesdahl, 2005).

King Harald's rune-stone (Fig. 4) was most prominently placed and must have been conceived for this position. Although basically a traditional monument, it was also innovative – with its horizontal text lines, set out as though in a book and not produced with the vertical lines common to contemporary rune-stones, and with its huge images, originally undoubtedly painted in bright colours. The stone is clearly inspired by the illuminated books of the new religion – a 'book of stone'. Moreover, its innovative grand pictures, which were executed in a new art style, the Mammen style, were to inspire many later rune-stones. The text sends a powerful message about a powerful king's legitimacy and achievements, linking the monuments to his dynasty and to Denmark (Wilson, 1966, pp. 119–133; Moltke, 1985, pp. 202–223; Roesdahl, 1999).

But why were all these monumental, dynastic and religious symbols of power built, and why at this particular time, with these particular Scandinavian forms, and at this place? The answer must lie in Europe, where kings and emperors built powerful monuments for themselves and to their Christian God, in the light of their own culture and religion. Germany is clearly particularly relevant in this context, for this was the time when the Ottonian emperors developed Quedlinburg and Magdeburg on a grand scale as imperial monuments with royal burial churches, which, particularly in Magdeburg, had over-arching references to imperial Rome. Jelling may be seen as a grand Danish counterpart, with distinct reference to Scandinavian culture and particularly to Danish history and identity (*Otto der Grosse, Magdeburg und Europa*, 2001; Meier, 2002; Roesdahl, 2005).

The various monuments at Jelling were superbly designed to emphasise a place of power and of dynastic memory. The site, however, was also well chosen as a place for grand assemblies. Here is a powerful blend of the idea of Denmark, of royal power, of religion and presumably law. Jelling is situated quite near the main north-south road through Jutland – the Army, or Ox Road – at a place where monuments could stand proud, dominating the landscape and be seen from the Road (pers. comm. Jens Andresen). It was also fairly near – but not too close – to the German border which, as has already been pointed out, was the source of the main political problems of the time. The long, wide and well-constructed bridge over Ravning Enge was probably built not only to ease traffic to and from the south, but also for symbolic religious and prestigious reasons. The immediate functions of the burial mound, the great rune-stone and the church are self-evident, while the meaning of ship-settings is an enigma (Vestergaard, 2007). But the huge flat-topped mound to the south, the meaning of which has been much discussed, together with the recently found enclosure, may provide major clues to the practical function and *raison d'être* of the whole site.

With reference to features of other assembly- or thing-sites, such as Thingvellir in Iceland, Tynwald in the Isle of Man, the Anundshög complex in Västmanland in Sweden, and others, I would suggest that Jelling was planned as a place for major thing meetings. It combined visual elements of royal power and legitimacy with structures of religion and law (Þorsteinsson, 1987; Brink, 2004; Sawyer & Sawyer, 1993, pp. 80–91; Brink, 2008a; Wilson, 2008, pp. 122–127; Sanmark, 2009). Jelling was easily accessible, with apparently no important settlement, and its palisade would define the physical extent of the thing-site. It would be a place where fighting and brawling were forbidden and the king's peace was paramount during a formal assembly, while the strong palisade would even provide physical protection to an assembled company and to the monuments at all times. The flat summit of the South Mound would provide ample space and visual exposure for the leaders of the formal proceedings and of their chief men. Pagan as well as Christian religious features were represented in the form of the ship-setting(s), the burial mound, the church (which was probably dedicated to Saint John the Baptist) and the picture of Christ on the rune-stone. The site may also have been a place for mass baptisms, like that recorded by Bede (II, 14) which took place at Yeavering in Northumbria nearly three centuries earlier. Blair (2005, pp. 54–57) discusses the mass baptism at Yeavering and draws the parallel to Scandinavian assembly places.

It is generally accepted that thing-sites were 'constructed' and that their location might change by decision of the magnates. In the light of Harald Bluetooth's politics and achievements it seems entirely plausible that he had a major thing-site designed at this place and constructed in this manner, perhaps to serve the whole of Jutland or even the whole kingdom. In later times – first known from King Valdemar's cadastra of 1231 – Jelling gave its name to a *herred* (now Tørrild herred), implying that it was then an assembly site; but the division of the country into such administrative units is centuries older. Indeed, the oldest known seal of Tørrild herred, from 1535, shows Jelling church between the two mounds (Skovgaard-Petersen, 1977, pp. 102f., 89f.; Sawyer & Sawyer, 1993, pp. 84–89; *Trap: Danmark*, Vejle Amt, 1964, pp. 1085f., 1113f.). No evidence for Viking Age 'thing-booths' or a royal manor has yet been recognised in the immediate neighbourhood; the latter may have been situated at some distance from the site. Based on its place-name a candidate for a royal manor might be Husby, some kilometres to the northeast.

Jelling and the Ravning Bridge, like the circular fortresses, had a short life. King Harald was not even buried at Jelling and no great monuments were built there after his death. Times and politics had changed during the 980s and 990s; Germany was no longer a threat or even a challenge after 983. The centre of Danish power moved east, to Sjælland and Skåne, and England became the centre of attraction for those in search of wealth and power. Meanwhile, the growing strength of Christianity, together with new European influences, had changed taste and outlooks by the turn of the millennium. The fashion for old monument types was fast disappearing.

Centralisation of power

In Denmark the second half of the tenth century was, then, a time of unusual experiment, initiative and display, linked to centralisation of power. The same trends were apparent in the rest of Scandinavia – and in Europe (for example Nelson, 1999). In the north of Norway, a dynasty from Hålogaland who had established themselves as earls of Hlade, near Trondheim, probably acquired some new form of overlordship over the wealthy magnates of Lofoten, which may help to explain why the chieftain's residence at Borg (Fig. 5) was finally destroyed. The earls became major players on the political scene in Scandinavia and were often allied to Danish kings and opposed to Norwegian rulers (Krag, 2003; Näsman & Roesdahl, 2003).

In Denmark the concentration of prestigious and innovative royal monuments built by Harald Bluetooth demonstrates an entirely new focus on the king and his power, and also indicates a new royal control of huge resources. The mere construction of the circular fortresses and the Jelling monuments, not to speak of extensions to the Danevirke and to town ramparts, demanded enormous resources of manpower and building materials. How these resources were achieved has been much discussed. At one time it was suggested that the fortresses were paid for by silver taken from England, but for chronological reasons such an argument cannot be upheld; the fortresses had probably fallen

Fig. 5. Reconstruction of the 81 m-long house at Borg in Lofoten. The house was violently destroyed in the tenth century. Photo: David Wilson 2002.

into disrepair before the raids on England had even begun. Other scholars have suggested that they were built by slave labour. It is, however, more convincing to believe that both building materials and the labour for these huge building enterprises came from converted military obligations.

Such obligations are well documented in England and on the Continent (Reuter, 1985; Brooks, 1991), but they may well have been new to contemporary Denmark, at least on this scale. It may have become possible to establish and maintain them during the years of constant threats from Germany, but the whole system would probably be difficult to maintain after this threat had disappeared. These various circumstances may be part of the reason for the revolt against Harald Bluetooth in *c.*987. Laurits Weibull (1911, pp. 277f.) and others have drawn attention to stories related by the Danish twelfth-century historians Saxo and Svend Aggesen; they say that part of the reason for the revolt was that Harald ordered an enormous stone dragged to his mother's burial mound. Perhaps it enshrines a folk-memory of his huge building programmes and overreaching ambitions.

Harald Bluetooth may be seen as an iconic figure of this period. His reign saw unprecedented changes to society, and his achievements comprise large-scale and innovative responses to military, cultural and religious challenges from the south. His death marked the end of an era, and few of his achievements outlasted him.

Late paganism

The middle and second half of the tenth century appears to have been a time of great pagan revival, undoubtedly as a response to the advance of Christianity. Pagan symbols in the form of pendants, especially Thor's hammers (Fig. 6), became immensely popular. These were made in many materials and must have been used at all social levels (Wamers, 1997; Pedersen, 2004; Gräslund, 2008).

New burial-customs for the aristocracy of both sexes were also introduced, and graves were now richly furnished according to specific rituals. This is particularly true of male graves in Denmark, with their weapons and riding-gear, and of the socially equivalent women's graves, in which wagon bodies were used as coffins. The pagan monuments at royal Jelling also belong to this period. Linked to this was almost certainly a new focus on the cult of Odin, which was particularly important to the military aristocracy (Roesdahl, 1983; idem, 2006). According to the poem *Eiríksmál*, for example, Eric Bloodaxe, killed in 954, went to Odin's Valhalla. In Norway king Hákon Athelstansfostre, who had had a Christian upbringing in England, was forced to participate in pagan rituals, and, according to the poem *Hákonarmál,* he was given a pagan burial *c.*960. He too went to Valhalla. This was exactly the time (958/9) when king Gorm was buried in pagan splendour in the North Mound at Jelling. The

Fig. 6. Pagan Thor's hammer (unprovenanced, from Skåne) and a Christian cross (from the Tolstrup hoard, North Jutland, deposited *c.*995). Height: 5.1 and 4.1 cm respectively. Both are of silver, with a characteristic loop in the shape of a prominent head of a bird-of-prey. Such pendants became fashionable in the second half of the tenth century and are probably a symbol of vernacular power. Photos: Historical Museum, Stockholm and National Museum of Denmark. Not to scale.

Norwegian Hákon Jarl, who had fought so bravely at the Danevirke in 974, is known to have been a particularly zealous pagan (Meulengracht Sørensen, 1991; *Medieval Scandinavia. An Encyclopedia*, 1993: 'Eiríksmál', 'Hákon góði ("the good") Haraldsson', 'Hákon jarl ("earl") Sigurðarson).

Conversion

But about 965 Denmark officially converted to Christianity. On his runestone in Jelling king Harald claims that he 'made the Danes Christian'. The German chronicler Widukind confirms this statement and explains that Harald became convinced of the strength of the Christian religion by the actions of a certain bishop called Poppo, who carried hot iron without damage to his hands. Seen in a wider context, Harald must indeed have taken an active part in the Conversion. He was at the height of his power, and kings throughout Scandinavia were deeply involved in the conversion to Christianity. Where there was no king, as in Iceland, the leading political figures had a big say in the Conversion and ultimately made the decision to convert. Neither was such an involvement in religion new; there is ample evidence from literary and archaeological sources that kings and other magnates were closely involved in the practice of religion and cult in pagan times (e.g. Sundqvist, 2008; Steinsland, 2008). Major sites throughout Scandinavia – such as Tissø and Lejre in Denmark, Borg in Norway and Uppåkra and Gamla Uppsala in Sweden – also linked secular and religious power (for example Christensen, 2004; Gräslund, 2008).

However, the Danish Conversion could not have been accomplished without the consent of the aristocracy and of the main thing assemblies. There is no concrete evidence for this, but the Conversion of Iceland may provide a useful analogy. Here, after much debate, and according to the advice of important men, and after the acceptance of certain exemptions from Christian rules, which, we are told, were soon abandoned, Christianity was accepted as the official religion at a meeting of the Althing (summaries in, e.g., Foote, 1993; Brink, 2008b, pp. 624f.). This decision is supported by archaeological evidence; grave-goods in the pagan tradition were, indeed, very quickly abolished (Eldjárn 1956/2000, pp. 609–610).

Some exemptions must have also been part of the deal in Denmark. At Jelling, for example, religious tolerance was signalled by the augmentation of the pagan monument with Christian elements. Everything points to a gradual transition to Christian rites, including the ritual of burial. Changes were, then, probably not achieved quite as quickly as they were in Iceland. The Mammen grave, for example, is dated by dendrochronology to 970/71, that is some five years after the official Conversion. The grave was laid out in pagan style with many grave-goods, including the well-known axe; furthermore, in pagan fashion, it was covered by a mound. At the King's own fortress of Fyrkat traditional pagan burial customs were in use as late as the late 970s or the 80s, which is up to twenty years after the Conversion. Even a pagan *völva* (according to Neil Price and I believe him) was buried here and had probably lived here. But the Fyrkat cemetery also included a number of children's graves, an exclusively Christian rite in Denmark; the Christian attitude to the burial of children was thus fairly quickly accepted. Before the turn of the millennium pagan burial customs were generally abandoned in Denmark, and Thor's hammers were substituted with pendent crosses (Fig. 6) (Price, 2002; Pedersen, 2004; Roesdahl, 2004a; idem, 2006).

But why did the Scandinavian lands convert? In Denmark pressure from Germany must, again, have played an important part. Otto I was crowned emperor in Rome in 962, and saw the spread of Christianity as an imperial duty (for example Müller-Mertens, 1999; Refskou 2004). The Danish decision to convert only a couple of years later must have been affected by this. Conversion would remove religious arguments for German aggression against Denmark at a time of severe political tension. In Iceland, pressure from the Norwegian king played some role, and in all countries the reasons for Conversion must have been mixed and complicated, comprising at least some religious conviction. Furthermore, Christianity was the religion of 'the future'. At the time there was a spate of conversions in Europe: Poland in 966; Russia in 988 and Hungary *c.*1000. Conversions in the Scandinavian world were part of this process.

Effects of the Conversions

By 1000 much of western Scandinavia was at least nominally Christian, and all Scandinavian kings were Christian. The Swedish lands had begun the process, although it took some time before paganism was abolished. According to Adam of Bremen, writing *c.*1075, there was still good work to be done there by missionaries, while the pagan centre at Gamla Uppsala continued to function. Conversion, naturally, brought considerable changes to Scandinavia and to its people – some were quick, some slow. It was seen by contemporaries as a change of ways and customs, of culture including religion, as expressed by the Norse word *siðaskipti* – so well explained by the late Preben Meulengracht Sørensen (1997).

One of the important practical effects of the Conversion was that Christian Scandinavia was fully accepted by Christian Europe. Four exquisite objects decorated in the Scandinavian Mammen style may be explained as gifts from Scandinavian royalty (perhaps even Harald Bluetooth himself) to Christian colleagues in foreign lands. There they have been preserved in churches which were closely under the patronage of princes or royalty. The objects in question are the Cammin casket, preserved in present-day Poland until the end of the Second World War; the Bamberg casket in south-east Germany; the so-called St. Stephen's sword in Prague; and the small reliquary in León in northern Spain (Roesdahl, 1998).

Changes included the visual and symbolic environment as well as settlement patterns. Pagan monuments, such as burial mounds and ship-settings, were abolished. But in Denmark, Norway and Sweden a boom in the raising of rune-stones occurred during the Conversion period of each country – for some reason this did not happen in Iceland, the Faeroes and Greenland. Rune-stones had been raised sporadically for a long time in Scandinavia and in Scandinavian societies abroad, and some are definitely pagan. But the Conversion would have created a need for a new type of monument, and one that was clearly visible (Roesdahl, 2005; Gräslund & Lager, 2008, pp. 634–36).

For some time to come the day-to-day ritual of the Christian cult would probably still have taken place in aristocratic halls and at home, as it had in

Fig. 7. Left: example of Harald Bluetooth's early coinage with its traditional motive, and of his innovative coinage *c.*975, bearing a cross. Right: Danish, Norwegian and Swedish coinages *c.*995, by Sven Forkbeard, Olav Tryggvesson and Olof Skötkonung, respectively; all are closely modelled on contemporary English coins which at this time poured into Scandinavia from Danegeld payments, and all show a cross on the reverse. Drawings: Brita Malmer. Not to scale.

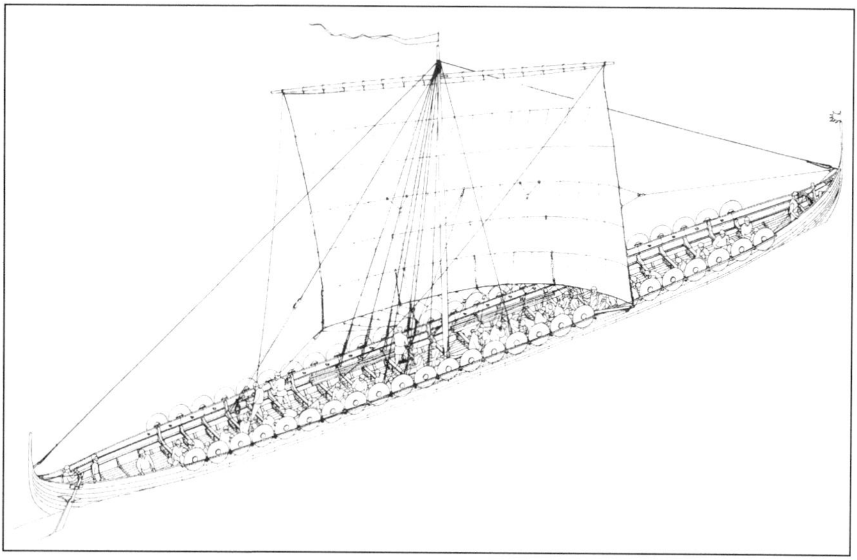

Fig. 8. Reconstruction of a warship excavated at the harbour of Hedeby. 30 m-long, it was built *c.*985. Of fine quality, it would have been fit for a king. After Crumlin-Pedersen, 1997, p. 93. Drawing: Sune Villum-Nielsen.

pagan times. But churches as places of worship naturally followed Conversion. In the early phases they were probably built only at certain very important places where people would gather on feast days, and where important rituals like baptism took place *en masse*. As elsewhere in Europe, such churches would be grand buildings – very unlike the former, fairly small pagan cult buildings which have been identified at some magnates' sites. It was probably not until the mid- to late eleventh century that smaller local churches became common (Roesdahl, 2004b; Skre, 2004; Gräslund, 2008).

Another striking feature of the latter part of the tenth century is the failure of a series of important sites which had a long history and which were often linked to both secular power and religion; sites such as Uppåkra, Lejre and Tissø (Hårdh, 2008; Christensen, 2008; Jørgensen, 2008). The decrease in their importance was often linked to the foundation and rise of a new site nearby, as at Lund and Roskilde. Such changes probably often relate to the Conversion. Some of these sites would have been so closely linked to pagan rituals that a clean break may have been considered appropriate.

Economy

The discontinuation, however, of Birka (Ambrosiani, 2008), one of Scandinavia's most important towns and the predecessor of Sigtuna, was probably based on economic and other practical reasons, which were part of a complicated pattern of dramatic economic changes which took place from about 970.

At this time the stream of Arab silver dirhems which had fuelled Scandinavian economy for so long, ceased rather abruptly, for reasons based on the situation in the East. This, together with the exploitation of new silver mines of the Harz in Germany, and, from 991, the influx of silver in the form of Danegeld from England, created an entirely new economic situation. Linked to this were the beginnings in parts of Scandinavia of a coin-based economy, which replaced the former bullion economy. In Denmark a substantial new coinage had already appeared *c.*975 and must have been issued by Harald Bluetooth. The coins had no legend but did have a new iconography – for the first time in Scandinavia coins showed the cross. This coinage ceased around the time of Harald's death in *c.*987, as did so many of his other initiatives. What followed from *c.*995 onwards was again different. Scandinavian coinages were now closely modelled on English coins (Fig. 7), while coin hoards also contained many English and German coins (Jensen (Ed.), 1995, nos. 1–4 *et passim*; Gullbekk, 2008; Moesgaard, 2008).

All this happened at a time which must have seen great economic expansion and increasing trade. I cannot here venture into the background, or how it affected town and countryside. However, I would point to one technological effect: the specialisation of ships into their various functions as trading-vessels and warships, which probably took place in the late tenth century. This crucial development must have been caused by a need for greater cargo capacity, as well as for more efficient war machines and thus demonstrates the interaction between trade and power. Cargo-ships were sailing ships and could not be rowed. They would therefore be easy prey for pirates when winds were slow – requiring that peace at sea be guaranteed by a strong power (Bill, 2008). This chimes in well with the suggested centralisation of power at this time.

Militarisation

Another striking feature of the late tenth century is the sense of an intense militarisation of society. This is demonstrated by the increased importance of the cult of Odin; by weapon graves and inscriptions on rune-stone; by skaldic poetry and the building of royal fortresses for the first time in Scandinavia; and by the specialisation of war-ships into extremely long, slender, elegant and fast man-carriers like the 30 m long 'royal' ship in Hedeby (Fig. 8), or Olaf Tryggvesson's legendary 'Ormen Lange'(Crumlin-Pedersen, 1997, pp. 81–95; Jesch, 2001, pp. 57–63, 180–265; Bill, 2008). All this, and more, tells of a fasci-

Fig. 9. Rune-stone from Aarhus with long inscription in memory of a warrior, laid out in complicated fashion on three sides of the stone around the prominent mask. It reads: 'Gunulfr and Eygautr and Áslakr and Rolfr raised this stone in memory of their companion Ful, who died … when kings fought'. It is not known in which battle Ful died, but the stone must have been raised just before or around 1000. The mask itself probably had a protective meaning and would have been acceptable in a Christian environment. Photo: Moesgaard photo and media lab.

nation with fighting and of the high status of those involved in it professionally, and of the importance of the matters at issue.

As happens so often in periods of great change, important battles were fought that would change society. Some of the most legendary battles in Scandinavian history took place at this time and were commemorated in runes, poems and sagas (Fig. 9). The battle at the Danevirke in 974; the revolt against Harald Bluetooth in *c.*987; raids by the Swedish king Erik the Victorious; the battle at the Fyris, near Uppsala, between Danes and Swedes; the battle at Hjørungavåg between Jomsvikingar and the Norwegian earls Haakon and Eric. These and the sea-battle of the three kings at Svold in the year 1000, where Olav Tryggvesson lost his life, were but some of the great military exploits related in literature.

Scandinavian power struggles continued for a long time to come, but from *c.*990 Scandinavian military might found a new and most profitable outlet in England. Continued raids and other means of exploitation, and the consequent levying of danegeld consisting of enormous quantities of silver, led to the final conquest of the whole country by Knut the Great in 1016 (Keynes, 1991; Lund, 1991). A new era had started in Scandinavia, and until the mid-eleventh century men from all countries and lands sought opportunities across the North Sea. Meanwhile, much of Scandinavia seems to have enjoyed a certain degree of peace.

CONCLUSIONS

With these examples I hope to have shown that during the second half of the tenth century Scandinavia changed dramatically. Christianity was an important element of this change, but does not provide anywhere near the whole story. Its introduction was in part a response to other challenges and changes. Complicated interactions also gave rise to efforts to centralise power, to create new economic enterprises, new settlements, a new art style and great buildings. There was also the settlement of new land in the north, militarisation, social movement and experiments, as well as the awareness of a new source of wealth and power in England. There was an outburst of 'true' Viking culture in various forms, and much of this may be seen as answers to challenges from Ottonian Germany.

But by the year 1000 much of the old cultural baggage had been shed. Not just pagan religion and monuments, but even the traditional female dress with oval brooches which had been worn for centuries. European fashions had taken over and a new era was dawning. Scandinavia had been in a melting-pot. People who lived through the previous half century would have experienced a *siðaskipti,* or a cultural revolution. One likes to think that the spirit of the time is caught in the splendid pagan poem Völuspá, *the Sayings of the Sibyl,* which may have been composed in Tröndelag, at the court of devout pagan Hákon Jarl (Meulengracht Sørensen & Steinsland, 2001).

Postscript

Our subject, the Viking Age, is in danger of being atomized among the different disciplines involved, and even among specialities within individual disciplines. Today it is difficult for one person to cover the entire Viking Age – the modern model of a synthesis is rather an edited collection of essays by various scholars, such as that recently published by Brink & Price (2008). But synthesis by a single person of the ever-increasing and much scattered evidence and detailed research is still just about possible for parts of the period, and, in my opinion, it is essential to produce such surveys from time to time. It provides broader views and some understanding of interactions, and may stimulate discussions and provide starting points for further work. For this reason I have tried here to present an overview of important developments in the second half of the tenth century, although admittedly with a focus on my own discipline.

I am most grateful to David M. Wilson for comments on various aspects of this article, and for adjusting my English.

BIBLIOGRAPHY

Albrectsen, E. (1994). Harald Blåtand og Danmark. In C. Due-Nielsen et al. (Eds.), *Struktur og Funktion* (Festschr. Erling Ladewig Petersen), (pp. 17–26). Odense: Odense Universitetsforlag.

Althoff, G. (1999). Saxony and the Elbe Slavs in the tenth century. In T. Reuter (Ed.), *The New Cambridge Medieval History, vol. III, c. 900–c. 1024* (pp. 267–292). Cambridge: Cambridge University Press.

Ambrosiani, B. (2008). Birka. In S. Brink (Ed.) in collaboration with N. Price, *The Viking World* (pp. 94–100). London and New York: Routledge.

Andersen, H. H. (1984). Die Haltung Dänemarks im Jahre 983. *Zeitschrift für Archäologie* 18, 1984, pp. 101–106.

Andersen, S. W. (2009). Bautasten og kæmpehegn. *Skalk* 2009 no. 1, pp. 11–17.

Andersen, S. W., Jessen, M. D., Holst, M. K. (2011). Jagten på kongens gård. *Skalk* 2011 no. 1, pp. 9–11.

Bede. *A History of the English Church and People* (trans., with an Introduction by L. Sherley-Price, rev. R. E. Latham). Harmondsworth: Penguin Books. Revised 1968.

Bill, J. (2008). Viking ships and the sea. In S. Brink (Ed.) in collaboration with N. Price, *The Viking World* (pp. 170–180). London and New York: Routledge.

Blair, J. (2005). *The Church in Anglo-Saxon Society*. Oxford: Oxford University Press.

Brink, S. (2004). Legal assembly sites in early Scandinavia. In A. Pantos & S. Semple (Eds.), *Assembly Places and Practices in Medieval Europe* (pp. 205–216). Dublin: Four Courts Press.

Brink, S. (2008a). Law and society: polities and legal customs in Viking Age Scandinavia. In S. Brink (Ed.) in collaboration with N. Price, *The Viking World* (pp. 23–31). London and New York: Routledge.

Brink, S. (2008b). Christianisation and the emergence of the early church in Scandinavia. In S. Brink (Ed.) in collaboration with N. Price, *The Viking World* (pp. 621–628). London and New York: Routledge.

Brink, S. (Ed.) in collaboration with N. Price (2008). *The Viking World*. London and New York: Routledge.

Brooks, N. (1991). The development of military obligations in eighth- and ninth-century England. In P. Clemoes & K. Hughes (Eds.), *England before the conquest* (pp. 69–84). Cambridge: Cambridge University Press.

Carver, M. (2001). Why that? Why there? Why then? The politics of Early Medieval Monumentality. In H. Hamerow & A. Macgregor (Eds.), *Image and Power in the Archaeology of Early Medieval Britain. Essays in honour of Rosemary Cramp* (pp. 1–22). Oxford: Oxbow Books.

Christensen, T. (2004). Fra hedenskab til kristendom i Lejre og Roskilde. In N. Lund (Ed.), *Kristendommen i Danmark før 1050* (pp. 191–200). Roskilde: Roskilde Museums Forlag.

Christensen, T. (2008). Lejre and Roskilde. In S. Brink (Ed.) in collaboration with N. Price, *The Viking World* (pp. 121–125). London and New York: Routledge.

Crumlin-Pedersen, O. (1997). *Viking-Age Ships and Shipbuilding in Hedeby/Haithabu and Schleswig*. Schleswig & Roskilde: Archäologisches Landesmuseum der Christian-Albrecht-Universität, Wikinger Museum Haithabu, National Museum of Denmark, Viking Ship Museum in Roskilde.

Dulinicz, M. (2002). Forschungen zu den Herrschaftszentren des 10. bis 11. Jahrhunderts in Polen. In J. Henning (Ed.), *Europa im 10. Jahrhundert. Archäologie einer Aufbruchzeit* (pp. 147–160). Mainz am Rhein: Philipp von Zabern.

Eldjárn, K. (1956/2000). *Kuml og haugfé úr heiðnum sið á Íslandi*. 2. ed., by A. Friðriksson. Reykjavík: Mál og menning.

Foote, P. (1993). Conversion. In P. Pulsiano (Ed.), *Medieval Scandinavia. An Encyclopedia* (pp. 106–108). New York, London: Garland Publishing.

Gräslund, A.-S. (2008). The material culture of the Christianisation. In S. Brink (Ed.) in collaboration with N. Price, *The Viking World* (pp. 639–641). London and New York: Routledge.

Gräslund, A.-S. & Lager, L. (2008). Runestones and the Christian Missions. In S.

Brink (Ed.) in collaboration with N. Price, *The Viking World* (pp. 629–638). London and New York: Routledge.

Gullbekk, H. (2008). Coinage and monetary economies. In S. Brink (Ed.) in collaboration with N. Price, *The Viking World* (pp. 159–169). London and New York: Routledge.

Henning, J. (2002). Der slawische Siedlungsraum und die ottonische Expansion östlich der Elbe: Ereignisgeschichte – Archäologie – Dendrochronologie. In J. Henning (Ed.), *Europa im 10. Jahrhundert. Archäologie einer Aufbruchzeit* (pp. 131–146). Mainz am Rhein: Philipp von Zabern.

Hårdh, B. (2008). Viking Age Uppåkra and Lund. In S. Brink (Ed.) in collaboration with N. Price, *The Viking World* (pp. 145–149). London and New York: Routledge.

Jensen, J. S. (Ed.) (1995). *Tusindtallets danske mønter. Danish coins from the 11th century*. København: Nationalmuseet.

Jesch, J. (2001). *Ships and Men in the Late Viking Age. The vocabulary of runic Inscriptions and Skaldic Verse.* Woodbridge: The Boydell Press.

Jørgensen, L. (2008). Manor, cult and market at Lake Tissø. In S. Brink (Ed.) in collaboration with N. Price, *The Viking World* (pp. 77–82). London and New York: Routledge.

Keynes, S. (1991). The Historical Context of the Battle of Maldon. In D. Scragg (Ed.), *The Battle of Maldon AD 991* (pp. 81–113). Oxford: Basil Blackwell.

Keynes, S. (1999). England, *c.*900–1016. In T. Reuter (Ed.), *The New Cambridge Medieval History, vol. III, c. 900–c. 1024* (pp. 456–484). Cambridge: Cambridge University Press.

Kornerup, J. (1875). *Kongehøiene i Jellinge,* København.

Krag, C. (2003). The early unification of Norway. In K. Helle (Ed.), *The Cambridge History of Scandinavia* vol. 1. *Prehistory to 1520* (pp. 184–201). Cambridge: Cambridge University Press.

Krogh, K. J. (1982). The Royal Viking Viking-Age Monuments in Jelling in the Light of Recent Archaeological Excavations, *Acta Archaeologica* 53, pp. 183–216.

Krogh, K. J. (1993). *Gåden om Kong Gorms Grav. Vikingekongernes Monumenter i Jelling*, vol. I. Herning: Poul Kristensen.

Krogh, K. J. & B. Leth-Larsen (2007). *Hedensk og Kristent. Fundene fra den kongelige gravhøj i Jelling. Vikingekongernes Monumenter i Jelling*, vol. II. København: Carlsbergfondet og Nationalmuseet.

Lund, N. (1991). The Danish perspective. In D. Scragg (Ed.), *The Battle of Maldon AD 991* (pp. 114–142). Oxford: Basil Blackwell.

Medieval Scandinavia. An Encyclopedia (P. Pulsiano Ed.), (1993). New York & London: Garland Publishing, Inc.

Meier, T. (2002). Magdeburg zwischen Aachen und Jelling: Repräsentationsarchitektur als semiotisches System. In J. Henning (Ed.), *Europa im 10. Jahrhundert. Archäologie einer Aufbruchzeit* (pp. 311–322). Mainz am Rhein: Philipp von Zabern.

Meulengracht Sørensen, P. (1991). Håkon den Gode og guderne. Nogle bemærkninger om religion og centralmagt i det tiende århundrede – og om religion og kildekritik. In P. Mortensen & B. Rasmussen (Eds.), *Fra Stamme til Stat i Danmark*, vol. 2 (pp. 235–244). Højbjerg: Jysk Arkæologisk Selskab. – Reprint, in Meulengracht Sørensen, P. (2001). *At fortælle Historien. Telling History* (pp. 151–167). Trieste: Edizioni Parnaso.

Meulengracht Sørensen, P. (1997). Religions old and new. In P. Sawyer (Ed.), *The Oxford illustrated history of the Vikings* (pp. 202–224). Oxford: Oxford University Press.

Meulengracht Sørensen, P. & Steinsland, G. (2001). *Vølvens Spådom*. København: Høst og Søn.

Moesgaard, J. C. (2008). Udbredelsen af reguleret møntøkonomi i geografisk perspektiv ca. 600–ca. 1150, *hikuin* 35, pp. 133–150.

Moltke, E. (1985). *Runes and their Origin. Denmark and elsewhere*. Copenhagen: The National Museum of Denmark.

Müller-Mertens, E. (1999). The Ottonians as kings and emperors. In T. Reuter (Ed.), *The New Cambridge Medieval History, vol. III, c. 900–c. 1024* (pp. 233–266). Cambridge: Cambridge University Press.

Nelson, J. L. (1999). Rulers and government. In T. Reuter (Ed.), *The New Cambridge Medieval History, vol. III, c. 900–c. 1024* (pp. 95–129). Cambridge: Cambridge University Press.

Näsman, U. & Roesdahl, E. (2003). Scandinavian and European Perspectives – Borg I:1. In G. Stamsø Munch, O. S. Johansen, E. Roesdahl (Eds.), *Borg in Lofoten. A chieftain's farm in North Norway* (pp. 283–299). Trondheim: Tapir academic press.

Nørlund, P. (1948). *Trelleborg*. København: Det Kgl. Nordiske Oldskriftselskab.

Olsen, O. (1999). *Da Danmark blev til*. København: Fremad.

Olsen, O. & Schmidt, H. (1977). *Fyrkat. En jysk vikingeborg. Bd. 1. Borgen og bebyggelsen*. København: Det Kgl. Nordiske Oldskriftselskab.

Otto der Grosse, Magdeburg und Europa (2001). Bd. I Essays, Bd. II Katalog (M. Puhle Ed.). Mainz: Philipp von Zabern.

Pedersen, A. (2004). Religiøse symboler i vikingetidens arkæologiske materiale. In N. Lund (Ed.), *Kristendommen i Danmark før 1050* (pp. 60–74). Roskilde: Roskilde Museums Forlag.

Pedersen, A. (2006). The Jelling Monuments – Ancient royal memorials and modern world heritage site. In M. Stoklund, M. Lerche Nielsen, B. Holmberg, G. Fellows-Jensen (Eds.), *Runes and their Secrets* (pp. 283–313). København: Museum Tusculanum Press.

Pedersen, P. & Otto, T. (2005). Disentangling Traditions. Culture, Agency and Power. In T. Otto & P. Pedersen (Eds.), *Tradition and Agency. Tracing cultural continuity and invention* (pp. 11–49). Århus: Aarhus University Press.

Price, N. (2002). *The Viking Way. Religion and War in Late Iron Age Scandinavia* (AUN 31). Uppsala: Uppsala universitet.

Refskou, N. (2004). Ottonernes missionsvirksomhed. In N. Lund (Ed.), *Kristendommen i Danmark før 1050* (pp. 28–42). Roskilde: Roskilde Museums Forlag.

Reuter, T. (1985). Plunder and tribute in the Carolingian Empire, *Transactions of the Royal Historical Society* 5th ser., 35, pp. 75–94.

Roesdahl, E. (1977). *Fyrkat. En jysk vikingeborg. Bd. 2. Oldsagerne og gravpladsen,* København: Det Kgl. Nordiske Oldskriftselskab.

Roesdahl, E. (1981). Aggersborg in the Viking Age. In H. Bekker-Nielsen, P. Foote, O. Olsen (Eds.), *Proceedings of the Eighth Viking Congress* (pp. 107–122). Odense: Odense University Press.

Roesdahl, E. (1983). Fra vikingegrav til Valhal. In T. Kisbye, E. Roesdahl (Eds.), *Beretning fra andet tværfaglige vikingesymposium* (pp. 39–49). Højbjerg: Hikuin og Afdeling for middelalder-arkæologi.

Roesdahl, E. (1987). The Danish geometrical Viking fortresses and their context. *Anglo-Norman Studies* 9, pp. 208–26.

Roesdahl, E. (1996). Fyrkat. In *Reallexikon der Germanischen Altertumskunde*, vol. 10 (pp. 295–301). Berlin-New York: Walter de Gruyter.

Roesdahl, E. (1998). Cammin – Bamberg – Pragh – Léon. Four Scandinavian objects d'Art in Europe. In A. Wesse (Ed.), *Studien zur Archäologie des Ostseeraumes. Von der Eisenzeit zum Mittelalter (Festschr. M. Müller-Wille)* (pp. 547–553). Neumünster: Wachholtz Verlag.

Roesdahl, E. (1999). Jellingstenen – en bog af sten. In O. Høiris et al. (Eds.), *Menneskelivets mangfoldighed. Arkæologisk og antropologisk forskning på Moesgård* (pp. 235–244). Århus: Aarhus Universitetsforlag, Moesgård Museum.

Roesdahl, E. (2002). Harald Blauzahn. Ein dänischer Wikingerkönig aus archäologischer Sicht. In J. Henning (Ed.), *Europa im 10. Jahrhundert. Archäologie einer Aufbruchzeit* (pp. 95–108). Mainz am Rhein: Philipp von Zabern.

Roesdahl, E. (2004a). En gravplads fra tidlig kristen tid – Fyrkat. In N. Lund (Ed.), *Kristendommen i Danmark før 1050* (pp. 153–158). Roskilde: Roskilde Museums Forlag.

Roesdahl, E. (2004b). Hvornår blev kirkerne bygget? In N. Lund (Ed.), *Kristendommen i Danmark før 1050* (pp. 201–206). Roskilde: Roskilde Museums Forlag.

Roesdahl, E. (2005). Jordfaste mindesmærker i Danmarks yngre vikingetid. *hikuin* 32, pp. 55–74. – French version (2005): Monuments archéologiques de l'âge viking au Danemark. In R. Boyer (Ed.), *Les Vikings, premiers Européens*, (pp. 27–51). Paris: Éditions Autrement.

Roesdahl, E. (2006). Aristocratic Burial in Late Viking Age Denmark. Custom, Regionality, Conversion. In C. von Carnap-Bornheim, D. Krausse, A. Wesse (Eds.), *Herrschaft – Tod – Bestattung. Zu den vor- und frühgeschichtlicen Prunkgräbern als archäologisch-historische Quellen* (pp. 169–183). Bonn: Verlag Dr. Rudolf Habelt.

Sanmark, A. (2009). Administrative Organisation and State formation: A Case Study of Assembly Sites in Södermanland, Sweden. *Medieval Archaeology* 53, 2009, pp. 205–241.

Sawyer, P. (1988/2002). *Da Danmark blev Danmark. Fra ca. år 700 til ca. 1050.* Gyldendals og Politikens Danmarkshistorie vol. 3. København: Gyldendal & Politikens Forlag.

Sawyer, B. & Sawyer, P. (1993). *Medieval Scandinavia. From Conversion to Reformation circa 800–1500.* Minneapolis, London: University of Minnesota press.

Schou Jørgensen, M. (1997). Vikingetidsbroen i Ravning Enge – nye undersøgelser. *Nationalmuseets Arbejdsmark* 1997, pp. 74–87.

Skovgaard-Petersen, I. (1977). Oldtid og vikingetid. In I. Skovgaard-Petersen, A.E. Christensen, H. Paludan, *Danmarks historie* vol. 1 (pp. 16–209). København: Gyldendal.

Skre, D. (2004). Kristning, misjon og konversjon i Norges vikingtid. In N. Lund (Ed.), *Kristendommen i Danmark før 1050* (pp. 235–252). Roskilde: Roskilde Museums Forlag.

Steinsland, G. (2008). Rulers as offsprings of gods and giantesses: on the mythology of pagan Norse rulership. In S. Brink (Ed.) in collaboration with N. Price, *The Viking World* (pp. 227–230). London and New York: Routledge.

Sundqvist, O. (2008). Cult leaders, rulers and religion. In S. Brink (Ed.) in collaboration with N. Price, *The Viking World* (pp. 223–226). London and New York: Routledge.

Svanberg, F. & Söderberg, B. (1999). *Den vikingatida borgen i Borgeby* (Arkeologiska studier kring Borgeby och Löddeköpinge 1). Lund.

Tesch, S. (2008). Sigtuna ca. 980–1200 – det maktpolitiska och sakrala stadsrummet. In H. Andersson, G. Hansen & I. Øye (Eds.), *De første 200årene – nytt blikk på 27 skandinaviske middelalderbyer* (pp. 323–340). Bergen: Universitetet i Bergen.

Trap: Danmark (1964) = Trap, J.P.: *Danmark.* 5th ed. Vejle Amt. København: G.E.C. Gad.

Vestergaard, F. (2007). Monumentale skibssætninger i Danmark og Skåne. *Kuml* 2007, pp. 145–190.

Wamers, E. (1997). Hammer und Kreutz. Typologische Aspekte einer nordeuropäischen Amulettsitte aus der Zeit des Glaubenswechsels. In M. Müller-Wille (Ed.), *Rom und Byzanz im Norden*, Bd. 1 (pp. 83–107). Mainz-Stuttgart: Franz Steiner Verlag.

Weibull, L. (1911). Kritiska undersøkningar i Nordens historia omkring år 1000, reprint in L. Weibull (1948). *Nordisk Historia* I (pp. 245–360). Stockholm: Bokförlaget Natur och Kultur.

Wilson, D. M. (2008). *The Vikings in the Isle of Man.* Århus: Aarhus University Press.

Wilson, D. M. & Klindt-Jensen, O. (1966). *Viking Art.* London: George Allen and Unwin. 2nd. ed. 1980.

Þorsteinsson, B. (1987). *Thingvellir. Iceland's National Shrine. A Visitors Companion.* Reykjavík: Örn og Örlygur.

Aspects of Settlement Structure and House Construction in Hedeby

JOACHIM SCHULTZE

ABSTRACT

The structural analysis of the large-scale excavations in Hedeby yields various possibilities of research into the early development of a proto urban town in Northern Europe[1]. This article intends to give an overview of the state of research into the structural remains in the low-lying settlement areas close to Hedeby's harbour as well as highlighting perspectives of further analysis[2]. In favourable conditions, the excellent preservation of constructive timbers can enable far-reaching and detailed insight not only into house construction but also into the settlement layout and its change. By combining structures and find material it might in future even be possible to arrive at conclusions about the former socioeconomic structure of the excavated settlement parts.

Keywords: Trading place, Viking Age, urbanisation, house construction, settlement development, socioeconomic structure.

In the settlement zone close to the Haddebyer Noor excavated by Herbert Jankuhn and Kurt Schietzel a structural analysis is based mainly on the large amount of preserved constructive timbers. In an excavated area of 1.300 m^2 which has been picked for a first analysis, nearly 12.000 timbers have been preserved in cultural layers of up to two metres depth. Projected onto the excavated trenches of about 5.500 m^2 this means that probably up to 40.000 timbers were recorded by H. Jankuhn (1935–1939) and K. Schietzel (1963/64; 1966–1969). In order to handle the enormous amount of data, the documentation is presently transferred into a Geographical Information System (GIS), which is interlinked with a database. This allows a fast selection of individual timbers along various criteria and helps to single out individual structures. This is facilitated further by a simplified 3D-model (created by the ArcGIS component ArcScene), which shows layers and timbers in their excavated position.

1 This has always been one of the main interests in the research of Hedeby (e.g. Jankuhn, 1984, pp. 12 or Jankuhn, 1936, pp. 98 for the first time).

2 The results presented are mainly based on the author's studies of the last few years (see also Schultze, 2008).

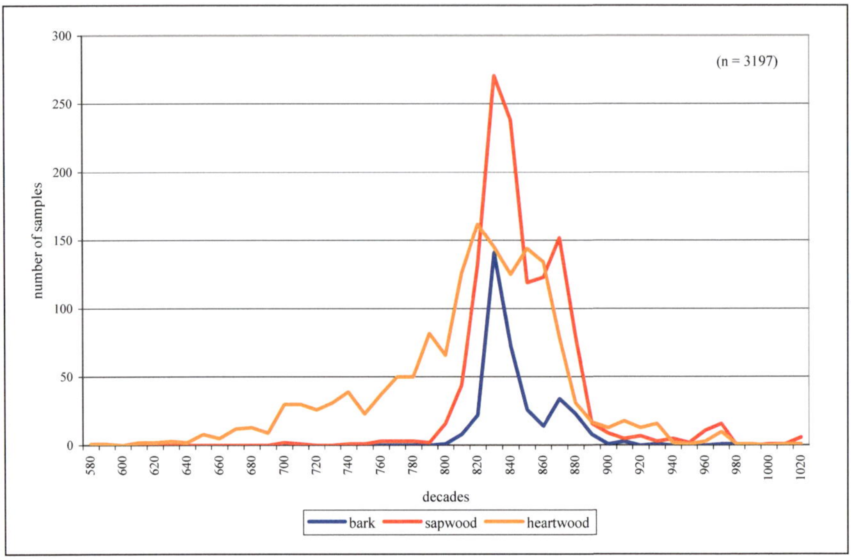

Fig. 1. Chronological distribution of dendrochronological datings.

The model allows the placement of structures into their relative chronological order. The absolute date of a structure may then be established with the help of dendrochronology.

Dendrochronology was introduced into research in Hedeby in 1966 (Eckstein, 1969; Eckstein, 1976; Eckstein & Schietzel, 1977, pp. 151; Eckstein & Schietzel, 1984; Schietzel, 1981, pp. 61) and about 4300 samples were taken. More than 90% of the samples which could be dated more precisely (sapwood and bark datings) could be dated into the 9th century (Fig. 1). Few timbers with precise dates before 830 and a large number of timbers dating to the 830s indicate that the excavated settlement areas were probably not intensively settled before that time (Schultze, 2005). There are only a few timbers dating to the 10th and 11th century. This reduction is caused by worse preservation conditions in the upper layers and can not be taken as a criterion for settlement reduction. On the contrary, the dendrochronological dating of the wells (Eckstein & Schietzel, 1977, p. 159, Fig. 11a) and fireplaces found in the upper layers, as well as recently recovered coins and jewellery (von Carnap-Bornheim & Hilberg, 2007, pp. 211; Hilberg, 2007; Hilberg, 2008), prove continued habitation. This fits well with the data from the harbour, which must have functioned well into the 11th century (Kalmring, 2010, pp. 329; Kalmring in this volume).

The structural analysis may be subdivided into different fields of research: the construction, the settlement structure as well as its development and the

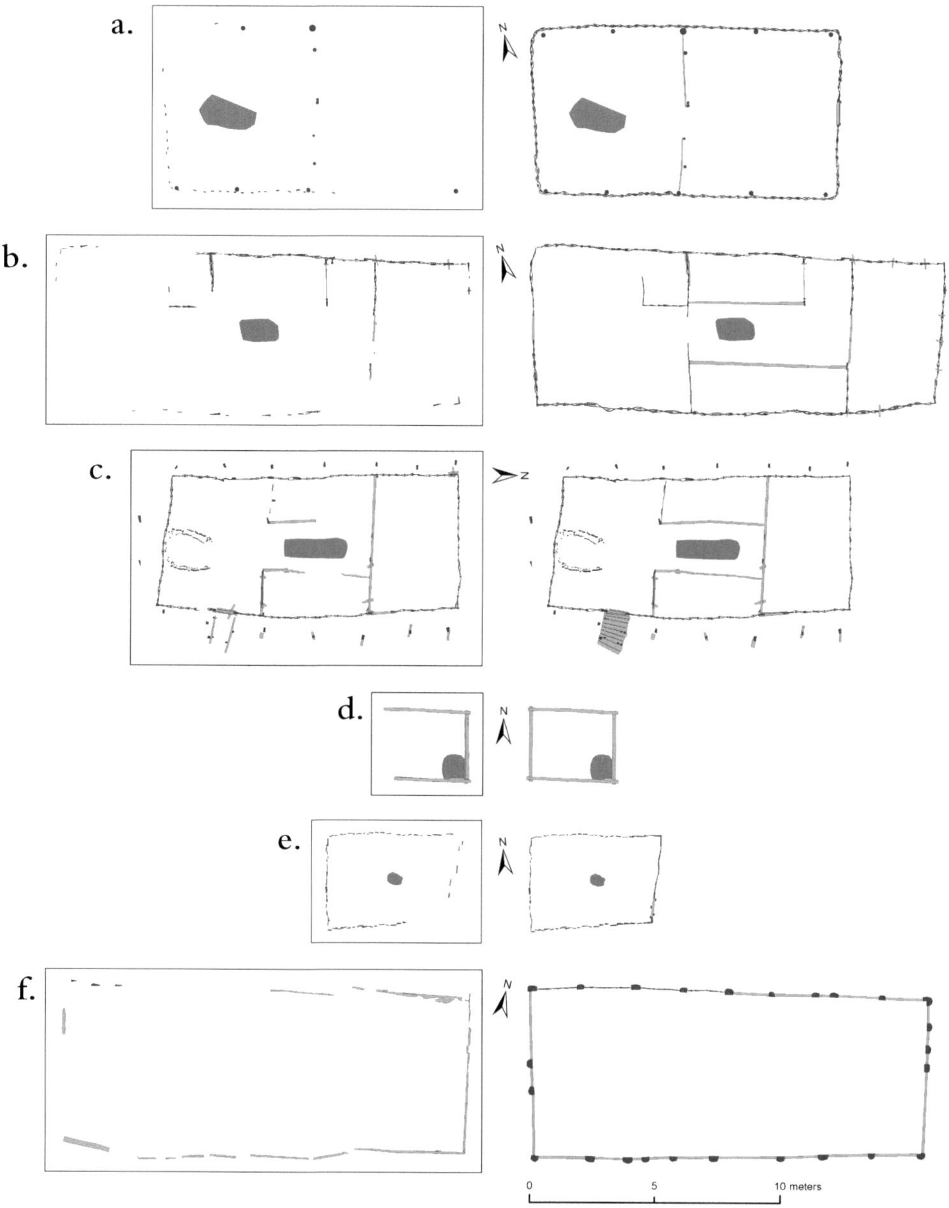

Fig. 2. Different types of house construction in Hedeby. Excavated (left) and completed (right) groundplans. a) internal frame construction, b) wall frame construction, c) wall frame construction with outer slanting posts, d) log construction, e) palisade construction, f) post and beam construction.

Fig. 3. The best preserved house in Hedeby so far. a) during excavation.

socioeconomic structure. Below is an overview of these different aspects, indicating the state of research of the last few years, the main research aims and the prospects of research.

CONSTRUCTIONS

Against the background of the main research aim of finding out about the early urbanisation in Northern Europe, the wooden constructions seem of special interest, as they might hint to the origins of urban architecture.

In the low-lying areas close to Hedeby's harbour various types of ground-level buildings of differing size can be recognized during the 9th century.[3] However there are two features, which are in common with all of the buildings. Firstly oak was primarily used for all frame posts (Behre, 1969, Tab. 1; Behre, 1983, p. 101, Tab. 41; Eckstein, 1977, p. 114, Fig. 2), due to its long durability, and secondly trunks were mostly split up into halved, quartered timbers or planks. The reason for this probably is the fact that this emporium had

[3] For preliminary reports and the older state of research on house constructions in the area close to Hedeby's harbour see Jankuhn, 1935a, pp. 58; Jankuhn, 1935b, p. 243; Jankuhn, 1936, pp. 102; Jankuhn, 1937, pp. 70; Jankuhn, 1938, pp. 102; Jankuhn, 1949, p. 73; Jahkuhn, 1956, pp. 98; Jankuhn, 1986, p. 95; Rudolph, 1936a; Rudolph, 1936b; Rudolph, 1939; Schietzel, 1969; Schietzel, 1981, pp. 31; Schietzel, 1984a.

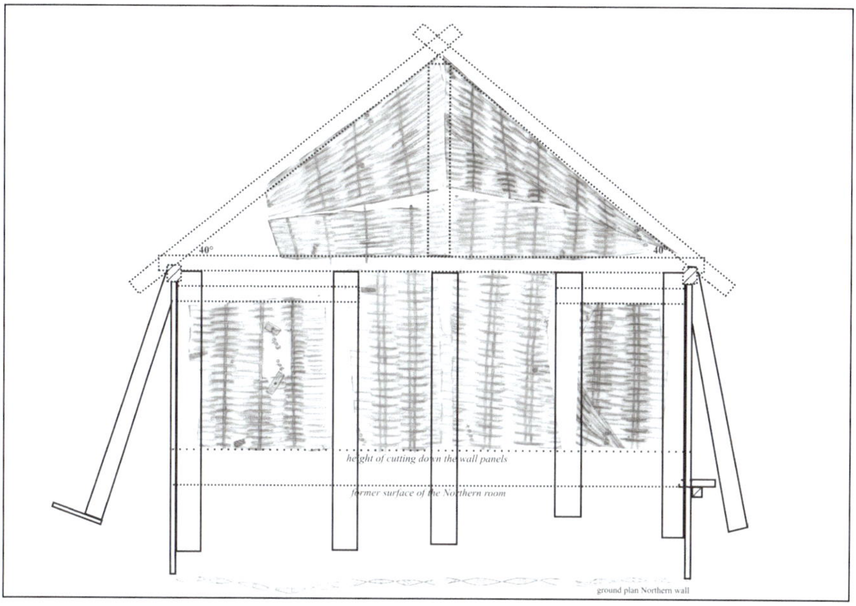

Fig. 3. b). The north wall as a reconstructed drawing.

Fig 3. c) reconstructed in full scale.

huge needs for wood (e.g. buildings, crafts, fire-wood) and the resources had to be used economically.

Compared to houses in the rural countryside, where those with an internal frame are predominant in the older Viking Age (e.g. Ethelberg, 2003, pp. 346; Meier, 1994, pp. 94; Skov, 1994, pp. 141; Skov, 2002), buildings without internal posts seem to be typical in Hedeby. As the analysis has not been completed yet, building types can not be weighed statistically but up to now only one building with an internal frame has been recognized (Fig. 2a). It suggests that this building represents a typologically late form, as its frame posts are positioned inside the building but directly in front of the outer walls. As the line of planks holding the wickerwork of the long wall is running directly along the wall plate, it seems that the planks were originally nailed to the wall plate in order to prevent the wall sinking into the soft ground. Therefore this building works rather like the typical wall frame construction in Hedeby, but with the difference that the frame posts consist of sturdy roundwood instead of split planks, which were normally incorporated into the wattle wall and left the inner room free of posts (Fig. 2b). The best known house from Hedeby so far (Schietzel, 1981, pp. 43; Schietzel, 1984a, pp.152; Schultze, 2008, pp. 160) shows a special form of a wall frame construction as outer inclined posts are leaning towards the frame posts of the wattle wall (Fig. 2c). Probably these outer posts can be interpreted as hints for the introduction of a simple rafter roof without tie-beams. In this case their function was to absorb the roof's thrust, which was transferred to the walls by the rafters. Up until now, this is the only evidence of this type of construction in Hedeby. Houses with outer slanting posts seem to have developed in Westphalia and the Frisian Rhineland during the Early Middle Ages (Huijts, 1992, pp. 115; Waterbolk, 1982, pp. 104; Waterbolk, 1992, pp. 69; Waterbolk, 1999, pp. 107) and then spread northwards in the Viking Age, the example in Hedeby (built in 874 or shortly afterwards) being one of the earliest in the North (Schmidt, 1992; Schmidt, 1999, pp. 99 & pp. 124; Skov, 1994; Skov, 2002; Waterbolk, 1999, pp. 110; Zimmermann, 2002, p. 164). While this building accounts for personal contacts to the Frisian area, a small log building might rather indicate inhabitants of Slavonic or Baltic origin (Fig. 2d). As spruce, fir and pine – trees

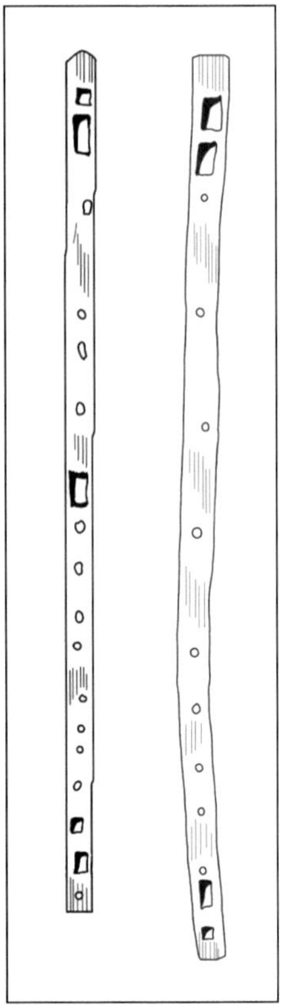

Fig. 4a. Possible wall plates drawing in scale 1:50.

Fig 4. b) A reconstructed wall plate.

with straight growing trunks – were not growing in this region in the Viking Age (Behre, 1969, p. 12; Behre, 1983, pp. 103) the builders used oak and dressed it carefully into squared timbers which were stacked horizontally upon one another, with their notched ends interlocking at the corners. The extra pains the builders had to take might indicate that they originated from an area, where log-building was traditional (Schietzel, 1981, p. 42; Schultze, 2008, pp. 132)[4]. Another building technique, which can be particularly observed with small buildings, is palisade construction (Fig. 2e). The walls of these buildings consist of timbers of various lengths, which have been so driven into the ground that the top edge, upon which the roof is placed, is level. Here, in contrast to the other types of construction, the roof is borne equally by all the timbers. While all of the types of buildings mentioned above are accounted for in the 9th century,there is another construction that can so far only be recognized in the upper layers, and that is post and beam constructions (Fig. 2f). Although the remains of these buildings are rather poorly preserved, it is possible to reconstruct these buildings with confidence as the same type of construction is characteristic of the earliest houses in the old town of Schleswig of the late 11th century (Vogel, 1992). In these buildings the frame of the house

4 It has to be kept in mind though, that log-building was not totally unknown in this region as is shown by the foundation works of the Danevirke (Andersen, 1998, pp. 45 with Fig. 27; Kramer, 1995a; Kramer, 1995b).

is provided by massive posts comprised of half-logs, which are dug into the ground. Between the posts sills were tenoned, upon which the wall filling rests consisting of either horizontal or vertical planks.

Besides reflections on different house types, the splendid preservation allows for further thoughts on the reconstruction of the upright parts of the buildings and of constructional joints[5]. The exceptional feature of a torn-down house in which the wall panels were left lying in the ground to provide a better foundation for its successor, allows the reconstruction of the height of the wall (2 m) and the roof pitch (40°) (Fig. 3). At the same time reused constructional timbers permit the study of the joints. Long timbers with regularly spaced mortises, which have been found in a reused position as runners for plankways, might be interpreted as wall plates and give an indication that posts and wall plates were connected via mortise and tenon joints (Fig. 4).

Even practical matters of building might be pursued. Issues like reuse of timbers, construction sequences and demand for wood are currently being researched by a project, which aims at identifying tree-individuals with the help of dendrochronology (Mom, Schultze, Wrobel & Eckstein, 2010). The first results of the computational research to group year ring sequences according to their similarity and to find criteria to define tree-individuals are promising. Applying the results to the wall-frame-constructed building (Fig. 2b) the method suggests that only two massive trunks were needed for the 30 to 40 cm wide planks used as the main supporting posts. At the same time timbers of various other trees were used as non-supporting posts of the wall panels and the inner partition walls.

SETTLEMENT STRUCTURE AND ITS DEVELOPMENT

The analysis into the structure and the development of the settlement aims for the core of Hedeby's main research objective of the genesis and formation of an early town, asking whether this place was planned, naturally grown or whether foreign influence can be identified and how the place was structured internally. Naturally these issues aim at the whole site and all elements – harbour, settlement areas near and far from the harbour – have to be contemplated.

According to the area under investigation this paper focuses on the low-lying zone close to the harbour where the large scale excavations permit a detailed view into the small scale structure and its change within this settlement

5 With the help of this knowledge it was possible to reconstruct from 2005–2008 a small section of the emporium including seven houses, fences, wells, roads, river enforcements and a jetty in full scale (von Carnap-Bornheim, 2005–2006; Drews, 2008; Drews, Schultze & Zich, 2005; Kalmring, 2008; Schultze, 2007; Schultze & Zich, 2007).

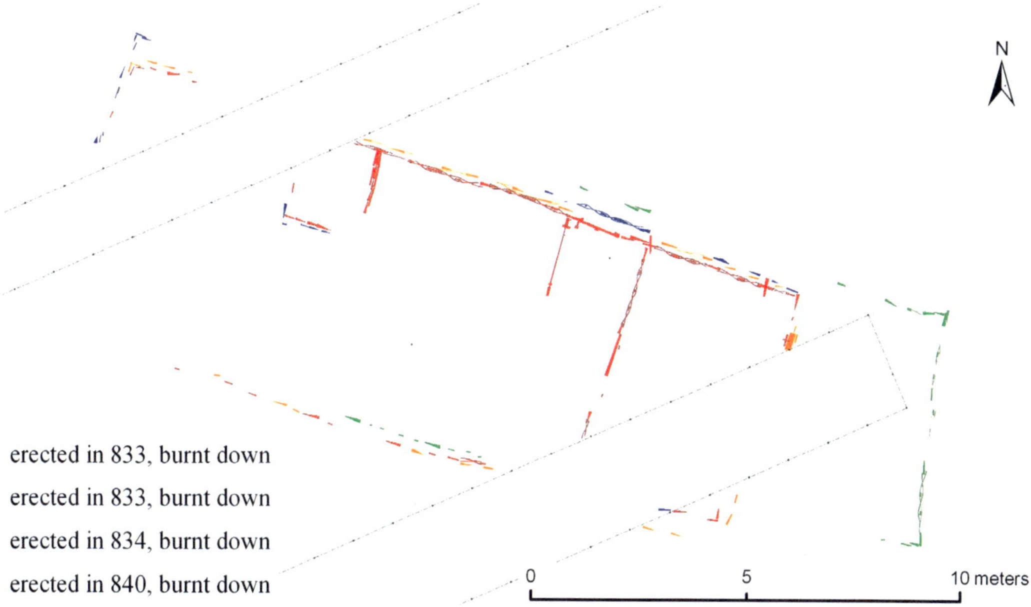

Fig. 5. The nightmare: the building was erected four times and burnt down every time. Scale 1:200.

area[6]. But not even in the excavated trenches can the settlement structure and its development be analyzed in all areas. On the one hand, the preservation condition of wood and the potential to date the preserved wood varies, and on the other hand older constructions were quite often demolished during the building processes. Up to now it was only possible to reconstruct the settlement structure and its nearly full development within the comparatively small trench 5 (Schultze, 2008, pp. 217). The main traits recognized in that trench could however be observed in other excavated parts, but how far they might be generalized as typical for the whole settlement area close to the harbour has to be proven in the further analysis.

6 For the recent research on the site as a whole and on the other parts see von Carnap-Bornheim & Hilberg, 2005; von Carnap-Bornheim & Hilberg, 2007; von Carnap-Bornheim, Hilberg, Kalmring & Schultze, 2007; von Carnap-Bornheim, Hilberg, Kalmring & Schultze, 2010; Hilberg, 2003; Hilberg, 2007; Hilberg, 2008; Hilberg, 2009; Kalmring, 2010 (summing up for the harbour); Kalmring this volume.

Up to now two traits stand out. First of all a quick succession of buildings could be observed. In trench 5 seven building phases could be recognized between 831 and the middle of the 10th century. One of the reasons for the frequent rebuilding is obvious, as scorch marks were recognizable in all parts of the settlement. In trench 8 in an extreme case, one house had to be rebuilt four times within only seven years and each was destroyed by fire (Fig. 5). Other buildings, like the wall frame construction with outer slanting posts (Fig. 2c and 3) obviously had to be torn down after only about ten years as it was erected on soft ground.

The second trait observed is a small-scale change of the settlement structure. Especially in trench 5 it could be seen that not only the position of houses shifted, but also that roads were overbuilt. The same seems to have been true in other parts of the settlement, as for example the house that burnt down, was rebuilt four times nearly at exactly the same place. At a later time, the orientation of the houses in this area seems to have changed to north-south and the road running along the north wall of the house was blocked. Up to now the parts analyzed are too small to comprehend what position they had within the settlement and how they relate to structures with long consistency. It seems likely that these small-scale changes happen within larger units – perhaps farmsteads.

In terms of change of the settlement structure, the central trenches where H. Jankuhn started excavating in 1935 seem of special interest. In both the lower (Schietzel, 1969, pp. 51 with folding map) and the upper (e.g. Jankuhn, 1943, p. 19, Fig. 4; Jankuhn, 1986, plan II) layers the timbers suggest a settlement layout which is characterized on the one hand by the small stream crossing the trench in west-east direction, and on the other hand by the north-south directed road. On both sides of it larger and partly smaller houses were erected and directed towards it. As hardly any dendrochronological data for this trench are available, it must be presumed that as in the other trenches, nearly all of the timbers and therefore both layouts date to the 9th century, although the date of the bridge over the stream – 819 – might indicate that this settlement area was settled a little earlier than the adjacent areas. In the geomagnetic survey conducted in 2002 the road can be traced to the north as well as to the south. It does however suggest that the road was lined only by very small houses (von Carnap-Bornheim & Hilberg, 2005, pp. 468; von Carnap-Bornheim & Hilberg, 2007, p. 208; Hilberg, 2007, p. 196; Hilberg, 2009, pp. 89; Schultze, 2008, pp. 235). Augering of the geomagnetic anomalies and the measurement of the earth's magnetic susceptibility have shown, that the anomalies are caused in the upper layer without wooden preservation. This fits well with the comparison to the excavations in the adjacent trench 4, where features of the same size as the anomalies could be recognized and interpreted as houses (Fig.

Fig. 6. Synopsis of the geomagnetic survey and the excavation showing a part of the north-south road, that runs parallel to the waterfront. In the bottom the artificial layer 5 of trench 4 excavated by K. Schietzel is displayed. The features excavated match in size and spacing the geomagnetic anomalies. The features are interpreted as houses standing on both sides of the road.

6). Material found from the layers affiliated with these houses seem to indicate a date of the late 9th or probably 10th century. At that time the settlement layout along this street has obviously changed fundamentally from large, middle and even smaller buildings to very close standing small houses directly on both sides of the road.

SOCIOECONOMIC STRUCTURE

The attempt to analyze the pattern of functional and social aspects aims at the internal functioning and organization of an early town. The main question behind this research is to find out, what was happening where and who was doing it.

For the excavated areas this means combining structures and finding material. Naturally, these studies can only be followed up systematically at the end of the structural analysis, when the house constructions and the settlement development have been distinguished and the associated former surfaces have been reconstructed. Moreover, the material found has to be entered into databases in order to be able to map it in the GIS. Therefore only preliminary studies have been carried out so far, which were too small scale to generalize. However, it seems that to find out about defined activity areas is challenging[7]. In one case the distribution of slag rather indicates a former surface (Fig. 7). In another case the spreading of raw material, refuse, fractions, half products and products of ambers might point to an amber working area, but up to now the former surfaces and the simultaneous buildings could not be identified with confidence. The situation is further complicated by the fact K. Schietzel has

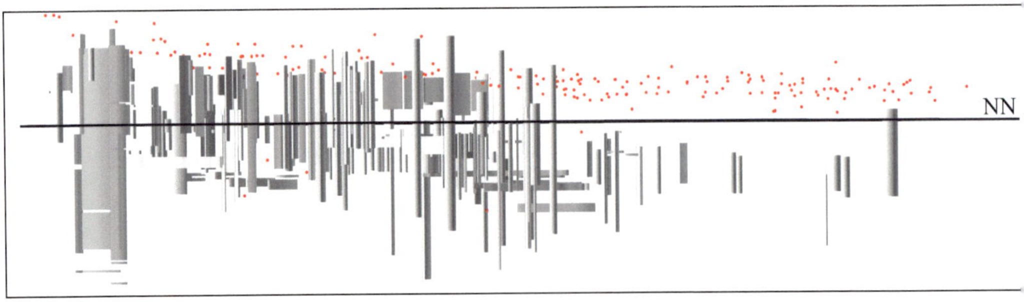

Fig. 7. Slags (red dots) and constructional timbers (grey) in trench 5 in a simplified 3D-model. The distribution of the slags indicates a former surface.

[7] This has already been pointed out earlier e.g. Schietzel, 1968; Schietzel, 1981, pp. 51 & pp. 81; Schietzel, 1984b.

already pointed out that buildings and the surrounding plots seem to have been kept free of refuse (Schietzel, 1981, p. 53).

Even if the small-scale functional analysis is difficult and only in its early stages, a striking change of the artefact distribution which goes along with the mentioned change of the settlement layout along the north-south road is conspicuous. In trench 4, where the features similar to the geomagnetic anomalies were excavated (Fig. 6), a high increase of discovered material from the lower to the upper layers is conspicuous and it seems that it might be paralleled with the change of the settlement layout. Great numbers of artefacts like moulds, slags, glass, amber and antler as well as whetstones, soapstone and ceramics were unearthed in these upper layers[8]. Even though slag (Westphalen, 1989, pp. 48 with Fig. 50) and moulds for trefoil brooches (Maixner, 2005, p. 70 with Tab. 2–3), the only two groups of discoveries which are mapped exactly up to now, are not concentrated within the features excavated, the increase of found material and the number of artefacts connected with craft activities is conspicuous. In a current project, the carrier of the high magnetic susceptibility is sought and the material obtained by augering is analyzed. It will be examined whether the separated magnetic material in the size, often well below a millimetre, might hint towards handicraft activity as well. Unlike the other finds these small particles would not be cleaned out, and might therefore well indicate the activity areas themselves. In that case the small houses on both sides of the road might then be classified rather as workshops than as living houses, especially as they seem to lack fireplaces. If that is true, one might wonder, whether a new functional differentiated plot layout along this road might have developed, with workshops on the roads front.

In summary it could be demonstrated that the structural analysis of the excavations of H. Jankuhn and K. Schietzel in combination with the geomagnetic survey, as well as the investigations of my colleagues (see Kalmring in this volume as well as footnote 6), in the harbour area, and the other parts of the site, yield various perspectives with which to approach the development of this early town.

[8] For quotations see Schultze, 2008, p. 242.

BIBLIOGRAPHY

Andersen, H. H. (1998). *Danevirke og kovirke. Arkæologiske undersøgelser 1861–1993.* Århus.

Behre, K.-E. (1969). Untersuchungen des botanischen Materials der frühmittelalterlichen Siedlung Haithabu (Ausgrabung 1963–1964). In K. Schietzel (Ed.), *Berichte über die Ausgrabungen in Haithabu 2.* Neumünster (7–55).

Behre, K.-E. (1983). *Ernährung und Umwelt der wikingerzeitlichen Siedlung Haithabu. Die Ergebnisse der Untersuchungen der Pflanzenreste.* Die Ausgrabungen in Haithabu 8. Neumünster.

von Carnap-Bornheim, C. (2005–2006). Denkmal, Museum, Landschaft – Das Wikinger Museum und die Wikinger Häuser Haithabu bei Schleswig. *Jahrbuch der Stiftung Schleswig-Holsteinische Landesmuseen Schloss Gottorf* N.F. 10, 47–51.

von Carnap-Bornheim, C., & Hilberg, V. (2005). Haithabu – ein frühstädtisches Zentrum in neuem Licht. *Archäologisches Nachrichtenblatt* 10, 465–471.

von Carnap-Bornheim, C., & Hilberg, V. (2007). Recent archaeological research in Haithabu. In J. Henning (Ed.), *Post-Roman towns, trade and settlement in Europe and Byzantium.* Vol. 1. The heirs of the Roman west. Millennium-Studies 5/1. Berlin – New York (199–218).

von Carnap-Bornheim, C., Hilberg, V., Kalmring, S., & Schultze, J. (2007). *Hedeby's settlement and harbour: recent research in a Viking age trading center.* C.J.C. Reuvenslezing 19. Amsterdam.

von Carnap-Bornheim, C., Hilberg, V., Kalmring, S., & Schultze, J. (2010). *Hedeby, the settlement and the harbour: old data and recent research.* In J. Sheehan & D. Ó. Corráin (Eds.), The Viking Age: Ireland and the West. Papers from the proceedings of the fifteenth Viking Congress, Cork, 18–27 August 2005. Dublin (511–524).

Drews, U. (2008). Wikinger Häuser Haithabu – Das didaktische Konzept. *Archäologische Nachrichten aus Schleswig-Holstein,* 14, 102–105.

Drews, U., Schultze, J., & Zich, B. (2005). Wikinger Museum Haithabu – Schaufenster einer frühen Stadt. *Archäologie in Deutschland* 2005/6, 70–73.

Eckstein, D. (1969). *Entwicklung und Anwendung der Dendrochronologie zur Altersbestimmung der Siedlung Haithabu.* PhD thesis unpublished. Hamburg.

Eckstein, D. (1976). Absolute Datierung der wikingerzeitlichen Siedlung Haithabu/Schleswig mit Hilfe der Dendrochronologie. *Naturwissenschaftliche Rundschau,* 29(3), 81–84.

Eckstein, D. (1977). Holzanatomische Untersuchungen an Befunden der frühmittelalterlichen Siedlung Haithabu (Ausgrabung 1966–1969). In K. Schietzel (Ed.), *Berichte über die Ausgrabungen in Haithabu 11.* Neumünster (112–119).

Eckstein, D., & Schietzel, K. (1977). Zur dendrochronologischen Gliederung und Datierung der Baubefunde von Haithabu. In K. Schietzel (Ed.), *Berichte über die Ausgrabungen in Haithabu 11.* Neumünster (141–164).

Eckstein, D., & Schietzel, K. (1984). Dendrochronologische Gliederung der Baubefunde von Haithabu. In H. Jankuhn, K. Schietzel & H. Reichstein (Eds.), *Archäologische und naturwissenschaftliche Untersuchungen an ländlichen und frühstädtischen Siedlungen im deutschen Küstengebiet vom 5. Jahrhundert v. Chr. bis zum 11. Jahrhundert n. Chr.*, Vol. 2. Weinheim (171–184).

Ethelberg, P. (2003). Gården og landsbyen i jernalder og vikingetid (500 f.Kr. – 1000 e.Kr.). In P. Ethelberg, N. Hardt, B. Poulsen & A. B. Sørensen, *Det sønderjyske landbrugs historie. Jernalder, vikingetid og middelalder.* Haderslev (123–373).

Hilberg, V. (2003). Geophysikalische Prospektion des Jahres 2002 in Haithabu. *Archäologie in Schleswig – Arkæologi i Slesvig* 10, 157–173.

Hilberg, V. (2007). Haithabu im 11. Jahrhundert. Auf der Suche nach dem Niedergang eines dänischen *emporiums* der Wikingerzeit. In M. Posselt, B. Zickgraf & C. Dobiat (Eds.), *Geophysik und Ausgrabung. Einsatz und Auswertung zerstörungsfreier Prospektion in der Archäologie.* Internationale Archäologie Naturwissenschaften und Technologie 6. Rahden/Westf. (187–203).

Hilberg, V. (2008). Auf der Suche nach dem Niedergang eines Handelsplatzes. Haithabu in der jüngeren Wikingerzeit. *Archäologische Nachrichten aus Schleswig-Holstein,* 14, 53–55.

Hilberg, V. (2009). Hedeby in Wulfstan's days: a Danish *emporium* of the Viking Age between East and West. In A. Englert & A. Trakadas (Eds.), Wulfstan's voyage. The Baltic Sea region in the early Viking Age as seen from shipboard. *Maritime Culture of the North* 2. Roskilde (79–113).

Huijts, C. S. T. J. (1992). *De voor-historische boerderijbouw in Drenthe. Reconstuctiemodellen van 1300 vóór tot 1300 na Chr.* Arnhem.

Jankuhn, H. (1935a). Die Ausgrabungen in Haithabu 1934. *Nordelbingen* 11, 45–66.

Jankuhn, H. (1935b). Die Ergebnisse der Grabung in Haithabu 1935. *Nachrichtenblatt für deutsche Vorzeit* 11, 242–244.

Jankuhn, H. (1936). Die Ausgrabungen in Haithabu 1935/36. *Offa* 1, 96–140.

Jankuhn, H. (1937). *Haithabu. Eine germanische Stadt der Frühzeit.* Neumünster.

Jankuhn, H. (1938). *Haithabu. Eine germanische Stadt der Frühzeit.* Neumünster (2nd edition).

Jankuhn, H. (1943). *Die Ausgrabungen in Haithabu (1937–1939). Vorläufiger Grabungsbericht.* Berlin-Dahlem.

Jankuhn, H. (1949). Ergebnisse und Probleme der Haithabugrabungen 1930–1939. Ein Beitrag zur Frage der Stadtentstehung im Norden. *Zeitschrift der Gesellschaft für Schleswig-Holsteinische Geschichte* 73, 1–86.

Jankuhn, H. (1956). *Haithabu. Ein Handelsplatz der Wikingerzeit.* Neumünster (3rd edition).

Jankuhn, H. (1984). Die Geschichte der Haithabuforschung und die Entwicklung der Fragestellung. In H. Jankuhn, K. Schietzel & H. Reichstein (Eds.), *Archäologische und naturwissenschaftliche Untersuchungen an ländlichen und frühstädtischen Siedlungen im deutschen Küstengebiet vom 5. Jahrhundert v. Chr. bis zum 11. Jahrhundert n. Chr.*, Vol. 2. Weinheim (3–15).

Jankuhn, H. (1986). *Haithabu. Ein Handelsplatz der Wikingerzeit.* Neumünster, (8th edition).

Kalmring, S. (2008). Archaeology visualised – The Viking houses and a reconstructed jetty in Hedeby. In Lehtimäki, M. (Ed.), *Cultural Heritage and Tourism: Potential, Impact, Partnership and Governance.* Vilnius (42–43).

Kalmring, S. (2010). *Der Hafen von Haithabu.* Die Ausgrabungen in Haithabu 14. Neumünster.

Kramer, W. (1995a). Das Seesperrwerk beim Reesholm in der Schlei. *Archäologische Nachrichten aus Schleswig-Holstein,* 6, 42–53.

Kramer, W. (1995b). Das Seesperrwerk beim Reesholm in der Schlei. Ein Arbeitsbericht. In Landesdenkmalamt Baden-Württemberg & Kommission für Unterwasserarchäologie im Verband der Landesarchäologen in der Bundesrepublik Deutschland (Ed.), *Archäologie unter Wasser* 1. Archäologische Informationen aus Baden-Württemberg 33. Stuttgart (135–143).

Maixner, B. (2005). *Die gegossenen kleeblattförmigen Fibeln der Wikingerzeit aus Skandinavien.* Universitätsforschungen zur prähistorischen Archäologie 116. Bonn.

Meier, D. (1994). *Die wikingerzeitliche Siedlung von Kosel (Kosel-West), Kreis Rendsburg-Eckernförde.* Offa-Bücher 76. Neumünster.

Mom, V., Schultze, J., Wrobel, S., & Eckstein, D. (2010). Allocating archaeological wood samples to a common source tree and its use for analyzing wooden settlement structures. In B. Frischer (Ed.), *Making History Interactive. Computer Applications and Quantitative Methods in Archaeology (CAA). Proceedings of the 37th International Conference, Williamsburg, Virginia, United States of America, March 22–26, 2009.* BAR Int. Ser. 2079. Oxford (234–239).

Rudolph, M. (1936a). Die Grundlagen der Holzbauweisen von Haithabu. *Offa* 1, 141–149.

Rudolph, M. (1936b). Grundsätzliches von den Holzbauten in Haithabu. *Nachrichtenblatt für deutsche Vorzeit* 12, 248–254.

Rudolph, M. V. (1939). Der erste Fund einer wikingerzeitlichen Tür in Haithabu. *Nachrichtenblatt für deutsche Vorzeit* 15, 31–34.

Schietzel, K. (1968). Zur Frage einer wirtschaftlichen und sozialen Gliederung Haithabus. In Claus, C., Haarnagel, W., & Raddatz, K. (Eds.), *Studien zur europäischen Vor- und Frühgeschichte.* Neumünster (253–257).

Schietzel, K. (1969). Die archäologischen Befunde der Ausgrabung Haithabu 1963–1964. In K. Schietzel (Ed.), *Berichte über die Ausgrabungen in Haithabu* 1. Neumünster (9–59).

Schietzel, K. (1981). *Stand der siedlungsarchäologischen Forschung in Haithabu – Ergebnisse und Probleme.* Berichte über die Ausgrabungen in Haithabu 16. Neumünster.

Schietzel, K. (1984a). Die Baubefunde in Haithabu. In Jankuhn, H., Schietzel, K., & Reichstein, H. (Eds.), *Archäologische und naturwissenschaftliche Untersuchungen an ländlichen und frühstädtischen Siedlungen im deutschen Küstengebiet vom 5.*

Jahrhundert v. Chr. bis zum 11. Jahrhundert n. Chr., Vol. 2. Weinheim (135–158).

Schietzel, K. (1984b). Stratigraphie und Chronologie in Haithabu. In Jankuhn, H., Schietzel, K., & Reichstein, H. (Eds.), *Archäologische und naturwissenschaftliche Untersuchungen an ländlichen und frühstädtischen Siedlungen im deutschen Küstengebiet vom 5. Jahrhundert v. Chr. bis zum 11. Jahrhundert n. Chr.*, Vol. 2. Weinheim (162–171).

Schmidt, H. (1992). Vikingernes huse. *Nationalmuseets Arbejdsmark*, 122–132.

Schmidt, H. (1999). *Vikingetidens byggeskik i Danmark*. Højbjerg.

Schultze, J. (2005). Zur Frage der Entwicklung des zentralen Siedlungskernes von Haithabu. In Dobiat, C. (Ed.), *Reliquiae gentium. Festschrift für Horst Wolfgang Böhme zum 65. Geburtstag.* Internationale Archäologie. Studia honoraria 23. Rahden/Westf. (359–373).

Schultze, J. (2007). Wo die Wikinger wohnten – die Wikinger Häuser Haithabu. In von Carnap-Bornheim, C., & Segschneider, M. (Eds.), *Die Schleiregion. Land – Wasser – Geschichte.* Führer zu archäologischen Denkmälern in Deutschland 49. Stuttgart (73–76).

Schultze, J. (2008). *Haithabu – Die Siedlungsgrabungen. I. Methoden und Möglichkeiten der Auswertung. Die Ausgrabungen in Haithabu* 13. Neumünster.

Schultze, J., & Zich, B. (2007). Wikinger Häuser Haithabu. In Fansa, M., & Vorlauf, D. (Eds.), *HOLZ-KULTUR. Von der Urzeit bis in die Zukunft. Ökologie und Ökonomie eines Naturrohstoffs im Spiegel der Experimentellen Archäologie, Ethnologie, Technikgeschichte und modernen Holzforschung. Wissenschaftlicher Begleitband zur gleichnamigen Sonderausstellung 4. Februar – 28. Mai 2007 im Landesmuseum für Natur und Mensch Oldenburg. Ergebnisse der Vorbereitungstagung vom 24.–25. November 2005 in Oldenburg.* Schriftenreihe des Landesmuseums Natur und Mensch 47. Oldenburg (281–288).

Skov, H. (1994). Hustyper i vikingetid og tidlig middelalder. Udviklingen af hustyperne i det gammeldanske område fra ca. 800–1200 e.Kr. *Hikuin* 21, 139–162.

Skov, H. (2002). The development of rural house types in the old Danish region 800–1500 A.D. In J. Klápště (Ed.), *The rural house from the migration period to the oldest still standing buildings. Ruralia IV. 8.–13. September 2001 Bad Bederkesa, Lower Saxony, Germany. Památky archeologické – Supplementum* 15, *Ruralia* 4. Prague (30–33).

Vogel, V. (1992). Profaner Holzbau des 11. bis frühen 13. Jahrhunderts in Schleswig. In H. W. Böhme (Ed.), *Siedlungen und Landesausbau zur Salierzeit.* Vol. 1. RGZM Monographien 27. Sigmaringen (2nd edition) (263–276).

Waterbolk, W. T. (1982). Mobilität von Dorf, Ackerflur und Gräberfeld in Drenthe seit der Latènezeit. Archäologische Siedlungsformen auf der nordniederländischen Geest. *Offa* 39, 97–137.

Waterbolk, W. T. (1992). Das mittelalterliche Siedlungswesen in Drenthe. Versuch einer Synthese aus archäologischer Sicht. In H. W. Böhme (Ed.), *Siedlungen und Landesausbau zur Salierzeit*. Vol. 1. RGZM Monographien 27. Sigmaringen (2nd edition) (47–108).

Waterbolk, W. T. (1999). From Wijster to Dorestad and beyond. In H. Sarfatij, W. J. H. Verwers & P. J. Woltering (Eds.), *In discussion with the past. Archaeological studies presented to W.A. van Es. Amersfoort* (107–117).

Westphalen, P. (1989). *Die Eisenschlacken von Haithabu. Ein Beitrag zur Geschichte des Schmiedehandwerks in Nordeuropa. Berichte über die Ausgrabungen in Haithabu* 26. Neumünster.

Zimmermann, W. H. (2002). Kontinuität und Wandel im Hausbau südlich und östlich der Nordsee vom Neolithikum bis zum Mittelalter. In J. Klápště (Ed.), *The rural house from the migration period to the oldest still standing buildings. Ruralia IV. 8.–13. September 2001 Bad Bederkesa, Lower Saxony, Germany. Památky archeologické – Supplementum* 15, *Ruralia* 4. Prague (pp. 164–168).

'Bullion-Rings' in Viking Age Britain and Ireland

JOHN SHEEHAN

ABSTRACT

This paper examines a simple type of silver ring, here termed the 'bullion-ring', that occurs in several Viking Age contexts in Britain and Ireland. It is proposed that the type may be dated to the later ninth and early to mid-tenth century, and that it developed in Ireland as a convenient way of storing silver as a result of inspiration from southern Scandinavia. Its distribution patterns suggest that it may have developed in one of Munster's Scandinavian settlements rather than in Dublin, the core of the Hiberno-Scandinavian silver-working tradition.

Keywords: Silver hoards, bullion-rings, Ireland.

INTRODUCTION

A 'bullion-ring' may be defined as a small penannular ring made from a thick band of silver of approximately rectangular cross-section, often with a concave outer face; examples are invariably plain, that is unornamented (see Fig.1). The majority of examples vary from 4–6 mm in thickness and taper in width towards the terminals, which may end convexly or angularly and frequently overlap for a short distance. They are too small to function as arm-rings and are generally too large and cumbersome for use as finger-rings. This simple type of ring, over twenty-two examples of which have been found in hoards in Ireland, has previously been known both as the 'penannular ingot' (Sheehan, 1998b, 155–6) and as 'Irish ring-money' (Graham-Campbell & Briggs, 1986; Graham-Campbell, 1995, 30, Fig. 16), though neither of these terms should now be considered appropriate. The term 'penannular ingot', for instance, is too suggestive of a relationship between these rings and standard ingots, while the term 'Irish ring-money' not only suggests a specific cultural attribution (which, in any case, is probably incorrect) but also implies that the primary function of these objects was to serve as a form of currency (which cannot be satisfactorily demonstrated). The new term 'bullion-ring' is more neutral and acceptable, implying no more than that these rings – like ingots – served first and foremost as convenient way of storing bullion.

Fig. 1. 'Bullion-rings from the 'Ireland no. 2' hoard. (Photo: National Museum of Ireland.)

HOARD OCCURRENCES IN IRELAND

'Bullion-rings' are known to occur in at least five hoards in Ireland, those from: Castlelohort Demesne, Co. Cork (Graham-Campbell & Briggs, 1986); Derrynahinch, Co. Kilkenny (Graves, 1852; Graham-Campbell, 1976, 50, 67, 68, note 3); Cushalogurt, Co. Mayo (Hall, 1973); Carraig Aille II, Lough Gur, Co. Limerick (Ó Ríordáin, 1949, 62-4, Fig. 7; Sheehan, 1998b, Fig. 15.2); and an unprovenanced find (Fig. 1), known as 'Ireland no. 2' (cf. Graham-Campbell, 1995, 30, Fig. 16). In addition, one further hoard, an unlocalised find from Co. Kilkenny (Windele, 1851, 332), now lost, may also have been composed of such rings, though the suggestion that a 'bullion-ring' formed part of the hoard from Ballyadams, Co. Laois (Sheehan, 1998b, 155), is now withdrawn. The total number of objects of this type represented in these hoards is at least twenty-two, though this is a minimum estimate given the incomplete records that exist for several of the finds (Fig. 2). In addition, there are four apparent single-finds from Ireland, all unprovenanced nineteenth-century discoveries. When the hoards and single-finds are combined, it appears that there may be between at least twenty-six and thirty rings of this type represented amongst Ireland's Viking Age silver finds.

Provenance	Number	Complete	Hack-Silver	Associated Material
'Ireland', 2	6–10	•	–	–
'Co. Kilkenny'	2+	•	–	–
Castlelohort Demesne	6	•	–	–
Derrynahinch	2+	•	?	•
Cushalogurt	3	•	–	•
Carraig Aille	1	•	–	•

Fig. 2. Hoards containing bullion rings from Ireland.

Castlelohort Demesne (Lohort), Co. Cork

This hoard was discovered in 1848 during quarry work near Lohort Castle, a late medieval tower-house. A contemporary account, by John Windele, recorded that the find comprised six rings, linked together, their average weight being 'about two oz each, but some exceeded and others were less'. On this basis it appears that the total weight of the hoard amounted to *c.*310 gm. Windele's records also feature sketches of several of the rings, from which it is clear that they are 'bullion-rings'. The find was dispersed sometime following its discovery, with most of its components being acquired by local Cork antiquarians. Some of these individuals later sold on the rings into the antiquities trade through London auction houses, though some were acquired either then or subsequently by museums. Five of the six original Castlelohort Demesne rings may now be identified in museum collections; at Tullie House Museum, Carlisle, the Pitt Rivers Museum, Oxford, and the National Museum of Ireland.

Derrynahinch, Co. Kilkenny

In March 1853 the Rev. J. Graves reported the acquisition of a plain silver ring by the museum of the Kilkenny Archaeological Society (Graves, 1852, 355–6). He described it as the 'sole remaining, or at least discoverable' piece from a hoard 'which consisted of about a quart full of rings and pieces of silver' that had been found at Derrynahinch in 1851, during the construction of a railway cutting. He noted that the hoard consisted of about 'twelve or fourteen rings, some of them flat', similar to the one acquired by the Society's museum, and others 'twisted like a curb-chain', as well as 'many flat pieces of silver, some square, about the size of a shilling, others of different sizes, and amongst them were oblong flattened pieces, tapering at the end, exactly like the ring which has been preserved, but straight'. He furthermore recorded that 'when the hoard was thrown out of its hiding-place, the pieces of silver being oxidized, and consequently black, attracted little attention, the greater part of them were shovelled into wagons and 'tipped' over the embankment'. He finally noted that the surviving ring was 'picked up by an intelligent ganger ... who placed it on his finger, where it gradually assumed its pristine lustre'. Described as comprising 'about a quart full of rings and pieces of silver', the Derrynahinch find was undoubtedly one of Ireland's largest hack-silver hoards. The records indicate that it comprised twelve or fourteen penannular rings, some of which were of 'bullion-ring' type and some, possibly, of twisted-rod arm-ring form, as well as 'many' pieces of hack-silver, derived from ornaments or ingots, or both. Its weight is unknown, but it appears to have been quite substantial. The townland is a large one within which, and close to the railway line, is located Derrynahinch church. It has recently been suggested that this hoard may have ultimately derived from the Scandinavian *longphort* at Woodstown, Co. Waterford (Sheehan *forthcoming* c).

Cushalogurt, Co. Mayo

This hoard was discovered by a farmer in 1939 while moulding potatoes about half-way along the northern shore of Urrisaun Point, a small peninsula located within the inner reaches of Clew Bay, in the west of Ireland (Hall, 1973). The find was made close to the shoreline. The finder noted, in a letter (NMI topographical file: Cushalogurt), that 'when found they were linked into each other', indicating that the rings in the hoard had been suspended within one another. He also noted that 'there were broken bits fourteen, a farm implement coming close will account for the bits', though it is clear from an examination of the fragments in the hoard that most of them had been reduced to this form prior to the hoard's deposition. The hoard comprises one complete Hiberno-Scandinavian broad-band arm-ring, a further six arm-rings of this type with a small portion of one or both terminals cut off, fourteen hack-silver fragments of such rings (of which four join with the terminals of incomplete broad-band arm-rings in the hoard), one penannular rod arm-ring, and three 'bullion-rings'. The total weight of the hoard, one of Ireland's largest, is 594.84 gm.

Carraig Aille II, Co. Limerick

This hoard was discovered in 1948 during the archaeological excavation of a stone ringfort known as Carraig Aille II, part of the Lough Gur archaeological complex. It had been concealed in an interstice on the inner face of the ring-fort's enclosing rampart (Ó Riordáin, 1949, 62–4). Excavation demonstrated that the site's occupation possibly started in the eighth century, and continued until after the remains of the enclosing stone ramparts were covered with debris. This indicates that occupation continued well after the deposition of the hoard, which had been inserted in the rampart while it was still exposed. The hoard comprises one 'bullion-ring', two ingots, one hack-silver fragment derived from an ingot, one hack-silver fragment derived from a rod of lozenge-shaped section, and two hack-silver fragments derived from Hiberno-Scandinavian broad-band arm-rings. One component of the hoard, an ingot, cannot currently be located in the National Museum of Ireland. This, however, was somewhat smaller than the other ingot in the find, and, if it weighed proportionally less, the overall weight of the hoard would be *c*.90 gm. Comber has recently interpreted the find both as representing 'possibly a stockpile of silver intended for use in the manufacture of items on site' and as 'merely fragments of objects broken after loss' (2004, 38–9), though it seems far more likely that it is a hack-silver hoard of standard Viking Age type.

'Ireland no. 2'

This unprovenanced hoard (Fig. 1) is known to have been discovered sometime prior to 1837. It comprises at least six, but possibly as many as ten, rings. Six of these are illustrated in Sir William Betham's ms., *Sketch-Book of Antiquities* (Nat. Lib. Ireland: Tx.1959, p. 26), where they are assigned individual weights, amounting to a total equivalent of 278.46 gm. The drawing probably dates to before 1837, when Betham published an illustration of the group of four linked rings together with the weights of all six illustrated in his *Sketch-Book* (1837, 15; Graham-Campbell & Sheehan, 2007). Information in the 1841 *Dawson Catalogue* and in the Royal Irish Academy's *Museum Register of Antiquities 1846–1853*, under registration nos. 558c–566c, gives rise to the possibility of there originally having been a hoard of ten such rings. The records relating to this hoard are, obviously, rather unsatisfactory and it is not possible, at present, to conclude how many rings actually constituted the find or, indeed, to ascertain if it originated as two separate finds. As Graham-Campbell observed, 'until the history of these groups can be more satisfactorily resolved, it would seem wisest to accept the existence of only one such hoard' (1976, 69). Based on the information supplied concerning the weights of the rings in the nineteenth-century sources, and given that the hoard comprised at least six and possibly as many as ten rings, its overall weight appears to lie within the range of *c*.270 gm to *c*.440 gm.

Co Kilkenny

The evidence for this find, which possibly was comprised exclusively of 'bullion-rings', is contained in the writings of Windele who recorded: 'Silver rings have been rarely found in Ireland. Several specimens, about the thickness of the little finger, were found in 1840, in one of the ancient *lioses*, in the County of Kilkenny, as Mr. Lindsey informed me; but they appear to have been soon after melted down' (1851, 332). The 'Mr. Lindsey' referred to was the renowned numismatist, John Lindsay. From Windele's description of the size of these rings, it seems probable that they were 'bullion-rings'. The find was made in a ringfort, the term *lios* usually being used to refer to ringforts of the earthen variety.

Occurrences in Britain

In Britain, 'bullion-rings' are only definitely represented in one recorded hoard, that from Cuerdale, Lancashire. This find contains almost twenty complete and hack-silver fragments, making it the largest known collection of such rings (Sheehan *forthcoming* a). The occurrence of such a large proportion of the total number of 'bullion-rings' from Britain and Ireland in this single hoard is not surprising given the immense size of the non-numismatic element of this find and the fact that its culturally diagnostic bullion contains many fragments of other Hiberno-Scandinavian and Irish types of ornament, suggesting that a considerable portion of the hoard originated in Viking Age Ireland, probably in Dublin (Graham-Campbell, 1987, 339–40). The presence of such rings in Cuerdale, deposited *c.*905–10, is of special significance given that this find represents the only coin-dated hoard context for 'bullion-rings'.

The Isle of Skye (no. 3) hoard, from Scotland, now lost, was composed of three linked rings. It has been proposed by Graham-Campbell that these rings may reasonably be identified as 'bullion-rings' on the basis of details contained in a mid-nineteenth-century account of their discovery in 1850 (1995, 30, 105, no. 20). Again, as in the case of the Cuerdale find, it is possible that the Isle of Skye hoard derived from a Hiberno-Scandinavian milieu in Ireland, as most of the hoards deposited in Scotland during the period between *c.*850 and *c.*950 display such connections.

The Torksey find

An example of what is to be considered, at least, a prototype 'bullion-ring' forms part of the large assemblage of metalwork that has emerged in recent years from Torksey, Lincolnshire. Like the Hiberno-Scandinavian 'bullion-rings', this somewhat misshapen object is a small, plain, penannular ring made from a rather thick band of silver (illustrated in Blackburn 2011, fig. 4). Torksey was the location of the winter-camp of the Danish 'Great Army' in 872–3, and Blackburn has drawn attention to the wide range of finds from the site, which includes coins, polyhedral weights and hack-silver. The ring find is of significance, despite having no formal archaeological context, because, firstly, of the apparent likelihood that it was deposited in 872 or 873 and, secondly, it provides an indicator of the potential occurrence of prototype 'bullion-rings'

Provenance	Broad-Band Arm-Ring	Penannular Rod Arm-Ring	Plaited Ring	Lozenge-Sectioned Ring	Ingot
'Ireland', 2	–	–	–	–	–
'Co. Kilkenny'	–	–	–	–	–
Castlelohort	–	–	–	–	–
Derrynahinch	–	–	?	–	?
Cushalogurt	•	•	–	–	–
Carraig Aille	•	–	–	•	•

Fig. 3. The hoard associations of 'bullion-rings' in Ireland.

within ninth-century cultural contexts in southern Scandinavia, from where most of the Torksey silver must ultimately derive. The only parallel known to the author for the 'bullion-ring' form within Viking Age Scandinavia lies within a small, coinless hoard from an unlocalised findspot on Gotland (Stenberger, 1947, 258–9, pl. 189.4, no. 676; SHM:12884). In terms of its overall form, closely-spaced rounded terminals, dimensions and weight, it conforms very well with 'bullion-rings' from Britain and Ireland, though its transverse-hammered marks do not (though this feature does occur on several items in the Torksey assemblage and the Cuerdale hoard). Its date, however, is unknown, though the date of deposition of the hoard, on the basis of the presence in it of a brooch of Stenberger's Rn Type 1 (1958, 65ff; Graham-Campbell 1984, 32–4), is unlikely to be much earlier than the mid-tenth century.

The date and location of the Torksey assemblage probably indicates both the main period and the route by which prototype 'bullion-ring' material travelled to the west and initiated the development of the type in Ireland, where by far the dominant Hiberno-Scandinavian arm-ring type, the broad-band type (Sheehan, *forthcoming* b), was also of southern Scandinavian inspiration. This reinforces the connections that existed between the ninth-century Hiberno-Scandinavian and southern Scandinavian silver-working traditions, connections which, ultimately, were due to the primary importance of the southern Scandinavian and Baltic regions as a source for the silver that was used to supply the silver-working tradition that developed in Ireland (Sheehan, 2001, 58–9). The Torksey find, therefore, is of major significance in that it provides a potential indicator of the origins of the Hiberno-Scandinavian 'bullion-rings', as well as an indication that the ultimate origins of the type lie in the 870s.

DATING

It is unfortunate that 'bullion-rings' are not recorded from coin-dated hoards in Ireland. The Cuerdale hoard, deposited *c*.905–10, therefore, represents the only coin-dated hoard context for the currency of this type of object. The only other method of establishing its date range is by associative dating but, here too, problems arise from the fact that in four of the remaining seven hoards the 'bullion-rings' are not known to have been associated with other material. We are, therefore, confined to a consideration of the associated objects in the hoards from Derrynahinch (now lost), Carraig Aille II and Cushalogurt (see Fig. 3).

The Cushalogurt hoard, in addition to its three 'bullion-rings', comprises one complete and six almost complete Hiberno-Scandinavian broad-band arm-rings, fourteen hack-silver fragments of such rings, and one penannular rod arm-ring. The Carraig Aille II find, as well as a single 'bullion-ring', comprises two broad-band arm-ring hack-silver fragments, two ingots, one ingot hack-silver fragment and one hack-silver fragment derived from a rod of lozenge-shaped section. Thus, apart from the 'bullion-rings', these two hoards both share the occurrence of broad-band arm-rings in common. Broad-band arm-rings represent the most important product of Ireland's Hiberno-Scandinavian silver-working tradition and form the largest and most impressive group of silver arm-rings known from Ireland, where they occur in twenty-nine hoards. However, only three of these finds are known to have contained coins, those from Dysart Island (no. 4), deposited *c*.907(+), Co. Antrim, deposited *c*.910(?), and Magheralagan, deposited *c*.910(?). The type is also known from Viking Age hoards in Britain and Scandinavia where they occur in thirteen coin-dated finds, the great majority of which were deposited between *c*.900 and *c*.930. On this basis the currency of the broad-band arm-ring type is broadly datable to the period between *c*.850 and *c*.950, though the majority appear to have been produced during the fifty-year period of *c*.880–*c*.930 (Sheehan, *forthcoming* b).

The penannular rod arm-ring from Cushalogurt is too simple in form to be of any real use in dating. The fragment of a lozenge-sectioned rod from Carraig Aille II is also of limited value in this regard, though lozenge-sectioned rings do occur in hoards from Ireland that date from the later ninth and tenth centuries. The only other object type found in association with 'bullion-rings' are ingots, where they are found in the Carraig Aille II hoard and, possibly, in the Derrynahinch find. Ingots occur, in either complete or hack-silver form, in at least half of the Viking Age hoards from Ireland that contain non-numismatic material. Seventeen of these finds also contain coins, and in each instance these are of tenth-century date.

Little is known about the content of the Derrynahinch hoard apart from the fact that it contained an impressive amount of silver, including hack-silver. It is possible, however, that it featured plaited rings of some form as a contemporary antiquarian account of its discovery noted that among the twelve or fourteen rings that formed part of the find were some that were 'twisted like a curb-chain' (Graves, 1852, 356). This term, of unusual occurrence in the antiquarian literature, may have been meant to denote a chain formed with loops linked end-to-end, with each loop being angled slightly so that they fitted together smoothly, and Viking Age twisted-rod arm-rings could reasonably be described in this manner. Although twisted-rod arm-rings originated in the ninth century (Graham-Campbell, 2006, 74-6), these are largely a tenth-century phenomenon and of rare occurrence in Ireland's hoards, with hack-silver fragments of silver rod showing evidence of torsion occurring in the Dysart (no. 4) hoard, with its coin-dated deposition of *c.*907(+), and, possibly, in that from Magheralagan, deposited *c.*910(?). The limited evidence of the Derrynahinch hoard, therefore, indicates that this find may have been deposited in the tenth century.

Note should be taken of the broad context of the Isle of Skye (no. 3) hoard. Containing only three probable 'bullion-rings', it is not independently datable. Graham-Campbell, however, has noted that its presence in the Isle of Skye recalls the Irish connections of another Skye find, the Storr Rock hoard, 'with which it must be broadly contemporary' (1995, 30). This latter find, a coin-dated example that was deposited *c.*935–40, is comparable with hoards from Ireland on the basis of both its numismatic and bullion contents. A date for the Skye hoard towards the mid-point of the tenth century would be in keeping with the evidence from Ireland.

In overall terms, therefore, it may be proposed that 'bullion-rings', on the basis of a single coin-dated occurrence combined with associated material from a limited number of finds, were in circulation during the later ninth and early to mid-tenth century. Graham-Campbell has suggested that the type was a 'relatively short-lived development during the first half of the tenth century' (1995, 30), though the new evidence from Torksey raises the probability of a later ninth-century horizon.

FUNCTION

In his consideration of the 'bullion-rings' in the Cushalogurt hoard, Hall suggested that they are 'most plausibly explained as ingots cast from small fragments, such as also occur in the hoard, as a more convenient way of carrying them' (1973, 83). Apart from the fact that they are formed by hammering, after casting, this is a reasonable suggestion. Since 'bullion-rings' may have func-

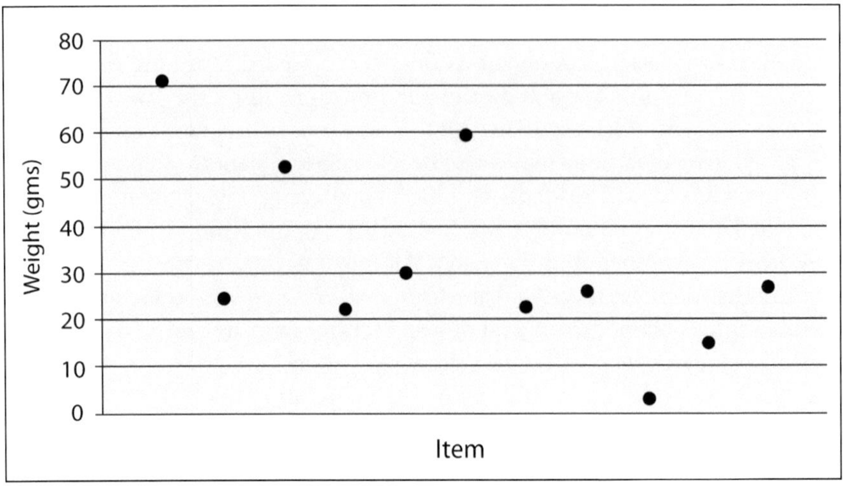

Fig. 4. Scatter diagram of the weights of 'bullion-rings' from Ireland.

tioned primarily, like ingots, as convenient ways of storing bullion, they may possibly have been made to a specific weight standard. A number of metrological studies of various types of Viking Age silver ornaments and ingots from Britain and Ireland have been undertaken in recent decades. Kruse conducted a study on ingots from hoards from England and Wales, and while no obvious standard could initially be ascertained there was a focus between 20 and 30 gm, with a basic 'fuzzy' unit of *c*.25–26 gm seeming possible (1988, 294). Warner performed quantum analysis on complete examples of Scoto-Scandinavian 'ring-money', searching for a basic weight unit within the data, and concluded that the material suggested a standard of 24.0±0.8 gm (1975–76, 141). Sheehan examined the weights of a sample of complete Hiberno-Scandinavian broad-band arm-rings and suggested a weight range of *c*.25.9±0.4 to *c*.27.3±0.9 gm; quantum analysis on this material suggested a weight target of 26.15 gm (1998a, 178–9). Kruse, however, has pointed out that problems may arise from the use of quantum analysis if multiple weight standards are present in the material (1988, 293). Several other Viking Age units or multiples around figures in the mid-20 gm have been proposed following studies on scale balance weights and silver artefacts from various areas of the Viking world. On this basis, therefore, although for various reasons it is incapable of statistical and mathematical proofs, it seems a reasonable proposition that a target weight of *c*.25–26 gm was in operation in the Viking Age bullion economy.

Too few 'bullion-rings' are known to exist, however, to permit any sort of statistically-meaningful analysis of their weights. Nevertheless, the recorded weights of all extant complete examples from Ireland, both from hoards and single-finds, are plotted in a scatter diagram simply in order to note what, if any, trends emerge from the exercise (Fig. 4). The results show that the majority of examples lie within the 20–30 gm range, as is the case with studies of other forms of non-numismatic silver of the Viking Age. The suggested function of 'bullion-rings' as a convenient way of storing silver is supported, in a general way, by this exercise.

DEVELOPMENT AND BACKGROUND

'Bullion-rings' have occasionally been culturally attributed as 'Irish' (as Graham-Campbell & Briggs, 1986), though without clear justification. While it is clear that Scandinavian activity in Ireland resulted in significant quantities of silver becoming available to Irish craftsmen for the first time, particularly from *c.*850 onwards, and that this led to the development of novel Irish types of objects, such as penannular brooches of the bossed and ball types, it is also evident that there are differences between the specific find-contexts of these Irish types and those of Scandinavian-type hoards, including those containing 'bullion-rings' (Sheehan, 1998b, 156). There are instances of the former entering the Hiberno-Scandinavian pool of silver and occurring as hoard components, but these are remarkably few in number. Indeed, these brooches are usually only found as single-finds rather than within hoards, the characteristic context of Scandinavian and Hiberno-Scandinavian material. On this basis alone it seems rather unlikely that the 'bullion-rings' are of Irish origin. It is worth noting, furthermore, that the form of these object types are without precedent in Ireland, and that when Irish craftsmen did experiment through the medium of silver they tended to produce highly decorative and sophisticated forms that were far removed in technical accomplishment and style from these plain 'bullion-rings'. It seems more likely that these rings derive from a Hiberno-Scandinavian milieu. As has been demonstrated above, they tend to occur in hoards of Scandinavian character, sometimes in association with diagnostic Hiberno-Scandinavian object-types and, most importantly, in a number of instances they exhibit the nicking that is characteristic of Scandinavian-type hoards.

The practice of nicking and pecking silver objects, bullion as well as coins, is a feature of some Viking Age silver hoards in Britain and Ireland and was presumably carried out to check silver purity (Graham-Campbell, 1995, 33). It is not a feature of native Irish silver artefacts, apart from a few examples that appear to have been deposited in Scandinavian-type hoards. It is difficult to ascertain to what extent nicking is truly a feature of 'bullion-rings', partly because a fairly large proportion of the material is known only from the antiquarian sources. Of the six relevant hoards from Ireland, three are problematic: the find from Co. Kilkenny and all but one of the objects from Derrynahinch are lost, while only two of the six rings from Castlelohort Demesne are available for inspection. Nevertheless, a significant proportion of the remaining rings from the Irish finds do feature nicking: four of the eight rings that currently constitute the 'Ireland no. 2' find exhibit this phenomenon, generally comprising a single slice on the edge of the rings, near their mid-points; one of the two available rings from Castlelohort Demesne is nicked, comprising two nicks and four slices; and five of the seven objects in the Carraig Aille II hoard are nicked, with the 'bullion-ring' featuring a slice, on the edge, near its mid-point, in the same manner as the 'Ireland no. 2' rings. On the other hand, nicking is not a feature of the three 'bullion-rings' in the Cushalogurt hoard, though it is noteworthy that only one of the twenty-five items in this hoard is nicked (and that only once). At the very least this pattern of evidence demonstrates that 'bullion-rings' formed part of the circulation of silver represented in Scandinavian-type hoards.

It, therefore, appears reasonable to suggest that the cultural background of the 'bullion-rings' is Hiberno-Scandinavian rather than Irish. The recent Torksey find, noted above, provides an indicator that the ultimate origins of the type lie in southern Scandinavia. The distributional pattern of 'bullion-rings' in Ireland is unusual, it being noteworthy that no example is represented amongst the many silver hoards on record from the midlands, north Leinster and Ulster. Of the five find-spots that have at least a county provenance, four are located in the southern third of the country (in counties Cork, Limerick and Kilkenny). This distribution appears to be significant, focused as it is on the early medieval province-kingdom of Munster, and suggests that 'bullion-rings' may have originated, not in the Dublin core of the Hiberno-Scandinavian silver-working tradition, but rather in one of the Hiberno-Scandinavian settlements of Limerick, Cork or Waterford (Sheehan 1998b, 155). The presence of examples of this ring type in the Cuerdale hoard, along with the Isle of Skye find, demonstrated that it gained some circulation outside the Munster area, both in Ireland and the Irish Sea region.

ACKNOWLEDGEMENTS

The author is grateful to Professor James Graham-Campbell, University College London, for comments on an early draft of this paper, to the late Dr Mark Blackburn, Fitzwilliam Museum, Cambridge, for informing me of the Torksey find, and to Nick Hogan, Department of Archaeology, University College, Cork, for preparing Figs. 2–4.

BIBLIOGRAPHY

Betham, W. (1837). On the ring-money of the Celtæ, and their system of weights, which appears to have been what is now called Troy weight. *Transactions of the Royal Irish Academy,* xvii, 7–17.

Blackburn, M. (2011). The Viking winter camp at Torksey, 872-3. In M. Blackburn, *Viking coinage and currency in the British Isles,* British Numismatic Society, Special Publication No. 7, London, 1-44.

Comber, M. (2004). *Native evidence of non-ferrous metalworking in early historic Ireland.* British Archaeological Reports, International Series 1296. Oxford.

Graham-Campbell, J. (1976). The Viking-age silver hoards of Ireland. In B. Almqvist and D. Greene (Eds.), *Proceedings of the seventh Viking congress, Dublin 1973.* Dublin, 31–74.

Graham-Campbell, J. (1984). Western influences on penannular brooches and ringed pins. In G. Arwidsson (Ed.) *Birka II:1. Systematische Analysen der Gräberfunde.* Stockholm, 31–8.

Graham-Campbell, J. (1987). Some archaeological reflections on the Cuerdale hoard. In D. M. Metcalf (Ed.), *Coinage in ninth-century Northumbria: the tenth Oxford symposium on coinage and monetary history.* British Archaeological Reports, British Series 180. Oxford, 320–44.

Graham-Campbell, J. (1995). *The Viking-age gold and silver of Scotland (AD 850–1100).* Edinburgh.

Graham-Campbell, J. (2006). The rings. In S. H. Fuglesang & D. M. Wilson (Eds.), *The Hoen hoard: a Viking gold treasure of the ninth century.* Acta ad Arch. et Art Hist. Pert. 14; Norske Oldfunn 20. Rome/Oslo, 73–81.

Graham-Campbell, J., & Briggs, C. S. (1986). Some neglected Viking-age silver hoards from near Athlone and Co. Cork. *Peritia,* 5, 309–16.

Graham-Campbell, J., & Sheehan, J. (2007). A Viking-age silver hoard of 'ring-money' from the Isle of Man re-discovered. *Proceedings of the Isle of Man Natural History and Antiquarian Society,* XI (4), 527–40.

Graves, J. (1852). Proceedings of the Kilkenny archaeological society 1853. *Transactions of the Kilkenny Archaeological Society,* ii (1852–53), 349–90.

Hall, R. (1973). A hoard of Viking silver bracelets from Cushalogurt, Co.Mayo. *Journal of the Royal Society of Antiquaries of Ireland,* 103, 78–85.

Kruse, S. E. (1988). Ingots and weight units in Viking Age silver hoards. *World Archaeology,* 20 (2), 285–301.

Ó Ríordáin, S. P. (1949). Lough Gur excavations: Carraig Aille and the "Spectacles". *Proceedings of the Royal Irish Academy,* 52C, 39–111.

Sheehan, J. (1998a). Early Viking Age silver hoards from Ireland and their Scandinavian elements. In H. Clarke et al. (Eds.), *Scandinavia and Ireland in the early Viking Age.* Dublin, 166–202.

Sheehan, J. (1998b). Viking Age hoards from Munster: A regional tradition? In

M. A. Monk & J. Sheehan (Eds.), *Early medieval Munster: archaeology, history and society*. Cork, 147–63.

Sheehan, J. (2001). Ireland's Viking-age hoards: sources and contacts. In A.-C. Larsen (Ed.), *The Vikings in Ireland*. Roskilde, 51–9.

Sheehan, J. *forthcoming* a. 'Bullion-rings'. In J. Graham-Campbell, *The Cuerdale hoard and related Viking-age silver and gold, from Britain and Ireland, in the British Museum*. London, forthcoming, 87–8.

Sheehan, J. *forthcoming* b. Hiberno-Scandinavian broad-band arm-rings. In J. Graham-Campbell, *The Cuerdale hoard and related Viking-age silver and gold, from Britain and Ireland, in the British Museum*. London, forthcoming, 94–100.

Sheehan, J. *forthcoming* c. The Woodstown silver, in context. In I. Russell & M. F. Hurley, *Woodstown: A Viking Age Settlement in County Waterford*, Dublin, forthcoming.

Stenberger, M. (1947). *Die Schatzfunde Gotlands der Wikingerzeit II: Fundbeschreibung und Tafeln*. Stockholm.

Stenberger, M. (1958). *Die Schatzfunde Gotlands der Wikingerzeit I: Text*. Stockholm.

Warner, R. (1975). Scottish silver arm-rings: an analysis of weights. *Proceedings of the Society of Antiquaries of Scotland*, 107, 136–43.

Windele, J. (1851). On the ring-money of ancient Ireland. *Transactions of the Kilkenny Archaeological Society*, 1 (1849–51), 328–33.

Urban Crafts and Oval Brooches
Style, Innovation and Social Networks in Viking Age Towns

SØREN M. SINDBÆK

ABSTRACT

This paper discusses technological and stylistic variations in copper-alloy workshops in Viking Age towns. In the decades around year 800 a cluster of new technologies, art styles and object types, including the characteristic oval brooches, were adopted across Scandinavia. Shared details of technology indicate close communication between workshops in Ribe and Birka, yet craftspeople cultivated styles which were specific to the particular town. However, the distribution of the products is not confined to specific regions. The persistence of the stylistic choices is suggested to be a marker of professional identity among craftspeople. This could indicate that the first urban craftspeople in Scandinavia were communities with a sense of civic identity, rather than itinerant cosmopolitans.

Keywords: Crafts, brass ornaments, oval brooches, style, innovation, social networks, towns, urbanism, Ribe, Birka.

Crafted products, along with the refuse from workshops, are among the richest and most informative categories of archaeological evidence pertaining to the urban sites of the Viking period. They allow rare insights into the cultural knowledge and communication of people in Scandinavia's first towns. Debate surrounds the character of these places: Were Viking Age town-dwellers a supra-regional society of itinerant cosmopolitans, or relatively settled communities with a sense of civic identity? The technological and stylistic similarities of products crafted in urban workshops across the Viking world have gained ground for the former view. This paper draws attention to some observations, which move the balance towards the latter.

In the early Viking period a cluster of new technologies for copper-alloy working were adopted in urban workshops in Scandinavia. The reception of these innovations, and the styles they inspired, created a new range of ornaments, including the characteristic oval brooches of the traditional Scandinavian female dress. Finds from urban workshops indicate that despite close communication and shared technology, craftspeople cultivated styles which were specific to particular towns. The persistence of these choices in individual sites contrasts with the randomness that characterises the regional distribution of the products. This may indicate that styles were markers of localised, professional and perhaps civic identities among the first specialised urban craftspeople in Scandinavia.

TOWNS, CRAFTS AND COMMUNICATION

Towns were a marginal phenomenon in Viking-period Scandinavia and the Baltic Sea Area. In all the lands north and east of the Elbe, there were hardly ten sites in the eight, ninth, or even tenth centuries, which might be described as such. They lay scattered far apart in a seemingly non-urban world. What importance could these places have in the wider fabric of society? One answer is that precisely by being few, far apart, and infrequently visited, they achieved an ability to "bind" the wider world together. Acting as destinations of long-distance travel, they funnelled exchange and communication into predictable, navigable routes (Sindbæk, 2007a).

The majority of Viking-period Scandinavians may never have visited one of these places, yet many must have been aware of their existence. Archaeology suggests that in each hamlet or community, there were people in possession of objects that had been produced in, or acquired through, an urban settlement, or who were involved in producing things that were eventually to be marketed in such sites. Towns were distant, but they were gateways to resources and opportunities. Marginal as they were, they were the sort of margin from which social change happens.

How were these relations maintained? Communication is an implicit condition for many subjects studied by archaeology, yet even today it is mostly termed and approached as "contact" or "exchange", that is, as infrequent points of coming together. To get at a more informed view, we need approaches that highlight not only communication as such, but its content in terms of cultural knowledge and learning. The adoption of new practices and technologies are instances which offer rare insights into the dynamics of cultural communication (Latour, 2005, p. 75). By studying how technologies and codes of practice are distributed in time and space, we can trace close, even personal links between sites or regions, or appreciate distinctions between otherwise similar places.

The question of how craftspeople transmitted, adopted or invented new practices is often raised in archaeological studies (e.g., with particular reference to Viking-period copper-alloy casting: Callmer, 2003; Eilbracht, 2004; Kleingärtner, 2007). Yet comparative investigations are hampered by the fact that most assemblages are analysed on a single-site basis. Most basic research, as a consequence, is concerned with identifying techniques, rather than exploring the process of their dissemination. A thorough explanation of these issues is beyond the scope of this paper, which shall aim, instead, to discuss some observations relating to a particular example.

OVAL BROOCHES

The form of oval brooches, a characteristic accessory of Viking Age female dress in Scandinavia, crystallised during the last decades of the 8th century. They developed from a combination of inspirations, including earlier, smaller oval brooches, which were mostly decorated with line ornaments indicating the outline of a crouched quadruped. Brooches of this description were produced in a variety of styles across Scandinavia. In the decades before year 800 they were among the first common metal ornaments in Scandinavia to be produced in large numbers in a serial mode of manufacture. This production demanded a high level of skills as well as steadily available raw materials. For these reasons it is widely recognized that the production of the majority of these brooches took place in towns (a.o. Almgren, 1955, pp. 81f; Jankuhn, 1977; Drescher, 1983; Fuglesang, 1987, p. 219). Waste materials from their production have been excavated in Ribe, Birka, Åhus, Hedeby and Kaupang (cf. below). The brooches are thus a tangible example of an innovation that emerged within the network of early towns.

In 1985 Ingmar Jansson estimated that as many as 3.600 finds of oval brooches were recorded across the Viking World; yet he stated that no clear local groups could be established from their distribution (Jansson, 1985, p. 12). The remarkably wide distribution of similar types seems to imply that the long-distance communication between early towns fed a rapid establishment of pan-Scandinavian designs. Yet in the evidence from actual urban workshops, which has become known in better detail in recent years, an important counterpoint to this picture has emerged.

RIBE AND THE BERDAL BROOCHES

The best studied copper-alloy workshops of the early Viking Age are those from Ribe, thanks to the work of Claus Feveile (2002; Feveile & Jensen, 2006) and Helge Brinch Madsen (1984). Some 10.000 fragments of moulds are known from all excavations in the town, and more than 2000 pieces bear impressions of the cast objects (Feveile, 2002, p. 17). The most common form among these objects is oval brooches.

Different workshops in Ribe have produced different selections of moulds, and new excavations would presumably add further variation. However, almost

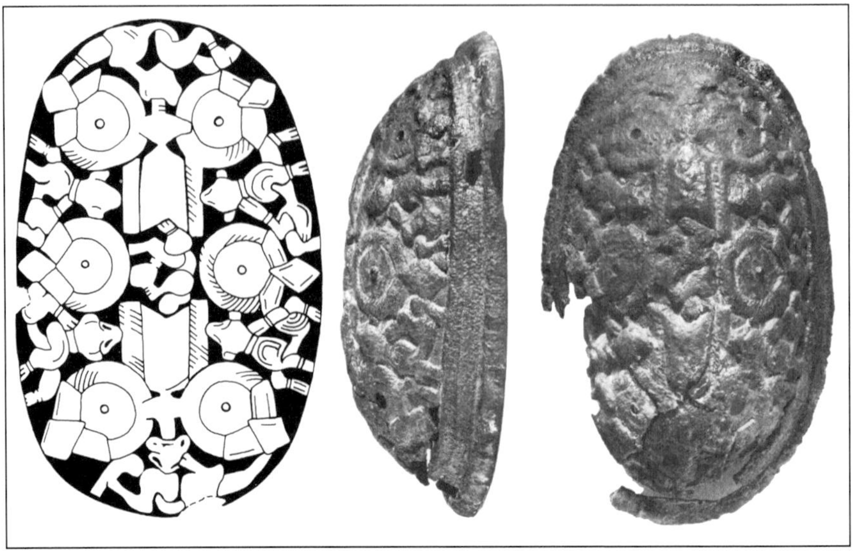

Fig. 1. Oval Brooch of the Berdal group, type P15. Birka grave Bj 557, Björkö, Uppland (After Jansson, 1985, Fig. 11).

all identifiable moulds for oval brooches are of a particular range of forms, the so-called Berdal-type series: Jan Petersen's types P11 to P17 (Petersen, 1928, p. 12ff). The designs of all these types are composed around a similar scheme, consisting of a central bar, each side of which is divided by three smaller features (Fig.1). These traits are the vestiges of the spine, legs and eyes of the crouched quadruped motive of mid-8th century brooches. Compared to these earlier types, however, the casting technique, and apparently the technique for producing the models, is greatly improved, allowing an increasing use of plastic ornaments (Brinch Madsen, 1984; Lønborg, 1994; Hedegaard, 2002; 2005). In response to this new technology a novel style of ornament leaps into the design: the earliest examples of that icon of Viking art, the Gripping Beast.

A remarkable aspect of the brooch moulds from Ribe is that the archaeological stratigraphy from which they have been recovered can be divided into short, successive phases, some lasting little more than a decade. The exact chronology of these phases was the focus of an intense debate during the 1990s, controversy being raised by an apparent mismatch between the date of oval brooches and *sceattas* in the layers (Bencard, 1990; Bencard & Jørgensen, 1990; Frandsen & Jensen, 1990; Myhre, 1993, pp. 186f). The problem was resolved by Feveile and Jensen (2006), who were able to present a consistent and convincing chronology of the entire series.

The key evidence is summed up by Feveile with reference to the phasing

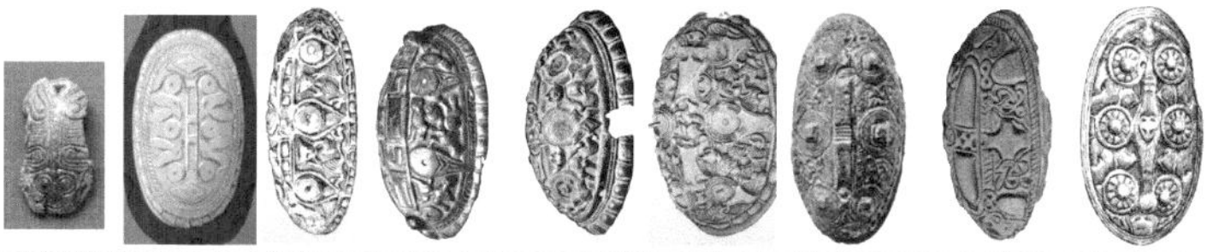

	N	RI9	P14	P16	P15	P17	P13	P11	P12
H/I 820-850				1	102	17	46		1
G 800-820		1	3	2	27	30	21	17	22
F 790-800		12	5	31	31	4	3	2	3
E -780-790		11			1		3		
D 760-780	1								
C 725-760	12								

Fig. 2. Distribution of identified mould fragments for individual types of oval brooches in the site 'Posthuset', Ribe (Redrawn after Feveile & Jensen, 2006).

of the site "Posthuset" (Fig. 2). The earliest phases contain mould fragments from small oval brooches of pre-Viking type (type N). The first evidence of the large Viking Age brooch types appears in phase E, shortly before *c.*AD 790. A number of different design variants, comprising RI9 and the Berdal types from P11 to P17, appear almost simultaneously in the late 8th century, and experiments continue in the first decades of the 9th century. Then gradually one or two of the original forms come to dominate the production – at least in the assemblages found so far (Feveile, 2002, p. 24). Further assemblages from Ribe confirm these general trends, albeit the chronology is less detailed (Madsen, 1984; Feveile, 2002, p. 24).

Berdal-type brooches appear widely across Scandinavia. Despite the serial mode of manufacture, it is highly unlikely that all these brooches were produced in Ribe. Feveile notes that only a small number of the known finds correspond exactly to details of the designs seen in the moulds found here (Feveile, 2002, 21). Other subtypes may have been produced in other production centres, including Hedeby, where mould fragments for type P15 are known (Drescher, 1983, 180). Presumably Kaupang in Vestfold was another production centre, since a notable concentration of Berdal Brooches is known from Vestfold (Madsen, 1984). At least three moulds from oval brooches are attested in Kaupang, although the finds are too fragmentary to identify the designs (pers. comm., Unn Petersen). Signe Horn Fuglesang points out that other brooches appear to have been produced by less experienced craftspeople, presumably working outside the urban production centres (Fuglesang, 1987).

BIRKA AND THE LATTICE BROOCHES

Another contemporary workshop producing oval brooches was excavated in Birka. No less than 25.000 mould fragments were recovered here in the 1990s. 6.000 of these are reported to contain identifiable impressions. Most of these finds came from a series of workshops, which were active for several generations in a single plot near the waterfront.

As in Ribe, the material could be separated into chronological units of comparatively short duration (Ambrosiani, 1998). The exact date of these phases, however, is ambiguous. At the time of the excavation, the dating of the Birka series was based on comparison with the Ribe stratigraphy and thus affected by the controversy surrounding the latter. The earliest levels of the town were dated to the mid 8th century, based on finds of so-called wasp beads, which were then believed to occur in Ribe between *c.*760 and 780 (Ambrosiani, 1998, p. 35). That date has since been postponed by some two decades, at least regarding the main occurrence (Feveile & Jensen, 2006, p. 150).

Another piece of evidence put forward in favour of dating Birka's foundation to the mid-8th century, is the location of the earliest excavated pier in relation to a geological curve of shore-line displacement (Ambrosiani, 1998). This method cannot, however, be regarded as sufficiently precise to distinguish between dates as close as two or three decades. Following the later revisions of Ribe's chronology, Birka's foundation can therefore be placed most plausibly in the last quarter of the 8th century. The metal workshop apparently began to operate shortly after the foundation – about the same time as the Berdal brooch-series emerged in Ribe.

A detailed study of the Birka moulds has yet to be published, although several surveys of the finds are presented by Björn Ambrosiani. The Birka metalworkers produced oval brooches of a like form and size, and using a similar technique to those in Ribe. They also adopted a version of the newly bred gripping beast, so similar to the Berdal subspecies that only a detailed taxonomic study, like that recently published by Michaela Helmbrecht (2007),

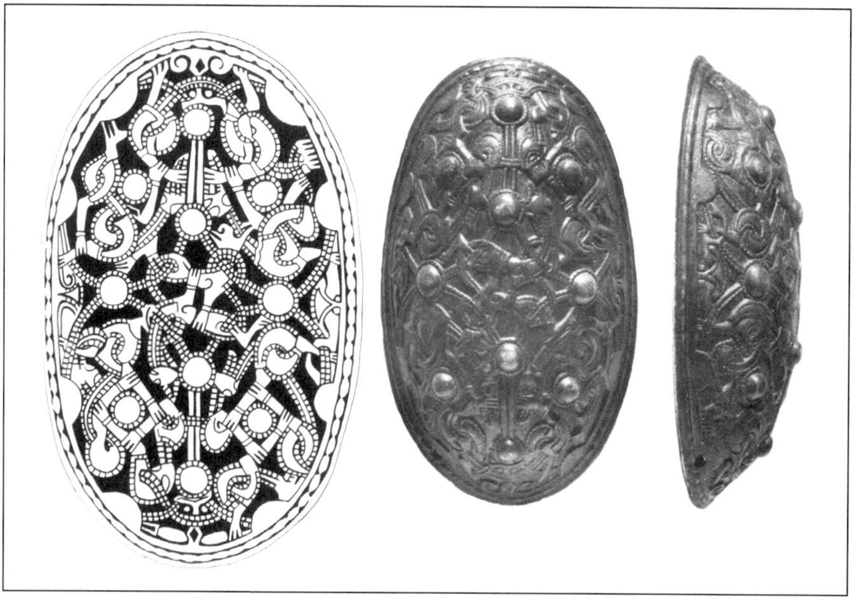

Fig. 3. Oval brooch of the Lattice type P27A. Västanå, Älvkarleby parish, Uppland – UMF 4176 (After Jansson, 1985, Fig. 25).

can tell them apart. Yet remarkably, they integrated this beast into ornamental designs that were substantially different from those used in the south.

The vast majority of moulds in the early phases belong to brooches of Petersen's type P27, later followed by the P37, P41 and P42 (Ambrosiani, 1994, p. 21; 1996, p. 29; cf. also 1992). The P27 type bore little resemblance to the Crouched Beast motive, which lived on in the Berdal design (Fig. 3). Instead, the design stems from a lattice of four ovals, typically encorporating a total of nine Gripping Beasts. Because of the occurrence of these beasts, the Birka moulds are sometimes assigned to the Berdal group. However, to avoid confusion, I shall here refer to them, together with other near-contemporary types, as the Lattice Type of brooch designs.

A number of brooches with similar design but with decoration in Vendel style III are known across Scandinavia, with some concentration of finds in Sweden and on Bornholm (Petersen, 1928, pp. 27f; Paulsen, 1933, 52; Jansson, 1985, pp. 19ff; Rundkvist, 2010, pp. 143f). From the context of some of these finds, they must be regarded as immediately preceding and overlapping with P27 in Birka. Their design with the four ovals bears some affinity to pelta-shaped pendants with animal motifs, which form a characteristic type of

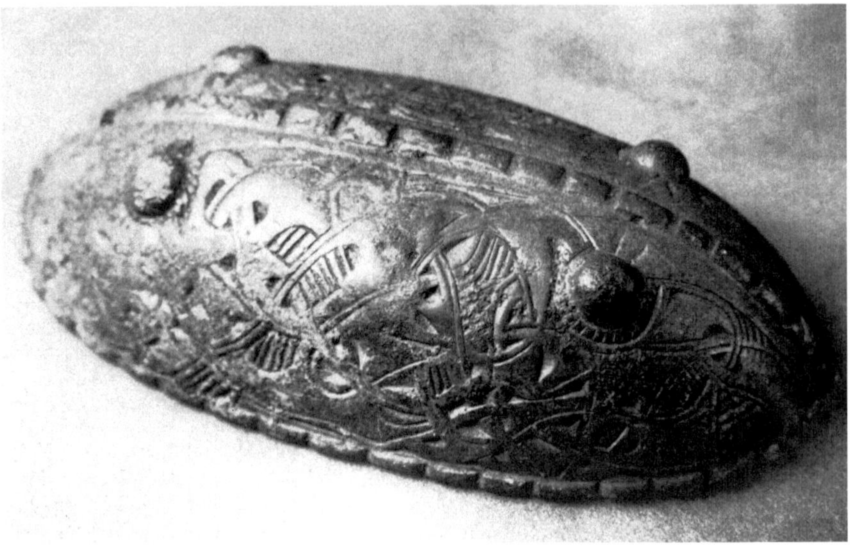

Fig. 4. Examples of a brooch of the Transitional type, which does not incorporate gripping beasts in the design. Lousgaard grave 47, Bornholm (after Almgren 1955, pl. 44).

women's ornaments in East Scandinavia in the 8th century (Callmer, 2008, p. 195). The early production of P27 brooches in Birka thus seems to refer to a local ornamental and iconographic tradition.

Unlike the situation in Ribe, where several different workshops are testified, only a single workshop is thoroughly identified in Birka. A question remains therefore, whether different brooch moulds would be encountered elsewhere in the town. It can be noted, however, that finds of Berdal-type brooches occur conspicuously rarely in central Sweden, with the exception of a group among the highly international finds collection from Birka (Jansson, 1985, p. 25). This rarity argues against this group having been produced regularly in Birka.

The important point to make here is that craftspeople in Birka developed and maintained a distinct tradition of design. This happened despite the close contacts between the production sites, and despite the wide distribution of the products. Notwithstanding the ease with which existing brooches could be used as models for new moulds, it was not these which were taken up in Birka. Nor are any moulds for Birka's Lattice types noted in Ribe. Workshops in each town adhered staunchly to their own types.

OTHER TRADITIONS

The observation that these two centres seemingly maintained distinct traditions of oval brooch production raises the question whether further traditions existed in other, contemporary production centres. A possible example would be brooches of Petersen's type P23 and P24, which mark a distinctive 9th century "speciation" from the Berdal line. Their design is based on a rectangular grid with a central ornamental field framed by two horizontal and two vertical bars. While moulds for this type are unknown in Ribe and Birka, they are confirmed among the relatively few mould fragments identified in Hedeby (Paulsen, 1933, p. 27; Capelle, 1968, p. 43; Jankuhn, 1977; Drescher, 1983, p. 180). The material known from Hedeby is too limited to decide whether the production of P23/P24 brooches here was on a substantial scale, but the fact that they occur marks a noteworthy contrast to Ribe and Birka.

Another group of oval brooch designs from this period are the so-called "Transitional Types" (*övergångstyper*), so called by Bertil Almgren (1955, p. 82). The Transitional Types are a highly heterogeneous group, comprising of pieces from at least 2–3 generations during the second half of the 8th century and into the early 9th. They were previously believed to belong to a period before the arrival of the Berdal series, but according to the revised dates assigned by Ribe's stratigraphy, some of the Transitional brooches must now be regarded as partially contemporary of the early Berdal and Lattice types.

A comprehensive study of the Transitional oval brooch types was recently presented by Martin Rundkvist (2010). This study appeared after the initial presentation of the present paper, but it has been possible to incorporate some key results. Among the wider group of 8th century oval brooches, Rundkvist assigns a total of 127 finds to the Transitional types. Correspondence analyses of grave finds confirm that the size of the oval brooches increases gradually through the 8th and 9th centuries (Pedersen, 1999, pp. 189f, cf. also Høilund Nielsen, 1987 and Rundkvist 2010, pp. 173f). Hence the size of brooches can be regarded as a tentative indication of their date. Among the Transitional brooches listed by Rundkvist, 25 examples are within the same size range, *c.*96–113 mm long, as seen in the Berdal and Lattice types. In many cases these large Transitional brooches contain design elements which correspond to these types (e.g. moulded ornaments or a thick rim).

Most of these large, Transitional brooches bear designs which are descended from the same Crouched Beast that lived in the Berdal design; yet they have evolved along a separate line and, characteristically, have not interbred with that new species, the Gripping Beast (Petersen's type P7-9, cf. Petersen, 1928, p. 9f). Brooches of this appearance occur most frequently in the Baltic Sea area, particularly in Bornholm (eight finds), with further finds from Öland

(Kåtorp – SHM 11680:2) and Fyn (Tranekær – NM 10774). Some of these brooches are found in grave-assemblages, which contain segmented metal-foil glass-beads and other types, making their first appearance in the same phases in Ribe which sees the first production of Berdal-type brooches. For example: Lillevang-Melsted, grave 2 – NM C 6593; Lousgård grave 47 – NM C 5706-7; and Bækkegård grave 166 – NM C 31086 (Ørsnes, 1966, pp. 246ff; Jørgensen, 1990, pp. 135f; Feveile & Jensen, 2006, p. 150). This adds further weight to the conclusion that these types must be regarded as contemporary.

Examples of the Transitional group of brooches, like the Berdal types and the Birka Lattice types, are found across Scandinavia. Yet the concentration of finds in Bornholm and adjacent regions is a pattern which departs from the other main groups. This might suggest the existence of another workshop tradition, and another principal site of production. By far the most likely candidate within Bornholm is the long-lived Iron Age centre Sorte Muld on the north coast of the island. Famously rich in Merovingian period finds, it still shows up among Scandinavian productive sites in the early Viking Age (Aarsleff, 2008, p. 119). However, there is little in the assemblage to suggest that Sorte Muld was a centre of specialized production compared with Ribe or Birka. Possibly an island location was less attractive for the increasingly specialized production centres of the Viking Age: Islanders from Bornholm, always reliant on maritime transport, could easily reach a port on the mainland, while the opposite might not have been true of the populations from the interior of Skåne or Småland.

There are at least two production centres in the western Baltic Sea area which might qualify as a production site for Transitional type oval brooches. Gross Strömkendorf ("Reric") in the Wismar bay, and Åhus in eastern Scania both give evidence of late 8th century copper-alloy working on a relevant scale. The finds from Gross Strömkendorf have yet to be presented in detail, but the evidence for copper-alloy working appears to be rather moderate (cf. Tummuscheit, 2003, p. 213). Geographically, Åhus is a more obvious centre to the known distribution of Transitional type brooches. If Transitional brooch types were cast in Åhus, they would presumably belong to the earlier of the two sites identified here, Åhus I. Extensive refuse from copper-alloy working was found here, though due to the state of preservation of the deposits, virtually no mould fragments were recovered (Callmer, 1982, p. 151). This site was followed in the 9th century by Åhus II, from which mould-fragments for a production of the very common mid-9th century type P37 are found in four different contexts (Callmer, 2002, p. 138).

CONCLUSION

Despite the unmistakable evidence of close communications, a shared technology, and reliance on similar supplies of imported raw-material, the metalworkers of the early urban network in Scandinavia maintained regionally specific design traditions for a surprisingly long period of time. Distinct designs were produced in Ribe and Birka, and arguably in other production sites. In addition to the examples discussed above, one might also mention the tradition of animal head shaped brooches maintained in Gotland, where oval brooches were never commonly adopted (Carlsson, 1983).

Previous studies have pointed to distinct stylistic regions in the Vendel-period and early Viking-period Scandinavia (Ørsnes, 1966; Nielsen, 1991; Callmer, 2008). Yet the wide distribution of the oval brooch types testifies that non-local types were apparently accepted across regional boundaries. This may imply that users made no important distinction between the various designs, as also suggested by the fact that different brooches are sometimes found in the same grave. By contrast, the workshop evidence shows that urban craftspeople certainly did discriminate. The reason for this must remain for the present, a matter of speculation. The consistent choices may reflect community spirit or peer-pressure, or simply professional pride. Perhaps a master craftsperson of this period would not be seen dead paying symbolic tribute to a different centre by copying its models. Copying its tricks and technologies was a different matter.

Regardless, these traditions imply the existence of maintained and visualised group-identities among the craftspeople in any particular centre. Rather than being itinerant cosmopolitans, these masters must have belonged to some form of a civic community. This community was sufficiently entrenched to persuade craftspeople to follow stylistic practices, which distanced them from colleagues – some in all probability, teachers and kin who worked in different sites.

For several decades these site-specific traditions were maintained intact. Yet eventually, before the mid-9th century, they were all abandoned in favour of a common type, Petersen's type P 37, which now became a standard type throughout Scandinavia and beyond. Some 600 examples of this type are known, and mould fragments for their production are found in Birka, Åhus and Hedeby (Fuglesang, 1987). Whether this change reflects changing stylistic or iconographic preference, new modes of workshop interaction, or even a changing political embedding of exchange and production, must be considered elsewhere. However it is to be explained, that this shift presumably took place in the second quarter of the 9th century, and marks the true beginning of the international production patterns that are seen through the rest of the Viking Age.

Further details of these relationships could emerge from direct, comparative investigation into the much broader evidence of crafting offered by the archaeological record. This would have to include scientific characterization of the raw materials, and identification of the operative process implied by refuse materials. By comparing a full range of practices within a number of crafts across the early urban network, we might develop a more appropriate vision of communication, as a field in which interaction occurred by dynamic movements of knowledge, cultural resistance and thresholds.

BIBLIOGRAPHY

Aarsleff, E. (2008). Fund fra Vikingetiden. In C. Adamsen, U. L. Hansen, F. O. Nielsen & M. Watt (Eds.) *Sorte Muld* (pp. 118–121). Rønne: Bornholms Museum.

Almgren, B. (1955). *Bronsnycklar och djurornamentik vid övergången från Vendeltid til vikingatid.* Uppsala: Appelberg.

Ambrosiani, B. (1992). Gjutformar i Birka – en sensation. In B. Ambrosiani & B. G. Erikson (Eds.), *Birka Vikingastaden* 2 (pp. 34–42). Stockholm: Sveriges Radios Förlag.

Ambrosiani, B. (1994). 1993 – långt men inta ända fram. In B. Ambrosiani & B. G. Erikson (Eds.), *Birka Vikingastaden* 4 (pp. 7–33). Stockholm: Sveriges Radios Förlag.

Ambrosiani, B. (1996). De två sista grävningsåren 1994–95. In B. Ambrosiani & B. G. Erikson (Eds.), *Birka Vikingastaden* 5 (pp. 6–43). Stockholm: Sveriges radio.

Ambrosiani, B. (1998). Birka and the Beginning of the Viking Age. In A. Wesse (Ed.), *Studien zur Archaeologie des Ostseeraumes. Von der Eisenzeit zum Mittelalter. Festschrift für Michael Müller-Wille* (pp. 33–38). Neumünster: Wachholtz Verlag.

Bencard, M. (1990). The stratigraphy and dating of 8th-century Ribe, *Journal of Danish Archaeology,* 7, 225–28.

Bencard, M., & Bender Jørgensen, L. (1990). Excavation and stratigraphy. In M. Bencard (Ed.), *Ribe Excavations 1970–76,* vol. 4 (pp. 15–167). Esbjerg: Sydjysk Universitets Forlag.

Callmer, J. (1982). Production site and market area. *Meddelanden Lunds universitets historiska museum. New. ser.*, 4, 1981–1982 (1982), 135–165.

Callmer, J. (2002). North-European trading centres and the Early Medieval craftsman. Craftsmen at Åhus, north-eastern Scania, Sweden ca. AD 750–850+. In B. Hårdh & L. Larsson (Eds.), *Central Places in the Migration and Merovingian Periods.* Papers from the 52nd Sachensymposium, Lund, August 2001. Uppåkrastudier 6. Acta Archaeologica Lundensia Ser. in 8° no. 39 (pp. 133–158). Lund: Almqvist & Wiksell.

Callmer, J. (2003). Wayland. An Essay on Craft Production in the Early and High Middle Ages in Scandinavia. In L. Larson & B. Hårdh (Eds.), *Centrality – Regionality. The Social Structure of Southern Sweden during the Iron Age.* Uppåkrastudier 7. Acta Archaeologica Lundensia Ser. in 8° no. 40 (pp. 337–361). Lund: Almqvist & Wiksell.

Callmer, J. (2008). The meaning of womens' ornaments & ornamentation. Eastern Middle Sweden in the 8th and early 9th Century. *Acta Archaeologica*, 79, 185–207.

Capelle, T. (1968). *Der Metallschmuck von Haithabu. Studien zur wikingischen Metallkunst.* Die Ausgrabungen in Haithabu 5. Neumünster: Wachholtz verlag.

Carlsson, A. (1983). *Djurhuvudformiga spännen och gotländsk vikingatid.* Stockholm Studies in Archaeology 5. Stockholm: University of Stockholm.

Drescher, H. (1983). Metallhandwerk des 8.–11. Jahrhunderts in Haithabu auf Grund der Werkstattabfälle. In H. Jahnkuhn et al. (Eds.), *Das Handwerk in vor- und Frühgeschichtlicher Zeit*, Band II. Abhandlungen der Akademie der Wissenschaften in Göttingen, Phil.-Hist. Kl. 3. flg. bd. 123 (pp. 174–191). Göttingen: Vandenhoeck und Ruprecht.

Eilbracht, H. (2004). Feinschmiede und Münzmeister – Ein Forschungsprojekt zum wikingerzeitlichen Metallhandwerk in Nordeuropa. In W. Melzer (Ed.), *Schmiedehandwerk in Mittelalter und Neuzeit. Beiträge des sechsten Kolloquiums des Arbeitskreises zur archäologischen Erforschung des mittelalterlichen Handwerks.* Soester Beiträge zur Archäologie 5 (pp. 33–46). Soest: Stadtarchäologie Soest.

Feveile, C. (2002). Støbning af ovale skålspænder i Ribe – type- og teknikvariation. In M. B. Henriksen (Ed.), *Metalhåndværk og håndværkspladser fra yngre germansk jernalder, vikingetid og tidlig middelalder. Rapport fra et seminar på Hollufgård den 22. oktober 2001.* Skrifter fra Odense Bys Museer vol. 9 (pp. 17–26). Odense: Odense Bys Museer.

Feveile, C., & Jensen, S. (2006). ASR 9 Posthuset. In C. Feveile (Ed.) *Det ældste Ribe. Udgravninger på nordsiden af Ribe Å 1984–2000.* Ribe Studier bd. 1.2 (pp. 119–191). Aarhus: Jysk Arkæologisk Selskab.

Frandsen, L. B., & Jensen, S. (1990). The dating of Ribe's earliest culture layers. *Journal of Danish Archaeology*, 7, 228–31.

Fuglesang, S. Horn (1987). "The Personal Touch". On the identification of workshops. In C. Blindheim & J. E. Knirk (Eds.), *Proceedings of the Tenth Viking Congress, Larkollen, Norway, 1985* (pp. 219–230). Oslo: Universitetets oldsaksamling.

Hedegaard, K. R. (2002). Yngre jernalders stempelornamentik. Teknik og formål. In M. B. Henriksen (Ed.), *Metalhåndværk og håndværkspladser fra yngre germansk jernalder, vikingetid og tidlig middelalder. Rapport fra et seminar på Hollufgård den 22. oktober 2001.* Skrifter fra Odense Bys Museer vol. 9 (pp. 41–48). Odense: Odense Bys Museer.

Hedegaard, K. R. (2005). Casting Trefoil Brooches. *Viking Heritage Magazine*, 1/05, 8–13.

Helmbrecht, M. (2007). Der frühe nordische Greiftierstil. Studien zu einer stilistischen, räumlichen und chronologischen Gliederung. *Offa*, 61/62, 239–307.

Jankuhn, H. (1977). Das Bronzegießerhandwerk in Haithabu. In L. Gerevich (Ed.), *La formation et le développement de métiers au moyen âge (Ve-XIVe siècles)*. Colloque International. Budapest: Akadémiai Kiadó.

Jansson, I. (1985). *Ovala spännbucklor : en studie av vikingatida standardsmycken med utgångspunkt från Björkö-fynden*. Archaeological studies / Uppsala University Institute of North European Archaeology, aun 7. Uppsala: Institutionen för arkeologi, Gustavianum.

Jørgensen, L. (1990). *Bækkegård and Glasergård. Two Cemeteries from the Late Iron Age on Bornholm*. Arkæologiske Studier VIII. Copenhagen: Akademisk Forlag.

Kleingärtner, S. (2007). *Der Pressmodelfund aus dem Hafen von Haithabu*. Die Ausgrabungen in Haithabu, Band 12. Neumünster: Wachholtz Verlag.

Latour, B. (2005). *Reassembling the Social: An Introduction to Actor-Network-Theory*. Oxford: Oxford University Press.

Lønborg, B. (1994). Fremstillingen af vikingetidens skålformede fibler. *Kuml*, 1991–92, 151–164.

Madsen, H. Brinch (1984). Metal-Casting, Techniques, Production and Workshops. In M. Bencard (Ed.), *Ribe Excavations 1970–1976*. vol. 2. Esbjerg: Sydjysk Universitets Forlag.

Myhre, B. (1993). The Beginning Of The Viking Age – Some Current Archaeological Problems. In A. Faulkes & R. Perkins (Eds.), *Viking Revaluations. Viking Society Centenary Symposium 14–15 May 1992* (pp. 182–204). London: Viking Society For Northern Research.

Nielsen, K. Høilund (1987). Zur Chronologie der jüngeren Germanischen Eisenzeit auf Bornholm. Untersuchungen zu Schmuckgarnituren. *Acta Archaeologica*, 57, 47–86.

Nielsen, K. Høilund (1991). Centrum og perifieri i 6.–8. årh. Territoriale studier af dyrestil og kvindesmykker i yngre germansk jernalder i Syd- og Østskandinavien. In P. Mortensen & B. M. Rasmussen (Eds.), *Fra Stamme til Stat i Danmark 2. Høvdingesamfund og Kongemagt*. Jysk Arkæologisk Selskabs Skrifter XXII:2 (pp. 127–154). Aarhus: Jysk Arkæologisk Selskab.

Nielsen, K. Høilund (1999). Typological and chronological analysis of female equipment from South and East Scandinavia. In J. Hines, K. Høilund Nielsen & F. Siegmund (Eds.), *The Pace of Change: Studies in Early Medieval Chronology* (pp. 160–194). Oxford: Oxbow Books.

Paulsen, P. (1933). *Studien zur Wikinger-Kultur*. Neumünster: K. Wachholtz.

Petersen, J. (1928). *Vikingetidens smykker*. Stavanger: Dreyers grafiske Anstalt. Available online from Oslo University: http://rosalie.uio.no./minuskel/00kj34448/

Rundkvist, M. (2010). Domed oblong brooches of Vendel Period Scandinavia. Ørsnes types N & O and similar brooches, including transitional types surviving into the Early Viking Period. In B. Hårdh (Ed.), *Från romartida skalpeller till senvikingatida urnesspännen*. Uppåkrastudier 11. Acta archaeologica Lundensia. Series in 8 (pp. 127–200). Lund: Almqvist & Wiksell.

Sindbæk, S. M. (2007). Networks and nodal points: the emergence of towns in Early Viking Age Scandinavia. *Antiquity*, 81, 119–32.

Tummuscheit, A. (2003). Gross Strömkendorf: a market site of the eight century on the Baltic Sea coast. In T. Pestell & K. Ulmschneider (Eds.), *Markets in Early Medieval Europe. Trading and 'Productive' sites, 650–850* (pp. 208–220). Windgather: Macclesfield.

Ørsnes, M. (1966). *Form og stil i Sydskandinaviens yngre germanske jernalder*. Copenhagen: Nationalmuseet.

The Vikings as a *Diaspora* – Cultural and Religious Identities in Early Medieval Iceland

STEINUNN KRISTJÁNSDÓTTIR

ABSTRACT

As portrayed in this paper, the available material expressions of religious practices in Iceland represent a much more complicated picture of the settlement and the Christianisation, than the literary sources present alone. The Christianisation of Iceland should thus simultaneously be studied through archaeological sources, along with the concepts of mobility and interaction, as the process must have begun long before the time of the colonisation of Iceland among those who settled there. By the time the island was colonised, there had been contact between Pagans and Christians for centuries, resulting in inter-cultural exchanges following the Viking crusades in Northern Europe during in the 8th century. Therefore, the generation of the Vikings that settled in Iceland was most likely comprised as a disperse unit, raised in an environment of migration and interaction; a world compounded of multi-faceted worship, highly influenced by the Christians. For this reason, it may be relevant to regard the Vikings as a Diaspora, that stretched over large areas of Northern Europe and America.

Keywords: Vikings, Diaspora, identity, hybridization, interaction, deconstruction, Christianization, medieval Iceland.

According to medieval literary sources, Iceland was colonised during the late 9th century by Pagan-practising Vikings who adopted Christianity as a national religion at the Icelandic general assembly, Alþingi, in AD 999 or 1000 (Ólafia Einarsdóttir, 1964: Íslendingabók 1968). Interpretations of these literary conceptions have profoundly influenced the historical memory of the Icelandic nation as holding a uniform inner structure, originated from the Pagan Norse Vikings who are supposed to have arrived primarily from Norway to Iceland. Besides this, the Conversion to Christianity as a well-defined event is usually regarded as having marked the beginning of the Christianisation process in Iceland (see for example Jón Jóhannesson, 1956; Orri Vésteinsson, 2000).

In contrast to these interpretations, the author proposes that the Christianisation spanned a more prolonged period of time, as the process must have begun long before the time of the colonisation of Iceland among those who settled there. By the time the island was colonised, there had been contact between

Pagans and Christians for centuries, resulting in inter-cultural exchanges following the Viking crusades in Northern Europe during in the 8th century. Those who settled in Iceland had thus most probably a much more diasporic background than commonly has been supposed, embracing assorted cultural and religious identities, although unifying as the descendents of the Vikings.

This view will be supported by the various archaeological sources, dating to both pre-Christian and early Christian times in Iceland. It will be demonstrated here that these sources express more similarities to the other Norse societies in Northern Britain and Ireland, than those found in the Vikings' supposed homeland in Scandinavia. The church buildings in Iceland even display blended religious elements, caused by the merging of different ethnical identities during the Viking Age. In that manner, the remains of human habits and cosmology, mirror in fact, how complex and fluid cultural and religious identities are. They are far from being static, as they steadily go through the process of hybridisation and transformation in accordance with their contemporary contexts.

PAGAN BURIALS AND THE ORIGIN OF ICELANDERS

It may be stated that the process of the Christianisation is characterised by a coming together of different cultures, due to the increasing mobility on behalf of the European population during the Viking Age. On their crusades from late 8th to the 11th century, the pre-Christian Vikings left their markings over large areas extending from Newfoundland to Russia and from Greenland to France (see for example Price, 2003). At the same time, the different branches of Roman-Catholic traditions were flourishing in large areas of Europe (Lane, 2001, p. 149). However, clear regional differences are visible in the archaeological records, regarding the performance of rites among both the practices of the pre-Christian Norse faith and the early Christian religion, within the Nordic countries as well as outside them (Jón Hnefill Aðalsteinsson, 1999, p. 26; Hjalti Hugason, 2000, p. 54f; Andrén, Jennbert & Raudvere, 2006, p. 12).

As expressions of religious and cultural identities, burial practices give the opportunity to investigate how the early medieval society in Iceland may have been compounded during the settlement period. Assuming that the pre-Christian faith was practiced in early Icelandic society, settled by the Vikings, it may be stated that it was only in a vague manner. This is because only 316 pre-Christian graves have been found in 157 locations in Iceland, despite the fact that as many as 40,000–50,000 Pagan-practicing people are believed to have migrated and lived in the country during the Viking Age (Byock, 1988, p. 2; Kristján Eldjárn, 2000, p. 255f).

Moreover, the pagan graves examined so far do in fact resemble more closely those found in settlement areas of the Viking on the British islands. Cremations were not practiced in these areas, nor do they display any richly furnished burials, as the inner social structure of the colonised settlements in question did differ a lot from those in Scandinavia.

Even though a systematic survey of Pagan graves has not yet been performed in Iceland, it is not likely that many more will come to light. It may rather be stated that the Pagan-practicing population in Iceland was smaller and composed differently from that hereto claimed, as those who settled there had already integrated new or blended burial customs resulting from encounters during wayfaring. At least, it is justifiable to criticise the sweeping generalizations that describe the newly settled Icelandic nation as having had homogenised social, cultural and political structure, that existed across the other Nordic countries during the Viking period. Those that settled the island must have gained knowledge of, and even inherited, different practices that they learned on their crusades.

Recently, an investigation was made of mtDNA sequences in order to estimate Gaelic and Scandinavian ancestry in the population of Iceland. According to information gleaned from this investigation, the matrilineal lineage ancestry was 62% Gaelic and 38% Scandinavian. Conversely, the matrilineal lineage ancestry in the country was found to be 80% Scandinavian and 20% Gaelic (Helgason, Sigurðardóttir, Gulcher, Ward, & Stefánsson, 2000, pp. 999–1016).

Another intriguing study in 2000 showed that the modern population of Icelanders is among the most variable Europeans at the mtDNA level (Árnason, Sigurpálsson, & Bendikz, 2000, pp. 373–374). Furthermore, investigations made in 1973 on the ABO blood types indicated that 75% of Icelanders belonged to blood type O. This was the highest proportion of this blood type in the Northern world and is similar to the proportion of type-O inhabitants of Wales, Scotland, Ireland, and the Faeroe Islands. In Norway, Sweden, and Denmark, blood type A is the most common (Bjarnason, O., Bjarnason, V., Edwards, Friðriksson, Magnússon, Mourant, & Tills, 1973. See also Aðalsteinsson, 2007).

The results from the DNA and blood type testing have nevertheless been interpreted as supportive of the literary sources, which state that the male settlers of Iceland were mainly of Scandinavian origin but that the female settlers were brought there as slaves from other areas in Northern Europe, such as the British Isles and Ireland. However, neither DNA nor blood type testing unveils any information other than the biological, as it gives no information about the cultural, social, religious or geographical background of the people involved. The results may therefore rather highlight the close contacts of the

Scandinavian Vikings with other populations in Europe during the Viking Age. Such transfer among the population must certainly have involved material, cultural and social encounters as well. The encountering of two cultures does not necessitate the survival of one at the demise of the other, as they can be visualised as a hybrid form of a society that is mutually foreign and local (see for example Bhabha, 2004).

DIFFERENT CHURCH BUILDING TRADITIONS IN EARLY MEDIEVAL ICELAND

The results of mobility and transformation can not only be traced through the Pagan burial customs and genetic studies, as this may even be detected through the earliest church building tradition in Iceland. In fact, church buildings dating from the period spanning the late 10th to the late 11th century display at least two distinct types that may be interpreted as results of the coming together of different branches of the Christian faith in the newly colonised country (Steinunn Kristjánsdóttir, 2004; 2007, pp. 113–130).

It is though, worth underlining here, that no two churches look exactly the same, more than any other construction of that time, because of the presumed individually based characteristics emerging in their own contemporary context. Still, regardless of the individual characteristics, the earliest church buildings excavated so far in Iceland display at least two main distinct building traditions known from the societies of the North-Atlantic.

TIMBER CHURCHES

One of the two main types of the church building traditions in early medieval Iceland represent the earliest generation of the so-called *timber churches*, characterised by noticeably large corner posts dug down into the ground. Timber churches of this type have solely been identified through excavations in all of the earliest Viking settlement areas in Northern Europe and date exclusively to a short period of approximately 100 years, from ca. AD 1000–1100s. This early type of timber church was the predecessor of the stave churches, a type that emerged later in Norway (Jensenus, 2001). The early timber churches[1] disappeared as the Christian religion developed; in fact, simultaneously, as the Church turned from being an unorganised entity into an institution in the

1 The early timber churches are called *stolpe-kirker* in Norway for to distinguish them from the stave-churches that were built with almost the same technique but appeared at first during the 12th century.

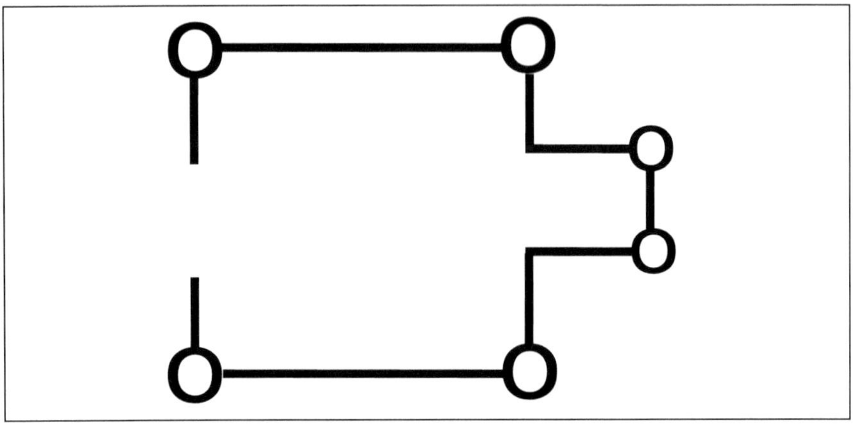

Fig. 1. A schematic drawing of the early timber church at Þórarinsstaðir in Seyðisfjörður, phase I (© Steinunn Kristjánsdóttir).

respective countries of the former Viking world (Christie, 1981, p. 174f; 1982, p. 69f; McNicol, 1997, p. 229f).

The architecture of the early timber churches – and later, stave churches – was featured by the vertical timber walls with a framework of sills, beams and their characteristically earth-dug roof-supporting posts located in the corners. The early timber churches' plan was also branded by their simplicity, although varying in size: it usually consisted of a rectangular nave and a narrower square chancel. At later stages, the simple timber churches became larger in size and more complex in structure. Most likely during the last decades of the 12th century, the earth-dug posts were replaced with posts resting on sills, as the walls themselves, and the second generation of timber churches – the so-called stave churches – developed (Christie, 1982, p. 68f, 73; Anker, 1997, p. 18, 182, 190f; Jensenius, 2001, p. 10f, 29f, 71).

Originally, the stave construction technique is thought to have developed from customary building practice which can be traced back to the Stone Age. Generally, it had its heyday in the early medieval era but in pre-conversion times it was common in large areas of Europe, where it was widely used for the construction of numerous types of secular buildings. It was only later, that the technique was used to build the first churches in Northern Europe, as it was perhaps brought to the area together with Christianity (Christie, 1982, p. 73; Jensenus, 2001, p. 11f).

The timber church, notably of the tradition described above, discovered at the farm Þórarinsstaðir in Seyðisfjörður represents this type in Iceland. An excavation in 1998–1999 at the farm revealed two phases of a church building (Fig. 1). These have been dated to the early and late 11th century respectively but both built according to the same form and technique. The interior size of the older building phase is estimated at 2.70 x 4.80 metres. The church belonging to the younger phase measured 4 x 6 metres in its interior, as it had been enlarged to the north. A choir was added to the eastern gable of both the church buildings, which were east-west orientated. Similarly, the both phases were built of driftwood, with earth dug corner posts that measured up to one meter in diameter each (Kristjánsdóttir, Macchioni & Lazzeri, 2001). During the excavation, three stone crosses were found outside the northern gable of the church and sixty graves were exhumed in the surrounding graveyard (Steinunn Kristjánsdóttir, 2004, pp. 39–95).

In Iceland, timber churches, with the early characteristics of the dug-down corner posts, have also been identified archaeologically in at least two other locations; at Mosfell in Mosfellsdalur and Keldudalur in Skagafjörður (Byock, Walker, Erlandsson, Holck, Zori, Guðmundsson, & Tveskov, 2005, pp. 194–218; Guðný Zoëga, 2009, pp. 30–43). Large corner post holes were also identified earlier by accident at the church site at Stóraborg in Eyjafjallasveit but these were not investigated further (Hörður Ágústsson, 1988, pp. 56–62). Other church buildings found with earth-dug posts, such as the merchants' church at Gásir in Eyjafjörður, is of a different type and age than the early timber churches (Orri Vésteinsson, 2009). The earliest version of the stave construction technique, notably with earth-dug down corner posts, has not yet been determined archaeologically in secular buildings in Iceland.

TURF CHURCHES

The other type of the early church building tradition, that will be classified here as *turf churches*, seems in fact to have been quite common in Iceland during early medieval times as regards building material and technique; i.e. they resemble most other contemporary buildings found in the country. This type is characterised by the use of turf in the outer walls, and sometimes stones as well, as the principal building material. They are usually less than 18 m^2 in size, and the length is usually two times the breadth. In later stages, Icelandic turf churches were panelled with wood in the interior.

What predominantly segregates the turf churches from timber churches, are the walls that are the main structural element supporting the roof, except in some that have a row of posts along the centre, whereas the large earth-dug corner posts perform the roof-bearing function in turf churches built according to the stave construction method (Christie, 1982, p. 73).

Of these, it is useful to use the church found at the farm Stöng in Þjórsárdalur as a representative example of the turf churches. The church

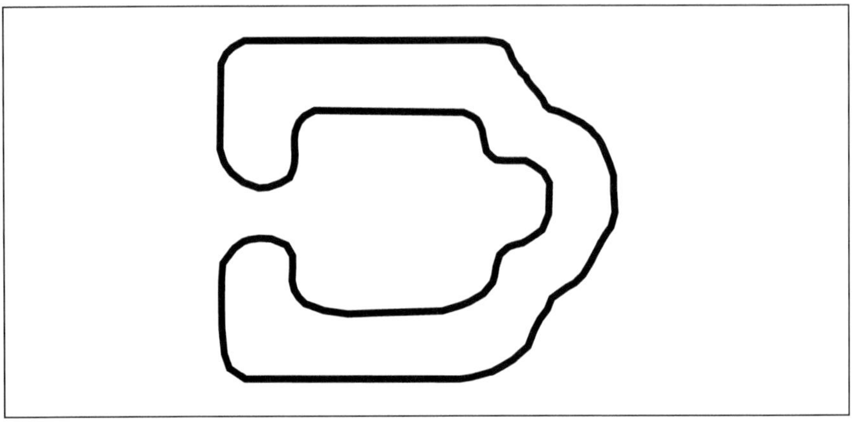

Fig. 2. The A schematic drawing of the ground form of the church building at Stöng in Þjórsárdalur (© Steinunn Kristjánsdóttir).

was discovered during an excavation that was performed there in periods in 1986 and 1992–1993. This particular building was first excavated in 1939 and interpreted as a smithy (Vilhjálmur Örn Vilhjálmsson, 1996, p. 119–139). The church at Stöng was built of turf and stones, and its interior measured 2.5 metres wide and 5 metres long. A choir was added to the east side of the church, which had an east-west orientation (Fig. 2). Several graves were exhumed. A fragmented stone cross of Irish origin was also found during the excavation of the church. The excavator suggests that the farm at Stöng was established in the 10th century; radiocarbon results date the church to the early 11th century (Vilhjálmur Örn Vilhjálmsson, 1996, p. 129f).

So far, turf churches of this early type have been excavated in at least six locations around Iceland, dating from the early medieval times. Similar turf churches as at Stöng have also been found at Geirsstaðir in Hróarstunga, Kross on Skarðströnd, Varmá in Mosfellsbær, Kirkjuból in Skutulsfjörður, and Neðri-Ás in Hjaltadalur (Steinunn Kristjánsdóttir, 2004, pp. 128–132). In some of them the western gable was of timber.

Descendants of this type of church, notably regularly panelled with wood in the interior, can still be found standing at several locations in Iceland. These are Gröf at Höfðaströnd (Fig. 3), Víðimýri in Skagafjörður, Saurbær in Eyjafjörður and Hof in Öræfi, beside the chapel at Núpsstaður also located in Öræfi.

CRUSADING IDENTITIES

The Merovingian period and the Viking Age are characterised by rapidly increasing contact between the pre-Christian inhabitants of Northern Europe and the Christians on the mainland (see for example Hedeager, 1998; 2007). The earliest Christian influences, notably those stemming from missions in Scandinavia, Iceland and the Faeroes, are considered to have originated from various areas of Europe: the Continent, France, Britain, and the Baltic region. According to literary sources, the Anglo-Saxon mission in Britain assumed a leading role in the process. In all of these geographical areas, however, the initial stage of the process was coloured by intensive international contact resulting in Christian infiltration, which was certainly not limited to missionary activities (Skre, 1997, p. 3, 9; Hjalti Hugason, 2000, p. 28 f; Gräslund, 2001, p. 20f: Lausten, 2002, p. 7f, 12f; Jón Viðar Sigurðsson, 2003, p. 20f).

Several scholars state that, in some areas of Sweden, the infiltration process may in fact have begun on an individual basis as early as the 4th century. In spite of the clear regional differences in Sweden, archaeological sources prove that there was early contact with Christian people on the continent and in Britain (Staecker, 1997, p. 419f, 447; Lausten, 2002, p. 5f; Gräslund, 2001, p. 29; Teliander, 2005).

Studies of the Nordic societies lying near the North Atlantic Ocean support the theory that there was greater Celtic-Christian impact than heretofore assumed. In Norway, for example, the Christian infiltration may have begun in the 7th century. Despite clear regional characteristics in the eastern and western parts of the country, the early Christian influences in Norway can be traced

Fig. 3. Turf church at Gröf in Höfðaströnd. Photo: Guðmundur L. Hafsteinsson.

to contact with both the Anglo-Saxon and the Celtic branches of Christianity (see for example Birkeli, 1973; Keller, 1989; 1990, pp. 126–141; Crawford, 1996, pp. 7–30; Myhre, 1998, pp. 3–36; Brink, 2004, pp. 163–175; Morris, 2004, pp. 177–195).

Moreover, archaeological resources indicate clearly that the second generation of the Vikings in Britain had abandoned Pagan customs and had begun to bury their dead in accordance with Christian customs, as the Germans did (Hernæs, 1995, p. 112; Krag, 1995, p. 30; Jørgensen, 1995, p. 101). Additionally, archaeological evidence from a site in Leirvík in the Faeroe Islands suggests that the Celtic branch of Christianity may have been introduced to the inhabitants there approximately 150 years before their formal Conversion (Stummann Hansen, & Sheehan, 2006, p. 29).

The early stage of the Christianisation process in Iceland may thus not have required much effort on the part of missionaries because of the increasing contact between the pre-Christians and Christians of Northern Europe during the Viking Age, and perhaps earlier. As illustrated above, the early Christian church material in Iceland displays, in fact, blended religious identities that were thriving in the newly colonized country. The church building, as an important material expression of Christianity, testifies to its divergent practices (Steinunn Kristjánsdóttir, 2004, p. 20f).

As both an individual and collective occurrence, the Christianisation process must inevitably have involved crucial influences on the social and political structures of the society. It is, therefore, important to consider the material remains from the past as representing equally the physical expression of thoughts, ideas, memory and knowledge, resulting in inter-cultural exchanges and interactions. They may in other words be regarded as symbolizing certain cultural and religious identities, which were organized and manipulated through the constant interplay and encountering of people, their social and natural environment.

Although it may be stated that the Conversion to Christianity in Iceland was a rather clear and simple event, the process of Christianisation must have been much more complex than has hereto been interpreted. As depicted above, the process involved an intensive spread of beliefs and practices, taking place in the world of mobility and migration lasting from the Merovingian period throughout the Viking Age.

As this interaction certainly meant a bonding between people and cultures, it must simultaneously have involved the construction and deconstruction of knowledge and thoughts. As acknowledged, the crusades resulted in the construction of the Viking identity; but notably an identity that nonetheless lacked a certain homeland, determined by geographical or artificial borders. For this reason, it may be relevant to regard the Vikings as a dispersed unit, a Diaspora, that stretched over large areas of Northern Europe and America. A Diaspora is here understood to mean a population sharing common ethnic identity, but that left freely or forced their settled territory and became residents in new areas.[2]

CHURCHES AS THE PRODUCT OF CULTURE

Architecture does not come out of nothing. It is a product of culture, although it is neither a static entity nor some sort of an end product, as it continues to develop through further encountering and transformations (see for example Anna Lísa Rúnarsdóttir, 2006, p. 6).

Consequently, as products of culture and religious expressions, the turf churches and the timber churches may respectively be interpreted as an indication that at least two different branches of the Christian faith were practised in early medieval Iceland. They can, in this manner, be regarded as the material expressions of distinct origination and cultural roots. In fact, through closer examination, the early turf churches resemble the church building tradition commonly found in Ireland, Scotland, the Faeroe Islands, Greenland, and some areas of Western and Northern Norway (Fenton, 1979; Keller, 1990; Ó Cróinín, 1995).

In support of this, a piece of a cross of Celtic origin was found during the excavation of the turf church at Stöng (Vilhjálmur Örn Vilhjálmsson, 1996, p. 123, 133). Accordingly, Iceland's early turf churches, those found archaeologically at Stöng in Þjórsárdalur, Geirsstaðir in Hróarstunga, Kross on Skarðströnd, Varmá in Mosfellsbær, Kirkjuból in Skutulsfjörður, and Neðri-Ás in Hjaltadalur, may therefore be representatives of the Celtic or Irish-Scottish branch of Christianity, or at least a blended version of it, as those that settled in Iceland may have gained knowledge of this faith through infiltration from Ireland, perhaps via Norway, as seems to have been the case in the Faeroes.

In contrast, as the exact prototypes of the timber churches as found at Þórarinsstaðir have been excavated in all of the Nordic countries, it can be suggested that they were visual manifestations of Anglo-Saxon missionary activity on behalf of the Vikings; special missionary churches physically expressing the integration of the Christian faith in these countries. At least they have been reported as being brought to Scandinavia with the spread of Christianity (Christie, 1982; Jensenius, 2001).

Furthermore, three crosses resembling early Christian crosses discovered in Britain, Normandy, and the west coast of Norway were found during the excavation at Þórarinsstaðir (see for example Birkeli, 1973; Fisher, 2001;

[2] For further discussion of Diaspora, see for example Lowe, 2003, pp. 132–155; Hall, 2003, pp. 233–246.

Sawyer, 2003, p. 129). The piece of the cross of Celtic origin that was found during the excavation at Stöng presumably had the same symbolic function as did the crosses found at Þórarinsstaðir, but each type representing the different branches of Christianity.

During the initial period of the organisation of the Church as an institution in Iceland, in the 12th century, Christian beliefs and their visual characteristics must have undergone further transformation, through further assimilation and new emphases. Both of the early Christian church types appear to have disappeared in Iceland during the process of organising, and a hybrid type of church developed: turf churches with timber structure in the interior (Fig. 3). This became the dominant type of parish churches and chapels in Iceland and remained so until late 19th century. In Norway a second generation of stave churches developed at the same time, but in Denmark and Sweden the stone churches became the dominant type (Christie, 1981).

CONCLUSION

The colonisation of the Vikings in Northern Europe surely left visible traits in the archaeological record; for example, in burial customs and the building of churches. This episode, along with the emerging of Christianity, was later memorised exclusively by Christians through their writings.

As portrayed in this paper, in Iceland, the available material expressions of religious practices represent a much more complicated picture of the settlement and the Christianisation, than the literary sources present alone. The Christianisation of Iceland should thus more successfully be studied through contemporary archaeological sources, along with the concepts of mobility and interaction, as the process concerns the cultural and religious identities of the settlers. This is likewise based on the fact that the generation of the Vikings that settled in Iceland was most likely comprised as a disperse unit, raised in an environment of migration and interaction; a world compounded of multifaceted worship, highly influenced by the Christians.

The pagan graves, the mtDNA testing, and blood types all support the idea of hybridisation, mobility and interaction among those who colonised the island. The vague appearance of the pagan burial customs in the archaeological record, explained above, indicates also that a larger portion of the Icelandic population had become acquainted with the Christian faith before the Conversion in the year 1000 AD. The possible diversity of the different branches of the Christian faith points even further towards a blended population in the newly colonised country, than has hereto been assumed. Thus the two distinct church types excavated in Iceland relate to dissimilar building traditions flourishing in the North-Atlantic area during the early Christian period.

As products of culture and identity, the pre-Christian burials as well as the early medieval church buildings found in Iceland, may be regarded as a material creation of such intensive interaction. However, both categories must have unavoidably undergone the process of hybridization and transformation depending on their own contemporary contexts. Consequently, along with the institutionalizing of the Icelandic church, around the turn of the 12th century, the different religious traditions finally became more homogenized, although they were still encountering changes.

BIBLIOGRAPHY

Aðalsteinsson, S. (2007). Possible changes in the frequency of the human ABO blood groups in Iceland due to smallpox epidemics selection. *Annals of human genetics* 49, pp. 275–281.

Andrén, A. (2006). A world of stone. Warrior culture, hybridity, and Old Norse cosmology. In A. Andrén, K. Jennbert & C. P. Raudvere (Eds.), *Old Norse religion in long-term perspectives. Origins, change, and interaction. Vägar till Midgård* 8, pp. 33–38. Lund: Nordic Academic Press.

Andrén, A., Jennbert, K. & Raudvere, C. (2006). Old Norse religion. Some problems and prospects. In A. Andrén, K. Jennbert & C. P. Raudvere (Eds.), *Old Norse religion in long-term perspectives. Origins, change, and interaction. Vägar till Midgård* 8, pp. 11–14. Lund: Nordic Academic Press.

Anker, P. (1997). *Stavkirkene, deres egenart og historie.* Oslo.

Anna Lísa Rúnarsdóttir (2007). Material Culture and Social Space in the Icelandic Turf House. In Edward H. Huijbens & Ólafur Páll Jónsson (Eds.), *Sensi/able Spaces. Space, Art and Environment*, pp. 6–24. Proceedings of the SPARTEN Conference Reykjavík 1st–2nd June 2006. Newcastle: Cambridge Scholars Publishing.

Árnason, E., Sigurpálsson, H. & Bendikz, E. (2000). Genetic homogeneity of Icelanders: fact or fiction. *Nature Genetics*, 25, pp. 373–374.

Bhabha, H. (2004). *Location of Culture.* Routledge, London.

Birkeli, F. (1973). *Norske steinkors i tidlig middelalder. Et bidrag til belysningen av overgangen fra norrøn religion til kristendom.* Skrifter utgitt av Det Norske Videnskaps-Akademi i Oslo II. Hist.-Filos. Klasse. Ny serie nr. 10. Oslo: Universitetsforlaget & Det Norske VidenskapsAkademi.

Bjarnason, O., Bjarnason, V., Edwards, J. H., Friðriksson, S., Magnússon, M., Mourant, A. E. & Tills, D. (1973). The Blood Groups of the Icelanders. *Annals of Human Genetics* 36, pp. 425–458.

Brink, S. (2004). New perspectives on the Christianization of Scandinavia and the organization of the early Church. In J. Adams & K. Holman (Eds.), *Scandinavia and Europe 800–1350: Contact, Conflict, and Coexistence*, pp. 163–175. Turnhout: Brepols.

Byock, J. (1988). *Medieval Iceland. Society, Sagas and Power.* London: University of California Press.

Byock, J., Walker, P., Erlandsson, J., Holck, P., Zori, D., Guðmundsson, M. & Tveskov, M. (2005). A Viking-Age Vally in Iceland: The Mosfell Archaeological Project. *Medieval Archaeology*, XLIX, pp. 194–218.

Christie, H. (1981). Stavkirkene – Arkitektur. Chapter 3. In Knut Berg et.al. (Eds.), *Norges kunsthistorie*, bind 1, pp. 139–253. Oslo: Gyldendal Norsk Forlag.

Christie, H. (1982). Stavkirkene som tradisjonsbærere og fornyere i middelalderens norske byggemiljø. In B. Myhre, B. Stoklund & P. Gjærde (Eds.), *Vestnordisk byggeskikk gjennom to tusen år*, pp. 68–79. AmS-skrifter 7. Stavanger: Arkeologisk museum i Stavanger.

Crawford, B. E. (1996). Holy Places in the British Isles: some Parallels to Selja. In M. Rindal (Ed.), *Two Studies on the Middle Ages*, pp. 7–30. KULT skriftserie no. 66. Oslo: Research Council of Norway.

Fenton, A. (1979). *Continuity and Change in the Building Tradition of Northern Scotland.* Fyrirlestrar Minningarsjóðs Ásu Guðmundsdóttur Wright. Reykjavík: Þjóðminjasafn Íslands.

Fisher, I. (2001). *Early Medieval Sculpture in the West-Highlands and Islands.* Monograph series 1. Edinburgh: Society of Antiquaries of Scotland.

Gilchrist, R. (2008). Magic for the dead? The Archaeology of Magic in Later Medieval Burials, *Medieval Archaeology* 52, pp.119–159.

Gräslund, A.-S. (2001). *Ideologi och mentalitet. Om religionsskiftet i Scandinavia från en arkeologisk horisont.* Occasional Papers in Archaeology 29. Uppsala: Institutionen för Arkeologi och Antik historia.

Gräslund, B. (Ed.) (1999). *Arkeologi i Norden.* Vol. 2. Stockholm: Natur och kultur.

Guðný Zoëga (2009). Fólkið í Keldudal. In Guðmundur Ólafsson & Steinunn Kristjánsdóttir (Eds.), *Endurfundir*, pp. 30–43. Rit Þjóðminjasafns Íslands 19. Reykjavík: Þjóðminjasafn Íslands.

Hall, S. (2003). Cultural Identity and Diaspora. In A. E. Braziel & A. Mannur (Eds.), *Theorizing Diaspora*, pp. 233–246.

Hedeager, L. (1998). Cosmological Endurance: Pagan Identities in Early Christian Europe. *European Journal of Archaeology*, vol. 1:3, pp. 382–396.

Hedeager, L. (2007). Scandinavia and the Huns: An Interdisciplinary Approach to the Migration Era. *Norwegian Archaeological Review* 40:1, pp. 42–58.

Helgason, A., Sigurðardóttir, J., Gulcher, J., Ward, R. & Stefánsson, K. (2000). mtDNA and the origin of the Icelanders: Deciphering signals of recent population history. *American Journal of Human Genetics* 66, pp. 999–1016.

Hernæs, Per (1995). Kristen inflytelse i Rogalands vikingtid. In Lidén, H.-E. (Ed.), *Møtet mellom hedendom og kristendom i Norge*, pp. 80–120. Oslo: Universitetsforlaget AS.

Hjalti Hugason (2000). Frumkristni og upphaf kirkju. In *Kristni á Íslandi I*. Reykjavík: Alþingi.

Hörður Ágústsson (1988). Minnisgrein um kirkjugarðsleifar á Stóruborg. *Árbók Hins íslenzka fornleifafélags 1987*, pp. 56–62.

Íslendingabók (1968). Íslenzk fornrit I. Ed. by Jakob Benediktsson. Reykjavík: Hið íslenzka fornritafélag.

Jensenius, J. H. (2001). *Trekirkene før stavkirkene. En undersøkelse av planlegging og design av kirker før ca. år 1100*. Context. Avhandling 6. Oslo: Arkitekthøgskolen.

Jón Hnefill Aðalsteinsson (1999). *Kristnitakan á Íslandi*. Reykjavík: Háskólaútgáfan.

Jón Jóhannesson (1956). *Íslendinga saga I. Þjóðveldisöld*. Reykjavík: Almenna bókafélagið.

Jón Viðar Sigurðsson (2003). *Kristninga i Norden 750–1200*. Oslo: Det Norske Samlaget.

Jón Viðar Sigurðsson (2008). *Det norrøne samfunnet. Vikingen, kongen, erkebiskopen og bonden*. Oslo: Pax forlag.

Jørgensen, T. (1996). Fra Wessex til Vestlandet. Noen perspektiver på kristningen av Norge. J. F. Krøger et. al. (Eds.), *Nordsjøen – Handel, religion og politikk*, pp. 99–108. Karmøyseminariet 94/95. Karmøy: Dreyer bok.

Keller, C. (1989). *The Eastern Settlement Reconsidered: some analysis of Norse Medieval Greenland*. Oslo: s.n.

Keller, C. (1991). Vikings in the West Atlantic: A Model of Norse Greenlandic Medieval Society. *Acta Archaeologica*. Vol. 61, pp. 126–141.

Krag, C. (1995). Kirkens forkynnelse i tidlig middelalder og nordmennenes kristendom. In H.-E. Lidén (Ed.), *Møtet mellom hedendom og kristendom i Norge*, pp. 28–50. Oslo: Universitetsforlaget AS.

Kristján Eldjárn (2000). *Kuml og haugfé í heiðnum sið á Íslandi*. First publ. 1956. Second publ. extended by Adolf Friðriksson. Reykjavík: Mál og menning.

Kristjánsdóttir, S., Macchioni, N. & Lazzeri, S. (2001). An Icelandic medieval church made of drift timber, – the implications of the wood identification. *Journal of Cultural Heritage* 2, pp. 97-107.

Lane, P. (2001). The archaeology of Christianity in global perspectives. In Timothy Insoll (Ed.), *Archaeology and world religion*, chapter 6, pp. 148–181. London and New York: Routledge.

Lausten, M. S. (2002). *A Church History of Denmark*. Translated by Frederick H. Cryer. Hampshire: Ashgate Publishing Ltd.

Lowe, L. (2003). Heterogeneity, Hybridity, Multiplicity: Marking Asian-American Differences. In Braziel, A. E. & Mannur, A. (Eds.), *Theorizing Diaspora*, pp. 132–155.

McNicol, J. (1997). *Plasseringe av de første kirkene i Norge i forhold til de første kultstedene*. Kult's skriftserie nr. 98. Oslo: Norges forskningsråd.

Morris, C. D. (2004). From Birsey to Brattahlíð: recent perspectives on Norse

Christianity in Orkney, Shetland, and the North Atlantic Region. In J. Adams & K. Holman (Eds.), *Scandinavia and Europe 800–1350: Contact, Conflict, and Coexistence*, pp. 177–195. Turnhout: Brepols.

Myhre, B. (1998). The Archaeology of the Early Viking Age in Norway. In H. B. Clarke, M. Ní, Mhaonaigh & R. Ó. Floinn (Eds.), *Ireland and Scandinava in the Early Viking Age*, pp. 3–36. Dublin: Four Courts Press.

Ó Cróinín, D. (1995). *Early Medieval Ireland 400–1200*. London and New York: Longman.

Ólafia Einarsdóttir (1964). *Studier i kronologisk metode i tidlig islandsk historieskrivning*. Bibliotheca historica Lundensis XIII. Copenhagen: CWK Gleerups.

Orri Vésteinsson (2000). *The Christianisation of Iceland. Priest, power and social change 1000–1300*. Based on the author's thesis (Ph.D.), University of London 1996. Oxford: Oxford University Press.

Orri Vésteinsson (2009). A medieval merchants' church in Gásir, North Iceland. *hikuin* 36, pp. 159–170.

Price, N. (2003). *The Viking Way. Religion and war in late Iron Age Scandinavia*. Uppsala: Uppsala University.

Sawyer, B (2003). *The Viking-Age Rune-Stones. Custom and Commemoration in Early Medieval Scandinavia*. First published in 2000. Oxford and New York: Oxford University Press.

Skre, D. (1997). Missionary Activities in Early Medieval Norway. Strategy, Organisation and the Course of Events. *Scandinavian Journal History*. Vol. 23. Nos. 1–2, pp. 1–19.

Staecker, J. (1997). Legends and Mysteries. Reflections on the Evidence for the Early Mission in Scandinavia. In C. Andersson & Lars Ersgård (Eds.), *Visions of the Past,* pp. 419–454. Lunds Studies in Medieval Archaeology 19. Lund: Central Board of National Antiquities.

Steinunn Kristjánsdóttir (2004). *The Awakening of Christianity in Iceland. Discovery of Timber Church and Graveyard at Þórarinsstaðir in Seyðisfjörður*. GOTARC serie no 31. Gothenburg and Reykjavík: Department of Archaeology, University of Gothenburg.

Steinunn Kristjánsdóttir (2007). Kristnitakan. Áhrif tilviljanakennds og skipulegs trúboðs. *Saga* XLV:1, pp. 113–130.

Stummann Hansen, S. & Sheehan, J. (2006). The Leirvík „Bønhustoftin" and the Early Christianity of the Faroe Islands, and Beyond. *Archaeologia Islandica* 5, pp. 27–54.

Teliander, C. (2005). *Västergötlands kristnande. Religionsskifte och gravskickets förändring 700–1200*. Gotarc Serie B. No. 41. Gothenburg: University of Gothenburg.

Vilhjálmur Örn Vilhjálmsson (1996). Gård og kirke på Stöng i Þjórsárdalur. In J. F. Krøger et. al. (Eds.), *Nordsjøen – Handel, religion og politik*, pp. 119–139. Karmøy: Karmøyseminariet 94/95.

Haugbrot, Haugbúar and Sagas

DANIEL SÄVBORG

ABSTRACT

It has been common among scholars to explain the *haugbrot* and *haugbúi* episodes in Íslendingasögur, like *Harðar saga* and *Þorskfirðinga saga*, as borrowed from the fornaldarsögur. Such motifs have been considered typical for the fornaldarsögur, and the alleged influence has been seen as common of a general influence from the fornaldarsaga genre on the alleged late, "post-classical" Íslendingasögur. At least in the Íslendingasögur, these motifs have been seen as generally late. This article examines where the *haugbrot* and *haugbúi* motifs occur in Old Norse tradition, and in what forms they occur. The conclusion is that both *haugbrot* and *haugbúi* motifs in general, are old and frequent in Old Norse tradition. They are though, especially in the form they have in the Íslendingasögur, rare in the fornaldarsögur. It is unlikely that *Harðar saga* and *Þorskfirðinga saga* at this point are influenced by the fornaldarsaga genre. The occurrence of the motif cannot be used for dating them as late.

Keywords: Fornaldarsögur, Icelandic saga, Old Norse Literature, *haugbrot*, ghosts, Harðar saga, Þorskfirðinga saga, folklore, supernatural motifs.

This article originated from the study of two Íslendingasögur, *Harðar saga* and *Þorskfirðinga saga*. The traditional view was that they were late "post-classical" sagas from the period after 1300. This classification and dating have been almost entirely based on their supernatural motifs, mainly haugbrot and undead haugbúar, or mound-dwellers. These are motifs that have been seen as typical late, "post-classical" features, borrowed from the fornaldarsaga as a written, literary genre, that is usually claimed to have emerged quite late, after the "classical" period, at the end of the 13th century.[1]

1 The "post-classical" Íslendingasögur are usually claimed to have originated under the influence of the written fornaldarsögur. This view is clearly expressed by several scholars. Sigurður Nordal says about the family sagas from the time after 1300: "de efterhaanden blev mindre realistiske, stærkere paavirket af de flittigt dyrkede oldtidssagaers smag" (1953, 261). Jan de Vries also comments the family sagas from the 14th century; one of their typical features is that they "zeigen besonders stark den Einfluß der zur Vorherrschaft gelangten Fornaldarsaga." (1967, 529). Einar Ólafur Sveinsson describes one of the most typical features of the saga literature after 1300: "the influence of Heroic Sagas on Family Sagas" (1958, 124–125). The same view is still expressed in Jónas Kristjánsson 1997, 285 and 219. I find the traditional notion of a group of "post-classical" sagas doubtful, and here I will use the term with quotation marks, referring to the traditionally alleged group and its representatives.

Anthony Faulkes points out "the raiding of the grave-mound and the fight with its occupant" in *Harðar saga* as an episode in the style of the fornaldarsögur[2]. For example Finnur Jónsson, Paul Schach, Sigurður Nordal, Björn Sigfússon, and Sture Hast have expressed similar opinions[3]. This is not surprising. The haugbrot is generally considered to be a typical fornaldarsaga motif. This is clear from Heinrich Beck's words: "Ihr eigentlicher Ort ist die Fornaldarsaga" (Beck, 1978, 227). A. Le Roy Andrews says about the haugbrot motifs and Viking adventures: "Besonders reich an beiden motiven sind die fornaldarsögur" (Andrews, 1909,78). But is this true?

I decided to examine where the haugbrot motif occurs in Old Norse literature and in what different forms and patterns it occurs. Is it really a typical fornaldarsaga motif and is it justified to see it as a "post-classical" one? Can we use this motif as a criterion for fornaldarsaga influence and for a late dating of a saga?

By "fornaldarsögur" I mean written mediaeval sagas taking place in Scandinavia before the settlement of Iceland.[4]

In *Harðar saga* Hörðr and his friends go to the mound of the Viking Sóti in Gautland. They break the mound and inside the tomb chamber Hörðr fights with the undead Sóti. Hörðr defeats Sóti and takes all the treasures in the mound (pp. 39–43).

In this episode, we have to deal with two different motifs which have been combined: 1) the haugbrot motif, a break-in in a mound, to get treasures and/or weapons from it; 2) the motif of an encounter with an undead haugbúi.

2 Faulkes 1983,14. In another work he is also commenting the adventures in Gautland (where the haugbrot is the main event) mentioning "crude folklore motifs that link the story with *fornaldarsögur* and romance." (1993, 269).

3 Finnur Jónsson mentions "höjbrudet, vikingetogene" in *Harðar saga* and comments: "Det er, som påvist, fornaldarsagamotiver og -stil" (1935, 333). Paul Schach claims about the haugbrot episode in *Harðar saga*: "This part of the story is told in the manner of the fornaldarsögur." (1985a, 101). Sigurður Nordal claims that it is a characteristic feature in *Harðar saga* that it is "stærkt præget af fornaldarsagaer" (1953, 263), and he has already mentioned "højbruddet i Harðar s." as an example of the general influence from the fornaldarsögur on the "post-classical" family sagas (ibid p. 262). Björn Sigfússon mentions the Gautland episode when he ascribes *Harðar saga* a large "kvantitet av fornaldarsagostoff." (1961, 230). Sture Hast claims that *Harðar saga* in its existing form is characterized by interpolations of "motiv från fornaldarsagor." (1960, 102).

4 This is basically C.C. Rafn's original definition of fornaldarsögur. His criterion was that these sagas told about events that took place "hèr á Norðlöndum, áðr enn Island bygðist á 9du öld" (1829, v). Rafn does not mention that the sagas should necessarily be mediaeval, which leads him to include post-mediaeval works like *Hrómundar saga Gripssonar*. The notion of such a group is not older that Rafn and it has been questioned. But most scholars have accepted it, and my aim here is to test the validity of their theories, which makes it necessary to use the concept. To avoid circular argument I stick to the simple definition mentioned and do not include sagas taking place in other times or places but with alleged motif parallels with the fornaldarsögur (i.e. the occurrence of haugbrot).

The combined motifs which we find in *Harðar saga* is a haugbrot resulting in a direct fight between the living intruder and the undead haugbúi. This combination is also found in some other works. Gestr in *Bárðar saga Snæfellsáss* breaks a mound in Helluland and fights a violent battle with the haugbúi, the Viking Raknarr (pp. 165–168). He succeeds in decapitating Raknarr and to get away with a lot of treasures which he has taken from the mound. In *Grettis saga,* Grettir breaks a mound in Norway, fighting against the haugbúi Kárr inn Gamli and taking the treasures from the mound (p. 58). *Landnámabók* (the Hauksbók-redaction) says that Miðfjarðar-Skeggi broke into Hrólfr kraki's mound in Denmark. He gets into a battle with the undead and has to fight against King Hrólfr and his champion Böðvarr, but succeeds in stealing some great weapons, including the sword Sköfnungr (p. 213). In these three works, we meet the same motif as in *Harðar saga.* In none of the cases, it is a fornaldarsaga.

The combination of haugbrot and a violent confrontation with a haugbúi appears in a few more cases, although the reality of the combination is somewhat different. In *The legendary Óláfssaga* Rani breaks into the mound of Óláfr Geirstaðaálfr, decapitates him and takes away the treasures from the grave (pp. 32–34). Here, there is no regular struggle, and both the decapitation and the haugbrot itself take place at the invitation of the haugbúi. In *Heimskringla* Snorri Sturluson tells that Óðinn opened grave mounds and with magic words bound those who dwelled in the mounds, and then took the treasures from the mounds (p. 19). There is no direct fight, but even here there is haugbrot followed by a confrontation in which mound-breaker defeats the undead haugbúi and takes his treasure. Saxo tells in *Gesta Danorum* about a haugbrot in the mound of the Norwegian prince Asuitus in order to steal the treasures. At this haugbrot it turns out that Asuitus has become an undead haugbúi who fights a violent battle against the living visitor in the mound before the visitor succeeds in decapitating the haugbúi (V.11, 3; p. 346). The story is reminiscent of the one we found in *Harðar saga* and the other earlier sagas mentioned. But in Saxo's work the haugbrot and the fight with the haugbúi are two separate motifs, although they are found in the same episode. The struggle is fought between Asuitus and his friend Asmundus, who has not broken into the mound, but followed his friend to the funeral for three days of vigil. This is revealed due to the fact that a group of Swedes shortly after the haugbúi struggle, commit a real haugbrot in Asuitus' mound to steal the treasures.

These episodes are so similar to the episodes in *Harðar saga* and the three other works that they should be seen as variations of the same motif. One may also note the parallels in several details. The haugbúi is depicted as buried seated in *Harðar saga* as well as *Bárðar saga*, *Grettis saga,* and *The legendary Óláfssaga.* The living mound-breaker decapitates the haugbúi in *Bárðar saga, Grettis saga, The legendary Óláfssaga*, and Saxo's *Gesta Danorum.*

The combination of the two motifs 'haugbrot' and 'haugbúi confrontation' that we find in *Harðar saga* is thus found in several works belonging to various genres of Old Norse literature. The motif, in its combined form, is old, as shown by the evidence of Saxo and *The legendary Óláfssaga*, both from around 1200. But one fact is remarkable: *The motif in this combination does not occur in any fornaldarsaga.*

There are also several cases where the haugbrot motif is combined with a more peaceful meeting with the haugbúi. These include a story in *Reykdœla saga* about Þorkell who takes a sword from a grave-mound before a battle, and when victory is won returns it; then the haugbúi comes to him in his sleep and gives him the sword (p. 213). In *Kumlbúa þáttr* the haugbúi has been robbed of his sword by Þorsteinn Þorvarðsson and comes to him in his dream expressing his anger (pp. 454–455). Neither this variant of the motif is found in any fornaldarsaga.

The *Harðar-saga*-episode has as its central element a combination of the two motifs 'haugbrot' and 'encounter with an undead haugbúi'. We have seen that this motif combination is well established in Old Norse literature. We have several occurrences in the family sagas. Through the cases in *The legendary Óláfssaga* and *Gesta Danorum* we know that the motif combination is old and not created in the "post-classical" period. *The motif combination can hardly be said to be typical of the fornaldarsaga. It does not occur there at all.*

But the haugbrot motif occurs in several cases in Old Norse literature unconnected with the motif of the undead haugbúi. *Þórðar saga hreðu* tells about Miðfjarðar-Skeggi's haugbrot in Hrólfr kraki's mound and mentions no undead haugbúi in this context (p. 169). The purpose of the episode is to explain why Skeggi owned the sword Sköfnungr. The same haugbrot is also mentioned in *Laxdœla saga* (p. 229), *Landnámabók* (pp. 212–213), and Haukr Valdísarsons *Íslendingadrápa* (st. 21; Skj BI, p. 544). In Saxo Grammaticus' *Gesta Danorum* king Haraldus breaks into the mound of Balderus to steal the treasures from it (III. 3,8). In *Sturlunga saga* (*Þorgils saga ok Hafliða*) there is a description of the entertainment during a party in the early 12th century. A man tells stories, including one about Hrómundr Gripsson's haugbrot in Þráinn berserkr's mound (p. 27).[5] *Flóamanna saga* mentions that some slaves broke into graves to steal treasures. In the late riddarasaga *Viktors saga ok Blávus* two young men break into a mound to get famous weapons from it (p. 108). *Hálfs saga ok Hálfsrekka* mentions briefly that a Viking band "braut haug með stafnbúa, ok fengu þar mikit fé" (p. 99). This is all the story tells about it, but is an impor-

5 Hrómundr's haugbrot is described in detail in a saga, *Hrómundar saga Gripssonar*, which sometimes is included in the genre of fornaldarsögur. This saga is, however, not mediaeval, but a reconstruction from around 1700 (cf. Einar Ól. Sveinsson 1959, 500).

tant fact, because *it is the only certain example we have of a haugbrot in a fornaldarsaga*. The short notice completely lacks all similarity with the adventures in *Harðar saga*. Haugbrot was not only a literary motif, but was also seen in the 13th century as a real problem that had to be stopped: in Magnús Hákonarson's law haugbrot is explicitly forbidden (p. 102).

In the analysis above, I have confined myself to cases where the mounds have been broken and treasures or weapons have been taken, which is usually seen as constitutive of a haugbrot. However, there are also some cases where graves are opened with the sole purpose of removing a body. The situation is thus quite different from those in the cases above. One of the cases, however, has clear similarities with the actual haugbrot episodes above, since the episode about the opening of the mound includes the motif with a haugbúi contacting a living person: the undead Ásmundr Atlason in *Landnámabók* comes to his wife one night asking her to remove his grave companion from the grave, which is then done (p. 105). In *Laxdœla saga* (two different episodes, pp. 39–40 and 69) and *Eyrbyggja saga* (pp. 169–170) too, the motif of grave opening is linked to the motif of an undead in the grave; the purpose is to remove the bodies of the undead villains, Víga-Hrappr and Þórólfr bægifótr to prevent them from continuing to walk. In *Ragnars saga loðbrókar* William the Conqueror has Ívarr inn beinlausi's corpse removed from his grave (p. 280), but in this episode, there is no undead haugbúi. Since both the motif of grave robbery and the motif of an undead haugbúi is missing here, this episode deviates so much from all the other cases that it seems doubtful whether it can possibly be described as a haugbrot at all.

Let us consider the haugbrot motif in Old Norse literature. Several scholars described the haugbrot in general as typical of the fornaldarsaga. What do we find if we look at all the haugbrot instances?

It can hardly be argued that the predominance of haugbrot-episodes in the fornaldarsögur is particularly striking, neither proportional nor absolute. The number of instances amounts to one or two (*Hálfs saga* and possibly *Ragnars saga*), and here there are no undead haugbúar nor any similarities at all with the pattern from *Harðar saga*. This can be contrasted against at least 21 instances in works from other genres: eleven cases in the family sagas, two in *Landnámabók*, two in kings' sagas, two in *Gesta Danorum*, one in *Sturlunga saga*, one in a riddarasaga, one in the skaldic poetry, and one in a law. We remember Heinrich Beck's words about the haugbrot motif: "Ihr eigentlicher Ort ist die Fornaldarsaga." We can also remind ourselves of Le Roy Andrews' words that the fornaldarsögur should be "Besonders reich" of this motif. In light of my review of all the cases this description does not seem to be correct. The connection between haugbrot and the fornaldarsaga is a myth.

⋆

Another "post-classical" family saga that has been associated with the fornaldarsögur by means of similar arguments is *Þorskfirðinga saga*. Paul Schach argued explicitly that the story "shows influence from the fornaldarsögur" (Schach, 1985b, 27), and so have several other scholars, pointing mainly at the motif of the undead haugbúi. Sigurður Nordal mentions it as an example of how "post-classical" family sagas are influenced by the fornaldarsögur (Sigurður Nordal, 1953, 262). According to Björn Sigfússon *Þorskfirðinga saga* has "assimilerat icke så litet fornaldarsagostoff" (Björn Sigfússon, 1960, 595). The same view is expressed by Jan de Vries: "Das ist also ganz wie in der Fornaldarsaga", is his comment after a summary of the story of Þórir's dealings with an undead haugbúi and of Vikings transformed into dragons, motifs that Vries uses to date the story to the 14th century (Vries, 1967, 533). I discuss the dragons in another work (Sävborg, forthcoming). Here, I shall stick to the motif of the encounter with the haugbúi.

Þorskfirðinga saga tells that Þórir and his men plan to break into the mound of the berserk Agnarr. But before they begin to break in they fall asleep, and in the dream Þórir is visited by the haugbúi. He asks Þórir to give up the haugbrot and instead he gives him advice about stealing gold from a dragon cave. Then he gives Þórir several precious gifts. When Þórir wakes up the gifts lie beside him, which – so to speak – confirms the reality of the haugbúi (pp. 184–185).

Here we don't have an actual haugbrot, but still an encounter with an undead haugbúi. So is this a motif borrowed from the fornaldarsaga genre? Is it a fornaldarsaga motif at all?

The motif of the undead haugbúi visiting a person in his dream occurs in a number of sagas. *The legendary Óláfssaga* from about 1200 tells, as already mentioned, the story of how Óláfr Geirstaðaálfr appears for Rani in a dream and gives him instructions for a haugbrot in his own grave, including how he should take treasures there (pp. 32–34). There are close motif parallels with the episode in *Þorskfirðinga saga*. In both sagas the haugbúi gives the living person gifts in the form of a sword, splendid clothing and further treasures. In both sagas the haugbúi gives the living person advice and instructions about how to get treasures.

The same motif is found in some family sagas which I have already mentioned in connection with the haugbrot motif. In *Reykdœla saga*, too, a haugbúi appears in a dream because of a haugbrot; he gives the hero Þorkell his sword, which Þorkell previously borrowed from the mound and then put back there, and when Þorkell wakes up the sword is there (p. 213). The sword gift is a motif that links the episode with that in *Þorskfirðinga saga*. In *Kumlbúa þáttr* the visit of the haugbúi is also motivated by a grave robbery. Þorsteinn Þorvarðsson has taken a sword from a mound, and in his dream at night he is visited by the kumlbúi who reclaims his sword (pp. 454–455).

In these three cases, we have clearly the same motif as in *Þorskfirðinga saga*. But there are still some saga episodes which belong to the same type of motif, even if the visit of the undead is not motivated by any haugbrot. In *Þorsteins þáttr uxafóts* Þorsteinn falls asleep at a mound, and in the dream he meets several haugbúar. As in the previous cases, the living person gets precious gifts from the haugbúi in the dream and finds them beside him when he wakes up, and as in *Þorskfirðinga saga* the haugbúi is "rauðklæddr" and "mikill" (pp. 352–354). In *Þorleifs þáttr jarlsskálds* the wannabe-skald Hallbjörn falls asleep on Þorleifr jarlaskáld's mound. In the dream he is visited by the haugbúi who talks to him. Here, too, the haugbúi is described as "mikill" and he also gives him a kind of gift: he gives Hallbjörn the gift of poetic skill (pp. 228–229). *Landnámabók* (Hauksbók version), tells about Ásmundr Atlason who is buried in a mound with his slave. Ásmundr's widow Þóra is visited in the dream by Ásmundr who complains about his grave companion (p. 105).

It is clearly a recurring motif we are dealing with: the haugbúi visiting a living person in the dream giving him a message. In most cases he gives him gifts, and in most cases the visit is connected with a haugbrot. This motif occurs in a number of family sagas, both "classical" – as *Reykdœla saga* – and "post-classical" – as *Þorsteins þáttr uxafóts*. And the motif is old. It occurs in fully developed form already in *The legendary Óláfssaga* from around 1200. The motif is found in both family sagas and kings' sagas. In contrast, *the motif does not occur in one single fornaldarsaga*. This genre has, at least in this respect, *not* influenced *Þorskfirðinga saga*.

There are some more instances of haugbúi encounters without haugbrot in the Old Norse literature. Snorri Sturluson tells in *Heimskringla* (*Ynglinga saga*) that Óðinn used to wake up dead, buried men (p. 18). *Egils saga einhenda* tells how a certain Ásmundr at the funeral of his dead foster-brother stayed in the tomb for three nights of vigil over the dead body; there he is suddenly attacked by his undead friend (p. 338).[6] Waking up of dead haugbúar is not solely a literary motif. In the Norwegian Gulating law certain acts are forbidden as pagan, including "freista draugha up at ueckia æða haughbua" (pp. 326–327).

In the family sagas *Þorleifs þáttr* and *Þorsteins þáttr uxafóts* the undead haugbúi opens his own grave. This is also the case in another family saga, *Njáls saga*,

6 The episode is clearly a version of the same story as in Saxo's story about Asuitus and Asmundus. In *Egils saga* there is, however, no haugbrot in this context.

where the dead Gunnarr á Hlíðarenda appears in his open mound reciting stanzas (pp. 192–193). But this motif also occurs in two fornaldarsögur. Hervör in *Hervarar saga* comes to her father's mound, calling him to wake up. He opens the mound himself and gives the daughter his sword (p. 17). In *Göngu-Hrólfs saga* king Hreggviðr twice opens his mound and gives gifts to Hrólfr (pp. 203–205, 253–255). These three sagas show a common pattern in their haugbúi episodes. At least the last two episodes have often been described as haugbrot by scholars, but they differ in several respects clearly from the haugbrot-haugbúi episodes that were discussed initially. In *Njáls saga, Hervarar saga* and *Göngu-Hrólfs saga*, as well as in the dreams in *Þorleifs þáttr* and *Þorsteins þáttr uxafóts*, the haugbúi opens the mound himself, in a magic way; there is no one who breaks into the mound. Here the mound-dwellers are basically friendly disposed to the living visitors, not hostile as in the earlier cases. The Eddic poem *Helgakviða Hundingsbana II* tells how Helgi after death opens his mound and he and his widow Sigrún spend a night there (st. 42–51).

The encounter with the haugbúi in *Þorsteins þáttr bæjarmagns*, a saga which is difficult to classify generically, but rather should be linked to the konungasögur[7], differs on some points from the other cases. Jarl Agði has gone alive into his mound and later returns to the settlement – probably dead – and a little later he tries to harass his enemy Þorsteinn. When Agði returns to his mound the Christian Þorsteinn puts a cross on the door, and then Agði can never come out (p. 344). The episode is the only instance throughout the material of a haugbúi whose undead life is not primarily linked to his mound. He is one of the few haugbúar who leaves his grave in his physical form. His activities as an undead are to go to settled areas and terrorize and destroy. He is much more like the usual revenants in sagas like *Eyrbyggja saga* and *Laxdæla saga* than the haugbúar in *Harðar saga* etc.

Among the descriptions of haugbúi encounters without any haugbrot we have three instances from fornaldarsögur – *Hervarar saga, Göngu-Hrólfs saga, Egils saga einhenda.* But most of the instances, eight, are, even in this case, found in other genres: in family sagas like *Njáls saga, Þorskfirðinga saga, Þorleifs þáttr jarlsskálds* and *Þorsteins þáttr uxafóts*, in a kings' saga like *Heimskringla*, in a saga of no clear genre like *Þorsteins þáttr bæjarmagns*, in a Eddic poem like *Helgakviða*

7 This saga is sometimes considered a fornaldarsaga in modern works (but not in e.g. C.C. Rafn's original collection), but it is set during Óláfr Tryggvason's time and therefore does not meet the basic *fornǫld* criterion for a fornaldarsaga. It has been included in the group only with reference to certain alleged motif similarities with the fornaldarsögur – namely, the supernatural elements and above all the haugbúi motif. It would thus be fundamentally wrong in this context to include the saga among the fornaldarsögur and it would be a circular evidence to conclude that the case of *Þorsteins þáttr bæjarmagns* proves that this motif also occurs in the fornaldarsögur. One can not examine whether a specific motif occurs in the fornaldarsögur and in the same time include a saga in this group with the argument that it contains this specific motif.

Hundingsbana II, and in a legal work like Gulatingsloven. The connection with the fornaldarsaga genre is not striking here either.

To summarize: The motif in *Harðar saga* that has been described as a late and typical loan from the fornaldarsögur, haugbrot with haugbúi confrontation, was old and frequent in the Old Norse literature. It did not occur at all in the fornaldarsögur.

The motif in *Þorskfirðinga saga* which has been described as a typical loan from the fornaldarsögur, encounter in a dream with the undead haugbúi, was also old and well-known in the Old Norse literature. This motif too did not occur at all in the fornaldarsögur.

The haugbrot and haugbúi motifs in general were not typical of the fornaldarsögur either. The majority of the many cases were found in other Old Norse genres, mostly in "classical" sagas. The instances that occurred in the fornaldarsögur lacked all similarities with the episodes in *Harðar saga* and *Þorskfirðinga saga*.

It seems impossible to claim that *Harðar saga* and *Þorskfirðinga saga* are influenced by the written fornaldarsögur in their use of haugbrot and haugbúi motifs. These motifs are not late or "post-classical". The occurrence of the motifs cannot be used as an argument for dating them later than the alleged "classical" Íslendingasögur.

BIBLIOGRAPHY

Andrews, A. Le Roy (1909). [Notes to:] *Hálfs saga ok Hálfsrekka*, (Altnordische Saga-Bibliothek 14).

Beck, Heinrich (1978). *Haugbrot* im Altnordischen, *Zum Grabfrevel in vor- und frühgeschichtlicher Zeit*, (Eds.) Herbert Jankuhn et al. Göttingen, pp. 211–228.

Björn Sigfússon (1960). Gull-Þóris saga, *Kulturhistoriskt lexikon för nordisk medeltid* 5. Malmö.

Björn Sigfússon (1961). Harðar saga Grímkelssonar ok Geirs, *Kulturhistoriskt lexikon för nordisk medeltid* 6. Malmö.

Einar Ól. Sveinsson (1958). *Dating the Icelandic Sagas: An Essay in Method.* London.

Einar Ól. Sveinsson (1959). Fornaldarsögur Norðrlanda, *Kulturhistoriskt lexikon för nordisk medeltid*, 4, Malmö.

Faulkes, Anthony (1983). Introduction, *The Saga of Hord and the Holm-Dwellers.* (Tr.) Alan Boucher. Reykjavík.

Faulkes, Anthony (1993). Harðar saga, *Medieval Scandinavia: An Encyclopedia.*

Finnur Jónsson (1935). Harðar saga Grímkelssonar, *Arkiv för nordisk filologi* 51, pp. 327–345.

Hast, Sture (1960). [Introduction to:] *Harðar saga*, Editiones Arnamagnæanæ A 6, pp. 13–115.
Jónas Kristjánsson (1997). *Eddas and Sagas*. Reykjavík.
Rafn, C. C. (1829). Formáli, *Fornaldar sögur Norðrlanda*, 1. Copenhagen.
Sävborg, Daniel [forthcoming]. Klassiskt och efterklassiskt i Þorskfirðinga saga: Om relationen mellan fornaldarsagor och islänningasagor.
Schach, Paul (1985a). Harðar saga Grímkelssonar (ok Geirs), *Dictionary of the Middle Ages* 6. New York.
Schach, Paul (1985b). Gull-Þóris saga, *Dictionary of the Middle Ages* 6. New York.
Sigurður Nordal (1953). Sagalitteraturen, *Litteraturhistorie: Norge og Island.* (Nordisk kultur 8 B). Stockholm/Oslo/Copenhagen.
Vries, Jan de (1967). *Altnordische Literaturgeschichte* II. Berlin.

Bárðar saga Snæfellsáss. →*Harðar saga* etc.
Egils saga einhenda. →*Fornaldar sögur Norðurlanda* III.
Eyfirðinga sǫgur. (Ed.) Jónas Kristjánsson. (Íslenzk fornrit 9). Reykjavík 1956.
Eyrbyggja saga. (Eds.) Einar Ól. Sveinsson & Matthías Þórðarson (Íslenzk fornrit 4). Reykjavík 1935.
Flóamanna saga. →*Harðar saga* etc.
Fornaldar sögur Norðurlanda I–IV. (Ed.) Guðni Jónsson (Íslendingasagnaútgáfan). Reykjavík 1954.
Göngu-Hrólfs saga. →*Fornaldar sögur Norðurlanda* III.
Grettis saga Ásmundarsonar. (Ed.) Guðni Jónsson (Íslenzk fornrit 7). Reykjavík 1936.
Gulatingsloven. In *Norges gamle Love indtil 1387* I. (Eds.) R. Keyser & P.A. Munch. Christiania 1846.
Hálfs saga ok Hálfsrekka. →*Fornaldar sögur Norðurlanda* II.
Harðar saga etc. (Eds.) Þórhallur Vilmundarson & Bjarni Vilhjálmsson (Íslenzk fornrit 13). Reykjavík 1991.
Heimskringla I. (Ed.) Bjarni Aðalbjarnarson. (Íslenzk fornrit 26). Reykjavík 1941.
Helgakviða Hundingsbana II. In *Edda: Die Lieder des Codex Regius nebst verwandten Denkmälern.* (Eds.) Gustav Neckel – Hans Kuhn. Heidelberg 1962.
Hervarar saga. →*Fornaldar sögur Norðurlanda* II.
Íslendingadrápa. In *Den norsk-islandske skjaldedigtning.* B: *Rettet tekst* I. (Ed.) Finnur Jónsson. Copenhagen 1912.
Kjalnesinga saga etc. (Ed.) Jóhannes Halldórsson (Íslenzk fornrit 14). Reykjavík 1959.
Kumlbúa þáttr. →*Harðar saga* etc.
Landnámabók. In *Íslendingabók, Landnámabók.* (Ed.) Jakob Benediktsson. (Íslenzk fornrit 1). Reykjavík 1968.
Laxdœla saga. (Ed.) Einar Ól. Sveinsson (Íslenzk fornrit 5). Reykjavík 1934.
Legendary Olaf saga. In *Olafs saga hins helga: Die „Legendarische saga" über Olaf den heiligen (Hs. Delagard. saml. nr. 8 II).* (Eds.) Anne Heinrichs et al. Heidelberg 1982.

Ljósvetninga saga etc. (Ed.) Björn Sigfússon (Íslenzk fornrit 10). Reykjavík 1940.

Magnús Hákonarson's law. In *Norges gamle Love indtil 1387* II. (Eds.) R. Keyser & P.A. Munch. Christiania 1848.

Njáls saga. In *Brennu-Njáls saga*. (Ed.) Einar Ól. Sveinsson (Íslenzk fornrit 12). Reykjavík 1954.

Ragnars saga loðbrókar. →*Fornaldar sögur Norðurlanda* I.

Reykdœla saga. →*Ljósvetninga saga* etc.

Saxo Grammaticus, *Gesta Danorum: Danmarkshistorien* I–II. (Ed.) Karsten Friis-Jensen. Copenhagen 2005.

Sturlunga saga 1. (Eds.) Jón Jóhannesson et al. (Sturlunguútgáfan). Reykjavík 1946.

Viktors saga ok Blávus. In *Saga af Viktor ok Blávus: A Fifteenth Century Icelandic Lygisaga*. (Ed.) Allen H. Chappel. Mouton 1972.

Þórðar saga hreðu. →*Kjalnesinga saga* etc.

Þorleifs þáttr jarlsskálds. →*Eyfirðinga sǫgur.*

Þorskfirðinga saga. →*Harðar saga* etc.

Þorsteins þáttr bœjarmagns. →*Fornaldar sögur Norðurlanda* IV.

Þorsteins þáttr uxafóts. →*Harðar saga* etc.

L'Anse aux Meadows: Different Disciplines, Divergent Views

BIRGITTA WALLACE

ABSTRACT

The presence of the medieval Norse in North America has been hotly debated for more than 160 years. Work at L'Anse aux Meadows in northern Newfoundland by Anne Stine Ingstad in the 1960s furnished the first physical evidence of a Norse presence there *c.*AD 1000. Parks Canada added substantially to the evidence during excavations in the 1970s. Together with research in Iceland and Greenland the archaeology makes it possible to understand L'Anse aux Meadows within the context of the Vinland sagas. It is argued that L'Anse aux Meadows is Leif Eriksson's base in Vinland and the *Straumfjord* of Erik the Red's Saga. The Norse presence in North America was confined to exploration and exploitation of resources. Vinland lay around the coastal regions of the Gulf of St. Lawrence, stretching from L'Anse aux Meadows and the Strait of Belle Isle in the north and to New Brunswick in the south.

Keywords: Norse, L'Anse aux Meadows, Ingstad, Vinland, Newfoundland, Sagas, Leif Eriksson.

One thousand years ago, northern people from the Baltic in the east to Greenland in the west shared a language and many cultural traits. For a short while, this also included a small section of the Atlantic edge of North America. At this congress we are going to begin our journey of Viking settlements at this western edge of Viking expansion, in mysterious Vinland, vastly distant from its mother colony in Greenland, which was itself remote from the rest of the Viking world.

That Vinland lay somewhere in what is now called North America has been known since the Middle Ages, but it was not until the discovery and excavation of L'Anse aux Meadows in the 1960s and 1970s that the physical proof was at hand. But is L'Anse aux Meadows Vinland? No it is not *Vinland.* Vinland, like Helluland, Markland, Greenland and Iceland, was a large *region.* L'Anse aux Meadows is a *place*, hence it cannot be all of Vinland. The question then becomes: Is L'Anse aux Meadows *in* Vinland? Here opinions differ, mostly according to different disciplines. We will return to this later. First let us have a look at the site itself.

The L'Anse aux Meadows site is located in northernmost Newfoundland, at the edge of a peninsula extending to the north from the body of New-

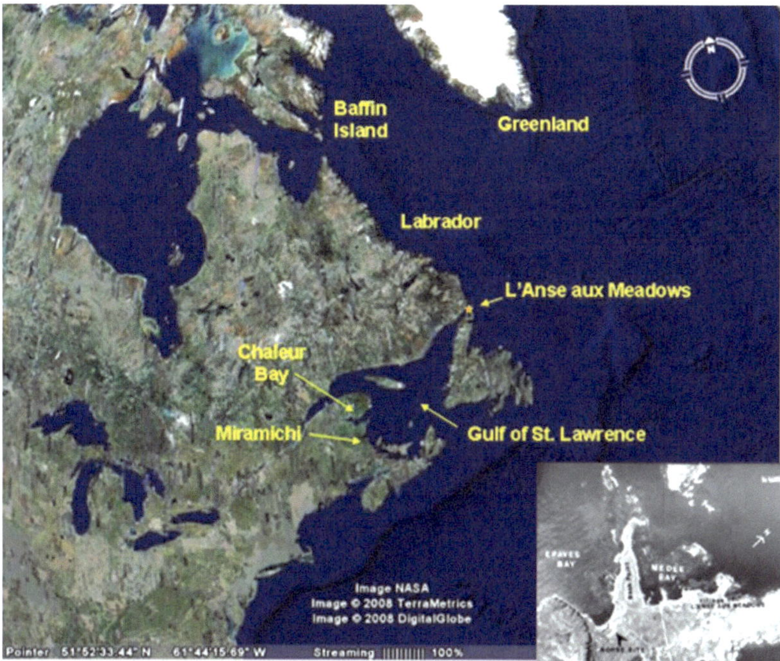

Fig. 1. Map of the Gulf of St. Lawrence and surrounding areas. Map based on Google Earth; insert on air photo showing the location of Epaves Bay and the L'Anse aux Meadows site, National Air Photo Library # 17543-55, Natural Resources Canada.

foundland, much like the pointing finger of a clutched fist (Fig. 1). The island of Newfoundland is slightly larger than Iceland. It is separated from the North American mainland by the Strait of Belle Isle, which, at its narrowest point is only 14 km wide. The site was discovered in 1960 by Helge Ingstad and excavated 1961 to 1968 by his wife Anne Stine Ingstad (A. S. Ingstad, 1977; A. S. Ingstad & H. Ingstad 1986). The Ingstad expeditions excavated the interior of eight buildings. The site was announced already at an early stage as the finding of Vinland (Fig. 2 – *New York Times* October 3, 1961; H. Ingstad, 1964). This evoked a storm of distrust. Similar claims had been made for over a hundred years, with all of them proven bogus. Contributing to the distrust was the fact that the site was so remote that few people could come and see for themselves. However, the Province of Newfoundland believed in the findings, appointing a caretaker[1] to protect them. He would guide the occasional visitor around the site where the excavated areas had been left open and covered with shelters in the style of Stöng.[2]

The site was declared a National Historic Site of Canada in 1969. It is administered by Parks Canada Agency, a government body that manages all National Parks and many of the National Historic Sites. An Inter-Scandinavian advisory committee[3] decided that additional excavations were needed to answer questions such as the function of the site, length of occupation, and relationship to native cultures. Anne Stine, having laboured on the site for seven years, declined leadership of these excavations, which came to be led by the Swedish archaeologist Bengt Schönbäck.

These excavations, which took place 1973-76, covered all the areas outside the buildings as well as large portions of other site areas.

I was fortunate to participate in the Ingstad excavations in 1964 and 1968, and I served as an assistant to Bengt during the first three seasons, becoming director when Bengt returned to Sweden in 1976. Since then the site has been one of my responsibilities at Parks Canada, even following retirement.

In 1964, when I first worked on the site, it lay at the end of the world. Going there was like going a century or more back in time. Electricity arrived only in 1974, telephones in 1975, and communication with the outside world was extremely limited.

.NYT Oct 3, 1961

TUESDAY,

'VIKING' RUINS DUG IN NEWFOUNDLAND

Norwegian Explorer Says Leif Ericson Settled in Remote Spot on Coast

5 SOD BUILDINGS FOUND

Excavations Indicate One Home Had a Great Hall—Carbon-14 Tests Due

By JOHN C. DEVLIN

A Norwegian explorer, Helge Ingstad, has discovered ruins on the northern tip of Newfoundland where he believes Vikings under Leif Ericson came to the North American Continent 500 years before Columbus.

Mr. Ingstad said the nearly buried ruins of seven "European-type" structures included one with a great hall in the Viking style. He said he believed Ericson, son of Eric the Red, had used this building as his home and headquarters in the period when he explored Vinland.

The ruins were found "a few miles west of Meade Bay" at a place shown on maps as Lance-aux Meadows, from the shoreline. It is an isolated area sometimes used by fishermen; there is no harbor nor bay. Mr. Ingstad said Viking ships were routinely hauled up on open beaches.

The discovery was made with the aid of the Icelandic Sagas and Newfoundland fishermen.

Bought 48-Foot Boat

Mr. Ingstad sailed from Norway on a Norwegian ship, bringing a forty-eight-foot motor sailer for his use. He, his wife and daughter sailed to the northern tip of Nefoundland in his boat, checking landmarks against descriptions in the sagas, inquiring as they went.

When fishermen told him they had been puzzled by the odd contours in the ground at Lance aux Meadows, Mr. Ingstad went

Fig. 2. New York Times October 3, 1961.

1 The caretaker was Lloyd Decker, son of George Decker who had made Helge Ingstad aware of the Norse ruins.

2 These shelters were removed 1973–1975 when it became obvious that they hastened the deterioration of the site.

3 The members of the committee consisted of Parks Canada directors and Helge and Anne Stine Ingstad as well as Sverre Marstander from Norway, Thór Magnússon from Iceland, Ole Crumlin Pedersen from Denmark, and Bengt Schönbäck from Sweden.

Fig. 3. The site, facing north. The building terrace is near the upper right corner. Photo by B. Wallace.

There was no road. I managed to get someone from a community 16 km away to take me in a boat. Although the day was beautiful, it was windy, and the boat owner did not want to round Cape Bauld, where waters can be dangerous. So he put me ashore about 10 km from the site, pointed across the moors and said, "L'Anse aux Meadows is that away" (Fig. 3).

In 1978 L'Anse aux Meadows became the first site to be declared a UNESCO World Heritage Site. Although situated 1000 km from St. John's, the capital of Newfoundland, the site is now easily accessible by road. It is open to visitors from June to mid-October and is visited yearly by *c.*30,000 people. It contains a visitor centre with a giftshop, guides, and archaeological displays. One Norse building complex has been reconstructed a short distance away from the actual archaeological remains.

The site lies about 100 m from the shore, facing the Labrador coast. It consists of four building complexes. Three are lined up on a narrow terrace, bordered by a slightly raised, "fluffy" sphagnum bog on its eastern side, and a funnel-shaped sedge peat bog to the west. The fourth complex is closer to the shore, at the bend of a brook cutting through the sedge peat bog. Its purpose was iron manufacture, which took place in an open-ended hut, cut into the steep brook bank. In its centre is a primitive low-shaft furnace. Nearby is a pit-shaped kiln for the making of charcoal (Fig. 4). A full-scale replica of the furnace hut was erected in 2001.

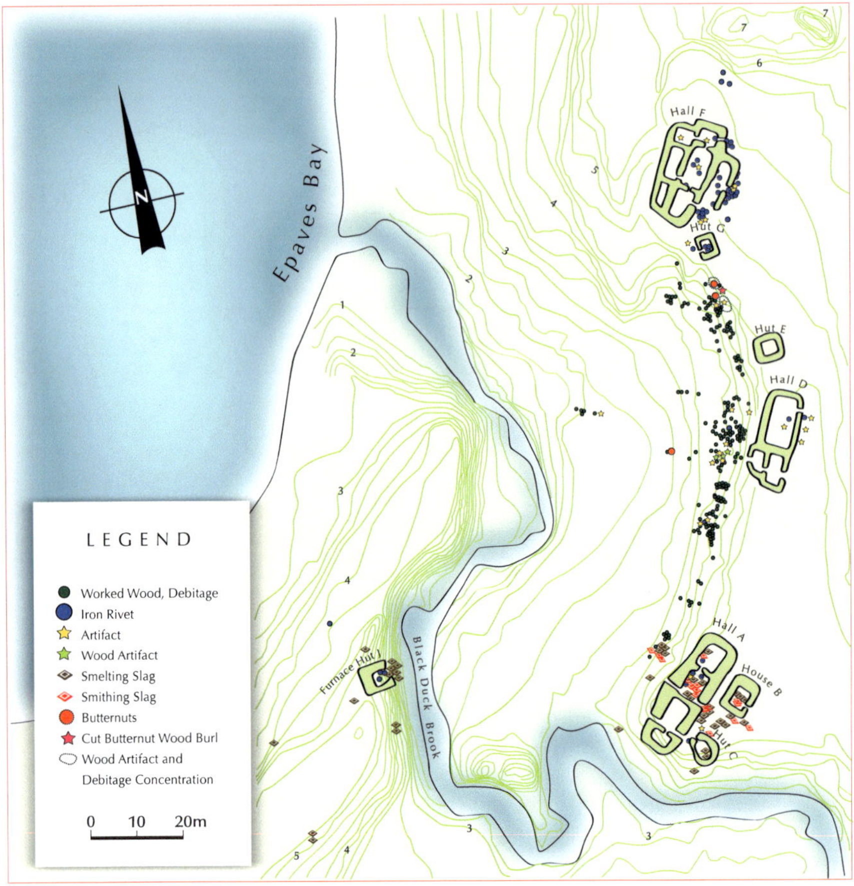

Fig. 4. Map of the site and the artifact distribution. Vis-à-Vis, Graphics, St. John's.

The site is on a shallow bay called Epaves Bay, which is a mix of French and English for Wreck Bay. A low cape extending northwest separates it from another, deeper bay called Medee Bay, which is French-English for Medea's Bay, named for the Greek goddess. This is where the modern village of L'Anse aux Meadows, founded in the 1830s, is located.

Pollen studies, chemical analyses and other botanical studies have shown that the vegetation had been much the same in the 11th century as today, that is primarily subarctic heath.[4] Although not clearly documented in the pollen,

4 For a summary of environmental studies made prior to 1976 at L'Anse aux Meadows see Gimbarzewsky, 1977. Later environmental studies are available in internal reports.

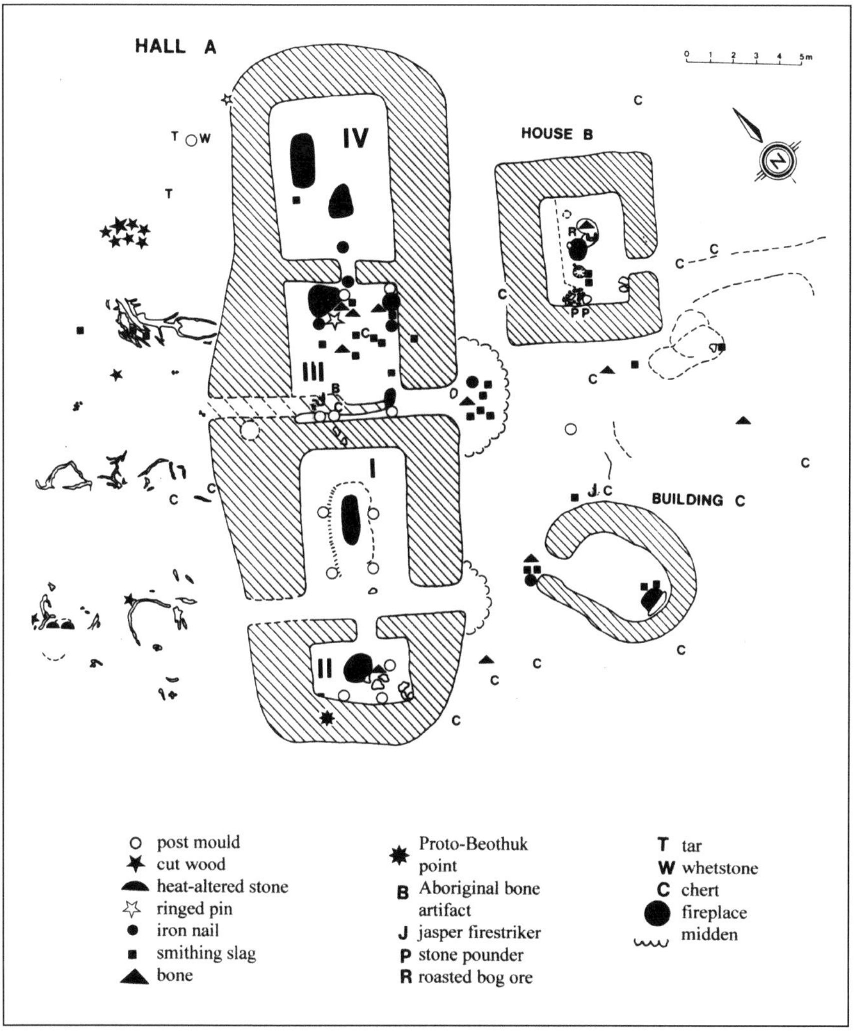

Fig. 5. Plan of the A-B-C complex. J. Gasparac & B.Wallace.

the area must have had nearby woods, primarily larch and Balsam fir. Area residents remember that stands of these woods were still present in the early 1900s.

What we have considered to be "normal" winters at L'Anse aux Meadows are winters with accumulations of up to 2 m of snow. Sea ice usually blocks the bays until June. A couple of unusual winters in 1998 and 1999 showed that this has not always been the case. During those two winters, the average temperature was about 2° C warmer than normal. To the surprise of everyone, there was no snow at all, and the sea ice was gone in April. Similar conditions with a relatively mild climate and low sea-ice incidence are thought to have been prevalent in the period AD 730 to 1100 (Astrid Ogilvie personal communication).

The Ingstads found mounds outlining the footprints of the buildings, in places rising as much as 35 cm above the ground. Three of them are large, multi-roomed halls. The smallest of the halls had a floor space of 89 m², almost twice the space in the presumed Eiríksstaðir in Haukadalur. The larger ones have floor spaces on par with what Orri Vésteinsson (2004, 74-75) has classified as Middle/High status halls. The thick walls had been of turf. Inner rows of posts had supported substantial roofs. The construction technique was the same in all of them. Huts flanking each hall were semi-subterranean, with thick built-up walls. Their floor space was minute compared to that of the halls. The smallest hut was irregularly rounded in shape. It had a fireplace, which suggests that it was intended for habitation. A small house next to this hut had only one room. It was considerably bigger than the huts but much smaller than the halls (Fig. 5).

The architecture of the buildings is clearly Icelandic and the same as the early buildings known from Brattahlíð in Greenland (cf. Albrethsen, 1982).

In the early excavations hardly any artifacts were found besides iron nail fragments, which led people to grumble that the site was probably a Portuguese or Basque whaling station (Mowat, 1965, 455-457). Then in 1964, Anne Stine asked me to dig a new trench by the largest of the halls. Working with me was a 16-year old American boy, Tony Beardsley, whose father had been instrumental in the protection of the site. It was Tony's first (and only) excavation, and he was very careful, asking me over and over again, 'Birgitta, is this anything?" My inevitable answer was, "No, Tony. That's a stone." The weather was miserable. We lived in double layers of sweaters and rain suits, and worked for the incentive of a hot cup of tea every two hours. When the afternoon was at its worst, Tony again held up something, asking if it was anything. This time my eyes widened. What he held in his hand was a soapstone spindle whorl, a flattened hemisphere type so common in the Viking Age. I called over to Anne Stine, "Anne Stine, *kom hit*!" She came, looked, and said, "*Er du gal*!" Whereupon we grabbed each other and danced around. Even if such a spindle whorl has a wide margin of dating, its clear association with the hall made it pretty certain that it was of Viking Age. Poor Tony did not know what had happened. He ran to our HQ shed telling the others that he had found something and that we were going crazy out there. Fortunately I had brought a bottle of aquavit so we could celebrate as soon as it was suitably cooled in the brook (Fig. 6).

Another even more exciting find was made four years later by Sigrid

Fig. 6. Anne Stine Ingstad in hall F in 1964. Photo by B. Wallace.

Kaland as she was brushing the walls of a firepit. As Anne Stine told it to me, an excited Sigrid called out to her, "Anne Stine, I am finding bronze!" "Oh no," said Anne Stine, "it is just a leaf." "No" insisted Sigrid, "it is bronze." And so it was. It was the now famous bronze pin, a Hiberno-Norse[5] type found primarily in Ireland and the Atlantic Norse area (Fanning, 1994, 34-36). An almost identical one was found in the 11th-century deposit on Fishamble Street in Viking Dublin (Fanning, 1994: Fig. 45).

The Parks Canada excavations[6] added some 2000 artifacts, about 600 of which were Norse, the rest from the five native cultures also present on the site. While most of the native artifacts are of stone, most of the Norse objects are of wood and were found in the sedge peat bog bordering the building terrace. The bog contained three distinct layers of wood, which we ingeniously termed the upper, middle and lower layers. The upper layer consisted mostly of

5 The term Norse used here is meant it in the broader sense of norroen. There is no other term for this concept in English.

6 All the Norse structures were excavated by the Ingstads. The Parks Canada excavations covered areas outside the buildings. The idea that Parks Canada removed the building remains is erroneous. With the exception of a couple of additional profiles through the walls, the Norse buildings remain as the Ingstads left them.

Fig. 7. Norse stratum in bog west of hall D. Facing west. Photo by R. Ferguson, 1976.

tree roots, with a sprinkling of small cut pieces of wood.[7] The lower layer was mostly trees which had died in situ as the bog formed, but among them were a few scattered cut or shaped pieces, including a harpoon shaft.[8] The middle layer consisted mostly of cut wood and discarded broken wood artifacts. This layer was thickest just outside the middle hall and clearly associated with it, as demonstrated by the radiocarbon dates. This was the Norse layer[9] (Fig. 7).

Putting together the results of the Ingstad and Parks excavations, certain idiosyncrasies became evident. The most striking was the artifact distribution. The artifacts form several distinct categories:

- A handful of small personal items such as the spindle whorl, the bronze pin, a needle sharpener, a glass bead, a broken bone pin or needle and the tiny fragment of a gilded and striated brass ring, the kind of pieces lost by their owners and never found again. There were also worn-out firestrikers of jasper. All of these were found in no particular pattern in and around the halls. The remaining four categories were all the result of particular work activities:
- Slag from iron manufacture. The iron production had been minimal, one single smelt, resulting in only about 15 kg of slag.

7 12 radiocarbon dates indicate that it developed from *c.*AD 1200-1500.

8 18 radiocarbon date the layer to *c.*1000-400 BC; the shank dates to 920±100 CalBC (S-1094).

9 Radiocarbon-dated to *c.*AD 1000 – see below.

- Slag from smithing, only about 1 kg.
- Wood waste from carpentry from cutting and shaping wood plus a few broken and discarded pieces, such as the split floorboard of a small boat, several treenails, pieces of rope made from spruce roots, a wooden lid, and pieces of unidentified use. A carved finial is of interest because it is of Scotch pine, a European species highly common in Scandinavia and North-Central Europe but not otherwise known from North America before the Colonial era.
- There were also about 80 boat rivets that had been snipped off and discarded.
- Each of the last four categories is associated with one particular complex (cf. Fig. 4). The smelting slag was found around the broken furnace in the open-ended hut in the brook bank. Most of the smithing slag came from one particular room in the southernmost hall. The carpentry waste lay in the bog below the middle hall. The boat rivets were found around a lean-to shed on the eastern side of the northern hall which is the largest and most complex building on the site. This shed also had the imprints of a frame to hold the boat in place, a strong-back, during repair. The boat in question would have been about 8 m long.

The work these categories represent was co-ordinated, each category contributing to the goal of boat repair. This co-ordinated distribution of the waste indicates that all three buildings were occupied at the same time.

There is little evidence of normal domestic activity. All the waste artifacts are associated with male work. From this, one may conclude that most occupants were men. However, women were present as shown by the spindle whorl, the needle hone and possibly the bone pin or needle. These are items usually representing female activities. The hone is a small item of quartzite with square cross-section, tapering towards the ends and no suspension hole, a type Else Roesdal (1977, 60, 133) has associated with women. The presence of a handful of women on an expedition is logical since house cleaning, cooking and clothing maintenance were primarily female tasks.

The house styles show that not everyone on the site was equal. This is not surprising. As stated by Orri Vésteinsson (1998, 261), the Icelandic economy was "geared towards equipping a chosen few with the means to eat, drink and show off". The two large halls are the dwellings of the elite, presiding over a large work force. The largest hall, which is also the most complex, was most logically for the leader of the expedition. The middle hall is more modest and housed fewer people. The small house is the kind used by tenants and workers on an estate (cf. Myhre, 1980, 392, 473). The sunken huts may have been work quarters,[10] but the small roundish hut, with its fireplace, was probably meant for slaves.

A few years ago lithic analyses were done by Kevin Smith (2000) in part sponsored by the Icelandic Ministry of Education, Science and Culture. He looked at 9 pieces of jasper fire strikers from the halls and 2 from Aboriginal features. Both the Aboriginal pieces were Newfoundland jasper. Of the other 9 all were Icelandic except for 4 in the largest hall. These were from Greenland, supporting the idea that the leader was Greenlandic, corroborating the Vinland sagas. Could this be the hall of Leif Eiríksson – providing of course that Leif Eiríksson was a historical figure? (Fig. 8).

Most of the floor area is living space, but there are also large storage rooms without organic deposits or features. The large food pantries found on most Icelandic farms are missing. The space could have accommodated between 60 and 90 people. This makes sense. Sending just a few individuals to a place as far away as L'Anse aux Meadows would not have been worth the investment, nor would it have been advisable for the sake of security.

In total there are 156 radiocarbon dates of which 56 pertain to the Norse establishment. The dates range all the way from the 7th century until the early 11th century. This was one of the first situations in which the effect of the wood age on radiocarbon dating was recognized. The stratigraphy made it obvious that the occupation was one single short episode, and yet the dates spanned about four centuries. The oldest date was obtained from the very centre of a spruce plank, a species that can become very old. It dated an early growth ring of the tree, not a fresh outer ring from the time it was cut down. Although dated to CalAD 640±90 BP (S-1092), it was closely associated with a young stem of Balsam fir, dated to CalAD 980±65 BP (S-1093) or the intercept date of AD 980. The most reliable dates are seven from small twigs which were very young when cut. All fall between about AD 990 and 1050, with a mean of AD1014.

The occupation was short, certainly not more than a decade. This is shown by

- The small size of the middens, the largest being 2 by 4 m and only 25 cm deep.
- Inside the houses, the cultural deposit is thin, with little more than charcoal and ashes from the fireplaces. Food remains are sparse, and there is a near-absence of domestic inventory.

10 Orri Vésteinsson's suggestion (2000, 168) that such huts may have been temporary quarters while the larger halls were constructed does not seem convincing, at least not at L'Anse aux Meadows. The construction of the three large halls would have required more people than could be accommodated in the small huts. It is more likely that tents or easily made *búðir* would have been used here during the construction.

Fig. 8. Hall F, facing south. The original building remains have been covered with new sod. Photo by R. Ferguson.

- And as stated previously, all the complexes were occupied at the same time, showing only one single settlement period.

The Norse were not the only occupants of the site. There were four native occupations before the Norse and one after them. Ecological data indicate that the shifts in cultures go hand in hand with climate (and presumably resource) changes (Wallace, 1989). It appears that there were no native people on the site during the time the Norse lived there.

Clearly, the site was not an attempt at colonization but a seasonal base for exploration. The absence of barns, byres or any structures associated with domestic animals and farming is striking. Of food bones, all are seal or whale, except for the vertebra of a very large cod. Two shoulder bones originally believed to be pig also appear to be seal. The Norse dependence on milk products makes it likely that at least some animals were brought, although no evidence of this was found.

The location of the site is unusual. It is in one of the most exposed spots in an area where more protected coves and harbours are nearby. Access to the sailing route through the Strait of Belle Isle appears to have been of greater importance than shelter and comfort, further indicating its connection with exploration.

The buildings are permanent structures, not seasonal *búðir.* Their solid construction, with walls more than 2 m thick, indicate that they were intended to be used throughout winter. They were built with care.

The most exciting finds on a site do not need to be spectacular artifacts. At L'Anse aux Meadows one of the most enlightening discoveries was the identification of three little nuts and a small burl of butternut wood. The burl had been cut with a sharp metal knife. The botanist doing the identification was amazed to find the nuts among the seeds submitted for identification. Butternuts, *Juglans cinerea*, are a North American variety of walnuts. They grow on high trees, require warm and long summers and are found primarily among stands of oak, maple, and other hardwoods. They do not grow north of eastern New Brunswick. Even the warmer temperatures of the 11th century would not have been enough for them to grow in Newfoundland. Nor are they native to nearby Nova Scotia and Prince Edward Island. They are not likely to have been brought in by currents as the currents reaching L'Anse aux Meadows are either from the north or other parts of Newfoundland (Farmer, 1981: Fig: 3-2). Furthermore, the nuts do not float for more than a short period, and they are too large to have been brought in by birds.

The implications of the nuts and wood burl are far-reaching. They show among other things that the Norse at L'Anse aux Meadows had visited regions at least as far south as eastern New Brunswick. This is fully 1000 km south of L'Anse aux Meadows. It clearly illustrates why the Norse required a winter base camp between Greenland and Vinland.

Walnuts were among the type of luxury food chieftains used to impress friends and foes (Elsner, n.d., 69). In Europe they do not grow north of Denmark, and yet are known to have been imported to Greenland where some were found at Brattahlíð (Nørlund & Stenberger, 1934).

The butternuts lead us to wine. They grow in exactly the same areas as wild grapes, in this case riverbank grapes, *Vitis riparia*. Northeastern New Brunswick is their northern limit in North America, and they grow in the same type of hardwood stands as the butternuts. Both butternuts and grapes ripen at the same time, in late September to early October. These river-bank grapes are quite sour and would not have made very good wine. This would not have been seen as a problem, however. After the Romans, Europeans did not have very good wine until the 17th century when proper seals were re-invented (Waugh et al., 1977, 14, 29).

Few aspects of the Vinland sagas have been so much discussed as the meaning of the name 'Vinland' and the concept of wine. Was Vinland pronounced with a short 'i' indicating the presence of pastures, or with a long 'i' meaning wine? Philologists consider the short 'i' and the meaning 'Grasslands' impossible (see e.g. Magnússon & Pálsson, 1965, 58–59; Wahlgren, 1969, 49–53;

Holm, 1997; Crozier, 1998).[11] Already Finnur Jónsson (1911–1912) pointed out that Vinland is even written with a long 'i' in Flateyjarbók.

As no grapes could ever have grown at L'Anse aux Meadows, even during the warmer temperatures of the 11th century, Helge Ingstad considered that the meaning 'Grasslands' made most sense, as livestock was the base of the Norse economy. However, L'Anse aux Meadows does not have much potential for grazing. The heath and grass there and in nearby coves are sufficient only for a few heads of cattle, sheep and goats, but they are not spectacular and were less so in the 11th century when most of the area was covered with dense forests. Besides, neither distant pastures nor new settlement areas were of interest to the 11th-century Greenlanders. Their colony was still in its settlement phase, with a work force barely sufficient to clear and maintain the pastures in the homeland.

The significance of the grapes cannot be overstated. Wine was not simply for pleasure. Norse Icelandic and Greenlandic societies were chiefdoms with prestige economies. Wine was associated with wealth, power and religious leadership. Ostentatious drinking and feasting ceremonies were means for exerting power. Wine was the type of luxury required for a chieftain to sustain his status. Both Erik and Leif were upstarts from *bændur* to chieftains. Wine, butternuts and fine lumber would serve their purpose well.

This is the archaeological interpretation of L'Anse aux Meadows. It is simple and relatively straight-forward. The big question: How does it relate to Vinland? is more problematic. The Vinland sagas have been studied for more than two centuries and can be read in many ways, according to one's perspective[12]. Early antiquarians viewed the Vinland sagas as accurate travelogues, which could be followed step by step as guides to Vinland. This view is now held primarily by Vinland enthusiasts in America. Although the late 19th-century historians P.A. Munch (1852-1859) and Gustaf Storm (1888) believed that the sagas contained a certain amount of myths, they saw them mainly as historical documents. Storm's work is still influential in this respect.

Fridtjof Nansen (1911) dismissed the Vinland sagas as legends inspired by Irish lore, such as The Tale of Moeldun's Voyage and The Voyage of St. Brendan. Vinland, with its wine, its self-sown wheat and its winters without snow, was Insula Fortunata, a mythical paradise in the western ocean. Nansen's views are once again winning adherents (cf. Keller, 2001, 79–85).

Literary historians have long argued that the Icelandic family sagas, including the Vinland sagas, are more creative art than history, based on inspiration from the European continent (Clover, 1982, 41). To the extent that they

11 The assertions by historians (Stefánsson, 1997; E. Lönnroth, 1997) that the 'i' was meant to be short do not carry the same weight.

12 For a more in-depth discussion see Ólason, 2001 and Wallace, 2009.

represent any historical reality, that reality would lie in the 13th and 14th centuries, not in the Viking Age (Nordal, 1953; Kristjánsson, 1988). Vésteinn Ólason (1998) has pointed out that we see the sagas through a double filter: the 10th century from the point of view of the 13th-century, and the 13th-century from a modern point of view.

From the folklore point of view, Gísli Sigurðsson (2004) has shown that the sagas are not straight-forward recordings of events but that there is reality behind them. They represent flexible oral traditions, told for specific purposes. Gísli has pointed out that only when we understand the essence of oral traditions can we begin to sort out what may be the historical core. As long as the traditions remained oral, they were in a constant state of flux, changing from one recitation to another, according to the audience and occasion. Old material was mixed with new, and subject to the interests of those in control – or what was topical at that particular moment. A well-known parallel is the Roskilde ship barrier which oral tradition associated with Queen Margrethe because her fame eclipsed earlier events to which it was actually related (Olsen & Crumlin Pedersen, 1969, 10–11). Joe Allard (2002) has compared the flexibility of the oral tradition to a jazz performance, which, although based on a general theme, contains individual improvisation, as opposed to a classical symphony adhering to a score.

Historians and others have also demonstrated that specific purposes affected the *content* of the sagas. Such a flexibility goes a long way towards reconciling the discrepancies between the Saga of the Greenlanders (hereafter GS) and Erik the Red's Saga (hereafter ES). Ólafur Halldórsson (2001) has pointed out that the motive for the ES version was glorification of the descendants of Gudrid and Thorfinn Karlsefni. Consequently Leif's role is reduced to that of accidental discoverer, and Karlsefni takes over, describing the expedition under his guidance as the only successful Vinland expedition.

As an archaeologist I would argue that with L'Anse aux Meadows we have in fact the key to the sagas. The archaeological findings give us a direct line to the real material world of 11th-century Norsemen temporarily settled in an establishment far from home. And this world has much in common with the world of the Vinland sagas: ES tells of a winter base at Straumfjord in the north and a summer settlement, Hóp, in the south. At this latter site, grapes were collected. In the GS, the winter and summer settlements have been combined into one, Leifsbúðir, with elements of both Straumfjord and Hóp. From the archaeological evidence, we can equate L'Anse aux Meadows with the base at Straumfjord, while Hóp probably lay in the resource-rich area of eastern New Brunswick where grapes grow wild. L'Anse aux Meadows, with its winter houses and large storage spaces, is indeed a base for the collection of resources to be brought back to Greenland, the same function as that of Leifsbúðir/

Straumfjord. This is a nearly universal model for the first stage of emigration into new areas where resources are exploited for the parent community (Anthony, 1990). The profit motivation is clearly stated in both sagas (Wallace, 2003, 214–215). Lumber formed the major part of the goods brought back to Greenland. Although the L'Anse aux Meadows area abounded in evergreens and birch, it is clear that the occupants visited areas of large richer hardwood forests. By the same token, the sagas do not tell of farming families settling in, but of labour crews contracted separately for each voyage, as spelled out in both sagas.

Both the sagas and the archaeological evidence indicate the presence of a male work force. In both there are a few women for female chores. And both show evidence of social ranking. The size of the saga expeditions is compatible with the number of people who could be accommodated at L'Anse aux Meadows. According to the sagas, living quarters were first *búðir*, later transformed into *skálar* or *hús*, when they decided to stay the winter[13]. Even though livestock was brought, no structures are mentioned for the animals.

Physical descriptions in the sagas can be made, and have been made to fit almost anywhere along the Atlantic seaboard. Still, the tall grass, islands, birds and whales of ES can certainly apply to L'Anse aux Meadows. The narrow Strait of Belle Isle is very much a fjord with a peculiar set of currents surrounding Belle Isle in the middle. The rapid Labrador Current coming in from the north collides with currents from the Gulf of St. Lawrence rushing in from the south, causing flows in several directions around the island, creating Straumfjord, the "Fjord of Currents". As for Hóp to the south, eastern New Brunswick is known for its long, protective sandbars along the entire coast and the warm sheltered tidal lagoons and rivers behind them.[14] Butternuts and grapes grow along the Miramichi River and in Chaleur Bay. This is a rich area, with large hardwood forests, inviting meadows, grapes and walnuts, similar to southern Europe and very different from northern Newfoundland, Greenland and Iceland.

Although the wine of Vinland may well be a universal symbol for paradise, it cannot be disputed that the Norse at L'Anse aux Meadows did observe grapes first-hand. Another matter, often overlooked in the discussion, that speaks for the discovery of grapes being based on physical observation, is the fact that the sagas speak of *vínvið* and felling trees on which the grapes grew. Wild grapes do not grow on low vines, as in the vineyards of medieval Europe, but in woods among trees. There they wind themselves up the tree trunks, looking indeed

[13] The terms *skálar* and *hús* here obviously refer to something more substantial than *búðir.*

[14] The sagas' statement that when the tide was out "their ship was soon stranded and the sea looked far away to those aboard ship" (*The Complete Sagas of Icelanders* I, 22) does not necessarily imply tidal differences as drastic as those in the Bay of Fundy, as has been suggested by many.

like grape trees. In the Miramichi and Chaleur Bay area, these include valuable lumber such as oak and maple (Fig. 9).

Eastern New Brunswick also harboured the densest populations of native people in Atlantic Canada, the ancestors of today's Mi'kmaq.

The description of native canoes gives a parameter for how far south the Norse could have gone. The Mi'kmaq used canoes from moose and deer skin (Wallis & Wallis, 1955), as well as birch bark. Canoes were rarely used south of central Maine, and not at all south of Boston, where dugouts were common (Snow, 1978; Salwen, 1978). This all but rules out New England as a place for Hóp.

Aside from closely fitting the sagas' model of Straumfjord, L'Anse aux Meadows is too substantial and complex to be a site *not* mentioned in the sagas. The construction itself represented a significant investment. It would have taken a labour crew of sixty about two months to build the whole settlement (Wallace, 2005, 31). This is the better part of a summer.

On the basis of L'Anse aux Meadows, I suggest that Vinland is the coastal areas around the Gulf of St. Lawrence, and the islands inside it. The location of L'Anse aux Meadows directly on the Strait and not on the more sheltered eastern side of the peninsula, indicates that the focus was on access to the Gulf. The map gives an idea of how the Strait of Belle Isle is literally a funnel into the Gulf for anyone arriving from the north along the coast. This leads me to suggest that L'Anse aux Meadows is Straumfjord in the north, and that Hóp is to the south, in the Miramichi or Chaleur Bay areas of eastern New Brunswick

L'Anse aux Meadows was abandoned after about a decade. Again the accordance with the sagas, which say that the Vinland voyages stopped after just a few years, is undeniable. So why did L'Anse aux Meadows and the Vinland experiment fail? There are reasons:

- The distance from Greenland. The sailing season was short, from June to October, even assuming that the sea ice was less than today.
- From Brattahlíð in Greenland it is almost 2500 km to New Brunswick where the wine and good lumber were. That is, if one sails in a straight line, which of course a sailing ship cannot do over such a distance. It was actually much farther to New Brunswick than to Norway. It was also more difficult as the Norse could not determine longitude.[15]
- Vinland had grapes and timber, but the Norse could get that in Europe. Vinland, on the other hand, lacked other essentials: luxury metals, spic-

15 To determine longitude, it is necessary to have an accurate clock or chronometer to establish the time of a known fixed location. Reasonably accurate clocks were not made until the 17th century, and accurate marine chronometers were not available until the mid-18th century.

Fig. 9. The Miramichi River in New Brunswick about 30 km from the estuary. Hardwoods dominate the area. Photos by R. Ferguson.

es, fine textiles, weapons, and armour – and family, political, religious, and personal connections.

- Unlike Iceland and Greenland, Vinland also had large native populations, and the Norse were not ready to stand up to them.

The most important reason was the small size of the Greenland settlement. According to current calculations, Greenland at the beginning of the 11th century probably had no more than about 500 inhabitants (Lynnerup, 1998, 116–118; 2003). Another distant settlement of the magnitude of L'Anse aux Meadows would not have been a likely option for such a small colony, especially as lumber could be had at a closer range. Furthermore, at this time Greenlanders did not *need* more land. The Viking settlements had reached their western limit.

BIBLIOGRAPHY

Albrethsen, S. E. (1982). Træk af den norrøne gårds udvikling på Grønland. In AmS Skrifter 7, Myhre, B., B. Stoklund & P. Gjærder (Eds.), *Vestnordisk byggeskikk gjennom to tusen år. Tradisjon og forandring fra romertid til det 19. århundre* (pp. 269-287). Stavanger: Arkeologisk museum.

Allard, J. (2002). Oral to Literary: *Kvöldvaka*. Textual Instability, and All That Jazz.

Sagas and Societies. International Conference at Borgarnes, Iceland, September 5–9, 2002. Retrieved from http://w210.ub.uni-tuebingen.de/portal/sagas

Anthony, D. (1990). Migration in Archaeology: The Baby and the Bathwater. *American Anthropologist*, 92, (4), 895–914.

Clover, C. J. (1982). *The Medieval Saga*. Ithaca, NY: Cornell University Press.

The Complete Sagas of Icelanders. (1997). Hreinsson, V. (Gen. Ed.); R. Cook, T. Gunnell, K. Kunz, B. Scudder (Ed. team), 1–5. Reykjavík: Leifur Eiríksson Publishing.

Crozier, A. (1998). The Vinland Hypothesis. A reply to the historians. *Gardar*, XXIX (1998), 37–66.

Elsner, H. (n.d). *Wikinger Museum Haithabu: Schaufenster einer frühen Stadt*. Schleswig: Archäologisches Landesmuseum der Christian Albrechts Universität.

Fanning, Th. (1994). Viking Age Ringed Pins from Dublin. *Medieval Dublin Excavations 1962–8*, Series B, (4). Dublin: Royal Irish Academy.

Farmer, Geoffrey H. (1981). The Cold Ocean Environment of Newfoundland. In MacPherson, A. G. & MacPherson, J. B. (Eds.), *The Natural Environment of Newfoundland, Past and Present* (pp. 56–82). St. John's: Memorial University of Newfoundland.

Gimbarzevsky, Ph. (1977). *L'Anse aux Meadows National Historic Park Integrated Survey of Biophysical Resources.* Information Report FMR-X-99, Forest Management Institute. Ottawa.

Halldórsson, Ólafur (2001). The Vínland Sagas. In Wawn, A. & Þ. Sigurðardóttir (Eds.), *Approaches to Vínland. Proceedings of a conference on the written and archaeological sources for the Norse settlements in the North-Atlantic region and exploration of America, held at The Nordic House, Reykjavík 9–11 August 1999*, (pp. 39–51). Reykjavík: Sigurður Nordal Institute.

Holm, G. (1997). Vinland: 'Vinrankornas land', *Gardar* 28, (1997), 47–53.

Ingstad, A. S. (1977). *The Discovery of a Norse Settlement in America: Excavations at L'Anse aux Meadows, Newfoundland, 1961–1968.* Oslo: Universitetsforlaget. Reissued 1986 as Ingstad, Anne Stine & Helge Ingstad, 1986, *The Norse Discovery of America*. Vols. I and II. Oslo: Norwegian University Press.

Ingstad, H. (1964). Vinland Ruins Prove Vikings Found the New World. *National Geographic*, Vol. 126, No. 5, 1964, 708–734. Washington, D.C.: National Geographic Society.

Jakobsson, S. (2001). 'Black Men and Malignant-Looking': The Place of Indigenous Peoples in North America in the Icelandic World View. In Wawn, A. & Þ. Sigurðardóttir (Eds.) *Approaches to Vinland* (pp. 88–104). Reykjavík: Sigurður Nordal Institute.

Jónsson, F. (1911–1912). Erik den rødes saga og Vinland. *Historisk Tidsskrift*, 5:1, 116–147. Kristiania.

Keller, Chr. (2001). Vinland etter Ingstad. In Hagland, J. R. & S. Supphellen (Eds.). *Leiv Eriksson, Helge Ingstad og Vinland. Kjelder og tradisjonar. Innlegg ved eit seminar i regi av Det Kongelige Norske Videnskabers Selskab 13–14 oktober*

2000, (pp. 67–90). Det Kongelige Norske Videnskabers Selskab, Skrifter 1. Trondheim: Tapir Akademisk Forlag.

Kristjánsson, J. (1988). *Eddas and Sagas: Iceland's Medieval Literature.* Reykjavík: Hið íslenzka bókmenntafélag.

Lönnroth, E. (1996). The Vinland Problem. *Scandinavian Journal of History*, 21 (1), 39–47.

Lynnerup, N. (1998). The Greenland Norse: A Biological-Anthropological Study. *Meddelelser om Grønland, Man and Society*, 24. Copenhagen.

Lynnerup, N. (2003). A Paleodemography of the Greenland Norse. Pp. 133–144. In S. Lewis-Simpson (Ed.), *Vinland Revisited: the Norse World at the Turn of the First Millennium, selected Papers from the Viking Millennium International Symposium, 15–24 September 2000*, Newfoundland and Labrador, St. John's: Historic Sites Association of Newfoundland and Labrador.

Magnússon, M. & H. Pálsson. (1965). *The Vinland Sagas. The Norse Discovery of America.* Hammondsworth, Middlesex, U.K.: Penguin Books.

Mowat, F. (1965). *Westviking. The Ancient Norse in Greenland and North America.* Boston and Toronto: Little, Brown and Company.

Munch, P. A. (1852–1859). *Det norske folks historie*, 1–8. Christiania: Chr. Tønsbergs Forlag.

Myhre, B. (1980). *Gårdsanlegget på Ullandhaug I. Gårdshus i jernalder og tidlig middelalder i Sørvest-Norge. AmS Skrifter* 4. Stavanger: Arkeologisk museum i Stavanger.

Nansen, F. (1911). *In Northern Mists. Arctic Exploration in Early* Times 1–2. Translated by A. G. Chater. New York, NY: F.A. Stokes Co.

Nordal, S. (1953). Sagalitteraturen. *Nordisk Kultur* VIII:B, Litteraturhistorie. B. Norge og Island. pp. 180–273.

Nørlund, P. & M. Stenberger (1934). Brattahlid. Researches into Norse Culture in Greenland. *Meddelelser om Grønland*, 88, (1). Copenhagen.

Ólason, V. (2001). Sagatekstene – forskningsstatus. In Hagland, J. R. & S. Supphellen (Eds.), *Leiv Eriksson, Helge Ingstad og Vinland. Kjelder og tradisjonar*, (pp. 41–64). Trondheim: Tapir Akademisk Forlag.

Ólason, V. 1998. *Dialogues with the Viking Age: Narration and Representation in the Sagas of the Icelanders.* Translation by Andrew Wawn. Reykjavík: Heimskringla, Mál og Menning Academic Division.

Olsen, O. & O. Crumlin Pedersen. (1969). *Fem vikingeskibe fra Roskilde Fjord.* Roskilde: Vikingeskibshallen.

Pálsson, H. (2000).Vinland Revisited. *Northern Studies. The Journal of the Scottish Society for Northern Studies* 35, 11–38.

Roesdahl, E. (1977). Fyrkat. En jysk vikingeborg. II. Oldsagerne og gravpladsen. *Nordiske Fortidsminder,* Serie B (4). Copenhagen: Det kongelige nordiske Oldskriftselskab.

Salwen, B. (1977). Indians of Southern New England and Long Island. In *Handbook* *of North American Indians.*15: Northeast. Sturtevant, W.C. (Gen. Ed.), Trigger, B. (Vol. Ed.). (Pp. 160–76).

Sigurðsson, G. (2004). *The Medieval Icelandic Saga and Oral Tradition. A Discourse on Method*. Publications of the Milman Parry Collection of Oral Literature No. 2. Translated by Nicholas Jones. Cambridge, Massachusetts: The Milman Parry Collection of Oral Literature, Harvard University.

Smith, K. P. (2000). Jasper Cores from L'Anse aux Meadows. In Fitzhugh, W.W. & E. I. Ward (Eds.), *Vikings. The North Atlantic Saga*, Washington, D.C.: Smithsonian Institution Press and National Museum of Natural History.

Snow, D. R. (1977). Late Prehistory of the East Coast. In Sturtevant, W. C. (Gen. Ed), Trigger, B. (Vol. Ed.), *Handbook of North American Indians*, 15: Northeast. (Pp. 58–69).

Stefánsson, M. (1997). Vinland or Vínland. *Scandinavian Journal of History*, 23, 3–4.

Storm, G. (1888). Studier over Vinlandsreiserne, Vinlands geografi og ethnologi. *Aarbøger for nordisk Oldkyndighed og Historie* 1988, 293–372. Copenhagen.

Vésteinsson, O. (2000). The Archaeology of *Landnám*. Early Settlement in Iceland. In Fitzhugh, W.W. & E.I. Ward (Eds.), *Vikings. The North Atlantic Saga*. (Pp. 164–174). Washington, DC: Smithsonian Institution Press and National Museum of Natural History.

Vésteinsson, O. (2004). Icelandic farmhouse excavations: Field Methods. *Archaeologica Islandica* 3, 71–100.

Vésteinsson, O. (1998). Patterns of Settlement in Iceland: A Study in Prehistory. *Saga-Book*, XXV (1) (1998), 1–29.

Wahlgren, E. (1969). Fact and Fancy in the Vinland Sagas. In Polomé, E. C. (Ed.), *From Old Norse Literature and Mythology: A Symposium*. Austin, Texas: University of Texas Press.

Wallace, B. (1989). *The Native Occupations at L'Anse aux Meadows*. Unpublished manuscript, National Historic Parks and Sites. Halifax, NS: Environment Canada-Canadian Parks Service, Atlantic Region.

Wallace, B. (2003). L'Anse aux Meadows and Vinland, An Abandoned Experiment. In Barrett, J. (Ed.), *Contact, Continuity and Collapse: The Norse Colonisation of the North Atlantic*. (Pp. 207–238). Studies in the Early Middle Ages. Turnhout, Belgium: Brepols Publishers.

Wallace, B. (2005). The Norse in Newfoundland: L'Anse aux Meadows and Vinland. *Newfoundland Studies* 19, 1 (2003), 5–43. St. John's, NL.

Wallace, B. (2009). L'Anse aux Meadows, Leif Eriksson's Home in Vinland. *Journal of the North Atlantic*, Special volume 2, Selected Papers from the Hvalsey Conference 2008.

Wallis, W. D. & R. Sawtell Wallis. (1955). *The Micmac Indians of Eastern Canada*. Minneapolis, MN: University of Minnesota Press.

Waugh, A. & the Editors of Time-Life Books. (1977). *Wines and Spirits*. Foods of the World. New York: Time-Life Books.

The Archaeology of Rimbert The Churches of Hergeir and Gautbert and Borg in Birka

TORUN ZACHRISSON

ABSTRACT

In *Vita Anskarii,* Rimbert describes the Christian mission to the port of the Swedes in the 830s. He mentions two churches there, one built on the family estate of the port bailiff, the other built in the seaport itself by Bishop Gautbert. The locations of these churches have long been discussed. Thanks to archaeological research excavations it is possible to offer a new suggestion regarding the church of Gautbert. It is argued that the hillfort of Birka, Borg, may be the site of this church and the bishop's fortified precinct. This would make the Viking Age town Birka structurally similar to a number of contemporaneous cities on the Continent, where there was a fortified cathedral hill and a market town at its foot. 9th century finds in and around Borg open up for such a possibility.

Keywords: Birka, Helgö, Christian mission, church, town plan, Gautbert, Hergeir, earls, town rampart.

The Birka mission began in 829 when Ansgar, accompanied by Witmer, arrived in a port city in the Swedish kingdom, *portus regni* (*Boken om Ansgar*: note 126). Emperor Louis the Pious had opted for a nationwide religious mission directed against the Scandinavian kingdoms, perhaps in response to inquiries received by the Nordic kings Harald and Björn (*Boken om Ansgar*, ch 7 and 9, note 105). Ansgar's first trip was a part of those procedures. He stayed in Birka for one year and a half.

In Birka there were already many Christian prisoners. Others became interested in the Christian faith. The bailiff of the town Hergeir agreed to be baptized a Christian. Shortly "thereafter he built a church on his estate …" (*Boken om Ansgar*, 28, note 134). Rimbert does not give us any information as to where this estate was situated, but it ought to have been in the vicinity of Birka.

According to Rimbert, Hergeir became 'praefectus vici', which the latinist Eva Odelman who has translated Vita Ansgarii, interprets as the bailiff of the site (*Boken om Ansgar*, note 132). Literally, this would have been the bailiff of the town. Hergeir was highly appreciated by, and advisor to the king, *consiliarus regis* (see note 132). The title *praefectus* is translated consistently with the bailiff, the king's overseer, and trustee of Birka (see *Boken om Ansgar*, note 132), but *jarl* – earl – might have been what Hergeir would have been called by his contemporaries.

In the Danish sources earls are first mentioned in the 15th century, and before that, the earls are probably hidden behind the Latin expressions *praefectus* and *comes*, as well as *dux* and *custos* (Nielsen, 1962, 565). In the Norse texts it is hinted that there were several contemporaneous earls in Sweden linked to different regions, although in the Swedish sources the earl of the Svear is only one at a time (Jerker Rosén, 1962). The Swedish sources mention earls in different contexts from the 1100s; for example, Ulf Jarl Gamle and Guttorm jarl, men from different aristocratic families (Rosén, 1962, 563, cf Ståhle, 1949). Peter Sawyer is of a different opinion. During the Viking Age and early Middle Ages the position of earls can best be illustrated by the Norwegian earls of Lade, local independent rulers who were subordinate to another ruler's sovereignty (Sawyer, 1991, 10).

HERGEIR'S ESTATE AND CHURCH

Rimbert's text states that Hergeir erected a church on his hereditary property, *hereditas* (Arbman, 1939, 35). Wilhelm Holmqvist, the leader of the Helgö excavations, thought that this might be identical to the settlement on Helgö (Fig. 1), situated 9 km by waterway from Birka (Holmqvist, 1980, 60). In the hall of the central building group, objects had been found that Holmqvist interpreted as the physical remains of a Christian congregation on the island (Holmqvist, 1969a, 179–181; 1969b). The objects are spectacular: an Irish crozier, a Coptic ladle, a silver bowl with cruciform decoration, used when celebrating the Mass, and a bell cover (Holmqvist, 1980, 60).

The objects were found on the same terrace where around 20 gold foil figures, guldgubbar, also had been found (see Fig. 2). Holmqvist saw this as a sign of the continuity of the cult in a hall building (1980, 59). On Kristina Lamm's distribution maps the guldgubbar, as well as most of the broken glass, the beakers and vessels, were found in the building called 1A. The Christian objects, however, were all found in another building called 1B (K. Lamm, 2004, 10, 53 f, Fig. 8 and 9). Probably, they were not found in the same hall building as Holmqvist thought, but in two separate buildings (Figs. 3 and 4).

Åke Hyenstrand had a similar idea to Wilhelm Holmqvist, but suggested that the Christian objects on Helgö would have come from the church that Gautbert erected (1988, 70 f; 1996, 118 f). This seems to me less likely. There is nothing in Rimbert's text suggesting that Gautbert's church was built elsewhere than in Birka. And Rimbert clearly states that Hergeir's church was

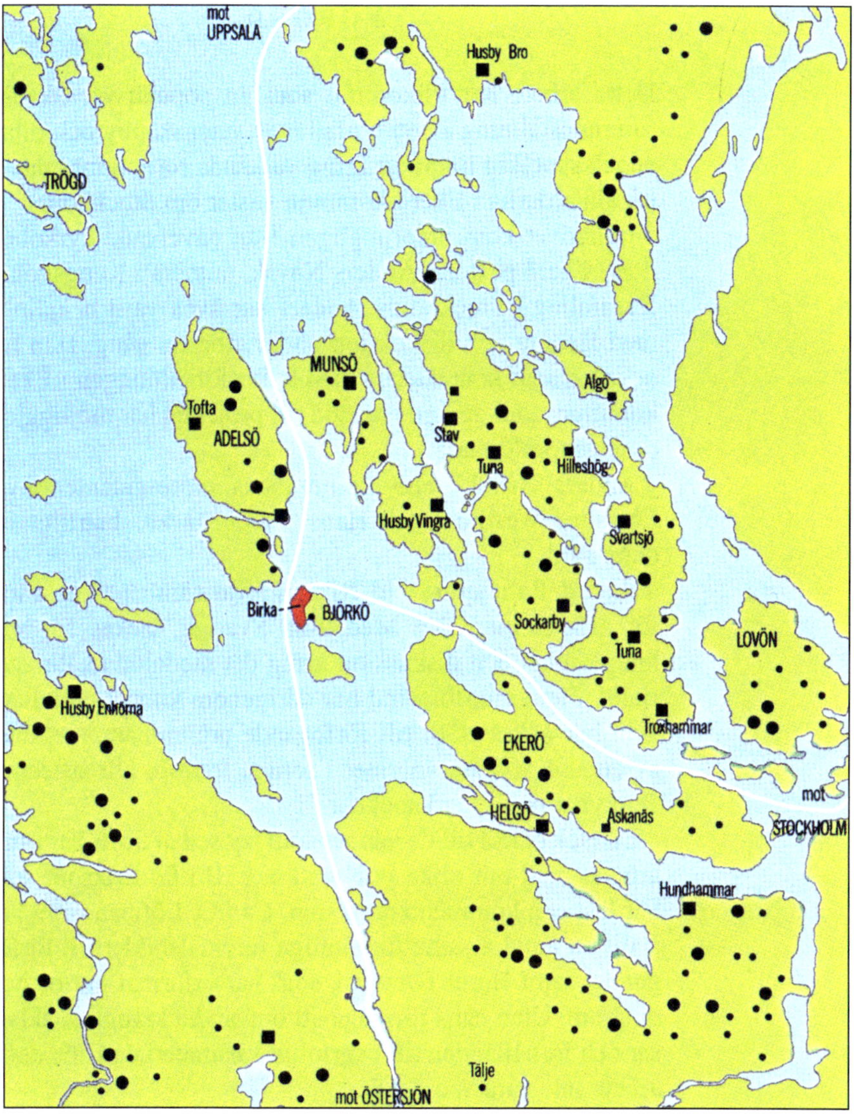

Fig. 1. The region Mälaröarna with Viking Age shoreline and Late Iron Age settlements and graves. Map: Björn Ambrosiani (2002, 6).

Fig. 2. The main settlement of Helgö. The hall building with the guldgubbar is in the centre of the picture. (Drawing: Mats Vänehem, Stockholm County Museum, following instructions by Kristina Lamm & Torun Zachrisson).

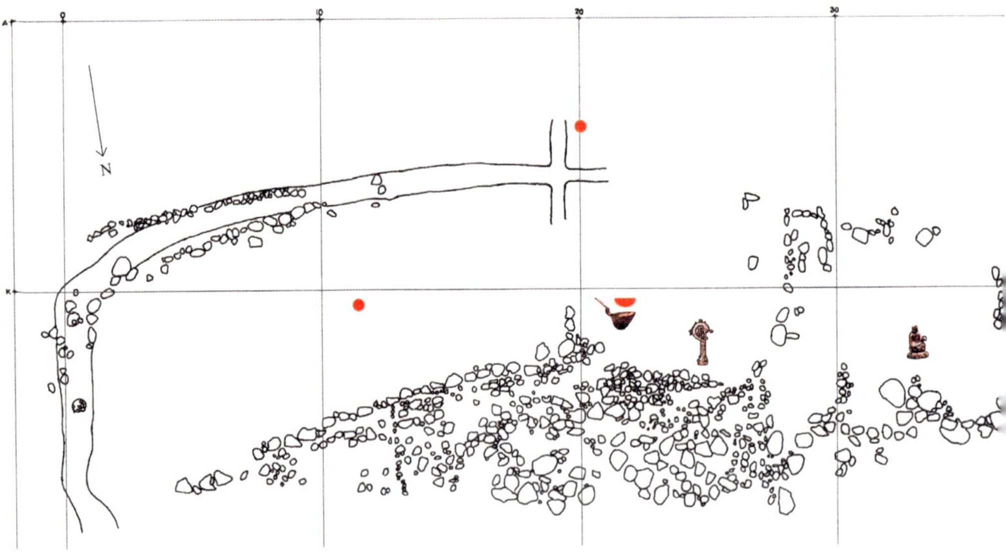

Fig. 3. The building, IB, with liturgical character, ladle, crozier and crescent showing silver bowl (circles are bracteate, by K. Lamb, 2004, 10).

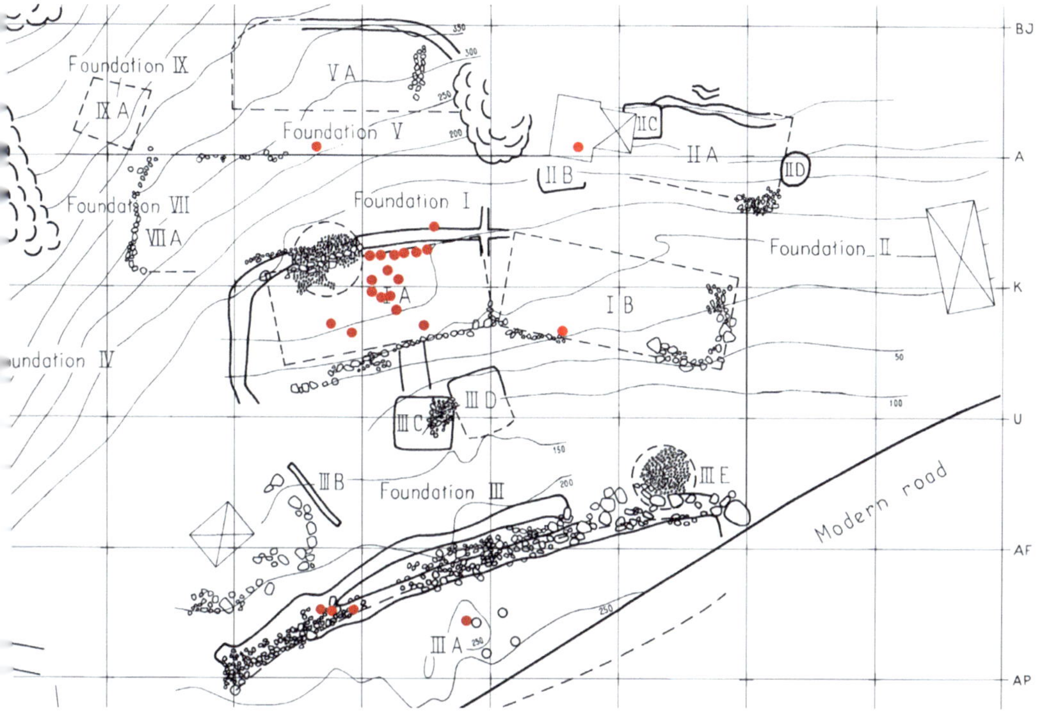

Fig. 4. The earlier representation hall IA with the finds of gold foil figures marked (K. Lamb, 2004, 52).

built on his hereditary property. Adam of Bremen (IV, 20) uses the term Birka concerning the town itself, but also with a broader geographic meaning referring to the Birka diocese that Bishop Adalbert wanted to establish, where Birka would be a metropolis for the people of the surrounding regions (Nyberg, 1984, 337 ff; Hallencreutz, 1984, 377 f, cf Holmquist Olausson, 1993, 34 f). In my opinion, this Birka Concept with its extended meaning relates to another time, the 11th century, and is not mirroring the time period that Rimbert depicts (Hallencreutz, 1984, 377).

Wilhelm Holmqvist imagined that the crozier found on Helgö could have been Ansgar's. The first bishop in Bremen was English, Willehad. He could very possibly have had a crozier like the one found on Helgö. The crozier would then have been given via Ansgar to Hergeir who was the king's representative at Birka. Furthermore, Ansgar looked upon him as his spiritual son, since he had baptized him (Holmqvist, 1980, 60; *Boken om Ansgar*: note 209).

Christian objects of high importance have been found not only in the central building group. A fragment of a glass chalice in blue, with gold decorations was found in the building group to the west (Lundström, 1971b, 58–59). This kind of glass chalice has also been found in Uppåkra in Skåne and in Borg in Lofoten (Stjernqvist, 1999, 79 ff). The Helgö chalice, *c.*6 cm, is the size for a chalice that was used when travelling. Agneta Lundström has shown that this chalice with gold decoration, can be identified with what in the sources is called, 'cuppa vitrae auro ornata' (Lundström, 1971, 58 f). The decoration on the chalice is similar to that of the Frisian jugs, the Tatinger ware, with cruciform tin- or gold decoration. Fragments of at least two jugs have been found in the audience hall (I) and the residence hall (III) in the central building group on Helgö, as well as in the filling of a grave in the adjacent cemetary 116, in graves and cultural layers on Birka, in a grave in Kunsta on Adelsö, in Ytterby in Täby and in Vällingby in Spånga ((Hus Ia and III, BG 2; Arrhenius, 1961, 184f, 1964, 289, grf 116, 31; Ullén, 1980, 39; Gräslund, 2001, 61; Rydh, 1936, 37, 163; Lundström, 1971, 55). Some researchers have suggested these as jugs used for wine or water in the Christian rituals (see Gräslund, 2001, 60f for references).

The idea that a Christian congregation existed in Helgö is appealing, and there are additional aspects put forward by other scholars, which justifies further work on Wilhelm Holmqvist's hypothesis. To Holmqvist himself, it was logical that a Christian congregation was evident on Helgö due to the central position that the island had as a pre-Christian site, as well as a trade and manufacturing location (1980, see also Lamm, 1999). Helgö's role as a religious center has been stressed by Lars Wernersson (1996). This I have built upon and enhanced (Zachrisson, 2004a, b, 2011a, b) when I analyzed the different material aspects of the sacred in Helgö. One of these was to discuss Helgö as a place where one could be cured (Zachrisson, 2004a, 368 ff, 2004b, 157 f). Surgical tools, such as scalpels and tweezers, have recently been analyzed by Annette Frölich (in press). These traces of surgery was something that Holmqvist also discussed (1961).

The historian Adolf Schück drew early attention to certain Helgö-islands specific location on the boundaries between different territorial districts, and thought that these holy islands were the meeting places for ancient ritual gatherings (Schück referenced in Calissendorff, 1971, 7, 9). The place-name scholar Karin Calissendorff considered that Schück had overemphasized the cultic aspect and therefore modified his idea of Helgö-islands as venues not only for religious gatherings, but judicial ones in the form of thing meetings and thus also market events (1971, 7). She thought that the Helgö-islands were enhanced by a certain kind of peace and suggested that certain Helgös might have marked the boundaries for the naval levy system, where a different kind of legislation occurred (Calissendorff, 1964, 123, 1971, 5 f, 1991, 14). At the holy islands, a new kind of legal regulations occurred and fines were doubled (cf Calissendorff, 1995, 54, cf Vikstrand, 2001, 234). In the Upplandic Law this right is called '*roþar raetter*' (UPL, 49). Place-name scholar Per Vikstrand emphasizes the holy islands' role as gathering places and boundary markers. At the Helgö-islands "the normal rules and laws governing human conduct changed" and the passage past them was probably ritualized (2001, 234, 252).

Helgö is mentioned in medieval sources in 1287 as 'curiam nostram Helghø' and later also as Boo, estate, alternative Bona (DMS 2: 1, 106 f). The place-name scholar Carl Ivar Ståhle has drawn attention to the Bo-settlements that are situated along the water routes towards Stockholm. He has suggested that Bo on Lidingö might have been an estate allocated for the disposal of an earl (Ståhle,1946, 177 f. 1954, 20, cf Ambrosiani, 1988, 16 ff). Ståhle, as well as Nils Ahnlund, thought that the steward of such estates probably was the king's or the earl's representative (Ståhle, 1946, 177 f; Ahnlund, 1953, 75 f). Similarly, place-name scholar Lars Hellberg thought of the Bo estates in the archipelago of Stockholm and along the east coast of Sweden, as representing Rod's bo, the part of the royal property Uppsala öd that was assigned for the disposal of an earl (Hellberg, 1979, 148; Vikstrand, 1993). Bo farms during the Middle Ages often represented the main farm in an aristocratic domain, whose origin would then be the one delineated Ståhle. Bona on Helgö could thus have been an estate allocated for the use of an earl.

The archaeologist Björn Ambrosiani, like his collegue Birger Nerman wanted to connect Helgö with Hundamra (see Fig. 1), while Per Vikstrand would like to link Helgö to Asknäs (Nerman, 1961, 107; Ambrosiani, 1988, 14, 2002, 34, 48 ff; Vikstrand, 2001, 241). Both Hundhamra and Asknäs are associated with earls. The estate Asknäs is mentioned in the Erik's Chronicle as the place where Earl Jon was slain. His wife fled across the water to Hundhamra and gathered together people, so that the invaders could be defeated and killed (*Erikskrönikan*, 43). Asknäs was probably Earl Jon's seat (Ahnlund, 1953, 93). The national antiquarian John Hadorph writing in 1673 on the occasion of Karl XI's eriksgata by Hundhamra states that there "äro dhe gamble Järlars höga Grafbackar", "en af dem heter Hunnehögen, af en som heter Hune Jern, den der synes ligga begrafwen, men Järn är Järl, det är Hune Järl ok till äfwentyrs hafwer gården fått sitt nampn af den Hunen och Hammar det är stora Stenbacken och bergen som der näst liggia". There "are the high mounds of the Old Earls", "one of them called the mound of Hunne, named by Hune Iron, that seems to have been buried there. But Iron is Earl, it is Hune Earl, and possibly the farm has got its name from that Hune and Hammar is the large stony hillside and the hills close by (manuscript quoted in Nerman, 1961, 106, cf Ahnlund, 1928, 155, 1953, 93 f, translation by the author). Both Hundhamra and Asknäs were around 1200 owned by the same family, probably the folkunga family (cf Nerman, 1961, 106 f; DMS, 2: 1, 55; Ambrosiani, 2002, 35). One of the farms in Hundhamra was called Borgh, today Norsborg (DMS 2: 1, 50), located at the cemetary with large grave mounds (RAÄ 8). Hundhamra resembles an old estate of an earl in the view of historian Nils Ahnlund (1953, 93).

Hergeirs title *praefectus* can be interpreted as earl. The earl, together with the bishop, was entitled to the second highest penalty after the king. According the Östgöta Law he received a part of the tax from the coastal districts, as well as 1/3 of the tribute from the island Gotland. The earl also had a part of the crowns estates in Östergötland (Rosen, 1962). The Östgöta Law separates districts (härader) that pay taxes only to the king from other districts that pay tax to both the king and the earl (Wessén, 1943, 17). He was the commander of the naval levy and possessed Rod's bo. In the Svea laws the earl is mentioned indirectly in connection with naval levy, which Hans Hildebrand noted (1892, 109, 1940, 17 Wessén, 1940, note 2). Here also the earl is associated with the coastal districts (skeppslagen), and it is stated that everyone should give harbour berth to the earl (Wessén, 1940, 17).

It is questionable whether Roden reached into the lake Mälaren during the Viking Age (Strauch, 2003, 348, cf Andersson, 2004). But the Hovgård stone on Adelsö close to Birka with the inscription which speaks of the king's steward in Rod, carved on behalf of Hakon, as well as the now vanished Nibble stone on Ekerö that tells of the best farmer in Hakon's rod, are signs that this might have been the case (Wessen, 1940, U 11). During the Middle Ages, the major islands in the lake Mälaren belonged to Roden: Lovö, Munsö and Färingsö while Adelsö and Björkö were part of Trögd (Wessén, 1940, 17, cf DMS 1: 7, 25, cf Strauch, 2003, 348). Birka is located where the coastal districts (skeppslagen) of Roden met several important territorial boundaries (Ahnlund, 1953, 10). If we take the premise that Hergeir's title may have been earl, and that the earls were later associated with the naval levy, the ports and with taxes from the coastal districts, we can presume that a town of Birka's dignity was the responsibility of an earl. Overall, there is much to suggest that Helgö by Ekerö might have played a role in naval levy organization as a gathering place and place for rituals. Hergeir, who was in charge of Birka, could according to this reasoning be identified with an earl that also had control over Helgö.

But there is of course another possibility, namely that Hergeir's family estate was situated on Björkö itself, as Anne-Sofie Gräslund suggested (1980, 83). For anyone who was responsible for the control of Birka, perhaps Helgö – 9 km away – lay at too great a distance. In this case, Björkö village will definitely be a potential future candidate for Hergeir's estate, further research will perhaps solve this question. During the excavations of a cultural layer in Björkö village by the National Board of Antiquities (2005–2006) an unusually large amount of oriental Viking Age pottery from the late Birka period was discovered, something that completely distorts the previously known amount of such ceramics in Mälardalen (Bäck, 2009). This was unexpected. These oriental ceramics could be a sign that Björkö village was a settlement of a particular kind. The rune stones found in the village highlights the late Viking Age history of the settlement (Wessén, 1940, see U5–9).

THE APOSTLE OF THE NORTH AND GAUTBERT

After 18 months in Birka, Ansgar returned back home and became archbishop. Ansgar's appointment as a bishop was reaffirmed by Pope Gregory in St. Peter's Chapel in Rome. This, comments Eva Odelman, who translated Rimbert's Vita from Latin, marks the apostolic nature of Ansgar's missionary mandate (*Boken om Ansgar*, note 159). Archbishop Ebo had already been given the same task (*Boken om Ansgar*, note 161). Therefore Ebo and Ansgar conferred and as assistant to Ansgar they chose one of Ebo's relatives – Gautbert. He would serve as a bishop situated in Sweden (*Boken om Ansgar*, note 165). Gautbert was sent to the Swedes. The king and the people received him honourably. With everybodys consent, he started to build a church and preach in public. After some time, the people became furious, and a devilish rage came upon them. It was all a plot by the people. Gautbert's assistant was killed and he himself was driven out of the country. The incident took place towards the end of the 830s (*Boken om Ansgar*, note 191).

The district was without a priest for seven years. So Ansgar sent a hermit called Ardgar, to assist the bailiff Hergeir, who continued to be a Christian (*Boken om Ansgar*, ch 19). At about the same time the Swedish pretender, Anund came with eleven ships, assisted by the Danes with twenty ships, to raid the town of Birka. Here Rimbert uses the word *vicus*, town, and Hergeir is said to be *praefectus loci*, the bailiff of the site (*Boken om Ansgar*, note 232). The king was far away, the chieftains could not get there in time. Hergeir and the merchants fled *ad civitatem*. Hergeir is central to the events and he wants to get merchants to respond. He tells them that the civitas and vicus will be burnt. It seems that these are parts of the city, urbs, concludes Bjorn Ambrosiani (2005, 26). Previously early Birka was perceived as a town without fortifications, believing that the town rampart built first in the 900's (e.g. Arbman, 1939, 70). But archaeologist Lena Holmquist could, through her excavations show that it has been built in several phases starting in the 800s (Holmquist Olausson, 1993, 134). Björn Ambrosiani believes that the older town rampart, but not the rampart of the "hill-fort" Borg, was built as early as the 800s, and thus he

Fig. 5. Birka with the town rampart and the large cemetary Hemlanden in the foreground. The rampart of Borg stands out in the upper left corner, with the gate to the right. On the natural slope below the gate is the Christian burial ground that Anne-Sofie Gräslund identified (1980, 74, 83F). Aerial photo: Jan Norrman, Riksantikvarieämbetet, 1986 from Ambrosiani 2002, 20).

believes that this is where the urban population fled. "This would mean that Hergeir's and the merchants' rapid flight into the civitas at Anund assault need not refer to Borg, but refers to the town (rampart) itself" (Ambrosiani, 2005, 26). And Ambrosiani imagines that civitas aimed more specifically at a religious enclave within the town itself (2005, 26).

Eva Odelman comments especially in her detailed note 148, that Rimbert writes that the population took refuge *ad civitatem*, "which would usually be understood as referring to a defense work in the vicinity of the town itself. But, she continues, Rimbert's text can possibly be perceived differently. Civitatis may designate an area of ecclesiastical immunity, over which a bishop has special jurisdiction, or the bishop's seat itself. Rimbert may have meant that the Birka inhabitants took refuge in the ecclesiastical area (the sanctuary) that was left from Gautbert's time, see note 170, but that was not very resistant against attacks 'jf non multum' (= it was not very strong)" (*Boken om Ansgar*, note 236). My proposal is accordingly that the hill-fort Borg in Birka encloses Gautbert's church and its defensive works.

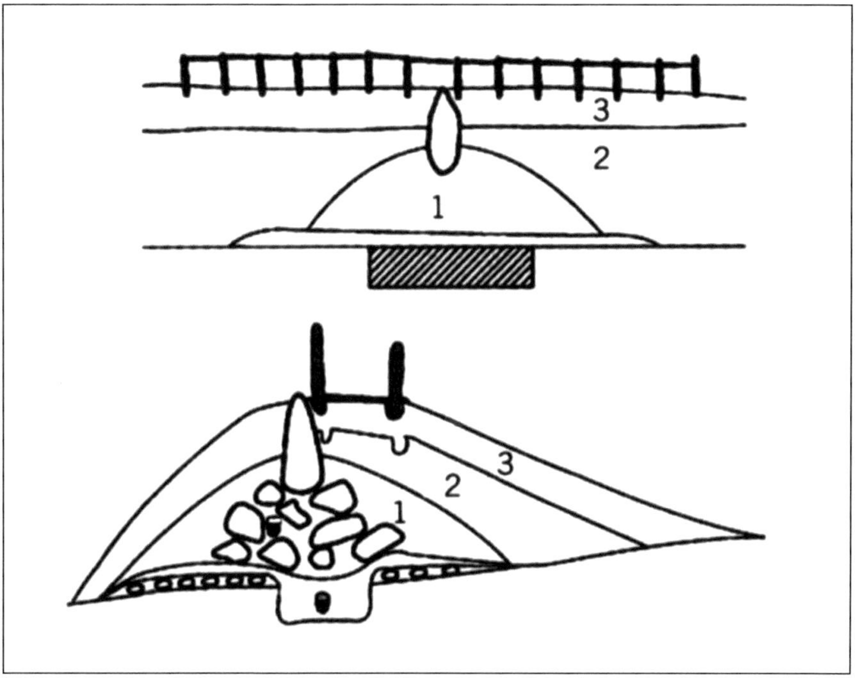

Fig. 6. Sketch showing the construction of the rampart of Borg. Drawing: F. Sieurin-Lönnqvist. A burial mound (1) is built into the older rampart (2) that after a fire is re-built to the double height (3) forming the younger rampart (Holmquist Olausson 2001, 11).

My suggestions are based on Eve Odelman's comment. I think the defense works near the town and the area of ecclesiastical immunity are the same – Borg (Fig. 5). This is identical to Gautbert's church with surrounding ramparts and it was located, like the cathedrals on the continent, on the cliff, above the lower-lying dense settlement of the urban character. The word civitatem et vicum of Rimbert, may refer to this topographical and functional difference.

When Rimbert describes Birka as a rich and well-supplied market town, he uses the concept of *vicus* (town, see *Boken om Ansgar*, note 232). The Birka residents had taken refuge in *urbem* (= to the town or fortification works in the town, note 240). Further in the text he writes that the Danes will destroy *civitatem et vicum* (the fort and town in general, *Boken om Ansgar*, note 242, see note 240). Also in Hamburg, Rimbert makes such a contrast, Hallencreutz & Odelman point out, between *civitas* and *urbs* on the one hand and *vicus*, the unfortified market town, on the other. *Civitas* Rimbert sometimes uses for an "episcopal town", such as Cologne, Konstanz and Worms (Hallencreutz & Odelman, 1986, 127).

The fort at Birka is truly visible in the landscape of today. It is one of the mightiest constructions in Viking Age Scandinavia. And it is hitherto the only hillfort in the Mälar valley dated to the Viking Age (Holmquist Olausson, 2001, 11). The word hill fort guides our thoughts, and Holger Arbman for example, has suggested that the hill fort may be older than the town and that it controlled Birka's location (Arbman, 1939, 58). Generally speaking, fortifications from the Viking Age are absent in Scandinavia, which in itself is puzzling, notes Michael Olausson (2009, 60 ff). In Sweden, these fortifications are represented by the hill fort and town rampart at Birka, but also the late phase of the hill fort Torsburgen on Gotland and the rampart Götavirke in Middle Sweden. In Norway, Viking Age fortifications as a whole are missing, while they predominantly occur in Denmark in the form of Trelleborg forts, as well as the fortifications around Hedeby and Aarhus and the rampart Danevirke (Olausson, 2009, 65).

If Borg on Björkö housed the remnants of Gautbert's church and its defensive works, it would also make Birka's urban structure more similar to continental cities such as Muenster. Before I touch upon this I will look at the results from the excavation at the fort and its rampart, of the garrison, and the hall building located next to and beneath Borg towards the seaside, to see if it seems at all plausible.

The fortification Borg was built some time after Birka was established. The rampart of the fort is 350 m long and 2–3 m high. On top of the palisade, there has been a 2 m wide arched walk, with a parapet built in horizontal-planking technique (see Fig. 6). It was built in two phases (Holmquist-Olausson, 2001, 11). If we examine the idea that the Borg houses Gautbert's church, it becomes important to scrutinize the rampart dating. Could it have been constructed as late as the 830s? When Lena Holmquist and Michael Olausson excavated the rampart, an imposing grave mound with an erected stone at the top was found, that had been built into the rampart. The grave had been attached to the construction when the rampart was built, so that the erected stone had stuck up and was visible from the outside of the rampart (see reconstruction in Holmquist Olausson, 2001, 11). This gives a *terminus post quem* to the rampart of the fort. The grave, one of the oldest in Birka, contained a man and his horse buried in the middle of the 8th century (Holmquist-Olausson, 2001, 11), but which I believe should be laid out later (see below). He was equipped with a knife, a belt with a clasp and mountings, tweezers, a box and a leather purse with silver fittings (Fennö Myuingo, 2000, 7 ff) and including silk fabric (Holmquist-Olausson, 2001, 11). The textile remains have been further analyzed by Anita Malmius, who believes that the man was not dressed in silk clothes, but that silk fabric was placed in the grave (Anita Malmius, Archaeological Research Laboratory, orally, July 8, 2009). Tweezers are a rare object in graves from the Merovingian period, although some have been found on the island of Gotland (Nerman, 1969, taf 290, No. 2302, 2303). In the cultural layer surrounding the grave a wasp bead and a piece of a Tatinger jug was found, as well as skeletal remains of another man and remains of a meal consisting of grain and bones of cattle, pigs, sheep and goats (Myuingo, 2000, 11). A horse tooth from the grave has been ^{14}C-dated to 667–776 AD, which I have calibrated anew OxCal (68.2%, UA 13239). In Ribe (the Posthus excavation) in Denmark the number of wasp beads 'explodes' in the phase 780–790. The distribution of wasp beads in the different phases are: 725–760 12 pc, 760–780 2 pc, 780–790 91 pc, 790–800 11 pc and 800–820 1 pc (Feveile & Jensen, 2000, 22 where the term 'explodes' occurs, see table p. 20). This may indicate that the grave was built towards the end of the second half of the 700s, perhaps the 780's.

The rampart of Borg was ^{14}C-dated to 786 AD, according to Helena Fenno Muyingo, who wrote the excavation report (2000, 9). But when I recalibrated this by OxCal the ^{14}C-dating for the bottom layer of the rampart is 766–871 AD (layer L9 50.2%, the range is 669–895 AD [94.8%], Ua 12,728, OxCal). In this layer a rim fragment of a light green funnel beaker was found, which can be dated to around 800 (Muyingo, 2000, 6; 1993, 146; Henricsson in Holmquist Olausson, 1993). The dating framework is thus broad and only the male grave indicates the time limitation. But it is possible to bring forward further arguments that the rampart was built some time after Birka's establishment. There were graves inside the fortification. Five of the seven graves were dated to older Birkatid and contained among other things, a Carolingian funnel beaker, fragments of a Tatinger jug and early oval brooches (Bj. 455–4588, 460–462). These were all cremation graves and the grave superstructure was missing (Gräslund, 1980, 64). The Birka scholar Anne-Sofie Gräslund believes that they originally should have been covered with mounds, which were leveled out when the rampart was built, or destroyed when the fortification was in use (Gräslund, 1980, 74). Birka scholar Ingmar Jansson also believes that the grave mounds were leveled off when the rampart was built (verbally July 14, 2009). Some burial mounds with a general dating to the Viking period were investigated by the Archaeological Research Laboratory (Hedenstierna-Jonson, 2000, 6). Inside the fort there are no later graves. It is therefore a strong case that the rampart of the fort was built sometime into the 800s. After having been burned, the rampart was rebuilt into the double height, so that the male grave with the erected stone was completely enclosed in the rampart wall and no longer visible. This younger rampart was rebuilt on at least two occasions towards the end of the 900s or beginning of the 1000s (Holmquist-Olausson, 2001, 11). Thus, the fortification mentioned in Rimbert as being not so strong, could include the older and lower wall. This as well

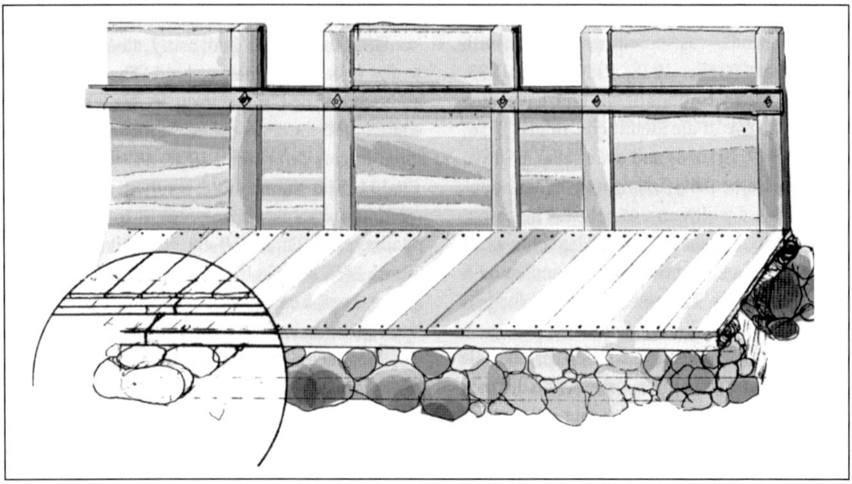

Fig. 7. Reconstruction of the younger rampart at Borg (drawing by Johan Lindeberg, after an idea of Lena Holmquist). In front is the 2-meter-wide shooting gangway, which is crowned by a breastwork (in Lund, Hedenstierna-Jonson & Holmquist Olausson, 2009, 112).

was fitted with a parapet and breastwork. During the excavation of the oldest rampart of Borg, four clamps were found, which were interpreted as part of such a design (Fenno Muyingo, 2000, 6).

Lena Holmquist links the construction of the two ramparts, the town rampart and that of Borg, and argues that they were both built at the same time (2002, 164). Thermoluminscens datings and ^{14}C datings suggest that Borg and the town rampart were burned in the first half of the 800s (Olausson, 2009, 65). Michael Olausson is of the opinion that both Borg and the town rampart were already constructed in 829 when Ansgar visited king Björn in Birka (a.a.). The stratigraphic relationship that could prove this, however, is missing today.

BORG

The surfaces inside Borg have been phosphate mapped and geophysically mapped by the Archaeological Research Laboratory as part of the project *Strongholds and Fortifications* (see Stavrum, 1997). In particular, the phosphate analysis, but also the electromagnetic analysis, showed increased levels along the rampart and inside Borg, which has been interpreted as indications of a cultural layer and a foundation (Stavrum, 1997, 18). Borg is about 180 x 100 m (NNW-SSE) and the wall enclosing an area large enough to accommodate the proposed episcopal church.

THE GARRISON

Northwest of the fortification is an area with terraces that were investigated by Holger Arbman in the 1930s, the so-called likbränningsplatsen, with an upper and lower terrace (1939). Lena Holmquist and Michael Olausson's investigations into this garrison, and Charlotte Hedenstierna-Jonson's analysis of it, has enhanced the picture of Birka and Birka warriors (Olausson (Ed.), 2001; Hedenstierna-Jonson 2006). This is an area, partially fenced, with several buildings and activities from the mid 700s to 900s (see Fig. 8). At the top, and just northwest of the fort is a hall building 19 x 9 m large with curved, double walls and strong postholes – a heavy and compact hall, probably the high building appeared from the water way below. The only parallel to this building is the great hall building on the terraces in Gamla Uppsala (Holmquist-Olausson, 2001, 13 ff). The picture sketched by the project *Strongholds and Fortifications,* is that of a group of professional warriors, who were supplied with food and other necessities from the outside. They were well equipped, some of them

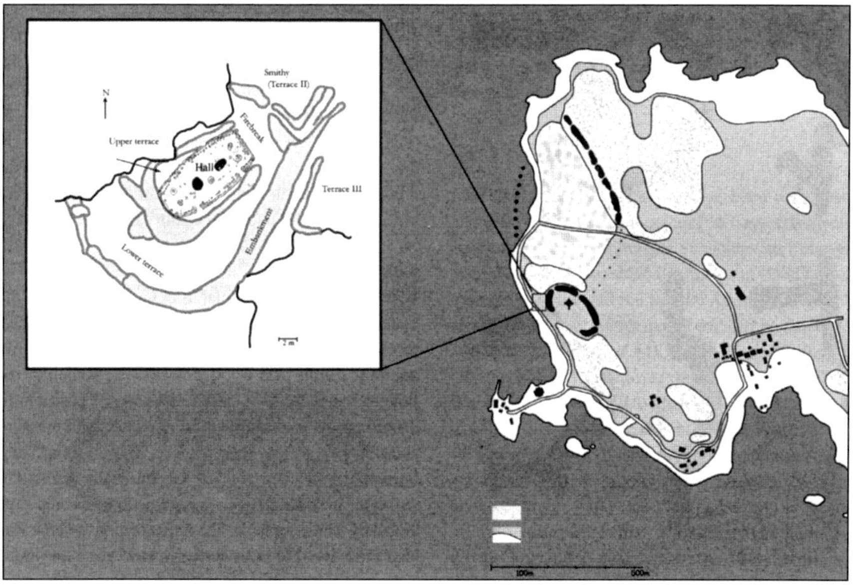

Fig. 8. The garrison with the soldiers' house and fenced area © Hedenstierna-Jonson, L. Kitzler-Åhfeldt & M. Olausson in Lundström, Hedenstierna-Jonson & Holmquist Olausson 2009, 105).

with lamella armour, with access to the eastern archery techniques and influenced by Magyar dress and equestrian ideals (Olausson (Ed.), 2001; Lundstrom, Hedenstierna-Jonson & Holmquist Olausson, 2009, for the dress, see Larsson, 2008). It is important to remember that this is a 10th-century image. For the older Birka period the cultural influences and expressions are different. Fedir Androushchuk remarks that from the whole of the Early Birka period there is only one man buried with a sword. This grave contains continental grave gifts and has been erected over a wealthy man, perhaps Frankish. All the other swords in graves belong to the 900s. Androushchuk goes so far as to call the 9th-century Birka, a merchant and crafts town in contrast to the 10th-century town of Vikings (Androushchuk, 2009, 97).

There are older cultural layers in the garrison and Lena Holmquist makes clear that the warriors' house is not excavated to the bottom (2001, 13 ff). There are remnants of an older building with a slightly different orientation (Lena Holmquist, verbally 2009). The numismatist Kenneth Jonsson suggests that the coin finds from the garrison and the terraces next to the castle must be interpreted as if there has been extensive activity there in the 800s, while the 10th-century coins are very few. He imagines that the coins from the 800s come from older layers used when the warriors' house was built in the 900s (Jonsson 2001, 33). This is remarkable, because Ingrid Gustin's analysis of the use of coins in Birka, is that coins occur from Birka's oldest time, but they are very few and very seldom put in graves as a gift, before the year 890 (Gustin, 2004, 100). The garrison area stands out, therefore, because there are many coins deposited from the older Birka period.

In the garrison during Holger Arbman excavations several fragments of the Frisian jugs/Tatinger ware were discovered (SHM 21064:21, 60, 131). These jugs are directly linked to the ecclesiastical top locations on the Continent, according to Mathias Bäck, and only the Nordic countries lack this connection (Mathias Bäck, orally).

Near the fence that enclosed the garrison area, a building sacrifice in the form of unusual kinds of tanged spearheads were found close to the original ground surface. Laila Kitzler wanted to connect them with Oden, but acknowledged that they could also be Christian sacrifices (Kitzler, 2000, 13 f, 19). In the building from around 900, there is a sacrifice in the center of the hall, consisting of a Thor's Hammer and 40 comb cases. This is an interesting and important deposition, but one has to bear in mind that it belongs to the building from the Late Birka period. What types of deposits were linked to the lower not yet excavated building we do not know. The tanged spearheads seem anyway to belong to a different chronological horizon than the other building sacrifices and lie next to the fence that enclosed the area.

In the article "The Defender of the Faith in Birka", Gustav Trotzig high-

Fig. 9. Tatinger jug (Birka grave 551. Photo: Christer Åhlin, The National Historical Museum in Sweden, 2001).

lights the shield-shaped pendants that have been found in various graves (2004). These pendants can be connected to a conception of defender of faith. Raban Mauer, the abbot of the monastery of Fulda, later archbishop of Mainz, was an instigator of the heathen mission in the North. Trotzig points out that there was a direct link between Raban Maur and Birka. He did, surviving letters indicate, equip Gautbert before the mission trip to Birka, including one sakramentarium and garments for the Mass (*Boken om Ansgar*, 91, note 167). In the

Black Earth a possible sepulcral stone of marble was found from a portable altar used when travelling (Gustafsson, 2008). It may have been among the objects Gautbert was equipped with before his trip to Birka, or it may have belonged to Ansgar who was bishop of Hamburg-Bremen when he returned to Birka, on his second trip 852 (Gustafsson, 2008, 164).

Anne-Sofie Gräslund has identified a Christian cemetery with closely spaced graves, known as Area B2, outside and north of Borg (1980, 74, 83F). Most of these graves were constructed in the 800s and Anne-Sofie Gräslund has put them in the context of the Ansgar Mission (1980, 83, see 2001, 70). This burial ground is similar to the continental Reihengräber (Gräslund, 1980, 44). Already found at the gate of the fortification in the excavations in the 17th century, though misinterpreted, was a broken part of a fetter. It may have been part of a hand or alternatively a foot fetter as Ny Björn Gustafsson recently has shown (2009, 90). It is not impossible that it was used to fetter one of the Christian slaves who were in Birka that Rimbert mentions.

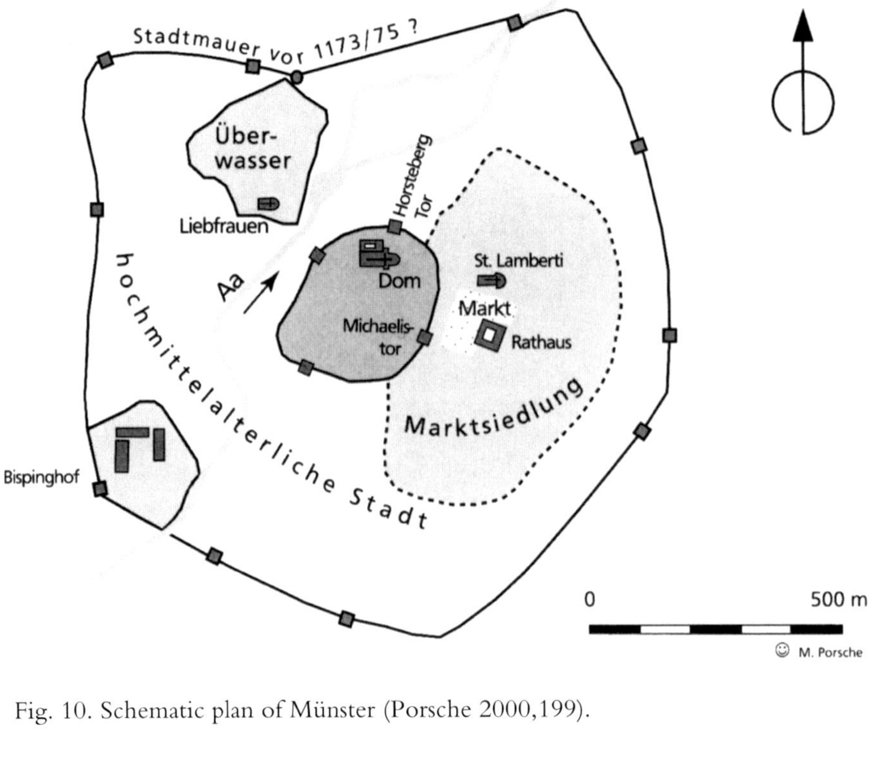

Fig. 10. Schematic plan of Münster (Porsche 2000,199).

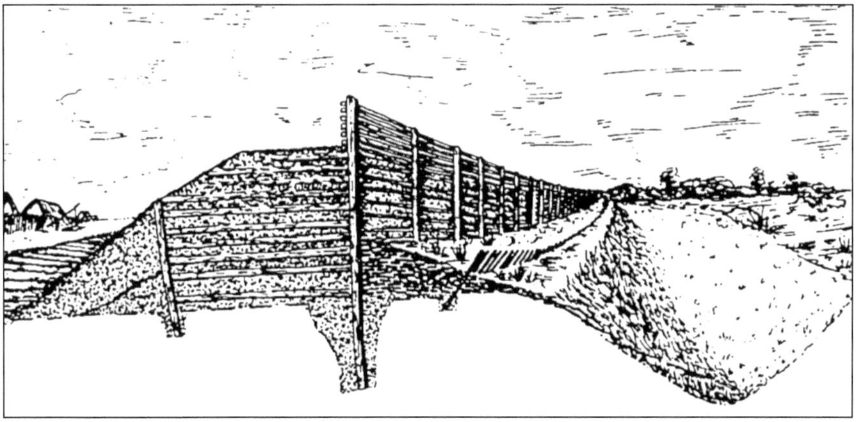

Fig. 11. The Carolingian rampart made of earth and wood that surrounded the Münster "Domburg" (Porsche, 2000, 204, after a reconstruction by Hömberg, 1997).

BIRKA'S URBAN TOPOGRAPHY – A COMPARISON

If we assume that the hill fort of Birka may be the site of Gautbert's church and bishop's fortification, this would mean that Birka is structurally similar to a series of continental and contemporary cities, where there is a higher cathedral hill with a fortification and an adjacent and lower positioned market town. Monika Porsche gives in her thorough review of the fortifications around the medieval German cities (2000) a series of fruitful parallels from the Birka period. In several of these cities there are older cultural layers. A first church was erected on the site of a missionary and then a bishop's seat was founded in the late 700s, early 800s, such as in Halberstadt, Minden, Münster, Bremen and Paderborn (Porsche 2000, 200). Rarely, but occasionally, it is possible to draw back the fortification works to Charlemagne and his son Louis the Pious' times (Porsche, 2000, 201). The geographic orientation of the cathedral mountains of the various continental examples vary (cf the Porsche in 2001, ENE-WSW, NNE-SSW or NNW-SSE). Borg would correspond to the size of the domburg, for example, in Minden (Porsche, 2001, 200).

The most complete picture is given by Münster (Fig. 10) where the rampart around the episcopal fortress – a rampart made of wood and earth – had been reconstructed (see Fig. 11 above, cf Hömberg, 1997). Münster, which was a city, with an area of 8–9 hectares, since Roman times, was elevated to a bishopric in the year 805. Already in the 7th–8th centuries, Münster had a craft production which was significant compared to other contemporary urban milieues (Porsche, 2000, 199 f the foregoing references). The reconstruction of the rampart around the domburg in Münster is interesting to compare with the one (see Fig. 7) that Lena Holmquist has made for Borgs rampart (in Sahlstedt, 1997, 7 and Lundström, Hedenstierna-Jonson & Holmquist Olausson, 2009, 112).

SUMMARY

The memorial cross of Ansgar and his mission was erected in 1834 and was placed on the hill in Borg. From the site one has a wide view, since it is the highest point of Björkö. The fortification Borg itself is an odd feature of the Viking era and Lena Holmquist has described it as the connecting link between the prehistoric hill fort and medieval fortifications (in Sahlstedt, 1997, 18). In this article Borg is interpreted as the site of an episcopal church with surrounding fortifications. The archaeological finds from the 800s may be opened up for such a possibility. The church would then have been erected on the cliff. From a symbolic perspective, it is a natural choice for the rock is synonymous with Christ himself (letter to the Corinthians 10: 4, Psalm 92: 16, Luke 6: 47–48, see Bibelfrågan). Quite logically, it was also here that Archbishop Nathan Söderblom once would have liked to see the Ansgar chapel erected.

The foundation, cultural layers and the levelled burial mounds that are inside Borg, may be the remains of activities within such a church area. Archaeologist Dagmar Selling has proposed that the Tatinger jugs would be connected to the 9th-century Birka Mission (Selling, 1951, 289 f). In Borg, as well as in the garrison, many fragments of Tatinger jugs have been found, close to the ecclesiastical environment where they were in use. The Garrison area below the fortification/church contains the remains of an older building, which may have been linked to the proposed church. Likewise, the cemetery at Birka that Anne-Sofie Gräslund identified as Christian, is located just off Kungsporten, the main gate into Borg (2 B).

Birka is so well known that it is easy to become blind as to what the site actually represents. At the Jelling Conference in 2008 I was asked to present Birka and Adelsö. The idea above emanated from the thoughts that I got, that evolved into a lecture that I held at the XVIth Viking Congress, in Iceland 2009. Thanks to generous contributions from Berit Wallenberg Foundation my trip to Iceland became possible.

ACKNOWLEDGEMENTS

Many thanks to Anders Andrén, who drew my attention to Monica Porsche's book, Ingmar Jansson, Ingrid Gustin for dating discussion, Mathias Bäck for discussions on the ceramics, Ulf Fransson for the location on Borgaskog and to Gustav Trotzig for the information on Nathan Söderblom's opinion on the location of Ansgar chapel.

BIBLIOGRAPHY

Adam av Bremen. (1984). *Historien om Hamburgstiftet och dess biskopar.* Translated by E. Svedberg. Stockholm.

Ahnlund, N. (1928). *Svensk sägen och hävd*. Stockholm.

Ahnlund, N. (1953). *Stockholms historia före Gustav Vasa*. Monografier utgivna av Stockholms komunalförvaltning. Stockholm.

Ambrosiani, B. (1988). Helgö or Bona on Helgö. *Thirteen studies on Helgö*, 14–19. Statens historiska museum studies 7. Stockholm.

Ambrosiani, B. (2002). *Mälaröarna. Från fornkungar till folkungar.* Stockholm.

Ambrosiani, B. (2005). *Birka under Ansgars tid*. Stockholm.

Andersson, Th. (2004). Svethiudh, det svenska rikets kärna. *Namn och bygd* 92, 5–18.

Androushuck, F. (2009). Vikings and Farmers. *The Martial Society. Aspects of warriors, fortifications and social change in Scandinavia*, 93–104. (Eds.) L. Holmquist Olausson & M. Olausson. Theses and papers in archaeology B: 11. Archaeological research laboratory. Stockholm.

Arbman, H. (1939). *Birka. Sveriges äldsta handelsstad*. Från forntid och medeltid 1. Stockholm.

Arrhenius, B. (1961). Pottery. *Excavations at Helgö* I, 182–221. (Eds.) W. Holmqvist, B. Arrhenius & P. Lundström. KVHAA. Stockholm.

Bibelfrågan. Var Petrus kyrkans klippgrund? www.alltombiblen.se/bibelfragan/grunden.htm jan 2010.

Boken om Ansgar. (1986). Rimbert, Ansgars liv. Translated by Eva Odelman. Stockholm.

Bäck, M. (1995). Importkeramiken i Birka. *META* 95/1, 4–21.

Bäck, M. (2009). Vikingatida bebyggelse funnen utanför Birkas stadsvall. *Fornvännen* 104, 262–273.

Bäck, M, Orally, November 2009.

Calissendorff, K. (1963). Vitulsö. Ett försvunnet ortnamn. *Ortnamnssällskapets i Uppsala årsskrift*, 3–8.

Calissendorff, K. (1964). Helgö. *Namn och Bygd* 52, 105–152.

Calissendorff, K. (1971). Place-names denoting centres. *Early Medieval Studies 3. Antikvariskt arkiv* 40, 2–12.

Calissendorff, K. (1991). Helgöforskningens dagsläge. *Ortnamnssällskapets i Uppsala årsskrift*, 9–15.

Calissendorff, K. (1995). Ortnamn och rättshistoria: två praktiska exempel. *Saga och Sed* 1994, 49–60.

DMS 1:7. (1992). *Bro hd, Adelsö sn, Färingsö tingslag och Sollentuna hd.* Ferm, O. Johansson, M. & Rahmqvist, S. Riksantikvarieämbetet. Stockholm.

DMS 2:1. (2002). *Tören. Svartlösa och Sotholm*. Janzon, K. & Rahmqvist, S. (Eds.). Riksantikvarieämbetet. Stockholm.

Erikskrönikan. (1991). Reviewed, introduction and commentary Sven-Bertil Jansson. Stockholm.

Fennö Muyingo, H. (2000). *Borgvallen II. Utvidgad undersökning av Borgvallen och underliggande grav 1997. Arkeologisk undersökning 1997, Uppland, Adelsö sn. Raä 34.* H. Fennö Muyingo med bidrag av E. During, M. Klockhoff & Ch. Hedenstierna Jonson. Archaeological Research Laboratory. Stockholms University.

Feveile, C. & Jensen, S. (2000). Ribe in the 8th and 9th century. A contribution to the archaeological chronology of North Western Europe. *Acta Archaeologica* 71, 9–24. København.

Frølich, A. i tryck 2011. Helgö – a place for surgical treatment, offering – or both. *Excavations at Helgö XVIII.* (Ed.) B. Arrhenius. Stockholm.

Gräslund, A-S. (1980). *Birka IV. The Burial customs. A study of the graves on Björkö.* KVHAA. Stockholm.

Gräslund, A-S. (2001). *Ideologi och mentalitet. Om religionsskiftet i Skandinavien från en arkeologisk synpunkt.* OPIA 29. Uppsala.

Gustafsson, N. B. (2008). A Sacred Stone from Björkö's Black Earth: On the Benefits of a Second Examination. *Viking and Medieval Scandinavia* 4, 159–168.

Gustafsson, N. B. (2009). För folk och få. Om vikingatida fjättrar och deras användning. *Fornvännen* 104, 89–96.

Gustin, I. (2004). Islamic coins and eastern contacts. Eastern connections. Part two. (Ed.) B. Ambrosiani. *Birka studies* 6, 96–120. Stockholm.

Gustin, I. Manus (2010). Coin stock and coin circulation in Birka. *Silver Economies, Monetisation & Society in Scandinavia, 800–1100. 5–6 December 2008 at the University of Aarhus, Denmark.*

Hadorph, J. (1687). Biärköarätten, printed in Ambrosiani, B. & Eriksson, B. G. 1994. *Birka – vikingastaden* Vol. 4. Höganäs.

Hallencreutz, C. F. (1984). Adam, Sverige och trosskiftet. Adam av Bremen. Historien om Hamburgstiftet och dess biskopar. Translated by E. Svedberg, 355–378. Stockholm.

Hallencreutz, C. F. & Odelman, E. (1986). Rimbert som ärkebiskop och författare. *Boken om Ansgar. Rimbert, Ansgars liv,* 115–132. Translated by Eva Odelman. Stockholm.

Hedenstierna-Jonson, Ch. (2000). *Borg. Arkeologisk undersökning 1998/99.* Borgar och befästningsverk i Mellansverige. Rapport 2. Archaeological Research Laboratory. Stockholms University.

Hedenstierna-Jonson, Ch. (2006). *The Birka Warrior – the material culture of a martial society.* Theses and papers in scientific archaeology 8. Stockholm.

Hellberg, L. (1979). Forn-Kalmar. Ortnamnen och stadens förhistoria. Kalmar stads historia 1. *Kalmarområdets forntid och stadens äldsta utveckling. Tiden intill 1300-talets mit,* 118–166. (Ed.) I. Hammarström. Kalmar.

Henricsson, L. G. (1993). Appendix 4. In Holmquist Olausson, L., *Aspects on Birka. Investigations and surveys 1976–1989.* Theses and papers in Archaeology B: 3. Stockholm.

Hildebrand, H. (1894). *Sveriges medeltid.* Bd 2. Städerna. Stockholm.

Holmquist Olausson, L. (1993). *Aspects on Birka. Investigations and surveys 1976–1989.* Theses and papers in Archaeology B: 3. Stockholm.

Holmquist Olausson, L. (2001). Birkas befästningsverk – resultat från de senaste årens utgrävningar. *Birkas krigare.* (Ed.) M. Olausson. Borgar och befästningsverk i Mellansverige, 5, 9–16. Archaeological Research Laboratory. Stockholms University.

Holmquist Olausson, L. (2002). Patterns of settlement and defense at the proto-town of Birka, Lake Mälar, Eastern Sweden. *The Scandinavians from the Vendel to the tenth century. An ethnographic perspective.* Studies in Historical Archaeoethnology. Vol. 5, 167. (Ed.) J. Jesch. San Marino.

Holmquist Olausson, L. & Kitzler Åhfeldt, L. (2002). *Krigarnas hus.* Arkeologisk undersökning av ett hallhus i Birkas Garnison. Borgar och befästningsverk i Mellansverige, Rapport 4. Archaeological Research Laboratory. Stockholms University.

Holmqvist, W. (1961). En vikingatida sjukstuga på Helgö. *Lychnos, lärdomshistoriska samfundets årsbok 1960–61*, 24–36.

Holmqvist, W. (1969a). *Helgö – den gåtfulla ön.* Uddevalla.

Holmqvist, W. (1969b). Comments on Hans Emil Lidén. From Pagan Sanctuary to Christian Church. *Norwegian Archaeological Review*, 22–24. Vol. 2. Oslo.

Holmqvist, W. (1980). *Vikingar på Helgö och Birka.* Stockholm.

Hömberg, Ph. (1997). Die Burgen des Frühen Mittelalters in Westfalen. *Hinter Schloss und Riegel. Burgen und Befestigungen in Westfalen*, 120–159. Münster.

Hyenstrand, Å. (1988). Helgö, Birka and the church of St Gautbert. *Thirteen studies on Helgö*, 64–71. (Ed.) A. Lundström. Statens Historiska museum Studies 7. Stockholm.

Hyenstrand, Å. (1996). *Lejonet, korset och draken. Sverige 500–1000.* Lund.

Jansson, I. Orally July 2009.

Jonsson, K. (2001). Mynten – en fyndkategori som speglar Birkakrigarnas internationella kontakter. *Birkas krigare.* (Ed.) M. Olausson. Borgar och befästningsverk i Mellansverige, 5, 29–34. Archaeological Research Laboratory. Stockholms University.

Kitzler, L. (2000). Odenssymbolik i Birkas Garnison. *Fornvännen* 95, 13–21.

Lamm, K. (1999). Helgö. *Reallexikon der germanischen Altertumskunde.* Band 14, 286–291.

Lamm, K. (2004). Distribution and context of the figural gold foils. Helgö, Uppland. *Excavations at Helgö XVI*, 50–56, 10. (Eds.) H. Clarke & K. Lamm. KVHAA. Stockholm.

Larsson, A. (2007). *Klädd krigare: skifte i skandinaviskt dräktskick kring år 1000.* OPIA 39. Uppsala.

Lindeberg, J. (2008). *Krigarnas hus i Birka – ett rekonstruktionsförslag av en vikingatida hallbyggnad.* Seminar paper. Archaeological Research Laboratory. Institute of Archaeology & Classical studies. Stockholms University.

Lundström, A. (1971). *Cuppa vitrea auro ornata. Early Medieval Studies* 3, 53–68. Antikvariskt arkiv 40. KVHAA. Stockholm.

Lundström, F., Hedenstierna-Jonson, Ch. & Holmquist Olausson, L. (2009). Eastern archery in Birka´s garrison. *The Martial Society. Aspects of warriors, fortifications and social change in Scandinavia*, 105–116. (Eds.) L. Holmquist Olausson & M. Olausson. Theses and papers in archaeology B:11. Archaeological research laboratory. Stockholm.

Malmius, Anita, Archaeological Research Laboratory, orally 8.7.2009.

Nerman, B. (1961). Till vilken ätt ha de stora gravhögarna vid Norsborg i Botkyrka hört? *Fornvännen*, 97–109.

Nerman, B. (1969). *Die Vendelzeit Gotlands*. KVHAA. Stockholm.

Nielsen, H. (1962). Jarl. *Kulturhistoriskt lexikon för nordisk medeltid*. Bd 7. Malmö.

Nyberg, T. (1984). Stad, skrift och stift. *Adam av Bremen. Historien om Hamburgstiftet och dess biskopar.* Translated by E. Svedberg, 295–340. Stockholm.

Olausson, M. (2001). *Birkas krigare*. (Ed.) M. Olausson. Borgar och befästningsverk i Mellansverige, 5. Seminar paper. Archaeological Research Laboratory. Stockholms University.

Olausson, M. (2009). At peace with walls. Fortifications and their significance AD 400–1100. *The Martial Society. Aspects of warriors, fortifications and social change in Scandinavia*, 35–70. (Eds.) L. Holmquist Olausson & M. Olausson. Theses and papers in archaeology B:11. Archaeological research laboratory. Stockholm.

Porsche, M. (2000). *Stadtmauer und Stadtentstehung. Untersuchungen zur frühen Stadtbefestigung im mittelalterlichen Deutschen Reich*. Hertigen.

Rosén, J. (1962). Jarl. *Kulturhistoriskt lexikon för nordisk medeltid*. Bd 7. Malmö.

Rydh, H. (1936). *Förhistoriska undersökningar på Adelsö*. KVHAA. Stockholm.

Sahlstedt, M. (1997). *Analys av fyndmaterial från Birkas borgvall*. Seminar paper. Archaeological Research Laboratory. Institute of Archaeology. Stockholms University.

Sawyer, P. (1991). *När Sverige blev Sverige*. Translated and reviewed by B. Sawyer. Alingsås.

Schück, A. Heliga öar och vatten. Paper held at the Royal Academy of Arts and Letters, cited in Calissendorff 1971.

Selling, D. (1951). Problem kring vikingatida keramikkannor. *Fornvännen* 46, 275–297.

SHM + nr. Statens historiska museum, website. Digital museum catalogue.

Stahre, N-G. (1986). *Ortnamn i Stockholms skärgård*. Stockholm.

Stavrum, B. (1997). *Förhistoriskt markutnyttjande i Borg på Björkö – en prospektering med fosfatkartering och elektromagnetisk kartering*. Seminar paper. Archaeological Research Laboratory. Institute of Archaeology. Stockholms University.

Stjernquist, B. (1999). Glass from Uppåkra: A preliminary Study of Finds and Problems. *Fynden i centrum. Uppåkrastudier 2*, 67–94. (Ed.) B. Hårdh. Acta archaeologica Lundensia. Series in 8°, 30. Lund.

Strauch, D. (2003). Roslagen. Geographisches. Rechtliches. *RGA* 25, 346–351.

Ståhle, C. I. (1946). *Studier över de svenska ortnamnen på -inge på grundval av undersökningar i Stockholms län.* Studier till en svensk ortnamnsatlas, 3. Skrifter / utg. av Kungl. Gustav Adolfs akademien för folklivsforskning, 16. Uppsala.

Ståhle, C. I. (1949). Om vår äldsta jordebok. Vårfruberga klosters godsförteckning. *Namn och Bygd* 36, 3.

Ståhle, C. I. (1954). Lidingö under forntid och medeltid, en namn- och bebyggelsehistorisk studie. *Ortnamnssällskapets i Uppsala årsskrift* 1954, 3–31.

Trotzig, G. (2004). Trons försvarare i Birka. *Fornvännen* 99, 196–208.

U+nr. 1940. *Upplands runinskrifter. Sveriges runinskrifter.* Band 6, häfte 1. Reviewed and interpreted by E. Wessén. KVHAA. Stockholm.

Ullén, I. (1980). *En jämförande belysning och diskussion av förhållanden på Helgö och Birka under vikingatid.* Seminar paper in Archaeology. Stockholm university.

UpL. Upplandslagen. 1979. Granskad och tolkad av Å. Holmbäck & E. Wessén. *Svenska landskapslagar.* Bd 1. Stockholm.

Vikstrand, P. (1993). Bo. Manuscript in Institutet för språk och folkminnen, Uppsala.

Vikstrand, P. (2001). *Gudarnas platser. Förkristna sakrala ortnamn i Mälarlandskapen.* Acta Academiae regiae Gustavi Adolphi LXXVII. Studier till en svensk ortnamnsatlas utgivna av Th. Andersson, 17. Uppsala.

Wernerson, L. (1996). *Helgö som religiöst centrum. En hypotes.* Seminar paper. Institute of Archaeology. Stockholms University.

Wessén, E. (1940). *Upplands runinskrifter. Sveriges runinskrifter.* Band 6, häfte 1. Reviewed and interpreted by E. Wessén. KVHAA. Stockholm.

Zachrisson, T. (2004a). Det heliga på Helgö och dess kosmiska referenser. *Ordning mot kaos. Världsbild och kosmologi. Vägar till Midgård 4,* 343–388. (Eds.) A. Andrén, K. Jennbert & C. Raudvere. Lund.

Zachrisson, T. (2004b). The Holiness of Helgö. *Excavations at Helgö XVI. Exotic finds,* 143–175. (Eds.) H. Clarke & K. Lamm. KVHAA. Stockholm.

Zachrisson, T. (2011). Helgö – mer än ett vi. *Makt, kult och plats. Två seminarier arrangerade av Stockholms läns museum under 2009 och 2010,* 69–78. Stockholm.

Zachrisson, T. Forthcoming 2011. Holy places as cosmic mirrors – the examples Helgö and Uppåkra. *Myth and theory in the Old Norse World,* conference held at the University of Aberdeen. (Ed.) S. Brink.

Settlements and Agrarian Landscapes Chronological Issues and Archaeological Challenges

INGVILD ØYE

ABSTRACT

The main topics examined in this paper concern chronological aspects of agrarian settlements and land use in the Viking Age and the Middle Ages, and the methods for ascribing farms to these periods. Traditionally, prehistoric and medieval place names, especially farm names, and Iron Age burials have played an important role in assessing the development of rural settlements in Norway and the rest of Scandinavia. The validity of these criteria can, however, be questioned. The paper presents some recent archaeological case studies of eleven farms in western Norway to assess this question. The selected farms represent different physical conditions for subsistence in relation to topography, available resources and territorial extent, located in different landscapes at different altitudes from coast to inland. These investigations showed that farms that have been considered as medieval or from the Late Iron Age may have a considerably longer history than earlier recognised and that the place name chronology and other traditional criteria for dating the origin and development of farms is less reliable than commonly thought.

Keywords: Rural settlements, agrarian landscapes, dating, place name chronology, western Norway.

INTRODUCTION

In the Viking Age and the following Middle Ages, farming communities worked profound changes in the rural landscape. Main characteristics of this period were the clearing of new land, the subdivision of old farms and important changes in the way farms were organised, indirectly signifying a substantial demographic increase. In Norway, the process appears to have started in the eighth century or perhaps even earlier, and to have followed parallel developments in other Scandinavian and many North European countries. In some Norwegian areas, the settlements have been calculated to have doubled and even tripled, although there was also extensive emigration in the Viking Age (Øye, 2004, pp. 93–95).

In Norway, as in other Scandinavian regions, such calculations have been based on archaeological and botanical (pollen) evidence, combined with toponomy and inferences drawn from later and better documented conditions. The dating of medieval and earlier farms has traditionally depended on the existence of prehistoric burial monuments or other datable traces of settlement, such as farm names, farm sizes, and topographical assessment. Such evidence is not always indisputable, and will be examined in this paper, the main topics of which are the chronological aspects of agrarian settlements and land use in the Viking and the Middle Ages, and the methods for attributing farms to these periods.

Traditionally, the rich heritage of prehistoric and medieval place names, especially farm names, has played an important role in assessing the development of rural settlement in Norway and the rest of Scandinavia. To a large extent, the place name typology and chronology established in the late nineteenth and early twentieth century still depend on archaeological dating, especially prehistoric burials. Recent archaeological research has, however, shown that Iron Age burials and farm names do not necessarily reflect the origin and age of a farm (e.g. Salvesen, 1990; Ringstad, 2000; Vikstrand & Zachrisson, 2006). The location of the prehistoric burials should also be assessed spatially and related to the oldest known farm territories, as the present farms are often the results of later subdivisions. Conversely, the absence of prehistoric burials in present farm territories does not exclude early settlements. Archaeological and botanical investigation has shown that farm territories without physically marked burials can be prehistoric. It is therefore necessary to look more closely at the criteria that have been used for dating farms to the Viking Age and the Middle Ages and discuss their validity.

The concept 'farm' should also be defined more precisely, as it seems to be understood somewhat differently within various disciplines and national frameworks. In Norwegian research, the definition put forward by the historian Jørn Sandnes (1979) has been commonly accepted. It denotes the farm as a location with its own name, and buildings housing people and livestock permanently or at least in winter, at the same time utilising land for plant production. This concept comprises the whole resource area of a farm, at least partly physically demarcated. The question, then, is whether it is possible to identify archaeological remains of house constructions and settlements with farms without taking into consideration a wider context, such as the resource area and the use of its land? To shed light on this question, some fresh archaeological case studies from the western part of Norway will be presented – a rather diverse landscape including lowland, valleys and more high-lying mountainous areas from the coast to the inner fjords. As Norway stretches over 13 degrees of latitude in varying altitudes, agricultural conditions diverge accordingly. Consequently, regional diversity in settlement patterns and land use should be expected and taken into account.

THE STATE OF RESEARCH

Until the 1970s, archaeological investigations of prehistoric and medieval agrarian settlements dealt mainly with small abandoned and rather marginal single farms, especially in the south-western and western part of Norway, focussing on house constructions and the layout of the farmhouses (e.g. Petersen, 1932; 1936; Hagen, 1953). In the 70s and 80s, ecological and environmental issues were increasingly taken into consideration and studied by help of interdisciplinary approaches and methodologies. Farm structure, access to resources and the character of local topography gained more interest, and structures such as clearance cairns and lynchets became new fields of research, but still limited to single site analyses or abandoned farms (e.g. Salvesen, 1977; Randers, 1982; Kaland, 1987; Martens, 1989). Deserted farms with their fossilised structures and landscapes are undoubtedly important archaeological study objects. Yet, as abandonment was generally a fate that befell marginal farms that had been run for limited periods, such farms are hardly representative of prehistoric and medieval farms in general. Studies from the 1960s into the 80s of so-called farm-mounds in northern Norway – accumulated masses and deposits of household refuse and ruins of buildings – have for instance demonstrated strong continuity in settlement and land use, in many cases from the Early Iron Age to the present (Munch, 1966; Bertelsen, 1979). Similar continuity should also be expected in western Norway and other topographically scattered and demarcated agrarian landscapes. Long term continuity from the Bronze Age to historic times was for instance documented in such landscapes in Sunnmøre as early as the 1950s (Johnson & Prescott, 1993).

In the last few decades, large scale rescue excavations based on mechanical stripping of topsoil have been carried out in more central agricultural landscapes, most extensively in the Oslofjord region (Bårdseth, 2008; Gjerpe, 2008). Larger expanses of features and structures have been exposed, such as postholes outlining buildings, hearths, pits and other features, both in seemingly 'blank' spaces and beneath more obvious earthworks. Plough-marks, cultivation layers and clearance cairns have also been uncovered. Such large scale excavations based on surface-stripping have clearly demonstrated that earthworks and structures visible above the surface, such as house grounds and/or burial monuments, do not give a representative expression of prehistoric and medieval settlements and land use. Revealing structures over larger areas beneath the surface, they indicate both stable and shifting land use and settlements in a long time perspective from the late Stone Age to the Middle

Ages. In many cases such structures are located within the territories of historic farms, but the settlements have, to some extent, also moved within these areas, as shown in southern parts of Sweden and in Denmark. At the same time, continuity of land use has been documented within the catchment area of historic farms. Some of these excavations, both in western Norway (e.g. Ringstad, 1998; 2000; Diinhoff, 2005; 2008; 2009) and in other regions (e.g. Rønne, 2005), have also revealed house structures and prehistoric settlements close to the historic farm settlements, signifying continuity from the Early Iron Age, if not earlier. However, only a few medieval house grounds have been uncovered, which may be explained either by stability in settlement, or that present buildings cover older structures (Martens, 2009).

Altogether, archaeological studies of agrarian landscapes and settlements have been carried out on different scales and with different techniques in different landscapes. Generally, they have been associated with individual sites as parts of smaller or larger rescue excavations and have been published as reports. They have given a more diverse and complex picture of prehistoric settlements and of processes that may vary regionally, and do not always appear synchronically in all types of landscapes. So far, analyses of the survey data have not provided regional syntheses of agrarian settlements.

CASE STUDIES FROM WESTERN NORWAY

The case studies I focus upon have been carried out as small scale investigations. Rather than studying long-deserted farms in marginal areas or sites as part of rescue excavations, the goal has been to investigate farms and agrarian landscapes that have been used until the present. This approach is based on the presumption that such farms and landscapes may provide information on more sustainable farming over time, and in space. By studying different natural environments in western Norway, a regional perspective has been developed.

A precondition for the investigations has been that the farms have largely been run on traditional methods that have left fossilised structures in the landscape that make it possible to study them archaeologically – such as lynchets, clearance cairns, fences and other features. The archaeological focus has thus shifted from the settlement area to the farmland and its usage, and may only indirectly throw light on the settlements as such. A methodological starting point has been that agrarian settlements and land use should be seen as an integral entity and as social constructions, not only influenced by topography but also formed by varying socio-economic conditions and shifting farming methods. Consequently, the resource area of a farm has to be studied in order to trace both changes and stable features in a long term perspective.

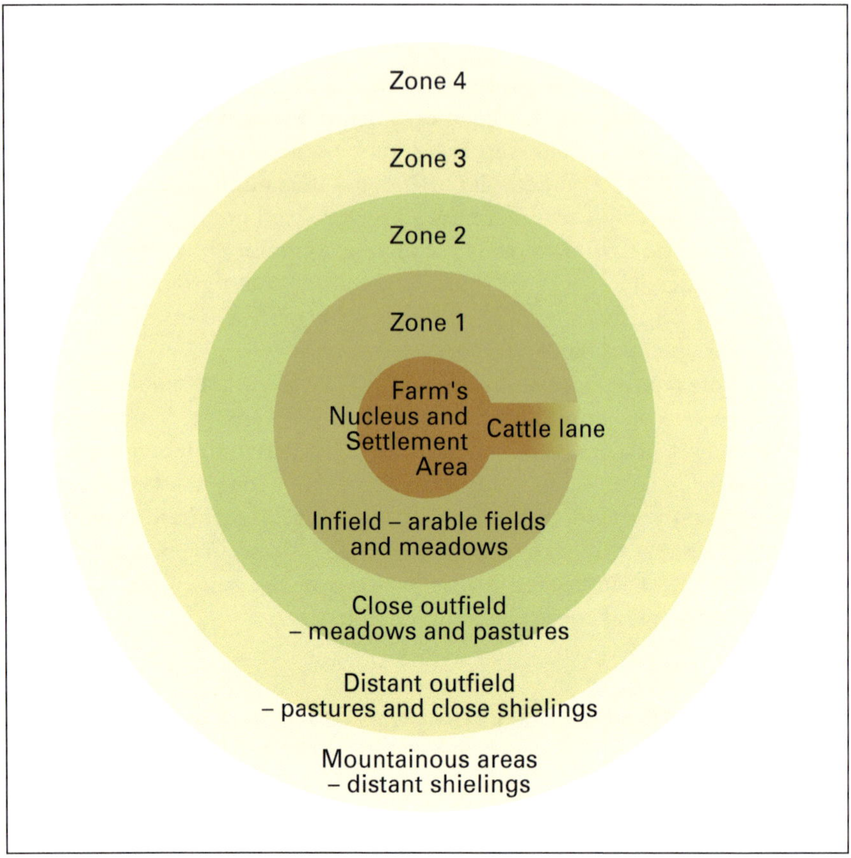

Fig. 1. Different zones within the farm's territory according to use and use rights.

Seen in its historical context, farmland seems to have been structured according to proximity to the settlements, with the home-fields and arable land closest, and the pastoral activities in more distant areas. Correspondingly, the effects of cultivating labour become less and less visible as the distance from the inhabited centre increases; in western Norway increasing altitude is part of the picture. As an analytical tool, the study areas have been divided into zones around the oldest known historical settlement (Fig. 1), within which fossilised elements have been mapped and spatial arrangements assessed in relation to height, land use and socio-political geographical features. This spatial division is used to compare the land use of different areas over time with a view to both stability and change.

The case studies started out as an interdisciplinary research project 'The

Fig. 2. Recent research projects at farms in western Norway.

traditional farm in western Norway', comprising of four different farms. The project was supported by the Norwegian Research Council (1995–1998) and included archaeology, botany (palynology) and history. Its aim was to gain a broader and more holistic outlook on the landscape development in the region (Austad & Øye, 2001; Øye, 2002). The historic farm demarks the territories of the fieldwork. Combining historical information with landscape surveys and archaeological small scale excavations (trenches and test pitting), scientific dating and pollen analyses, the area was studied as an integrated unit based on the oldest known farm structure and in relation to topography, changing land use and socio-economic conditions.

The archaeological part of the project has later been followed up by several similar studies as part of master projects (Stang, 2003; Lia, 2005;

Sivertsen, 2006; Sætre, 2008; Foyn, 2008) and a PhD project (Zehetner, 2007). Altogether, eleven farms have been investigated. Two are from the county of Hordaland and nine from the Sognefjord area (Fig. 2). The research areas have been chosen to represent different physical conditions for subsistence in relation to topography, available resources and territorial extent. They are located in different landscapes at different altitudes from coast to inland, with settlement areas varying from *c.*40 to 450 masl. The farming areas include: terraces in a fjord mouth (Indre Matre) or close to a fjord with access to vast outfields and pastures (Havrå, Rønset, Sæsol, Grinde, Ornes and Kroken), a remote valley (Jostedalen in Sogn with the farms Nedrelid and Kruna) or high-lying mountain plateaus (Lee and Ormelid). Some of them have prehistoric burial mounds, others do not. Some have old farm names, while others have younger names. Although some have a central location, others are in more marginal areas, as they were known in historic times. They represent single farms and agglomerations as well as freehold farms and subordinate farms within larger estates. In this way they represent different types of historic farms and supplement investigations of deserted farms and rescue excavations of more random areas.

Using the traditional criteria for assessing the genesis of farms – mainly prehistoric burials, farm names, relative size and earliest historic records (Table 1), six farms and probably also a seventh, would be classified as prehistoric (marked in bold), either from the Early (500 BC–570 AD) or Late Iron Age (570–1000 AD). Four farms have visible traces of burials close to the historic settlement areas or as demarcations of the historically known borders of the resource areas. Only two of the farm names are of a prehistoric type, as shown by their suffixes: Rønset (set-name) and Lee (vin-name). The other names refer to topographical or cultural features, and can hardly be dated on this basis. Two are mentioned in documents from the early fourteenth century (Sæsol and Havrå). According to the relative value (r.v.) of the farms in the Early Modern Period, they vary from smaller farms, clearly below the average, to units about double the average farm sizes of the surrounding districts. Some of them must, however, have included larger areas at an earlier stage, while others have more permanent topographical borders. According to this criterion, a seventh farm, Havrå, would probably be classified as prehistoric, and only one (Sæsol) as medieval. The rest, Nedrelid, Kruna and Ormelid would be seen as possible or probable medieval farms, as they are first mentioned in the late sixteenth century.

The archaeological investigations can be used to test these criteria. As indicators of farms, traces of permanent or stable farming in the inner zones can be counted. Altogether 222 trenches, some of them trial pits were excavated, and altogether 291 14C-datings were taken from different layers showing agricultural activities (Table 2). Without going into the empirical results in more

Farm name	Muni-cipality	Farm no	Burials	Name Class	Size – productivity r. v. 1647	Earliest records in written sources
(Indre) Matre	Kvinn-herad	250	IA grave-field)	Culture	0.81	1314
Havrå	Osterøy	68	–	Nature	1.75	1303
Rønset	Hyllestad	71	–	-set	1.2	1520
Sæsol	Hyllestad	78	–	—	0.7	c.1320–60
Grinde	Leikanger	2	BA (?)	Culture	1.7	c.1360
Nedrelid	=	191	–	Nature	1.28	1596
Kruna	Luster	208	–	Culture?	–	1596
Ormelid (Lid?)	Luster	1	–		0.56	1596
Ornes	Luster	91	BA/EIA	Nature	1.98	1308/09
Kroken	Luster	69 & 182	–	Nature	1.9	1298
Lee	Vik	54	–	–vin	0.7	c.1360

Table 1. Traditional criteria for dating farms to the medieval period or earlier. The average farm is given the value of 1.

detail, some trends should be mentioned. Ten out of eleven farms show traces of agricultural land use at an earlier stage than the burials and names indicate.

The oldest traces of agricultural activity in the Late Neolithic period (LN; 2400–1750 BC) and Early Bronze Age (EBA; 1750–1100 BC) probably reflect periodical use of wider areas which did not require more permanent settlement and cannot be directly connected with the later farms. Recent open area excavations have, however, uncovered traces of houses connected with arable cultivation and agricultural activities from the Late Neolithic, the Bronze Age (BA) and Early Iron Age (EIA) in western Norway (e.g. Ringstad, 2000; Diinhoff, 2005; 2007). Excavations in other regions in Norway and Scandinavia (e.g. Rønne, 2005) also open up for sedentary farming at a very early stage.

Another interesting observation is that intensification, identified as thicker layers of artificial and modified soil, repeatedly dug over and fertilised with dung and otherwise improved, started in the Late Bronze Age (LBA; 1100–500 BC) at some of the farms, and in the Early Iron Age at others. Traces of the most intensive use at all farms have been located in the inner zones, indicating sedentary farming and long term continuity of land use.

Farm	Munici-pality	Farm no	Trenches (N=222)	14Cdatings (N=291)	Oldest traces	Farm-indicating traces	Intensi fication
Indre Matre	Kvinnherad	250	31	29	LBA	EIA	LIA
Havrå	Osterøy	68	27	31	LN/BA	EIA	LIA
Rønset	Hyllestad	71	14	30	BA	EIA	LIA
Sæsol	Hyllestad	78	13	31	LN	MP	EMA
Grinde	Leikanger	2	25	24	LN	BA/ EIA	LIA
Nedrelid	Luster	191	12	12	LBA	MP	EMA
Kruna	Luster	208	9	9	–	EMA	MA
Ormelid	Luster	1	28	19	BA	EIA	LIA
Ornes	Luster	91	14	37	LN/BA	BA/EIA	LIA
Kroken	Luster	69&182	42	34	LN/BA	EIA	LIA
Lee	Vik	54	17	25	LN/BA	BA/EIA	LIA

Table 2. Results from the excavations at the eleven farms.

Through the archaeological investigations, a different picture emerges from that based on the traditional criteria. While four or five of the eleven farms would traditionally have been counted as medieval (*c.*1000–1500 AD) or probably medieval, the investigations indicate that two of them (Sæsol and Nedrelid) date back to the Merovingian Period (MP), to the seventh, perhaps the sixth century, and that only one farm (Kruna) seems to be medieval, from the eleventh century. The two farms with names of the Late Iron Age type (Rønset), and more vaguely from the transitional phase between the Early and – Late Iron Age (Lee), both show indications of farming in the Late Bronze Age and Early Iron Age, respectively.

Another interesting result is that seemingly marginal farms today, situated at high altitudes (Ormelid and Lee at 450 and 300 masl. respectively), appear to be just as old as farms with better conditions for arable farming. Outfields, grazing land, and proximity to other valuable resources seem to have played a significant role and may have been of equal importance (Øye, 2009). The investigations have also shown that the Late Iron Age and Early Middle Ages (EMA; *c.*1000–1150 AD) were periods of intensification and extension of the arable land, underlining the dynamic character of these centuries. Whether the areas have been used continuously, however, is difficult to prove by means of the methods used and the laconic information provided by the radio-carbon datings. The results of the pollen analyses that were carried out generally correspond to and confirm the archaeological results.

It should be noted that only four of the ten farms with apparent prehistoric origins have burial mounds or burial cairns within their historic resource areas. Where burials occur, they are located close to the historical habitation area or close to borders of the infield that were visible from roads and sea routes – a pattern also known from other parts of the country (Ødegaard, 2010). If one interprets burial monuments as demarcations of ancestral freehold land and indicators of land rights and social stratification (cf. Skre, 1997; Iversen, 1999; 2005), it is interesting to observe that the cairns are located to the three larger clustered farms in the project, of which Ornes and Kroken were nuclei in larger medieval estates. As demonstrated by Iversen (1999), there is a significant statistical concurrence of burial mounds and historical records of freehold farms or main farms of larger estates in western Norway. There is also a general lack of burial mounds on medieval tenanted farms and farms that were parts of larger medieval estates. The absence of burial monuments on tenanted farms in the Middle Ages and the Early Modern Period may therefore indicate some kind of subordinate status even at an earlier stage.

CONCLUSIONS

The studies referred to, open up new perspectives, not only with regard to agricultural land use, but also to the dating of farms and settlements and the understanding of the social landscape. Farms that have been considered as medieval or from the Late Iron Age may have had a considerably longer history than hitherto recognised. The implication being that the place name chronology and other traditional criteria for dating the origin and development of farms is less reliable than commonly thought. This should be taken into consideration when assessing the timing of the expansion of settlements and demographic development in the Viking Period and Early Middle Ages. At the same time the studies confirm that this was a period of intensive farming and subdivisions, but often within older agricultural landscapes.

Only further archaeological examinations of rural landscapes and historical farms can confirm whether the trends observed in western Norway are representative of other regions. The split up topography of western Norway would seem to limit the farming areas and a pattern of burial mounds close to historical farm nuclei and boundaries make it easier to discover the tendencies mentioned. Results from rescue excavations using open air stripping do, however, to a large extent concur with the trends of the case studies referred to, although in a more random way. Different methodologies and different landscapes and regions all show the similar tendency that the agrarian landscapes and settlements are older than earlier reckoned, even in marginal landscapes. Without depending on each other, the different approaches and methods that have been used, complement each other and strengthen the validity of the results.

The combined use of archaeology, written sources and later structures thus holds a large potential for understanding the development of land use, settlement and social organisation.

BIBLIOGRAPHY

Austad, I., & Øye, I. (2001). Den tradisjonelle vestlandsgården som kulturbiologisk system. In B. Skar (Ed.), *Kulturminner og miljø. Forskning i grenseland mellom natur og kultur* (pp. 135–205). Norsk institutt for kulturminneforskning. Oslo.

Bertelsen, R. (1979). Farm mounds in North Norway. A review of recent research, *Norwegian Archaeological Review* 12, 48–56.

Bårdseth, G. A. (Ed.) (2008). *Evaluering og resultat. E6-prosjektet Østfold. Band 5*, Varia 69. Kulturhistorisk Museum Fornminneseksjonen. Oslo.

Diinhoff, S. (2005). Tidlige jordbrugsbosætninger på Vestlandet med spor efter toskibede Langhuse. *Primitive tider* 7, 41–48.

Diinhoff, S. (2007). *Evebø, en førromersk bosætning fra Sandane i Nordfjord. Rapport fra arkæologiske undersøgelser 2000.* Arkeologiske rapporter fra Bergen Museum Nr. 1/2007. Bergen.

Diinhoff, S. (2009). *En ældre jernalders storgård i Nordfjord. Arkæologiske frigivningsundersøgelser ved Eide gnr. 76/77, Gloppen kommune, Sogn og Fjordane. 2000.* Arkeologiske rapporter fra Bergen Museum Nr. 5/2009. Årgang 3. Bergen.

Foyn, S. Ø. (2008). Rønset i Hyllestad. Arkeologisk undersøkelse av innmark-utmark på Rønset i Hyllestad, Sogn og Fjordane. Unpublished master thesis in archaeology. University of Bergen.

Gjerpe, L. E. (Ed.). (2008). *E-18-prosjektet Vestfold, bind 3. Hus, boplass- og dyrkningsspor*, Varia 73, Kulturhistorisk museum Fornminneseksjonen. Oslo.

Hagen, A. (1953). *Studier i jernalderens gårdssamfunn.* Universitetets Oldsaksamlings Skrifter IV. Oslo.

Iversen, F. (1999). *Var middelalderens lendmannsgårder kjerner i eldre godssamlinger? En analyse av romlig organisering av graver og eiendomsstruktur i Hordaland og Sogn og Fjordane.* Arkeologiske avhandlinger og rapporter fra Universitetet i Bergen, 4. Bergen.

Iversen, F. (2005). Royal manors and estates in Western Norway in the late Iron Age and Middle Ages. In T. Iversen & J. R. Myking (Eds.), *Land, lords and peasants: Peasants' right to control land in the Middle Ages and the early modern period – Norway, Scandinavia and the Alpine region. Report from a seminar in Trondheim, November 2004.* Skriftserie fra Institutt for historie og klassiske fag (pp. 133–144). Trondheim.

Johnson, T. & Prescott, C. (1993). Late Neolithic houses at Stokkset, Sande in Sunnmøre. In Solberg, B. (Ed.) *Minneskrift til Egil Bakka. Arkeologiske Skrifter Historisk Museum, Universitetet i Bergen No.* 7, 70–89.

Kaland, S. H. H. (1987). Viking/medieval settlement in the heathland area of Nordhordland. In J. Knirk (Ed.), *Proceedings of the Tenth Viking Congress.* Universitetets Oldsaksamlings skrifter. Nye rekke nr. 9 (pp.171–190). Oslo.

Lia, V. (2005). Ornes i Luster: En arkeologisk landskapsanalyse med punktundersøkelser i innmark. Unpublished master thesis in archaeology. University of Bergen.

Martens, I. (1989). Middelaldergårder i Fyresdal. Arkeologiske registreringer og historiske kilder. *Collegium Medievale* 2, 73–91.

Martens, J. (2009). Middelalderens jordbruksbebyggelse i de sentrale strøk. In J. Martens, V. V. Martens & K. Stene (Eds.) *Den tapte middelalder? Middelalderens sentrale landbebyggelse* Varia 71 (pp. 7–22). Kulturhistorisk museum Fornminneseksjonen. Oslo.

Munch, G. S. (1966). Gårdshauger i Nord-Norge. *Viking XXX*, 25–54.

Petersen, J. (1933). *Gamle gårdsanlegg i Rogaland. Fortsettelse. Institutt for sammenlignende kulturforskning. Serie B. XXXI.* Oslo.

Petersen, J. (1936). *Gamle gårdsanlegg i Rogaland. Institutt for sammenlignende kulturforskning. Serie B. XXIII.* Oslo.

Randers, K. (1981). Høybøen – en ødegård på Sotra. En undersøkelse av bruksperioder og erverv basert på bosetningsspor fra eldre jernalder og middelalder. Unpublished master thesis in archaeology. University of Bergen.

Ringstad, B. (1998). Fra territorium til gård – eksempler fra Møre og Romsdal, Vest-Norge. In T. Løken (Ed.): *Bronsealder i Norden – Regioner og interaksjon. Foredrag ved det 7. nordiske bronsealdersymposium i Rogaland, 3. august – 3. September 1995.* AmS – Varia 33, 75–84. Stavanger.

Ringstad, B. (2000). Gårdsnavn og gårdsbosetning sett i lys av senere års 'flateavdekkings-prosjekt'. In B. Sandnes, J. Sandnes, O. Stemshaug & J. F. Stenvik (Eds.), *Oluf Rygh. Rapport fra symposium på Stiklestad 13.–15.mai 1999.* NORNA-rapporter 70 B (pp. 189–212). Uppsala.

Rønne, O. (2005). Hus og gard i senneolitikum på Svinesund. *Primitive tider* 7, 61–69.

Salvesen, H. (1977). The Hoset project: An interdisciplinary study of a marginal settlement. *Norwegian Archaeological Review* 10, 109–119.

Salvesen, H. (1990). Forholdet mellom gårdsnavnforskning og bosetningshistorie. In T. Schmidt (Ed.). *Namn og eldre busetnad. Rapport fra NORNAs femtende symposium på Hamar 9.–11. juni 1988.* NORNA-rapporter 43 (pp. 17–30). Uppsala.

Sandnes, J. (1979). Ødegårdsprosjektet og tallet på gårdsbruk i Norge i høgmellomalderen, *Historisk Tidsskrift 1979/4*, 397–410.

Sivertsen, A. K. (2006). Jordbruks- og busetnadsutvikling i Jostedalen med utgangspunkt i punktundersøkingar i innmarka på gardane Nedrelid og Kruna. Unpublished master thesis in archaeology. University of Bergen.

Stang, G. B. (2003). Kroken – gard og grend. Arkeologiske punktundersøkingar i Kroken, Luster, Sogn og Fjordane. Unpublished master thesis in archaeology. University of Bergen.

Sætre, A. N. (2008). Sæsol. Jordbruk i et kvernsteinslandskap. En arkeologisk punktundersøkelse av en gård i drift. Unpublished master thesis in archaeology. University of Bergen.

Vikstrand, P. & Zachrisson, T. (2006). Lerslätterna och sta(d)-namnen. Om relationen mellan äldre järnålderns lerslättsboplatser och sta(d)-namn i Mälardalen. In I. Særheim, P.H. Uppstad & Å. K. H. Wagner (Eds.), *Bustadsnamn på -staðir.* Rapport fra NORNAs 33. symposium på Utstein kloster, 7.–9. mai 2004. NORNA rapporter 81(pp. 173–212). Stavanger.

Zehetner, J. L. (2007). Fra sted til gård. En agrararkeologisk analyse av Indre Matre i Kvinnherad, Hordaland. Unpublished doctoral thesis. University of Bergen.

Ødegaard, M. K. (2010). Graver og grenser – territoriell inndeling av jernalderens jordbrukslandskap i Vestfold. *Primitive tider* 12, 27–39.

Øye, I. (Ed.). (2002). *Vestlandsgården – fire arkeologiske undersøkelser: Havrå – Grinde – Lee – Ormelid* ved L. Julshamn, R. L. Bade, K. A.Valvik & J. Larsen. Arkeologiske avhandlinger og rapporter fra Universitetet i Bergen 8. Bergen.

Øye, I. (2004). Agricultural conditions and rural societies c. 800–1350. In R. Almås (Ed.), *Norwegian Agricultural History* (pp. 79–140). Trondheim: Tapir Academic Press.

Øye, I. (2009). On the margins of the medieval farm – Norwegian cases. In J. Klapste and P. Sommer (Eds.), *Medieval rural settlement in marginal landscapes. Ruralia VII 8th–14th Sept. 2007, Cardiff Wales, UK* (pp. 99–107). Brepols.

Authors

Eva Andersson Strand is Associate Professor of Archaeology in the Faculty of Humanities at the Danish National Research Foundation's Centre for Textile Research, SAXO Institute, Copenhagen.

Colleen Batey is Senior Lecturer in Archaeology in the School of Humanities at the University of Glasgow.

Barbara E. Crawford is President of the Society of Antiquaries of Scotland, Kincaple Cottage, Strathmartine Centre, St. Andrews.

Kristoffer Dahle is a county archaeologist at the Møre og Romsdal county in Molde, Norway.

Clare Downham is Lecturer in Irish Studies at the Institute of Irish Studies, University of Liverpool.

Stephen T. Driscoll is Professor of Historical Archaeology at the University of Glasgow.

Kevin J. Edwards is Professor of Geography & Environment and Archaeology at the School of Geosciences, University of Aberdeen.

Egill Erlendsson is a post-doctoral researcher at the Faculty of Life and Environmental Sciences, University of Iceland.

Silke Eisenschmidt is Curator at the Museum Sønderjylland – Archaeology Haderslev.

James Graham-Campbell is Professor Emeritus at the Institute of Archaeology, University College London.

David Griffiths is a reader in archaeology at the University of Oxford.

Anne-Sofie Gräslund is Professor Emeritus with the Department of Archaeology and Ancient History at Uppsala University.

Guðrún Gísladóttir is Professor in the Faculty of Life and Environmental Sciences at the University of Iceland.

Guðrún Sveinbjarnardóttir is Honorary Lecturer at the Institute of Archaeology, University College London.

Svein H. Gullbekk is Associate Professor in the Department of Archaeology, Museum of Cultural History, University of Oslo.

Gunnar Karlsson is Professor Emeritus of History at the University of Iceland.

Dawn M. Hadley is FSA Professor of Medieval Archaeology in the Department of Archaeology at the University of Sheffield.

Jane Harrison is a PhD candidate at the University of Oxford.

Helgi Þorláksson is Professor of History at the University of Iceland.

Frode Iversen is a researcher at the Department of Archaeology, Museum of Cultural History, University of Oslo.

Sven Kalmring works at Zentrum für Baltische und Skandinavische Archäologie, Schloss Gottorf, Schleswig.

James E. Knirk is Professor at the Museum of Cultural History, University of Oslo.

Gavin Lucas is Associate Professor in the Department of Archaeology, University of Iceland.

Thomas H. McGovern is Professor of Anthropology at Hunter College, City University of New York.

Else Mundal is Professor of Old Norse Philology at the Centre for Medieval Studies, University of Bergen.

Sæbjørg Walaker Nordeide is a researcher at the Centre for Medieval Studies, University of Bergen.

Olwyn A. Owen is Head of Scheduling and Marine at Historic Scotland in Edinburgh.

Else Roesdahl is Professor in the Section for Medieval and Renaissance Archaeology, Institute of Culture and Society, Aarhus University.

J. Edward Schofield is Lecturer in Geography at the Department of Geography & Environment, School of Geosciences, University of Aberdeen.

Joachim Schultze is Archaeologist at Archäologisches Landesmuseum in der Stiftung Schleswig-Holsteinische Landesmuseen, Schloß Gottorf, Schleswig.

John Sheehan is Senior Lecturer at the Department of Archaeology, School of the Human Environment, University College Cork.

Søren M. Sindbæk is a lecturer in the Department of Archaeology at the University of York.

Steinunn Kristjánsdóttir is Associate Professor in Archaeology in the Department of Archaeology, University of Iceland & National Museum of Iceland.

Daniel Sävborg is Professor of Scandinavian Studies, Department of Scandinavian Studies, University of Tartu.

Kim Vickers is Honorary Research Fellow in the Department of Archaeology at the University of Sheffield.

Birgitta Wallace is Senior Archaeologist (Emerita) at the Atlantic Service Centre, Parks Canada Agency, Halifax.

Torun Zachrisson is Associate Professor of Archaeology and Classical Studies at Stockholm University.

Ingvild Øye is a professor in the Department of Archaeology, History, Cultural Studies and Religion at the University of Bergen.

1. Else Roesdahl, 2. Sven Kalmring, 3. Jane Kershaw, 4. Guðmundur Ólafsson, 5. Birgitta Hårdh, 6. Anne-Sofie Gräslund, 7. Ragnheiður Traustadóttir, 8. Guðrún Sveinbjarnardóttir, 9. Dagfinn Skre, 10. Elizabeth Pierce, 11. Volker Hilberg, 12. Unn Pedersen, 13. Nancy Edwards, 14. Þórgunnur Snædal, 15. Kevin J. Edwards, 16. John Sheehan, 17. Christina Lee, 18. Søren Sindbæk, 19. Neil Price, 20. Torun Zachrisson, 21. Ingvild Øye, 22, Hildur Gestsdóttir, 23. Marjolein Stern, 24. Arne Kruse, 25. Erin-Lee McGuire, 26. Frans-Arne Stylegar, 27. Mogens Skaaning Høegsberg, 28. Gunnar Karlsson, 29. Sarah Croix, 30. Rúnar Leifsson, 31. Silke Eisenschmidt, 32. Jón Viðar Sigurðsson, 33. Claus Feveile, 34. Dawn M. Hadley, 35. Frode Iversen, 36. Símun V. Arge, 37. Anne Pedersen, 38. Patrick F. Wallace, 39. Anton Holt, 40. Donnchadh Ó Corráin, 41. Lasse Sonne, 42. Joachim Schultze, 43. James Graham-Campbell, 44. Barbara E. Crawford, 45. Judith Jesch, 46. Lesley Abrams, 47. Kenneth Jonsson, 48. Julie Bond, 49. Helgi Michelsen, 50. Eva Andersson Strand, 51. Máire Ní Mhaonaigh, 52. Birgitta Wallace, 53. Christopher Callow, 54. Richard Hall, 55. Thomas McGovern, 56. Staffan Fridell, 57. Poul Baltzer Heide, 58. Gísli Sigurðsson, 59. Svavar Sigmundsson, 60. John Hines, 61. Colleen Batey, 62. Alan Lane, 63. David Griffiths, 64. James E. Knirk.

1. Birgitta Wallace, 2. Olwyn Owen, 3. Neil Price, 4. Joachim Schultze, 5. Eva Andersson Strand, 6. Staffan Fridell, 7. Alan Lane, 8. Richard Hall, 9. Else Roesdahl, 10. John Sheehan, 11. Svein Harald Gullbekk, 12. Gareth Williams, 13. Lesley Abrams, 14. Claus Feveile, 15. David Griffiths, 16. Gísli Sigurðsson, 17. Ragnheiður Traustadóttir, 18. Mark Blackburn, 19. Unn Pedersen, 20. Daniel Sävborg, 21. Sven Kalmring, 22. Volker Hilberg, 23. Dawn M. Hadley, 24. Nancy Edwards, 25. Dagfinn Skre, 26. Kenneth Jonsson, 27. Christina Lee, 28. Máire Ní Mhaonaigh, 29. Silke Eisenschmidt, 30. Steinunn Kristjánsdóttir, 31. Else Mundal, 32. Helgi Þorláksson, 33. Guðrún Nordal, 34. Anton Holt, 35. Elizabeth Pierce, 36. Sólveig Georgsdóttir, 37. Birgitta Hårdh, 38. Elisabeth Ward, 39. Patrick F. Wallace, 40. James Graham-Campbell, 41. Sarah Croix, 42. Guðrún Sveinbjarnardóttir, 43. Marjolein Stern, 44. Þór Magnússon, 45. Erin-Lee McGuire, 46. Kevin J. Edwards, 47. Søren Sindbæk, 48. Frans-Arne Stylegar, 49. Anne Pedersen, 50. Þóra Pétursdóttir, 51. Arne Kruse, 52. Lasse Sonne, 53. James E. Knirk, 54. Barbara E. Crawford, 55. Donnchadh Ó Corráin, 56. Kari Egeland, 57. Gunnar Karlsson, 58. Margrét Hallgrímsdóttir, 59. Guðmundur Ólafsson, 60. Geir Waage.